LD

Roses and rain

a biography of

James Elroy Flecker

Heather Walker

Published by

MELROSE BOOKS

An Imprint of Melrose Press Limited
St Thomas Place, Ely
Cambridgeshire
CB7 4GG, UK
www.melrosebooks.com

FIRST EDITION

Cover designed by Geoff Hobbs Design

ISBN 1 905226 06 3

Printed and bound in Great Britain by:
CPI Antony Rowe, Bumpers Farm, Chippenham,
Wiltshire, SN14 6LH, UK

ACKNOWLEDGEMENTS

My first acknowledgement is to James Flecker, James Elroy Flecker's nephew and Literary Executor, for permission to quote and publish from the work of James Elroy Flecker

also:

Bodleian library, University of Oxford for permission to make use of the material in its Flecker collection.

The University of Texas at Austin, Harry Ransom Humanities Research Centre to quote from the Flecker materials in the HRHRC collections.

The Houghton Library of the Houghton College Library, Department of Manuscripts, Harvard University, Cambridge, Mass., for permission to quote and publish manuscript material of James Elroy Flecker, including poems, letters to Max Goschen and cards to D. Goldring, with the call numbers MS.Eng 972 and MS Eng 972.1; manuscript material by Saadi, translated by James Elroy Flecker, with the call number Autograph File S; a letter by Mathews Elkin to Cheltenham, with the call numbers Autograph File F; a letter by Flecker to Goldring with the call number Autograph File F; a letter by Flecker to Elkin with the call number *EC9 F6227.9076; and a letter by TE Lawrence to Flecker, with the call numbers bMS Eng 1252 (7)–(9)

The National Library of Scotland for permission to include quotations from Acc. 8264

The Archivist, New College Oxford, for permission to quote extacts from their typed manuscript of the biography of Cheesman (Ms 14,603) Original of biography in the Bodleian.

Department of Special Collections and University Archives, Raynor Memorial Libraries, Elizabeth W. Houghton Collection University, Marquette University, Milwaukee WI for permission to quote from the Minute Book of the Fabian Society, 1906–1913

The Poetry Collection of the University Libraries., The State University of New York at Buffalo, to quote from the James Elroy Flecker papers at the Poetry Collection.

Special Collections, Main Library, Edinburgh University, for permission to quote from the Sarolea Collection

Manuscripts Division, Department of Rare Books and Special Collections, Princeton University Library for permission to quote and publish from the Richard Halliburton Papers: Three letters from Flecker to Rupert Brooke, general manuscripts (misc.), two letters by Flecker, manuscript of Flecker's poem 'Golden', two manuscripts of portion of Flecker's exam papers (Final examination Oriental Tripos, at Caius College, Cambridge), seven letters by Flecker, seventeen letters from Flecker to Grant Richards.

The Permission of A. P. Watt Ltd., Literary Agents on behalf of the copyright holder of John Sherwood author of *No Golden Journey* to quote from *No Golden Journey*.

The Permission of Polly Bird, Literary executor of Douglas Goldring to quote from the work of Douglas Goldring.

The Permission of John Robinson (Arthur Waley Estate) to quote from the poems and plays of Arthur Waley.

The Society of Authors for permission to quote extacts from *Letters to X*.

Peter Mavrogordato for permission to quote from the published work and private papers of his grandfather, John Mavrogordato.

E.S. Turner to quote from his book *Boys will be Boys*.

Dr. Caroline Grigson to quote from the work of her father, Geoffrey Grigson.

Jeremy Wilson to quote from his book *Minorities*.

Wolfgang Gortschacher Editor Salzburg Studies in English Literature, University of Salzburg, Austria for permission to quote from the works of Mary Byrd Davis and Ronald Gillanders.

I would like to thank all those who have helped me by sharing their recollections of meeting with or hearing about Flecker's family and friends. In particular, Roger Dobson of The Arthur Machen Society, the late Kathleen Secker who knew both Hellé Flecker and Flecker's sister, Joyce. The late Martin Booth who gave me much encouragement in the early stages of my writng the Flecker biography and whom I met when he talked about Flecker and read Flecker's poetry at the Parish Church of St. Peter's Leckhampton, during the Cheltenham Literary Festival 1985. Also Basil Ashmore who helped and encouraged in the early stages.

Thanks are due to the following:

John Jealous of the Laurence Hope Newsletter for information about the life and work of Laurence Hope. David Sutton of the Location Register of Twentieth Century English Literary Manuscripts for help and advice. The staff of the London Library, The Public Record Office at Kew.

Also Jeanne Conn, editor of *Connections* magazine, who published my work and who read the typescript and made helpful suggestions and with her husband, Vic brought useful information to my attention. Nick Clarke of *Poetic Hours* magazine who also published my work, and gave help and encouragement. Brenda Watkinson who typed and helped with the preparation and delivering to me of the manuscript, from start to finish.

CONTENTS

CHAPTER ONE

The Isle of Wight in the high summer of 1885 was honoured by the visit of Queen Victoria. When the Royal Yacht sailed to East Cowes, the marines on board presented arms, and the band mustered on the high deck at the stern played the National Anthem. In the sovereign's honour, the harbour ships were dressed with masthead flags.

For those of Her Majesty's loyal subjects fortunate enough to be holidaying, there was sea-bathing, boating and fishing to enjoy. Further down the coast at Shanklin, residences with sea views could be rented for three to twelve months. These houses had adjoining Swiss cottages, similar to the one built as a playhouse for the Royal children at Osborne House, the Queen's residence on the Isle of Wight. If seeking health, recreation and pleasure (stated an advertisement in *The Times*), one could not do better than stay at adjoining Sandown where 'the sands are splendid and easy of access'.

It was to Sandown that same summer that Sarah Flecker came to stay with friends, with her baby Herman Elroy (who was always known as 'Roy'[1]). Her husband, William, was in Switzerland, where, to help with expenses he had taken a chaplaincy. He kept in touch with his wife and sent her long letters:

> 'I can look back on the past four years [they married on 1August 1881] and thank God for them. We will pray that the future may be free from anything that should mar our life together, or with God.'[2]

The only immediate factor that could mar their life (while apart) was the battle of wills that was already manifesting itself between their first-born, Herman Elroy, and Sarah. An early example of the baby's 'obstinacy'[3] was his reaction to Sandown when Herman Elroy was said to have screamed 'till he was taken out of sight and sound of the sea'.[4]

Sandown was a fashionable resort; its genteel atmosphere not spoiled by the presence of numerous day-trippers of the sort who crowded into Brighton or Margate. These seaside resorts were nearer to London by rail, and attracted city-dwellers. Scenes like those between the infant Herman Elroy and his mother would have attracted less attention there, while at Sandown the heads of nursemaids with their young charges could have turned to see who, or what, was making such a disturbance. The bathers emerging from the bathing machines would be (thankfully) out of earshot.

At the same time as his baby son was reacting badly to his first sight of the seaside, his father (despite his delight at this first sight of the Alps, the green slopes and sparkling rain) was reacting badly to unfavourable weather when the dark fir trees looked 'black and frowning'.[5]

In case his wife thought that her husband was enjoying only the grand sights that were new to him (he had described the interior of a palatial hotel, newly built for four hundred guests), he also wrote of a small church that was far from outstanding: 'There was no floor, save the ground – mother earth itself – the turf just scraped off and benches (very, very rough) put on instead. It is a Protestant Church, and one service per annum is held here, on Ascension Day.'[6]

Was this lack of a proper floor a reminder of some of the rooms in a little unfurnished house at Eastbourne to which the Fleckers had moved early in their married life? The coming of the holiday season had resulted in the Fleckers' landlady demanding double rent, a sum they could not afford, and they had had to move out and stay with friends. Then they moved to the unfinished house that was to be their first home.

This house was a long way from the church, St. John's Meads, where William Flecker was an unordained parish worker. The location of the new home meant that they could not return between William's preaching of the two sermons. A picnic had to be eaten in the church until a member of the congregation invited them to his home. In turn, the parishioner's employer, a former Governor of Assam, invited the Fleckers to lunch and to spend the rest of the day with him. The site of St. John's Meads was not so welcoming. The church was surrounded by trees, and the coastal winds brought branches crashing onto the roof and drowned out the voices of the choir and congregation, which were unlikely to be very loud. William's flock did not attend church regularly and he had to do a lot of walking to find out the reasons for their absence. William had been used to long walks in his childhood in order to get to school; it was not a new experience to find his way through farms and fields.

William Herman Flecker, the second of five children, was born on 10 December 1859, at Roade, Northamptonshire. His father, Issacher Flecker (a Polish Jew who converted to Christianity), had come to England from Austria. Issacher married Elizabeth Pardon, daughter of William Pardon, of Huguenot descent. At the time of William's birth, Issacher was a Baptist minister. Until William was in his twenties, his father (except for a three-year period) was not in charge of a church, but earned his living in other ways. These may have included teaching; Issacher was, for a short time, a schoolmaster in Constantinople.

Sarah was not so familiar with country ways. She was born at Hulme, Lancashire, at 36 Embden Street on 3 January 1861. Her father, Henry Ducat was, at the time of her birth, a silk mercer and her mother, Mary was formerly Miss Fox. Both Sarah's parents became naturalised British subjects; they were, like William's father, Polish Jews. They had to flee persecution because of their conversion to Christianity. Before his conversion, Henry Ducat was said to be deeply read in the Talmud (the fundamental code of Jewish civil and canon law). Sarah grew up with sufficient knowledge of Hebrew to take classes if called upon to do so.[7] Henry and Mary Ducat were equally dedicated to the Christian way of life, as were Issacher and Elizabeth Flecker.

Sarah was enrolled as a student at the Royal Academy of Music, where she followed a course of instruction that included composition, organ playing (if students paid for the cost of blowing), pianoforte and languages. William had a powerful singing voice and he was to become a performer and an accompanist. This mutual interest in music had drawn William and Sarah together, when William was taken by his father from their home in Finsbury Park to hear Sarah play the piano. At that first meeting, William fell in love with the sixteen-year-old Sarah Ducat. Sarah and her sister Rachel, two years younger, were not impressed at first with the tall, bearded, almost eighteen-year-old teacher. He was employed at a local private school in Stoke Newington. After an initial objection by the Ducat parents, the two young people began to write to each other and an understanding arose whereby they would get engaged in three years' time. Their objection is understandable on account of Sarah's age; they could not object on the grounds of family connections. The Ducats and the Fleckers had much in common. The Flecker parents could have found it hard to raise objections to their son's marriage plans but they came at an awkward time. Issacher Flecker, it was said, 'took his son to the Ducats' house';[8] no mention is made of William's mother, Elizabeth. It could be that she accompanied her husband and son to the Ducats' home, but one reason why she could not, would be her health, which was said to be frequently 'poor', although the reasons are not given.[9] While in her late forties (around the time William Flecker fell in love with Sarah Ducat) Elizabeth Flecker gave birth to a son, James. Elizabeth Flecker had a daughter, Isadora, who was ten at the time of her baby brother's birth, but she could not be called upon to give her mother the financial or emotional support they would need at this time. Elizabeth Flecker's widowed father, now retired from his work as a printer and aged over eighty, could not be called upon either to help his daughter's family. But William was old enough to be looked upon to help the rest of his family and at the same time too young, his parents might think, to begin to plan a home and family of his own.

William Flecker's determination to marry and the changes he must make in his life if this were to happen (and the difficulties he faced, which could have been avoided by giving himself longer to consider them) mirror the doubts he was to have about his own son at the same age. 'Flecker (Herman Elroy) always tended to expect "things" to right themselves, even to suit any complete and abrupt change he might make. The sagacious and prudent (William Flecker?) are often vexed when this peculiar kind of improvidence is justified, as it is occasionally, of its child.'[10]

But if William were to contemplate marriage in four or five years' time, he now needed to be much more ambitious in the pursuit of better academic qualifications. As a first step, he won a scholarship to read mathematics at University College, Durham. If he had been able to choose the classics, music, literature or theology, he would have been ultimately more successful and under less of a strain. Also, if he had won a scholarship to a university nearer home he would have felt the separation from Sarah less acutely.

The reason for suggesting that William would have found it advisable to choose another subject was that he made a success of preaching sermons in villages and singing at concerts at Durham. He did not approach his mathematical studies with the same zeal. Nobody at Durham, it would appear, could inspire him with a love for solving the mystery of mathematics. Mathematics was a subject that could be studied without much involvement with the outside world. It could have been this sort of isolation, after he had left his busy teaching life, that added to his dislike of mathematics as a subject. But there may not have been much of a choice for William. Mathematics, it may have been thought, would provide for him a much better chance of a well-paid teaching career. This could have been at the back of his father's mind when he influenced his son in the choice of mathematics. It was not surprising that, once on his degree course, and under more pressure from his father, William was not successful in an attempt he made in January 1880 to get into Oxford. William found, on his arrival at Oxford to take the necessary examinations, that the dream that had sustained him until then faded quickly. He faced long walks through snow-clad streets and hours of study in order to prepare for the scholarship examinations. He soon found that he was only one of a great many men with similar expectations. Even so, William felt that he could have done better in the examinations, nightmarish as he discovered them to be. The realisation these examinations gave him was that he would not get a First, and if he did not, he wanted to give up mathematics. He told himself that men he admired, such as Charles Kingsley (1819–75) were not mathematical geniuses. If he was to continue to grind away at mathematics 'let it be at the proper place, Cambridge.'[11] This reference to Cambridge (although it is not explained further) could refer to a system of non-Euclidean geometry. This system was not favoured by mathematicians at Oxford such as Charles Dodgson (1832–98) who advised a friend that Cambridge would be preferable to Oxford for anyone with a serious interest in the subject [mathematics].[12]

Added to all the intellectual pressures during his short time at Oxford was a vague social unease. William found he had to 'make, or try to make myself, agreeable to seven ladies ... '.[13] At Oxford he complained also of a 'fearful headache' and his need for 'a safety valve of some sort ... '.[14] These problems were a continuation of those he had suffered while at Durham, brought on by his heavy working schedule and a lack of sleep. He continued to worry about problems outside his own immediate sphere, such as the 'horrid opium question', and he opened a debate in the Union Rooms. He condemned the 'national position on the subject'.[15] In this respect, he was in line with the Anglo-Oriental Society for the Suppression of the Opium Trade, one of whose vice-presidents was the Right Rev. the Lord Bishop of Ripon.[16] The 'national position', as outlined in *The British Opium Policy and its results to India and China*, was seen as:

> 'Great Britain, by its sovereignty of India and pre-eminent influence in China, wields a mighty influence over the destinies of more than half the human race. For a little while (who can say for how long?) the hegemony of the world is ours. For the time being, we are peaceful, rich, and powerful – better fitted than any other people to meet the demands of this vast empire and influence upon our resources. Never since mankind began has any nation had so splendid an opportunity to pour our life-blood

of religion, our liberty, our commerce, our science, our education, into the stagnant veins of the dying East.'[17]

The *Spectator* suggested that 'if the opium revenue had to be abandoned, a tax upon tobacco might supply the deficiency, though at the risk of great unpopularity'.[18] William would not, therefore, take laudanum for his headaches, although he admitted, while preparing for the debate, that his dreams 'have been opium-y'.[19]

William returned to Durham and awaited the inevitable news that he had failed to win a place at Oxford. He soon realised that he needed to continue to work hard for his Durham Finals, which would not be any easier than the recent Oxford examinations. He hoped for a First, but while sitting the papers in June 1880, the months of overwork took their toll and his health broke down. He was forced to retire, but remained optimistic about his future. He wrote to Sarah in July, 'It would be madness to lose a First which I can easily get at Christmas'.[20] This optimism about his future was something maybe William felt he needed to maintain for his fiancée's benefit, so that she would not lose faith in him. But the optimism contained an element of self-deception, over-confidence, arrogance, call it what you will, which William appeared not to recognise. The real reason why he had reached this point of failure was his inability to set aside his preaching and other activities for a while in favour of his studies. If William had not been over-confident at this stage, he would have seen the wisdom of concentrating on his studies and nothing else, but he decided on another course. The postponement of his Finals resulted in William deciding that he needed to get a job in the interval before he could re-sit them.

William applied for a post of Vice-Master at a public school in the elegant East Sussex seaside resort of Eastbourne. The school for boys, New College, was founded by the South African-born Frederick Samuel Schreiner who first turned down William without an interview on account of his being only twenty years old. William went in person to see Schreiner, who could see that William looked older and more confident than the facts on paper might have suggested at first reading of them. It could have been that Schreiner saw through the air of confidence to the more vulnerable interior of William Flecker, and used it to his advantage. The First at Christmas might not be achieved. William needed the post, and if Schreiner was not fully aware of the nervous collapse that had brought his interviewee to this point, he may have seen that William's weaknesses could be overcome.

Not everyone had approved of William's confidence and youth in the pulpit,[21] but it was a valuable attribute when dealing with boys in a school.

Schreiner, forty years old, with heart problems, was in need of a partner to help him run the school; one who would, in time, be able to take over completely. A man several years older and more experienced than William Flecker (if one had presented himself from amongst the present New College teaching staff) would seem to have been a more realistic choice. It was a choice (the oldest member of his present staff, was only thirty-five) Schreiner did not make. Instead, he appointed William Flecker to the post of resident Vice-Master at New College at a salary of £150 per annum. This was an example of what could be described as 'Flecker's luck', but also the advantage of Flecker's outward air of confidence in his own abilities, which then and in the future allowed him to obtain a post over more experienced and better qualified rival candidates. ('Flecker's luck' would run out when, much later, he would collapse again.) But Flecker's lack of experience (which no amount of outward confidence could replace) could also be an advantage; he could be moulded into the ways of his headmaster. This, Schreiner was entitled to do; New College was his sole creation. Schreiner arrived at Eastbourne in the 1870s and built up the school (which was situated in fine grounds). At the time William joined the staff, New College had over one hundred pupils, including Schreiner's only child, Wilfred, who was doing well at the school (but whose strong will, even at this early stage, may have ruled him out as his father's future successor).

During the summer vacation, William spent time with Sarah who was staying with friends in Norfolk. Her health, too, was suffering, and doctors had advised that she live permanently out of London.

Life as Vice-Master of New College was a busy one, but unlike Durham, where William's activities had been scattered, now all his interests were situated in one place.

Any doubts about the confidence of William Flecker that arose in Schreiner's mind would soon be removed by the new Vice-Master's obvious strength as an all-rounder. He was ready to involve himself in any aspect of running the school, whether it was teaching, sporting activities, music (singing, choral and organ practice) duties in the chapel, Bible classes, taking part in debates, the Literary Society, the New College magazine or carving the mutton for lunch on Sundays. Sundays were not days of rest. The Vice-Master was on duty on alternate Sundays, which meant overall responsibility for all the boys in the schoolroom for half an hour, at a time he loathed, before breakfast, as well as teaching in the afternoons.

In the same way as differences arose about the value of William Flecker's air of confidence (whether it was desirable in a young man when it appeared excessive), so would his ability to involve himself in all aspects of school life be called into question. In time, this strength could be seen as a weakness; he was not so eager to 'decentralise or delegate authority'.[22]

William Flecker and Frederick Schreiner together must have looked an unusual couple. The headmaster was not much over 5 foot 5 inches in height, and he was black-bearded and wrapped in the black gown of a BA of London University, while the Vice-Master was much taller and half his age. But in the headmaster's study, where Schreiner would retire to smoke a cigar, they would find that they had more in common that their respective birthplaces and early upbringing would at first indicate.

Frederick Schreiner could not be seen entirely in isolation from his South African roots, although he had left Cape Colony for good at the age of thirteen. The remainder of the Schreiner family still lived in South Africa and, from time to time, visited England and used New College as a convenient staging post. Schreiner's youngest surviving brother, Will, was a law student at Cambridge when William started at New College. Frederick Schreiner was the second of twelve children, of whom seven had survived to adulthood.[23] Frederick Schreiner's father, Gottlob, was born in Germany in 1814, and ordained in London in 1838, the same year as he married Rebecca Lyndall, a teacher and linguist. Gottlob, with his wife, was sent out to South Africa in 1838 by the London Missionary Society. He broke regulations (by trading) and had to resign from the Wesleyan Society, which had employed him as a missionary.

Gottlob then opened a general dealer's store, but this was not a success, nor was he a success at any further ventures. In this respect, Gottlob was not unlike Issacher Flecker, William's father who was only in charge of a church for three years. It is not known what sort of work Issacher did outside the church[24] (except, as has been seen, teaching).

The periods when both fathers were out of work could also have been times when the fathers found work away from the family home. The absence of the fathers meant that Fred Schreiner's English mother and Elizabeth Flecker were both seen as the stronger partners and the greater influence upon their respective sons. The deep religious faith of both mothers was a necessary requirement of ministers' wives. Rebecca Schreiner educated the youngest children herself. She gave birth to her last child in her mid-forties and it was the death of this child, Ellie, at the age of three that had a profound effect on her nine-year-old daughter, Olive. The Flecker and the Schreiner families both valued education for their sons. Both families experienced the harshness of life, and faced a lack of money in their early years.

New College, with its middle- and upper-class pupils, meant that William had no direct contact with the poverty of the 'Waifs and Strays' type which had vexed him so while at Durham: 'On this Sunday I am to speak to the Waifs and Strays. I hope to speak to them from my heart to theirs. Poor things, they lead fearfully wretched lives: it seems almost a mockery to go from a well-spread table and speak to them of the Bread of Life, when they may be all the time hungry.'[25]

How 'well-spread' (on a regular basis) William's table was at Durham would be a matter for debate, but on the evidence of the amount paid for his college meals (generally not over the equivalent of £1.50 per week) he was certainly able to enjoy a standard of living much above the average 'Waif and Stray'.[26]

William's ambivalence, when faced with extreme poverty and what could be done to alleviate it, would prove no barrier to his getting along with his headmaster. Schreiner had a particular horror (not unusual in his day) of the work of the Salvation Army. He had expressed alarm at the prospect of his brother, Theo and his sister, Het feeling the urge to join. William Booth and his wife, Catherine, formed the Salvation Army in 1878 to help the physical and spiritual welfare of the very poor. But Booth would not have welcomed a favourable view of his work from someone like Schreiner or William Flecker. Booth had contempt for the Higher Education of his day and would not agree to his son going to university.

The fathers of the boys at New College had no objection to their sons going to university. and many former pupils had already gone on to London University, Oxford and Cambridge. New College pupils excelled at football, cricket and swimming, and old boys went on to posts in America, Canada, New Zealand and South Africa. All this information was to be found in the New College magazine, which included details of the academic achievements of the present staff such as in December 1880: 'Mr. W.H. Flecker has also taken his degree at Durham gaining Mathematical Honours'.

The truth behind this announcement was that, despite the Mathematical Honours, the BA degree was a Second and (as a result) any hopes of a Fellowship at Cambridge would be unfulfilled. The Oxford scholarship had not been gained, and it was doubtful by 1880 (as it drew to a close) that even if W.H. Flecker had obtained a First he would have still wanted to go on to Cambridge. This did not mean that he did not want to gain better academic qualifications in the future.

He had abandoned the idea of a scholarship to Cambridge[27] (although the exact date was not given) but, at New College (while he was still feeling sure of gaining a First) his dream of a Cambridge Fellowship could have been broken by the reality of the experience of Fred Schreiner's brother, Will. Will Schreiner MA ML was already a success at Cambridge when William Flecker knew him, and what he knew could have influenced William Flecker against taking a similar sort of step. He could see that if he had modelled himself on Will Schreiner's life and gone to Cambridge, his difficulties might have been more than if he had failed to do so.

Will Schreiner was the youngest surviving son, and he benefited much by leaving South Africa at the age of twenty-two and coming to Eastbourne and New College. Despite the warm welcome from Fred and his wife Emma, Will did not feel particularly happy at first. He worked for his scholarship to Cambridge in bachelor quarters at New College (and were these the same quarters that William Flecker was to inhabit?). Like William Flecker, Will Schreiner wanted to train for the medical profession, but financial considerations prevented him and he settled for a career in the law. Will would also, like William Flecker, have been happier settling for a longer time in the academic world. He, too, was a born teacher. But before Will left South Africa he had got engaged and, like William Flecker, if he wanted to marry, he had to consider entering a well-paid profession as soon as he could. Will soon found what life was like for an undergraduate who was not from a well-to-do background. Hard work was necessary if he was to survive financially, and even if he had come from a family with money, the fact that he was a Colonial would still have made him an outsider. Will Schreiner excelled at rowing, and he approached the sport with as much energy and zeal as William Flecker was to approach preaching, while at Durham. But Will's rowing activities had to be put aside in order to work for examinations. It is here that the parallels that could be drawn between Will Schreiner and William Flecker's lives ceased. William Flecker had put aside his studies of mathematics in order to concentrate on his outside interests, including an effort to 'reconcile the two great factions, Low and High Church, represented here in all bitterness, so that something unanimous may be done. At the same time I try to keep in the background as much as possible myself.'[28] William Flecker was Low Church.

Lofty ideals, such as endeavouring to reconcile High and Low Church, would need to be less of a priority as William faced the New Year. Now that the Cambridge Fellowship prospect was no longer viable for William, the main aim in 1881 was his wedding. The first priority to further that aim was the idea of living out of New College and taking on private pupils. It seemed that William did not relish the idea of living at New College with his bride. The reasons for alternative arrangements would seem obvious; the newly married couple would have more privacy. Sarah would not be involved in the domestic running of the school (although it is not clear just how much involvement in the running of the domestic side of New College Emma Schreiner could take credit for, if William had the task of carving the mutton at Sunday lunch). If Sarah was living outside New College, she could earn money more easily than if she was resident. It may have suited Fred Schreiner to have William and his bride living out of College, because, by the early weeks of 1881, he knew that his sister Olive was coming to stay.

On 30 March 1881, Fred Schreiner's unmarried sister, who had until then been earning her living as a governess, arrived at Southampton from South Africa. Olive Schreiner, aged twenty-six, and born at Cape Colony after her brother left South Africa for good, was meeting him for the first time. She was fulfilling a long-held dream of coming to England, and of seeing her novels published alongside a career in medicine.

A photograph taken shortly after Olive Schreiner's arrival at New College is dated April 1881.[29] It shows Olive with her brothers Fred and Will, sister-in-law Emma and Olive's nephew, Wilfred. Olive, like Fred, is small in stature and dark, while Will is tall and fair. Will took after the German side of the family. Olive Schreiner did not stay long on this first leg of her journey. She attempted a nursing career at Edinburgh Royal Infirmary soon after her arrival, but this venture proved to be almost as short-lived as William Flecker's interest in medicine after his visit (while still at Durham) to Newcastle Infirmary. William had gone through the wards with the doctors 'But could not bear to see the operations'.[30] He heard a man weeping in agony and could not bear that either. The experience had cured him of wanting to train to be a doctor. William's attempts to oppose the 'horrid opium business' appeared not to see that, for all its dark side, opium did relieve pain. (Olive Schreiner was prescribed opium for her asthma and heart problems.)[31]

Olive Schreiner's enrolment as a nurse probationer did not last even for the month she had planned. Her brother Fred brought her back to Eastbourne by 5 May. Her poor health was supposed to have been the reason for the curtailment, but the hospital's strict regime was just as likely to have caused her abrupt withdrawal. But that need not be the whole story. Olive did not mention on her application form that she had previously suffered from poor health, but this could have greatly improved on the long sea voyage from Cape Town. The distress and suffering that she witnessed at the Infirmary would not have turned her against a career in medicine. Unlike William Flecker, she was used to the illness of others, and she had already nursed patients in her native land, where the nearest doctor or hospital was always hundreds of miles distant. She was not squeamish; she had been able to dissect animals. Olive Schreiner, only that year, on 3 January, 'helped a poor coloured woman in the road when her baby was born ... I hope I cut the string quite right'.[32] She had been encouraged by a doctor friend and his wife in South Africa, who said that she would 'very likely get on at the R.I.'.[33] The doctor friend and his wife had tried to help Olive with the publication of one of her novels, *The Story of an African Farm*. Olive had, while she was at the Royal Infirmary, 'nursed for a little while & saw my beautiful girl.'[34] This image of a girl 'almost dying of inflammation of the lungs',[35] contrasts with William Flecker's memory of a patient, who was sobbing in agony. Olive Schreiner's dying patient gave her pleasure to nurse, and she recalled the way the girl opened her 'sweet' eyes; they reminded her of stars.

Olive Schreiner had more down-to-earth considerations in her life; she was financially dependent on her brother Fred, and by early May she needed coaching for her medical examinations. She needed to acquire knowledge of algebra, arithmetic and Latin.

At this time, William Flecker was dependent on Fred Schreiner agreeing to his idea of living outside New College after his marriage. He needed a salary of £175 per year rising to £200, which Schreiner agreed to reluctantly; he doubted his Vice-Master's ability to get to the start of the school day before breakfast. William needed to take on private coaching as soon as he could. He intended to spend no money between May 1881, and 10 August when the summer term ended, which would suggest that he was a suitable candidate to coach Olive Schreiner. He was already coaching a young man, and this would continue until July, and would bring him in £12. 'Then there is another three guineas I am sure of for next Term.'[36]

But by 30 June 1881, Olive Schreiner, who only a month previously had been happy 'sitting in my nice little study was writing in her diary: 'I am sitting in my bedroom trying to do my Latin but my heart is heavy. Oh God, so heavy. When will it be morning the shadows flee away! Yesterday we went to the athletic sports. I will work hard when I am in London.'[37]

Olive Schreiner was described by the Fleckers as 'always' having 'an air of great sadness'.[38] The use of the word 'always' indicates that the sadness was evident from her arrival at New College, when William Flecker first met her. Olive Schreiner's melancholy could have been due to a number of reasons, not least the fact that she was at heart a writer with three novels to try and get published, and she had no paid occupation. She was realising that neither nursing on the hospital wards nor the grind of examinations was for her. But there could have been a particular reason why her sadness was pressing upon her in the summer of 1881.

It was said that, during the first few months after her arrival at New College, Olive Schreiner had a sexual encounter with an unnamed man, 'possibly an instructor from Fred Schreiner's school in Eastbourne'.[39] It is difficult to guess the identity of this 'instructor' at New College; the teaching staff consisted of a dozen unmarried men, all under forty years of age. The affair was also said to be 'heavy with sado-masochistic overtones'.[40] A further difficulty arises when reference is made to Olive Schreiner falling in love again (she had previously broken off her secret engagement in 1872 for reasons that are unclear; one suggestion was that she found that she was not pregnant after all[41]), and the sexual encounter taking place at her brother's school in the 'Isle of Wight...' [sic].[42]

It is true that Olive Schreiner did go to the Isle of Wight, but she went in November 1881. Her brother Fred took her to Rose Cottage, Ventnor, a seaside resort further down the coast from Shanklin. Again, Olive was upset because she felt that she was letting her brother down. The extent of her distress is outlined in an extract from her diary written in a hotel in Norfolk Street, London, on 18 October 1881: '.... I got sick at Endell Street. My chest is very bad. My poor old brother is heartsore and tired. I wonder if he will ever come and see me ..'.[43]

The reference to 'Endell Street' was to Olive's abortive attempt at nursing at the Women's Hospital, Endell Street, London where, after five days, she got an inflammation of the lungs.[44] On 22 October, she wrote in her diary: 'Yesterday my Dadda [her brother Fred] came to see me. I was not expecting. He says he will come again on Monday week and take me to the Isle of Wight ...'.[45]

The decision to resume a nursing career at the Women's Hospital was thought to be a result of Olive's disappointment with the unnamed 'instructor'. In October 1881, William Flecker was safely married, but he and the other 'instructors' would be back at New College after the summer vacation. William Flecker could be described as an instructor.[46] Olive Schreiner was not a woman that men overlooked, and many men were to fall in love with her and wanted to marry her. If she had any interest in William Flecker before his marriage, the fact that he was five years younger than she was would not have prevented her becoming attracted to him.

Havelock Ellis (1859–1939) was four years younger than Olive Schreiner. They first met in 1884 and this age difference was no handicap to Olive Schreiner's attraction to Ellis and a lifelong relationship.[47] But Ellis was not the strong male partner that Olive Schreiner was seeking. Karl Pearson (1857–1936),[48] to whom she was attracted, was two years younger. The man Olive Schreiner eventually married, Samuel Cronwright, was eight years younger than his wife. The man whose love she did not return and whose offer of marriage she turned down, Bryan Donkin (1845–1927) was ten years older.[49]

Speculation on the feelings, if any, Olive Schreiner might have had for the young and confident William Flecker, albeit an engaged man, is pointless without any record of the feelings he might have had for his headmaster's sister. However, one important event in Olive Schreiner's young life was the death of her sister, Ellie. From that moment, Olive became a freethinker, and she rejected the authority of religion. She could not believe that her baby sister was living somewhere without her earthly body. Olive did not share (like Sarah Ducat and her fiancé) a devotion to the Church, and without this Olive Schreiner was unlikely to have any future with William Flecker, if such a thought ever crossed his mind. The identity of the 'instructor' must remain an unsolved mystery, unless he was an invention, much later, by Ellis to 'explain' why he and Olive were never lovers. Ellis could not reveal the real reason, namely that he was unable to love Olive physically, but rather that she was strongly attracted to another man – the unknown 'instructor' at her brother's school.

If the last term before the summer vacation was a difficult time at New College for Olive Schreiner, then it was an equally difficult time for William Flecker. His parents thought that their son was too young to think of marriage and to give up his ideas of Cambridge. But William threatened to go to South Africa for four years, by way of revenge, if he could not get his own way.

How serious the disagreement over the timing of the wedding, and how lasting this was, is difficult to assess, but Issacher Flecker did not sign the wedding certificate; instead the signatory is Ernest Hope Flecker alongside Henry Ducat.

The marriage of William Flecker and Sarah Ducat took place at the Church of All Saints, Hatcham, Surrey on 1 August 1881. A week of term remained, and the bridegroom was back on duty at morning school the day after the wedding. No honeymoon was possible; it would be twenty years before they enjoyed a 'real' honeymoon. The honeymoon period in August 1881, was given over to William's plan to engage in study in order to take 'my London degree in October'.[50]

The first weeks of married life were spent in rented rooms facing the church in the Old Town, but these (or the landlady) were not to their liking. A move to a nine-bedroom house not far from New College brought financial problems, although they took in lodgers. These lodgers were Sarah's two younger sisters whom she coached for examinations.

The Fleckers had to move out yet again in order to save money, this time to a smaller house, where they rented rooms. William had given up some of his work at the school in order to study and, as a result, their income would be even lower. Sarah took a post as a daily governess, but when summer approached they were forced to move out once again when their landlady demanded double rent. The summer season was short, but it was not unusual for landladies to take financial advantage of the popularity of the seaside resort in the high season. The Fleckers had to stay with friends until they were able to move to a house still in the process of construction. All this upheaval did not disturb William's concentration and he passed his examinations in Theology. On 19 May 1883, William Flecker was ordained by the Bishop of Chichester.

Early married life for the Fleckers had, of necessity, been a time for sacrifice so that William could attain good examination results. They rose early and maintained absolute silence while William concentrated on his studies. The hard work for examinations was over for a time; they could enjoy musical evenings and had frequent visits from Olive Schreiner, who brought flowers.

No dates are given for these visits, but the impression must be one of her still residing at Eastbourne, where she could drop by without too much trouble during the period when the Fleckers were together at Eastbourne (from August 1881 to August 1884). In reality, during this period, Olive Schreiner was seldom at Eastbourne. She spent the winter of 1881 until March 1882 on the Isle of Wight. She had gone there from London, and would return to the city in an attempt to get publishers interested in her novel, *The Story of an African Farm*. But the fogs of London drove her to the healthier climate of St. Leonards and Bexhill, along the coast from Eastbourne, but not near enough for visiting the Fleckers.

The Story of an African Farm was accepted for publication in 1882, and published early in 1883, under the nom de plume 'Ralph Irons'. It was instantly hailed as a work of genius, and compared by critics to *Jane Eyre* and *Pilgrim's Progress*. Olive began to move in literary circles. She became friends not only with Havelock Ellis but also with Eleanor Marx and her circle. Eastbourne and the people she knew there would appear to be less interesting by comparison. Olive admired Heinrich Heine

(1797–1856), Shelley and Ibsen. She was involved with the Women's Movement. She returned to Eastbourne for family celebrations such as her brother's birthday in November 1883, when a party was held for the headmaster at the school. But she was eventually banned for a time from New College because Fred Schreiner thought that the book revealed too much of their family life to the outside world. Fred Schreiner had read the novel in proof and it was strange that he only banned his sister in 1885. He could not have realised that his sister's novel would be soon selling thousands of copies. He encouraged Olive in her writing (she published stories anonymously in the New College magazine) because it was something she excelled in, unlike her recent attempts at nursing.

It is not revealed what the Fleckers thought of *The African Farm*, especially its freethinking element. The real difficulty in trying to find out the extent of any friendship, and how deep that was, between the Fleckers and Olive Schreiner is the references to Olive, Fred and Will Schreiner made many years later. In the LIFE reference is made to 'F. Schreiner, brother of the well-known authoress'. In the life of William Flecker, Fred Schreiner is referred to as 'brother of Olive Schreiner, the writer, and William Schreiner, the South African statesman'.[51] When William and Sarah Flecker first knew Olive Schreiner she was not yet 'the well-known authoress' nor was William Schreiner as yet a 'South African statesman'. Frederick Schreiner could have been more correctly described as a well-known headmaster, Olive as a not-yet-published writer, and Will Schreiner as not yet a South African statesman.

The Fleckers would have shared Olive Schreiner's interest in Heine, Shelley and Ibsen, and they may have also found a bond through her love for her nephew Wilfred. Olive was convinced that there was sadness in the life of a woman if she never had a child of her own. The pregnancy of Sarah Flecker and the birth of her child in 1884 would be an occasion for Olive to bring flowers. The Fleckers, like Olive Schreiner, were beginning to feel the need to move away from Eastbourne; their ambitions lay outside its environs. The Vicar of Holy Trinity, Lee (then a village south-east of London), was in Eastbourne and he interviewed William for the post of curate. The City of London College School was about to open and William also applied for the post of its first headmaster. He was appointed to the post.

In August 1884, the Fleckers took a house in Gilmore Road, Lewisham, near to Lee. The doctors' insistence, the year before her marriage, that Sarah 'should live permanently out of London'[52] appeared to be no longer necessary. The early years of marriage saw an improvement in the health of both husband and wife, although in Sarah's case moving house while pregnant would not have been recommended if it could have been avoided.

The last two months of her pregnancy were bound to be difficult for Sarah. William would be too busy to give her support. He had to settle into his new post as headmaster of the City of London School, as well as dealing with the needs of his congregation in the evenings, and preaching sermons on Sundays. William was more accessible to his flock than he had been at St. John's Meads and, as a consequence, an abundance of gifts were given to his son, born on 5 November 1884. If the parishioners had a chance to look into the cot they would have noticed that the newborn child was no lightweight. He had thick black hair and blue-grey eyes, which his mother thought gave him an elfin look. Sarah wanted her son (and any future children) to have one biblical name. The baby was baptised Herman Elroy by the Vicar of Holy Trinity Church, Lee on November 30th, 1884. 'Herman' after his father William Herman who had in turn been named after an old friend of the baby's paternal grandfather, Hermann Liebstein. 'Elroy' is a Hebrew word *el-roi*, the name given by an angel to Ishmael, the son of Hagar (the handmaid of the barren Sarah) and Sarah's husband Abraham. In translation Ishmael is 'thou God seest me' or 'hearest me'. The baby made himself heard, if not to God then to his mother, who endured nights of her son's outbursts of relentless screaming and growing demands for her attention. The baby had the full attention of his mother, especially at the Isle of Wight the following year, when his father was in Switzerland. In 1886, pressures grew on Sarah and William, when it was known that the City of London College School was going to move from Moorfields to nearby Catford. The plan was that the school would do better there, although William did not agree. A further pressure was the suggestion by the Governors that fifteen of the pupils would board with the Fleckers, and, if necessary, a bigger house would be found. This suggestion was not acceptable to the Fleckers, and William was determined to resign. His congregation urged him not to do so.

William had already been interviewed for the post of headmaster of a school at Cheltenham, which was to open in May 1886. This school had re-advertised the post of headmaster early in 1886, and out of the eighteen candidates William was chosen.

Herman Elroy was just eighteen months old when he left Lee with his parents for Cheltenham. Much later, he was to write:

'Though I was born a Londoner
And bred in Gloucestershire.'[53]

CHAPTER TWO

Links with the previous life in London were not entirely broken by the Flecker family's departure for the opening of Dean Close Memorial School in May 1886.[54] Most of the fourteen pupils arriving for the first summer term came from the City of London School: their fathers were Evangelical clergymen who were personal friends of the Fleckers. Assistant master, J.H. Harvey, was a 'warm friend'.[55] He was to teach classics and was destined to take Holy Orders; a destiny shared by large numbers of Dean Close School Old Boys. The establishment of Monthly Missionary Meetings would inspire many pupils.

Two women from the congregation at Lee came also to work at Dean Close School. One was to be cook and the other, nurse. A nurse would have more time to spare for Master Roy than his parents, who both had to apply themselves to getting the school up and running. As well as headmaster, William was also bursar and chaplain. Sarah had sole control of the school catering and the domestic staff. None of the masters in the early years of the school were married men. The low salaries and lack of suitable accommodation prevented the presence of wives, who could have helped Sarah with the domestic running of the school. Two married masters were later appointed to be in charge of Houses, but they soon resigned. The House system was not continued under the Fleckers' rule. In order to have structure and competition within the school for athletics, divisions into north, south, west and south-west were introduced. The domestic side of the school remained under Sarah's sole command until her husband's retirement in 1924. But a matron, Matilda, was employed in the 90s, and her appointment was to be a permanent fixture. This would have relieved Sarah of some of her school duties. This arrangement, whereby the headmaster and his wife took so much responsibility themselves for running the school, could be seen as a means to save money. Early in the life of Dean Close School, financial difficulties in the School Capital Account were soon to be evident.[56]

In the early months, a school cricket side (masters also took part in it) was ready to compete in the summer term of 1886. The area around the school was also cleared to provide for the eventual establishment of flower and vegetable gardens. In all this upheaval, the muddy grounds of Dean Close School would not be a safe place for Master Roy to try and explore. However, he would not be safer inside the newly built Headmaster's House, adjoining the school, where, first, it was the ceiling of the headmaster's study that caved in. Luckily, this took place when the study was empty, but Master Roy narrowly missed injury on one occasion when ceilings elsewhere continued to fall.

A caving in of Master Roy's emotional life took place shortly after his third birthday at Christmas, 1887. This was brought about by the birth of sister (Naomi) Claire. The new baby was poorly in health and needed her mother's constant attention, which until then her brother had demanded (not unreasonably) for himself alone. He responded to this new situation with naughtiness and aggression towards his sister. Sarah would have little time to understand or comfort her first-born, as well as her sick baby daughter. She needed a quick solution and this was, it is supposed, to be physical punishment for her toddler son.[57] His mother was also still responsible for the day-to-day welfare of one hundred boys attending Dean Close School. She was to be known by countless pupils as the 'mother of the school'.[58]

Her husband would have even less time in which to help his young son with his outbursts of jealousy. By the next year (in December 1888) William had worked hard, and obtained the degree of Doctor of Civil Law for a thesis on 'The History of Roman Civil Procedure to the time of Justinian'. Physical punishment took place on a daily basis at Dean Close School. Dr. Flecker would see no reason why this form of punishment should not be given to his son. William Flecker had a reputation as a 'flogger', which was said to have given Dean Close School a 'good reputation'[59] – in Cheltenham, at least. This reputation was largely as a result of William giving one older pupil 'a good thrashing' for no immediate misdemeanour, in front of other pupils, after bedtime. William had laughed at the idea put to him by a nervous Sarah that the pupil ('a big fellow for his age') would turn on him. But when the father ('a distinguished man') of the thrashed pupil (who had previously been expelled from his public school) asked William if he would flog the boy again because of something done during the holidays, he replied, 'I don't punish for what is done in the holidays'.[60]

Roy Flecker was not so fortunate. He would have to endure, when at Dean Close School, a double set of punishments; at home and at school. It was said that William Flecker would administer the cane on pupils at the slightest provocation, but that he did not inflict much pain.[61] However, whether this evidence was brought to light by the punisher, or the one punished, is not given. The humiliation of such punishments and the effect on the one punished and spectators are not speculated upon. But Dr. Flecker was of the opinion that such punishments were necessary because 'he needs to feel he is not the master' (and in the case of the son of the distinguished man, that the father was frightened of his son). Dr. Flecker 'enforced his will on his son in school as well as at home'.[62] Roy Flecker also had to endure more day-to-day pressure from his father who 'always provided him with extra help in any subject when he seemed to be failing or lagging behind'.[63]

In 1889, suffering of a different kind overcame the young Master Roy, when he caught diphtheria. It was said[64] to be on medical grounds that his mother was told to keep away from her son in order to prevent the risk of infection passing to his sister, Claire. (But it would seem necessary also to keep the infection away from the Dean Close School pupils, unless the infection did not arise in term time. In 1896, the school had to break up two weeks early due to an outbreak of measles.) Master Roy's distress during this illness was recorded as being due to the prolonged separation from his mother. His grandmother and nurse were said to have very generously given nursing care. But the physical pain of the illness (the swelling and feeling of suffocation when his muscles and nerves were attacked), which the young child would experience, were not sympathised with or given as the cause of the distress. The underlying impression was that the child ('his life was endangered') might have borne the isolation with more fortitude and not cried in vain for his mother (the only explanation given for his tears). In this account of Master Roy's diphtheria, the statement was made that 'Antitoxin was unavailable'. Antitoxin, a drug that eventually brought about a welcome diminution of childhood deaths from diphtheria, was not pioneered until Christmas 1891 (in Germany). It was stated that when Master Roy recovered 'his exasperation remained'.

Convalescence and more exasperation continued in the big south-facing nursery, where the walls were papered with pictures from *Pears* and other children's annuals. A pet parrot and a piano were also in the nursery. Aggression towards his delicate sister continued, once her brother's strength returned. It was therefore decided that Master Roy would be sent to the kindergarten department of Cheltenham Ladies' College at the age of six, but he was removed in a matter of weeks. The reasons for this decision were strange; namely that the teachers at the kindergarten were full of praise for their brightest pupil, who was Roy Flecker. This praise was repeated often and in all innocence to his parents: 'the teacher says I do it best of everybody'.[65] Most parents would be pleased to realise that they had not given birth to the class dunce. But the Flecker parents were not happy to hear this repeated good news of their son's prowess. They thought it was not good for their son 'to measure his abilities against other children in this way'.[66] His mother thought that he would get 'accustomed to praise'. 'There he was *facile princeps*';[67] so he was sent to preparatory school.

In case it could be concluded that Cheltenham Ladies' College was a new school with inexperienced staff, and therefore not in the same category of worthiness as Dean Close, it is as well to realise that Cheltenham Ladies' College was founded in 1853. The headmistress was Dorothea Beale (1831–1906), who was to found St. Hilda's Hall, Oxford, in 1892. The Cheltenham College Kindergarten had been in existence since 1882 and it catered for fifty boys and girls between the ages of three and eight years old. In case it could also be concluded that at Dean Close School the boys were discouraged from measuring their abilities against each other, it is as well also to realise that this was not the case. Dean Close pupils were not placed in forms according to their age, but in eight classes according to their abilities and progress in certain subjects. One class was for Maths and another for Latin, English, etc. The pupils in the First Class for Latin, for example, knew they were the best Latin pupils in the school.

The preparatory school where Master Roy was sent after kindergarten was also not satisfactory to his parents but for a different reason – they thought that their son was being 'forced'. But this objection to being 'forced' was not thought to be wrong by his parents when he was 'forced' to learn to swim at the age of five. The 'forcing' took place at Bournemouth rather than at the Town Baths at Cheltenham, where the Dean Close pupils learned to swim, or in the heated swimming baths built at Dean Close School in 1889. His hatred of the sea had first manifested itself at Sandown, where the low temperature of the seawater could have added to the shock of the experience. At Bournemouth 'he was made to learn to swim', and the 'remedy' was described as 'drastic' and 'little less than torture to him'.[68] It was stated that this hatred of water had to be overcome, and an underlying message was that this hatred of water was something he chose not to overcome. This was illustrated by describing how he was guilty at this time of crossing a stream while fully clothed. It was thought that he could do this because he had a 'passion' for going straight ahead 'which overruled his hatred of water'. If this particular stream was cold, then being fully clothed would help, or it may have been fairly shallow and warmed by the sun and so not as frightening and icy as an expanse of ocean. The sea at Sandown and Bournemouth could be cold even in summer.

The young William Flecker had briefly attended a boarding-school at Clevedon 'but this school was closed owing to a bathing fatality, from the mental effects of which the headmaster [of Clevedon] never recovered'.[69] This memory could have explained why the headmaster of Dean Close School wanted so badly for his son to learn to swim that he was prepared to use force, and why Sarah Flecker donated a Senior Diving Prize to the school.

In another sphere of his education, the Natural Sciences, Roy Flecker was eventually to resent that he had not been forced.[70] The emphasis on the faults of the kindergarten and the preparatory school gave the impression that educational establishments other than Dean Close School were not up to the desired standards required for their first-born, and any other schools they might consider sending him to might have similar faults. Dean Close School would appear to be the only educational establishment worthy of consideration. (Financial advantages are not referred to, but these must have been taken into consideration in the decision.) The drawbacks in sending their son to his father's school would be obvious to an outsider, but at no time did his parents admit to any fault being on their side or that of the school. It was concluded that the unsatisfactory relationship between Roy Flecker and Dean Close School was due entirely to Roy Flecker's personality. His parents though that '... his sensitiveness to his position as son of the headmaster grew to an almost morbid fancy, ...'.[71]

Roy Flecker continued to be portrayed (before he reached Dean Close School as a pupil) as a child with a hot temper. It was recalled that he had battered his sister's head against a lamppost and cut her forehead because (it was said) he resented being collected by his nurse and young sister. But Claire, as the younger child, could have been spared the physical punishment meted out to her brother. She would have been spoiled a little, due to the fact that she was a pretty and delicate little girl. Her brother, young as he was (or as his parents would describe, as 'in a dim childish way'[72]) could have resented the unequal treatment. Claire's jealousy, if she showed any when her sister, Joyce, was born in 1892, was not recorded. If her brother resented the birth of yet another contender for his mother's love and attention, it also was not recorded. Both his sisters were born at Dean Close, and had no disruption in their early lives, unlike their brother; born in London and then moving to Dean Close. His sisters had no experience of going to school in their early years, unlike their brother, who had entered three different education establishments by the age of eight. Joyce and

Claire's early education was in the hands of governesses at home in the Dean Close nursery. (Dean Close school did not admit female pupils until 1968.) An understanding of how their eldest child came to be seen as difficult does not appear to emerge from his parents' account of his young life.

The Fleckers determination (and the reasons behind it) that their son and, subsequently, the rest of their children (a son, Oswald, was born in 1896), should not become conceited or take a pride in his abilities is hard to fathom. His parents discovered that their son, at an early age, had taught himself to read, when he accompanied his mother in the pony-trap on daily shopping trips to Cheltenham. He had asked her to read out the names above the shops. It was said of this achievement that his pre-school education was 'informal' and nothing else. No great pride appears to be attached to this milestone, and others, reached by so young a child. 'He was never regarded as a genius by his family'.[73] It was left to Master Roy to hold up one of his own letters and remark, 'That is not a bad letter for a little boy'.[74]

For this 'little boy' the teaching of religion was something that was 'not bad' because there appears to have been no early source of conflict, or a desire on his parents' part to prevent any showing off of religious knowledge. The Dean Close pupils, masters and domestic staff marched two by two twice every Sunday to hear long sermons preached by Canon Griffiths, another friend of the Fleckers. Master Roy would be too young to join the school procession to the parish church of St. Mark, but he could attend church with his mother from an early age. Or learn at her knee the Bible stories, and be shown pictures of biblical characters in flowing robes smiting rocks in far-away, barren lands. The Flecker parents experienced behaviour from their first-born that could not be classed as 'not bad'. The battle of wills erupted early, but the inevitable punishment would not remove the problem.

Some sort of solace was available in Master Roy's young and turbulent life; something that was beyond his parents' control. From the nursery window a view of the rose-garden, of which his mother was so proud (two photographs of it appear in the LIFE), was eventually to be visible. Beyond the rose-garden lay a row of elms, the Cotswolds and Leckhampton Hill. The beauty of this view was recalled in Roy Flecker's adolescent poem: 'No more his waking eyes will see/ Leckhampton bathed in light,/' (From 'Flakes' published in *Decanian*, September 1899). In adulthood he wrote of '... queer winds like Harlequins/ That seized our elms for violins/ And struck a note so sharp and low/ Even a child could feel the woe./'[75]

Master Roy's horizon was not confined to the view from his nursery window; this was not the limit of the world as he perceived it. He was to hear about the countryside of Wales from 'Your loving daddy', when he got a letter dated 1892 from the Castle Hotel, Brecon, North Wales. His father had just come back from church and was homesick for his 'dear ones'. His son had asked him to tell him 'all about the mountains'.[76] How this initial interest in the Welsh mountains arose is not explained, but the young Roy Flecker would be already familiar with the Welsh lilt in the voices of the Dean Close chambermaids, all of whom came from the same Welsh valley. In his letter, Dr. Flecker did not dwell on the mountains because that would be 'a long business'. Instead, he described to his son the swift-flowing streams and rivers, as well as the valleys. His father also told him of a railway journey and included a railway map. This is in keeping with the space devoted (in the LIFE) to the assertion that the young Roy Flecker had an intense interest in railways and that, when older, he had a desire to be an engine-driver. Much attention is given to the railway line, which ran near to Dean Close School, and his greeting the signalman in the signal-box. Roy Flecker also experienced the rapture of being allowed to get up and inside a railway engine for a brief while. 'Best of all', it was alleged, 'Dr. Flecker, sometimes, had leisure to take him on to the [railway] bridge, on dark winter afternoons...'.[77] The space devoted to the young Roy Flecker's love of the railways near his home gives the impression that he shared this fascination with some of his schoolfellows and boys in general. One reference in the school magazine, to the Banbury line, which ran near Dean Close, was that it was a vantage point from which to catch the first glimpse of the Prince of Wales on his way to visit Cheltenham. In the General Knowledge Prize awarded to Roy Flecker on 26 July 1900, the examiners remarked on the great weakness shown by the entrants on the question of railways. If Roy Flecker shared a love of railways, his schoolfellows would not see him solely as a 'swot' and nothing else. The idea of the headmaster and his elder son sharing an interest outside the internal life of the school suggests a closeness only possible when Dr. Flecker 'had the leisure'. As well as the shared interest in railways, Dr. Flecker superintended his son's learning of Greek. The reason for this was dissatisfaction with the teaching at the local preparatory school, where his parents thought that he was being 'forced'.[78]

It was at this time, in 1893, that Roy Flecker entered Dean Close School as a pupil, where he was known as 'Roy' (not Herman) by the masters, unlike all the rest of the pupils who were addressed by their surnames. He was a day boy, although, unlike the other small number of day boys (known as 'day-bugs'), he was not able to get away from the school buildings when lessons ended. He had to disappear into the Headmaster's House. He ate all his meals during the school day at a table set aside for the Flecker family. He was dressed in a sailor-suit, while all the rest of the pupils wore suits, white shirts and ties.

No privileges were granted to him, and he had to endure a double standard of being under the strict eye of his father at school and at home. He was also supposed to present problems to his masters. It was said of his position at Dean Close School in relation to his masters: 'Passionate and lacking in self-control, he was a trial to his masters since he could not take rebuke in any form and his hastiness, inaccuracy and carelessness often got him into trouble'.[79]

What sort of 'trouble' is not outlined. In addition to the risk of a caning, all pupils were liable to detention every day after morning and evening school. The length of detention could be up to six hours. If four hours of detention were undergone then the 'Monthly Holiday' could be forfeited.

On one monthly holiday, Flecker and another pupil, T.S. Mercer (who also had Huguenot forebears and was the son of a Church of England clergyman 'with extremely narrow evangelical views')[80], both not having been in 'trouble', spent a memorable day looking for fossils in the quarries at Leckhampton. Dr. Flecker did not share this interest with his son, perhaps because of the conflict between the dating of fossils (billions of years old) and the making of the world by God in six days (thousands of years ago). On Darwinian Evolution, Roy Flecker was quoted as saying: 'Surely it makes it all the more wonderful that God should have revealed His love to the world in Christ'; and the conclusion made about this utterance was 'a remark which suggests that his attitude was not merely borrowed and conventional, but had in it some personal interest and thoughtfulness'.[81]

Mercer was invited to tea with some of the Flecker family and, afterwards, he was shown around the rose-garden. He also saw the rose-garden from the window of Roy Flecker's new study, which he was shown around. Mercer was next to encounter the famous rose-garden in the adult Flecker's early poem 'Roses and Rain', the later poem 'From Grenoble' and in prose at the start of *The Last Generation*.

The study, Mercer recollected, was crammed mainly with schoolbooks and dictionaries. This reinforced the view of Mercer and most of the boys at Dean Close; that their headmaster's son was a 'swot'. But Master Roy, before he put away childish things such as picture-books and got his own study, was read to by his mother. She chose the works of Dickens, George Eliot, Carlyle, Thackeray, Longfellow, Tennyson and Browning to read to her children. Copies of these particular works would not, as a result, be in Roy Flecker's study, although Longfellow, Tennyson and Browning were lasting influences. He acquired a copy of *Tales of the Crusades* from his Aunt Rachel around 1893 and it remained a favourite book, as well loved as his little bookcase with red dragons painted on it. *Tales of the Crusades* was published in 1861, and in one chapter, European slaves are treated with great cruelty.

Roy Flecker was appointed librarian during his time at Dean Close School. The school boasted an extensive library and the headmaster encouraged the donation of books. *The Arabian Nights' Entertainment* was one. Books were Roy Flecker's passion: his books, which later he stored at Dean Close School, were so numerous that they began to overflow their allotted space and could be found in a cupboard outside the headmaster's study.[82]

The reputation Roy Flecker acquired amongst his schoolfellows of being a 'swot' is at odds with the complaints made by his parents and schoolmasters that his work was careless at times and he did not like to practise for his music lessons. The books Roy Flecker loved and collected added to the impression of a swot, but, like the recollections of those who took part in his education, it was not the full picture.

Creative activities for the Flecker children were not confined to the nursery, study or drawing-room. Encouragement was given to them and their cousins to try and compose their own poems out loud while on walks with their parents. This method was in the best tradition of past poets such as Wordsworth, who used the stimuli of the open air and countryside to compose out loud with family and friends, and then go home and write the verses down. The Flecker poetry-composing walks differed from those of the great poets in that the theme was decided beforehand by the parents and would be religious. Two lines of a poem composed by a young cousin on one of these walks were published in the LIFE:

> The goats shall go to hell below
> The sheep to heaven above.[83]

Whether or not the children were then encouraged to write the poems down is not made clear but what remained is the memory of the quality of them: 'Oddly enough Roy's were seldom the best...'.[84]

The Flecker parents did not think that the set themes explained for what they described as their first-born's 'rather odd inferiority' in this connection. They went on to state, 'because Roy's fluent capacity for turning out verse on anything was marked at Oxford'.[85] This was not entirely true, because he worked on the set subject for the Newdigate Prize at Oxford in 1906, which was 'Ode on the Death of Shelley', but set it aside uncompleted. 'Fragments of an Ode to Shelley contains the lines:

> Forgive, thou calm and godlike shade,
> The drooping wreath, the flowers that fade,
> This passionless pale offering
> From one who scarcely dares to sing
> His love and praises, being afraid
> At the sweet brilliance of thy spring,

The young Roy Flecker, when he was composing on family walks, may have felt that he was 'one who scarcely dares to sing'. His parents were not afraid that their 'love and praises' on walks might cut down the delicate buds of their son's early verse before they had time to flower. If this was their reason, then it would have been more readily understood. Instead, lack of parental praise it was hoped, would prevent conceit. His parents decided that 'he was far from being the most precocious of the [Flecker] children'.[86] But the lines from Flecker's 'Fragment of an Ode to Shelley' ('This passionless pale offering') illustrate that he knew his efforts could not be compared to Shelley. He did not appear to be conceited when it came to evaluating his own verse, at this stage. When he was still Master Roy he had learned that it was unwise to try and earn praise. This lesson could have been applied to his first attempts at spoken verse. If he spoke some inferior lines then everyone who was listening would be kept happy. Or, even if he gave of his best, someone else in the party would be judged to have done so much better. 'But then I was not a brilliant child', he wrote to his young brother and sister.[87] But it was also said of Roy Flecker that his 'genius developed slowly and surely till it was prematurely cut off'.[88] The use of the word 'genius' suggests that the Flecker parents did not recognise it in their young son at the time, because it was a slow and hidden quality that they could not have been expected to recognise and nourish.

The poetical cul-de-sac in which the young Roy Flecker found himself while on the family poetry-composing walks, and the verbal straitjacket he was fitted with, may have done him no immediate harm. As a result he began to write his poems on loose sheets of paper. One poem was 'The Story of Christopher', described as 'a semi-religious poem'.[89] The poems that followed were mainly 'tinged with religious conviction and feeling'. An untitled poem is described as 'with a subdued religious strain':

Rude Frost! what brooks it that thy breath be chill?
Wild Wind! who fretteth for thy fury fierce?
Rude Frost well-tended flower ne'er may kill,
Wild Wind the cheery cottage ne'er may pierce.[90]

The poem continued by telling the reader 'forget not prayer'. The date of this poem is given as 1897, when the poet was thirteen. and thus written in the winter of that year. The reference to the 'well-tended flowers' would be his mother's prize roses in the Dean Close rose-garden, and the 'cheery cottage' a reference to the small house built in the 1890s at Southbourne, near Bournemouth. The house at Southbourne-on-Sea (to give Southbourne its full name) was built by the elder Fleckers near where a doctor had acquired land on which to build a new health resort. (It was this doctor who called the area Southbourne-on-Sea.) He thought that the air was more bracing than Bournemouth and also suitable for asthma patients. The need for the Fleckers' south coast house may have arisen partly because of the delicate health of Claire Flecker and also the throat operation performed upon their elder son in 1895. This last may have needed a period of convalescence by the sea when the surgeon had done his work.

The Flecker parents tried to play down their son's early ability to write good poems, but they did not use a similar tactic when describing his early capacity for dramatic improvisation. 'Roy's dramatic ability showed early, and stage-plays of a sort abounded in the nursery.'[91] These plays (or games) were based on Bible stories. While demonstrating the Judgement of Solomon, Roy Flecker threatened to cut in half his sisters' beloved rag doll. No praise was forthcoming for this use of props to heighten the drama. It was the same rag doll that he let down from the nursery window in a basket.[92] [93]

The Flecker parents encouraged their children to engage in theatricals, although acting was a form of showing-off and this was something that they had tried to curtail in other spheres of their offsprings' upbringing. It is to be supposed that it was the learning of the biblical stories that was the main outcome, and if this involved a little showing-off then no real harm would be done. But, once again, no credit was given to their first-born's ability as an actor. He was described as an 'indifferent' and it was said: '... constrained to play the Prince in Cinderella he achieved, through natural boredom and vexation, a success which was not histrionic'. [94]

This was not a verdict on an enacted scene from a Bible story, so the Prince might have been uneasy in that particular role. But 'indifferent' as his acting abilities were judged to be, this verdict could have resulted in the development of a play-constructing ability, which did not bore or vex him, but fascinated him and came more easily to him. Much of the published recollections of the Flecker parents' views of their eldest child's abilities are not dated, so the reader has no idea of when he achieved or failed to reach desired standards. It would seem better to look for the records under the name of H.E. Flecker (the name under which they were recorded) in the school magazine. But even in that publication, it was said that references to the headmaster's elder son were deliberately kept to a minimum. It was Mercer who made this observation and it was the Flecker parents who stated that their son never won a prize for English verse while a pupil at Dean Close. But they failed to recall that H.E. Flecker won the Fifth Class prize for English in 1895. In 1897, H.E. Flecker was second in English and, according to Mercer, H.E. Flecker reached the highest place in almost every subject. Mathematics, also according to Mercer, was Roy Flecker's worst subject. It would have created more family difficulties if the son had shown early signs of turning out to rival his father in mathematical ability. Music was the subject in which Sarah Flecker excelled (and one where her husband too had considerable ability), and her son was not likely to exhibit early signs that he would overtake his mother.

It was said that Roy Flecker disliked music practice (which did not make him at all unusual). Sarah Flecker could have become impatient with her son, who took time to master the skills that came so easily to her, or she had practised her musical skills at his age with more diligence and liking. The Flecker children were taught to play both the piano and violin. They joined in action songs until old enough to play more sophisticated music in the drawing-room. But when Roy Flecker graduated to playing in a string quartet in a school concert, it was noted in the school magazine that he 'did well but could have put more work into it'.

Sarah's impatience with her son could have been similar to the way her husband was said to be impatient with pupils (and perhaps his son also) who were perceived to be 'non-mathematical'. The headmaster wrote screeds of figures on the blackboard, and then tried to bully his pupils into understanding what he was trying to prove to them. Dr. Flecker may have been a born teacher who could turn his hand to teaching any subject, but he lacked the necessary patience with less able pupils.

Born teachers (or even those not born, but made) have a tendency to take their teaching skills into their family life. When involved with adults outside school, they can find it hard to throw off their mantle of authority. One of the Dean Close school masters, who was said not to be a born teacher, managed to be a friend of Roy Flecker's out of school hours. This master was T.M.A. Cooper, who joined the teaching staff of Dean Close School in 1890 as the physics master. Cooper was a well-read man, with special knowledge of a variety of subjects including Russia. He was said to be a shy man, which was something his young pupils could easily exploit. Because Cooper was not seen as a born teacher he could throw off his teaching hat, once he had left the school grounds, more easily than some of his colleagues. He was able to form a bond with his headmaster's son, and hold long conversations with him on their walks together. Cooper recalled that Roy Flecker had the ability to translate texts into English and also to produce his own texts in selected subjects. Cooper also remembered Roy Flecker's ability to translate Molière's work. Flecker's sisters thought that, as a child, their elder brother spoke French 'rather badly'.[95] But no mention is made of their brother's ability to translate French into English. In all fairness, their elder brother did not have the advantage, as his sisters did, of having a French governess. The date that this governess and a German governess joined the Flecker household is given as 1895. At that time both sisters were under seven years of age. They would (if this date was accurate) have had an early opportunity to speak French with a native speaker, while their brother did not, to the same extent. Their brother's interest in modern languages 'may have been stimulated' by his sisters' governesses.[96] Cooper took Roy Flecker in early classes in Latin and also geography when his pupil remarked (quite rightly) on the poor geography textbook available. Out of school hours Cooper noticed that his pupil began to take an interest in astronomy. One lecture on astronomy was given by Dr. Flecker, President of the School Field Club. Cooper was Vice-President and Mrs. Flecker donated a magnificent case of butterflies to the club. Lantern lectures accompanied the talks, which included one on 'The Anatomy of the Human Body'.

In order to try and redress the balance of his favourable recollections of Roy Flecker (and at the time of writing down his memories for publication, Cooper was still a master at Dean Close), Cooper commented also on his pupil's inaccuracy and untidiness. Cooper felt that the punishments for this unsatisfactory work were justified. But, without Cooper outlining any examples of these faults and the nature of the punishments (and given by whom?), it is not fair to conclude whether or not Cooper was completely right in his views.

Those who described Cooper as not being a born teacher were not entirely right in their views of him. In allowing Roy Flecker out of the tight bonds and safety of Dean Close School and stimulating his young mind with views of the world outside, Cooper could be seen as well ahead of his time and a true teacher. Cooper wrote: 'He [Roy Flecker] made too much of them ['occasional troubles'] far more than those at whose hands they were inflicted, ever intended'.[97] Cooper continued: 'But they did not amount to anything more that what we all have to put up with and remedy, and in another school, perhaps, neither he nor anybody else would have taken any special notice of them'.[98]

'In another school, perhaps,' is the nearest Cooper came to suggesting that Roy Flecker was bound to be influenced in his behaviour and reactions to punishments by the fact of his being the son of the headmaster of Dean Close School. Cooper's reference to 'that what we all have to put up with' could refer to what Cooper himself, as a shy man, had to endure as a master at Dean Close School. His headmaster was well known for 'an unwillingness to decentralise or delegate authority'.[99] This caused tension with the school prefects and, it is to be supposed, with the masters, who also would feel that they were not fully trusted. It was concluded:[100] 'Flecker, then, ran the School according to his own lights. He taught practically every subject without any special preparation and expected others to do the same. He delegated no responsibility, transacting bursarial business in his own hand. He hired and fired staff, admitted and dismissed boys without consultation.'

Cooper managed, during his many years at Dean Close, not to get himself sacked, or to leave of his own accord, as did many masters under Dr. Flecker's rule. Cooper, along with Edward Ellam, the Senior Classics Master and Heller Nicholls (who took over from Green as Music Master, in 1894) were known as 'the great triumvirate' and 'the heart, soul and body of the School'.[101] These three masters could not have served for so long if they had opposed their headmaster's methods or entertained any new-fangled notions that frequent canings and lack of delegation of authority were not in the best interests of the school.

Shy as he was supposed to be, Cooper (out of the many who helped the young Roy Flecker with his education) was the one who appeared to come closest to understanding him at school and beyond its boundaries. Cooper, many years later, wrote about Roy Flecker and his teachers, although without naming any names. But Cooper, who had spent most of his teaching life at Dean Close School, could not help but including Dr. Flecker in his mind, when expressing these views in print:

> He [Roy Flecker] had no absorbing interest in questions of scholarship, ancient history, philosophical or otherwise, and could not devote systematic study to these things. Anyhow, he never came across the teacher who

could inspire him with such an interest. In fact, in these days, many teachers seem to think that self-interest is the only kind of interest that their pupils require as a spur to industry, forgetting the origin and aim of the studies which is their business to promote.[102]

Whatever would be the real outcome of any future debate about the strengths and weaknesses of the young Roy Flecker while he was in an educational system dominated in all its aspects by his father, much could be made of the fact that it appears that Roy Flecker did well at Dean Close, despite being the son of the headmaster and not because of it. Roy Flecker was recalled on one occasion, when he arrived late for a lesson, as dodging back into a doorway to avoid detection by his father.[103] Roy Flecker could not avoid detection at the Debating Society. Dr. Flecker was president of the School Debating Society, thus his son's participation in the debates could be monitored. The weekly meetings of the Debating Society, particularly those which took place in 1898–9 are of interest. There, Roy Flecker's contribution was recorded in the school magazine on such motions as: Conscription, Freedom of the Press, Fashion, and the Decaying Power of England.

On the motion of Conscription, Roy Flecker thought that a conscripted army would not be as efficient as a voluntary one. He opposed the motion 'That the Freedom of the Press be curtailed' because he considered that this meant slavery to the nation. He saw no harm in cartoons.[104] He supported the motion 'That Fashion is a form of slavery and ought to be abolished'. During the debate on the motion 'England has become a Decaying Power', he opposed the motion because he thought that this was not possible with the fleet to protect England. In a limited sphere in the Debating Society, Roy Flecker gained confidence to speak in front of an audience and to express his views. This was an audience of his peers and masters, and he could have expected toleration, if not praise. But when he was up against pupils from other schools and examiners he did equally well, if not better.

Roy Flecker did well in the Cambridge Local Examinations in 1899 where his work was judged, not by the staff of Dean Close School, but by outside examiners, and he was measured against other entrants, both boys (who were not all from Dean Close School) and girls. The results were published in the school magazine. Roy Flecker was third in religious knowledge, seventh in Greek, nineteenth in Latin and he also gained distinction in these subjects. Dr. Flecker was so pleased with his pupils' results that he added an extra day to the school holidays.

Days off school were valuable in fostering Roy Flecker's interest in fossils, plants and wild life. Longer holidays were even more rewarding, especially those spent at the house at Southbourne, where a love of pine trees began. There he would blend into the background when wearing his sailor-suit.[105]

Roy Flecker also blended into the background when he was old enough, in the summer of 1899 (when the Southbourne house had been given up), to go by himself to a Public School Camp along the coast from Southbourne, at Highcliffe. Here, he could still enjoy the bracing sea air and the Camp's evangelical atmosphere. He was no longer standing out in the crowd solely because he was a son of a headmaster, or having to refrain from showing off due to possible family disapproval. It was said that he was 'the life and soul of the party',[106] which indicated that some form of showing off there was acceptable. He joined in the games and enjoyed himself. He would talk of Christianity 'with deep fervour'. Many of the impressions of Roy Flecker at the Camp were supplied by Cyril Edward Roberts, whose friendship with Roy Flecker lasted beyond Camp days. Cyril was younger (born 1886), and he came from the Isle of Man where he attended a Public School. Roy Flecker would not be the sole representative of Dean Close School – other members of the school would also attend.

When Roy Flecker had scarlet fever in the winter of 1899 he was not able to convalesce at Southbourne because the Southbourne house had been given up. In the period before the house had been given up, its advantage for the Flecker children was its new freedom for them to play at times, unsupervised. This was not to say that the nurse did also not go to Southbourne. Mr. Cooper recollected visiting the Fleckers at Southbourne where the habit of going for walks with his headmaster's son was continued. They went together to nearby Hengistbury Head. In his recollections, Cooper refers to 'the Southbourne home'[107] instead of 'house', which importantly this place was for a brief while for the Flecker family. Cooper also thought that Southbourne had not made an impression on the young Roy Flecker. It was not until Cooper read the adult Flecker's prose and poetry that he realised how far Southbourne had entered the poet's imagination.

It was said that Roy Flecker preferred to wander alone at Southbourne, but he may not have had a great deal of choice when it came to holiday companions. In his poem 'Brumana' he described himself at Southbourne as: '.... lonely boy beneath the tree/ I listened with my eyes upon the sea.' This feeling of loneliness is understandable when for most of his young life up until then, he had lived at Dean Close School. He did not have the freedom to be alone, even when he was old enough to walk to and from school. The reference to 'chosen tree' may have meant that he had a set path at Southbourne and a particular tree he returned to time after time because it afforded him a certain sense of security.

It was at Southbourne that the Flecker family made a long-lasting friendship with Mr. and Mrs. Arthur Bell and their children. The Bell parents were described as 'the one an artist, the other a writer'.[108] It was said that 'Mrs. Bell soon recognised Roy's brilliant gifts, and she dedicated one of her books to him'.[109] This accolade was something the Flecker parents did not strive to play down or tell Mrs. Bell that their eldest child should not be picked out from the rest in this way. This is a rare glimpse of parental pride in their son's 'gifts'. However, in referring to Mr. and Mrs. Bell simply as 'an artist and a writer' readers could not be blamed if they concluded that Mr. and Mrs. Bell were on the fringes of some bohemian crowd, or that they had by chance been encountered by the Fleckers on the sands at Southbourne, while either painting the local scenes or writing about them. Or, even, that Mrs. Bell wrote books for children and not much else. But that was far from the case, as the Fleckers must have known. The Bells were not in the area for health purposes, like Robert Louis Stevenson who resided at Skerryvore between 1885 and 1887. Mrs. Nancy Bell, née Meugens, judging by her body of work, must have enjoyed better health. In addition to her children's books, Mrs. Bell (also under the nom de plume 'D'Anvers') wrote books on Christian art, and science and translated works of Sanskrit and many more. The Bells were well-qualified to recognise the brilliance of the young Roy Flecker. The brilliance of the Bells, in this context, does not appear to have been highlighted by the Fleckers.

In view of all the conflicting opinions on the gifts (or lack of them) expressed about the young life of Roy Flecker, it is as well to record this description of him as 'having been born within a few days of the School's foundation ceremony, spent seven years there during the 1890s before becoming the most distinguished of pre-war Old Decanians.'[110] This group had previously been known as the Dean Close Society. Its president had been Dr. Flecker, who attended regularly the bi-monthly meetings in London.

Southbourne, in adulthood, Roy Flecker felt was a place to build a school. This idea may have been in his mind when he attended the Public School Camp and enjoyed the opportunity to have an extension of school life and the seaside at the same time. Southbourne was, as a boy, the place he 'loved of all places'.[111] When at Southbourne, he grew in confidence; he was able to venture further along the dunes and to the cliffs. But it was the view of the Solent, the Isle of Wight and the Needles that would draw him back.

The notion of building an ideal school could have been further inspired by another stay at yet one more Public School Camp, at Fritton, in 1900. Here, he met up again with Cyril Roberts with whom he had been in correspondence since their last meeting. Cyril looked up to Roy Flecker and told him that he prayed for him and that the older boy was 'a mentor and model'[112]. But what Roy Flecker would appear to need was a mentor and model for himself. He was fortunate to meet someone who was not from the world of evangelical clergymen and schoolmasters. The person who fitted the role was Mr. Locker Lampson.[113] [114]

Locker-Lampson was educated at Eton. He was editor of the *Camp Magazine*, and Roy Flecker was asked to assist him in editing this publication. It was concluded that this was 'a tribute to his literary ability'[115]. This praise for their son's 'literary ability' contains another element of rare parental pride; a person who was to become well known had picked their son out from the crowd. But no further details of Mr. Locker-Lampson are given.

Locker-Lampson, too, had 'literary ability', which had been encouraged by his late father. His second wife (Locker-Lampson's mother) had given birth to his sons when he was in his fifties, and thus was not (unlike William Flecker, in his early twenties, when his wife gave birth to their first son) hampered by a career or other pressures. He could spend more time with his young family. Eleanor was the only child of his first marriage (which took place in 1840). Despite his career in the Admiralty and ill-health, Locker senior still found the time to encourage his daughter's literary education. It was said that Locker 'loved poetry as few men have ever done.'[116]

Locker loved poetry so much that he not only wrote it, but copied out on loose sheets Eleanor's favourite poems. He then stitched the leaves together and bound them in leather. He got the poets who were still alive to sign the various verses.[117] Thus Locker-Lampson's father had friendship, kinship, acquaintance or correspondence with some of the greatest writers of his day; those whom the young Roy Flecker only knew from the printed page. The Locker-Lampson family were aware of Browning, Thackery, Ruskin, George Eliot, Matthew Arnold, Charles Dickens, Swinburne, Walt Whitman, Thomas Hardy, R.L. Stevenson, W.E. Henley and many others. Alfred, Lord Tennyson and his family were perhaps the most important of these literary people. Eleanor married Tennyson's son, Lionel. Above all, with these literary influences Locker-Lampson's father knew how best to tackle the discipline of rhyme, metre and content of poetry and pass this knowledge on to his son in the form of detailed letters.[118]

When the time came to publish details of Roy Flecker's habit of copying his own poems into small manuscript books, his parents do not take any credit or indicate that this habit was acquired entirely by their son without any outside help. They wrote: 'His own attitude to poetry is indicated by his custom, from school-boy days, of copying his poems into small manuscript books with the utmost care'. A few on sheets of notepaper he made into tiny books. But, as a rule, he preferred well-bound manuscript books: these were given a title and an index. One of these,[119] which he sent to his mother from Uppingham, contains a dedication to her, which was probably, however, written at Cheltenham, when he was about fifteen and a half, just before he left Dean Close.[120]

The mention of 'about fifteen and a half' relates to the Easter or summer of 1900 when Roy Flecker was helping Locker-Lampson to edit the *Camp Magazine*. This could be the time when the 'custom' or idea began in Roy Flecker's mind of collecting his poetry together, or it was influenced or encouraged by someone at the Public School Camp, such as 'Mr. Locker-Lampson'.

One of these early notebooks he entitled *Olla Podrida* (a Spanish Stew) and in this he wrote that he had chosen the title because it sounded 'classy'. The notebook does not have a preface in verse because he thought that it would be too much trouble. In the prose of this notebook there continues to run a current of modesty mixed with the showing off, which his parents elsewhere had tried to suppress. Roy Flecker thought that the notebook would be admired by millions, including the Queen, the Prime Minister, the Colonial Secretary and the Poet Laureate. This vision of the universal acceptance of his work as a poet is not so wide off the mark as might be supposed.[121] He described himself as 'a boy of extreme modesty', stated that he did not like praise for his poems and acknowledged that some of the poems were borrowed from other poets but that others were his own work.

The notebook contains an early reference to what was to be a lifelong source of conflict between the poet and his parents. He was guilty of extravagance by spending a shilling on a notebook in which to write 'rubbish'. The description of his poetry as 'rubbish' ties in which the verdict given about his early work, that it was 'deplorable doggerel',[122] but reading through the notebook *Olla Podrida* this cannot always be said. In his poem 'Hymn of the East' (which he later changed to 'Song of the East') there is the immediate feeling that the young poet has managed to begin to capture some of the magic and the rhythms of the East in the lines such as: 'The Eastern Clouds pass the Empurpled mountains of dawn'. The use of 'Empurpled' demonstrated once more the young poet's fascination with colour. But his parents would not entirely agree. They wrote: 'One poem, 'Song of the East', not remarkable for anything else, shows that already, in his schoolboy days his mind was at work on Eastern countries and things'.[123]

It was not remarkable that the young poet's mind was 'at work' on Eastern countries because he would encounter references to them in biblical studies and his geography lessons. But Eastern countries were not remote in their influence. English people returning to Gloucestershire from India or Japan brought to gardens in locations such as Sezincote, near Moreton-in-Marsh, many reminders of the Indian landscape.[124] This garden and another at Stancombe Park, near Dursley, Gloucestershire, had temples, bridges and statues in the Indian style. If the young Roy Flecker did not visit these places himself, he would surely have heard about them in the same way as he heard about the mountains, valleys and rivers of Wales – from those who visited or knew and loved them.

Of later poems in this notebook, his parents referred to a 'Triolet' as 'hardly more than a jest'[125,126] and then stated that: 'The undated Villanelle is a more serious, but only passably successful effort in a kind of composition which is never very easy, and was too artificial and fettering to be really congenial to Flecker'.[127]

Less serious, and written with a good deal of humour, was a poem entitled 'Solemme Tragedie of Miss Brown and Miss Smith'. This was a story of two neighbours, one of whom owned a pet parrot while the other owned a pet cat that killed the parrot. Written in 1899, this narrative poem owed much to Longfellow, although the parrot Roy Flecker knew was the one in the Dean Close nursery, which was often banished by nurse from her domain because it was a source of irritation to her.

The notebook also contained a list of magazines to which the young poet's verses were sent for possible publication. He did not list the poems sent to children's competitions in magazines such as *Chums*, a children's magazine that first appeared in 1892 and cost one penny. *Chums* was not an exclusively fiction magazine, but the stories it did contain were about bravery in strange lands, men and boys battling with eagles and snakes and descriptions of burning ships. *Chums* used Latin phrases in its editorials and was generally thought by parents to be the type of publication (along with *Boy's Own* paper) that their sons could safely read.[128] But this did not appear to be the case in the Flecker parents' eyes. It was emphasised that Sarah Flecker did not encourage her son in the *Chums* enterprise. Her son's poems for *Chums* were described as 'poems on a post-card', which gave the impression that they were inferior to those demanded for competitions for pupils of Dean Close. The Flecker parents could not take any credit for the *Chums* poems that were said to have won him watches amongst other prizes.[129]

Some of the early poems young Roy Flecker copied into *Olla Podrida*, such as 'The Brook' (which he later added to) could come under the 'doggerel' heading. It was written in 1899 but with no more precise dating, it cannot be decided whether or not the influence of someone such as Locker-Lampson later helped him to master the technique of writing poems that could no longer be thought of as 'doggerel'. The mastery could also have been acquired by the translation work undertaken during classes at Dean Close School.

One poem that is more precisely dated (March 1900) is 'Villanelle', which shows a remarkable improvement on the poems given earlier. 'Villanelle' echoes the young poet's view of his Dean Close School masters and his studies of Plato. 'It begins:

Once there was a learned don
Who, wrapped in Plato all the day,
Oft sighed for avro ro ka ov... [130]

Roy Flecker also attempted a 'Triolet' and translations such as Catullus III ('Lesbia's Sparrow') are in the copybooks of 1900, where the influence of his studies at Dean Close could be at work.

If, for Roy Flecker, the printed pages of books (and meeting someone who knew the authors in the flesh) were a source of wider knowledge of the literary world, it was also a book that inspired him to explore the Cotswold countryside. In his notebook *Olla Podrida*, dated Easter 1900, he refers to *A Cotswold Villa* by J. Arthur Gibbs, who died, aged thirty-one in 1899, and was a relative of Arthur Hallam's. The first edition of *A Cotswold Villa* (*Country Life and Pursuits in Gloucestershire*) was published in 1898 and the third edition in 1899.

At Easter, 1900, Roy Flecker wrote in *Olla Podrida* of starting out late in the morning by bicycle and 'shaking the dust of Cheltenham from our feet' (Dean Close had a Bicycle Club, which may account for 'our'). He cycled past 'undesirable freehold villas' until he came to the reservoir, where 'the fresh zephyr made quite respectable foaming wavelets on the waters'. He had a 'right hearty lunch on a grassy bank by the roadside, near the shelter of a wall 7 miles from Cheltenham'. The 'favouring breeze' allowed him to coast on the level for a mile and a half. He could stop for 'good ginger beer' at an inn.

The poems that Roy Flecker wrote in *Olla Podrida* before his venture into the Cotswold countryside are of a less down-to-earth nature. One poem, written in 1899, 'The Dream Child' (A Fragment) has the lines which are amongst the earliest on the poet's lifelong subject, death:

The father lay awake that night heavy was his heart
Mourning his treasured darling from whom he had to part.

'The Dream Child' could be based on the death of one or other of his grandparents. Another poem also written in 1899 was 'The Brook', and it would be one of the poems he admitted 'borrowing' from other poets, two lines of which are:

From the mountain crag I gush
Down the mountainside I rush.

His fear of water appears in this poem to have been overcome.

Even if Roy Flecker never won a prize for English verse while he was a pupil at Dean Close School he was later to write: 'The Age when such poems are written precludes their being good: still more the necessity of writing at length on a subject dictated by another'.[131]

The *Decanian* quoted in August 1900 some lines from his poem 'The Dying Century' (the set subject for the school poetry prize), which was unsuccessful in the eyes of the adjudicator, subsequently known to be Mr. Cooper. One (unwritten) reason for the lack of a prize could be that the son of the headmaster wrote it. The lines quoted were:

Red rose the sun a hundred years ago;
Red rose the sun upon a troubled main:
With blood-red stain
He streaked the sullen billows far and wide,
And gorgeously he dyed
The sapphire robe of heaven with scarlet hue;
And o'er the surging sea, the petrel flew,
Emblem of rising restlessness and might,
Within the ocean breakers flaked[132] with white. [133]

'The Dying Century' is set alight by the poet's use of bright colours. But this use of red, scarlet and even the 'sapphire robe of heaven' could seem to be extravagant, and in his parents' eyes a more subdued approach and reverence for the passing of time would be acceptable; not only in this poem but in others of their son's.

War was in progress between the Boers and the British in South Africa, a country Dr. Flecker was familiar with after his association with

39

the Schreiners at Eastbourne. A former Senior Prefect, R.G. Brooke was killed at the Relief of Mafeking in 1900.

1900 was Roy Flecker's last year at Dean Close School, and a decision was taken by his parents to send him to Uppingham School. There, he would no longer stand out in the crowd because he was the son of the headmaster or be known by his Christian name. At Uppingham School, he would be known as Flecker.

CHAPTER THREE

Queen Victoria died at Osborne House on the Isle of Wight in the evening of 22 January 1901. On 24 January, despite the grief and the uncertainty as the nation entered a new age, on his arrival at Uppingham School, Flecker appeared to be concerned only with mundane matters. After he had been taken round and shown his study, he sent his parents a telegram: 'Arrived safe. Please send eggs and jam'.[134]

He needed the jam for tea, after which he mixed with his fellow pupils in Meadhurst, the house he had been assigned to, and for that evening at least he 'got along grandly'[135] with the rest, in his first experience of the House system. That night he slept in one of 'those pernicious partitioned dormitories, which so obviously foster vice'.[136] On his first night he was disagreeing with the ideals of Edward Thring, headmaster from 1853 to 1887, who had installed the cubicles in an effort to give the boys more privacy.[137] Thring's idea that privacy gave boys an opportunity to behave well was not one which was borne out in practice.

Next morning he awoke to electric light; Mr. Haines, his housemaster, owned a dynamo as well as two peacocks, 'which wake me up at 6.30 with a noise like a fog horn with a cold'.[138] After chapel, which was at 8 a.m. because it was a Saint's Day – ('That everlasting chapel with its murky Gothic ritual – and before breakfast too, what a fearsome way of beginning the morning')[139] – he had breakfast (for which he needed the eggs). Flecker then faced a long talk with his housemaster.

Reginald Haines, MA, FSA Hist., formerly of St. Catherine's College, Cambridge, had arrived at Uppingham in 1887, from a post of assistant master at Dover College. He had been in charge of Meadhurst since the closing of Red House in 1894, and he taught the Lower Sixth. He had a keen interest in writing poetry and the works of Housman and Edgar Allan Poe, but he suffered from ill health of an unspecified nature, and as he was tall and thin, he had earned the nickname 'Hungry Haines'. He was one of 'Those withered trees ... usually surrounded by the fair and delectable shrubs of youth: they look ill in a forest by themselves'.[140]

Haines, during this interview, offered Flecker the prospect of looking after a dormitory, later in the term. The only sixth former in Meadhurst, he was slightly older than the dozen new boys who had arrived with him, and as the son of a clergyman and headmaster, he had an added advantage over most of his fellow pupils; he had experienced a strict religious upbringing and religion was the school's means of instilling moral principles. Religious priggishness, Flecker thought, was the only way to deal with 'compulsory vice'[141] in schools, and this compensated for his lack of prowess at games, which was the main qualification for any sort of leadership post. Haines, who was said to believe what he was told by pupils on their word of honour,[142] initially may have been taken in by Flecker's attitude to dormitory discipline, not seeing that the priggishness was a necessary cover for his immaturity in such matters, and that his knowledge on the subject of vice had been obtained at second-hand.

After the interview with Haines, Flecker went down to the school at 10.30 and 'colonnaded' until 11. This, he afterwards wrote to his parents, consisted of 'standing in the colonnade and being cold and trying to talk'.[143] Like chapel before breakfast, this tradition was uncomfortable and not likely to improve the pupils' health, especially on cold damp mornings.

He went next with his violin under his arm to see the music master, and, as he had done with colonnading, found himself up against a tradition that he did not feel happy with. 'I know there are some who consider music to be the purest and best of arts, because it requires for its comprehension no external intellectual effort, but makes a direct appeal to the emotions'.[144] But whatever he thought, music was more firmly woven into the fabric of Uppingham School than any subject at Dean Close, where, as yet, traditions were few. Thring had been especially interested in music, which he had said 'was the only thing that every country, both sexes could do equally well'. Music and games at Uppingham had been part of Thring's plans for boys to gain self-respect. As Thring himself had no musical ability, the music master had, since his appointment in 1865, built himself an empire with several assistant masters. Thring's German wife had brought the love of, and interest in, music.

Herr David, violinist, who was the son of a famous violinist, a former pupil of Liszt, and from Mendelssohn's School in Leipzig, not surprisingly told Flecker that he had not been under a strict enough teacher, and that he needed training in technique. When relating this to his parents, Flecker made fun of Herr David's accent and added, 'So I'm going to get it hot evidently'.[145] It was obvious that he was not going to get the better of the situation, or be allowed some praise for the talent and work he had put into his violin playing, or be allowed to enjoy music for its own sake. Flecker kept 'forgetting' to practise, and on more than one occasion he 'forgot' a music lesson. If he was not going to be praised highly then he was not going to co-operate in the music field. Underlying this rebellion, or the result of it, was Flecker's feeling 'that my enthusiasm for music is not so great as my enthusiasm for the arts of representation'.[146] Flecker had already got 'an ear for the subtle music of words'.[147]

At first, schoolmasters at Uppingham could not win his approval. Herr David, who could be seen as a success in his chosen profession, was mocked for his mannerisms: 'I have known only too many good musicians, especially those who were simply good performers, who outside this one specialised atmosphere were not only stupid, but exhibited the most appalling mental vulgarity'.[148]

Haines, whom Flecker did not see as a success, was also mocked. Haines and Flecker continued to be locked in a tug of war that neither had the strength to win. 'If Haines should make me a praepostor, which there is no earthly reason why he shouldn't, I might do even more.'[149] Flecker also could not resist poking fun at the earnestness of the headmaster, the Rev. Dr. Edward Carus Selwyn, in a way that he could not have done to the headmaster of Dean Close.

In mocking the headmaster and writing about him to his parents in a derogatory fashion, he was letting them know that he was still loyal to his old school and its Head. In one letter he wrote to his parents and told them that he had 'nothing really terrible to do as yet, except Sunday Qs, for the Rev. Carus.... I enclose a copy of the questions'. He then asked his parents if the Museum would 'like them to put with the other antiquities?'[150] Sunday Questions were designed by Dr. Selwyn to stimulate his pupils' intellects and had to be searched out in the library, a task that took most of the day. Even if a pupil was eventually going to follow a deeply religious path, 'Sunday Qs' were not a pleasant memory. A pupil remembered them as 'of fearful difficulty'.[151]

Sundays at Uppingham were the busiest days of the week, but were always going to prove irksome. First, Flecker needed a tail-coat for Sundays, then he discovered the service was chanted from end to end, and that he had to endure two chapels, one without a sermon and one with a sermon.

The rest of the school week consisted of three half-holidays, which was one of the pieces of news relayed to his parents in his first letter home. It might have been expected that this amount of freedom during the week, would be welcome, but Flecker saw the advantage of a different sort of arrangement of free time, which would also help with the tedium of Sundays, and the need to remain indoors on cold, wet winter afternoons when the light faded early: 'There should be two half-holidays a week in the winter terms with a short and interesting hour's work in the late afternoon, but three full half-holidays a week in summer; and every opportunity should be given to boys for spending their Sundays in excursions over the country side...'.[152]

The letter about the half-holidays contained a request for pictures for his study. He also needed picture-hooks; a rule forbidding the use of nails was in force. His own study was bare, with only a few photographs and very small china pots. His parents sent some framed reproductions and more photographs, which he thought would do for that term. Next term he intended to take more from home and some ornaments. He told his parents about a shop nearby (Uppingham Village had a market square with small shops). He would have gone there for his possible purchases 'but I fear you would think it foolish'.[153] In case his parents thought that they had right on their side, he told them of a fellow pupil who had more than sixty framed pictures in his study. This was more a case of blackmail than a desire to be the same as his fellow pupils; his parents were inclined to think of him as extravagant.

The telegram on his day of arrival should have warned his parents of more demands to come, but if differences began to crop up, they could be seen as due to defects in the catering arrangements at Uppingham, which were open to abuse. Mrs. Flecker, more than most mothers, would know how to deal with them,[154] but even she did not appear to be entirely successful. It was easier at first, and then became a habit, to blame their son for extravagance, rather than take up the cudgels with the school authorities over such small matters. However, their son was not going to take it lying down. He wrote: 'What is life without jam? Nothing for breakfast, nothing for tea: and how long does a pot of jam or even marmalade last?'[155] The tussle with his parents over what was necessary and what was an extravagance also started over very small matters, such as football shorts; he explained to his parents that wearing these four times a week for seven weeks meant that 'the said shorts are apt to get, ahem, inconvenient'.[156] As he could not play in trousers, which would hamper him and get dirty, and he could not play in bathing drawers, his parents would have to supply the remedy. He thanked them with 'unbounded gratitude' for having clean stockings on his feet.

He did appear in the matter of laundry to be conforming, but the rest of his fellow pupils, it was said, thought him to be 'simply a 'freak'.[157] In a school where the herd instinct was inevitably fostered, the title of freak, for a number of reasons (the starting-off point being physical appearance), was not hard to acquire. There had been at least one other recent contender for this title, (Arthur Annesley) Ronald Firbank (1886–1926), who was shy and ill at ease with his own appearance, and could be seen as strange. Firbank had arrived at Uppingham in the summer term, 1900, and had been so unwell that he had survived the school regime for only two terms, leaving at Christmas to continue, when his health improved, his education with a private tutor. His family could afford this financially. Ronald Firbank, born in London, was the son of Sir Thomas Firbank, MP.[158] His father had been one of the largest railway contractors, who had started his working life, aged seven, as a coal-putter, then coal miner. ('But you know well enough that our best and most venerable public schools contain numbers of boys whose grandfathers were, shall we say, shoeblacks.')[159,160] The fact that Firbank's family was nouveau riche, and Firbank, homosexual, added to the lack of success that Firbank experienced with the rest of the pupils.

The recollection about Flecker being a freak, was supplied[161] by Charles Raven (1885–1964) who had been born and brought up in London. He was the son of a barrister (who had been brought up in New Zealand) and a mother who had, with his father, given him a love of the countryside. Raven had been sent to Uppingham in 1898 after winning a scholarship. Raven needed the scholarship or he would not have been able to attend Uppingham, where he was in his uncle's house, Fircroft. In a sense, Raven suffered from being under the eye of a relative, as Flecker had been at Dean Close. Thus, Raven might have been just a little more understanding of why Flecker tended to stand out from the crowd. It was a case of his always having been the odd one out on account of his dress and appearance at school, his 'remarkable literary power' (which was how Raven described it) and also his genius, which all the boys were supposed to have recognised instinctively, although it is difficult to conclude that they would have liked him for it. But in all fairness to Raven, he may have found it impossible to compare of the life that Flecker had led at Dean Close, as the headmaster's son, and the life he himself led at Uppingham under his uncle's eye. Even if he had, the comparison would not have found its way into the LIFE, or after the passage of time he may not have made the connection. Although Raven described Flecker as a 'freak', he did not make any direct reference to Flecker's appearance, which was much more likely to have provoked such a description.

Raven's autobiographical writings[162] paint a better picture of how he felt as a sensitive pupil at Uppingham. Although he came to Uppingham at the age of thirteen, rather than sixteen like Flecker. Raven's experience of unhappiness at Uppingham would be nearer to Flecker's than many of the others who came up to Uppingham in the same period. Raven and Flecker had a religious upbringing but Raven did not stand out because of his appearance; he had good looks. The fact that Flecker and Raven were in different forms and Houses, and that the Houses were not close together, were part of the reason why they did not become close friends at Uppingham. Raven was not outstanding at games either, he was a self-confessed bookworm and he continued his interest in the natural world. From the sanatorium where Raven was incarcerated during his first spring term, he had been fascinated by the abundance of birds, not only the common sparrows, hedge sparrows, and blackbirds, but also the chaffinches and finches, robins and thrushes. Raven learned to observe the wild life accurately and he had friendships for a time with boys who had the same interests.

Raven was well aware of the interpretation that Dr. Selwyn put on close friendships at his school, and how strict a disciplinarian he appeared to be in such matters. Raven went as far as to say that 'indeed if two boys of unequal age and different houses were seen speaking, immorality would be taken for granted'.[163] Flecker was older than Raven. So, if Flecker was to rebel against the somewhat blinkered regime of Dr. Selwyn, he would have to do it in a less conventional mode, if he was to avoid the fate of some of his fellow pupils.

Dr. Selwyn's punishments did not always achieve what he had intended, when he decided to stop what he saw as immorality and other sins taking place in his school. But it was possible that he did not act entirely alone, as it was said that one housemaster used to creep about in his carpet slippers in order to spy on pupils and catch them out.[164] As this particular housemaster went on to be a headmaster of another well-known school, the practice (and the memory of it) could have been one for the other masters to copy and so curry favour with Dr. Selwyn. Eight expulsions had taken place in one term and Flecker told his parents, 'I need not tell you what the fellows were sacked for'.[165] The particular sin is not mentioned by name, but it demonstrated that vice was a problem that must have been dealt with at Dean Close, and that Dr. Selwyn and Dr. Flecker had similar views. Flecker told his parents that his House Captain, on Dr. Selwyn's instructions, addressed the House, which he described in terms 'to move you to tears, but nothing further'.[166] Dr. Selwyn, he went on to tell his parents, was going to preach a 'vehement sermon' to masters and boys. Whether

Dr. Selwyn attached any importance to the partitioned dormitories and vice in his school, is not known. Not all dormitories were thus, as they are described as being 'open' in Raven's day.[167] The idea of the House system at Uppingham, whereby the Houses were apart from each other and supposed to resemble a family rather than an institution, posed problems of co-ordinating the system so that the headmaster knew what went on in each House.

Flecker did not agree with Selwyn's decisions in the matter, 'We shall not expel boys; and we shall not, like the conventional headmaster, pretend to faint with horror when we discover others acting as we might perhaps with a little temptation have acted ourselves, had we ever been members of so monastic an establishment as a public school'.[168] Flecker's own feelings on the question of vice were remarkably detached: 'Emotional purity in the young is to my mind an insidious form of indecency. It is laying too much stress on things. The normal boy troubles as little about the matter as possible: and he is perfectly and entirely right'.[169] He did not agree with Selwyn expelling boys for smoking 'if they are caught smoking ... we will not weep over the enormity of the offence, but deal with it succinctly'.[170] Yet he was not against maintaining discipline with the rod. He admitted that there was 'a certain peril of the flagellant vices, but a risk could be run for the sake of 'considerable advantages'. He would not lend himself to the 'sentimentalists who consider it degrading to endure physical pain'.[171] He considered punishment to be absolutely necessary in a large school. He was also in favour of detention, but not the giving of 'lines'. He would not go as far as returning to the days of floggings, which he thought 'were a real and serious evil'.[172] He did not want to return to the days of *Tom Brown's Schooldays*, but he felt that the school system he knew about was much better than the Continental system, especially the German – 'the lives of German schoolboys, embittered by the deadly gymnastics, the huge classes, the incessant cram, the perpetual and ruinous horror of the final examination. Think of the ghastly statistics of child suicide in Prussia. Is it not this appalling system that is making the modern German so different a man from the old – is making him the great brutalising force of the world?'[173] Some pupils of German origin were at Uppingham in Flecker's time.

Flecker appeared to blame the system, but a contemporary, a German poet Georg Heym (1887–1912), who wrote to his provincial board of education about the child suicides, also complained to the board about his headmaster (known to his pupils as 'Bloodhound') who, like Dr. Selwyn, deplored his pupils' smoking and drinking and 'something else', which was not talked about. Heym did not think that the 'Bloodhound' was a fit person to be a teacher, and he pointed out that those pupils who left were those whose parents could afford to take them away and educate them elsewhere.[174] Although some of the 'Bloodhound's methods may not have found an exact parallel at Uppingham (Heym, as a sixth former, informed the board that pupils who owned up to their misdeeds were told that they would not be punished, but when they owned up they were nevertheless punished). Heym seemed to think that if a teacher had behaved like that in England, he would have been dismissed on the spot, but this was over-optimistic; it was usually the pupils who had to go. Selwyn at Uppingham gave his pupils the freedom of three half-holidays, but then punished them for taking too much freedom, such as 'the attendant evils of these excursions – the irate farmer whose horse has been ridden round a field, the boy with the catapult, the boy who goes to a public house to be grand and drinks a mug of beer, and the boy who surreptitiously buys Black Dog cigarettes – are not very terrible after all, and the attendant advantages are too great to be missed'.[175]

Both Heym and Flecker failed to realise that their development as writers of potential genius was partly due to the harshness of the education system that they endured. Had they been allowed to escape to a more tolerant regime, their reaction would not have been so extreme and their desire to be poets would not have been so immediate. In their condemnation of Dr. Selwyn and the 'Bloodhound' they were transferring to these two figures their own feelings about their fathers, who had sent them to the schools in the first place. The German educational system may have been responsible for brutalising the modern Germans, but Uppingham ex-pupils in the Boer War and in subsequent wars were not reluctant to join the army and fight. Selwyn made sure that all pupils knew how to shoot.

Norman Douglas (1868–1952), a diplomat and travel writer who had experienced Uppingham School and the German educational system, knew of the suicides in German schools, but he felt that he had 'a secret but healthy contempt for all education', which he had acquired in England and that he would not be caught attempting suicide for any lack of achievement at school.[176] Uppingham, it was said, under Thring and his wife who gave 'the help of a powerful mind trained with German thoroughness to high educational ideals', was therefore influenced by German educational methods.[177]

Selwyn's methods of tackling what he saw as immorality at Uppingham School were nothing new; he appeared to be following in the footsteps of Thring. Thring had tackled zealously the need 'to arm boys against the inevitable struggle against their own lower nature or against the influence of evil associates'.[178] Thring saw that ignorance was at the root of the evil and that the mystery in which sex was wrapped did nothing to help, although he did not want to go as far as educating the boys in matters of sex. So he made sure that every one of his pupils knew about the dangers of lust, and he divided the school into three different sets and warned them against indecency. Thring was in favour of severe floggings, always administered at noon precisely, to any of the boys who erred. If this failed, he expelled the pupils, objections of parents notwithstanding; mercy was not something he would agree to, although he admitted to 'slight mercy' if a pupil was what he described as 'wilful'.

One former pupil (and he would not be alone) told Thring that he frightened him so much that, although he tried his best, he got into 'an utter muddle'.[179] This particular pupil may not have been referring to sex, but all pupils must, as a result of Thring's views, have been in a muddle about sex – as much of a muddle as Thring himself must have been.

Although Flecker was rid of 'the great curse of day schools [which] is that boys should live perpetually with their parents',[180] he was still under his parents' influence, which he found to be 'deeper, finer, more pathetic when transmitted through loving letters and accepted in loving replies. The individual parent who, being human, must have foibles, is sunk in the ideal parent, the loving watcher over the destiny of his far-off child.'[181]

These feelings about his parents' supervision from afar were intensified by their complaint that he had sent five letters in ten days that merely outlined his wants. He took the broad hint, and told his parents about his progress in school-work. In doing so, he demonstrated how he was dealing with supervision at the Uppingham. He told them that he had forgotten to do some verses, 'which had to be shown up before breakfast'.[182] ('There should never be any work before breakfast at all.')[183] Dr. Selwyn was annoyed and said he wanted them done as soon as possible. Flecker rushed through the whole 16 hexameters in 25 minutes, which amazed the headmaster, who thought that the work must be very inferior, and was surprised that Flecker got 27 marks out of 30.

This method of defiance and then compliance seemed to work, as he then got 93 out of 100 for Latin Grammar; he had never got more than 90 before. As the first term came to an end he wrote to his parents: 'Selwyn the immortal set me for last copy of Latin verses *gratae vices*, the pleasures of change, metre according to choice ...'.[184]

He was making progress (he wrote to his parents) in understanding pictures and he had bought or 'invested' in a reproduction of a painting entitled *Ulysses deriding Polyphemus* framed – (original painted by Turner in 1829). This picture reminded him of Southbourne.[185] He also bought four of the 'excellent "hundred best" prints'.[186] He was also getting a better appreciation of music, and a whole day was devoted to a small Plato exam, rehearsal and concert.

Amid all this activity at school, he had some time to himself and 'for amusement', he told his parents, he had 'versified most of Pervigilium Veneris: and have concentrated my execrable habit of scribbling into a single effort, and have finished my long poem – nearly 700 lines!'[187] The poem was 'Phaon, A Tale of Days Gone By In Twelve Idylls', which he had written out in a pocket-book with a dark red spine and a brown, gold and red-speckled cover, measuring 5 by 3 inches. The poem's dedication was to the reader, but the poem Inscription at the back ended with the lines:

Yet strange to say
O Mother mine
I offer the tune to you.[188]

In case anyone thought that his mother would be pleased to receive this offering, the last sentence of his letter about 'Phaon' read: 'Which *sans doute,* especially if I ever read it to you, you will consider an utter waste of time'.[189] The pocket-book also contained a translation of 'The Vigil of Love' from *Pervigilium Veneris.*

In his versification and creation of 'Phaon', he had found the link with his own conflicting feelings of homesickness and love of exotic lands, and made some sense of them. 'Phaon' was the story of the search of Phaon for the father he had never seen, and Flecker wrote lines which were reminiscent of Southbourne: 'The sea, the cliffs, the escalading pines.'[190]

In 'Phaon' too he found a place to express his feelings about a lecture he had attended on Sicily, when he had watched on lantern slides good photographs of the eruption of Etna (which interested him more than the date of the eruption which he thought was about 1893). He wrote:

They sailed beneath Italia's pastured shore,
And saw the sable throne of night afire
Where, northward Etna flooded into flame
And cloaked the stars with whirl of sulphur cloud.[191]

The lecturer who had shown the pictures of Etna had, amongst other qualifications, FRGS, but he was sneered at by Dr. Selwyn because he had said that he had 'a gross ignorance of the classics'.[192] This indicated that Dr. Selwyn would not welcome a pupil's work in praise of the lecture; impressions of that kind were best left 'for enjoyment', and buried in 'Phaon' where Dr. Selwyn would not read them, but the poet might hope his parents would approve them. Two more poems written at this time showed the influence of another lecture; this time the subject was the Boer War and the titles were: 'The Warrior's Return' and 'The Warriors Return in Summer'. They contained the lines:

Home from the land of drought and parching sun,
Home from the hillside steeps where death is dealt,
Home from the great grey ocean of the veldt.[193]

Flecker told his parents about the Boer War lecture, and related how the lecturers had given 'a good clear account of the manoeuvres of Buller'. He had already told them in the letter about Dr. Selwyn wanting him to join the Rifle Corps. Dr. Selwyn did not pour scorn on the credentials of this lecturer, who was a Fellow of All Souls', and captain of the Oxford Cricket XI. The subject of the Boer War was of great significance to masters and pupils of Uppingham. Two hundred and twenty former pupils had fought in the Boer War, and nine had given their lives. One who had returned was Captain Jones, M.A., whose arrival at Uppingham was described vividly in a long letter to Flecker's parents: [194]

On Saturday the conquering hero, Captain Jones, came. By a stretch of unparalleled generosity we were let off half an hour school and a half on Monday. The Rifle Corps parade in vast solemnity down to the station; our drummer looks resplendent in his leopard skin. You will find him somewhere beneath the big drum. The fifes give a little squeak rather out of tune. The civilians line the palings, the élite of Uppingham keep the other side of the road discreetly. Punctual for once in its eventful and irregular life, the smoke is seen half a mile away. Someone suggests a luggage-train and we groan. But it is the proper sort after all. In ten minutes the half-mile is covered, and five astounding pop-guns proclaim its momentous arrival. A long wait in the station; we hope for the sake of the corps that it is the wrong train. But no, a slim figure in khaki emerges and a rather erratic wave of cheering arises. Captain H, after a soldierly embrace, gets him to walk at the head of the corps.

Then again the boom and squeak, and to the school march the glorious vermilion crowd, followed by a vast and seething throng of smart-clothed civilians. The masters assemble on the green in the quad. The chief robes himself in a great hood like a red ensign fluttering in the wind. The corps form an inner circle, we an outer. Sedgwick bawls forth his peroration – rather spoilt by a babe belonging to the élite who formed the inevitable rear. Captain Jones also bawls forth some soldierly words apropos of the corps, and there are more cheers, and one side sings *God Save the King*, and the other doesn't, and the solemn and impressive ceremony ends ....

'The Conquering Hero' (who was to take over from Mr. Haines and become housemaster of Meadhurst when Haines retired to the country in 1905) was someone Dr. Selwyn would wholeheartedly approve of, whilst the science master received none of the honour and glory, giving further proof of the headmaster's neglect of science as a subject, as did the crumbling buildings:

'Until very recent years, it was almost impossible for a boy of any ability to escape from the classical tradition or to get any sort of acquaintance with the sciences. In my own school, where Thring had lived and laboured, there was in my time only one science master, Howson, afterwards the second founder of Gresham's School, Holt. Yet he failed to secure any pupils except those incapable of progress in classics or mathematics, and ruined by years of unprofitable drudgery; and, when he left, his successor found his laboratory a bear-garden, his apparatus grossly defective, hardly a single microscope, and no balances that weighed accurately. We grew up totally ignorant not only of biology, but the whole scope, meaning and method of scientific studies.'[195]

In some respects, it was just as well that science was not a subject of great importance as Flecker had difficulty enough when it came to coping with the subjects already set before him. Whatever happened, he was going to get a bad report. The wet weather at the end of term did not help his mood of despair, as he tackled the much-disliked exams. He knew he was not going to shine as he had already done badly in the music examination and he had to prepare for a history examination. However, he told his parents that he did not mind about the form master's report; he thought that these marks did not count. This statement about the marks, which he followed by telling his parents 'I mind very little',[196] was more an act of bravado, even if the marks did not count, and success or failure depended on more important examinations, which would come at the end of the school year. It would have been better if the marks had been good and he would have pleased his parents too.

The difficulties he had in coping with school-work and what he described as 'weekly papers' reflected in some respects his being away from home for the first time, and adjusting to new masters and fresh ways of teaching in a form where he was the youngest.

During his time at Uppingham the body of Queen Victoria had lain in state until the funeral at the beginning of February. In January 1901, Flecker had written in each notebook (D243 and 244) separate versions of a poem 'Song' (the version was given the title of 'Le Nuit d'Hiver' in his notebook D244). The subject of these two versions was: 'The Queen who is Queen of the night'. The poem told how, in a peaceful and still night, when 'Deep lay the snow' quaint little elves in 'jerkins green' and 'dear little fairies' danced until they 'scurried away' when the 'cock crowed'.

The dating of the two poems, January 1901 for the first, written before he left home for Uppingham, and February 1901 for the second, provide a useful dividing line between Flecker's childish view of a Queen and the more sombre thoughtful one of death. Not only do these two poems form a useful connection for him between the Queen's life and death and his own life, which had changed as drastically, almost overnight, as had the life of the nation, but the world outside had a drama unfolding, while the life at Uppingham went on as before and any changes were of a very much slower and monotonous kind.

The versions of another poem[197] had images of 'hoary winter' and 'season of the dying year' and of a 'chilly vault' and contained the line 'Still the lumbering wheel must turn/Still the books upon me ply'.

At the Tercentenary of Uppingham School in 1887, the school choir had performed an elaborate cantata, 'Under Two Queens' with words by the Rev. J.H. Skrine and music by Herr Paul David. If Flecker had heard a repeat performance of this work, he could have drawn inspiration from it.

The death of Queen Victoria, although greeted with sadness and universal mourning, was the start of a new age under a king who was sweeping away past restraints, which to a certain extent was the case in Flecker's own life. In March he returned to his sombre mood in two poems, one called 'Truth' and the other 'To On'.[198] 'Truth' began with the line: 'Are we to live with never a to-morrow?'[199]

The long seclusion of Queen Victoria after the death of Albert, was also something he seems to be beginning to question when he wrote to his mother. 'And how would the true and sincere Christian look upon the passing away of one he loved? With unfeigned joy. He would not wear black, or shrink from festivity among his fellows. Only if the snapping of the string were painful might he be allowed a tear. Why do we mourn? Because we have lost the guidance, the counsel, the love of one who was dear to us? A selfish mourning. But we are not ideal Christians: we do need a physician, and therefore we must have our fill of sorrow.'[200]

His poem 'The Babes in the Wood' had a more final view of death, and to illustrate how he altered his versions which appeared in both notebooks, the last lines of each read:

But the kiss of sunshine found them clasping, dead. [201]
But the kiss of morning found them clasping, dead. [202]

Both versions were dated March 1901. Another poem with the theme of a queen, this time a Syren Queen,[203] is thought to be related to his time at Uppingham. The poem had the title 'The Shadow of a Dream' and the first line is 'Launch the fairy craft'. It includes the image of the mocking Syren Queen and the reader is told not to 'linger by the stream/'That follow/ the deep eternal sea.'

Flecker, as yet, was not able to demonstrate a surefooted path of excellence in writing his own verse, but was continuing to show a much more competent knowledge of the path he was taking in verse translations of Catullus. He polished and rewrote these in four of his notebooks, and by the time his Uppingham days were over he had translated sixteen poems by Catullus.[204] These verses (various versions of some of them found their way into print)[205] were not always easy to date with accuracy, as he usually just dated them with the year of their origin (between 1900 and 1904), but one at least contained a more precise date, 10 April 1901. This was his translation of part of 'Colonos, which began: 'Aged stranger, thou has come/To a land of noble horses,'.[206]

In these verse translations of Catullus, Flecker was following the route set by famous poets, in particular Byron, who owed a great debt

to the Latin poet.[207] The standard of these verse translations stood a
greater chance of being high, than did his own poetry, which did not
follow the same path. Another reason for the success of his translations
was that he had a love of Latin, which was bolstered by the fact that he
had the underlying discipline to prepare for examinations; he had an
aim in view. He also found a connection, as he had in writing his Phaon
translation, of finding a link with his own feelings. In Catullus One, he
wrote: 'My simple verses worthy of esteem', which echoed his feelings
about his verses and the sort of reception the writing of them would
receive from his parents.

Flecker's imposition of his feelings about his own life did not detract
from the translation and the spirit of the Latin. Nor did Flecker's
ambitious use of the Shakespearian sonnet form for Catullus III.[208] His
Sirmio poem (which he first translated into verse in 1900 and polished
and rewrote) owed something to Tennyson;[209] its lines have a connection
to his life at Uppingham, which consisted of being incarcerated at
school with the delight of homecoming ahead of him:

In we hurry through the doorway of our home of
long ago...
Hail then, hail! Thy master welcome, welcome him,
sweet Sirmio,
Leap for joy, ye tumbling waters, winking at the
summer's glow,
Gaily through the house resounding let the peals
of laughter go. [210]

An early version began with the line: 'My brother from afar I
come'.[211]

The high standard of Flecker's translations was a result, not only of
the teaching at Dean Close, but the high esteem in which the classics
were held at Uppingham. Death, patriotism, mourning and Christianity
were suitable subjects for poetry; science was not considered a subject
that would inspire the same sort of logical reasoning and style. Science
was, therefore, neglected. If the headmaster found it acceptable to be
ignorant of the sciences, but not of the classics, then his pupils could
do little but adopt the same sort of attitude towards science as a subject.
However, this was not a view of science that Flecker held after leaving
Uppingham.[212] At Dean Close a different sort of view towards science
was adopted; science buildings, begun in 1892, were completed in
1902. A chemistry laboratory was completed at Uppingham in 1907,
when Selwyn was reported to have said of those who had studied in

the dreary science rooms, the change was like coming out of the house of bondage into the promised land. Selwyn retired in 1907; he never explained satisfactorily why he had let the study of science sink into such a state of affairs.

The world outside Uppingham could not impinge so immediately on Flecker as the internal life of the school. First, there was the House system, which Flecker came to dislike: 'That is a pernicious system by which a boy only sees some thirty of his follows, and cannot get away from the aggressiveness of those school-fellows whom he dislikes'.[213] Flecker's being in charge of a dormitory did not bring him popularity: 'Few realise or remember that it is harder for the unpopular boy to manage his fellows than for an unpopular ministry to manage the State: no one is more relentless, ingenious, persistent in hatred, than the schoolboy who dislikes and despises those who are set over him.'[214]

Raven was guarded on the point of Flecker's popularity at Uppingham; he afterwards wrote: 'Boys recognised his power, but he never suffered any persecution or unpopularity, so far as I know'.[215] Raven, in a different House, was still under the constant eye of a relative, which made 'persecution' from other boys something he himself was unlikely to suffer to a great degree. Raven would be seen by the other boys as occupying a place of 'some privilege',[216] as it could be said, did a son of Dr. Selwyn, who had joined his father's school in 1900, at the age of twelve. His presence would have given Dr. Selwyn insight into what it meant to have been a pupil whose father was the headmaster. Selwyn was said to be a nephew of Matthew Arnold, who was at the school of his father, Dr. Thomas Arnold, Rugby, and so Selwyn could have had some knowledge of what that meant for Matthew Arnold. Selwyn's misunderstanding of Flecker's position could account for his cat and mouse behaviour. Selwyn had some inkling of the problems, but knew if he showed understanding he could be accused of favouritism.

Once Flecker had his return journey money in his pocket, he could write more optimistically on Easter Day, if not about examination results, then with news of his attending Communion. The attendance at Communion (or lack of attendance) had been a source of conflict between his mother and himself. He had previously excused himself attendance at Communion on the grounds that the surroundings were strange and so were his fellow communicants. After he had got over this strangeness, he had dug his heels in, and concluded that going to Communion more than once or twice a term was unprofitable. But he made an exception of Easter, when the music in the Chapel was sacred, and it was decorated with lilies.

It is interesting to realise that the conflict between Flecker and his parents arose over the attendance at Communion, but the actual fact of his confirmation (which must have taken place about this time) did not create conflict or feature in the LIFE. Raven's preparation for confirmation gave rise to dissatisfaction although the confirmation service itself 'thrilled me to the core'.[217]

Part of the Easter holidays was spent at Alresford, Hampshire, and the description he gave his parents of a church service he attended at Ovington, taken by his Uncle John, was in contrast to the splendour of the crowded Easter services at Uppingham. The rectory at Ovington he described as tumbledown: 'it was darned and patched all over, just like one of my stockings'.[218] He thought Ovington pretty, it had 'lots of little streams running all over the place like a spider's web'.[219]

He also walked to the village of Armsworth and saw 'the Hs' who had 'chirped like a pair of old canaries'[220] and asked about all the Flecker family. The service at Armsworth in 'the wee little chapel-room'[221] was also in contrast to the Uppingham service: it had a tenth of the congregation. He did not express any discontent at having to attend this small gathering, but then he did prefer to worship in a smaller congregation. 'I would not go to Church once a year, unless I found some little place where worship was earnest and real.'[222] This gathering also would be free of those who attended 'to study fashionable dress'.[223] The rest of the holiday was spent at Cheltenham and 'the rambling old house by the waters of Ocean...'.[224]

On his journey back to Uppingham for the start of the summer term, he bought a *Golden Treasury* in very good condition, at Birmingham, but could not get a copy of Postgate's *Propertius* so asked his father to get one for him. He had read *The Woman in White*, part of *Barnaby Rudge*, and he had tried to 'wade through *Les Misérables* and also Kipling's *Departmental Ditties.....*'. He requested his family to search for a book (Mackail's *Greek Anthology*) and the tone of this letter indicated that, whatever conflicts there had been in the first term over his schoolwork and his religious views, the holiday had been relatively free of conflict over school-work. He had wanted the *Anthology*, which he had originally got out of the library, for work not directly concerned with his school course, as he had explained to his parents:

> 'Apropos of verse there is a prize poem here – English as
> well as Greek and Latin – the subject of which is given out at
> the end of term. Of course I shall enter. There is no chance
> of my getting it here ... The fellow who got it last year (he
> is not allowed to compete again) is second in the school

and second XV. football. As he is in the house next to ours,
I often go up and down with him. He is most literary for a
boy, and a nice fellow all round.' [225]

Flecker did not care for de Quincey or Tyrrell's *Latin Poets*, but
praised Myers' *Classical Essays*, which had quite converted him to Virgil.
He was also reading Charles Kingsley. It is too easy to conclude that his
reading list, and the comments, represented Flecker's true feelings; a
certain amount of allowance had to be made for the fact that he had
to win parental approval and he did not change his mind about writers
who he had admired very much, at Uppingham. He had written to his
parents about de Quincey: 'I have read de Quincey – about murder and
nuns, and mail-coaches and Levana; very pretty but rather useless.' [226]

He changed his mind about Ruskin (he was allowed to read some
letters of John Ruskin to the mother of the Captain of the House) and
Stephen Phillips whose *Ulysses* he had read, and admired, although
he did state that the first scene was 'like a pantomime'."[227] He was to
change his mind about Stephen Phillips. During the term he longed
for summer: 'Will summer never come? Not with fitful gusts of sunshine
and mornings chill as January, but real languorous summer when one
can actually lie in the sun and long for the shade. Not but what even
to-day I was constrained to drink ginger-beer in the lucid intervals of
cricket.' [228] He wanted to know if the roses were in bloom and, if they
were, he wanted some sent to him.

On 8 June he sent his parents a letter that began with details of an
offer of £15 made for his violin (without bow and case). A sum of £15
was also mentioned as being offered by a publisher for a translation of
Pliny's *Letters*.[229] Whether he ever received the money for his violin or
the letters is not clear, but the rest of the pupils were lost in admiration
for his method, whereby he took down the translation in form, thus
making a member of staff do the work for him and turn a dull subject
into financial gain. The problem of turning a writer's own work into
financial gain was a problem on which he had gained insight from an
unexpected quarter – the previously despised Herr David. He told his
parents that having seen Herr David's name in his Boosey alongside
Rubinstein 'and a lot of other great pots' he had had a conversation
with him after the lesson. He learned that David had written a great
deal, including an opera, which (although it had not entirely failed)
had not exactly found success. It was, he told his parents, called *Hans
Wacht* ('John Wakes'). The critics had said, 'John wakes and the audience
sleeps'. Flecker commiserated with David, who had had this experience
'after four years' toil'. It was not surprising that it was in this letter that

Flecker went on to extol the virtues of the returning hero from the Boer War.

In June, he wrote a poem he called 'The Sea: Two Visions' (in his note book D244) in which he outlined two moods of the sea, one calm and one stormy, ending with the lines, 'And a grey spectre of death floats on the wind's wild breath'. In this poem he also seems to outline his own feelings about his life and revives his old theme of fascination with death.

In the same June, he wrote to his parents that he had seen a 'MOTOR-CAR' in Uppingham, and, what was even more unusual at the end of term, he got an hour from Selwyn because his was the best and most industrious sixth form. In case his parents thought that he would get big-headed, he told them that he thought Selwyn wanted to go up and see the Haileybury Match.[230] Despite the lack of the school's confidence in his abilities, Flecker won at the end of the summer term, 1901, the school prize for English Verse and was noted as distinguished in Latin Translation.[231] His activities in the summer vacation were to indulge his interests in photography and bicycling. One day, he rode 160 miles and, another day, he managed, with his bicycle, to get over Helvellyn.

Flecker, on his return to Uppingham had no school to attend on his first day, so he did nothing but unpack and read. He got to the end of *Paris Sketches* and through a great deal of *Old Mortality*, he told his parents. Some of this letter is left out, and although this may have been done so as not to bore the reader with details, it may also have been because it gave the news of the death in September 1901, of one of the boys in his House, William Mordaci Lewis, who had been just sixteen.[232,233]

He continued in this letter to ask for books to be sent to him from Dean Close, and subsequent letters belonging to the autumn term of 1901 show a settling down process, which was remarkable compared to the rebellion and fun-taking moods of his arrival in January of the same year. In music, too, he seemed to be settling down, he was trying to master a 'Fantasia of Bohemian Melodies' by Hans Sitt. He was also reading and discussing poetry once a week in the rooms of some of the masters in a small literary society, which had been recently formed.

He told his parents that Haines had given him a 'slight lecture' for helping a boy with Latin Prose, but this seemed a small matter as Flecker's mind was already on the prospect of winning a university scholarship. He was studying Stichus with Selwyn. It appeared then, that Flecker was sailing in calmer waters at school, and that he did not need to try and swim against the tide. However, he was still facing storms at home over religion. A long letter on the subject of religious beliefs was written to his mother on Sunday, 27 October 1901.[234]

He analysed first his reasons for going right through term to a prayer-meeting. He had not gone to get help or because he got a thrill in praising God, but only because he had a faint idea that if he attended he would go to Heaven, and also find favour with his parents. He had been told to believe in Christ but was not told what was meant by that particular faith. He felt the idea was: 'Feel a very enthusiastic Christian, set a good example and you will go to heaven'.[235]

The result of this teaching had only lasted two or three days, and he had come to the conclusion, after careful thought, that Church was a farce, and every Sunday he was further convinced. After he had discussed various Bible texts, he concluded that 'nothing will shake my convictions'.[236] He told his parents that these were not H.'s views, 'as you might accuse them of being: though perhaps *Fors Clavigera* suggested one or two to me'.[237] It is not clear who H. was (although the science master was called Howson), but this habit of blaming people outside the family for their son's rebellion against their religious views was one that was to recur.

It was easier to bring up the question of his plans to sit for a scholarship than to dwell on the conflict of differing religious views. He told his parents that the required subjects for the scholarship examination were Latin and Greek verse, an Unseen, an essay and general knowledge. Latin verse, he told his parents, was 'a thing of much chance, according to how a piece suits you, but if I keep clear of howlers I think I ought to manage as well as anybody'.[238] He felt that with Greek verse his vocabulary was at fault without the use of a dictionary. Although he was prone to howlers in Greek, he managed to get good marks generally.

Flecker already realised that style was at the root of his problems; he was inclined to 'rhapsody', which he thought might please 'the Oxford man' but he was trying to keep clear of it; he complained of the style they were required to write in, which he described as 'a cut and dry Johnsonian style' with no opportunity to cultivate their own style or ideas. He rebelled against this restriction. Haines, he told his parents, would describe such writing as 'balderdash' and another master, Mr. T., as 'bunkum', but 'T.' did not mind it much if it was to the point.[239] It was not likely that his masters at Uppingham would realise his reasons for wanting to embark upon more elaborate translations. 'Why mayn't I write as enthusiastically as Symonds or Myers?'[240] he had written to his parents.

Howlers continued to be a problem, and the strictness of Uppingham's method of dealing with them – no marks for a piece of work that contained them – meant that it 'has wrought wonders in me'[241] he wrote to his parents. The wonders were reflected in the marks he received, and Selwyn was so pleased with one copy of Flecker's Latin verses that he kept them. Flecker's Greek verses were not so well marked, even if he had done them without books; a small error meant low marks. He found the unseens so easy that he spoiled them by 'too elaborate translations'. Although he thought it strange, he caught the rhythms of his Ciceronian and Thucydidean style very well, but this nightmare of possible howlers and the restrictions on style were problems that would never go away when any sort of examination confronted him.

Selwyn had said that he wanted Flecker to wait another year because, as he told him, 'only a genius could get a schol. at my age'.[242] If he waited another year before trying for a scholarship, this would mean only another term at Uppingham, and the possibility was held out to him of being Head of the school and Head of his House. One advantage of taking the scholarship, besides the experience it would give him, was that he could end the term six days early, as it was hardly worth coming back to school after the examinations ended on the 13th.

The news of his winning an Open Classical Scholarship to Trinity College, Oxford, arrived during the Christmas holidays. Past holidays had been marred by rows and recriminations; these particular holidays must have been less tense as a result of the favourable, but no great praise would be heaped upon him, on case he became too conceited. His age, which Selwyn had thought a barrier to his winning a scholarship, meant that on this aspect alone, he had done well.

He had been the youngest but one of all the candidates for Open Scholarships, and of the Uppingham candidates to be successful, he was the youngest of six Exhibitioners. Two years separated him from the oldest and he was six months younger than the fifth in line. Leonard John Sedgwick, eighteen months older, was also an Exhibitioner. It was possible that Selwyn's reference to Flecker's age held a slight fear that he would show up the others, although the headmaster had never thought Flecker's age a barrier to his being expected to stop undesirable conduct when he was the youngest in his form.[243]

Back at school in the spring term, he told his parents that he had spoken successfully, but not in votes, on the Japanese Alliance.[244] More success followed when one of his poems was published in the June 1902 edition of the Uppingham School magazine. It was 'Danae and Perseus', which had won him the school prize for English verse the year before, and, like Flecker's description of the return of the Boer War hero, was full of colour, with such examples as 'silvered', 'violet cloud', 'Heaven's ensabled mantle', 'sapphire', 'fiery' and 'scarlet and saffron'.[245] Haines (who wrote poetry himself) wrote[246] (with benefit of hindsight) that Flecker at Uppingham had the root of poetry in him, but did not explain why the school did not encourage the talent to flourish beyond the root stage in the soil of Uppingham School.

Flecker realised that great poets were not made out of the school system, a great poet was made despite the school system: 'We shall not give a prize once a year for some absurd heroics on a set theme, but we shall very diligently teach the art of verse, initiating our boys by setting them to write verse translations from poems in other tongues. Our criticism will be ruthless: we shall point out vulgarity of idea, insufficiency of thought, staleness of metaphor, harshness of sound. We shall not necessarily produce great poets by this training, but we shall certainly produce young men who love poetry and (what is rarer still) who understand it.'[247]

Yet, in some ways, had Flecker not shown ability in his school subjects, his ability to write poetry not related to translations might have been better appreciated. Thring had once written:

> 'The most astonishing thing has happened today. There has been a fellow named —— at the school these eight years, an excellent good fellow, but so inaccurate through bad teaching, and apparent inability to fix his mind, that I have simply again and again given up his exercises in despair, doing nothing because I knew what a good fellow he was. Lately I have been able to give him some credit for trying in the right way. Well, that fellow has shown up the winning poem – full of tender, true feeling, and graceful diction. It is a marvellous triumph of goodness wakening into delicate power in him, and a marvellous reward to me for working at each boy hopefully. Thank God.'[248]

At this stage in his life, Flecker did not appear to attach any importance to the source of the poet's inspiration and the creative force, beyond the translations of other poets' works. Poetry, he believed, was a craft to be learned and practised, but he did not acknowledge (or even realise) that the conflict between his external and internal world, and the tension this produced, was essential for creating a poet's mind of any worth. How was the poet's mind first nurtured and how did the need arise to create another world beyond his own immediate horizon? He had written instinctively, and it was not the countryside around Uppingham that had inspired him. On his journey from Cheltenham to Uppingham, he had exchanged the silver-grey of the Cotswolds for the golden-brown limestone of the countryside around Uppingham, and it was not an exchange that had brought him profit. For Flecker it was the memories of the Cotswolds and Southbourne that were already part of his young soul, and the longing to be back there produced tension and conflict. He absorbed himself in these sources, which to some extent influenced his translations. At this stage, these were mainly brought to the attention of his schoolteachers and, like going to chapel, to gain the approval of his parents. He did write about the Uppingham countryside in letters to his parents: 'The countryside here annoys me. It seems to go like this ⁓⁓⁓ for ever: still, it is very pretty in parts by the brooks: there are no rivers unfortunately. [249] The lack of rivers was to be remedied later.[250] The Wardley Wood, the railway cutting where the bones of prehistoric animals could be found, the fields, the water meadows, red squirrels, the oaks and the butterflies appeared to make no lasting impression, as it had on others.

Flecker seemed to find his fictional ideas in the village of Uppingham and in the villages he visited during his holidays. Uppingham had a market-place and small shops, including a bookshop and an ancient wine and spirit business. Flecker eventually portrayed village life as somewhere to escape from, or, if he had to stay he would be a wine-merchant rather than the owner of a grocer's shop, interesting as these establishments were in the variety of goods they had to offer. 'Nearly everything was on sale in his shop – all groceries, also cloth, garden seeds, papers, books (the least flourishing part of the trade), and tobacco.'[251]

His scholarship to Oxford notwithstanding, the masters found his work had errors and was erratic in performance. But Flecker found that the teaching given to him at Uppingham had similar shortcomings. He had written to his parents to tell them that: 'There are not two masters who have the vaguest idea of the way to teach, or who can form a right estimate of, a boy's character.... Not that I have been misjudged.'[252]

This lack of stability in the teaching methods could have been at the root of Flecker's erratic scholastic performance. The drastic method employed to eradicate 'howlers' was unlikely to restore confidence in his abilities, and the unfairness of it would breed an inner resentment, even if he told his parents it had wrought wonders in him. His confidence to pass examinations would be undermined; he knew there was a risk that bad work and good work would be treated equally.

The dead hand of Thring could still be seen in the attitude towards marking examinations; a son of Thring was still a master at Uppingham.

Traditions at Uppingham were firmly entrenched and, as long ago as 1869, Thring had written on the subject of examinations:

> Many years ago I was examining at Eton, and set a paper in Greek translation. The boys had to read their work when done to the assembled examiners; I also looked over it all in private. When the first paper of these translations was read out, the then headmaster of Eton, Dr. Hawtrey, a man of great reputation, said, as soon as the boy had left the room, "How beautiful!" and gave the highest praise to it. I had observed that there was not a single point in scholarship given of those on account of which the paper was set, and I had accordingly marked the paper low. Dr. Hawtrey might fairly have held me up as an incompetent examiner from his point of view, and might justly have objected in his own school to my system of marking. We were, in fact, looking at two entirely different things. I thought, as I was examining in Greek, that I was sent down to see whether the boys knew Greek, and till they showed that they did, they got little or no credit for their English style. He was of opinion that a certain undefined literary power was the thing to prize, and so gave high marks for what, in his judgment showed this. Now, what is good translation has never been decided, and to this hour examiners are divided into two camps on the question. I belong to one camp, your examiner belonged to the other. [253]

In prose, Flecker wrote to his parents,[254] Haines found him to be all right, whilst another master found him to be 'all wrong' mainly because he did not keep close enough to the original to please him.[255] Flecker did keep to the original, however, in his Catullus translations. The pattern of the original poem, its stanza form and metre, was preserved as it should be and he approached very closely the form of the original length.[256] Matthew Arnold asserted that in a verse translation no original work is any longer recognisable.[257] It could be that Flecker's ability to get close to the real meaning and spirit of the Latin poet gave the impression that he was not being sufficiently accurate for his masters' liking. Flecker described one master who looked after the bottom half of the form's Latin verses as a 'disgracefully lazy animal, who will pass over eight lines with a "Yes, those are all right".'[258]

The trouble was that the ideals of Thring were waning by the time Flecker arrived. In addition, Selwyn, David and Haines already had retirement in their sights, and they were the masters with the main influence.[259] But Thring's waning ideals, plus some of Dr. Selwyn's ideas, had not really worked in practice, however enlightened they appeared in theory. Views on education were changing and Uppingham had not fully adapted to them.

But Flecker had stayed the course, however unsatisfactory it had appeared to him; he had little choice, unlike past pupils, who also had a leaning towards writing. Norman Douglas, for example, had been able to leave Uppingham of his own free will. Of his near contemporaries, Frank Savery had left prematurely after a row with Dr. Selwyn, and Ronald Firbank left before his time, without giving a term's notice.

Flecker must have had a certain inner toughness (although Dr. Selwyn had complained of an 'astonishing lack of backbone'[260]), covered by his priggishness, which had enabled him to stay the course, and keep out of severe trouble. He had kept his friendships at a prudent distance, although had he made one close friendship (as Norman Douglas had stated), he might have found Uppingham more to his liking. He had learned to stay around someone like Sedgwick, who was good at games and had a large following, so that his presence in the crowd would not attract the suspicious eye of Dr. Selwyn. Sedgwick might have been expected to have had a better time than most and to have enjoyed his schooldays, but nevertheless stated that he did not.[261]

In most things at school Flecker felt he had to account to his parents and he told them: 'I have no friend here: plenty of talking acquaintances, if you like: but I don't think many people here know what friendship means.'[262] He put the blame on the school and his fellow pupils, but the reasons were much more complex and varied.

However many misgivings his teachers might have expressed about his abilities as a scholar, Flecker won prizes at the end of his last term. He was awarded the Nettleship Prize for English Essay, on the subject of Urbanity, and the school prize for Latin epigram. The winning of the prizes and the doubts of those who taught him reflected the mixed feelings he expressed about his life at Uppingham. He wrote to his parents and told them that he was 'excessively glad I came here', but in the same letter he also wrote: 'I am excessively glad that I am leaving'.[263] When he wrote 'I have no friend here' it reflected his realisation that being put in a position of authority over some of his fellows (however humble that position was in the scheme of things) and retaining their respect was something he was not mature enough to achieve. He craved respect and praise; the last was denied him at home, on the grounds that if it was handed out, even in small measure, he would become big-headed. At school he was in the same position, or he felt that he was. He told his parents, 'Haines thought I was rather a fool when I came: and so I was: but though I hope I have become less of a fool, his opinion has not altered one jot. Were I some huge swell – Cricket XI, Football XV, or anything like that, then I might sorrow.'[264]

Prowess on the games field brought respect and admiration from masters and pupils alike. Flecker had tried hard with running. Together with the best runner in his House, who was the House Captain, he had run together to Oakham, a distance of six and a half miles there and back. Flecker told his parents he had done this with only three brief stops to ask the way and no stops on the way back, after which he ate a large tea. Despite this effort – he finished a fourteen-mile paper-chase, when few of his fellows did – he knew his parents saw running simply as his latest fad or craze, so much-needed encouragement did not come his way. However, in one sporting area, his rifle shooting, they could not make the same accusation, as it was Dr. Selwyn who wanted him to join the Rifle Corps. Even if Dr. Selwyn had gone about this in his usual cat and mouse manner, giving Flecker the impression ('Wait afterwards, Flecker') that he was in trouble over bad school-work and keeping him in unnecessary suspense, it was one of Dr. Selwyn's more imaginative gestures. It gave his pupil the chance to excel in a sport that did not depend on exhausting the body physically, but on the eye and hand. Yet Raven remembered that 'he [Flecker] mocked our schoolboy heroes unless they could show a truer title to respect than mere dexterity of hand and eye[265]...'

What was more likely to develop at Uppingham was his own inner voice, and one of the first instances of this was his poem 'The Chapel Bell', a copy of which he sent to his parents and which he tried on more than one occasion to perfect.[266]

Clangour of the long-releasing backward swinging Chapel bell,
Of the Summer's glowing gladness is the message that you tell
Laughing days on heath and mountain, or by Ocean's silver swell,
But for us there is a sorrow that no happy hope can quell,
As we listen to the thunder of the swaying clashing crashing
Clashing slow reverberated knell
Like the mocking of a demon, echoing, echoing Farewell. [267]

The 'laughing days on heath and mountain' referred to a holiday in North Wales with Cyril Roberts, at that time 'his greatest friend', who was not at Uppingham and to whom he wrote a farewell poem. The 'Ocean's silver swell' meant that the family would go back to

Southbourne again. The poem did not look forward to the delights that Oxford might bring him.

CHAPTER FOUR

On his journey to Oxford from Cheltenham, in October 1902, Flecker travelled past towns still bedecked for the coronation celebrations of Edward VII. As his train slowed down to enter the station it lurched between the melancholic Oxford Canal on one side and the view of the college spires and meadows on the other. Once he was out on the platform he needed a porter for the task of getting to his lodgings. He tipped an extra sixpence over and above the regulation 2d. for each piece of his considerable luggage.

Sixpence was a sum his parents considered far too much; he had to render accounts for all items of expenditure over and above his 2s. a week pocket-money. His parents, to his annoyance, called him green; he tried to justify himself by explaining that the porters expected extra money on 'coming-up' day. It was not an argument that he could win; his parents held the purse strings, even if the financial burden had been lightened by the scholarship. It would have been better if he had been left to learn from his mistakes, and his parents had rejoiced that he had not taken a hackney cab.[268]

His parents had failed to see that he was entering a world where most of his fellow undergraduates' parents had made them allowances of between £200 and £300 per year, but he did take the matter of the tip to heart.[269] He could have been forgiven for thinking that the management of money was more important to his parents that his mastery of his subjects for Greats. The immediate impact of Oxford, 'that curious world',[270] on the seventeen-year old Flecker, was bound up with the ready cash problems imposed on him by his parents, who still (despite his mature appearance that made others think he was older than he really was) regarded him as a child.

His very first letter home contained an objection; his parents had forgotten to put a stamp on their letter. He told them 'a penny means a lot of things' and he referred to 'strict economic principles'. He told his parents about the subjects he was taking – Catullus, Plato and Trilogy for Mods – and that he was 'very comfy'.

The next October letter told again of his circumstances, which were 'magnificently comfy', and that he had nothing 'particularly horrid to look forward to (except going surpliced to Chapel tomorrow because it is a Saint's Day)'. He mentioned rugger and rowing and wanting to join the Volunteers.[271] He would not then have time to join the Musical.[272] After all this reasonableness and amiability, he placed a request for ten guineas to join the Oxford Union, or he could pay a guinea a term. This approach of asking first about possible expenditure had a much better result; he became a member of the Union 'for all time'. News of his interview with the President of Trinity and his Tutor, and the presentation in state to the Chancellor, would wait until his parents made their visit, which was to coincide with his eighteenth birthday on 5 November. He signed his letter: 'Yours in serene and affectionate optimism. LE ROI'.

Trinity had a number of clubs and societies but Flecker appeared to have eschewed them all. The Savoyard Society for Gilbert and Sullivan lovers did not have him as a member, nor did he join the Trinity Club for play-reading, the Gargoyle Club, or even the Boat Club. The strict economic principles may have influenced his decision not to join.

The subject of how to spend money did not go away. In a letter home in November he told his parents that he had got a copy third-hand of Ellis Catullus for 15s. from a fellow undergraduate, and he aimed to sell the book when he had finished with it. He admitted that he should have got his parents' views first (but they could hardly have quibbled over the cost of a book that he needed for his studies). Flecker used the word 'robbed' when explaining the 10s. needed to pay for the Freshers' Dinner, which he assured his parents was not just an excuse to get drunk. He had not joined the Claret Club, a dining society at Trinity. He told his parents about getting a better dinner at the Union for so much a night, and that it was a better dinner than any of the commoners got. The commoners were those students whose fathers paid for them to attend College. So the Union Society served a useful purpose; he could mix with his fellow undergraduates outside his own college. He told his parents that he had spent 2s. (his weekly pocket-money) on cigarettes for other people. Like the 6d. tip he was justifying his expenditure by letting his parents know that he was conforming to what was expected of him in his circle; a fairly familiar form of blackmail used by all young people to get what they wanted from their parents.

He was used to standing out from the crowd, and at Oxford it appeared he was still going to be the odd one out. He would need to apply himself to his studies, more so than those who came from the upper and more leisured class, or those from the less well-off classes who had the minds of true scholars, or those who had also won honours on the playing field. He was used to isolation, first as the son of the headmaster when there was more pressure on him to succeed than on his fellow pupils, and then at Uppingham when he was older than his fellow pupils and a late arrival. His parents seemed determined to add to his feelings of being different by making sure he was short of ready cash, and this was not because they could not afford to give him a little extra. Dr. Flecker did not need to buy himself a house, as other parents did. Mrs. Flecker, by merging her household expenses during term-time with the pupils of Dean Close, may not have fully appreciated the day-to-day expenses needed in the world outside Dean Close.

What really mattered was that he had no set allowance from his parents; they did not make him one because they thought he would not learn to handle money as they saw fit. Instead they gave him sporadic handouts, expenditure for which had to be submitted for approval with weekly accounts. The obvious weakness of such a plan was that it would lead to endless arguments about what were necessities and what were luxuries.

Some of his fellow undergraduates at Magdalen were known as 'Demys' because of the amount they received each year – £80 or half the value of a Fellowship. They kept themselves to themselves, as a result. The Fleckers did not want their son to pursue a life of scholarship; they wanted him in time to enter one of the well-paid professions. To do this, he needed to participate in university life in order to make the right contacts. Since the Fleckers were not from the upper classes this would be difficult, but if they had allowed him a little more money then a little less conflict would have resulted.

Flecker's eighteenth birthday in November was an unexpected source of extra cash, but he lamented the fact that an uncle had forgotten to send him anything. The day after his birthday he was due to play fives and attend a Logic lecture. He relayed this information to Sedgwick, his friend from Uppingham, who was now at Pembroke, Cambridge, studying amongst other languages, Hindustani and Sanskrit. Flecker wrote his letter on 6 November, during what he described as an incomprehensible Logic lecture. He had already realised he could give the outward sign of being a diligent student, while following his own private interests. He asked Sedgwick to excuse the weird paper, which was 'provided cooking paper' and hoped that Sedgwick would not be insulted. [273]

The letter to Sedgwick was long and involved; he put down on the greaseproof paper his feelings about poetry and his growing doubts about the wisdom of holding religious beliefs. He also outlined what he thought were his own emotional needs. He placed great importance on friendship, but because Sedgwick was an 'unemotional character' he could not ever enter into a friendship in the way that Flecker did. He told Sedgwick that he had two such friendships already, but did not name the friends. Stanley McKelvie from Evangelical camp days, who was now at Exeter, reading Theology, could be one contender, and also Frank Savery, formerly at Uppingham, now at Hertford, reading Classics, could have been the other.

Flecker told Sedgwick that he 'may possibly add two more to the list. But not for a long time'.[274] These two 'possibilities' he did not name either. One possibility was John Mavrogordato (1882–1970), also at Exeter, a Greek, born in London, the second son of a merchant. Mavrogordato, a former King's scholar at Eton, and now an open classical scholar, came up to Oxford in 1901, so was already established in a group of friends, one of whom he introduced to Flecker, E.M.C. Mackenzie (1883–1972) of Magdalen. Compton Mackenzie or 'Monty' was born the son of touring actors. He had been educated at St. Paul's, London, and had refused to try for a scholarship to Oxford. He had wanted to read History at Magdalen, but first he had taken Pass Mods. Of much greater interest to Flecker was the flamboyantly dressed Mackenzie's accomplishment in starting a new magazine called the *Oxford Point of View*. The first issue had been published in May 1902. Contributors were not paid. The magazine, which came out quarterly, by the standards of the university was successful. The first number sold 1,500 copies, costing 1s. a copy, and the President of Magdalen judged it to be 'one of the handsomest magazines Oxford has ever produced'. The President wrote to Mackenzie's father to praise this very creditable enterprise. Mackenzie was for Flecker a model to try and emulate, not that he thought much of the magazine; he described 'the stilted gravity and intolerable motherliness of the *Oxford Point of View*'. He was not picking out Mackenzie's magazine for particular criticism; he thought that the *Varsity* had 'cheap sensationalism' and he referred to 'the heavy commonplace' of the *Isis* magazine.[275] It was the achievement of bringing out a magazine that made money and got the attention of the President of the College, to say nothing of a letter of praise to parents, that Flecker took note of for the future.

Someone else referred to in the same letter as 'a man here who writes excellent sonnets' and who he said 'takes a thought and rounds it off and elaborates it and turns out the complete article like a copy of

Latin verse' is also not named, but in case this man became conceited, Flecker took him down a peg or two: 'He writes very good sonnets, but will never rise above the level of sonnets. He is a good critic of my poetry, discovering absurdities that I should never have found out. But he will never be a Keats or Shelley. I intend to be, if poetry can work a mission.'[276]

1902 to1903 was a lean time for Flecker's verse, an indication that settling in to his new life and work took up a lot of his time and attention, although his only scholastic goal on the immediate horizon was to satisfy the examiners in divinity; he had to pass 'Divvers' at the end of his first year.[277] Compton MacKenzie, however, said that students were considered 'honour bound to fail' Divvers the first time.

Another friend might have been Humbert Wolfe (1885–1940) [278]who was Jewish by birth, born in Milan, and educated at Bradford Grammar School. He was two months younger than Flecker, and he too had entered the scholarship examinations in 1902. He was asked by the Chairman who had conducted the Viva (who unbeknown to him was the President Pelham of Trinity) why he had chosen Wadham, and he had replied that he had been told it was a better college than Trinity. He was awarded a scholarship to Wadham; he too, like Mavrogordato and Mackenzie, was a would-be poet. He was certainly glad he was not selected for Trinity, of which he said: 'if anyone mentioned to the hearties of Trinity College that they had in Flecker a real poet amongst them, they would reply (with truth), "We kick him about a good bit".'[279]

'Hearties' was a term that originated at Trinity, according to Compton Mackenzie.[280] Humbert Wolfe agreed about the 'hearties' but stated, 'Flecker was not a second Shelley'.[281] This remark could have been made about Flecker's appearance, as much as the nature of his verse.

Wolfe also showed no signs of rivalling Shelley, and if he harboured such thoughts he was soon disillusioned one evening, by Flecker, in a darkened room after he had listened with a group of people, to Mozart. Wolfe was asked by Flecker to recite aloud one of his many poems which he did with a thumping heart in a sing-song tone:

> They chose an island for her dwelling-place –
> the goddess with the sorrow in her eyes;
> where the slow waters of the ocean pace
> to seek a distant dawn, that island lies.[282]

Wolfe thought that Flecker had fallen asleep in his chair, but suddenly in a soft, deep voice he had begun to repeat the verse slowly, lingering on the line 'the goddess with the sorrow in her eyes'.

'You have no technical accomplishment at all,' Flecker said to Wolfe, 'your thought is shallow – but you have an ear. Continue to use it. You may overhear something. And one thing more,' he added, rising to leave, 'read the French, particularly Verlaine. What you need above all is a healing touch of corruption. Come and see me soon' he concluded, and took his leave.[283]

Flecker's attack on Wolfe's poetry and his way of life was something that future poets would echo when Wolfe's verse was published.[284]Flecker's desire to appear superior to Wolfe was cruel, although in fairness, Wolfe's recollection, like many of his others of Flecker, was tempered by factors enhanced by the passage of time, such as Wolfe's desire to make his recollections startling and amusing.

The two young poets had much in common but also much to set them apart. Both disliked the names given to them at birth. Wolfe at one time decided to change his name from Umberto Wolff and Flecker had changed his baptismal name from Herman to James.[285]Wolfe appeared to fit the role of poet alongside the role of aspiring civil servant, without too much conflict within himself or with his father who was in trade in Bradford. Wolfe knew that failure at Oxford would lead to a working life in his father's warehouse. Flecker was said to have mocked Wolfe at one stage for these sorts of ambitions, but Flecker tended to mock what he really did not understand, and he may have secretly envied Wolfe because he could balance his twin aims in his life.[286] Wolfe's poetry, as a result, tended to be on the popular side, as if his nature would not let him write more serious poetry.

Wolfe realised that Flecker had many ambitions, which he saw as 'philosopher, novelist, politician, man of the world, playwright and poet all in one, and at the same time'.[287] Wolfe had similar ambitions, but he felt able to poke a little fun at Flecker's studies of philosophy, his novel writing and his attempts at politics. Flecker had failed to join a plan to organise blanket-makers at Witney and had spoken against Socialism at the Union.

Wolfe was a Jew whilst Flecker was Jewish in looks. Wolfe had a merry-eyed lean face, while Flecker had a swarthy complexion; a fact Flecker discussed with Wolfe and others. 'Take jaundice, for example.' 'Not if I can help it,' interposed Flecker. 'I am swarthy enough anyhow.'[288]

Wolfe's appearance did not put people off, whilst Flecker's did, although his 'man of the world' pose was something Wolfe was not able to acquire. Wolfe's recollections provide a picture of Flecker's behaviour in the company of people he wanted to impress with his supposed knowledge of the world outside Oxford, while he drank port and listened to Mozart, or *The Moonlight Sonata* on the pianola.

Wolfe had realised that Flecker often posed, and that once a guest had gone he threw off the elegant facade as easily as he poured back into the bottle the contents of his glass of white curaçao. Wolfe had not liked the amount of curaçao that Flecker pressed upon him, imagining it tasted of a mixture of cheap scent and ink. He was told that his host imported it himself from the Boule Miche, and it was not possible to get it anywhere else in England – a piece of news that his guests would welcome as they tipped the odious liquid out of the window when Flecker left the room. All poets had weaknesses: Verlaine's (Flecker told guests) was absinthe. Flecker boasted that he drank six glasses to a stanza, and that writing poetry required 'finger-exercises' for six hours a day, which meant a good deal of drink must have been consumed; nobody really believed him. Discipline was what every artist needed, he told Wolfe, which contradicted his image of the poet prey to drink.

Wolfe did not penetrate far beneath the mask that Flecker put up to impress his audience, and Wolfe did not recall, in any great detail, Flecker's real doubts about his religious beliefs. Sedgwick had mistakenly thought that Flecker was still calling himself evangelical; but he was soon corrected, as Flecker wrote in his 'greaseproof' letter that he 'hated (no slighter word would suffice) all Church divisions, and all divisions into sects'. He conceded that if Sedgwick meant that to be evangelical was to like 'Mission-work' he thought he had 'as every man has, a mission in life to fulfil, about which I hold a high ideal'. Flecker wanted to be called 'purely, plainly and simply, a Christian'. So what he was turning his back on was not Christianity, but the narrow sect to which his parents belonged. No question of his joining another sect was entertained. He disliked 'the ineffectual obsolete gabble of the Prayer-Book' he told Sedgwick, an opinion which he realised would not go down too well with his father who was publishing a book on the subject for students.[289]

He went, despite his feelings about religion, to the Christian Union with Stanley McKelvie, whose rooms were close enough to his for them to shout messages to each other. McKelvie had been asked to have lunch with Flecker's parents when they came up to Oxford, and it was obvious that McKelvie was someone whose friendship they would not frown upon. McKelvie's parents approved of their son's choice of friend. Mrs. McKelvie felt that Flecker had a very warm place in her heart. McKelvie, who was destined for the priesthood, [290] eventually came to think of his friend as something of a Bohemian, and to find that they did not have much in common in the life they wanted to lead as undergraduates. They had enough in common to remain friends, but there was much in their respective interests that held them apart.

His other friend from former days was Frank Savery, who was born on 27 September 1883, at 37 Newhouse, Huddersfield, Yorkshire, the son of Frank Pasmore Savery, a woollen merchant, and his wife Mary Hannah (née Brooke), now living in Leeds. Savery had been a pupil at Uppingham.[291] He was at Hertford, to study classics, on £100 scholarship. Savery did not appear to concern himself with Flecker's shifting religious views (he himself converted to Catholicism) but he saw great merit in the verse Flecker was writing at Oxford, more so than most people Flecker first encountered there. Savery would see that even if Flecker's early efforts at poetry-writing had faults, he would eventually write verse that would last. Savery had faith in Flecker's work; so vital at this stage in his development as a poet. Savery remembered: 'Hence there was a certain piquancy in the exuberant flow of passionate verse which issued from Flecker's ever-ready pen, in spite of his entire innocence of any experience whatever'.[292]

Savery recollected that Flecker was 'a great wit, but no humourist' who 'talked best when someone baited him'.[293] It was a popular habit to invite Flecker to lunch and dinner parties just to listen to him talking. Savery refers to 'bad taste' and it is possible that some of the talk verged on the obscene. From Flecker's point of view, a free lunch or dinner was a very useful help to his finances, when he could simply repay hospitality by giving a performance. At Dean Close he had lacked rich praise, and so admiration was very sweet to digest. His family, on the other hand, saw him as someone who had a 'rather shy and modest nature'. They felt that he undermined his health with 'idiosyncrasies of diet', without mentioning what these might be or realising that an emotional diet lacking in praise would need to be supplemented by something richer, for the sake of his mental and spiritual health.

What Flecker thought of Savery was summed up best in a ballade he wrote:

THE BALLAD OF CAPTAIN SAVERY THAT CAUGHT A DODO

I will tell you the tale of honest Captain SAVERY,
A man of merit and of good behaviour; he
Was neither blathery not yet palavery;
And, since he watched, but did not often pray, very
Prone to discountenance religious reverie.
For he was one whose words were full and flavoury, –
A sound man, who was never known to shave awry –
In fact, averse to every form of knavery,

He hated niggers, and he hated slavery.

So here's the tale, in brief, of Captain Savery:

HE CAUGHT A DODO WITH CONSPICUOUS BRAVERY AND KEPT IT SEVERAL WEEKS INSIDE AN AVIARY.[294]

Savery encouraged Flecker's poetry composition, and was most important to him as critic, friend, and admirer. Flecker soon realised that once up at Oxford, his life was almost a continuation of his schooldays:

> But to me it appears still worse that after this public-school life a boy should pass on to Oxford and Cambridge, where instead of entering on a new life he will merely continue in his former ways. If it meant influence to be a good cricketer at school, why so it does in college; if chapel was compulsory at school so it is at college; if independence meant unpopularity at school, so it does in most colleges. No new society arises to entertain the mind, no women enable him to understand the proportion of things in this world; no freedom of town life, no rousing interest in art or politics, will ever encroach on the monotony of a protracted schoolboy existence, wherein smoking, drinking and cards are only occasionally restrained by authority.[295]

As far as the influence 'to be a good cricketer' was concerned, Trinity was the place to excel. For the past seventy-five years Trinity had stood third in all colleges, in the number of cricket blues. Vice-President, Robert William Raper (1842–1915) was a very good cricketer, and also excelled at horse-riding and skating. Raper, who came from an army background, had been to Cheltenham College (1857–9). He had published a very good imitation of Walt Whitman in 'Echoes from the Oxford Magazine' (1890). He lectured in Homer, Virgil and Aristotle, amongst others, and he had been Bursar from 1887, until he had taken over the post of Vice-President in 1894. Flecker, who was not an outstanding cricketer, was unlikely to be taken notice of for his sporting activities, and Raper's notice-board style bore out the protracted schoolboy existence theory: 'Gentlemen coming from homes where bread throwing at the dinner table is habitual and finding it difficult in conforming suddenly to the unfamiliar ways of higher civilisation will be permitted to continue their domestic pastime at 5s. a throw, during their first year. After that the charge will be doubled.'

The president between 1897 and 1907 was Henry Francis Pelham, formerly a Fellow of Exeter College and Camden Professor of Ancient History. His interests were also in the sporting side of college life and Flecker described him as 'the amiable Pelham' after his interview with him soon after his arrival. Flecker found difficulty in conforming 'to the unfamiliar ways of higher civilisation' as McKelvie related how he was 'walking along in cap and gown and cigarette and dreams of Utopia' when he was fined on the spot after bumping into the Proctor. For him there was 'no freedom of town life'.

It was obvious that university life imposed its own restrictions but it also gave new freedoms. As a pupil at Dean Close, Flecker always had to push open a green baize door in order to find friends, and then these were from a rather limited selection. At Oxford he had access to a wider world and although he complained about University life as having 'no rousing interest in art or politics' he also wrote: 'returned the fire of his Oxford days: for long ago no one more often than he had sent the sun – and the moon too – to bed with talking. Social qualities, said his friends, had spoilt his chances (never too brilliant, it must be confessed) of academical distinction.'[296]

It is not explained why, for his first year at least, Flecker did not have rooms in College. If it was for financial considerations this was a pity. He would have been more comfortable and would also have had the chance to mix with his fellow undergraduates, and sometimes the Dons, and in the long run would have spent less money socialising outside college. Flecker changed rooms several times for reasons that appear rather superficial. His first rooms had no view, but despite his mother's efforts to improve the outlook by means of her horticultural expertise, he left and moved to rooms which had once been lived in by Dr. Johnson. Sharing the space once used by a famous person did not persuade him to remain. Saying the rooms did not get any sun, he moved again. Another set of rooms had the same wallpaper as the sanatorium at Dean Close, where, isolated by scarlet fever, he had written 'The Ballad of Blue Carnations'. He moved even when the wallpaper was changed. The real truth lay between the idea of looking for an ideal room, so that he could express his own personality more easily, and finding a room at a more reasonable cost.

The state of rooms available at Oxford was outlined in a letter to *The Times*, written by an American woman whose son had gone to Harvard before he studied at Oxford: 'Is it necessary in order to turn out the well-dressed Englishman we admired so much in America, to subject the youth to half-painted floors, ragged carpets, shabby furniture, shockingly greasy cushions, untidy wallpaper, dirty mattresses and blankets and extraordinary discomfort.'

Flecker did not aspire to be the well-dressed Englishman, but the letter demonstrated the wide gap that existed between those people who could afford to rent rooms, and the working-class people who rented out the rooms. They were not in a position to offer rich furnishings in exchange for the few shillings rent they were offered. Undergraduates who rented rooms could escape from them into the rooms of friends who had rooms in the colleges, or they could dine out. Flecker managed, in his many moves, to impose his personality on the rented rooms, even if he appeared to be modelling himself on Huysman's famous character, Des Esseintes, who carried a light cane, whose rooms were hung with rich tapestries and crowded with works of art and literature, and who drank curaçao.

This was borne out by Stanley McKelvie's recollections of Flecker's rooms: 'Curious knick-knacks, strange fruits, rare liqueurs, choice tobacco, and strange books were all around'[297], as well as by a passage from Flecker's *The Grecians*:

> They entered a low and obscure doorway, toiled up a painful staircase, turned a corner, and found themselves in the sitting-room of Smith. It was a small room, but comfortable beyond all an Italian's dreams, and beautiful enough to satisfy the most exacting of Cambridge aesthetes. A dim, reddish light suggested[298] tapestried hangings, surprising pictures, and innumerable books; yet for all the display of furniture and fabrics in a little space, the room was mysteriously cool. Hofman, turning his eyes to the bookshelves, as reading men will, was delighted to find his beloved moderns, Teutonic and Scandinavian, bound in pigskin and arranged in order; while Edwinson marked with delight the rows devoted to the classics, for he was a devoted scholar, although so pathetically second-class. Smith let them busy themselves with inspection while he prepared an excellent coffee: soon they drank it, not unaccompanied by seductive liqueurs. The pipes were lighted with English tobacco, glasses filled with Scotch whisky, and there sank into armchairs worthy of the noblest university traditions ...[299]

This room, although not supposed to be a room in Oxford, was nevertheless, a room of a writer's dreams, shorn of the chaos that existed in his rented rooms. Flecker furnished his rooms with gifts from home, and objects his parents regarded as necessary. This fictional room, with its shelves of books all bound and in order, was not something he achieved, but at times he aspired to it. He did spend money on getting some of his books bound; an extravagance that his parents objected to when they found out. The rooms of his friends or college staff, where he visited and had happy times, are more likely to have resembled the rooms of his fiction. The friends who visited his Oxford rooms always came away with the impression of clutter, but their recollections gave a more accurate and human view of their host. The life of a scholar was for a man with a true scholar's mind. Flecker did not possess that sort of mind needed to maintain it: the picture he saw was clear, but well out of reach.

Flecker needed to hide his more serious side, and many who encountered him at Oxford did not know that it existed. He had realised that being a swot (a role that he could hardly escape as the son of the headmaster) had not made him popular with his fellows, and that it was better to try and hide this side of his character from all but a few close friends – at least until he found his feet around the social scene during the first terms. It was even more prudent to hide the fact that he was an aspiring poet and instead concentrate on the sporting side.

At the beginning of the Oxford term, he took a football team home, made up of friends from the old days, and some he had met whilst up at Oxford. This infiltration of new faces alarmed his parents, who feared that the new friends would flatter their son. However, he learned the art of telling his parents that whatever praise came his way he took with a pinch of salt.

Flecker had spoken at an evening debate on Luxury (of all subjects), something that his parents would have hoped he was not an expert on. Flecker told them that he was congratulated by the Secretary, who had said that he had made the best speech of the evening. He also told them that he thought that his was the formula adopted to boost the morale of new speakers.

Flecker did not make holiday plans with any of his new friends; he spent the Easter vacation of 1903 with Cyril Roberts in a cottage in Capel Curig, North Wales. The cottage had no running water, and the camp bed felt very hard. The weather was cold and very wet, and he had to light a fire (a task he did not complete at the first attempt) before preparing his own breakfast and washing up. He had to do this all alone, as Cyril had already left. Amid all the descriptions of his domestic chores, which he outlined in a letter to his parents, it would have been as well for them to note that he was also having difficulties with his attempts to study. He admitted that the logic notes he had brought with him were 'badly scrawled' (if these were the notes he had written while writing a long letter to Sedgwick, then it was not hard to see how the problem had arisen). He did not enjoy solitude or studying on his own; life at Dean Close and evangelical camp holidays had not prepared him for this short period when he had to be self-reliant. The picture he wanted to present to his parents was that he could not work in the cottage and that he was homesick, as well as having too much to study. But the real problem was that he had a growing feeling that a classical education was a waste of time, as he told Sedgwick (but not his parents) in a letter dated May 1903. To his parents, in case they thought he was complaining too much, he said that he enjoyed the solitude 'because I enjoy everything'.

He was no happier in Germany, where he was sent after his holiday in Wales to study at a crammer's called Tilleys. The noise of the Germans, who never stopped talking, was as bad as the silence in the cottage in Wales. The Germans always shouted instead of talking, and were rude to one another. Flecker told Sedgwick that he wanted to learn German, because 'Germany has a fine literature' and 'because the Germans are a fine people'. But he also accused the Germans of talking rubbish and pointed out that they did not keep any cats. This letter demonstrated that he was beginning to realise the difference between reading about a country and visiting it and meeting the people.

Sedgwick had thought that Flecker had the Civil Service in mind when choosing to learn German, but was told that he would not ever do anything 'half so steady as that'. Flecker felt his temper was restless and his ideas of the future were very vague.

It was in this letter that he told Sedgwick that he did not dislike classical education; he found it quite entertaining, but he was 'absolutely convinced that it is so much time, to a great extent, wasted'. His ideas were 'not all the outcome of Germany'. His views were 'entirely contrary to that of all other opponents of classical education'. He thought it should be preserved at school as a mental training. He thought that verse composition was one of the finest trainings in existence. He thought too that a university classical education should be done away with, because by that time the undergraduate should have attained self-consciousness. As for what classical literature had done for him, he told Sedgwick, 'it is only just now that I am thrusting off its unmanly despondency'. He did not elaborate any further on that point.

Three of the world's greatest poets – Shakespeare, Goethe and Keats (he informed Sedgwick) – had not known any classics, but gained their knowledge from translations. This statement implied that Flecker saw a classical education as a barrier against joining the ranks of the greatest poets.

He was trying to rid himself of the influence of Ruskin, as he felt it was 'dangerous'. Ruskin was 'far too excitable and his character not very strong'. He was turning to 'that magnificent book, *Two Years Ago*, because it preached 'healthy manliness' (it had just been re-issued). Flecker had written to his parents and told them: 'I don't want to get my instructions from sermons: because my views are fixed now, for ever and through eternity'. (Although Kingsley's book preached sermons of a kind, they were from viewpoints and on subjects that Flecker found more to his liking than anything from Dean Close.)

Two Years Ago reflected Kingsley's views on sanitary reform, of which he was a zealous exponent. Kingsley described the outbreak of cholera and denounced the evangelicals who took the opportunity to scare the local people with rants about divine judgment and the prospect of burning in Hell.

In contrast to the horrors of the cholera outbreak, the novel had wonderful descriptions of the beauty of North Wales. These Kingsley used with great effect in a book in which the characters, and their deeds and exploits, are not so convincing or so spectacular. Flecker used the North Wales countryside in his novel, with the same result.

One of the characters in *Two Years Ago*, was the artist, Claude Mellot, who was described as: 'a delicate featured man with a look of half-lazy enthusiasm about his beautiful face, which reminds you so much of Shelley's portrait; only he has what Shelley had not, clustering auburn curls, and a rich brown beard, soft as silk. You set him down at once as a man of delicate susceptibility, sweetness and thoughtfulness'.

Mellot's companion (described in the Introductory) was tall, dark and handsome, with a very large forehead, but the size of his mouth was described as a fault (in his case, too small).

Kingsley's novel had a series of heroic characters, amongst them an Anglican curate, Frank Headley, and Tom Thurnall. Tom's friend is not heroic, he is a decadent, the poet who starts off as John Briggs, a chemist's assistant but quits this humble post for an unknown future, as does Norman Price in *The King of Alsander*, who worked in a grocer's shop, owned by his father.

John Briggs, like Norman Price, owed everything to a gentleman. In Briggs's case, it was a doctor, the father of Tom Thurnall. Briggs feels unappreciated and misunderstood, and the doctor urges him not to turn his back on the quiet country life in which poets such as Wordsworth have been content to live and grow old.

The eighteen-year old Briggs would have none of this advice, as this sort of progress was too slow for him to contemplate. He did not want long years of obscurity, misconception and ridicule. He wanted everything at once, and if necessary he would die like Chatterton.[300] Briggs did not want to continue living in the village of Whitbury, and aspiring to the post of correspondent on a country newspaper.

Briggs was handsome, with a bad complexion due to the life he led, which was not active enough; he wrote verses or worked in the shop, where he felt himself above learning the business. But Kingsley did let the poet have large, dark eyes and a dreamy look, even if he 'moped at home like a yard dog'. Briggs vanished from Whitbury, and re-emerged as Elsley Vavasour, author of 'A Soul's Agonies', and other Poems, and married to the former Lucia St. Just, by whom he had children. He was not happy, despite living in a sumptuous house at his wife's expense.

Vavasour had a fatal habit of taking opium. Although he conquered it for a while, he took it up again after a flight through the Welsh mountains. Claude Mellot had said that the poet would go crazy one day, and it was thought that he had done so when he took the Capel Curig road to the mountains, pursued by two 'hearties'. The descriptions of North Wales were after Flecker's own heart, and he, too, used the North Wales countryside in his own novel. Vavasour on the run, saw in front of him: 'Glyder Vawr, its head shrouded in soft mist, through which the moonlight gleamed upon the chequered quarries of that enormous desolation, the dead bones of the eldest born of time'. Vavasour climbed and saw, 'On the right hand Snowdon rises'.

The 'hearties' were two Cambridge boating men who were risking their lives in order to save Vavasour. They were described by Kingsley as far more 'poetic' than Vavasour 'or any dozen mere verse-writers' because they were prepared to risk their lives. When the 'hearties' found the poet, he wanted to be left alone. He escaped when the 'hearties' slept, intending to reach London and then go to the Continent and be at peace, like Byron and Shelley. Vavasour reached the bottom of an enormous slope 'till he stopped at the top of a precipice, full six hundred feet above the lone tarn of Idwal'. He then ran along the 'boggy shore of Idwal'. Vavasour reflected that he had married a fine lady who did not understand him, and then took opium again to help with hunger pangs and the railway journey to London.

Vavasour, the poet, who is not depicted as a noble figure or even a worthwhile one when compared to the men of action, gave Flecker ideas that in their turn made him try to fill both roles of 'hearty' and poet.

Flecker had good news to impart at the end of his first year; he told his parents that he was through 'Divvers' and he was optimistic about his future. He thought he could get into the ICS, win prizes and get a second in Mods. In the summer of 1903 he was back again in the Wales he loved, at Colwyn Bay, mid-way between Chester and Holyhead. Flecker had suggested that he and Sedgwick might meet at the evangelical camp at Colwyn Bay when he had written to him in May.

The town of Colwyn Bay 'was encumbered by the adjectives marine, sylvan, mountainous and recreative. Country lanes overhung with briar, berry and honeysuckle but these might disappear beneath the advance of the speculative builder. Colwyn Bay had no streets, drives or avenues or garages, but had higher than average sunshine, a pebbly beach with a pier and promenade and well-wooded hills.'[301]

Flecker was happy in the evangelical camp, where he was involved in the production of a painfully witty magazine, but this carefree feeling was soon to disappear beneath the burden of returning to Oxford for more serious work for Moderations.

Classical Honour Moderations represented an arduous path through Latin and Greek and stretched before him when be began the Michaelmas term in 1903. He was also continuing to study French because he had told his father he wanted to take the examination for the Taylorian Scholarship in French in December, 1903.[302] He told his parents that he felt a first-class certificate in French almost as important as a good class in Mods 'now that classical education is being shoved into its right place'.[303] In order to get his parents' acceptance of this course of study, he told them 'Prof. Ellis approves'. Professor Robinson Ellis (1834–1913) was the author of the book on Catullus, the purchase price of which had been the subject of discussion with his parents soon after his arrival. A distinguished classical scholar who lectured on Propertius and Latin verse composition, as well as Catullus, he was reclusive and eccentric, and he may have already decided that Flecker was not going to get a First in Moderations. Even a second, at this stage might be in doubt, and so a certificate in French might be a helpful life-raft thrown into what could prove to be a troubled sea of future failure.

Knowledge of a second language, such as French, could be a more liberating experience than the translation of Latin and Greek. Here was an escape from the dominant language, English, to a language where the images produced were much less restrained. But learning French had a practical use, as he pointed out to his parents: 'Surely for a schoolmaster nowadays, a first-class certificate in French is almost as important and useful as a good class in Mods.'[304]

He continued to study German as modern languages, he felt, would be more useful should he reconsider views that he had about joining the Civil Service. The study of two more languages also meant that he could enjoy the poetry of Germany and France. He especially like Gautier and he had been to the lecture on him given by Professor George Saintsbury.

Théophile Gautier (1811–72) appealed to Flecker, as he had appealed to Swinburne. Both Swinburne and Flecker had French forebears, and Gautier had been 'imported' into England by Matthew Arnold of Balliol. Flecker was already taking the path followed by all young aspiring writers in adopting the literary life and style of writers they admire. Flecker was so influenced by Gautier, a southern Frenchman, that he may have gone so far to imitate his mode of dress by wearing 'a white knitted waistcoat that will simply eclipse you'.[305]

The influence of Gautier went beyond clothes and style. Gautier was morbidly absorbed by the subject of death and dread that the dead continued to be conscious and in despair at being no longer remembered by those still living. The life of Gautier was something to copy. Gautier's earliest collection of poetry was *Poesies*, published, at his father's expense, in 1830. Few copies were sold. In September 1833, Gautier signed a contract for a novel to be called *Mademoiselle de Maupin*.

The novel, when first published, was thought to be scandalous. The heroine, like the hero of Flecker's novel, appeared to inhabit a different dimension, and there was an aura of lesbianism and hermaphroditism. Gautier was also commissioned to write a series of articles on writers whose works had been long neglected, an idea that also appealed to Flecker. Gautier started his journalistic career in 1833, and because, like Flecker, he had no private income, he prompted Flecker to see the advantages of journalism as a career.

Gautier later published *Voyage en Espagne* and, with others, a scenario for the ballet *Giselle*. He met Baudelaire and mutual esteem was established. In 1850, Gautier visited Italy and wrote his *Voyage en Italie*, and later made voyages and published books on Malta, Smyrna, Constantinople, Athens and Russia. He was also interested in the Middle East, and his interests began to influence Flecker's writings. Gautier was not anti-Christian, according to Saintsbury, but in favour of classical paganism. Gautier and Flecker shared the view that they disliked Christianity because it had given rise to guilt and anxiety.

All Flecker's mental conflict about his future, alongside his extra work for Mods brought on 'a horrid sore throat' in the early days of 1904. Despite this, he wrote in not very serious vein to his parents about his belief in Fate and ideals and his literary abilities. He gave them a list of posts that might come his way, ranging from Vice-Chancellor of the University to a second Shakespeare. Once again, he appeared to be putting red herrings in his parents' way, for although they could argue that the posts he was suggesting were unrealistic in aim, they could not say it was unrealistic to aim high. Neither Flecker nor his parents took the view that if he stopped worrying about a future career and concentrated on his studies, he would be better prepared to make a good choice when the time came.

Fate took a hand, and, as a result, his future professional prospects took second place in his life. One day in March, at a lunch in Savery's rooms, he met John Davidson Beazley. Jack Beazley was the living counterpart, in appearance, of Claude Mellot in *Two Years Ago*. Like Mellot, Beazley was a 'delicate-featured man', who had 'a look of half-lazy enthusiasm about his beautiful face', which also reminded Flecker of Shelley's portrait. Beazley was not 'tiny' as Mellot was, but had his 'clustering auburn curls' (although Beazley's hair could be described as red-gold). The resemblance to Mellot was striking, even if Beazley had not grown 'a rich brown beard, soft as silk'.

The merging, in Flecker's mind, of the fictional Mellot with the real-life Beazley was a powerful mix. Although Beazley was not the same sort of person as Mellot, their similarity in appearance meant that Flecker invested Beazley not only with the qualities that all who fall in love invest the beloved with (that is qualities they do not possess), but also an extra dose of perfection. Beazley not only had to live up to a fictional hero but also to Flecker's dream, held ever since he had come up to Oxford, that he would find a friendship that would never pall, and of such a character 'that the longer it lasts the firmer it becomes'.[306]

Beazley was 'only nineteen; a handsome and strong young man,' 'whose beauty of person and brilliance of mind made one forget his unfortunate connection with trade'.[307] He was not the son of a professional family.[308] The first child of Mark and Mary Beazley, John Davidson Beazley was born at his grandparents' home, 51 Grant Street, Glasgow, on 13 September 1885 at 5.45 a.m. At the time of his son's birth, Mark Beazley had risen from Club Steward to be a Club Secretary, like his own father. By the time Jack Beazley's brother was born, the family had moved to Newcastle-upon-Tyne, where Mark Beazley was a Club Manager. Mark James Robertson Beazley was born on 25 March 1887, at 29 Malcolm Street, Newcastle-upon-Tyne.[309]

In his very early years, Jack Beazley had an unsettled life. By the time he was four, his maternal grandfather was dead (at the age of sixty-five on 16 December 1889) and Mary Davidson, his grandmother, was head of the household. Jack Beazley was back in the five-room house he had been born in, his aunt Jemima was still unmarried, and the household took in an Inland Revenue officer as a lodger. Beazley was surrounded by female relatives; his father appeared not to have made a permanent home for his wife and two sons. This sort of background, although not one of great poverty and deprivation, was not one where the expected path for the elder son would be university, even allowing for the higher regard for education in Scotland. Beazley's achievement was not unique,[310] but his path to Christ's Hospital, where he won the Richard's Gold Medal for the author of the best set of Latin Hexameters in 1902 and the Thompson Classical Gold Medal for the most proficient in classics, leading to his becoming the senior scholar of his year at Balliol, when he came to Oxford, in 1903, must have meant financial sacrifices for his family that he could only repay by not failing to succeed in academic life.

The clue to how Beazley reached his university status (apart from his undoubted ability to win scholarships and prizes) is found in *The King of Alsander*. Flecker, when referring to the origins of Norman Price, said: 'If young Price appears in this story so strangely different from his father and from the other villagers of Blaindon, and indeed from all grocers whatsoever, we need not accept the explanation of some, that his father was "a deeper man than you think", or the assertion of others that he "got it from his mother,".....The lad's singularity was much more likely due to this curious and close intimacy with a gentleman: and I hope that those who read history will not close the book without a sigh of remonstrance against all those who insist on giving the lower classes thoughts above their station.'[311]

The lunch, where Beazley and Flecker were Savery's only guests, was enlivened by discussions about Sir Richard Burton (1821–90), a volume of whose work Flecker was said to have brought with him.

The particular work under discussion was a long nine-part poem, *The Kasidah*, first brought out in 1880 in a privately printed edition. A *kasidah* is an early type of Arabic poem, consisting of thirteen or more rhyming couplets. Although the full title was *The Kasidah of Haji Abdu El-yezdi, a Lay of Higher Law Translated and Annoted by his Friend and Pupil FB*, Burton was the sole author both of the poem and the annotations. Although it was claimed to predate the *Rubiayat of Omar Khayyam* by Edward Fitzgerald (1809–83), published in 1861, it was, in fact, written after the publication of Fitzgerald's popular work. Flecker, it was said by Savery, was fascinated by the wide and not very deep ponderings on different religions, in *The Kasidah*, while Beazley remarked that the line 'the lovely Gods of libertine Greece' was in poor taste, and that the best part of the entire poem, except for the refrain, was the part that dealt with the death of Pan.[312]

The refrain was in the first of the nine parts, and was about the dawn coming up over the desert:

> Sad falls upon my yearning ear the tinkling
> of the Camel-bells:

The last part of the ninth part of *The Kasidah*, which was about Faith and Death, has the final line: 'The whispers of the Desert-wind: the Tinkling of the camel's bell.' Flecker copied some of it out into his copy-book as *The Kasidah* was difficult to obtain.[313]

Burton had translated *The Arabian Nights*; not in a version that was suitable for children, but one that was strictly for adults. It was not the first; the standard authority had been written by Edward William Lane (1801–76) who published *The Thousand and One Nights*. Burton had risked prosecution for obscenity by publishing his version outside academic boundaries. Ten volumes had come out in 1885 and a further six volumes between 1886 and 1888. Burton had made a substantial profit from this enterprise, unlike the commercial failure he had faced over the publication of *The Kasidah*. *The Arabian Nights*, unlike *The Kasidah*, treated frankly all aspects of sex, including male and female homosexuality, which greatly shocked most of the critics. Burton tried to excuse his work on the grounds that he treated what others regarded as obscenity with laughter and wit to make it a matter of manners rather than morals. Sex was not the only subject dealt with in great detail; death was one of the main topics, including murder and suicide, as was the making of hashish. [314]

The life and work of Sir Richard Francis Burton KCMG (1821–90) could not fail to intrigue Flecker. Burton had also been an undergraduate at Trinity, going up in 1840 to study Latin and Greek for Greats. He did not see eye to eye with the college authorities on their teaching. Oxford had failed to appreciate the linguistic gifts of Burton, and after only a year Burton had gone to India to become an interpreter. Burton was no poet, but an expert in languages, including countless dialects.

'*The Carmina of Gaius Valerius Catullus*. Now first completely Englished into Verse and Prose, the metrical Part by Captain Sir Richard F. Burton' was published in 1894. As Burton was better at spoken languages, his was a flawed and rhymed translation, and not successful.

Flecker had himself translated Catullus, and he would discover on reading Burton's translations that his grasp of metre and rhyme was not in the same class as Flecker's. Flecker's translation was much superior, but both men were drawn to Catullus for the same reasons; they appreciated his decadence and obscenity.[315]

Burton was also the translator, from the French, of *The Perfumed Garden of Cheikh Nefzaoui*, a manual of Arabian erotology, published for the Kama Shastra Society in 1886. A German edition of *The Perfumed Garden* was available in 1905.[316]

In *The Perfumed Garden*, as in *The Arabian Nights*, sex was humorous. Beazley and Flecker continued to read and enjoy Burton's works together. 'Beazley brought sex out into the open and indeed made it seem uproariously funny.'[317]

It could have been that Beazley was already interested in Burton before they met, and that was the reason why *The Kasidah* was brought to the first meeting. If Burton's books could not all be read in the original, then there were pirate copies available, as well as editions in German, which Beazley could translate. Passages from *The King of Alsander* could apply to Beazley:

> But the sudden wide prospects opened up by all
> that golden world – all those enchanted gardens
> that hid between pasteboard covers – had dazzled his eyes
>   and made him a most exceptional person.[318]
> He liked his literature garish and vivid, and
> with his insistent passion for all the decadent stuff
> that used to be in favour ten or twelve years ago,...."[319]
>
> the delicate shades of metre and language, lay
> beyond his sphere.[320]

Flecker's description of Norman Price applied to his own love of books:

> But he loved all the books that are not generally read;
> he could feel that such books were peculiarly his own
> property or his own discovery, and had a habit of always
> reading books that no one else has read is not a bad guide
> to literature.[321]

Burton's life and work showed Flecker that even if Burton was regarded as a failure at Oxford, he could use his knowledge of languages and his travels to gain fame that even Oxford would acknowledge. Oxford could be deceived by what they supposed were genuine translations, when in fact they were the original work of the author.

The mystique surrounding the great adventurer could not fail to excite Flecker's interest and admiration as someone he could model himself upon: much more so than the fictional poet Elsely Vavasour, from *Two Years Ago*. Burton was a figure to admire in this respect; he was like Beazley, whose intellectual scope of mind, attractive appearance and air of mystery immediately drew Flecker to him. Beazley was from a class below the one that the Flecker family now aspired to; the Beazleys had not risen further in society by marriage or by the change in status of their work. Flecker, like most people, was intrigued by the class just below his own, as well as the one just above. Beazley did much to conceal his origins throughout his life.[322] Flecker described Beazley's voice as being 'like a bell', which would seem to rule out the accents of his native Glasgow, betraying his working-class origins.

In a letter dated 14 March 1904,[323] Flecker wondered what Sedgwick would think of Jack. He told Sedgwick that Jack reminded him of Shelley, 'as portrayed by Hogg, especially when he lies on the hearth-rug, his head almost in the fire, with his long light hair, slight frame and pensive face'. Flecker admitted that the description sounded as if it was out of a novel, but 'such a fellow' was not often to be encountered outside the pages of 'a novel, or romance'. Flecker did not admit to Sedgwick which novel he had in mind. He told Sedgwick that Jack was very like 'E' only more so, without the cynicism. Flecker mentioned that he had another friend 'H', an Etonian, the fourth Trinity Scholar of his year, and Flecker gave a description of 'H'.

He is large, solid, imperturbable, and lazy; in his grey eyes are libraries of humanity and mirth. His great charm is his talking, which is slow and deliberate. The least jest of his is most marvellously funny from his lips. He is a true aristocrat, cousin of Lord G., etc., etc., a fact it would be unnecessary to mention, were it not that he possesses all the peculiar virtues of the English nobility, with none of their vices. I have never heard him laughed at, never heard anyone talk ill of him. He is a friend of young S. and knows Uppingham well.

His bent is not so much to poetry as to art, social history and problems, and Church questions, in which, though an agnostic, he takes great interest. I know you would like him because I never met anyone who disliked him and have met many that know him. He represents sensible refinement, and true broad mindedness to a wonderful degree.[324]

The fourth Trinity scholar of Flecker's year was Granville Hamilton (1883–1947) who had been admitted to Trinity on 17 October, 1902.

The first son of Major Douglas Hamilton, Irish Guards, he was born at 2 Draycott Place, London, of a Scottish background. 'Aristocrat' referred to the fact that he was a grandson of the Earl of Donaghue. At Eton he had been in the same group as Maynard Keynes and Bernard Swithinbank, who could have been the 'young S' referred to by Flecker, or this could have been Savery. Hamilton was a close friend of Keynes and Swithinbank. Of him, Flecker had written in his *Book of Kara James*: 'Again how Proby, glorious but mute/Would not be happy in a parachute.'[325],[326]

Beazley, unlike 'H' (who Sedgwick was 'far surer to like'), was not of the aristocracy and he did not have money; he was worse off financially than Flecker. Beazley was going in for university scholarships; these were the Ireland and the Craven, both of which he won. Like 'H', Beazley was an agnostic and interested in Church questions. This letter to Sedgwick, which extolled the virtues of Jack Beazley, also contained important news. Flecker, too, had become an agnostic. He told Sedgwick he had become an agnostic because he felt bound to reject Christianity 'not so much from the improbabilities of Bible narrative, although it is very doubtful, of course, that Christ Himself claimed to be more than man (see *Erehwon Revisited* by Butler, for an amusing account of the growth of a false worship), as by a feeling that its ideals are not the highest possible, e.g. justification by faith, the system of reward and punishment, the excessive altruism, precluding strength of character, etc. Charles Kingsley is not so true a type of Christian as S. Francis of Assisi'.[327] It is hard to be sure how much this professing of agnosticism at this particular time was due to his blossoming friendship with Jack Beazley, or to the fact that it was bound eventually to stir up more conflict with his parents and divert attention away from his inability to handle money and his growing dislike of learning Latin and Greek. The chances were that he wanted to please Jack and upset his parents at the same time.

The main news in the letter to Sedgwick was to tell him that, after his exhausting work for Mods, he was off to the Welsh mountains with Jack to stay in an old lady's cottage, and live on £1 each a week. Sedgwick had been invited to Capel to meet Jack, but his silence on the matter was taken as indicating he was declining the invitation. Sedgwick may have decided that two was company, three a crowd, and the travelling arrangements more in the nature of a marathon than a holiday. Jack Beazley travelled by train to Betwys-y-Coed, where Flecker met him, having cycled to Leominster, and taken his cycle on the train to Corwen, where he cycled on a messy road, with a head wind, to Betwys-y-Coed, a journey of seventy miles. They then faced a five mile walk to Pont-y-

Cyfind, where Jack (in much better shape, as he had not had the long cycle-trek) after cooking supper, worked for an hour. Jack Beazley had to read *Prolegomena to Greek Religion* by Jane Harrison.

Jack insisted on taking texts to read in Conway Castle and these descriptions of hard work and physical exertion were outlined for his parents' benefit, in a letter. Sedgwick, in his letter, got a much jollier picture as Flecker described to him 'a three miles' ride at a rattling pace over the sands, of Red Wharf Bay, with the wind behind us'.[328]

Flecker and Beazley also stayed with Cyril Roberts at the same cottage in mid-Wales that Flecker had shared the previous year with Cyril. This stay brought no grumbles about the work involved or even about cooking their own meals. Flecker summed up the holiday: 'Chiefly of all, I learnt what work really is.'[329]

This concentration on work was due to the friendship with Beazley, but his influence on Flecker's handling of money was not nearly so beneficial. They ran out and had to borrow from the postman, but repaid him. Flecker described the holiday to Sedgwick as 'the pleasantest and most useful vac. or holiday of my life'.[330] It was useful to learn to concentrate on work, and pleasant to have the beauty of Wales forever in his mind, as he wrote:

> The boy swung round a corner of the highway, and suddenly beheld the valley far below. He saw quiet forests of tall golden trees and meadows so rich with gentian and wild pansy that even at that far height he could see them shine. To his left, at the edge of the of the plain, lay spear-sharp mountains, a little darker than the skies, whose distant hollows and tortuous cones ever hinted at the mystery of the next valley and the joy of things unseen. He saw the thin torrent which tumbled down in cascades behind the wall become a quiet and solemn river below leading to a curved strip of sea, of an intense unearthly colour, southern, fantastic, beyond all belief, and the sound of rushing waters seemed the only sound in the world...

> 'Surely in those blue mountains lurked and lolled the devastating dragon who came down for his yearly toll of maiden flesh; surely in that blue sea swam all the shoal of nereids and dolophinous fishy beings whose song is dangerous to men.'[331]

The oblong Conway Castle, where they spent two hours reading, was washed on two sides by the river, which hurried down the mountains beyond Capel Curig and was refreshed on both sides by many swift flowing tributaries before it hurled itself into a chasm sixty feet wide, where jagged rocks broke it up and the stream erupted into three large falls. Flecker wrote to his parents about contemplating the Swallow Falls and Miner's Bridge in lovely weather.

It is not possible to demonstrate with any certainty which poems Flecker wrote before he met Beazley, and those he wrote immediately afterwards. All poems for that month are dated March 1904; so how much impact Beazley had on Flecker's poetry is uncertain. Also the exact date of their first meeting is not given. One exception is 'Lucretia, which was known to have been revised with Jack Beazley's help, as he mentioned the fact in letters to Sedgwick. The fragment of 'Lucretia' began with the lines that also conjure up Beazley and Flecker together in the cottage in Wales:

> *As one who in the cold abyss of night*
> *Stares at a book whose grey print meaningless*
> *Dances between the lamplight and his eyes,*

This was the first poem in his black copybook, and it is appropriate that its theme was that of the devastating effects of passion (although in this poem it is between husband and wife). It is in blank verse, on which Beazley was said by Flecker to be an expert, and the poem shows the influence of Tennyson and Swinburne. The lines '…with lash and terrible hiss/With lash and terrible hiss of steaming snakes, ' are pure Flecker.

Flecker's translations from Bierbaum included 'Munich Student Song', dated March 1904, in both copybooks, and 'The Throb of His Heart', dated March 1904 in the Kara James copybook, but April 1904 in the black notebook.

'Song', the poem that began 'Not the night of her Wild Hair', was also dated March 1904, in the *Book of Kara James*, and in the black copybook; it is a farewell poem and, although addressed to a female love, in a disguised way it refers to a brief parting between himself and Jack Beazley before the return to Oxford.[332] Flecker would have to go back by bicycle to Dean Close and Beazley by train to a separate destination. The poem read:

> Not the night of her wild hair
> Nor the remembrance of her eyes

Leave me in so deep despair
As her echoing good-byes.

Swift musicians of the air
Still repeat those [word unclear] idle sighs
And their violins prepare
Newer deeper melodies.[333]

Kara James Dean Close School

The Bierbaum translations, if not influenced directly by Beazley, at least must have been chosen because of the subject-matter or, once chosen, it became evident to Flecker that the subject had some bearing on his present state of mind and relationship with Beazley.

Flecker dated the fragment of his play *Nero and Acte – A dialogue in an Old Manner*, March 1904, in his BKJ copybook. A meeting with Compton Mackenzie may have helped him with the idea of writing a play. Mackenzie was planning to write a trilogy of plays, under the influence of reading *The Death of the Gods* by Dmitry Merezhkowsky (1865–1941), which had been translated by Herbert Trench (sometime Fellow of All Souls College) and published in 1901. The book was about the extraordinary career of the fourth century Apostate Julian who travelled through Asia and visited Constantinople and Syria. Compton Mackenzie hoped to make his name with plays, essays and a novel, and when he met Flecker in the Broad and told him about his proposed trilogy and the influence of Merezhkowsky, Flecker nodded slow agreement, but as far as Mackenzie was concerned the idea faded from his memory.[334] Merezhkowsky, who could be described as a Russian Nietzschean, had written a trilogy of novels which took historical figures as their fictional heroes. These superhuman characters embodied the Nietzschean philosophy, and in one case, one novella about Leonardo da Vinci, portrayed beauty and love.

But Flecker's memory may have recorded the idea that a play would bring in money and fame, as Mackenzie had heard of Hubert Henry Davies, who at the age of twenty-four had two plays running in the West End, *Cousin Kate* and *Mrs. Gorringe's Necklace*.

On Flecker's return from Oxford, he discovered he had got a third in Mods. He could hardly believe the facts when he saw them in black and white and he reacted melodramatically when he wrote to his parents and told them of: 'one of the most crushing blows that has ever befallen me – or you'.[335]

By way of softening the blow, he told them that nobody at Trinity had got a First, and there were three Seconds. (How many had also got a Third, he did not mention.)

'Yet in no way does my conscience prick me,' he wrote, and went on to say that he had worked conscientiously and in only one paper (which he did not name) did he feel he could have done better with more work. He concluded: 'The fact must be that my ability in comps. and verses has entirely failed.'[336]

From the point of view of Trinity College, no reason appeared to have been given or discussed for the poor results. But, as he had been taken on in the first place as a scholar of promise, and at that time his composition had required 'a great deal of improvement',[337] it has to be concluded that Blakiston[338], who had been reluctant to take Flecker on in the first place, now had the opportunity to prove that he was right in at least one respect.[339]

The meeting with Beazley could have been blamed for disrupting Flecker's concentration on his classical work only if Beazley himself had been an indifferent scholar. But Beazley was already a brilliant and dedicated scholar, and it was surprising that the close association with him had not helped Flecker to get better results. Although Flecker had 'worked' to gain Beazley's support and admiration, the meeting had come too late to help him make up for the time he had already lost. His conscience should have pricked him just a little. 'What am I to do?' he despaired. He told his parents that all the dreams he had formed 'of a life of study' had gone. He felt he must work and cram for the 'ICS or something'. He finished the letter: 'Anyhow, this last vac. closes to me for three years, at least, that education in poetry and literature and research I longed for – and now for a cram. I did expect a second.'[340]

His tutor Blakiston had expected five Firsts and he was worried that he would 'probably dock my schol.' He begged to be allowed to stay on in Oxford until he had taken the Taylorian. He ended his letter: 'Yours in vast disappointment, Roy'. What his parents thought of this failure was, surprisingly, not recorded. But, as the letter was sufficiently contrite and he told them that he was stirred to new exertion, his parents did not appear to have chided him too bitterly, although it was not their style to let a chance to air their views on their son's supposed shortcomings pass unnoticed. As he had told them, his failure had stirred him to 'new exertion', so, to some extent, the Third in Mods represented a temporary setback.

Flecker's letter in May 1904, from the Oxford Union, to Sedgwick (who was recovering from an accident) about his poor performance in Mods was along the same lines as the letter to his parents. It was much less melodramatic, and with a little more insight and detail and ended on a more optimistic note: 'How I managed to get a Third I don't know. It was not lack of work – things I worked hardest at I got C's for. My unseen, my pride! scored a B. My comps. were all bad, except the one that was ever accounted worst – Greek iambics – one that I all but dropped – which got a B+.

The reason, I expect, is that finding me woefully given to inaccuracy, whenever I attempted style, they sniffed for hedging. And the examiners have been unusually severe this year. I am now combating inaccuracy: fortunately it is not so grave a fault in Greats.'[341]

The comments about being woefully inaccurate and sniffed at hedging were the best clues to his failure in Mods. His translations of French and German gave him the opportunity to attempt a more romantic style, more so than his translations of Latin and Greek, which he may have found too restricting. The real roots of his failure lay in his studies and examinations at Uppingham, when his confidence had been undermined and he saw examinations as a means of rebelling and establishing his own views.

Flecker went on to extol the virtues of Greats which he described 'in a way the finest exam. there is. It consists of two parts, history and philosophy, as perhaps you know. Though I hate philosophy, it is excellent mental training, and my historical essays have been received with approbation.' He was 'carefully pruning my style, reserving outbursts for verse!'[342]

He went on to tell Sedgwick about his work for the Taylorian, that he had stopped reading English literature, except for his 'bible' *Sartor Restartus*,[343] and in his leisure time he was reading nothing but French literature, of which he had bought a great deal, alongside books for his Greats work. He was taking up a non-obligatory subject, 'the fascinating Mycenean Age'.[344] He also extolled the virtues of Frazer and asked Sedgwick if he had read *The Golden Bough*, which he described as 'a marvellous combination of delightful, often humorous style, with vast erudition: and it has been said that no one has a right to have an opinion on religion till they have read it'.

Frazer (1854–1941) was born in Glasgow. He first became interested in the classics and then in anthropology. Through primitive beliefs, the ancient world and folklore, he sought to explain the society he lived in and its religion. Sir James George Frazer was at Sedgwick's Trinity College, Cambridge, where he had been appointed a Fellow in 1880. *The Golden Bough* was first published in 1890. Of *The Golden Bough*, it was said by Jane Harrison,[345] whose book Beazley had been reading during the Welsh holiday: 'We Hellenists were, in truth, at that time "people who sat in darkness", but we were soon to see a great light, two great lights – archaeology, anthropology. Classics were turning in their long sleep. Old men began to see visions, young men to dream dreams" …. J.G. Frazer who was soon to light the dark wood of savage superstition with a gleam from *The Golden Bough*. The happy title of that book – Sir James Frazer has a veritable genius for titles – made it arrest the attention of scholars.'[346]

Flecker told Sedgwick he was also reading and enjoying the lovely style of Renan's *Life of Christ*,[347] but it was more than Renan's style that attracted him. The next sentence, the last in the letter, contained the sting, when he wrote: 'I am just going to write to my father professing agnosticism, and cutting the last thread of my double life'.[348,349]

This letter to his father no longer exists, although Dr. Flecker's reply is available in full. Its real value is lost because the reader can only guess at what Dr. Flecker refers to as 'the men whom you mention', meaning the men whom his son had brought into the argument to support his professed agnosticism. Renan and Frazer could be guessed at as possible contenders. Dr. Flecker was also capable of putting the sting in the tail of his letters; the emotional barb came when, after he wrote 'Your loving father', he stated, 'It seems to me equally unnecessary to allow either B. on the one hand, or the Camp Evangelicals on the other to influence you.'[350] This sideswipe at Beazley and the Camp Evangelicals showed that Dr. Flecker did not see how much his own influence had resulted in his son's professed agnosticism. He preferred to put the blame on men much younger than himself, and not to see that the agnosticism was a symptom of something wrong in the relationship between himself and his son.

His son was bound to rebel against his parents, if he was to stand any chance of being an individual in his own right. The religious teachings of his younger days would never really leave him, but he needed to bridge the gap between his childish faith and the belief of a mature person. Religious doubts had been in his mind long before he encountered Jack Beazley, or had met up again with the Camp Evangelicals. He had written to Sedgwick of 'cutting the last thread of his double life', but in reality his life was split in many ways that would trouble him, even if he could not fully express the nature of the divisions, even to himself. He had deep feelings for Jack Beazley, but he also had been associating with an Oxford shop girl.[351] Dr. Flecker found out, although it is not entirely clear whether his father's shock was due to the actual association, or to the girl's lowly occupation. Flecker had dealt with this confrontation in a light-hearted way, but he must have felt that he could not discuss this emotional matter in anything like the way he could discuss agnosticism.

He was split also between his desire to become a published poet and his parents desire that he should be a hard-working scholar, with a secure profession in front of him.

Professing agnosticism was another convenient red herring to draw across the path of conflict over the spending of money. If Dr. Flecker had tried to grasp that fact, the whole matter might have been a lot less painful for all concerned. But his father tended to treat the conflict over religion as an intellectual exercise, and suggested the reading of Ward's *Agnosticism and Naturalism*. It would also have seemed prudent not to have yielded quite so much to his wife's consternation over the growing friendship between Flecker and Beazley. His parents used their religious principles as a means of coping with discouraging what they saw as a threat to their power and influence.

Beazley was banned from visiting Dean Close. The answer to Dr. Flecker's letter about the professed agnosticism is shrouded in mystery. [Flecker's reply, if he made one, is not to be found.][352] The letter in which there was a possibility of Beazley visiting Dean Close was not published, nor was the one from his mother banning Beazley, but the letter from Flecker was published in full. Sufficient reference was found in Flecker's reply to produce some idea of what his mother's letter must have contained. She must have told him that she did not want as a guest 'anyone who was against Christ and His teaching'.[353]

Flecker argued that Beazley was not 'against' Christ; he had not at his age any settled convictions, and it was foolish of her to expect that Jack would. He went on to argue the point by saying that 'A genius like he is can scarcely accept things on tradition', Beazley had to have time to read 'and he has never yet had time to read both or even one side of the question'. Flecker asked his mother, 'Where, then, is your Evangelical spirit?'[354] She was losing the opportunity to convert Beazley, he told her. Beazley would come to church: he was the last person to make a parade of his beliefs. If converted by reasoning, Beazley would become an archbishop. Flecker outlined a whole host of his friends, who would be considered lesser men than Beazley, but who would be admitted to Dean Close simply on the grounds that they went to church. His mother did not admire intellect or refinement, he went on. The one Christian he had met at Oxford whom he could admire, he had got to know through Beazley. He wanted his letter shown to his father who he felt would be of the same mind in some things. This was strange as Dr. Flecker appeared to be under his wife's thumb when it came to dealing with their son's problems. It was even stranger that he did not realise that his extravagant defence of Beazley would not make his mother change her mind; she would dig her heels in even further.

This hostility from his mother was due to much more than Beazley's lack of settled convictions, or fear that Beazley's presence at Dean Close might have some impact on the religious faith of its younger members. It struck deeply at the core of her control and influence. She could not see that the result of banning Beazley was to make him even more desirable in her son's eyes. It would have been better, in the long run, to have let Beazley come to Dean Close so that there would be no reason to keep the friendship hidden from her. The banning meant that Flecker's feelings for Beazley had to be hidden deeply in poetry and prose; they took root and flourished in a way that could never be planned or pruned to look more respectable in the eyes of the outside world, like the rose-garden at Dean Close.

Mrs. Flecker could not object to Beazley on the grounds that he came from a lowly background. This would be unchristian and a case of the pot calling the kettle black. She might now be the wife of a headmaster and clergyman, but she had been the daughter of a furniture-dealer at the time of her marriage. 'Risen from the ranks' was how she had described Beazley, but this did not distract from her dislike of him. She saw that he was the one person who could steer her son along a different path to the one she had mapped out for him: 'We knew he had great gifts, but were anxious for him to develop great thoughts as well as beautiful words, and were perhaps too desirous that his character should become formed in the best and highest way. Our idea was that if he grew into a fine and noble manhood, his work and talents would be all the more worthwhile.'[355]

Did his parents acknowledge the great gifts? It was difficult for these to develop when the main topic of discussion between parents and son was money, as Flecker realised: '...this worrying about filthy lucre all day long is preying upon me ..... You are turning me into the most avaricious Jew. I begin to shape my life with a view to getting money. This does not agree with my aesthetic taste.'[356]

His mother thought that his friends were guilty of what seemed to her 'the grossest flattery'. Sarah Flecker's idea of grossest flattery would be another's help and encouragement or appreciation of his 'great gifts'. If she did not praise her son and show an interest in his verse then he would turn to others; but she seemed to ignore the fact that his friends (and the 'hearties') were capable also of quite ruthless criticism and of poking fun. He had written poetry and tried to get it published long before he met the Oxford 'flatterers'. If flattery existed, it was their son who tended to flatter Beazley, and, at first, be blind to his faults. Just as they transferred the agnosticism burden, so too did they transfer the flattery burden to Beazley's shoulders, as the leader of the flatterers.[357] As he had written in June 1905, in the *Book of Kara James*:

> I am the book of Kara James –
> The little book of moral lays –
> I rather like a word of praise –
> I do not greatly care who blames
> This moral book of Kara James.

This word of praise, if it only had been forthcoming from his parents at the right time, would have lessened the pain of all concerned. Praise was at the heart of the conflict. If only a word of praise had been given with real feeling, how much misunderstanding would have been removed.

Flecker continued to defend Beazley from any attacks from his parents and to counteract anything he saw as their nastiness about his friend. He told his mother that Jack thought him 'a prospective power in the world and a genius, but also a most charming and affectionate companion.'[358] This would do nothing to heal the rift.

The most damaging accusation against Jack Beazley was his agnosticism. Dr. Flecker made a living out of his religious beliefs, and his wife had a vested interest in religion; they were not going to shift their ground, whatever arguments their son put forward. Emotionally, they could not accept his shift of ground, although intellectually Dr. Flecker could be expected to get the upper hand.

Flecker continued to translate poetry, despite the conflict over his friendship with Beazley. In June 1904, he translated Bierbaum's 'A Woman Tells' and 'The Castle Mirabel'. These were typewritten in *The Book of Kara James*. He also translated Bierbaum's poem 'Violet'.

The sort of advice he was receiving about the wisdom of establishing himself as a published poet was best summed up in the first version of the poem entitled, 'Sound Advice Given and Received by a Minor Poet of To-day',' typed out in his Kara James copybook and dated July 1904.[359] The minor poet in the poem has been advised to write short stories, as these are what is said to pay. Although Flecker's attempt at a short story is not dated, the *Book of Kara James* contains a typed carbon copy, with alterations.

He had requested a typewriter from his parents in order to type out his badly organised notes and make study for Greats' work much better. The letter requesting the typewriter was at the end of the Trinity term, 1904, and he was sending poems typed on his new typewriter to Sedgwick in a letter dated July 1904. It appears that his parents were eager to do something to help their son get his work on course for Greats, although the letter also had an ominous reference to: 'More and more I feel that a literary life à la Andrew Lang would be the ideal one.'[360]

Andrew Lang (1844–1912) was a Scot who was much influenced in his childhood by the reading of *A Midsummer Night's Dream* and *The Arabian Nights*. He was educated at the Edinburgh Academy and St. Andrew's University, where he had poems published in the university magazine. After a spell at Glasgow University, Lang came up to Balliol in 1864, where he continued to write poetry and got a First in Greats. He went on to spend seven years as a Fellow of Merton College, Oxford. He pursued a journalistic career and married in 1875. He contributed many poems and essays to magazines, *The Illustrated London News*, for example, published hundreds of his works.

A prolific writer and a romantic, Lang had published fairy stories inspired by the legends and ballads of his childhood days in the Scottish Borders. His first collection of traditional fairytales, *The Blue Fairy Book* was published in 1889, and he had undertaken the preface and the editing of *The Brown Fairy Book* in 1904. Lang published in 1888 in his *Ballads of Books*, a verse translation of the first lyric of Catullus, which Flecker's translation most closely rivals.[361]

Flecker's short story was more on the lines of a fairy story, and as Andrew Lang's life of scholarship, journalism and criticism was in his mind, the idea of trying to follow Lang's success in the fairy-story world may have occurred to him.

Flecker's story[362] was called 'Boy and Girl', and is about two young people, identified as Boy and Girl because names had not been invented at the time the story took place. They had lived for five years in a firwood clearing since they were ten years old. They had been left alone, when their tribe went hunting, encountered another tribe and been killed. One afternoon the boy attempts to kiss the girl. This lovemaking it is suggested, then went further. The boy goes hunting and the girl finds the boy wounded in the breast by a great boar. Next morning, she cannot wake the boy. She does not know what death is, and the story ends: 'She could not cry. She leant against the tree: her jaw hung downwards and the light fled from her eyes.'

The story, with its aura of sexual awakening, stopped short of describing sexual intercourse, and the attempt to explain was scored through, it read: 'Then they began to understand. But you are not going to hear any more about this. Even ten thousand years cannot excuse our prying; we do not want to be rude.' This story was not one that he appeared to want to publish, but the carbon copy could indicate it was circulated amongst friends for their opinions.

Instead of a holiday à deux at Dean Close in July 1904 (having seen Beazley almost every day), Flecker parted from him to go to a country vicarage for two weeks to coach a not-very-bright young man for an examination. Aside from this unrewarding work, he also typed out on his new typewriter (which he must have carted with him, so although the exact location of the vicarage was not given, it could not be too far away from Cheltenham or Oxford) two poems with no titles, for Sedgwick to criticise. These two poems had the first lines: 'Launch the galley, Sailors bold:' and 'Not the night of her wild hair.'[363]

A draft of another poem he called 'Loneliness' was dated June 1904, in the *Book of Kara James*,[364] but he did not send it to Sedgwick. The poem reflected the feelings he had about the separation from Beazley:

> Long low levels of idle sand
> And Ridges of open sea
> Barren water and bitter land
> Keep him away from me.

The landscape seemed to be distorted by his unhappy feelings, which are then embellished by thoughts of love:

> I love those levels of sand
> I love that horizoned sea
> Stretching away like a mighty band
> To bind my beloved to me.

The memories come back to him in a verse he added in added in August 1904:

> Shapes that walk on the lonely land,
> Spirits that head on the sleepless[365] sea
> Breathe to my love my heart's demand
> Back little lover, come back to me."

Ultimately he trimmed the poem down left the sex of the lovers open to doubt, although he changed the title from 'Loneliness' to 'The Little Song of Sorrow', adding 'her' afterwards and the use of 'him' in the second last line. This made the poet's intentions clearer than in the version in the *Book of Kara James*, but despite the alterations, the indications are that the poem was inspired by his holiday with Beazley:

Long low levels of land
And sighing surges of sea,
Mountains and moor and strand
Part my beloved from me.
I love you, levels of land,
I love you, surges of sea;
You forge an eternal band
To bind my beloved to me.
Phantoms who pass on land
And move on murmuring sea.
Give him a quiet command –
Back, my beloved to me. [366,367]

Flecker did not go en famille to Switzerland, as he had written to tell Sedgwick in July 1904. His exact phrase was, 'We are going to Switzerland in August'. It is not clear who was referred to in the 'we'; it could have meant Beazley and himself, as the row over Beazley's ban from Dean Close erupted 'sometime in June' and his plans to go to Switzerland with a companion or companions were still on course in July. Flecker made the excuse of not wanting to come to Dean Close because the school would not have broken up for the holidays and Beazley would not be welcome. He refused to go the Chamonix at first, or take a course of French at Caen, but went to Lausanne to stay in a pension, which he did not enjoy. He wanted then to join the family – as he told his father, he wanted a companion, to be with the family and talk over his future. [368]

In a letter to his mother he tells his mother: 'Then, I have a friend with a big brain and a slender body, whom I want to teach to swim and ride and become strong, and also to give him some chance of a good healthy outdoor life and of seeing some fine country, and forsooth this friend may not enter the Precinct because he is not going to be an Evangelical parson, while any fool I cared to bring would be welcome – for you have been very kind about inviting my friends – provided that I assured you he went to church.' [369]

The reference to swimming and riding and 'seeing some fine country' also pointed to Switzerland as well as Cheltenham for the Flecker/Beazley holiday. Flecker's rebellion against going to Chamonix was perhaps made in a forlorn hope that his parents might reconsider their verdict when faced with the prospect of losing their son's company The strategy, if that was what it was, did not work. Because Beazley was unlikely to have the financial means to pay for a holiday of his own on the Continent (part of the attraction of the holiday chez Flecker could have been that it was free), Flecker had to spend his holiday on his own.

The poems that Flecker wrote at Lausanne, depicted his inner loneliness, now he was without Beazley, and his sense of isolation. The poem he wrote, 'Glion', made no mention of people; he was said to be depressed about his failure in Mods and had gone to Lausanne as a result. He wrote to his parents about being the only male in the pension and the company was dull. 'Dull' is the word he used in the second version of 'Glion – Evening' (the first version was in written in July 1904) written in August 1904:

> Like a dull bee the steamer plies,
> And settles on the jutting pier:
> The barques, like monster butterflies,
> Round idle headlands idly veer.[370]
> He scored through 'vast' and replaced it with 'dull'.

The words of the poem such as 'dull' and 'idle' echo his own loneliness, and the feeling that he was wasting his time, as he wrote to his parents, on the course he was undertaking. The poem ended with a reference to Gautier in a verse he wrote in pencil:

> From Glion at the close of day
> Vivid are the lands below:
> Oh if the poet Gautier
> Could grave them in a Cameo![371,372]

The cold, clear and sharp outlines of the mountains recalled for him the precise imagery of Gautier's poetry and the fact that Gautier made cameos. But Gautier was not the only poet he was thinking of during this lonely period; he was reading a copy of the Tauchnitz Swinburne.

One version of the companion poem to 'Glion – Evening' , 'Glion – Noon', began with the verse:

> From Glion on an August Noon
> I scarcely see the ripples shine,
> So brightly do the vapours[373] swoon
> In drifting clouds of cyanine.

He ended this draft with a verse that he scored through:

> Here I would dream away long years,
> Till with the mountain I was one,
> Knowing not loves, or hates or fears,
> Standing immutably alone. [374]

The Glion poems displayed a vision of a life free of the grip his love for Beazley had upon him and the hostility it drew from his parents. He would then have come to terms with his fears of being alone and isolated.

He did eventually spend part of the rest of the holiday with his family at Chamonix, until he was despatched on a walking tour with T.M.A. Cooper, the Dean Close master. He spent six weeks in all in Switzerland, a holiday, he told Sedgwick, that he 'did not enjoy anything like so much as my stay in Wales last Easter, which was, indeed, the best time I have ever had'.[375]

The general feeling of despair was further echoed in the drafts of his poem 'G.T.B. Drowned Among Reeds' (to which he eventually added 'At Wisbech'). The first 'G.T.B.' was written in the black notebook, July 1904. In the BKJ version (p.52) August 1904 he wrote:

> Thus far to Southward Shelley had his end
> Thus too he gazed through water to white sky.
> But you – Do you know all – or is it lie?
> Say, silent friend!

The identity of G.T.B. is not known.

He was beginning to tire of books and ideas, he told Sedgwick. He brought up again the subject of Gautier, and strongly recommended Francis Thompson 'as being remarkable, if not quite healthy'. Flecker wrote his poem 'To Francis Thompson' in September 1904. The reference to Francis Thompson demonstrated Flecker's ambivalent attitude towards religion, as he was praising a poet whose poems were mainly religious. Beazley with his Irish-Scottish Protestant background did not approve of Thompson, a Catholic mystic. Flecker, with his admiration of Beazley, not unnaturally had mixed feelings about Thompson's verse. in a letter to Sedgwick he 'confessed that every book he read made a return to Christianity an absolute impossibility'. He wrote: 'What makes me marvel is that any sane man can believe in Christianity: what makes me annoyed is the way clever men temporise with it, looking upon it as a philosophy, as a fulfilment of Plato, as an interesting relic of mediaevalism not to be disturbed, as a refuge from despair very convenient for the lower classes, as anything in fact but truth or a lie.

And the hopeless quibbles and shiftings!'[376]

He knew that his rejection of Christianity made a dream of his impossible, as he outlined in his letter to Sedgwick: 'All my sympathies, all my hopes are to be a headmaster of a school of my own.' He had 'an entire scheme of education: of course, immature as yet, but different to all others. I will not dilate on it, simply saying that its main idea is to make each boy "know something about everything, and everything about something".'[377]

He knew that money was needed for such an adventure, and that it was unlikely to be forthcoming. He would not attract pupils if he did not teach Christianity. He told Sedgwick: 'Yet I am sure it is the one thing I am really fit for'. An interesting aspect of this very long and rambling letter, written from Dean Close before he returned to Oxford for the start of the Michaelmas Term, was the small amount of space devoted to news of Beazley. The only reference to him was: ' "Lucretia" has been most carefully revised with J.'s aid – who knows all about blank verse: I am beginning to think it rather rubbish.' This piece of information had already been given in his previous letter to Sedgwick, dated July 1904.

The lyrical recital of what he saw as Jack's great attractions was beginning to be expressed in more realistic terms, or else he thought it prudent to appear to be more realistic when writing to his parents, as he admitted to them: 'He is a little bit selfish, very impulsive, not very serious about anything but his work, quite capable of being led into all sorts of things, but it is for this very reason that I like to keep a continual eye on him, and put him in the company of Cyril, if possible, and so forth.'[378]

The reference to Jack Beazley's single-mindedness in regard to his work was something that the Flecker parents could not hold against him; there were to be no half-measures when it came to working. Beazley's proposed profession needed an evenly balanced emotion, and a committed approach to scholarship.

At the end of the Trinity Term, in 1904,[379] Flecker had told his parents that he was not going to get them to ask Jack to stay, again; he left that to them to suggest. A hint was given that the end of the vacation would be best. The invitation was not immediately forthcoming, but he remained philosophical, as he wrote: 'Really life will begin to be worth living again at the Varsity next term, when both Cyril and J. are with me ....'[380]

As usual, when disputes were running with his parents, he put forward arguments that tended to obscure the real issue. The combination of

Jack and Cyril was not such a bitter issue as the one of he and Jack alone. He had already told them that he wanted Cyril in Jack's company. The Flecker seniors could not argue with the same certainty that Jack would influence Cyril too; even by their standards, this would be going a little too far. Even if they tried to raise the issue of Cyril and Jack, it would be a convenient red herring. He was continuing to see Jack but with Cyril, his friend from evangelical camp days, and surely that could not be a source of such great conflict?

When he started his third year at Trinity, in 1904, he had to get down to his studies for Greats; he had already stated that if he got a First, it would be by 'some absurd fluke'.

The practical difficulty of expenditure on essentials, was now under better control. When his birthday came he got a 'bewful sausage, about three ells long'[381] from his aunt and uncle in Lambeth. He found that flattery got a lunch from his landlady. He told her she was the best cook in Oxford, which (he told his parents) he believed to be true. The same landlady provided a new cushion for his sofa and a curtain over the door. The flattery was reciprocated: Mrs. Walker opined to Jack that Flecker's looks were getting better, and, as he had been told in childhood, he had beautiful eyes. 'I would rather be told that I had beautiful eyes than that I had pulled all the wires in the University.'[382] He could not remember who it was who had enquired about the 'saturnine oriental'.[383] On the debit side, he lost five overcoats while at Oxford. He saw a way of getting replacements. He told his parents he had breakfast with Neville Forbes (1883–1929) formerly of Marlborough, now a Taylorian scholar of Russian at Balliol; not someone whose background his parents could question: 'He has a new white overcoat which is the most vivid thing in Oxford. It came from Malta, and is greyish-white like a blanket and cost 18s. only. If only Miss S. would bring me one over! They are magnificent. Everyone stares, little boys say, "Yah!'" "Dressing-gown!" and so forth. N. cares not at all. He never cares what other people say. Would I could add '"*ni moi non plus*".'[384]

His mother wrapped her religious beliefs around her, and although little boys were unlikely to call after her in the street, she too did not care what others thought of her. So, his request for the outlandish overcoat could hardly be turned down on the grounds that people would stare and criticise. If his parents took that line, then he could argue that it would help him to overcome what his mother considered to be a fault of his; caring what others thought. The fact that the overcoat was not very expensive was also a point in its favour. He was not slow in employing devious methods of dealing with his parents and anyone else who could supply his material needs. It was not likely that, if such an overcoat came his way, he would wear it outside. He was known by his family to have a tendency to go in and out of heated rooms 'in bitter weather unsuitably clothed'.[385] The white 'overcoat' was really envisaged, it is more likely, as a dressing-gown. Compton Mackenzie had bought a crimson and silk Moorish caftan, which he wore at Oxford as a dressing-gown.

When it came to Flecker giving something himself, such as a present to his sister on her birthday, he wrote and told Joyce it would be impossible to know what to send her. He knew what she would really like (Murray's *Anatomy*, or a treatise on Conic Sections) but these would be difficult to obtain. The stress of packing (which indicated that combined efforts of his mother and old nurse had been dispensed with), he told her, had made him almost forget her birthday. His sister was allowed to choose a book of his, but since he specified that the book was in German and too hard for her to read, her 'choice' was no choice at all. It resulted in his not having to part with any of his own cash.

Material matters and his studies took up much of his time during this term, while Beazley was still his companion. He worked on his poetry as well; his mind on dream and tradition. A poem dated October '04, was 'The First Dream – Picture from Heine' and 'The Second Dream Picture' was dated December '04. 'This is the End of Everyman's Desire' was dated 27 November, and 'In a Life of Cellini', December 1904. He also completed 'Hylas' in December '04, when he gave the poem the title 'Propertius 1.20 A Prayer to the Brightness of the Day' and enclosed it in a letter to Leonard Cheesman, for his criticism, with his reasons for altering the title.[386]

George Leonard Cheesman (1884–1915) was the son of a Hove solicitor, George Cheesman, and his wife, who came from Lincolnshire. They also had a daughter Margaret. Cheesman had won a scholarship to Winchester in 1897, and although Sedgwick had thought that he and Flecker would have been better for having been at a school like Winchester 'where the intellectual life among scholars is so much higher ....',[387] if they had been sent there, Flecker would have gone through the same sort of misery as Cheesman, as a result of compulsory games. At Winchester, Cheesman had suffered bouts of depression, headaches and other illnesses, but he had managed to be a leading member of the Rifle Corps, and became a College Prefect in his final year. His verse writing and his interest in ancient history, specialising in Roman military history, may have served as a helpful retreat from the aspects of Winchester he had failed to enjoy.

Cheesman had been elected to a Classical Scholarship at New College in 1903, where he had a comfortable room and he found the Oxford atmosphere the only haven he needed from the world outside.

He felt he was 'of Oxford', unlike Beazley who he felt ultimately was 'of the world'. It was this feeling that gave him a better insight into the behaviour of his fellow undergraduates than most of them had of themselves. Moss-Blundell (who featured in the BKJ poem about Flecker's contemporaries) annoyed him because despite his interest in archaeology: 'He knows better but won't go further.'[388]

Cheesman was right, as L.A.B. Moss-Blundell of New College obtained a First in Mods, but only a second when he took his final degree. Cheesman was well on his way to a First in Mods, and although at first a loner, he made friends, amongst them Maurice Campbell of New College, whose younger brother Patrick became Cheesman's pupil and biographer. Cheesman, despite his ability to see to the heart of his friends, including Flecker, was not uncaring, and he found contentment in spending the night on the floor of a friend suffering from flu. He enjoyed discussing Latin and Greek translations with Flecker. The length of their lives was so nearly the same; it is useful to compare their respective approaches to life at Oxford and elsewhere and see how Cheesman coped more easily than Flecker.

Cheesman had rooms in New College, where he did not give way to chaos, but was able to dispense sandwiches and cake to the mothers and sisters of his friends. New College was not on the main thoroughfare; it was set back from the hustle and bustle of Oxford, which made it an easier place to study or relax.

Cheesman did not have any interest in seeking female company around his own age. Peter Pan was first performed in 1904 and Cheesman saw it five times. It could be that he identified with the main character and also sympathised with Peter Pan's inability to grow up and become heterosexually mature.

Flecker and Cheesman had a lot in common: Cheesman also was a born teacher with a desire to write. He was slim and good-looking without the dramatic good looks of Beazley. The friendship of Cheesman and Flecker was more of a sentimental one, at least on Flecker's side.

The sort of relationship which existed between Flecker and Cheesman is best illustrated in Flecker's letters to Cheesman: [389]

Dear Xees,

Have no time to write you a long letter. I enclose Hylas and a suggestion for the Cellini. I have not done all the poem on Hylas have still got 16 lines to render. Very hard at work now. Please send a frank verdict on both. I have got a white knitted waistcoat which will simply eclipse you.

Went through Birdlip on Sunday with male parent to open
(?) a new Sanatorium Chapel – saw I believe your future
residence. Was awfully pleased with a present of Wm.
Watson's complete works sent me for Xmas.
Take care of yourself.
Kara James

Can you guarantee to get all verses onto the Flyleaf?

This letter was undated, but it seems safe to say it was written after
Christmas 1904, as the version of 'Hylas' in the *Book of Kara James* is
dated December 1904.

The next letter, which Flecker wrote after receiving Cheesman's reply
is also undated, but as it is headed 'Headmaster's House, Dean Close',
it is also safe to assume that it was written during the same holiday.
Flecker wrote to Cheesman:

Most classical C,

Firstly as to Hylas. For indeed whereas you are for a
moment, Hylas is for posterity. Observe here that all such
things as may be safely entrusted to Mama Charisty's(?)
keeping.

I knew when I translated the lines that mine was not
the usual translation, but I thought it was a permissible
suggestion. But to take *officio* as a dative with *praebilit* is
easy and obviously correct, that to demur would be brazen
dogmatism. *Correcti facilis*: e.g.

Once he has picked, wherewith he childlike plays
The flowers are fair: his task he sets aside

Post haec meliora perhaps – this 'on the spur of' as I said
before, missing a syllable.

When I look out of my window, I can see forest-clad
Birdlip, quite in the distance, under the yellow sky. To think
that you are there, and I am here and rather that I am here
and you are there. So near and yet, so remote! And such
pains of hell are gathering hold upon m...

(in this interval I have relieved myself of a burden and
feel more cheerful) Absurdissine!

Surely on departing you shall behold me here yourself
named place and time, if you can afford to spend an hour
or so. or will I come with a ———— and elope with you.
Another thesis.

'Hylas', Flecker's translations of 'Propertius 1 20', told of the tale
of Hercules' love for Hylas; with its theme of homosexuality it can be
seen why he discussed it with Cheesman, who could also appreciate the
technical problems of its translation and the theme. The translation
was not undertaken for the purpose of publication.

What 'burden' Flecker had relieved himself of during this period is
obviously not stated clearly, but in his circle it was usual to write in some
sort of code, or to be obscure, in case someone else read the contents.
'Burden' could refer to virginity.[390]

If Cheesman had turned up at Dean Close, the fact that he was
agnostic would not surely have been a barrier against his being accepted
for a few hours within the Flecker family. Mrs. Flecker approved of
Cheesman (although this approval appeared in print, after Cheesman
had died for his country); she may not have been aware of his agnosticism
at the time she knew of him, but she would only have had to enquire
about his religious beliefs to have found something out. She would not
have encouraged him to be hypocritical about such an important matter,
but if it was brought to her notice she could not have turned against
Cheesman in the same way. The differing attitudes towards Cheesman
and Beazley only reinforce the idea that it was not Beazley's agnosticism
alone that made her hate him so much, it was only a convenient peg on
which to hang her dislike of him. The aristocratic Granville Hamilton
was agnostic, and should he have condescended to spend any time at
Dean Close, he would surely not have been turned away on the grounds
that he was an agnostic. The fact of the agnosticism was published in
the LIFE, although Granville Hamilton was only identified as 'H'.

Flecker summed up his outward view of Cheesman in a light-hearted
verse in part of his poem on his contemporaries, which featured in the
Book of Kara James copybook:

How Cheesman was invited after lunch
To Edit, or to understudy Punch
How he refused temptation, walked the world
To Ecuador, where pasteboard crowns are hurled
About, and how with some terrific whoops
He told his noble band of nincompoops
To use the diadem as croquet-hoops. [391]

The views of their lives and writing exchanged by the Flecker/Beazley circle were not renowned for their detachment, but one member did succinctly sum up his views about Flecker at Oxford: 'I liked some of his serious verse, but did not in this days take him very seriously, as a poet or otherwise....'[392]

The writer of these words was Bernard Winthorp Swithinbank (1884–1958), the son of the Rev. Herbert Swithinbank. Swithinbank had been educated at Eton, where he had become the best friend of Maynard Keynes (1883–1946). The close friendship continued (although Maynard Keynes entered King's College, Cambridge, in October 1902) when Swithinbank came up to Balliol, at the same time as Beazley. Swithinbank was a first-class scholar of Latin and Greek, and in appearance not unlike Beazley, although his face was often sick and pallid; he had a feline look. Swithinbank had a sense of humour as Flecker noted in his BKJ: 'Swithinbank produce his pretty wit/ (It makes his victim feel an awful nit).'

'An awful nit' could have been Swithinbank himself felt; as he fell 'unhappily in love'[393] with Beazley at the end of their second year. Swithinbank's love had consequences for the Beazley/Flecker relationship, even if Beazley did not return the love in the same way. Swithinbank brought Beazley in contact with Maynard Keynes, Lytton Strachey and other influential men at Cambridge. The visits Beazley made to Cambridge did not include Flecker, and Beazley moved into a circle of well-off, intelligent people he could not help but admire. In turn, they could not help but admire Beazley, who was well on his way to his First in Mods.

In the Cambridge circle feelings for each other were just as strong but pushed down much more below the surface, as was their genius and homosexuality. Maynard Keynes sometimes visited Balliol, where he met Beazley, and although not very close to him, he was anxious that he should join his circle. Swithinbank, Beazley and Dundas,[394] who was also a friend of Maynard Keynes, went over to King's in the autumn of 1904. Beazley caught a cold, and was nursed by Maynard Keynes 'like a mother'. Beazley recollected conversations he had with Strachey and Keynes, when Strachey was lying on the hearthrug saying that he had never read a book just for pleasure, and neither had Keynes. Beazley had said he read poems out of a *Greek Anthology* 'like eating chocolate creams out of a large box'.[395] When Beazley had expressed a liking for the classical revival of Canova and Ingres, he was immediately set upon by Keynes who was irritated and wanted reasons. Beazley felt he 'had trodden on sacred ground'.[396] Beazley always thought that they were 'the two cleverest men he had met'. Cleverness of this sort was not a quality of Flecker's, a fact that appealed to Beazley.

Flecker's mistake was that he did not 'mother' Beazley but instead seemed almost to be more of a 'father' to him. He had plans to alter Beazley. He told his parents that he wanted to teach Beazley to swim and ride and to introduce him to the good healthy life. He had told Sedgwick that he wanted to make all his friends ride a bicycle and force them to take daily exercise; it was no wonder that Beazley often preferred to be in front of the fire, to talk, and to follow in the footsteps of Jane Harrison. He could see the opportunities available to him, when he cultivated the right sort of people, and Beazley's good looks and intelligence meant that it was not hard for him to achieve, especially in a circle where beautiful, clever young women, also striving to obtain a good degree, were non-existent.

The separation from Beazley, when he went on his trip to Cambridge with Swithinbank made the writing of Flecker's poem 'South East and North' all the more revealing: the poem indicated a desire to escape reality through dreams and death, the version in the BKJ read: [397]

O call me, call me far away,
To black Carpathian woods, where vampires roam,
And further to the quiet midland sea,
To sungirt meadows of old Sicily,
To white Aegean isles among the foam –
O call me, call me, call me far away!

But call me, happy voices, farther, far,
Away to dreamy painted lands beyond,
Where idle censers swing the whole day long,
And all the night is mellow with a song
By splendid women, softly monotoned, –
O call me, voices, call me farther, far!

Call me, strange voices, call me yet once more:
Call me to silent lands of windy snow,
Where cold eyes of the immortal spheres
Immutably are open. But there peers
Death in the cold white [crossed through] empty desert
where winds blow,
And through my dream, strange voices call once more.
Kara James, XXXV p.60 BKJ typewritten
November 1904

This poem is reminiscent of his Glion poems, also written when he was separated from Beazley. Much longer separations were envisaged when Beazley's studies took him to different parts of Europe, and Flecker would hope to be called there – at least that is what, superficially, the poem could be said to mean. The 'black Carpathian woods' convey the feeling of returning to the country of his forebears and the vampires introduce a grotesque element, almost a means of introducing pornography, as he was to do in a poem 'In a Life of Cellini', also typewritten, in the *Book of Kara James*, in December 1904. It was dedicated to Cheesman:

> We never drink – it is not nice,
> We buy no women at a price –
> As for obscurer forms of vice.
>
> Be they but mentioned, we say – Ugh!
> Such things the Best Men never do:
> They are unfit to listen to:
> They are not done by me or you![398]

This poem he also wrote out in his black notebook.[399]

Although his output of poems was down in the New Year, he managed to translate 'The Painting of Love' from 'Propertius' and 'Maiden Mine' from Heine in January 1905.

Fleckers continuing interest in the cosmopolitan Heinrich Heine (1797–1856), a baptised German Jew, who could be described as the German Byron, is understandable. Heine, who wrote the famous ballad of the Lorelei, was an exile from his own land. He lived in Paris and found admiration in Spain. His poetry, with its themes of dreams and unrequited love, were written in a lyrical, fresh and supple style that would appeal to Flecker.

In February, he wrote two versions of a poem he called 'Garibaldi'. The version he wrote in his black copybook (D245) was a frivolous one entitled:

> Specimen for my great Newdigate Prize Poem on Garibaldi. (Meter unlimited)
>
> He is greater than Adam or Noah
> Than Joseph or Jacob or Jude
> When the hail of his hollow holloa
> Proclaimed him no end of a dude:

To Italy thunderously called he
And Italy came to a lad
To the gallant and gaunt Garibaldi;
(The biscuits are bad).

The Book of Kara James version was handwritten and 16 lines long. It began with the lines:

He was a man that men could love, – a friend
Of all that wept. He was a peasant-king
Not of our age. Perhaps should we descend
The stairs of Time in our imagining
We might find some Chieftan reverend
And find that Homer had been pleased to sing
So strong a man, that yet would, wondering, bend
In awe of each inexplicable thing.   [February, 1905.]

In March he typed out versions of his poem 'Idwal' in the BKJ copybook. Idwal, in North Wales, also featured in Kingsley's novel *Two Years Ago*. He sent a version of the poem to Cheesman, with a letter:

Dear Len,

    Thought I'd send you this as you think you know an awful lot about how classical metres should appear in English. It's quite legible enough for you. There is also much subtlety of repetition.

Yours ever

James

Idwal is in North Wales near Capel Curig if you don't know.

In Cheesman's version the first lines of 'Idwal' are:

Idwal among dark rocks, – wild lake in Welsh desolation,
Sullenly mocking the sun, shuddering under the moon!

The poem continued:

114

> Then 'twas a boy held rule upon all Glan Conway the
> lovely, –
> (Idwal's father was slain down the long white sea.)

The poem contained the folklore and legends from his Welsh holiday, but it remained unpublished.

In March he also wrote 'Juvenaeleum Prodgit The works of Juvenal' (a moral man, try to like him Mr. Beazley if you can)[400]

Flecker was also, during the early part of 1905, preparing a paper to be given to a college society in March. His subject was the major poet and prolific writer of plays, novels, essays and criticism, John Davidson (1857–1909). Davidson's *Selected Poems* had been published in 1904. He called his paper 'John Davidson; Realist, A Point of View', and began by stating that Davidson, Ibsen and Nietzsche all cried with one voice, and he quoted form Davidson's play *Smith* to illustrate his point: 'Think my thought, be impatient as I am,/Obey your Nature not Authority;'.

Flecker also quoted what he considered 'faultless lines' from a lyric from Davidson's 'Scaramouch in Naxos':

> The boat is chafing at our long delay,
> And we must leave too soon
> The spicy sea-pinks and the inborn spray,
> The tawny sands, the moon.
>
> Keep us, O Thetis, on our Western flight,
> Watch from thy pearly throne
> Our vessel, plunging deeper into night
> To reach a land unknown.

Davidson's success in the nineties had not continued into the early twentieth century, and Flecker's paper was, in a sense, an effort to bring Davidson to the notice of a wider circle. Flecker had corresponded with Davidson, whose handwriting, he noticed: 'sloped upwards to the right across the page at a terrific angle', which he thought showed egoism, as Davidson 'was in all ways a self-confident, ostentatious man'. Flecker met Davidson. After he had read the paper, Davidson edited it for eventual publication in the *Monthly Review* of July, 1905. Flecker said of Davidson 'his imperfections surpass the perfections of other men'. Davidson, he said, must be dealt with on a par with Keats, Shelley or Tennyson. Nevertheless, Flecker picked out faults in Davidson's works that could at the same time be shown in his own writings. He accused

Davidson of lapsing into the grotesque or 'an impetuousness that leads him to disregard the symmetry and form of his work'.

Now that Flecker had Beazley and others to criticise his work, it was possible for him to analyse the work of others writers and to try and see why Davidson, in his middle age, was living a life of ill-health and poverty with his family in London. He said of Davidson:

> Sometimes he will spoil a ballad with lines too colloquial for the hurrying metre; sometimes he will just mar a fine speech in blank verse by getting it involved, and hard to follow, or by the unnecessary introduction of some abrupt phrase from common parlance.[401]

Flecker thought that these faults were more common in Davidson's earlier works, and he put forward 'the great dying speech of Hallowes' in *Smith* as an example. Ballads like 'An Exodus of Houndsditch', or 'The Vengeance of the Duchess' he thought failed 'because their language is too commonplace for their thought'. Flecker had no experience of the fault he criticised. Davidson had worked as a clerk, which had influenced his writing of his poem 'Thirty Bob a Week'. The poem is no less moving because it employed the speech of common people, and how else would a clerk indicate his anger against a system of oppression, but in the speech he used every day?

Although Flecker suffered from a lack of cash, it was not in the same way that Davidson had experienced in his drudgery in the office of Clark's Thread Mill or that Humbert Wolfe had known, second-hand, from his father's warehouse. Davidson, too, was the son of a parson, but his parents had had a much larger family than the Fleckers. Unlike Beazley, who was one of only two sons, Davidson had not managed, by dint of hard work and scholastic achievements, to escape at an early age from the pressure of earning a living. The clerk had had a hard and difficult life, as would anyone who wanted to make a living by writing verse; a poet, too, would be lucky to earn more than 'thirty bob a week'. But, at this stage, Flecker still had hopes that life would be better for him, and that he would not make what he saw as Davidson's mistakes in his life and work. He failed to see that Davidson was travelling a new road, and he that was bound to take wrong turns or find himself in a cul-de-sac on occasion, but others would follow him and find the going much more straightforward.

Flecker did think Davidson's blank verse 'the best since that of Milton'. He thought that 'the most interesting point about Mr. Davidson's poetry is his extraordinary objectivity. Mr. Davidson was the first realist that had appeared in English poetry'. He felt that Davidson's work had only just begun, and he hoped for greater masterpieces from him. Davidson was approaching his fiftieth birthday and had written a great deal, so his work could hardly have 'just begun'. It had just begun, however, in the sense that it would impress young writers, especially the poems about urban life and the common people.

Davidson had published his first novel in the same year, 1885, his first play in 1886, and *Smith: A Tragedy* in 1888. Flecker quoted at length from the latter in his paper because it was 'clearly voicing the ideas of the dramatist himself'.

Flecker described the play, which opened in a public house. The characters are Brown, from Oxford, and Jones and Robinson who discuss the character of Hallowes, a poet. When Hallowes enters he is going to Garth, where he will write poetry even if it is one line a day. Although advised to let fame alone, the poet says that it is 'the breath of power' and he continues:

..... fame is worth its cost,
Blood-sweats and tears, and haggard homeless lives.

Flecker thought that *Smith* 'brought something strong and vital into our literature'. The 'most powerful and the best written' of Davidson's ballads he thought was 'The Ballad in Blank Verse of the Making of a Poet' (first published in 'Ballads and Songs' 1894). He realised that it was perhaps from Davidson's own experience. It is the story of a boy who causes his parents grief because of his refusal to acknowledge himself as a Christian. The mother dies of a broken heart, and in a moment of 'weak contrition' the boy takes the eucharist, but he finds no peace, and his father also dies of grief. He quoted from the boy who curses creed and dogma and proclaims the gospel 'Self's the Man'; the last lines of his quoted passage are:

...... Within my heart
I'll gather all the universe, and sing
As sweetly as the spheres; and I shall be
The first of men to understand himself....

Flecker also praised 'Ballad of Heaven'. It was about a musician who 'toils at one great work for years' and whose wife and child die because he cannot maintain them as he lives but for his music. Yet he is 'welcomed to Heaven by God himself, and by his wife and child'. A theme he himself tried to work out, although not so drastically, in a play that he did not finish.[402]

Flecker also praised other ballads of Davidson's including his version of 'Tannhauser' and the 'Testament of a Vivisector', which he realised many people would find 'repulsive' because the vivisector 'loves vivisection because it fills him with a pleasing sense of mastery, and because it satisfies his lust for inflicting pain. Few things more grimly straightforward have been written.'[403]

It is easy to see why Flecker had sympathy for many aspects of John Davidson's life and works, which were similar to experiences in his own life, but he does say: 'I doubt if the most ardent admirer would stand by this Reformer in his utter condemnation of Christianity, convention, and culture, and taking refuge in a Materialism that says body and soul are one. But more might be inclined to agree with the fascinating theory held unconsciously by the Greeks, and held very consciously by this least Greek of poets – the theory of Man's natural sinlessness. If Calvary has a meaning for Mr. Davidson, it means the death of sin.' Here it would seem that the influence of Jack Beazley, is creeping in. Shortly after this, Flecker brings in a reference, however carefully hidden, to his own father, when he states: 'Do we not know and hate the type of individual that takes Holy Orders out of a vague desire to improve humanity by his miserable assistance – that is, by preaching a creed which he neither firmly believes nor thoroughly understands?'[404]

Davidson's poems did not hide his feelings about his own life and family sufferings, although by the time the details of his sad life were in print, the family members concerned were already dead. Davidson wrote:

> You were his wife, his servant; cheerfully
> You bore him children; and your house was hell.
> Unwell, half-starved, and clad in cast-off clothes,
> We had no room, no sport; nothing but fear
> Of our evangelist, whose little purse
> Opened to all save us; who squandered smiles
> On wily proselytes, and gloomed at home.
> You had eight children; only three grew up;
> Of these, one died bedrid, and one insane,
> And I alone am left you. Think of it!
> It matters nothing if a fish, a plant
> Teem with waste offspring, but a conscious womb!
> Eight times you bore a child, and in fierce throes,[405]

For Davidson's mother, the 'fierce throes' took place in the afternoon of 11 April 1857, at Barrhead, Renfrewshire. 'Our evangelist' was Alexander Davidson, Minister of the Congregational Church at Barrhead. John Davidson was the fourth child, and the first son after three daughters, two of whom were still alive. Euphemia, the sister nearest in age, was born on 9 June 1855. Davidson's parents had married in 1851 in Glasgow, and moved to Barrhead in the autumn of 1853. The reasons for the 'little purse' were many.

Alexander Davidson was born on 20 September 1825, at Craighead Farm in the parish of Daily, in Ayrshire, where his father John was a tenant farmer. He was forced to leave the land when he grew old and live in Glasgow. After an education at parish schools, Alexander was sent to work as a draper's assistant. At the age of seventeen Alexander gave a speech on the evils of drink, which so impressed the minister of the Congregational Church that he advised Alexander to study for the ministry. After the death of his father, Alexander was able to study at Glasgow University. Although money was not plentiful he was able to marry, in 1849, Helen Crocket, whose father had been a schoolteacher and an elder of the church. The church in Greenock, where the Davidsons moved after the birth of John, was a new one formed as a break between the Congregational Church and the Evangelical Union. The latter had very little money, and as the family increased John Davidson was sent out to work at the age of fourteen. So it can be seen that the legacy of his father's poor farming background, his long struggle with little money to achieve his aim of becoming a minister, his marriage and increasing family (the Davidsons had eight children, although not all survived) made John Davidson, like his father, fear debt, and the consequences of spending money he had not earned. He had a short spell at Edinburgh University to study Latin and Greek. He resumed teaching and a spell in the offices of Clark's Thread Mill may have influenced his poem 'Thirty Bob a Week'. After marriage and the birth of two sons he came to London, when it may have been better, despite the toughness of life there, to have remained in Scotland. London in the nineties was not a place where John Davidson was going to fit in, any more than Flecker would fit into the educational system offered by his public schools and Oxford. The difference between an educational system and the life of nineties London was that one could attempt to change it. As previously mentioned, Flecker had already been considering 'an entire scheme of education'.[406] Education for girls was not uppermost in his mind, but a letter written from Dean Close to Leonard Cheesman, although not dated, most likely belongs to this period, and it gives details of Flecker's views on education as far as literature is concerned:[407]

Dear Les,

Your letter received so I will be less brief and more cutting.

I was not altogether for the Literature Paper. It seemed to me to promote desultory reading of second-rate authors. There should have been a question on characters in Hamlet or on Milton's Prosody – and why is Kipling's *Kim* necessary when there is no mention of Meredith or Hardy.

I know quite well that one can't have everything in a paper – but I think soundness and not desultory reading is what should be aimed at at school – not wide reading but deep reading of the right things, less poetry, more novels and drama. It may amuse you to hear me talk like this, but you see I am on my sound subject.

Of course all the best men would have begun with Tennyson thus:

"Our assent to the last half of the statement is only equalled in vehemence by our dissent from the first half."

I enclose a literary paper of the sort I think it should be.

Do write again.

PS Motor has just broke down – it is not bought yet. I suggest reforming the back of it into a horse-box, in order to have something to rely on.

ENGLISH LANGUAGE PAPER

A   Short Essay on one of these subjects

The benefits and defects of Augustan Age Poetry
Richardson in English Novelists
Marlowe

B   (to be answered briefly)

1. Sketch the character of Macbeth and contrast it with that of Hamlet and Iago.
2. Taking any novel of Meredith's point out how it conforms to accepted forms of the novel, sketch its plot and give brief criticism.

3. Discuss the truth of some apothegm of Chesterton on Browning.
4. Trace the literary ancestors and influences of either Swinburne or Tennyson.
5. Mention the most important symbolists in English literature and discuss the influence of symbolism in their poetry.
6. Criticise the style of Ruskin and Walter Pater.

In what works of what writers do the following characters occur.

More about author or where do the following quotations come.

All the work for the John Davidson article precipitated illness; on the back of a copy of a poem he sent to Cheesman there was a note: 'Have been ill with a chill etc., Work deranged. Motor bought, if it goes up hill. Am more cheerful. Send you verses – have written better – (none much) James.'[408]

The poem he enclosed was 'Ennui' (the version sent to Cheesman had no title, and it differed in some respects from the BKJ version) which was typewritten as follows: [409]

"The flat provincial town groans in the gloom:
Electric cars through dirty highways boom,
Go, day of muddy blood! Go, seek thy silent tomb!

Through watery greyness of the sordid street.
Phantoms of smoke inevitably meet,
Thronging[410] towards me formless, faceless, fleet.

With forms of unimaginable fears,
With sorrow of illimitable tears,
With staleness of immeasurable years.

Laugh, grandiose young man! The humble truth
Is stupid age awaiting silly youth,
A death, a birth, more like, an aching tooth.

Well, there are friends and fires and memories,
Pictures to gape at, pretty books to please, –
Perhaps a woman sitting on your knees.

Pull down the blind: switch on the light: all's done!
Better the gas than daylight with no sun!
I'll take a cigarette. Will you have one?

April '05. BKJ p.46

The 'Ennui' poem (which he never published) with its reference to 'dirty highways', 'muddy blood' and 'watery greyness' contained images that had connotations of anal intercourse, which meant that there had been furtive, casual encounters, real or imagined, in the group.[411] The poem was not sent primarily for the opinion of Cheesman, but to convey a message he could not put in a letter.[412]

An idea for a magazine was discussed with Cheesman to whom he wrote:

> You write things of course. The magazine would be a great success. It would be seismic, and spasmodic. A typical Bill of Fare would contain 'A Comparison of the Literary Methods of Jokai and Peacock' by LC. Poems, moral and others, no 1 by HEF and so forth.
>
> And we would have it bound in vivid yellow. The only worry is financial as always. That might be avoided by finesse. What we want is a wealthy patron. Carnegie might do, or Stead. If you do not see the point of my remarks don't trouble. There isn't any. Only really think that we might float a mag: I know some of the most surprising and paradoxical writers in the 'Varsity. I am perfectly sure the first number would pay; but I hear that the loss of the second number usually makes the second gain disappear......'[413]

Flecker went on to disparage the other Oxford student magazines that were in existence. It is interesting to note how he sees sponsorship from a wealthy person as the only means considered to get his magazine published. The vivid yellow binding is also intriguing as there is mention of a *Yellow Book of Japes*,[414] which would not get into print or get the sponsorship of wealthy people. The *Yellow Book of Japes* was said to have contained Flecker's witty sayings, and it was illustrated, as was a similar publication (also humorous and obscene) *ABC for the Children* illustrated by Trelawney Dayrell-Reed (born 14th September 1885).

Dayrell-Reed, who seemed like 'a survival of the Green Carnation days', was at Lincoln, he announced, 'for the purpose of popularising the use of drugs amongst non-conformist members. He used to attend

Benediction at St. Aloysius, in immaculate evening clothes.'[415] Dayrell-Reed did not take a degree, but he was interested in ancient history.[416]

In April 1905, in the *Book of Kara James* copybook Flecker wrote the poem 'Vigil of Venus', which he had first entitled 'The Vigil of Aphrodite'. He also wrote 'The Ballade of the Mycenaeans'. The subject was 'the fascinating Mycenean Age', the 'non-obligatory special subject' he was taking up and which he mentioned in a letter to Sedgwick in May 1904.[417] 'The Ballade' was in the old French form, which consisted of three verses of eight lines and a last verse of four lines with a refrain, which in 'The Ballade of The Mycenaeans' was: 'Older than Homer's oldest song.'[418]

In May 1905, he translated from Bierbaum 'The Tomcat's Song' and typed it out:

> My tomcat sings the whole night long –
> "The Spring has wakened to my song,
> Has wakened to my song;"
> O fair and fluty is his voice
> When he goes forth to take his choice
> Of tabbies still unwedded.
> 'My sweet' he sings 'my Mousamie,
> Let him who dares to look at thee
> Be deaded!
> I quite alee – ala – alone
> Must keep you, for my very own
> Till Morning rise, redheaded!"
>
> Sing Puss! In May the leaves are green:
> In May the lovesick cats are keen,
> And all young life is springing.
> Now men with hearts may hold their own,
> And men without – must go alone!
> Sing, Pussy! Go on singing." [419]

May '05

This translation, at first reading, gives the impression of simply being a humorous poem whose subject would appeal to Flecker. But it could be seen also as a not very flattering portrait of Swithinbank's activities, as many had remarked on his cat-like appearance. The 'red-headed' could have reminded him of Beazley's hair, which was reddish fair. Translations appealed to him not only because of their language

123

but because of the subject matter. They were an opportunity to put into verse other men's thoughts and ideas, which were similar to his own, and which would not, if he wrote them entirely off his own bat, have produced the same sort of admiration in the reader, from outside.

In May 1905, he typed his first draft of his poem 'To Turner's Polyphemus' in the *Kara James* copybook. He was following the ideas of Gautier, who had written poems that were directly inspired by looking at pictures, a sculpture, or reading works of literature. This draft began:

> Strange Painter, let my wandering spirit lie
> Near those Sicilian cliffs,[420] and gaze upon
> The daylight horses of Hyperion
> Riding the fiery stairs, that lead on high[421]

BKJ, p.67
The last line of 'On Turner's Polyphemus' is 'Of hyacinthine mist, and shining gold.'

These are the colours of Turner's painting which so shocked the critics when the painting was first exhibited at the Royal Academy Exhibition of 1829, and reminded the schoolboy Flecker of the landscape of Southbourne.

In the same month he wrote in ink in the *Book of Kara James*, 'Light, Shadow and the Moon'.

> Over purple seas of sunset, where waves fall
> rhythmically,
> Over iridescent hills, where firwoods climb,
> Travelling in forgotten pathways I have found
> a pleasant valley
> Past the twilight, in the continents of Time.
>
> Wander with me up the mountains where the
> bosomed valley quivers
> In the flashes of the brazen-hatted sun:
> Walk with me among the meadows, dream with me
> beside the rivers,
> Dream with me where lilies open, rivers run.
>
> Wait till night and we shall see them –
> how from every cave and hollow

Come the Dryads who had fled the gorgeous noon:
Wanton fauns come hurrying after: through the
trees the Dryads follow:
Here and there a white limb glitters in the moon.

Kara James,
May, 1905 p.81

In May 1905, he wrote his first version of his poem 'The Piper'.[422]
His fragment of a play *Nero and Acte a Dialogue in the Old Manner*, which
he had begun in March 1904, was revised in June 1905.[423] He did not
get encouragement to continue with this play's theme from Cheesman,
who urged him to leave the Roman emperors alone.[424] Cheesman,
who obtained a first in Mods in 1905, was an expert on Roman history,
and planned to write a factual account for publication,[425] displaying
the difference in their approach to ancient history. For Flecker, history
inspired plays and poems whereas Cheesman wanted to unearth facts
and make them readable to scholars who shared his interest. Flecker, in
his play, used a version of lines from his translation of Lucretia. When
Acte speaks she says:

Or out among the ploughlands: let us hear
The dim sweet echoes of the Linos song
Whispering through the drowsy sheaves of corn,
On summer evenings, when the harvesters
Come homewards, and the children wait for them. [426]

As well as lack of encouragement, another difficulty was that he was
also translating *Peer Gynt* from the Norwegian of Ibsen. Flecker's interest
in Ibsen, besides putting him alongside Davidson, and mentioning
Ibsen's *'Wild Duck'* to Sedgwick, had a Beazley/Swithinbank/Maynard
Keynes connection.[427]

Flecker had sent 'The Greatest Version of The Death of As' from *Peer
Gynt*, in a translation to William Archer (1856–1924) who had, with his
brother Charles, translated *Peer Gynt* in 1893.

The reason for Flecker's choice of the death of the mother when
scenes set on the coast of Morocco, in the desert of Sahara and in a
madhouse in Cairo, or the characters of the dancing-girls, female slaves
and Arabs, might have given him more scope for his poetic gifts, is
not clear. Nor why he chose to send his translation to Archer for an
opinion, when he might have realised that Archer would not want
another translation by a much younger man, following close on the

heels of his own. Tom Archer, William's only son, was the same age as Beazley. He had applied to Balliol, and failed to gain a place, but he was accepted for Christ Church, on a classical scholarship. Tom Archer was up at Oxford at the same time as Flecker. He abandoned the study of classics for law, but opportunities existed for Tom Archer and Flecker to know each other. The clue lies in the fact that Flecker's was a rhymed translation, and that Archer had thrown out a challenge in his introduction to *Peer Gynt*:

> Peer Gynt is written from first to last in rhymed verse. Six or eight different measures are employed in the various scenes, and the rhymes are exceedingly rich and complex. The frequency of the final light syllables in Norwegian resulting from the number of inflexions in e, en, et, er, es, ene, ende, etc. implies an exceptional abundance of double rhymes, and Ibsen has taken full advantage of this peculiarity. In the short first scene of the second Act, for example, 25 out of the 40 lines end in double rhymes, and there are three sets of three lines ending in the same double rhyme.[428] The tintinnabulation of these double rhymes then gives to most of the scenes a metrical character which might puzzle Mr. Swinburne himself to reproduce in English. Moreover, the ordinary objections to rhymed translations seemed to apply with exceptional force in the case of Peer Gynt. The characteristic quality of its style is its vernacular ease and simplicity. It would have been heart-breaking work (apart from its extreme difficulty) to substitute for this racy terseness the conventional graces of English poetic diction, padding here and perverting there. From such a task even a master of rhymes and metres have shrunk, as from a 'labor improbus' in a double sense; and we were the less tempted to essay it as we knew ourselves no masters either of metre or rhyme.
>
> XVI Peer Gynt by Henrik Ibsen Authorised translation by William & Charles Archer. Walter Scott Ltd., London p.XV, 1892

What poet could resist such a challenge? A challenge that not even Flecker's favourite poet was judged to be able to meet. He was naive; and Archer returned Flecker's typescript with the following comments: 'I am, no doubt, a prejudiced witness on the point, but I doubt whether

Peer Gynt, as a whole could with advantage be translated into English rhyme. It would be a work of the most extraordinary virtuosity; and the very ingenuity required to find the rhymes in our comparatively rhyme-poor language would vitiate the whole effect and make it, in the main, more grotesque than pleasing.'[429]

Whether or not as a result of Archer's comments, Flecker appeared to turn against Peer Gynt: '.....you take up that miserable Peer Gynt attitude "Let us think of the things that are pleasant, and forget those that hurt" – and you send our pupils, as he sent his mother, headlong through the gate of death with ancient folk-tales and sweet, lying harmonies in their ears.' [430]

Someone else who had an interest in the grotesque in Flecker's writing signed himself SNM[431] when returning manuscripts and wrote: 'At present there seems to be more stuff – more freedom and force and inventiveness – in your grotesque. But I don't know whether it is a real or pseudo-grotesque. You will decide for yourself, I suppose, whether it's to be the form or the grotesque. Perhaps you may unite the two: and that I am prepared to admire.'[432]

June 1905 was also the date given to poems based on his travels with Beazley. He gave the poems the title: 'Two Songs of Two Wanderers' and they contained the line: 'Two bristly tramps are we'. [433]

'The Song of a Lady with Bright Eyes' signed Kara James,[434] was also given the date June 1905.[435] This is a poem to an unknown love, and an encounter that may or may not have been in his own life. It began with the lines:

> You were not so surpassing fair
> You were not clever, were not wise:

and ended:

> How far the little wind would take
> Which way the wind would blow!

As the poem described a river trip, could the love be the Oxford shop girl he was said to have associated with?[436] The poem was handwritten in ink and not offered for publication.

A poem written in July 1905,[437] indicated that it was written against the background of the rose-garden at Dean Close. He gave the poem the title 'A Garden Where Love Died':

Evening: a garden's roses loveliness;
Trees that begin to threaten, shapeless, sombre;
Low hills beyond dim meadows – ah confess,
Here are more charms than one sad soul could number.
I feel them not: I heed no suppliant stress
From quiet winds, nor eye the well-girt dress
Of closing flower-tops waving into slumber.

I am young and lonely, but Love has fallen beside me;
He is weary as I, can bring no dear vision.
I am blind and longing and where I cannot see
I hear back there a sound of shrill derision,
As the white wind goes whirring through a tree.
The wizard garden moves away dreamily;
It seems a painted view of lawns Elysian.

Stir, stir your listless wings, sweet naked boy!
Fraught with my sad heart's burden shall wander:
Your feathered flight shall someday bring me joy:
Rest not, rest not, young Love, till you have found her.
Speed, pretty wings, lest heavy cold night cloy
Your nimbleness: Oh with your smiles decoy
Someone for me to love from the bright lands yonder!

I long for no night-passion of fierce sighs,
With rose-fires swiftly dying, swiftly burning;
Nor bring for me thin bodiless fantasies,
Ideal toys, meet for a strong man's spurning.
My love shall have deep laughter in her eyes.
Strong, graceful, sinful she shall be, and wise.
To cheer the road till there is no returning.

How soon the bastioned night has walled me fast:
The black-fleeced clouds shake dripping wings of terror:
With mocking silhouettes the world grows vast;
Poor love is dead, so I have lost my bearer.
Alone I walk where violet shades are cast.
'At last?' the great Wind whispers. Why, 'at last'
There's no more loneliness, no hope, no error.

This poem he signed HEF, and he used the same ideas in his 'Glion' and other poems when at first the background is distorted by his own unhappy feelings, although the roses, like the mountains, remain beautiful. The 'shrill derision' is something he might, rightly or wrongly, have felt he could hear when someone else fell in love with Beazley. Certainly there would be no sympathy from his parents if he felt unhappy over his relationship with Beazley. They could not possibly know of the Swithinbank/Beazley complication.[438]

His parents would have no real sympathy or understanding of what he was trying to say in his prose, especially in 'Potter', a story he wrote about a not very bright menial girl, who had embraced the Roman Catholic Church after her employers, a disagreeable Anglican curate and his spouse, had ill-treated her.[439] His parents held on to the 'Potter' manuscript, and he had to ask for it back. 'Wreckage', his sketch, was also anti-religion, and about a defeated Anglican priest. His short novel, *Jack Villars*, was completed around this time; his parents would not be impressed, although it was less on the anti-Anglican theme, and the hero, Jack Villars, was brought together once more with his elderly father, after the death by drowning, of his close friend, Francis.[440] Another hero of his, Dick Hamilton, who featured in his story 'An Evening Tale' brings grief to his old father, a widower, who was a missionary in China.[441]

Yet, despite any unhappy doubts that had grown in his mind in July, he went with Beazley to Scotland in August. Clues as to where the holiday took him are given in his poem 'Tramps'[442] (which he gave the new title: 'The Song of Two Wanderers') as this poem refers to Sutherland and Edinburgh. A letter to Sedgwick (September 1905) informed him that he had walked up many mountains in Scotland. Cheesman scolded him in a letter for not telling him about the scenery; instead he got an outline of the state of his mind.

His state of mind is not readily revealed in August 1905, as it usually was, by the poetry he wrote. 'Cradle Song', from the German of Richard Delumel, was dated 7 August and had no obvious clues in its four verses, one of which was:

Sh, my angel: diddly dums!
It is raining sugar-plums!
Golden eggs with rain to-morrow
(Snore oh, pretty dabchick, snore oh!)
Shining pennies the day after
Till the heaven cracks with laughter. [443]

His first version of 'The Lament of Danae' was typewritten in April 1902 (a second version was written in August, 1905 'in ten minutes'

– BKJ, p.63). The August 1902 version has lines that indicate sleep can heal, and which might have reflected his own experience:

> Lord of Lethe whose thin wand
> Fetters woe in welcome bond. [444]

It took him slightly longer (one and a half hours) to write 'The Second Scaefola', on August 12, which turned again to Roman emperors and cruelty:

> And some poor fool whom he had lashed
> Went in and slew him as he slept,
> So all the rest of us were thrashed
> By men peculiarly adept:
> And then in prison we were kept. [445]

He also wrote on the same day his poem 'Man and the Mountains – winds' but it is mostly scored through. It was headed:

> Wind of the West
> Wind of the North
>
> But a fire for the true man's breast
> Is the blast from the shuddering North;
> And the noise of his whistling flute
> Is a horrible sound and drear
> That the lonely mountains hear;
> They listen, moveless and mute
> But the firwoods shiver with fear.

'Man and the Mountains' is in contrast to his other poem with a similar theme, 'Light, Shadow and the Moon', which he wrote in May 1905, and also did not publish. The inhospitable mountains of 'Man and the Mountains' (which must have been the ones he told Sedgwick about as he uses 'I'; it would seem he was alone), reflect his feelings on the holiday. As with his 'Glion' poems, when he was unhappy, the landscape was cold and unfriendly. He used 'firwoods' in both poems, but in 'Light, Shadow and the Moon' the firwoods are pleasant places, while in 'Man and the Mountains', this is not the case. 'Man and the Mountains' has no legends and does not express the kind of love he felt for the Welsh countryside, the sea and the mountains. Wales, for him, had memories going back into childhood, while his Scottish holiday had no roots of that kind to draw upon. He did not find the ghosts of Walter Scott and his characters in the mountains of Scotland.

A poem he wrote on 14 August 1905 reflected the irony of his life and future as he saw it, in his 'Nonsense Rhyme of Life':

> Twenty is the time for doing
> Anything and everything
> Till world with our hallooing
> Ring.[446]

The age of thirty was the time to marry, at forty he would travel, at fifty study, and at sixty it was time 'you left this earthly pig-stye/For the fleshier pots of Heaven.' A legacy of his Scottish tour was that he continued to read or reread the Walter Scott novels, including *The Bride of Lammermoor* and *Redgauntlet,* which he thought 'about the best'. He asked Sedgwick if he had seen Swinburne's splendid eulogy to Scott in the preface to Swinburne's new novel? He told Sedgwick that Thomas Hardy was not so great as Scott, yet *Tess of the D'Urbervilles* was the finest novel in the English language. Flecker's admiration was embodied in his poem 'On Closing Tess', which he had written in July 1905, and signed 'Alroy Pardon', in the BKJ copybook. Opposite his Tess poem was an undated poem, which he called 'The Murderer'. It was about a nephew who suffocated his rich old aunt, and forestalled her will. He changed the poem's title to 'Aunt Murder' when it was published in *The Best Man*. It began:

> It is the simple truth that I relate:
> I never lie: I can't
> However, it is with regret I state
> That I have killed my Aunt. [447]

This humorous but macabre poem seemed to indicate yet again that Flecker did not see a future working for money, but that his hopes lay in the death of a relative who would leave him money in their will. He would not go as far as murder, but the possibility that the death of his parents, uncles or aunts might be an eventual source of revenue was not far from his mind.

He continued to discuss literature in his letters to Sedgwick, and asked him if he had read George Meredith's (1828–1909) novel *The Egoist,* and whether he did not find, as he did, that the hero's character was reflected in his own? *The Egoist,* a comedy in narrative, was first published in 1879, and the hero Sir Willoughby Patterne (Willow

Pattern) was someone with whom more than one person found a kinship of character.[448] The favourite image of the hero was *Le Roi Soleil*. Flecker, with his middle name 'Elroy' may have felt that part of the image fitted him. Sir Willoughby was handsome, well-off, generous and subject to great admiration, which is more fantasy Flecker than the real one. But the exceptional quality of the book is the theme of sexual obsession, which was more likely to be the reason why Meredith's book appealed to him. It was Willoughby's relationship with the three women that intrigued him and gave him the idea of his ideal woman.[449] Sir Willoughby was involved with Constantia Durham who had money, wealth and beauty. The Patternes married money; it was said that they were not romantic people, and Willoughby was susceptible to beauty. But Constantia jilted him for someone else, and Sir Willoughby went abroad for three years.

Clara Middleton had money, wealth and beauty. After a whirlwind courtship, Clara's youth eventually made Willoughby think of her as his future wife; the eventual mother of his children. But all this time, Laetitia Dale, a poet, admired him. She was the daughter of a battered army surgeon from India, a poor girl living with her father, a tenant in one of Sir Willoughby's cottages, but a clever girl, who was 'a modest violet to the queenly rose of Clara'. But Laetitia could also be bold 'as timid creatures are sometimes bold'. Eventually it is Laetitia he marries, he had put Clara on a pedestal, and she had someone else to marry.

He told Sedgwick about Meredith's poetry: 'If you want substance and thought, try and read his poetry.'[450] When he discussed Swinburne with Sedgwick, he wrote, 'Only Browning has ever made his words mean so much; and, in prose, Meredith.'[451] He accused Sedgwick of knowing very little about poetry or criticism, and he hoped that Sedgwick would know himself enough to see that fact. Sedgwick had referred to 'suffocating windbags of Swinburne' and stated that he preferred Tennyson. Flecker told him that he denied Swinburne 'the qualities of dignity, lucidity, and depth'.[452]

He asked Sedgwick if he had ever studied anything besides Swinburne's first volume of *Poems and Ballads*? He asked him if he had studied 'Mater Triumphalis', which he thought was perhaps was the 'most dignified and majestic lyric ever written'. He thought that the true sense of Hertha 'would tax a keener intellect than yours to discover'. Although Flecker was fond of Tennyson, especially 'The Lotus Eaters' and 'Maeldune', he could not be compared to Swinburne. 'In Memoriam' in Flecker's view 'is almost the worst thing he ever wrote'.[453] Flecker agreed that Lamb was preferable to Chesterton. He asked Sedgwick if he had read Walter Pater's 'wonderful criticism of Lamb in his *Appreciations*?'[454]

Flecker's interest in literary criticism was connected with a literary review called *Corybant*, which he wanted to bring out and sell on a co-operative basis in the first six months of 1905.[455]

The months away from the pressures of study and preparation for examinations released an imaginative energy to write and plan new works and absorb fresh ideas. Robert Barr, editor of the magazine *The Idler* (described as 'light and bright') published Flecker's poem 'Song' under the pseudonym Kara James, in the September 1905 edition. This was the poem with the first line 'Not the night of her wild hair', which he had sent to Sedgwick in a letter dated July 1905.[456] This publication of his poem in *The Idler* gave him confidence: he planned to publish a book of his own poetry.

While he was writing at great length to Sedgwick on 18 September 1905, from Dean Close, Beazley was composing a letter (dated 22 September) in which he told Flecker that he wanted to 'make a frieze of Gods'.[457] This was an idea similar to the one found in Jane Harrison's *Studies in Greek Art*, published in 1885, and her *Prologema to the Studies in Greek Art* published in 1903, which Beazley had read when on holiday with Flecker during the Easter of 1905. This idea of 'a frieze of Gods' was the trigger for the title poem of Flecker's book of poems *The Bridge of Fire*.[458]

In September, he translated Baudelaire's 'Litany to Satan'. Either the shadow of his return to study in Oxford and work for examinations meant that he wanted to write poems with a more serious theme, or if he wanted his book of poems to contain a poem about gods, then Satan would have to feature too. 'Litany to Satan' did eventually appear in *The Bridge of Fire*. He did not include a version of 'Felo De Se', which he wrote in October 1905, based on the subject of loss of faith and suicide. He also wrote a poem in BKJ, 'The Penny Poet' in September 1905, which began:

> Extravagance in books is my worst vice:
> I buy too many.[459]

His fortunes continued to rise, as *The Idler* published another poem in the November 1905 edition, also under the pseudonym Kara James. 'The Little Song of Her Sorrow' had originally part of *Dream Songs*. He had toned it down to make the sex of the lover either male or female and it differed from his versions in his copybooks. In *The Idler* version the last line was:

> Give him a quiet command..
> Back my lover to me!

One verse of his 'private version' was more lyrical:

> Breathe to my love my heart's demand
> Back little lover, come back to me. [460]

Flecker came of age in November, and he had reason to be more hopeful about his future. Part of the Christmas vacation of 1905 was spent with Beazley and, it was also said,[461] a mistress called Nellie. 'Mistress' may not have been the correct word to use about Nellie, who was said to frequent Carfax and Cornmarket Street, and to favour both Beazley and Flecker. The *Book of Kara James* told a slightly different story:

> Nellie, calm voiced and pleasant,
> You talked, and we talked too:
> We charmed you for the present,
> But others hove in view.
> Oh, naughty girl from Paris,
> What Tom's, what Dick's, what Harries,
> (Men that one never marries)
> Have driven a share in you?
>
> We talked like high-class novels,
> We were of noble house:
> But other men from hovels
> Dully fulfilled their vows,
> And we, whose education
> Demanded admiration
> Achieved no consummation
> Nor saw beneath the blouse.[462]

January 1906, brought a more optimistic note to his verse when he wrote his 'A New Year's Carol', the first verse of which was:

> Awake, awake! The world is young,
> For all its weary years of thought:
> The starkest fights must still be fought,
> The most surprising songs be sung.[463]

But his poem 'Prayer', which he dated January 1906, had a more sombre and realistic note:

> Let me not know except from printed page,
> The pain of bitter Love, of baffled Pride,
> Or sickness shadowing with long presage.[464]

His output of prose and poetry was not so prolific in the early months of 1906: he had to prepare for his Greats examination at the end of May. He was also in debt, and money-making ventures were much in mind. He and Beazley, helped by an Oxford bookseller, Hedley Vicars Storey,[465] embarked on a magazine that would sell in Eights Week, when as it was also the end of the term, there would be a lot of visitors. A visitor to Oxford in the middle of May, two weeks before the Greats examination, was certainly not interested in the forthcoming publication of *The Best Man* (as the magazine was to be named). This visitor was his mother who, by reading between the lines of her son's letters, had felt that something was wrong. At first he denied that anything was amiss and he had written to her: 'Why should you think I am worried over anything in particular? I should have thought that Greats and a misty future were sufficient?'[466]

Mrs. Flecker thought differently and concluded that he was worried because he was in debt; she was hell-bent in finding out more and making an issue of the amount. Was she in a sense working out her own feelings over her husband's spending of money? Dr. Flecker was buying a motor car. Did she approve of this sort of expenditure? Could they afford it? In the quarrel that erupted with her son over money was she side-stepping the money problems in her own marriage? Or was money a concrete problem to grapple with, while his lack of interest in work for Greats had been left so long without discussion, that a meeting-point could not be reached? He told his mother that he hoped to pay his debts with the money he would get from the publication of his article on John Davidson. He was worried about life 'which is a more serious thing'.[467]

He was not like the young man in his poem 'Felo-De-Se':

> Not mine to be weary of life
> As pallid poets are:
> My star was a rising[468] star
> My element, strife.[469]

'Life' was not a subject that mother and son would be able to talk about in a rational way, whilst strife was something that both could easily stir up. The relationship between mother and son was not like that between Peer and As in *Peer Gynt*:

> Now, Mother, we two can chatter
> Not of things that are crooked, and harm
> But of little things that don't matter
> Of things that won't grieve or alarm.
> Hallo, is that dear old Tabby?
> Can he really be living still?[470]

> Nay, Mother, we two must chatter
> No more of things crooked that harm;
> But of little things that don't matter
> Of things that won't grieve or alarm.[471]

Flecker's mother's visits had upset him so much that he went as far as stating that his chances of a Second in Greats had gone completely as a result. He had a fit of what he admitted 'was very near madness' (which had upset his father) when he had written in reply to a letter received after his mother's visit.

It would seem obvious at this stage, that when it came to failure in University life, it was a case of like father, like son. The son was treading on what had been his father's dream.

'At last I am at Oxford, trying not with much success, to realise the true position of affairs. It all seems strange to me. It only needed that I should come to this old city which for me had somehow or other, always had a great fascinating power; it only needed this to make me believe that I am in a great dream.'[472] Flecker's father had written after he had come out first in the examinations and sat for an Oxford scholarship, which he had not really wanted to obtain at the time; he felt he would have been happier 'at the proper place, Cambridge'.[473] He did not get the Oxford scholarship, gave up the idea of Cambridge and went instead on a scholarship to study for a degree in Durham, with a view to going on later to Oxford. Flecker senior chose mathematics instead of literature or history, so he knew from his own experience, the misery of choosing the wrong subject to study. Once at Durham, Flecker's father let himself become diverted along many different paths, so he knew again from his own experience just how easy this was. He had sung and played the piano at concerts, he had addressed meetings, he preached on Sundays and he had long discussions with people about religion.

In taking on the responsibility of deciding to get married, Flecker's father had suffered physical stress, tiredness and blinding headaches. His son had written that one hour's work had given him a headache. Flecker's father had continued with outside activities, such as speaking at meetings, visiting Newcastle infirmary, opening a debate in the Union Rooms on the opium question, and talking seriously to a man who was ruining his life with riotous living. Many more activities followed, and it was not surprising that he did not sit his final examinations. At least his son had sat his, but it seemed he was not able to let his son benefit from his own experience as an undergraduate – one who had set off with such high hopes and then 'knocked myself up so thoroughly'.[474] Debts may not have been at the root of Flecker senior's problems, but he had mortgaged his future financially by getting engaged to Sarah Ducat. Mrs. Flecker may have felt that she had been powerless, because of her own ill-health at the time, to make her fiancé into a more stable man with an immediate well-paid future. She could now appear to be more in control of events. Her husband's distress reflected his feelings about his son's behaviour, which meant that he was not going to fulfil the plans he had for him, in the same way as he himself had not fulfilled the dreams his father had had for him.

As usual when conflicts arose in the Flecker family, the pieces of evidence are hard to find and fit into the complete picture. The reply Flecker sent to his parents went back to him, and he destroyed it. It was recollected that he had told his father that, as he was under age when most of the debts were run up (with the bulk of them, he admitted later, building up in his third year), his father was responsible for them. They amounted to about £50, a modest amount compared with the sort of debts his contemporaries ran up, which ranged between £200 and £300. If his father did not pay his debts, his son would write against religion in his own name. A letter that has survived arrived at Dean Close on 30 May; it played down the idea that he had made a threat. He stated, 'All that I meant was not a threat by any means, but I simply thought that if I was to use a pseudonym (which is an extraordinary nuisance) I felt I was entitled to a little consideration.'[475] He did not want to be treated 'like a madman', he wrote to his father, because he had refused to enter upon a gamble with £100 of his father's money, which would have enabled him to get into the Home Civil Service. Flecker had given his name to a scholastic agency, where he had been advised to lecture and he had heard about a post in Russia.

The letter contained the real explanation for all his anguished feelings about his parents: 'Of course I feel, as I tried to explain to Mother, that you have no affection whatever for me at all. For your son, yes, but not for me. If I were not your son you would loathe me. You take no interest in anything except that your son should have an honourable and comfortable position: but you have never even troubled to enquire after my beliefs, never asked to read my works ....'[476]

His father still maintained that the refusal to discuss religious beliefs was at the root of the disagreement between them. Dr. Flecker took refuge in his religious beliefs when dealing with this conflict; the lack of affection was not one that he was prepared to battle over.[477]

Flecker still thought, despite making these allegations, his father might still get him 'an excellent post where religion need not enter at all'. This idea embodied Flecker's belief that whatever might befall him in a future career or with financial problems, his parents would provide a safety-net. He still hoped, he told his parents, that he would work in Russia. This threat, not so obvious as the one to write about religion, nevertheless held the message that if his parents would not help him financially, he would vanish from their lives in a far-off country. His parents, he was now beginning to realise, were not going to pay his debts. He ended his letter 'Your not unloving son Roy'.

Oxford experienced dull and gloomy weather, with very heavy rain in the second last week in May, which would do nothing to alleviate the storms raging between the Fleckers. Or encourage the sales of *The Best Man*. The damp chill also would not stimulate the desire to revise for examinations.

Flecker began his Finals on 29 May 1906, and for an insight into his deeper feelings about his life it is better to look at a poem he wrote at this time. His row with his parents over money was only a superficial irritation; not the cause of the deep unease he felt about 'life' as he had already told them. His parents had told him not to worry, which he told them was a useless instruction. He knew he was not going to get a good degree, and although his mother's visit upset him, she was not the real cause of his emotional turmoil. Later, he was to tell his parents that he was rather touched by his mother's visit. His despair was reflected in his poem 'Oxford Canal', which he wrote about this time. (The poem was not in the copybooks for this period, but was published first in *The Best Man*, before being published in *The Bridge of Fire*.) 'Oxford Canal' was consciously influenced by Flecker's 'bible' *Sartor Restartus*.[478] The poem described a transient experience; one without beginning or end. It was in blank verse, reminiscent of the poetry of Walt Whitman; Flecker had a copy of Whitman's *Leaves of Grass*. In 'Oxford Canal', the poet is tired of Oxford town, and is beside the canal when a train rushes by.

The image of the train resembled that found in Carlyle's *Sartor Restartus*. In the chapter called 'The Everlasting No': 'To me the

Universe was all void of Life, of Purpose, of Volition, even of Hostility: it was one huge, dead, immeasurable Steam-engine, rolling on, in its dead indifference, to grind me limb from limb.'

As the train rushed by, Flecker wrote: 'The sun veiled himself for a moment ...'. This reference to the sun had religious meanings[479], as in *Sartor Restartus*, where the man contemplating suicide would find that he held back because 'of a certain aftershine of Christianity'.

In Flecker's poem the lines:

> A savage woman screamed at me from a barge:
> little children began to cry;
> The untidy landscape rose to life; a sawmill started;

and

> The untidy, unfinished land began to move:
> a sawmill started! [480]

are also connected with *Sartor Restartus*. After the reference to the steam-engine Carlyle refers to: 'Of the vast, gloomy, solitary Golgotha, and Mill of Death!' which is explained in a footnote as: ' "Triumphant learning, said Novalis ... opposed itself to Religion," and changed the infinite, creative music of the Universe, into monotonous clatter of a boundless Mill .... turned by the stream of chance ... For nature too remains ... ever a frightful Machine of death: everywhere monstrous revolution, inexplicable vortices of movement.'

The reference in 'Oxford Canal' to a savage woman who screamed at the poet from a barge, workmen clanging over an iron foot bridge, an old man who nodded from the window of a house, and a pretty girl hanging up clothes, which he saw as a dance of death, also have an echo in *Sartor Restartus*.

In *Sartor Restartus*, Carlyle described the 'strange isolation' he had lived in, in Edinburgh (also a university town), where he wrote: 'The men and women around me, even speaking with me, were but Figures; I had practically forgotten that they were alive, that they were not merely automatic.'

Flecker was not entirely isolated in Oxford, but he might momentarily envy the working class of Oxford, who did not have worries about failing or passing examinations. The majesty of the buildings of Oxford did not inspire 'Oxford Canal', and the readers of *The Best Man*, if not familiar with the poet himself, could see it as reflecting the ironical style that was part and parcel of the Flecker/Beazley magazine and designed to undermine and poke fun at the city where he had arrived with such soaring hopes. He had swung like the train between the canal side of Oxford life and the spires and meadows.

It is possible that a real-life suicide had a bearing on 'Oxford Canal'. A suicide in the Cotswolds was recorded[481] of the son of Jacky Bridges, a road-mender, who had served in the cavalry in the South African War. Out of work and without money, he was near the railway line when he saw the express coming towards him and dived, just like a swimmer into the water. He went straight under the wheels of the engine. Marston, where the death took place, was on the Honeyborne and Stratford line, not far from Cheltenham, and the name of the man is said to have been carved on beeches at the side of a pool.[482]

The tragic death of the road-mender's son contrasted dramatically with the triumphal return of the South African war hero, Captain Jones, to Uppingham, which Flecker had described so vividly. Uppingham had constructed a splendid memorial in 1905 to the nine Old Uppinghamians who had died in the South African War: their public memorial so much longer lasting than that of the son of Jacky Bridges.

The Best Man's editorial set the tone of the magazine:

> Everyone knows that the Best Man, with his shining hat, his well-groomed hair, and massive diamond stud. For him we have expunged these pages. We trust him not to borrow the copy that he reads.
>
> Assistance has been afforded to the editorial staff by the Suffragen Professor of Ontology (whose grip in reality is so tremendous), by a well known Peer, by a Colonial Bishop, and by Archibald Pottles, Esq.,
>
> The Captain of Boats at All Souls has kindly revised the proofs.
>
> Humour is an abortive attempt at wit (epigram).

Flecker was said (by Wolfe) to have found correcting the proofs a bore. Beazley appeared not to have taken a hand in proof-correction, despite being brought up by a mother and a grandmother, who themselves had been brought up in the stationery and lithographic business. Flecker was also said by Wolfe to have the 'air of one who was constantly pursued by printers' devils'.[483] This air could have been mainly a pose to hide the first excitement of seeing his work coming to a wider audience. He told his immediate audience 'you should devote as much pains to a limerick as to an epic'[484] and he had worked for three weeks on one about the typical Balliol man'[485] This was:

Bar-Jesus McTingletock Han –
a typical Balliol man.
He went off to Spain
in a corridor-train
with a lily-white boy in the van.[486]

He had written this limerick, he told his audience, 'for the Club which I have had the honour to found, known alternatively, by reference to the appearance of its members, as The Praxiteleans' and, having regard to their morals, as *Les Fleurs du mal*.'[487]

Wolfe also quoted a poem, which he alleged took Flecker almost a week to write:

M. Zola
Would not wear a bowler
Because he said,
It would not fit his head. [488]

In fact, the poem actually printed in *The Best Man* was slightly different:

Emil Zola
Never wore a bola
Because (he said)
It would not fit my head.

The contents of *The Best Man* which Flecker had to proof-read, were:

1. Prince Bombadill
2. Oxford Canal
3. Mrs. Hemens' A Limerick
4. The Potato Ghoul
5. In The Backwater
   Poem Song 'I have read all Love's great songs'
   Poem: Roses and Rain
6. Advertisements
7. Limericks (2)
   King Cambyses I am confidential adviser to the Kaiser
   [– illustrated to resemble Flecker]
   Drawings by Jhon

8. Aunt Murder – Poem – (formerly 'The Murder')
   Overheard at the Theatre
9. The Last Generation
13. Limerick When I met the Pope
14. Emil Zola Limerick, also illustration, one Flecker
   look-alike, and Mrs. Beecher Stowe
15. The Penny Poet, p.16 Poem:
   (adapted from the French)
16. Our Grimmest Page and last for Greats Men Only.

None of the items gave the name of the contributors – Jhon was the name of the illustrator – but there were, in fact, only two, Flecker and Beazley. Flecker was asked if they took outside contributors but he gave assurance that: 'We could find nothing which satisfied our standards'.[489] Some of the contributions came from Flecker/Beazley's *The Yellow Book*.

The Best Man used many advertisements to cover its publication costs. Advertisements tended to give a picture of the Oxford life of the day. There were invitations to take tea in tea rooms and W.H. Walker, 2–25 Broad Street, advertised Panama Hats and fancy waistcoats. The 'mock' advertisements, which Flecker and Beazley made up about the Oxford Colleges (one for example was Pembroke 'opposite the post-office'), stuck in the memories of the friends who first read it.

'Oxford Canal' also stayed in the minds of friends such as Humbert Wolfe, as did his poignant poem 'Roses and Rain':

> Roses and Rain and scented mould
> (There is gladness in your garden)
> The ivies are shining, the lawn is rolled
> (The shadows have gone from your garden)
> The green box hedge is alive with gold
> (There are two seats in the garden)
> A red brick wall to keep out the cold
> (Why sit alone in your garden?).

Another garden featured in *The Best Man* was in Flecker's prose poem 'The Potato Ghoul'. It had nothing of the sweetness and joy of 'Roses and Rain', although both poems could owe their inspiration to the rose-garden at Dean Close, and the early memory of the time potatoes were planted there:

The mists of the garden began to strike a chill into me, the wall crooked into curious outlines: breathing and seeing seemed to become one: there was nothing to hear .... Luckily at this point the sound of my Scout poking the coals disturbed a reverie which might have gone far towards cracking the glass of my brain. [490]

'The Potato Ghoul' also showed the influence of Samuel Butler's *Erewhon.* [491]

The mists in 'The Potato Ghoul' reflected Flecker's use of 'mistiness' in his letters to his parents when referring to his future.[492] The feeling of the cracking of the glass in his brain reinforces the idea of an emotional breakdown around this time, which was only narrowly avoided.[493] The idea of a potato ghoul, which rose from the potato flowers, grey in colour, without expression and with flesh like dead fish, was similar to the potato in Butler's *Erewhon.* He wrote: 'Even a potato in a dark cellar has a certain low cunning about him which serves him in excellent stead.' [494]

Some sort of lull in the hostilities between Flecker and his parents began after he had sat his Finals at the end of May. After all, he might by some fluke get a good degree, or agree to study for the civil service. It was not so much a lull in hostilities, but more of an opportunity to try and get some of the forces in the opposite camp to persuade the main enemy to give in. Beazley and Savery were invited to Dean Close[495] so that their influence with their son could be turned to hidden advantage. The elder Fleckers wanted Savery and Beazley to persuade their son to cram for a year in order to get a place in the Civil Service. In a letter Beazley told Mrs. Flecker that, although he loved and admired Roy, he was not sure that he would achieve a place after a year's drudgery in London, and the whole conflict would mean so much energy and vigour draining from his character. Beazley emphasised that he himself was raw and youthful, and had no knowledge of the world, but he appeared to have protested too much, because he must have known that it was the elder Fleckers who had a too narrow view of the world. Their view of a poet's life was limited, and they believed that the security of a Civil Service post and the short hours might mean that he could still write. However, they hoped that the poet would vanish and the civil servant take over.

Savery was even less help. He thought that Flecker was a literary genius and that, if he had been older, Savery would have been inclined to advise that he was set adrift with £100 in London. The gift of £100 was most unlikely in view of the financial restrictions imposed upon their son while at Oxford.

Flecker applied for an evening post as an LCC lecturer in English Literature and was given a glowing reference by the Professor of Literature at Oxford, Sir Walter Raleigh (1861–1922). By the elder Fleckers' standards the text of the reference was excessive, but there is no reason to suppose that its contents were not carefully thought out and a genuine appreciation of Flecker's suitability for the post. Raleigh was able, alone of all the senior men at Oxford, to see that Flecker needed encouragement and to tell him that he was a poet. He was not put off by what others might see as an undisciplined person.[496] Raleigh, the first holder of the Professorship of English literature, appointed in 1904, was no worshipper at the shrine of Oxford scholarship. He held the opinion that doctorates were given every day to men who would not have got to be shop-walkers had they started off as drapers' assistants. He knew that the academic world was a small-minded affair. He did not think that failing to get a First could damage anyone for life.[497] If only the elder Fleckers had seen Raleigh as an ally instead of their foe. The reasons why Raleigh was so broad-minded compared with William Flecker, who was less than two years' older, was apparent in his life before he reached Oxford.

Walter Alexander Raleigh was born the fifth child of Dr. Alexander Raleigh, a Congregational minister and distinguished preacher and author of religious works. His mother was Mary Darnley Gifford of Edinburgh. After preparatory school in Highbury and the City of London School, he lived in Edinburgh with Lord Gifford and went to Edinburgh Academy, returning to University College School, and then to University College. Raleigh got a second at Cambridge, where he was a member of the Apostles and editor of the *Cambridge Review*. Cambridge was his real love. He was a professor of English in India, and he had a spirit of adventure and a fascination with the East.

At Liverpool University College, because his sister Ada had married a cousin of Lytton Strachey, Raleigh became the lecturer and friend of Lytton Strachey (1880–1932), who was a student there for two years. Raleigh had returned from India to the Chair of English at University College in Liverpool in 1889. He married Lucie-Gertrude, outspoken only daughter of editor Mason Jackson of the *Illustrated London News*, in the same year. So Raleigh had knowledge of the magazine world, and he knew how to advise Flecker on getting into print, the necessity of finishing submissions in time, and how to get work as a journalist, if that was a path he wanted to follow. Raleigh had published books on the English Novel, Robert Louis Stevenson and Milton before he took the Chair of English Language at Glasgow. In between his sojourn at Glasgow and his appointment to Oxford, he had written a book on Wordsworth. It may be too simplistic to see the tall imposing Raleigh (he was over six foot) as a father-figure to Flecker. It was easy for him to offer encouragement to Flecker; he did not need to support him financially. Raleigh knew the value of lecturing in English literature. A reference, to be of any use, has to flatter its subject, if the subject is to obtain the job. It is a pity that Flecker's parents could not see Raleigh's encouragement in a more positive light.

To Flecker's annoyance, a walking tour in Normandy with Beazley had to be cancelled because of lack of cash, so Flecker went home and worked on his novel, the outline of which he had already discussed with Wolfe.

I will tell you the plot of my novel. It deals with a young provision-merchant who travels in the East, and, as a result of ordeal by flogging in a town turreted with gold and rose-minareted, he wins a bride out of the Arabian nights and becomes a king. It will be a pot-pourri of musk and blood and roses, of suns on white flat houses and tortured triumphant lovers. I shall call it *The King of Alsander*, and there will never have been a novel like it in the English language.[498]

He also began a translation of the *Golden Ass of Apulieus* as 'he adored that mysterious wonder-story of the *Golden Ass*, and its glittering precious style',[499] but he did not finish it. 'He opened the *Golden Ass* and found he could not progress without looking up too many exotic words, and the dictionary was too heavy.'[500]

Compromise was reached about his future as a candidate for the Home Civil Service, and he went on a course to Grenoble to improve his French. He was away when his parents celebrated their silver wedding on 1 August 1906. On a postcard from Grenoble, dated Sunday 29 July 29 1906, he supposed his parents had heard of his third in Greats. He ought not to be annoyed but he was.

'I must be a frightful fool'[501] he wrote, and that was his only comment on his failure to get a better class of degree. He went straight on, in the letter, to tell them that the entire University had gone to the Grande Chartreuse: 'Like Derbyshire on an immense scale', they had lost their way. He avoided, as usual, the English and American students, but a lady from Scotland was not so vulgar or ugly as the rest. He was not going to take the exam, as he did not think the diploma 'worth obtaining'. His poor showing in Greats seemed to have sapped his confidence; not only did he think the diploma not worth having, he did not think he would pass. In a long postscript, he hoped he would not be a burden to his parents. He had heard nothing from the LCC or the address of his landlady in Hampstead where he was taking up his teaching post. He also told his parents: 'You are probably wondering about the poems. A reader recommended their publication and they are at last in the press. They have undergone a very careful revision.'[502]

Which poems and press he was referring to is not given at this stage, and why his parents would be wondering about the fate of the poems is unclear, when they had to digest the news of their son's poor showing in his examinations. He was envious of tours to Italy. He was due back on the 22 August, and he was going straight to Hampstead. He did not forget to send love and best wishes for the Silver Wedding.

One positive aspect of this sojourn in Grenoble was his admiration of the Faculty of Grenoble: '... the Faculté of Grenoble may be attended with profit, constructed as it is for the French language alone instead of being a complicated scientific universal affair which one can fit on to Czech and Turkish. This script from Grenoble clearly shows how words should be run together in reading French sentences, and how the accent and pause must come after groups of words pronounced without a break; yet it can be learned in ten minutes.'[503]

Flecker's poem 'From Grenoble', which was intended for publication in *The Bridge of Fire*, reflected his feelings:

> I hate this glittering land where nothing stirs:
> I would go back, for I would see again
> Mountains less vast, a less abundant plain,
> The Northern Cliffs clean – swept with driven foam
> And the rose-garden of my gracious home. [504]

He could not want to see 'my gracious home' again so soon, and this last line looks like some sort of sop to his mother and an idealisation of the home he would like to have been able to return to. He did not see the rose-garden on his return from Grenoble, as he went straight to his schoolmaster's post at Holly Hill, the junior branch of University College School.

A distinguished former pupil of this school was Walter Alexander Raleigh, who described the masters of his day as overworked and underpaid, and his fellow pupils as 'smart commercial boys'. The classes were large and the location in Hampstead gave it a certain 'esprit de corps'.

The headmaster from 1891 to 1919 was Charles Simmons, who encouraged the study of literature. He was also the founder of the Junior branch. The school had two outstanding female teachers, Miss Garlick, a naturalist, who taught between 1893 and 1922, and Miss Fuller, who taught between 1902 and 1939. One of these two teachers could have been the one who was startled by Flecker boasting that he had made a visit to the Oxford Music Hall. Despite the visit, Flecker made a success of his short spell as a schoolmaster, although in many respects it was a continuation of his own time at University. He played games, and he drafted a translation of 'Hjalmaar speaks to the Raven'. He was credited with starting the school library; his love of books and his extravagance with them may have found a useful outlet if the school paid for any of them. He was not to be paid his salary until the end of term. He had still to rely on financial handouts from Dean Close. On leaving, the boys in his form presented him with a 'charming ugly', enormous, leather pocket-book, which would have little money in it when he went home to Dean Close for Christmas. His expenses during the term had been his room near Mount Vernon Hospital, a trip to Oxford for the weekend (Beazley had come of age in September) and all the necessities of life, for which he had still to account to his father. His problems with his parents were temporarily smoothed over by a generous Christmas present. But despite his success as a teacher, his enjoyment of visits to London and Hampton Court, the Tate, the National Gallery and the British Museum he went back to Oxford early in 1907. He now badly wanted to earn his living by his pen. Difficult as this was going to be, Oxford held compensations – Jack Beazley was still there.

Like the great tree in the grounds of Trinity, which flowered only in the summer vacation, he had found interests and loves in subjects not dealt with in the university syllabus, and for which there were no honours. Compton McKenzie had suffered a similar fate; poor showing at the University but more hopes after he had left and with less guilt and anger on the parental front.

For Flecker, the smell of the lime trees in the Lime Walk at Trinity remained the most powerful memory; it was one that contained no sadness or regret. He would have answered the question:

> Would you really be content to plough fields or push barrows? 'No. Although in moments of depression I yearn for the thoughtless existence of the ignorant, I would not really abandon my little knowledge: it is too precious to me, and I would not barter it against animal happiness. In knowledge, as in civilisation, the further we advance the greater are our joys, the deeper our sorrows; but we cannot retreat.'[505]

CHAPTER FIVE

A total eclipse of the sun was visible on 13 January 1907, from Samarkand, where a gas-installation meant it could be viewed by balloon. Even if this project (organised in Europe) like Flecker's flight to Oxford, was destined to fail, the art of ballooning symbolised Flecker's brief escape from his earthly troubles. This is seen in his poem (with a decorative design by Trelawney Dayrell-Reed), which was published in Volume 1 of the January, 1907 edition of *Ballooning and Aeronautics, a Monthly Illustrated Record* (price 1s.).

BALLADE

Up through the amethystine air,
Above the silence of the sea,
Flew a young boy with golden hair,
But reached not home and Sicily.
A pioneer's catastrophe
Drowned Icarus. 'Twas long ago.
Wiser and not less bold are we:
There is no fear for those that know.

Yet worse than Icarus may fare
The rash and windy devotee
Who leaps, not having looked with care,
Who lets a fancy wander free.
Men tell how through infinity,
Small bags of gas incognito
Still navigate the nebulae:
There is no fear for those that know!

Of men that first of all did dare
The waters in a hollow tree

Montgolfier is the splendid heir;
Of Andre too my song shall be
Of chemist Charles, or those brave three
Zeppelin, Spencer, Dumont: so
We struggle on to victory:
There is no fear for those that know!

ENVOI

Prince, thou must leave to Poetry
Her dream of golden clouds below;
Forth from a bad world's trouble flee:
There is no fear for those that know.

James Flecker

The venture to get his poem into print was also an enterprise undertaken for reasons of self-advertisement as part of a letter to Dayrell-Read revealed: '...or something of the sort. His style would do admirably. If he is willing to undertake it you might ask him to do it as quickly as possible, as I want to get it in the first issue, which means that we ought to have it on Wednesday in good time to have the block made with sufficient care. Of course if drawing is suitable I shall be pleased to pay for it... Get this done, old bud, at once: it is a chance for advertisement, too. Dimensions (relative) of border. 10 by 6. I suggest you draw it 20 by 12, 2½–4 inches wide. You know the shape of Ballade.'[506]

This poem, rather solid in feeling for a poem about ballooning, bears the impression that it was written to order to earn ready money, and it has not been republished. It was not the only poem offered to magazines at this time, which he did not want republished.

An anonymous poem with the title 'Winter Roses', was published in the January 1907 edition of *The Idler*, a magazine that had already published two of Flecker's poems.[507] 'Winter Roses' uncannily echoed the feelings that Flecker had for Beazley at that time.

WINTER ROSES

Pale winter roses, the white ghosts
Of our June roses,
Last beauty that the old year boasts,
Ere his reign closes.

I gather you as farewell gift
From parting lover,
For ere you fade, his moments swift
Will all be over.

Kind ghosts ye are that trouble not,
Nor fright, nor sadden,
But wake fond memories half-forgot,
And thoughts that gladden.

O changeless Past! I would the year
Left of lost hours
No ghosts that brought more shame or fear
Than these white flowers!

A few pages on in the same edition of *The Idler* is a short poem, also in the black type of 'Winter Roses'; this was Flecker's poem 'Desire'. 'Desire' was the new title and version of his poem 'Dream Song', which he had first written in June 1904.[508]

DESIRE

Launch the galley, sailors bold!
Prowed with silver, sharp and cold,
Winged with silk, and oared with gold.

Silver streams in violet night;
Silken clouds in soft moonlight,
Golden stars in shadow height.

Stars and stream are under cloud;
Sinks the galley silver-prowed.
Silken sails are like a shroud.

H.E. FLECKER

The use of silver and gold, with death represented by the fairy boat, were familiar and safe materials for a published poem, but the publication of 'Desire' was not considered of sufficient importance to include at this stage in the LIFE.[509] If it had, it would have brightened the brief and gloomy scene they painted of their son's life during this period: 'After Christmas, for some weeks in the early part of 1907,

Flecker returned to Oxford, to make in that city he loved so well, the young, impecunious author's vain endeavour to support himself by writing. Though he kept the facts to himself, it is believed that he underwent some real hardship.'[510]

No mention was made of Beazley's presence in Oxford; and the impression is given that Flecker had cut himself off from his parents as a source of financial help, and that he was free to starve in Oxford.[511] It is obvious that he did not starve, and his parents already knew, from Beazley, that their son 'would not be too proud to pot-boil if he found himself in a strait'.[512] He suggested journalism.

It is likely that Flecker suffered the same fate as Slimber, his fictional poet: [Whose] 'articles to *Tit-Bits* and *Pearson's Weekly*, though the real source of his modest revenue, were even less well known than his poems. Yet his unsigned essay on 'How to make money by writing' was not only deservedly popular among that wide public to which *Tit-Bits* appeals, but also saved him from death by starvation."[513]

Even if he could deal with the financial hardships (and references to 'real hardship' in his parents' recollections referred to physical, rather than spiritual suffering) he could not have been entirely emotionally carefree, despite being reunited with Beazley.

Flecker would soon realise that he was not back in the Oxford of his undergraduate days and freedom from the purse strings of Dean Close did not make it a happier time. 'Vain endeavour' was a more accurate description of any attempt to try and recapture the spirit of their close friendship, than of his efforts to make a living by his pen. Beazley was now well ahead on the scholarship path, with an Honours Degree coming into view, together with more prizes, prospects of financial security and influential friends. Beazley's hopes of success in life depended on his now stowing away hopes of establishing himself as a published poet, or sustaining an open emotional attachment to James Elroy Flecker, or anyone else. This was not just a passing phase, as Beazley had already written in his own poem, 'Waste':

"Avoided sorrowing men and weary faces,
Afraid of thinking, and afraid of tears."[514]

Beazley was not in a position to offer Flecker any great emotional or financial support. A shared address and help with criticising his poetry was all that was on offer. The creative process continued, despite the emotional setbacks, and in order to understand Flecker's inner feelings, it is better to look at the work he attempted during this return to Oxford. Staring at the blank page while waiting for inspiration was avoided by translating other poets' work; the material and the rhythms were there already. The same could be said for the process of revising his own work. For drafts of his poems and prose, he possibly used the same notebook (as it is bound in 'art linen' and yellow in colour) that he had used for obscenely jocular rhymes. Although these pages had been torn out and discarded, heads in profile remained and little sketches of elephants. It could be *The Yellow Book of Japes* from Oxford days. He gave the notebook the title *The Second Book of the Prophet James.*

Flecker, in this notebook, turned again to translating Baudelaire. The reason for selecting Baudelaire was not that he was likely to get promptly into print, and gain wide acclaim, admiration and ready cash. If this is what he wanted, he would have selected a more traditional French writer. Translations of Baudelaire were undertaken at this time because Baudelaire's mood when writing the poems matched Flecker's own mood of despair.

Like John Davidson, Baudelaire (1821–67) was a writer whose emotional and family life formed a background similar to Flecker's own. Baudelaire's father, a former ordained priest, left the ministry for teaching and then resigned his priesthood when the opportunity came. Fewer than two years after the death of her husband, Mme. Baudelaire, when eight months' pregnant, married Major Aupick. The child was stillborn.

It is interesting to note that Flecker's January 1907 translation attempt was of a poem from *Les Fleurs du Mal* entitled: 'Je n'ai pas oublie, voisine de la ville...' It was written about a time in the poet's childhood, when he and his widowed mother lived together, with a servant. The very nature of Baudelaire's poem gave rise to confused and unhappy feelings within Flecker. He was cut off from Dean Close, and without an anchor in a sea of uncertainties. Jack Beazley, he knew, was only a temporary anchorage. Like Baudelaire, he longed for an ideal home, one that had existed long ago; such as the cottage he and Beazley had shared in Wales, and then, before that, the time when he had his mother all to himself.

Flecker was depressed to realise he had made a mistake in meaning as he translated a line of the poem. He had translated *gerbe* in the line: 'Qui, derrière la vitre òu se brisait sa gerbe' as 'The corn that flattened out against the pane,' instead of: 'Breaking its rays upon the window pane,'.

His unfinished translation read:

I shall never forget our small white house
Just in the country where we used to drowse.

Where Venus and Pomona tried to dress
In meagre shrubs their crumbling nakedness.
~~The corn that flattened out against the pane,~~
Or the evening sun behind with his proud train
Like a great eye that asked us to reveal
To curious heaven and a long and silent meal.
So grandly scattering his fiery froth
On our poor curtains and cheap tablecloth.

He crossed out his mistake and wrote underneath the poem: 'Mistake in meaning. O God.'[515]

Paradoxically, a poem about his endeavours entitled 'When I translated Baudelaire', written in February, 1907 was more satisfactory.[516] The noise of a children's game outside his window made him think of a dance of death:

They are as terrible as death
The children[517] in the road beneath.

The poem ended with the line: 'When all the ghosts go round and round.'

He was once again on familiar territory with the theme of death, and his old habit of sitting at an open window while working had been resumed. The noise of children playing took him back to his attempts to work at Dean Close, when he had complained that his university terms did not coincide: 'Can you wonder that I prefer the society of my friends, when the vac. falls in term-time? With everyone busy and worried, without having the time or capacity for assisting: sitting gloomily working in my room all the morning, my greatest treat being a game of tennis or football with the boys?'[518] He had no opportunities to play games; Oxford did not provide the peace and quiet for work, any more than his home.[519]

Flecker could work out for himself, in this bleak period, that poverty and writing poetry went hand in hand, just as Baudelaire had found. Both poets used extravagance as a means of rebellion and of treating their real, deep problems. Baudelaire's stepfather, like Flecker's father, treated him as a child, even when grown up. Baudelaire felt he had to repay his stepfather's investment in him by success in the outside world, but this did not mean in the realms of literature. In this respect, the same pattern in the Flecker father and son relationship is evident: comparison of Flecker and Baudelaire is limited to the Epilogue, which Hodgson wrote herself in the LIFE.[520]

As well as trying to write new work and continue with translating, Flecker revised and altered his poems in his notebook, 'Rioupéroux', 'Dorothy', 'Anapaests', 'The Old Poet' and 'We that were Friends'. These were destined for his proposed book of poems *The Bridge of Fire*, which was soon to be in the hands of the publisher Elkin Mathews, to whom he wrote in February 1907: 'Please give the poems to your reader to be added to the MS. I have only just discovered the omission which is important, as one of them is illustrated!'[521] The illustrated poem referred to is either 'The First or Second Sonnets of Bathrolaire', which were enclosed in a letter to Trelawney Dayrell-Reed, written when Flecker discussed the illustrations for 'Ballade'.[522,523]

John Mavrogordato, who had received a second in modern Greats, was a reader at Elkin Mathews. He came down from Oxford in 1905 and worked as a publisher's reader in London.[524] (He had hoped to join the Egyptian Civil Service in 1905.)

Everything was not going smoothly in this proposed publishing venture as a letter from Elkin Mathews showed: In the fourth line he changed 'a faint metallic stare' to 'a sullen stare' and 'Whilst din and drone of ghostly violins,' to 'Whilst drone and cry and drone of violins'. And in the next line, 'Drown the triumphant shriek of obscene sins was changed to 'Hint at the sweetness of forgotten sins'. The final version of 'The Second Sonnet of Bathrolaire' has the lines: 'Pass through strong portcullis brazen teethed,/ And enter glowing mines of cinnabar.'

Flecker put these sonnets in a category he referred to as 'my old style poems – the tourniquets, cinnabar, portcullis, and all the rest of it of Bathrolaire....' (p.186 SLA)

Mary Byrd Davis states: 'Flecker may have created "Bathrolaire from Baudelaire and the place name Bath". The poems answer questions which Swinburne asks in 'Ave Atque Vale'. The imagery suggests Baudelaire, although many writers used such terms for one poet to be the only source.'

It is not too difficult to see that an illustration of these two sonnets would not be acceptable to a publisher.

Mar.28 1907
Ms. & Illus taken by Mr. F.

To H.E. Flecker, Esq. 23.4.07

Poems

Dear Mr. Flecker,

In reply to yours of yesterday my answer is – 'I am waiting for you.'

When I returned your MS. with my reader's report on March 5th I said 'In order that you may profit by his suggestions I return your MS. for revision as soon as I get it back again I will get an estimate cost for your approval – I shall be glad to publish on commission'.

So it rests. I am only waiting the revised MS. I have the drawings here.

Yours sincerely, Elkin Mathews.

I addressed the above letter to James Flecker. What style of book do you like?[525]

Charles Elkin Mathews (1852–1921) came from a Gravesend ship-owning family with trading interests in the Orient. He had arrived in London from Exeter to open as a publisher, with John Lane, in 1887. The partnership was responsible for publishing Yeats, Oscar Wilde, John Addington Symonds, Arthur Symons, Lionel Johnson, John Davidson and Francis Thompson amongst others, as well as publications such as *The Yellow Book*. The partnership ended in 1894.

Charles Elkin Mathews had successfully published between 1895 and 1898, 'The Shilling Garland Series', which ran to ten slim volumes of verse by young and not very well-known poets. The idea of a series of books sharing the same design and format was suggested by the poet Laurence Binyon (1869–1943), who felt he was held back by the publishing system of his day, which charged 5s. for a book of verse. If the poet was unknown, the chances of making even a slender profit were remote, and the opportunity for people with little money to buy these books was equally remote. Binyon, who had come down from Trinity College, Oxford, with little money to spare, gained an advantage by getting into print through 'The Shilling Garland Series', as did Henry Newbolt (1862–1938).

Writers who followed Newbolt had less success with Mathews in the publication of their work. John Masefield (poet laureate from 1930) had his *Ballads* published in October 1903 by Mathews in his 'Vigo Cabinet Series', but the public response to his second book of verse was disappointing, and Masefield published nothing more until 1911.

James Joyce (1882–1941) had a book of poems entitled *Chamber Music*, published by Elkin Mathews on 6 May 1907. The selling price was

1s. 6d. and no royalties were paid on the first 300 copies sold. Despite favourable reviews, the book made no money for Joyce. Ronald Firbank, Flecker's contemporary at Uppingham, was first published by Mathews in June 1905 (at Firbank's own expense). Firbank's first published work was called *Odette d'Antrevernes* and sold at 2s.

Thus Elkin Mathews published new writers if he received guarantee against loss.[526] So if references made to poems 'in the press' (in Flecker's letter to his parents on the occasion of their silver wedding) the year before, meant that they never came off the press, the reason could have been financial. Hence a second attempt when money had been accumulated from journalism. He had emphasised the need to publish his poems, and he told his father that this could be done on a part-risk basis for £10 and a guarantee of a further £10. There is no evidence that his father would agree to put any money towards such a publishing venture. To love poetry was one thing, to subsidise a son while he established himself as a poet was something very different, and £20 was a considerable amount of money. Dr. Flecker loved poetry, especially the work of Donne. His wife too, loved poetry, although whether the Fleckers would love some of the poems destined for *The Bridge of Fire*, is doubtful. Their son's translations of poetry from the Latin, Greek, French, German and Italian would be much more to their liking. His father's brilliance at languages and his mother's competence in Hebrew meant that he had grown up against a background of many different languages. It was to gain their love and approval that Flecker used his natural aptitude for languages in this way. The Flecker parents were no exception to the rule that parents applaud their offspring's talents when they can claim the credit.[527] The translations he made of other poets' works were much to the fore at this time, while previously written poems of his own, of the 'Roses and Rain' type, were left out of publication plans. This sort of poem did not carry quite the same air of respectability as poems on the subject of religion or death.

The rift between his parents and himself was brought about by the difference between scholarship and literature and his translations went some way towards healing it. It is also possible to draw a parallel between Eastern poets and Flecker's translations of other poets' works.[528] Translation was a means of getting inside the mind of a fellow poet, and it helped to ease the isolation he felt in his present circle. His ability to speak and understand other languages made the idea of interpreting as a career the next logical step, and a further means of healing the rift between himself and his parents. As he wrote in *The Grecians*:

Nevertheless, very fine is the spirit of the true linguist, which I admit to be a very different thing from the mere spirit of literary curiosity which desires to learn just enough of a language to read some favourite or famous author in the original. The true linguist revels in fantastic grammars where the verbs open out in the middle to make themselves passive or negative, and numerals agree with singular masculine nouns in the genitive feminine plural.[529]

The idea of studying to be a student-interpreter came from a friend of both Flecker's and Savery's from Oxford days, Walter Divie Peckham. Peckham was the son of a clergyman, Henry John Peckham and his wife Edith (née Robertson). Walter Peckham (born 18 March 1883 at the Vicarage, Nutley, Maresfield, Sussex) had been at Corpus and had passed the examinations to be a student-interpreter in the Levant in February 1906. He moved to Trinity College, Cambridge, in Easter of the same year. Flecker saw the Levant Consular Service as an attractive proposition, not only would he find favour with his parents because he was embarking upon a career, but he would be at the foot of a ladder in what appeared to be a secure and respectable profession. As well as these advantages, as he prepared for entry into the service, he would be in London and on the Continent at the same time as Beazley, who would need to be in those locations in order to further his study of Greek vases.

The Levant Consular Service trained men for posts in Egypt, Persia, Morocco, Greece, Russia and Ethiopia. Greece was his preference, and he told his father the reason why. It was that he could talk a bit of modern Greek already. Beazley's ultimate destination would be Greece; he did not tell his father this.

Flecker went to stay with Peckham in Cambridge, and then went to Nutley Vicarage, for the weekend, where he got more details of the life of a student-interpreter. Time was not on his side, as the upper age limit for these posts was twenty-four. If he was to follow in Peckham's footsteps, he had to cram for the entrance examinations, which were due to take place at the end of the year. He explained to his father, by letter, that he had been to see the coach for the Consular Service, Dawson Clarke 'late Scoones'. Dawson Clarke was a 'bearded, somewhat Rabelaisian figure not likely to be forgotten by anyone at Scoones'.[530] Flecker told his father that it was absolutely necessary to take all optional subjects i.e. Ancient Greek, German, Spanish and Italian. As Dawson Clarke was a first-rate teacher of Latin and Greek, and a clergyman, his advice was not likely to go unheeded at Dean Close. Flecker was home and dry with his choice of career.

Flecker was sufficiently anxious to qualify as a student-interpreter that he himself proposed the financial arrangements and agreed them with his parents. £10 was to be put in his name in the bank to start an account and weekly statements of his expenditure were to be rendered, despite the agony caused by such arrangements in the past.

His father had to agree to paying a guarantee of £500, against his son leaving the service before a five- year period had elapsed. Although Dr. Flecker could have had this sum guaranteed through an insurance company, he chose to make the guarantee himself.

It would be too simple to see Flecker's decision to accept his father's terms for financing his studies and the choice of the career itself, as something he could not have avoided.[531] Flecker had managed to get poems published during his stay in Oxford.[532] Obviously, publication of some poems would not give him enough money to support himself, and he was still working on his novel , but this held out the promise of publication and more money for living expenses.[533] It was obvious that he needed a source of income and the Levant Consular Service provided this, by giving him a salary while he studied at Cambridge. It also provided the opportunity to have a career, which he could continue alongside Beazley's. He did not want to join the Home Civil Service, and the stay in Oxford had provided him with the opportunity to see how Beazley's career was shaping, as well as to test the strength of their relationship. Flecker's writing career, both from the point of view of work that he got published and work that he failed to finish or get published, profited from this brief period in Oxford. It showed him that he needed a secure base for a while from which he could write more than a few poems.

Flecker took lodgings in a Bloomsbury boarding house at 37 Torrington Square under the watchful eye of the landlady, Mrs. Elizabeth Evans. Torrington Square[534] had been the home of Christina Rossetti's family, who had lived at number 10 between 1876 and 1894 (the year of the poet's death). The unfussy Georgian houses of the narrow square overlooked trees, but as the character of a square changes more slowly than the tide of its inhabitants, the period from Christina Rossetti's death to Flecker's arrival can be seen as a period of slow decline, when its addresses were no longer considered to be 'good', but had not yet reached the stage when, during the Great War, rooms could be rented by the hour. A few houses of the square remain, including No.30, but the rest were demolished to make way for the extension of London University.

Flecker continued, despite his studies, to revise his poetry. One at least, has the date April 1907; this was 'The Ballad of the Student in the

South'. He decided to get his manuscript back from Elkin Mathews, and to try to persuade Grant Richards to publish his book.

Grant Richards (1872–1948), son of Franklin Thomas Richards, Fellow and Tutor of Trinity College, Oxford, had started in business as a publisher on 1 January 1897, at 9 Henrietta Street, in Covent Garden. In the ten years he had been in business he had persuaded George Bernard Shaw to let him publish his plays and had published G.K. Chesterton's first book. He had also become the friend and champion of John Davidson and published some of his works.

Richards had come to think, in the early years of the century, that publishing poems by new writers was not a profitable enterprise. 'Commercially, poetry was on the wane, when *Self's The Man* appeared, and there were few exceptions to the rule.'[535] Richards admitted that he had published 'an unusual number of poets: some of them I carelessly let go. Some of them went.'[536] One poet who 'went' was not entirely new or young with family responsibilities. He was A.E. Housman (1859–1936), who did not want any royalties paid to him on an edition of *A Shropshire Lad*, published by Richards in 1898. An American magazine published Housman's poetry without his prior permission, then sent him cheques, but he returned them. Housman had only allowed Richards to publish a second edition of *A Shropshire Lad* after the first edition (by another publisher) had been sold. Housman told Richards he was not a poet by trade, he was a Professor of Latin. Richards then included *A Shropshire Lad* in his 'The Smaller Classics Series', but during what Richards described as a 'crisis' in his affairs, Housman, in a letter dated 17 August 1906,[537] protested about the title of the series, and asked Richards to withdraw the book. Next, Richards had problems with a pictured *Shropshire Lad*; the rural decorations supplied by the artist were the cause of a rift. Housman found fault, this time, with the accuracy of the designs.[538]

The 'crisis' referred to by Richards was his own bankruptcy, which was said to have been in 1905.[539] The roots of this failure lay in the amount of money that Richards had put into his business when he had set up as a publisher at the age of twenty-four. He was not a writer, but he was not inexperienced, as he had first worked for seven years in the publishing world, and he had met literary people through his uncle by marriage, Grant Allen, a novelist and author of *Evolution of the Idea of God*, described by Flecker as 'published for 6d. by the admirable Rationalist Press Association'.[540] But Richards, now the son of a retired Don of Trinity College, Oxford, did not, for a number of reasons, have the soundest of financial backing for his publishing house, and this, although he was a lover of books and had the right connections, was the source of the trouble. It is not surprising, in view of Richards' financial problems, to find that some mystery surrounds the publication of poetry by hitherto unknown poets who approached Richards before Flecker did with his manuscript.

Richards had published in 1902, the first volume of poetry by John Masefield (1878–1967), for which Richards had suggested the title, *Salt-water Ballads*. Masefield's book of poetry, although on the same subject as Newbolt's, had quite a different approach. Over 500 copies of *Salt-water Ballads* were printed during 1901–3 but Richards said that a fire at the warehouse meant that the book was not available to a wider audience.[541] Masefield's book, which contained his most famous poem 'Sea Fever', was also thought to be handicapped by the title Richards had suggested because it was then associated with Kipling's *Barrack-Room Ballads*. Masefield's next book of poems was passed to Elkin Mathews, a fact much regretted by Richards. Elkin Mathews published Masefield's *Ballads* in 1903.

Another book of poems passed to Elkin Mathews, after first being considered by Richards, was James Joyce's *Chamber Music*, which Richards much admired. He held on to the manuscript, which he said he could not get access to because it was locked up in a warehouse. Arthur Symons, who had suggested Richards to Joyce, subsequently found out about Richards' bankruptcy and told Joyce.[542] Richards turned down *Chamber Music* in May 1905, unless Joyce could afford to pay for publication, which Joyce was not willing to do. It was then published by Elkin Mathews in 1907.

It is helpful to see how Richards handled the first books of two (later famous) authors, and how he played a game of hide and seek with both author and manuscript; his contention that poetry was on the wane commercially was mainly due to his own financial problems.

Flecker's book of poetry had a title decided beforehand, and he did not have to rely on Richards to supply an illustrator. He would have a better chance with Richards if he could pay towards the cost of publishing *The Bridge of Fire*.

Richards was now trading under his wife's name and his office was in Vigo Street, where Flecker sent his poems and the illustration after he collected them from Elkin Mathews on 23. On a sheet of Balliol College notepaper he wrote to Grant Richards:

> Dear Sir,
>   I had better tell the whole truth about this book of poems and the illustrations which I hope you will be able to publish for me soon.

They have been read and thoroughly approved of by another publisher's reader, and he has been willing to publish them. But his terms are so onerous that even if I could afford them, I do not think I should be justified in accepting them.

Some time ago Mr. Maurice Woods[543] recommended me strongly to apply to you, and I wish I had done so at once.

May I call between 5 and 6 on Wednesday and arrange terms, that is, if you are willing. I think the illustrations will sell the book.

Yours sincerely,

James Flecker.[544]

The illustrations referred to were by Trelawney Dayrell-Reed, who was in London at the same time. He introduced Flecker to Douglas Goldring at a crowded tea-party in a flat in Chelsea, given by the mother of Isabel Davidson.[545]

Douglas Goldring was born on 7 January 1887 at 36 Burney Street, Greenwich, the youngest of five children. His family background bore some resemblance to Flecker's own. Goldring's father, Frank, had wanted to be a doctor, but instead he had to train to be an architect. He turned out, not surprisingly, to be an unsuccessful one. Goldring's mother Constance Ann (née Norris) had lowland Scots forebears. She was a domineering and deeply religious woman, who was a convert from non-conformist to the Church of England. The Goldring family had moved to Brussels when he was two years old, but they returned to the English countryside. At ten years old, Goldring was living in Oxford, where he attended Magdalen College School, and then went to Felstead. He had poems accepted by the magazines *Country Life* and *The Academy*. The joint editor of both publications was P. Anderson Graham, and his secretary was Alice Head, who organised his disorganised office.[546] Goldring wrote to Graham to ask for a job; he was at a private crammer's in Oxford where he had amassed a large amount of bills.

Goldring was amazed to be offered employment on the editorial staff of *Country Life* at £2 per week, with payment at the usual rates for anything he wrote in the paper. He took over from Alice Head, who had accepted an offer to be secretary and sub-editor to Lord Alfred Douglas, newly appointed editor of *The Academy*, in May 1907. Goldring did the same sort of work as Alice Head, but at a better wage, although he did not have the same experience or skills. It was this work he had been enjoying, when he was introduced to Flecker and Beazley by Trelawney Dayrell-Reed, whom he had met at Oxford.

The tall blond Goldring was a self-confessed London addict, and he suffered acute withdrawal symptoms if away from the city for more than a few months. In London, Goldring felt he could live more than one sort of life and play many roles. This too, was Flecker's way of coping with his time in London, where it was easier to use this chameleon-like method, than it had been in Oxford, where it was usually a case of belonging to Town or Gown.

In London, Flecker could be admired for his having poems in the press and in magazines, or he could play the role of dutiful nephew, man about town, or even, after a case of mistaken identity, a 'foreign' tourist. He gained admiration as a cultural guide when he persuaded his uncle, a curate in Lambeth, and his aunt, a former art student, to visit the collection of old Japanese prints at the British Museum. He followed that with suggestions of books to read on Ancient Egypt, Russian art and music. It was doubtful that his relatives would see him in another role when his interest in Japan extended to wearing a brief Japanese style dressing-gown (a kind worn by both men and women); it is to be hoped that the long sleeves did not interfere with his piano-playing. The Kabuki Theatre of Japan played at the Criterion Theatre in 1907, this traditional theatre may have influenced his dress, as well as his artistic consciousness.

He played the piano, thus dressed, while Beazley, Goldring, and their hostess, Isabel Davidson, sang the choruses of Parisian cabaret songs. Besides singing for his supper, he also presented the hostess, as did Beazley, with handwritten copies of their poems in book form. Flecker is portrayed by Goldring as the life and soul of these parties, where admiration sparked off jollity, wit and the reading of verses.

Only at one dinner party was he said to have been handicapped in the conversation stakes: an ageing, diminutive, former showgirl, called Gertie, born a Londoner, but nearer to the sound of Bow Bells than Flecker, referred to his dark skin, which she hinted was due to a lack of washing, and also remarked on his Jewishness.

Another environment where he could, as others had found, be at some social disadvantage was in the crammers, Scoones, at 19 Garrick Street, Covent Garden.[547] Here the atmosphere was alive with the charm and courtesy of would-be diplomats and ambassadors, whose social life revolved round country balls. When at Scoones, they had lunch at the next door Garrick Club. The French, Latin and Greek teaching may have been first-class, but Flecker's social standing there was not high. Although he might not be the social equal of most of his fellow students, he was their intellectual equal, and if he could not aspire to attending country balls, he haunted instead the restaurants and cafes of Soho and Holborn in the company of Goldring, Beazley and Reed. The Cafe Royal was one of his favourites, where, according to Goldring, Flecker made drawings of not very recognisable monkeys, on the tables. The Vienna Cafe in New Oxford Street was where 'he liked studying the types'. Hodgson found it difficult not to laugh when she read this statement in Goldring's book, as she wrote[548] that the Vienna Cafe was frequented by 'respectable spinsters and even well-known educationalists', which she claimed was 'suspicion that Flecker's tastes were not wildly exotic after all.'[549] Goldring gave details of evenings he and his friends spent in a little Belgian cafe in Lisle Street, W.1, called the Ile de Java, which did not feature in the LIFE.

Flecker must have studied 'types' sitting in cafes and restaurants, and also the decor, as these impressions are in a fragment of a play he wrote (in his *Prophet James* notebook), which he set in the Ristorante Paige 'probably somewhere in Soho'. The evening there was a 'floating half-dozen' of the people who frequented 'this rather wicked tavern' whom he recognised as, 'the favourite actors, journalists, painters and other outcasts, ...'. After describing the interior of the Ristorante Paige he continued, 'Despite all efforts to be Continental an indescribably oppressive air of Suburban Sin haunts the place'.

The play, entitled *The Poet's Tragedy*, had the following characters:

David Rivers – A Poet. (he was going to be called David John Henry
    Rivers, but these names are crossed through)
Ivan Delamere – A Young Man from Oxford, a pupil of:
Professor – Professor of English at Newcastle Arbuthnot Huggins
    University
Edward Cambus – An editor of the *Review* (described later as 'the *Weekly Review of High Art*)
Dorothy – A Lady
Rose – A Prostitute

He outlined what would happen in this unfinished First Act: Mr. Cambus and Professor Huggins talk in a Soho Restaurant with Delamere about Literature (Poems etc.). A strange man talks to them (Rivers). Friendship of Rivers and Delamere. Delamere married. Rose and Rivers.' [550]

At the start of the First Act, Cambus and Huggins talk about Delamere before he comes in, and it is learned that he only got a second class degree in Literature due to the fact, according to Huggins, that he was so erratic and 'never shone at Philology'. He would also waste his time reading Swinburne (this is crossed out) and modern people like Thackeray and Disraeli, adding 'of course there is nothing in the school later than 1820' (this is altered to 1790). This conversation is broken off when they notice what they describe as a curious-looking man enter. Although the fragment does not continue for long enough to find out who this figure was, at a guess it was the poet Rivers. Cambus tells Huggins that he is surprised that Huggins seems so fond of Delamere, and Huggins replies that 'one gets fond of people at Oxford, very fond indeed'. Huggins does not know why he is so fond, but says that Delamere is very amiable 'such a delightful boy'. He confessed to taking a deep interest in him, and wished that he had children of his own and that he could have fathered the orphan Delamere. He says this just as Delamere comes in and here the fragment breaks off.

The fact that Huggins was a Professor, at Newcastle University, and not Oxford, is not explained. Trinity College, Oxford, was originally Durham College, founded by an order of monks from Durham, which may have been the origin of Newcastle. Flecker senior had been to Durham University. As plans for a career for Delamere are outlined, it is not too difficult to see that this fragment exposes Flecker's anxieties about his own future and regrets about his own immediate past. Delamere's appearance makes him more like Beazley in looks than Flecker. 'There is something so young about that boy,' Huggins says before Delamere comes in. But other characteristics of Delamere, such as the fact that he is without a career, and that reviewing as an occupation is considered for him, makes him more like Flecker. Delamere is not referred to as a poet, but Huggins has sent Cambus some of Delamere's essays, which Cambus thinks are very original.

Huggins is based on someone like Professor Raleigh, as Huggins is 'about forty' and Raleigh would have been that age when Flecker encountered him at Oxford. Also Cambus remarks that Delamere, judging from his writings, is not much like Huggins, in character, so to speak. It is more difficult to see who Cambus is based on, as his age is given as sixty.[551] It is easy to see that, as Raleigh had connections with the world of journalism, the chat between Cambus and Huggins was one that Flecker could visualise taking place between Raleigh and an editor. In an effort to get work for Flecker and introduce him to a useful contact, this was how he imagined they might talk together (as Huggins and Cambus did rather patronisingly in *The Poet's Tragedy*) about the Ristorante Paige as being a little Bohemian, but that it would do Delamere good to see a little life, and a spell in London would soon settle him down. The poet, John Henry Rivers, does not speak, but the original use of David and John indicates that John Davidson could have been the model. The fact that Delamere is married, and that there is mention of Lady Dorothy in the cast, makes it possible that Flecker had already seen that one means of securing a financial future, while he established himself as a writer, was to marry an upper-class woman with an income of her own. He had already written a poem 'Dorothy' in his *Prophet James* notebook, and he presented poems to his hostesses; the idea of Lady Dorothy had sprung from his socialising while he studied in London. The friendship between Delamere and Rivers would have revealed much, as would the Rivers and Rose relationship. It is interesting, too, to see how he classed actors, journalists, painters as 'outcasts'. He had no desire to be a full member of such a group, at present; he was, if anything, a part-time Bohemian. If he was ever going to make a living by his pen, he wanted financial help along the way, and to make use of his knowledge of classics. His ability to play the leading role in whatever group he found himself enabled him to observe groups of people in a detached and light-hearted way. This light-heartedness permeated the poems written under the influence of this particular period. Although light-hearted, the poems did not lack strength, colour, beauty and nostalgia and were just as impressive as many of his poems on more sombre themes.

Flecker's differing roles, and his enjoyment of them, explained why he did not deliberately seek out and settle into a group of struggling writers. As he had written in *The Poet's Tragedy*, he saw them (even if rather tongue-in-cheek) as outcasts. He needed his own group of younger friends, who admired him – Beazley, Goldring and Reed, amongst whom he was the undoubted master. Unlike Beazley, he wanted very much to get his book of poems off the press and into the hands of the public.

The result of his approach to Grant Richards was not favourable and he wrote to Richards: [552]

37 Torrington Square,

W.C.

Dear Sir,

I am very sorry indeed, but I am afraid that I must go against my own interests for the sake of my friend the artist. He has nothing to depend on but his work, and a debut, even with imitative work, is better than none at all.

Will you please be so kind as to send the poems and the drawings by return to me at 37 Torrington Square? I must get them published at once.

A friend has informed me by the way, that there is a custom of finishing <u>half</u> a novel, & shewing it to a publisher before it is completed. I also have a book of short stories I badly want published. If you would like to see these, and especially the novel, I will have it typed. I am certainly most anxious for you to publish for me in the future.

Yours truly,

James Flecker.

The picture of the artist, Trelawney Dayrell-Reed, having 'nothing to depend on but his work', was in stark contrast to the picture of Reed in London given by Goldring in this period when he knew Flecker, Beazley and Reed.[553] Reed is depicted as a man about town 'wan and precious' who lived in Bramerton Street, Chelsea (although Bramerton Street, off the King's Road, was in Chelsea, it was a small street, with apartment houses, where Reed could have rented a room) and who had arrived at Goldring's lodgings, around midnight, in tails 'and a particularly splendid topper'. The two friends, who had known each other at Oxford, spent some of the night in a small Chinese Restaurant in Limehouse Causeway, where Reed made 'fantastic Beardsleyesque drawings on the marble-topped table', while Goldring 'scribbled and talked about Verlaine and Dowson'. They finished the night having drinks in Covent Garden. Reed is depicted as having private means – Goldring was envious of Reed, as he could sleep as long as he liked, while Goldring had to be at his desk at *Country Life* by 10 a.m. Was Reed not prepared to pay his share of getting *The Bridge of Fire* into print? And without his share, was Flecker unable to find the money?

It could be that the fantastic Beardsleyesque drawings which were Reed's trademark, were at the root of the publication problem (one was to be a caricature of Flecker, just as Beardsley had caricatured Wilde, in one of his *Salome* illustrations).[554] The Beardsleyesque drawings by Reed did not reflect the theme of the opening poem in *The Bridge of Fire* – 'A New Year's Carol'. It extolled the reader to 'Awake, awake! The world is young,/For all its weary years of thought'. This was a message of hope for a New Age and not a turning back to old beliefs, old times or the past century. Grant Richards knew the difficulty of selling books illustrated by the real Beardsley; a book by an unknown poet, with illustrations that imitated Beardsley, would not only be difficult to sell, but impossible to sell at a reasonable profit. All was not lost by taking the poem and illustrations back from Grant Richards as a letter from him, dated 18 June showed:

June 18th, 1907
James Flecker Esq.,

Dear Mr. Flecker,

You will by now have received the manuscript of your poems and your friend's drawings.

It will certainly give us great pleasure to have the opportunity of considering your stories and the novel, which you tell me is partially completed. I shall hope to receive them from you shortly.

Sincerely yours,
Grant Richards.[555]

The poems and illustrations went back to Elkin Mathews, who had been willing in the past to publish both; his firm's 'terms' would now appear to have been better than the 'terms' offered by Grant Richards. Flecker did offer Richards the volume of stories, in a letter to him, he wrote: [556]

37 Torrington Square,
W.C.

Dear Sir,

I send you the volume of stories. I thought at first of writing a long letter to you about them. But I shall instead call in on Saturday morning.?

Yours truly,

James Flecker.

The Saturday appointment with Grant Richards did not appear to have been kept and Flecker wrote again and pressed for another appointment:

37 Torrington Square,
London, W.C.

Dear Sir,

I should be much obliged if you could give me an appointment on Thursday at latest concerning the stories I sent you, as I shall be leaving town for a week or two.

Yours truly,

James Flecker. [557]

Flecker was off to France, armed with a gun. Evidence of his revolver barrel glittering in the gaslight of his Bloomsbury room was supplied by Goldring, who visited Flecker just as arrangements had been concluded for the publication of *The Bridge of Fire*, and he was preparing for his journey to France. The fact that gaslight was needed in Flecker's room on a summer's evening when his window 'was wide open framing a square of dark blue night, and as an undertone of his conversation came the faint, thrilling tone of London',[558] meant that the hour of the visit was late, or that the atmosphere of those summer evenings in London, in the dingy room near the British Museum, played tricks with the memory and imagination, like Flecker's poem 'Oak and Olive', the third verse of which reads:

> And there's a hall in Bloomsbury
> No more I dare to tread,
> For all the stone men shout at me
> And swear they are not dead;
> And once I touched a broken girl
> And knew that marble bled.

In the second verse he found:–

> And when I stand by Charing Cross
> I can forget to hear
> The crash of all those smoking wheels,
> When those cold flutes and clear
> Pipe with such fury down the street,
> My hands grow moist with fear. [559]

He may have experienced moments of anxiety, but the main feeling of these weeks in London was of light-heartedness and joy. His room was dismal, but it was near the British Museum and Beazley, and a short distance away from the markets of Covent Garden, where the odour of fruit and vegetables and the scent of flowers in baskets mixed, as he made his way to the crammers of William Baptiste Scoones, or publishers' offices.

At this point in the summer, with his poetry in the hands of Elkin Mathews, his stories under consideration by Grant Richards and his course of studies at an end, he needed more physical activity than the social round offered him. He also needed more realistic challenges than that engendered by the ghosts of Bloomsbury and Charing Cross. He was due to enter the Diplomatic Service where conflicts were not settled by hand to hand combat.

Flecker was going to the south of France, against a background of conflict in the French wine trade (a consequence, mainly, of watering down the product), which had resulted in riots in which lives were lost. French troops were brought in to quell the disturbances, but the troops mutinied because they sympathised with the peasants' uprising. The crisis had thrown up an unlikely leader, known as Marcellin Albert, who confronted Clemenceau in his own office, after which the revolution largely collapsed. Flecker, with his companion, G.G. Knox, who was also on the student-interpreter path, were going out to make investigations.

Geoffrey George Knox (1884–1958) was born in Sydney, Australia, the son of George Knox and grandson of Sir Edward Knox.[560] He was at Trinity College, Cambridge, but according to Francis Toye,[561] who had already give up his student-interpretership, Flecker saw more of Knox in London than he had done in Cambridge. Knox was also a contemporary of Flecker's friend, Peckham, who was up at Cambridge.

Acceptance of an article by *The Monthly Review*'s last edition, June 1907, might have given Flecker sufficient cash, or promise of cash, to enable him to go to the Continent.

The article in *The Monthly Review* was on the subject of a woman poet, who wrote about the world of Islam and the Persian Poets. Laurence Hope (1865–1904) was, not surprisingly, often reviewed as a man, but her real name was Adela Florence Nicolson (nee Cory). She was born at Stoke Bishop, Gloucestershire, and her first book of poetry, *The Garden of Kama* was published by Wm. Heinemann. After her death, *The Garden of Kama* was described 'as a series of love lyrics from India, and their tropical luxuriance and Sapphic fervour attracted so many readers that a second and third edition of the book were demanded'.[562] But Flecker wrote in his article: 'It is hard to account for nine impressions of *The Garden of Kama*'. Her next book of poetry, *Stars of the Desert*, published in September 1903, reprinted. The reviews of *The Daily Chronicle* described Laurence Hope as 'one of the happy few who have created literature out of our occupation of India'. *St. James's Gazette* declared that 'passion beats and palpitates in every line'. ' *"The Queen"* spoke of Eastern quaintness and colour.' *The Academy* wrote of Laurence Hope's poems 'the measure of their literary fidelity concerns us as little as in the case of Edward Fitzgerald', and *The Athenaeum* 'He brings us into a region of native feeling and imagination never yet fully explored'. Laurence Hope killed herself two months after the death of her husband, which *The Athenaeum* of October 1904 stated was due to 'depression which had settled upon her since the loss of her husband...'. India was, above all, the theme of her poetry, which was about youth, love and death. Her last book, *Indian Love*, which contained a portrait of the author, was published in 1905. She is best remembered, now, for her poem 'Pale Hands I Love Beside the Shalimar'.

Most of these biographical facts were not in the article Flecker wrote for *The Monthly Review*, instead he concentrated on the fact that she was a woman poet, and popular. His article is interesting as it shows his thoughts about women poets and the two sorts of famous woman poets who had given 'force without grace or grace without force'. Even more interesting is that what really made him uncomfortable about Laurence Hope's works was that she had faults that he feared might reveal themselves in his own poetry; he complained in his article 'page after page of Laurence Hope's poetry is marred by lilts and jangling tunes and passages of sentimental prettiness that, so far from breathing of the East, savour of that most Occidental invention, the music-hall'.

He quoted from one of her poems at the end of his article: 'That thou may'st keep the stamp of thy love and shame.' The 'love and shame' elements he still had to come to terms with in the publishing of his own poems, but he wrote in this article: 'And very often the glow of passion transfuses lead into gold'.

Laurence Hope died in October 1904, and it was around this time that Flecker used the pseudonym Kara James. It has an echo of Laurence Hope, in that Laurence is a man's name, and Hope is a woman's name, just as Kara can be mistaken for a woman's name, while James is undoubtedly male. Flecker published poems under the name of Kara James; he called his copy book of poetry *The Book of Kara James*, but with his second notebook the name was changed to *The Prophet James*.

The article revealed his feelings about the writing of poetry, not only Laurence Hope's. As he wrote in his poem 'No Coward's Song': 'I am no coward who could seek in fear/ A folk-lore solace or sweet Indian tales:'. It is also revealing, as it bears out what Professor Huggins says to Cambus in *The Poet's Tragedy*: 'it is difficult to get these modern people into perspective, so very difficult to form judgment so soon on people who are hardly dead.'

Courage was needed for the Continental adventure, not least because it was prudent to keep the visit secret from his parents, or at least the reason why he was going.[563] Dean Close would hardly have been willing to finance such an expedition, and as Knox came from an affluent background the financing of the expedition would be safe in his hands. The adventure on Flecker's side was more a sentimental mixture of *Chums* and *Boy's Own Paper* exploits, coupled with a dream he had of being a wine merchant. A brief break from his studies would be welcomed, and a companion such as Knox was an advantage; with Beazley, he was unlikely to do anything as rash or expensive. Flecker was still missing the days of school sports when he was a first-class shot in the Uppingham Rifle Corps.

Another case of mistaken identity, much more dangerous than his previous one, occurred when a mob rushed up to Flecker and Knox when they were sitting in a cafe, and threatened to hang them, thinking they were spies. It was difficult for Flecker to convince the mob that he was English, and as Knox was a fluent French speaker, the spy theory was equally difficult to dissolve.

He was inclined later to brush off any suggestions that he was frightened during this expedition, but it made him oppose war, and this sort of encounter was as far as he was prepared to go. He wrote in *Don Juan* (Act II, Scene 1): 'It's modern war I hate – an ugly and stupid affair of money and mathematics. Give me that ancient bloody spear-jabbing tussle that poets call a fray.'

The 'fray' served as useful background material for his novel *The King of Alsander*, when troops confronted the rabble. He wrote in his novel about fermentation in Alsander, although the fictional riots were not about the over-production of wine. His next venture to the Continent was to go to Bonn, in August. He wrote to Grant Richards from Dean Close, before his departure:

Sunday

Dear Sir,

I am going abroad for a month on Thursday next to Coblenz, and will send you my address from there if I do

171

not hear from you before that date, about stories I have left in your hands.

I might well mention that I have made one story – the *Last Generation* – three times as long: and that I can add a tale if the book is too small. I do not send you the new version of the '*Last Generation*' until I hear generally your opinion with regard to the book.

My poems will probably be out in a Fortnight or less. I have had the proofs – and you might like to wait and see if they meet with any success before deciding re. the Stories.

Yours truly,

James Flecker. [564]

Call the stories for the present '*The Last Generation and Other Stories*' for convenience!

He also wrote to Elkin Mathews from Dean Close, before he left for Germany:

Dean Close School
Tuesday
Cheltenham.

Dear Sir, [565]

I send the revised proof, to supersede the list of errata I sent yesterday, which I should not have sent had I known that the revised proof would appear so soon.

I should like a final proof to be sent to me in Germany, especially as I noticed two slips in the last proof which were not in the first.

I will send my German address as soon as I know it.

Forgive the number of corrections, rather large for a second proof. I think everything is now discovered!

Yours truly,

James Flecker.

Flecker stayed in a pension, recommended by the Dean Close music teacher Heller Nicholls, at 10 Auguststrasse, Bonn. He wrote to his parents on 13 August, and told them that he had taken a programme of twenty Berlitz lessons (two a week of Spanish and one of French) for a period of six weeks. He said that Bonn was a very dull town indeed, but that he supposed this was better from his work's point of view.

The dullness was not relieved by the sunshine of a beautiful morning, which heralded the unplanned visit of Heller Nicholls, who found to his surprise that Beazley was also at the pension, working hard.

Flecker may, in one respect, have welcomed someone from home, in the same way that Harold Smith of *The Grecians* met two schoolmasters, as arranged, comparatively early the next morning, at a cafe. He found them ruefully consuming thin coffee and thick rolls, and pining for the fleshpots and teapots of England. He laughed at their dejected countenances and gleefully produced from his pocket a fine pot of jam, which he good-naturedly shared with the forlorn travellers.[566] Flecker, when away from home, always longed for jam.

Nicholls certainly had not come to spy, and although Flecker realised that the news of Beazley's presence amid the usual clutter of possessions would get back to his parents, at least he would be able to hide the amount of his own writing that he was doing, and that he was pursuing the aim of publication, alongside talking to German students in the pension to improve his German, which he found hard to write.

A letter from Grant Richards, which like Nicholls's visit was something of a mixed blessing, read:

August 19th, 1907

James Flecker Esq.

Dear Mr. Flecker,

I should like, if I may, to congratulate you on the interest and talent of your stories, but I do not quite see how they could be made a success in book form; I don't think, in fact, that they could be sold in sufficiently large numbers to pay the cost of their production.

Our reader has been especially pleased with the stories, which he describes as having great merit and originality.

Will you not let me see as much as you have written of the novel on which you told me you were at work? I am specially anxious to see this after having read your stories.

I am keeping the stories here until I hear from you as to their disposal.

I hope I am right in addressing you at Bonn. A postcard which I took to be from you arrived some days ago, but it was unsigned.

Sincerely yours,

Sgd. Grant Richards.[567]

Richards was wary about publishing a volume of short stories, as he had been sent James Joyce's *Dubliners* in December 1905, and had accepted the twelve short stories for publication early in 1906. But when Joyce sent him two further stories, Richards had changed his mind because of their content. Richards eventually agreed to publish *Dubliners* in 1914. Flecker wrote in reply:

> 22nd Aug. 1907
> 10 Auguststrasse, Bonn, Germany
> Thursday

Dear Mr. Richards,

Many thanks for your kind letter. I am very busy with the novel at present; I will send it to you in a week or so. Meanwhile, as to the stories, I can guarantee from 80–120 copies being sold within two months of publication. But I cannot cover any expenses. If you think you could do anything with them on those terms, write, and I will send you the longer improved version of the '*Last Generation*'.

If not, will you kindly keep the MS till I return to England: perhaps there will be more chance for the book if I publish it after the novel. Still, I wish I could get it off my hands.

The '*Last Generation*' is now 36 pages long, or thereabouts, more amusing and more detailed.

Please excuse a Postcard, as I have no envelopes at hand.

Yours truly,

Sgd. James Flecker.[568]

Two days after he wrote to Grant Richards, Flecker's poem 'The Piper' was published in the 24 August edition of *Country Life*. Two unpublished versions of this poem, one dated 5 May 1905, and the other dated September 1905, were first written in the *Book of Kara James*. The first verse in *Country Life* read:

> A lad went piping through the Earth,
> Gladly, madly, merrily,
> With a tune for death, and a tune for birth,
> And a tune for lovers' revelry.

The second verse began:

> He kissed the girls that sat alone
> With none to whisper, none to woo:

The next verse relates:

> And those that lay on beds of pain
> Went laughing through the gates of death.

Ending with the lines:

> I listened, but the street was still,
> And no one played for you and me!

His poems on the theme of death seemed to be favourites for magazine publication.

Flecker must have received and corrected the final proofs of the book of poems and returned them to Elkin Mathews. A letter from Mathews reached him just before he left for Florence with Beazley, as on his arrival he sent a postcard in reply:

> "Post-marked Florence
> 21st September, 1907
>
> Dear Mr. Matthews, [sic]
>
> Please publish my book as soon as possible, say on the 25th. I am sorry; I did not know that you were waiting for me to give a date. My address here, for two weeks is Pension Scandinavia, 14, Via Nazionale, Firenze.

Yours sincerely,

James Flecker" [569]

His impressions of Florence ('no Italian to be had' he had written to his parents from Bonn) were more agreeable than those of Bonn, although they too were tinged with disappointment: 'The melodious name of Florence calls up such delightful and extravagant memories that many wayfarers, [to those[570]] who have the love of books and pictures in their souls, have been disappointed with the austere appearance of the city, with her narrow yet straight and gloomy streets, her huge rectangular palaces, her vast and unsatisfying cathedral. [571]

But he was happier with the hill of Fiesole: 'But if on a summer afternoon a man should ascend, as our friends ascended, the hill of Fiesole, he would see from that famous eminence the City of Flowers, wonderfully set amongst her gardens and villas, and he would appreciate that tremendous dome which rises high above the plain of Arno, like some fabled antique emphalos of the world, and he might cry, perverting to himself that gentle ballad of old: 'Where will you bury me? In Saint Mary of the Flowers./Wherewith will you cover me? With violets and roses.' [572]

He embodied his feelings about these two weeks in Florence in his poem 'Looking Eastwards', which began: [573] 'The sacred bell of high Fiesole/Called the Etruscan ghosts to speech with me.' The fifth last line had the words: 'Wandering is sweet pain.'

These words sum up the travels in Italy with Beazley, happy as many of the days were when they were together, the happiness was marred by the pain of discovery, the tedium of studying, the anxiety of getting poems into print and the shortage of cash. Jack was left behind in Florence, he had to wait until friends, one of whom was Savery, later provided the fare home. Any extra cash that Flecker might have had to spare, was needed to treat his toothache.

The warm summer weather was prolonged well into October, but the emotional climate on his return to Dean Close was frosty. He cursed in a letter to Savery[574] that his father had heard Jack was with him on the Continent. The news of the publication (and the cost) of *The Bridge of Fire* would not melt the ice. His parents gave no outward show of pride in their son's first book of poems[575] and he had inwardly to sing his own praises until they surfaced in his prose piece *N'Jawk*:

'Slimber was a poet. He had published an exquisite volume of verse in the Doreskin Library of modern

Masterpieces. The volume, not fifty pages long, but fine in quality, was printed on one side of the page and was dedicated to a Lady.' [576]

The Bridge of Fire was not dedicated to a lady; he had dedicated the book to Jack Beazley. It was also sixty-four pages long, but it is easy to see that the name of his publisher Elkin Mathews, had been used with 'Elk' being changed to Doe or Doreskin. The word exquisite was a term he would use to describe his own book.

More evidence of the importance of his work was shown in an early draft of a poem he first called 'Dedication of a Story, To an Unknown Friend'. In this poem the poet sent his soul 'through time and space'. This idea is akin to those of Gautier, who wrote in an article in 1843: '... great geniuses also have a family, beyond time and space. If there is any consolation for death, it is the thought that when you are no more than a handful of dust, beings who suffer like you have suffered will pause in front of your works and feel their hearts swell and overflow, drawn towards you by some invisible force.'[577]

The letter to Savery in which he enclosed the draft of his poem was in reply to a letter that contained a draft of a dialogue, which Savery described as 'a somewhat indecent production of mine'. This was a meeting between Suckling[578] and Shelley in the underworld, in which Suckling was represented as being much shocked at some of Shelley's views on sexual morality. Flecker told him it was rather bad, something he had never said of anything Savery had sent him before. Flecker stated that Suckling was not a poet 'of very great significance'. He felt no comparison with Suckling, and he drew Savery's attention to his own poem, which he enclosed. Savery stated that it bore little resemblance to the final version of the poem 'To a Poet a Thousand Years Hence'. But there were resemblances to a poem of Baudelaire's entitled 'These lines I give thee so that if mankind...'

> These lines I give thee so that if mankind
> Recall me, happily in years to come. [579]

The poem enclosed with his letter to Frank Savery (probably November 1907) read:

> O dark and silent friend of mine,
> I who am dead a thousand years
> Salute thee, Prince of ancient line,
> Man with a heritage of tears.

Thou who art clad in robes unknown
And speakest strange this English tongue
Read out my words at night, alone,
Art thou a poet too, and young?

I hope that man whose friend am I
Is not less noble than before,
And dreads a little less to die,
And knows, perhaps, a little more.

Thou too hast converse, wine, and song
And statues and a a [sic] bright eyed Love
And foolish thoughts of right & wrong
And prayers to them that sit above.

Thus lived the nightingales of Greece
Who sung a thousand years ago
Man changes little: like a breeze
His fancies delicately blow

But this I tell you from the grave:
In golden fancy put no trust:
There are no ghosts or gods who save,
For I am utter, utter dust. [580]

Self-advertisement was necessary for a book of poems that had been published on commission. He sent copies of *The Bridge of Fire* to Professor Raleigh, John Davidson and Arthur Symons, [581] who all wrote him enthusiastic letters, Symons said he was haunted by the Dolly poem. Raleigh liked 'Rioupéroux', and 'Mary Magdalen' and 'The Ballad of The Student in the South', 'in which he caused me to alter one line'.[582] Raleigh, whose book on Shakespeare (published in April 1907) had received an unfavourable review in *The Academy*, may have felt the need to give support to a much younger writer, whose book was coming out in the same year, and might meet a similar fate. John Davidson 'was wildly enthusiastic about nothing in particular: most notable book by young man he had ever seen etc.' he wrote to Savery. Flecker wished 'these beggars' would print their opinions in *The Times* or the *Daily Mail*. 'Four lines in *The Times* by a man who has read three or four of the poems is not enough for me,' he wrote to Savery.[583]

The 'four lines in *The Times*' referred to were in the 20 September edition of *The Times Literary Supplement* and read: 'Mr. Flecker writes neat and polished little poems somewhat pagan in feeling, and regrets the time he spent at Oxford. Indeed in a Whitmanesque descriptive piece called Oxford Canal he clearly prefers the canal to the "country town with its red motors and lumbering trams and self-sufficient people".'

His grievance about the reviewer having read three or four of the poems is understandable, but to give the reviewer his due, he was obviously rather short of space. The impression is that he had just glanced through Flecker's thirty-four poems, and decided that they were 'rather pagan in feeling', without taking the trouble to illustrate this point. A number of the poems dealt directly with religion, and could not be described as pagan in feeling, not least the poem, which gave the book its title. The lines, which refer to:

Belus and Ra and that most jealous Lord
Who rolled the hosts of Pharaoh in the sea,
Giants and Trolls, in every hand a sword,
Gnomes and dwarfs and the Spectral Company,

may have been misleading, the poem 'The Bridge of Fire' has to be read many times before it can be appreciated and understood. Flecker subsequently made many alterations to it.

The reference to 'Oxford Canal' as a Whitmanesque descriptive piece gave the impression that this was the one poem that owed its inspiration to the work of another poet, but failed to mention that the book contained poems that could be described as 'Swinburnesque' or even 'Shelleyesque'. 'The Bridge of Fire' bore the influence of Swinburne, Leconte de Lisle, Oscar Wilde and Francis Thompson.[584] The reference to Flecker clearly preferring the canal to the county town, may have been influenced by the dedication to Jack Beazley which contained the lines:

With my friend in Oxford Town:

Since I so regret a time
So unprofitably spent.

The anger he felt about this review could have been because the reviewer failed to discover the poet's individual voice, which was revealing itself, despite the influence of other poets. The next review was in *The Academy*. Douglas Goldring's review of 19 October 1907, began by saying:

'The artistic revival which took place in the latter part of the 19th century, and cast *The Yellow Book* and *The Savoy* before a yapping and inappreciative England, has had an influence on the work of many younger poets which can still be easily traced. It has caused them, amongst other things, to see in France the Holy Land of their Art, and to accept Baudelaire and Paul Verlaine as impeccable masters. Thus far its influence has certainly been a good one, but it is a pity that out of all the poets of France it has brought two into special prominence whose poetry, whilst being extraordinarily fascinating, is also very dangerous to imitate. Much of the most interesting verse which has appeared of late years (saving that which hails from Ireland) has suffered considerably from having derived from one or other of the writers mentioned. Our poets, in too many cases, have loved to pose as Pierrot babbling to the moon, smiling cynically to conceal a broken heart and unutterable desires; and Mr. James Flecker, whose verse is before us, is no exception. He acknowledges Baudelaire as his master, and pour *epater le bourgeois* (rather a commonplace thing to attempt nowadays) he has chosen to make a translation of 'Les Litanies de Satan' thus paving the way for the poem at the end of the book, in which he describes his attitude towards life. Says he:

'Know me the slave of fear and death and shame,
A sad Comedian, a most tragic Fool ...'

and describes himself, with evident gusto, as the 'lean and swarthy poet of despair.' This factitious despair is a little absurd, and Mr. Flecker does not imitate his master with much success. Here and there, however, we can discover in his work, sufficient traces of a personal note to make us regret that they are so few. The feeble dedicatory poem at the beginning of this book, and the following self-revealing lines:

[He quoted from 'I Rose from Dreamless Hours' without naming the poem]

180

indicate a whole set of thoughts and emotions which might have been developed, and could not fail to have been more interesting than exercises, however clever, in Gallic modes.

When Mr. Flecker forgets to pose, and is content to be sincere, he is sometimes curiously effective, as in the following lines:

[He quoted all of the poem 'We That Were Friends', without giving the title: and finished by saying:]

From the point of view of sheer melody, the best thing in the book is the poem 'Pervigilium'. This is a remarkable performance as an exercise in metre, though the theme is, perhaps as little hackneyed. On the whole, Mr. Flecker's book has been something of a disappointment to us. He has a good ear, his verses are remarkably finished and he is extremely accomplished; but he seems to have some defect of temperament which wars against his success, and to lack entirely that magic touch which the Gods often give (in their perversity) to quite dull and stupid people. It is a pity, as he is very clever."

Flecker saw the poor public reception of his book of poems as a challenge and not a setback and he began revising the poems in *The Bridge of Fire* and writing new ones. He used for this purpose, a presentation copy of *The Bridge of Fire*, bound in terra-cotta buckram with 100 blank pages. He filled these pages with a list entitled 'Further Poems: 1907'. It included poems that had already been published in periodicals, such as *The Piper* and which had appeared in the *Country Life* (which he dated September 1907, although it appeared in the 24 August edition). This indicated that even poems accepted by periodicals needed revising, or that they were possibly to be included in his new anthology, which he was already planning.

It would have been advisable to have read what had already been stated under the heading 'More Verse' on 6 July 1907 by *The Academy* when reviewing six books of poetry, four published by Elkin Mathews:

'There are two ways of dealing with minor poets. One is praise them for writing any verse "in these materialistic days" as people are pleased to call this dark and fiery age:

to deal gently with their infirmities, and to remember that they have taken a lot of trouble and have had to pay some twenty pounds or so for the privilege of seeing themselves in print. The principle is a generous one, and I think one may say it is the one usually followed in *The Times* literary supplement.'

The review ended:

'Reading new poetry is like seeking for buried treasure – it is quite exciting, but there is a vast amount of earth to be sifted. With Mr. Swinburne still alive one hardly realises that writers such as Mr. Kipling, Mr. A.E. Housman, Mr. John Davidson, even Mr. Yeats, are not quite of the newest generation. We are suffering now from a pause: there is a young generation of poets preparing to startle the world.

Poets at present not old enough to pay a publisher; but in a year or two we shall hear of them. In the meanwhile we must wait patiently, buy patiently, and condemn patiently.'

Flecker was in the south of France when this piece was printed, and amidst riots and facing possible death he may not have had the opportunity to read this edition of *The Academy*.

The Academy review made him angry and he composed a reply to send to the editor. His anger and hurt were understandable; he could have hoped for something better from a publication of the standing of *The Academy*, to which he had sent contributions, and with whom he had been in contact.[585] *The Academy* described itself as 'A Weekly Review of Literature, Science and Art', and it has been described by other as:

'Aloof, superior stranger, like a Kingfisher among a colony of sparrows ... Group of contributors including GBS, Arthur Machen[586] and James Elroy Flecker.'[587]

Flecker had sent *The Academy* his poem 'The Young Poet', which the magazine had kept so long that, by the time it was published in the 2 November edition, it had already been published in *The Bridge of Fire*. Flecker referred to its publication, using its new title 'Dirge' in a letter to Savery, in early November.

Many suggestions have been made as to the identity of the young poet, who inspired Flecker to write the poem and why *The Academy* chose to publish it at that particular time.[588] The poem could have been chosen because of the seasonal lines which read in *The Academy* version:

> At falling of the leaf;
> It is when pale October,
> Relentless tree-disrober,
> Invade their[589] silent homes.

Subsequently this line altered to: 'Conceals the smokeless homes'.

So many poets died young in that era, that a case could be made out for many other poets.[590]

'The Young Poet' was not his only contribution to *The Academy* of 2 November 1907. He had an unsigned review of twelve books of poetry by the following authors:

More recent Poetry

Ballad of Victory and other Poems by Dollie Radford, (Alston Rivers) 1s.
Stray Sonnets by Lilian Street (Elkin Mathews Vigo, Cabinet Series) 1s.
Witcheries and other Verses by Margaret Maclean Bogle (Paisley: Alex Gardner) 1s.
The Dead God and other Poems by James Blackhall, (Greening) 2s.6d.
Istar and Tammuz, and other Poems by John Lewis Brown (Kegan Paul) 1s.6d.
A Vision of Armageddon and other Poems by Walter Terence Stace (Hodges, Figgis & Co.) 1s.6d.
The O'Donoghue and other Poems by Mr. D'Arcy, (Hodges, Figgis & Co.) 3s.6d.
Wayside Verses by Alec Joy (Elliott Stock) 1s.
Songs in Exile by Maurice Brown (Samurai Press)
Poems by Two Friends (J.M. Dent & Co.)
Voces Amoris by John B. Rankin (John Long) 3s.6d.
Poems by George A. Nicholson (C.W. Deacon) 2s.6d.

He began the review by stating: 'Ladies, Kelts, Religionists, amiable Wordsworthians, insipid Lovers, and bold Realists figure in this motley summer crowd, with pretty little books of pretty little poems. The ladies, as a rule, though imitative, write with much more delicacy and precision than the sterner poetasters, who, carried away by the violence of their ideas or passions, revel in a welter of dashes and mixed metaphors.'

It is interesting to note the emphasis he placed on the craftsmanship of writing poetry rather than whether the verse might be imitative. He began by criticising the poetry of Dollie Radford (1852–1920), wife of Ernest Radford (1858–1919), who with Maurice Browne (1881–1955) remain better known than the others on the list.

He compared Dollie Radford's verse to Bridges' poetry; he thought she had the same quiet charm and effective workmanship, 'the same power of making everything dull'. He liked the delicate and refined workmanship of Lilian Street, but felt that her idea of working her poems round a few thoughts from sermons was 'unpromising'. He liked a sonnet on the burning of love letters, and another one, which he quoted on hands:

> The eye and mouth may well deceivers be,
> And look and smile more than the heart doth hold.

but:

> None can change the likeness of the hands.

'It is,' wrote Flecker, 'a new, simple and rather beautiful idea.'

He expressed the notion that although Miss Bogle belonged to the 'new Celtic school of poetry, one could belong to no better school'. But he thought that Miss Bogle could not reach 'that exquisite and subtle simplicity which is rendering Mr. Yeats's work immortal'. He liked a poem she had written called 'The Watcher' (from the lines he quoted it had a foretaste of Walter de la Mare's 'The Listeners'). He felt Miss Bogle's verses were promising and vigorous but that they lacked cohesion. The same applied to the poems of James Blackhall and he was reminded 'not infrequently of Mr. John Davidson's most characteristic works'. He admired a ballad, which was about men who went to find Christ's grave, and he quoted some of this poem. He felt that this book of poems was best by far of the twelve he was reviewing.

He felt that Mr. Brown had translated the legend of Istar and Tammuz from the Chaldaic original into fairly elegant English verse. Again he warned on the use of words such as 'aeons', 'orbs' and 'galaxies'. The greatest prose poems he said are always concrete and clear in their images. Flecker writes that Mr. D'Arcy poems are also undistinguished, but he quotes one line, which he describes as 'rather haunting'.

She, like fair Nature, sleeps in balmy night.

Wayside Verse he thought contained a 'few pleasant poems' and he quoted a poem in full, in which the poet stated: 'For future poets, then, I care no jot,'.

Flecker's own poem, which he eventually named 'To a Poet a Thousand Years Hence', published in *The Nation* 11 January, took the opposite view of this poem.

He thought Maurice Brown's poems to be 'sumptuous in the style of Keats'. *The Poems by Two Friends* he described as 'a pale imitation of Mr. Watson's pallidities'.

Mr. Rankin's book is dismissed in one sentence as 'an unhappy document of love, sentimental, childish and uninspiring'.

From the last book of poems he quoted from a poem with the title 'The Ballad of the Mad Atheist'; he was not greatly impressed by the verses.

Under the heading 'Translating Molière', there was a review of *The Plays of* Molière in French. With an

English Translation and notes by A.R. Waller, which followed immediately after Flecker's poetry book reviews, and reference was made to Molière's play *Don Juan*. *The Academy* decided to publish Flecker's reply to the review of *The Bridge of Fire*, and this may have had an influence on their decision to publish 'The Young Poet' and his reviews. He was quite confident in his relationship with *The Academy*. In a letter[591] on Dean Close Memorial School notepaper to Alice Head dated October, Flecker wrote:

> Dean Close Memorial School
> Cheltenham
> October, '07

Dear Miss Head,

> Send further batch. I have done with these! Here is the last article.
>
> Please remember you have an article of mind on Carducci and Heine for the 'Library Table'[592] which you have not yet used, unless you put it in without sending a proof.
>
> This dreadful poem, saying how the sun 'upclomb'[593] is not mine and I shudder to think that you thought it was. Do forgive my rudeness to it: but I am piqued because Lord Alfred returned two of mine.

Yours sincerely,

James Flecker

This letter revealed the haphazard arrangements for dealing with contributions and contributors at *Country Life*, were just the same at *The Academy*. However, another letter to Alice Head from Flecker indicated that he was finding out about the system and he continued to address her, in a style that was both arrogant and diffident.

> Dean Close Memorial School
> November 1907

Dear Miss Head,

> Peccavi. Mr. Goldring, of *Country Life* is possibly responsible: he implied that you opened everything exercising a preliminary recension, weeding out the poems in the early throstle and the letters threatening suicide in event of non-publication. I therefore addressed you on the inside, as I have exchanged quite fifty words with you and only five with Lord Alfred Douglas.
>
> In future, then, I will send anything special to Lord Alfred Douglas, such as articles on Pentheus, and the reviews of books to you. Is that right?
>
> I fear the new volume of Mr. Stephen Phillips[594] work has been assigned by now. I should have liked it, as I have particular theories on the said writer.
>
> Please forgive my anomalous conduct, and tell me if I have, to use a plebeian phrase, hit the nail on the head. For instance is it right to ask you for Mr. Stephen?

Yours sincerely,

James Flecker.

The reference to Goldring in the letter to Alice Head is interesting; Flecker wrote to Savery: [595] 'Next week will contain a long letter by me defending myself from the attacks of their own critic of which

I enclose a copy, please return.' This was further proof that he did not know the critic's identity.

The letter was published on 9 November 1907, under the heading 'A Defence, even of Baudelaire'.[596] It was, therefore, as Goldring had stated, 'he contented himself with sending a rejoinder to *The Academy*, which was published a week after my notice – a rejoinder which showed great skill and the most exemplary good manners.' [597]

To the Editor of THE ACADEMY

Sir, – A poet has to apologise humbly, even in these self-advertising days, if he protests, however mildly, against the critic's scorn. If I were to write to the *Soapmakers' Weekly Journal* affirming that Mr. Pears' beautiful brown soap was made in France, Mr. Pears would make a protest, and I, not he, would apologise. My critic in THE ACADEMY has directly accused me of borrowing my poetical wares for "The Bridge of Fire" from France, from Baudelaire, and from Verlaine; and I should like (without the slightest attempt to value my wares) to declare that they are English made and not noxious in the sense implied, and to attempt to prove the same. And especially I should like to deprecate all reference to "The Yellow Book".

Art is good or bad; not healthy or unhealthy, French or non-French, "Yellow Book" or non-"Yellow Book". Will that unhappy periodical never be allowed to rest quietly in its grave? It contained some good early work by Mr. Yeats and others, some ephemeral witticisms by Mr. Beerbohm. Its only claim to immortality is founded on the drawings of Aubrey Beardsley; and they can illustrate my point. These drawings thought so sinful and alarming, are just amusing or severe satires that remind us of Leonardo da Vinci's admirable grotesques. But when Aubrey Beardsley drew attenuated people, it was considered a ghastly sign of mental disease. And when he drew dragons and other curious delights, and Japanese patterns, and ridiculous divinities:

Square heads that leer and lust, and lizard
shapes that crawl –

if I may quote from my book, everyone accused him of being decadent, or French, or cynical, or *fin de siècle*, while to me a love of pleasantly malformed beasts seems most delicately child-like and humorous. In such a fantastic mood it pleased me to call myself a "sad comedian and most tragic fool." "The despair of Mr. Flecker is rather absurd." Well, better a tragic fool than a dull fool. But can no one recognise any charm in a half-serious rhetoric? Rhetoric is true to life; we use it in moments of excitement, despondency, or passion, if we say anything at all; we cannot use such language as

Othello's for our miseries. Trammel rhetoric in verse, and the exaggeration, I thought, would appeal as at once sincere and humorous. Of such outrageous and great humour in prose "*Sartor Resartus*" is the example. I wanted humbly to say in verse. In this mood I called Oxford a "county town" and sighed for "the empty canal at noon"; in this mood I wrote a luxurious sonnet introducing such joyous words as "portcullis", "cinnabar", "catacombs" and "tourniquet"; in this mood I wrote of

The jealous Lord
Who rolled the hosts of Pharaoh in the sea,
and imagined Bacchus leading the dance on Hampstead
   Heath:
The 'busmen pranced, the maidens danced,
The men in bowlers gambolled.
And in this mood did I translate Baudelaire's rollicking
   ode to Satan:
Thou stretchest forth a saving hand to keep
Such men as roam upon the roofs in sleep.

Because I did this, and wrote a poem in a Baudelarian mood while I was translating it, I am said to have acknowledged Baudelaire as my master, and to have chosen to translate the poem "pour épater le bourgeois."

Now, with regard to the last charge, I did not think that any *bourgeois* read new books of poems, and it never occurred to me that among the few dozen readers I can expect to find anyone would be even startled to see an ode to Satan. I judged by my friends, but I suppose they must have been very wicked men, for they did not mind at all. And I did not feel that Mr. Shaw was episcopally denounced for making the D—, as I had perhaps better call him, utter words of wisdom in "Man and Superman".

But, to speak seriously, the accusation of having Baudelaire as master, the coupling of his name with that of Verlaine, and the sinister hints of insincerity, immorality, and cynicism, whispered by this accusation, seem to me first of all to imply a false notion of Baudelaire. Baudelaire was *not* a monstrous decadent, nor did he babble of Pierrots nor does his poetry resemble Verlaine's in the remotest degree. An essentially classical poet, a master of harmony and form, he was, unlike Verlaine, invariably careful to make his images correspond to his sense. His affinities are with Racine, Milton, and above all with Dante. Though his medieval sense of the taint of sin and his extravagant Christianity may have sometimes led him to be unfortunate in his choice of subject, yet in the choice of language he is infallible, and his poems are the most virile poetic productions of the nineteenth century in France. Call the tearful dirges of Lamartine, the slovenly and bombastic tirades of Hugo, the querulous and fugitive sentiment of Verlaine dangerous to imitate if you will. Baudelaire is beyond imitation, and, as Mr. Gosse has somewhere remarked, only one man, the unhappy Maurice Rollinat, has ever tried. And I no more attempt to imitate Baudelaire because I have translated the "Litany" than Goethe because I have translated "Mignon". If apart from love of jovial grotesques I have any philosophy, I have let my wandering student tell it to his lady beneath the moon:

[He quotes two verses of 'The Ballad of the Student in the South'.]

Perhaps some reader, if any there be, will see why this mention of "Yellow Book" sets me in arms for every horror, so that I could almost quote the epilogue to Asolando.

James Flecker

Goldring had shown great skill because it was obvious that Flecker did not know that his young friend had written the review. Goldring outlines how he came to write the review of *The Bridge of Fire*:

'I had arranged with the editor[598] to review it in *The Academy*. When I received my copy I found that, alas! it did not come up to my exaggerated expectations, and in my disappointment I proceeded to administer a perfectly sincere if rather jejune "slating". My notice, when it came out, caused surprise and wrath among our little circle. All my friends were indeed, extremely angry with me – except Flecker. I think Flecker must have been amused and interested to hear one note of honest criticism, however amateurish, amid a chorus of rather fatuous praise.' [599]

The reference to Goldring 'arranging' with the editor to review *The Bridge of Fire*, is ambiguous. Did he mean he arranged with the editor of *Country Life*, the magazine he worked for, to review it for *The Academy*? Or did he 'arrange' with Lord Alfred Douglas, to review it? This last conjures up a rather strange spectacle, as Goldring in the autumn of 1907, was not yet twenty-one and was not even sub-editor on *Country Life*. Goldring related that the one-time joint editor of both *Country Life* and *The Academy* 'was intriguing to get him the editorship of *The Academy*'. This 'intriguing' seems to be rather blurred in Goldring's memory if it took place, as he said, before he had been with the paper a year because Lord Alfred Douglas, previously assistant editor of *The Academy*, was appointed editor in May 1907. It is possible that Goldring meant sub-editorship of *The Academy*, as at twenty he had not yet been promoted to sub-editor, and had only been on *Country Life* for a matter of weeks in a very lowly capacity. *The Academy* was coming to the end of its long life (it was founded in 1869) and although Goldring was not aware of this fact, it was more than likely that Anderson Graham would realise that Goldring needed to get out while the going was good, and indeed got him the sub-editorship, later on, of *The English Review*, 'a position much more useful to me at that stage in my development!'. A senior contributor who was in no doubt about *The Academy*'s flagging fortunes was Arthur Machen (1863–1947), the chief contributor on religious matters. Although not all his pieces were on that particular subject, he was the authority on faith and morals, on the paper.[600] Machen never converted to Catholicism, although at one time he might have been expected to take this step. But his articles in The *Academy* 'were what first set Douglas on the way to Catholicism'.[601]

Goldring said of his childhood: 'At Brighton which in the 'nineties swarmed with ritualistic churches, I was induced, with my two elder brothers, to become an acolyte. I had to serve Mass in a red cassock and lace-trimmed cotta and, occasionally, I officiated as "Boat-boy" carrying incense for the thurifier and bowing at the appropriate moments to the altar and congregation.'[602]

These childhood influences, coupled with the fact that *The Bridge of Fire* had already been described as being 'somewhat pagan in feeling' by *The Times Literary Supplement*, could have influenced Goldring and the editor. Machen was soon to complain, on receiving his last cheque from *The Academy* that they had reduced his rate by 10s. per thousand words. Goldring's payment for his review in *The Academy* would have received the same treatment. He was in no position to complain or to resign his job.

Flecker's contention that 'the beggar in The *ACAD.* is really right; I do like Pierrot and his moon' was true because Goldring had already heard Flecker talk about his work in general and Pierrot and his moon could have been part of that conversation. The reference to the critic as 'the beggar' was further proof that Flecker did not know the critic's identity. In the same letter[603] he referred to 'their own critic'; if he had known the critic was Goldring, why not say so?

For Goldring to describe the dedicatory poem as 'feeble'[604] when he knew both Flecker and Beazley, to whom the dedication was made, is to mislead the reader. Did he mean that the poem should have been stronger in feeling? He knew Flecker could not do so, without revealing details of the relationship more clearly. Flecker himself wrote of the dedication: 'The dedication I knew appears superficially weak, But I think it is saved by its feeling and simplicity – and may pass for what it is – a dedication.' [605]

To say he thought 'Flecker must have been amused and interested to hear one note of honest criticism, however amateurish, amid a chorus of rather fatuous praise'[606] is strange. He does not say who would have voiced this type of praise; Savery or Beazley were not in the habit of voicing fatuous praise, as Flecker had written: 'My dearest Franko, you adopt perilous paths of criticism in which no one can tread better than yourself.' [607] When writing of both Savery and Beazley, he stated: 'Jack is a meticulous critic; you want the spirit of the thing.'[608]

Goldring admitted that he was determined not to be impressed by the Flecker legend, and he himself was 'rather contemptuous of Oxford wit and Oxford reputations'. Goldring had not obtained a university degree; so his insecurity, coupled with jealousy (he wrote about the toxins of jealousy in his autobiography and of his jealousy of Ezra Pound), had influenced his attitude towards Flecker's work.

His desire to get on in the magazine world led him to take on a reviewing job in which he could not distance himself sufficiently from Flecker, or have the courage to admit to Flecker what he had undertaken.

Goldring, in his review, described Flecker's reference to 'the lean and swarthy poet of despair' as 'this factitious despair is a little absurd'. Flecker would eventually challenge this statement[609] but the 'lean and swarthy' he could not dispute.

The review of *The Bridge of Fire* in *The Granta* (which it appears Flecker did not see), had similarities to Goldring's review, in that it was written by someone who must have known him personally. *The Granta* review, if not written by Charles Raven who knew him at Uppingham, was published under Raven's editorship. It was a much more perceptive review which stated:

October 12th, 1907 *The Granta* p.13

THE BRIDGE OF FIRE by James Flecker (Elkin Mathew 1907)

> The makings of a poet, or some of them, are in the author of these verses. But he has still to perfect the instrument whereby he expresses poetic thoughts. The lines "To Francis Thompson" and "The Ballad of Hampstead Heath" are, to our thinking, the most real expressions of the author's self in the book."

The less-than-satisfactory, and not very numerous, reviews did not deter Flecker from writing for publication, as was seen in the mention of 'such articles on Pentheus' in his letter to Alice Head.

He told Savery[610] that he was 'writing furiously in a state of such divine inspiration as I have not known for many a long day'. Savery was told that he was writing so fast as to be almost illegible and had written ten pages in an hour and three quarters. He had written 'a wondrous essay on Pentheus making him the type of all Philistinism'." The essay was inspired by his careful reading of 'Bacchae', which had 'thrilled me more than anything since I had first opened Swinburne....'.

'Divine inspiration' could be a force brought into being by his desire to get the essay into print so that he could provide himself with ready cash. 'Divine inspiration' combined with the desire to prove that he was a writer to be reckoned with, and that he was ready to emerge alongside those poets who were at getting their work commercially produced to greater acclaim and publicity. The 'divine inspiration' could be seen as due to the onset of tuberculosis, which it is said, does result in bouts of inspiration of this kind. The separation from Jack in Italy may not have been entirely due to lack of money for the fare.

The essay on Pentheus was about the conflict between the King of Thebes, Pentheus and the god Dionysus the Terrible, and has touches of satire. Pentheus 'was a man who hated all nonsense, and was not given to dancing or to drink. A religious man, no doubt, he was one of those who believe in the moral and social benefits that religion confers, and was not over-interested in miracles and myths. It is hard to persuade a man of sense that you are an angel.' The essay ended with the dialogue between Dionysus and Pentheus, who has survived down the ages, and who talks about the Civil Service pension (as no doubt Flecker himself had heard from his parents).

Dionysus says to Pentheus:

Thou does not see; thou does not know
What thou livest, nor who thou art.

Pentheus replies:

I am Pentheus, the son of Agave and Echion,
I am Hobson the son of Mr. and Mrs. Hobson! [611]

Dionysus tells Pentheus that he is 'feeding on the fat of the land, and oppressing the people so long as the air does not tremble to the faint echo of a madman's song.' Pentheus tells him he is a rational being with a cultivated imagination, a respectable member of society, 'my religion is the religion of all good men.' Dionysus says the poor man is right, he is always right. He finishes the essay by saying: [612] 'His humdrum days may be pleasant or painful; he has never tasted of our purple grapes of heavy sorrow, our golden grapes of super-human joy. Alas, poor Pentheus!'

The essay contained a number of themes, including state patronage of the arts and state education, dealt with in a satirical fashion. It is easy to see this essay as an echo of the conflict between Flecker and his father, when he had written: 'You would like a convenient and tidy appendage, conveniently evangelical, in a Government position, conveniently respectable, for a son.' [613]

The emotional aspects have to be considered alongside the 'enormous bills' and the fact that he reported to Savery that relations with his parents seemed to be going smoothly. Did they know the size of the bills? Pentheus was written quickly because he needed to make money, to cash in on the publication of his book, to help counteract the lack of publicity it had received and because *The Academy* was printing his reply to the critics.

In the lines of the next letter to *The Academy*, there is the feeling that the unkind review of *The Bridge of Fire* still rankled:

> ? November, 1907
> Dean Close,
> Cheltenham.

Dear Miss Head,

Lord Alfred Douglas has by now an essay called *Pentheus*[614] by me and a short poem. I hear no news of them. Would you as a great favour find out for me on the quiet, if I may put it, whether Lord Alfred Douglas intends to use either of them, and whether he is pleased at receiving verse. It is prose from my unskilled pen. I only want to know because I do hate troubling anybody, even editors with things they don't want.

Have the muses forsaken Poesy? What has happened to my old friends the minor bards.

Yours sincerely,

James Flecker

Poor Stephen Phillips. He is an inferior poet.
It would be such a pleasure to send with a notice
of his new book between Miss Lilac Smith and Miss
Dorothea Brown in the next batch of 'More Verse'"

Flecker put his ideas on the work of Stephen Phillips into an article, which he described to Savery as 'in the spirit of mod. poetry as exemplified in the *Shropshire Lad*'[615] He hoped that the article would be published in *The Albany*.[616] He wrote about Phillips in his article which he called:

THE NEW POETRY AND MR. HOUSMAN'S "SHROPSHIRE LAD"

'The English living imitators of Victorian style also claim a moment's notice. Of these Mr. Stephen Phillips is the most important. The grave sonority of 'Christ in Hades', the pleasant metrical variation of 'Marpessa' produced a certain impression. That 'Marpessa' is a *tour de force* is obvious upon close analysis: that Mr. Stephen Phillips is a close follower and rather slavish imitator of Tennyson can be proved.' [617]

The article spent a lot of space on the subject of metre, structure and verbal sounds, which he said 'are almost too sacred for explanation.. Stephen Phillips, who had the benefit of having his work published by Elkin Mathews and also by Lane, needed no self-advertising as Lane advertised Phillips' works in *The Academy*. There was an element of discontent in Flecker's criticism; that someone he considered an inferior poet should at the same time enjoy public acclaim and fortune.

In choosing A.E. Housman's *A Shropshire Lad* for the article, he was not choosing a poet whose work was, unlike Baudelaire's or Davidson's, unpopular. But he was still choosing a writer whose earlier emotional life had much in common with his own. 'A Shropshire Lad', a poem about a rejected lover, may have been read or reread by Flecker because he had fellow feelings with Housman. Housman, too, had fallen love at Oxford, in his case with a man called Moses Jackson, who was handsome and gifted. This relationship had much in common with the Flecker/Beazley relationship, in that the passion was not of equal intensity. However, it was of great importance in Housman's life, as was the friendship with Beazley in Flecker's life. Jackson, like Beazley, left behind little information about his personal life, which was hidden from view, although his scholarship was not. Housman took no degree at Oxford. He entered the Civil Service, mainly because Jackson had a job there.

His correspondence about his literary work with Alice Head was not the only correspondence he was undertaking at this time, as he wrote to Grant Richards in November: [618]

Dean Close School,
Cheltenham

Dear Mr. Richards,

It suddenly struck me that I might well send you the first part of my novel. The second part, which will be perhaps a little shorter than the first, will be ready in a month – that is, if you encourage me with it, for I have many other things to do, and am a very lazy writer.

I have not typed or corrected the first half; but it is quite legible enough, I imagine, for a first reading.

I will not say anything about the book, but I hope you will be able to let me have a favourable judgment, and that soon, for it is horribly dispiriting to write work that one knows to be literature, without the certainty of finding a publisher. But if any work I have written ~~deserves~~ is likely to be <u>popular</u> it is this novel.

Yours very truly,

James Flecker

I enclose a sketch of the 2nd half for the reader's benefit.

Grant Richards replied on 15 November[619] that the manuscript had arrived just as he was leaving on a business trip to the United States. He proposed to take the manuscript with him, and if it seemed promising he hoped to be successful in placing it with a publisher 'on the other side'. He was due back in England on 22 December.

Flecker answered Richards' letter in November: [620]

Tuesday

Dear Sir,

Many thanks for your letter. Would you be so very kind as to return me my bundle of stories, I see a faint chance of getting one or two of them printed.

Please excuse this scrap of paper.

Yours very truly,

James Flecker

Dean Close School,
Cheltenham.

The 'bundle of stories' must have been returned, as he wrote again:
[621]

Many thanks for sending me the extra ms. which was mine. I have an idea, which may quite well be mistaken that you have another Ms. of mine included in the same batch – a little play, called "*The Dead People*". Would you be so very kind as to look and see.

Also, would you tell me roughly when Mr. Richards will be back from America, or whether he has yet returned, as I am expecting to hear from him.

Yrs.

James Flecker.

His play was not returned, Richards' secretary wrote back on 2 January 1908:

James Flecker, Esq.,

Dear Sir,

I have made enquiries and I cannot find that we have the manuscript of your little play, "*The Dead People*".[622]

If by chance it should turn up I will immediately send it to you, but I do not think we ever had it.

Mr. Richards has now returned from America and will be writing to you shortly.

Faithfully yours,
Secretary [623]

A letter,[624] with no date, which Savery dated in the last days of 1907, summed up his feelings about life:

DCMS i.e. Dean Close School
Friday

Dear Franco,

a. What in H... are you doing?
b. Am still prisoned here, and sulky.
c. Read me on "Fiona Macleod" in to-day's
Academy [625] and tell me what you thought on it.
d. I think the *Witch of Edmonton* is a very fine play,
though rather wildly constructed. What say you?
The Virgin Martyr appeals to me less: pretty in places.
Have just finished a splendid Spanish novel; wish you
could read it. You ought to read a translation
(said to be bad) of one of Emilia Pardo Bazan's books,
published by Lane, and tell me what you think of it.
I haven't read it. [626]
e. Novel very near close and no news from Grant
Richards. Joyous New Year to you.
Xt. I am very weary of life. "

(There is no signature)

A letter to Alice Head dated 'late December' reads:

Dean Close Memorial School

"Dear Miss Head,

Here is the article revised. I do not think another proof will be necessary.

Please tell the Editor that 'From the Hills of Dream'[627] is not a reprint but a complete collection of Sharp's poems. About one fourth of them, which are starred in the Contents list were in the old volume: the rest are either new or have only been published in America.

It is the only title and a few poems that have been preserved from the older book.

Yours sincerely,

James Flecker " [628]

30 November had seen the publication of the book *Father and Son; a Study of Two Temperaments*, Heinemann published it anonymously. The reviewer in *The Academy* praised it very highly and ended by stating: 'The secret has not been kept for long, and we understand that Mr. Edmund Gosse does not deny that he is the writer of the book. It is a great book. But for our part we scarcely like this close atomisation by a son of a father.'

In *The Academy* of 21 December a letter was printed under the heading:

THE CURSE OF EVANGELICISM

To the Editor of The Academy

Sir,

I fear that your brilliant contributor, Mr. Arthur Machen, and the author of "Father and Son" – a book which your sympathetic review should much help to circulate among clever young persons in country towns – neither of them realises that hundreds of lads and girls of fine instincts are still being warped for life in our country cities and boroughs by an evangelicism which puts Sunday smoking on a level with highway robbery, and teaches that the world is ruled by a morose, capricious and spiteful Deity.

Let me assure such young persons through the medium of your columns, which they may contrive to see more or less surreptitiously, that their case deserves and has the sympathy of all right-feeling members of both the Roman and the Anglican Churches. Lads and girls who have such great trial to bear should remember that "absence of body is better than presence of mind" in many cases, and should concentrate their energies upon attempts to get altogether out of what is really a slightly insane social element.

The wickedness of evangelicism in our provincial towns lies chiefly in the fact that it is promoted by plausible knaves now, not by sincere fools, as it was when Spurgeons and Birrells came into being. If you could suddenly enter the study of an evangelical clergyman on a Sunday night, you would find him enjoying a large cigar and a volume of Punch, while unhappy lads and girls in his congregation are made to pore upon Old Testament prophecies or booklets about hysterical "conversion".

A CHURCH WORKER

This letter echoed Flecker's views on evangelicism, and the relationship between father and son. Dr. Flecker featured in the following week's edition of *The Academy*, 28 December, when he launched a friendly attack at the Headmaster's Conference, against the headmaster of a Cambridge School on the subject of conversational Latin, which he proposed should not aim in the teaching, alongside Greek, to enable boys to speak those languages.

The Nation published his 'A Christmas Carol' in the December 1907 issue.[629] The carol begins with the lines:

Three Kings have come to Bethlehem
With a trailing star in front of them.

Mary
What would you in this little place.
You three bright Kings?

Kings
Mother, we tracked the trailing star
Which brought us here from lands afar,
And we would look upon his dear face
Round whom the Seraphs fold their wings.

Mary
But who are you, bright Kings?

Then the three Kings each tell her who they are and there is a verse from Caspar, Balthazar and Melchior. Then there is the Chorus of Angels, and the poem ends with the lines: '"Who art thou, little King of Kings?"/His wondering mother sings.'

His Poem 'To the World and a Poet a Thousand Years Hence', an early version of which he had sent to Savery in November 1907, was published in *The Nation* on 11 January, 1908.[630] It is a poem with a note of optimism and hope for the future, despite the fact that his book of poetry had not received wide acclaim.

The Academy's review of fiction in the 18 January 1908 edition, began with a review of '*The Heart's Banishment*' by Ella Macmahon, in which the reviewer wrote: 'Mrs. Macmahon has succeeded in reproducing to an astonishing degree that subtle, indefinable spirit or note which is the hall-mark of Oxford men.'

The last review was '*The Marble Sphinx*' by St. John Lucas published by Elkin Mathews price 1s.6d. which began:

'When the Greek slave Alexis was thrown out into
the high road, bleeding from the whips of his
master's gigantic Nubians, he lay so still that
all the wild things of the woodland came and
looked at him and went away; he lay like a
broken flower until the dryad saw and loved him
with her magic herbs.'

The review goes on to describe the dryad and the slave living together in the forest until the dryad is told that she must choose between her woodland nature and her human lover. She chose her human lover and they passed out of the forest and 'among the eternal roses of the Marble Sphinx'. They were welcomed to the great feast, which Death is preparing in honour of his triumph of the gods of old.

The review ends: 'There is no heavy insistence on one interpretation, with the result that the allegory is instinct with fine meaning, which is as natural and potent and satisfying as is the smell of sweet-briar in early sunshine.'

Reviews in *The Academy* were unsigned, but as had already been seen in his letter to Alice Head, Flecker was writing reviews for *The Academy*.[631] St. John Lucas's book gave him an insight into prose fantasy, sadism, and also, if he reviewed it or read the review, inspiration for the writing of '*Hassan*'.[632]

He chose teaching as a means of bridging the gap between his period of study at Dean Close and the announcement by the Foreign Office of the date the examinations would be held. Obviously his father was not prepared to offer him the opportunity to coach pupils at Dean Close, or permit him to escape to be near Beazley. What was the relationship with Beazley at this time? Did it go through a period of estrangement, as Savery said it did from time to time? It is less clear why this spell of teaching precipitated the onset of TB,[633] unless it was also precipitated initially by a break in a close relationship.

If Flecker's deeper feelings are not easy to discover, there is no doubt that money was troubling him. One practical point in favour of filling in for an absent master at Mill Hill School, was the school's proximity to Grant Richards, to whom he wrote:

Haselmere,
Mill Hill,
London, NW

Dear Mr. Richards,

Could you give me an interview about the novel next week, or is it not worth it.

Sometime next Thursday week for instance.

I should like to have some word from you about it.

I shall be at this address for a week.

To which Grant Richards replied:

Dear Mr. Flecker,

I have this morning received an unsigned letter which I believe to be from you, asking for an appointment for next Thursday week. I shall be pleased to see you at eleven o'clock on the morning of the 6th.

Sincerely yours,

Flecker sent a postcard to Grant Richards 30 January, 1908:[634]

Thursday,
Jan. 30th.

Haselmere,
Mill Hill NW

I can hardly believe that I have for the second time sent
you an unsigned letter! I am very sorry.

If by any unlikely chance I cannot come on the 6th I will
at once write for another appointment. "

The appointment was not kept, the reason and his general state of
mind are outlined in a letter home:[635]

"Bust indeed!
have secured this place ... I imagine it will be about four
weeks. I am utterly worn out, so forgive briefness. The boys
... very respectful since I clouted one boy's head, first go-
off.

The work has been hard. I like old Maclure ...

Tomorrow I stop teaching at 12, leave Mill Hill Sta, 12.53
catch the 2.20 express at King's Cross and get in at 10.12. I
enclose address, and I appeal to Claire for clothes."

His new address was Aysgarth School, Newton-le-Willows, Yorkshire
where he wrote to Grant Richards: [636]

Dear Mr. Richards,

To my extreme annoyance I cannot come to see you on
Thursday, as I intended, because I have been wired for to
teach here for a Fortnight.

I shall certainly be in town after the 18th, and will call to
see you at once.

If you can tell me anything definitely, I should like to
hear from you: if not, I will wait till I can see you.

Yours sincerely,

James Flecker.

Aysgarth School in the North Riding ('very pleasant country' he
wrote to his sister)[637] was not much more to his liking than Mill Hill.

It may have had the sort of atmosphere that pervaded Dean Close at times, as it was a new school with teething troubles. Unlike Mill Hill, which had celebrated its centenary on 5 July 1907, Aysgarth had been founded by the Rev. C.T. Hales, and moved to Bedale outside the village of Newton-le-Willows, in 1890, to a building which, like Dean Close, had been purpose-built, near a railways station, Jervaulx. Hales died in 1900, having built up the pupils from 45 to 100. He was succeeded by George V. Brocklebank, who was not such a dynamic personality, and more used to Natural History than boys. He gave up in the last term of 1908 and was followed by Walter Chitty. The school could not have been at its best during Flecker's brief time there, and the number of pupils had dropped to 65; he complained of a hard time and weariness. Each master had two private rooms in a hostel, and meals were served by a resident housekeeper.

In the LIFE a letter is quoted and it is described as 'apparently the only one he wrote from Aysgarth School'. It may have been the only one he wrote to his sister Claire. A long letter was also written to Dr. Flecker, 'reviewing the financial situation'.[638] The letter to Claire asked for his clothes to be packed in the green bag he had got in Germany, including 'two more unfrayed 15.5 collars'. He wanted all his typewritten manuscripts, which included amongst others, '*Henderson felo-de-se Potter*', which was a prose-fantasy (the poem 'Felo-De-Se' was eventually published without the prose context). The fate of his play *The Dead People* is discovered; he tells his sister it is in his brother Oswald's room. He wanted his copybook, *The Book of Kara James*, sent on to him and his manuscript of *The Last Generation*, as well as dictionaries and books in German. He also wanted all copies of what he described as 'my own book'.[639]

The letter that was left out of the LIFE is more interesting than the one that was published, as it indicates the mental stress Flecker suffered at this time, due to the usual conflict over money with his father. One sentence in the letter[640] summed up the financial side of his schoolmastering. He told his father that he would leave Yorkshire as poor as when he came. He had debts to be paid off. They included doctors' bills, which proved that he could not have been in the best of health. The date of the Foreign Office examinations had yet to be announced and he needed Dr. Flecker to pay his £4 entrance fee. He knew his father, who worked so hard, could not understand why he had a son who had turned out to be a dilettante, or at least a person who only worked hard at things he liked.

In a postcard (which was the only one he had left) dated 17 February 1908 ('and the foolish virgin has covered it with lamp-oil'), he told his parents he would go straight to see people at Scoones when he got to town. He told them of the hard time he had had at the school. He got in touch with Grant Richards after his two weeks in Yorkshire: [641]

Sevilla House,
7 Colville Terrace,
London W Friday
Feb. 13th '08

Dear Mr. Richards,

Could you give me an interview some time on Monday? I enclose another third of the novel. You will understand I know that it is only scribbled; the very names of some of the characters have got altered from the first part. If Monday is impossible some time after 5.30 any day between Tuesday and Friday of next week would do.

If you accepted the novel, I could have it ready for you before the end of March.

Yours very truly,

James Flecker

There is no record of a meeting between Flecker and Grant Richards in February or March 1908. The reasons may have been due, on Flecker's side, to illness or the fact that he was out of town. He wrote to his father on the 25 March that he was suffering from feverish symptoms and that he had no money. If he did not get a teaching job, he would be coming home. The examinations must have intervened. He wrote two more letters to Grant Richards, which although undated, must have been written in this periods:

Dean Close Memorial School
Cheltenham

Dear Mr. Richards,

I am hoping to hear from you about the novel in a few days.

Meanwhile, will you return to me the first part of it. I now want to work on the whole of it together, to conceal the

joints in the harness, and to expand it considerably. That is, if you are willing to take the book.
Yours sincerely,

James Flecker

The second letter read:

Dean Close School
Cheltenham

Dear Mr. Richards,

Would you kindly send me my Ms. to the above address as soon as you possibly can, with any notes you like about alterations etc. I am very eager to finish it.

Yours faithfully,

James Flecker.

He finally got a letter from Grant Richards, which read:

April 7th, 1908

James Flecker, Esq.,

Dear Mr. Flecker,

I now return *The King of Alsander* and shall look forward to seeing it again when it has had the revision that you intend to give it. By then I hope it will be typewritten.

You asked me to give you any suggestions for its improvement that occurred to me. I do not know that

I have any definite suggestions to make, but I may as well deliver myself of the feeling that I have – that you have allowed a rather facile pen and invention to run away with you; that neither the writing nor the invention of incident is always as scrupulous as the manner demands and as your poems would have led me to expect. I confess that this feeling may be the result of difficulty of reading the book in handwriting.

Believe me, dear Mr. Flecker,

Sincerely yours

[Grant Richards] [642]

He replied to Grant Richards:

> Dean Close School,
> Cheltenham

Dear Grant Richards,

Many thanks for sending me my MS. I am already at work on its completion and will get it typed as soon as possible.

I think your criticism is very just, but in an extravaganza like mine it is very hard to find any rules to follow. I will have the MS looked over by the most competent critic of novels that I know.

Yours very truly,

James Flecker[643]

The 'critic of novels' was most likely to have been Frank Savery (or John Mavrogordato).

Despite the concentration on his novel, he passed a competitive examination on 16 April 1908 and entered the Levant Consular Service as a student-interpreter.

CHAPTER SIX

Flecker was appointed student-interpreter in the Levant, on 23 April 1908, at an annual salary of £200; the first instalment of which was not due until the end of the summer term. He would not be immediately financially free of Dean Close, as any attempt to work out a more flexible approach to joint finances had not yet produced any real result.[644]

He realised that, even if he was in sight of a regular income, ready cash to spend as he thought fit was more of a problem than it had been when he first arrived in Oxford. This time it was not a question of an extra sixpence but a possible three guineas for a duplicate copy of his completed novel *The King of Alsander*. He had still such high hopes of publication by Grant Richards that he had packed the manuscript for typing, alongside his books and pictures to take with him to his lodgings at 10 Jesus Lane, Cambridge. He wanted the second copy to send to Frank Savery for his opinion, as Savery could not afford, despite suggestions from Flecker, to travel to Cambridge at that particular time.

He wrote to Savery:[645]

> The Union Society
> Cambridge
>
> Dear Franko:
>
> Sorry you can't come here. You cld. take a return from Brum or somewhere and so use the whole of your Manchester ticket but it wd. be v. expensive. Alas Franko, I doubt if you will ever see the novel till it gets into print. The xpence of duplicating even a little of it shewed me I can't afford it. It would have meant a bill of about 8 guis for typing alone. As it is it will cost me about a fiver.[646]
>
> Besides I can revise no more. I am weary.

It is possible that my story starts in tomorrow's *NEW AGE*, if not next week's.[647]

James.

'My story' referred to '*The Last Generation*', a twice-as-long-again, revised version of the tale that had first appeared in the privately printed *Best Man* in 1906, now returned by Grant Richards. The first mention of '*The Last Generation*' in the *New Age*, was in the 6 June edition, 1908, in the form of an advertisement, which continued throughout the year, and eventually in July, contained the extracts from two reviews, one from *Country Life* and one from *The Globe*, which described 'The Last Generation' as 'a very weird and absorbing story'.

The New Age Press, an associated publishing house of the *New Age*, which brought out, in pamphlet form, the writings of well-known people. Flecker's '*The Last Generation – A Story of the Future*' appeared in May/June 1908, and cost 6d. a copy. The story was described by the publishers, quoting a review, in *Country Life*, as a thrilling story. They went on to say that the author was a grim disciple of H.G. Wells at his grimmest, and that his story contained a series of vivid snapshots portraying the events that would lead to the final extinction of the race of man.

Flecker was furious at being called a grim disciple of H.G. Wells,[648] although the tale did bear a resemblance to *The Time Machine*, published in 1895. Flecker's fury could be due more to the fact that he was no disciple; this sort of story fascinated many writers, and if there was a question of discipleship, '*The Last Generation*' was more influenced by G.K. Chesterton's fantasy novel, *The Napoleon of Notting Hill*, published in 1904. It had been very successful and, like '*The Last Generation*', had autobiographical elements. Flecker's story owed much also to Max Nordau's book *Degeneration*, which was much admired at Oxford.[649] M.P. Shiel's fantasy novel *The Purple Cloud*, published in 1901, in which the author annihilated the human race, and Arthur Machen appears, also is an influence on '*The Last Generation*'.

The Country Life review extract, should have mollified Flecker, as it described '*The Last Generation*' as 'a remarkable little story. Mr. Flecker is to a certain extent a disciple of H.G. Wells, and his prophetic vision of the future of the world is, in its way, as forcible as anything that writer has accomplished. His style is brilliant and polished, showing at times the influence of Swift, and he possesses a keen if somewhat sardonic sense of humour.'

'*The Last Generation*' begins pleasantly enough with the lines:

'I had been awake for I know not how many hours that summer dawn while the sun came over the hills and coloured the beautiful roses in my mother's garden. As I lay drowsily gazing through the window, I thought I had never known a morning so sultry, and yet so pleasant. Outside not a leaf stirred; yet the air was fresh, and the madrigal notes of the birds came to me with a peculiar intensity and clearness.'[650]

The narrator hears the wind which is to bear him into the future and who tells him:

'You whom others call dreamy and capricious, volatile and headstrong, you whom some accuse of weakness....'[651]
The narrator expects to see the upper air 'busy with aeroplanes' at the first stopping place in the future, but he is put down in Birmingham Town Hall, where a crowd is being addressed by a thirty-year-old man with a black beard and green eyes, who exhorts them to march on London. The next scene takes place ten years later when the leader, whose name is Joshua Harris, has conquered the world. He proclaims that no children are to be born, or if they are, they are to be killed with their father and mother. Next, the narrator is introduced to the Mutual Extermination Club in Germany, and he gets 'wildly excited' as a very handsome woman, in the prime of life, is shot. In the next episode the narrator is back in England, where a woman has given birth to a child. There is a discussion about the best means of killing it, but it is dropped by accident and its neck broken. The next episode is eventually less gruesome; although the background is a much altered Paris. The Time Traveller meets a member of the Florentine League. The members have been chosen for 'their taste and elegance' and they had 'an exceeding great delight in Poetry, Art, Music, and all beautiful sights and sounds'.

The Time Traveller described their walled garden: 'We walked out into the garden, which was especially noticeable for those flowers which have always been called old-fashioned – I mean hollyhocks, sweet-william, snap-dragons, and Canterbury bells, which were laid out in regular beds.'[652]

It is interesting to note that the Time Traveller says in the next episode: 'I passed many years in that sad enchanted place, dreaming at times of my mother's roses, and of friends that I had known before, and watching our company grow older and fewer.'[653]

The fantasy ends with a description of the end of '*The Last Generation*': 'I saw the vast Halls and Palaces of men falling in slowly, decaying, crumbling, destroyed by nothing but the rains and the touch of Time. And looking again I saw wandering over and above the ruins, moving curiously about, myriads of brown, hairy, repulsive little apes. One of them was building a fire with sticks.'[654]

The apes, including the one building a fire, were portrayed on the cover of '*The Last Generation*'.

'*The Last Generation*' contains a hint of prophecy about Flecker's own generation; if not the last generation, they were to be the lost generation, they were also to fall slowly, and to decay and crumble, many of them, before too long.

It is not known exactly what Savery thought of '*The Last Generation*', with its sado-masochistic sexual references in the 'Mutual Extermination Club' and the story's attitudes about the future of religion in the lines:

'and the church bells shall ring, and the Earth be
re-peopled with new miseries in God's own time.'[655]

Despite the references to Christianity as being of no help in the future of mankind, '*The Last Generation*' is still enjoyable to read, even if the present day reader is not fully aware of its irony. From Frank Savery's point of view he could not fail to appreciate the dedication which was: 'To Frank Savery, who taught, encouraged, and revealed.'

Flecker needed someone who was familiar and reliable, like Savery (Honest Captain Savery in the 'Ballad of Captain Savery')[656] when he first arrived in Cambridge. He complained to Savery in a letter[657] that there was no word from Peckham.[658]

Flecker was not one to enjoy being on his own or to endure solitude for its own sake.[659] His loneliness on arrival at Cambridge was not offset by the beauty of his surroundings, as it was when he was alone in Wales or Switzerland for a short period.[660] The town of Cambridge and the surrounding fenlands did not immediately appeal to him, but it could be that the limits of his situation made him dislike the background, just as he had been reminded of the school sanatorium by the wallpaper of his rented room. He would realise, as he had discovered at Chamonix,[661] that the surroundings would be more bearable, if there were familiar people around.[662]

Flecker was not now one of a great tide of undergraduates, as he had been when he first arrived in Oxford and he had Savery and McKelvie on hand to greet him and help him settle in. He was one of only six new student-interpreters (three of whom were still to come up), 'which will make things more lively',[663] who dispersed to their separate colleges for thirty-two weeks, instead of the usual twenty-four, to learn Persian, Arabic, Turkish and eventually Russian; they were equivalent in status to men in their fourth year.[664]

A man already in his fourth year was Charles Raven of Uppingham days, who was reintroduced to Flecker by the Dean and brought into the Bachelors' common room at Caius, where they sat next to each other at the BA table. They soon found Flecker's comfortable rooms, not far from the College, through the market, in the heart of the town in Jesus Lane, a more congenial place to sit and talk. Apart from old times at Uppingham, there would be much to talk about, as they had not been in close touch since they had left school, and their lives in the intervening years had taken such differing turns.[665]

Raven was no longer the shy and lonely person he had been when he first arrived at his father's former college. His interest in translating Latin verses and his love of the classics had changed, but his love of English literature and the natural sciences remained undimmed. His journalistic activities[666] were behind him, now that the possibility of a Divinity Tripos and ordination for the priesthood were on the horizon. Raven had fallen in love with the Master's niece, 'Bee' Buchanan-Wollaston, and got engaged to her. He also had a close male companion, so his leisure time was not empty, but there was still much to talk about as Raven felt that: 'Conventional standards in morals and religion had for the time broken down badly: the "New Hellenism" of Lowes Dickinson[667] and Gilbert Murray[668] was fashionable, and with it came an outburst of abnormality and a revival of something like the aestheticism of the "nineties".'[669]

At the mention of Gilbert Murray, Flecker's ears pricked up. Murray's work he had most probably been his inspiration for 'Pentheus', written at Oxford.[670] At this point he moved away from Raven's views in favour of Gilbert Murray's work on Greek poetry, which were inspired by Jane Harrison of Newnham, the brilliant scholar who had immersed herself in the study of Greek vases at the British Museum, under Sir Charles Newton. She had found, in scenes on vases and sculptures, similarities to primitive religions around the world. Jack Beazley was following in her footsteps.[671] 'The classics were turning in their long sleep; old men began to see visions and young men to dream dreams.'[672]

211

Young men at Cambridge did more than just dream dreams, and Raven came to judge Flecker not so much for his views, but by the company he kept.[673] This friendship with Raven followed the pattern of the McKelvie friendship at Oxford, as McKelvie, who was also destined for the priesthood, hinted at a 'so-called' scandal when he referred to Flecker at Oxford.[674] But Raven made no bones about what he really meant, which was the company of homosexuals.[675]

Raven, as an engaged man, had less need to mix with this particular group for friendship than his contemporaries, whose prospects of meeting a young woman to court were very limited during term-time, even if marriage was what they wanted, or could afford. Daughters of dons or sisters of their fellow undergraduates were the only women they met, and mixing with the women at the women's colleges was even more unlikely without a formal introduction, although this was gradually changing in the midst of the fight for women's rights. Also, a second generation of women students was now at Cambridge. 'Their experience seems similar to that of any second generation; once the pioneers had broken the barriers, their followers accepted the new opportunities as their due.'[676]

Early in June, coinciding with the VOTES FOR WOMEN march, when thousands of women marched through London, a motion in favour of Women's suffrage was carried by 83 votes to 70 at a Cambridge Union Debate. It could have been at this particular debate, which Raven attended and spoke at, that Kenneth Woollcombe-Boyce was astonished to see Flecker in front of him.[677]

Boyce, like Raven, was also at Caius and had met Flecker before but did not know he was now in Cambridge. Boyce, born a Londoner, but now at Minchinhampton, Gloucestershire, had been educated at Radley school (where Flecker had visited him) and was now studying classics. Boyce appeared fascinated by Flecker's flamboyant style, Flecker was inclined to find him dull at first. He wrote to his mother and told her he did not mind the dullards as much as he used to and 'besides, in one's college one should be tolerant'.[678] The friendship with Boyce resembled the friendship with Douglas Goldring (whom he continued to meet now and again) inasmuch as Boyce (who was four and a half years younger than Flecker and learning Italian at that time) remembered him reading aloud some of his manuscript, which was to be an Italian Grammar,[679] much as Goldring recalled with pleasure Flecker reading to him some of his poems in his Bloomsbury rooms. There was no need to read poems to Boyce as he already cherished a book of Flecker's poems; an inscribed copy of *The Bridge of Fire*.

Boyce had lunch and tea with him and they played bridge and tennis together. Boyce said of Flecker's style of tennis: 'What I recall of his tennis was just a quality which matched that of his mind – he was ambidextrous, and often took backhanders by shifting his racquet to his left hand.'[680]

Boyce, like Raven, was involved in the College Magazine, *The Caian*[681], and like Goldring, when he was editor of *The Tramp*, Boyce was useful to Flecker in mentioning him in the magazine and printing his material.[682]

Flecker may have thought it prudent to play down the extent of his friendship with Boyce, rather than make any reference to his magazine connections, which might have aroused suspicions in Dean Close that his literary ambitions were taking up too much time, as they had at Oxford. Although he wrote little poetry during this time, his desire to get into print was not by any means diminished. He wrote to Grant Richards:

10, Jesus Lane,
Cambridge

Dear Mr. Richards,

I sincerely hope you will let me have a definite answer about this novel in a week's time. I have revised it carefully, had it typed; and it represents the labours of a whole year. I am therefore anxious about it.

Good judges who have read it seem curiously pleased with it. I hope it may prove a popular success.

Yours sincerely,

James Elroy Flecker

There remains to send you

(i)   a dedicatio
(ii) a map of Alsander which you shall have as soon as you decide.[683]

Another person who might have been of help to him, in his desire to get into print, was Raglan Spencer, who had taken over from Raven as joint editor of *The Granta*, but when joint-editor Pattinson-Muir dropped out, Raglan Spencer became sole editor. However, Raglan Spencer was not impressed; quite the reverse. Flecker wrote to his mother on 25 May 25 1908: 'Under the heading, Derelict, the editor of *The Granta* (whom I met at dinner the other night) is publishing an editorial on me (quite absurd) as the typical Oxford man!!! Oxford, the part of it I hate, would explode with wrath at this representation.'[684]

On 30 May 1908, *The Granta* indeed published an editorial under the heading 'Derelict', and the piece, although it did not mention him by name, was obviously about Flecker:

" We speak a different language. We reverence different gods, names which are household words to us come to him with a strange unfamiliar flavour. Oxford has made him, Cambridge almost bores him. To Oxford if he is good he will return when he dies, where he will drink port and propound brilliantly superficial epigrams for all eternity. We met and drank together, and while I consumed new and fiery Chartreuse he read me his quasi-literary compositions. I have still a ticket bearing the magic legend of "Mesopotamia", for I, too, have helped to push a boat up the "Rollers", and drunk Moselle cup at midnight on the Cher. I look at that ticket and it reminds me of him. It is a stranger in a strange land, where men carry caps and gowns at night on the upper reaches of the Cam, and where drunkenness brings an almost permanent stigma.

The men he was up with have most of them gone down and drifted into strange habitations. One of them went out as secretary to a stray colonial minister, but his prospective employer heard of the coming trouble, guessed at the possible epigrams, and returned home. Their vessels passed each other in mid ocean, going different ways. Another was sent down for climbing a hitherto inaccessible college roof. Of that brilliant crowd, some are dead, which is bad; others are engaged, which is worse; others have written books – which is worst of all. Some have won a foretaste of Oxonian eternity by drifting into the Senior Common Rooms of lesser colleges, where they will in time come to be regarded as part and parcel of a great system.

Without exception they were "coming men," but the wheels of their chariots have tarried, and their arrival has been postponed, perhaps indefinitely. He alone has come to "the other place," and he misses things terribly. We do not make funeral orations in purest Attic over our friends who go down, and very few of us write papers on Death or kindred subjects. We give undue respect to no man's opinions. We put up our own like cocoanuts at a fair, where men can have as many cockshies at them as they choose. When our ideals are knocked over we leave the poor battered creatures lying about, or else pick them up, carry them home, and try to nurse them back to some semblance of their old beauty. In no case do we feel resentment against the successful iconoclast. In Oxford it is all so different. Oxford will contain the last Tory. He will keep very much to himself, and probably be cut by the Demos as exclusive and an outsider, but he will be a very great and antiquated gentleman who will sneer at the bad form of that generation for wearing their college blazers in the common street. In Oxford there are certain things no fellow can do, and others every fellow must do – one of these being to dress decently. An Ex-President of their Union Society once confided to me that he ascribed his success in the early stages of the cursus honorum to due attention to sartorial details, and a carefully considered colour-scheme.

Frankly, the general effect is more pleasing. Ancient and ugly attire crowned by a badly coloured calabash of alarming proportions, though fortunately not common in Cambridge, do, if seen, give an impression either of conventional unconventionality, or of some inherent moral depravity. Judge a man by his clothes; if they have the looks of being second-hand, it is quite probable that their owner is himself a second-hand creation, both mentally and morally. These are some of the things which strike 'the stranger' within our gates.

R.H.E.H.S. "

Vol. XXI, No.472 Saturday, May 30th, 1908

Raglan Spencer, a classical scholar of Queens' College, was a person who made enemies; Flecker was not the only one to fall foul of him, and to gain Spencer's friendship was a long and difficult business. According to *The Granta*[685] Spencer's 'his life-work has been attacking people who have been pushed into positions for which (in his opinion) their talents gave them no claim'. Raglan Spencer had requested Ronald Firbank, who was at Cambridge between 1906 and 1909, to get something from Lord Alfred Douglas for publication in *The Granta* at this time. After publication Douglas sued for libel. *The Cambridge Review* was also involved. Undergraduate editors of *The Cambridge Review* were dismissed from the university, and Firbank left Cambridge, feeling he was not welcome. Raglan Spencer had already left Cambridge[686] for Clifford's Inn.

Raglan Spencer appears to have done no research on his subject as, if he had, he would have had to look no further than his own publication of *The Granta* of 12 October 1907 when Charles Raven was editor. This edition contained a review of *The Bridge of Fire*. The review stated that the makings of a poet, or some of them, are in the author of these verses.[687]

In all fairness to Raglan Spencer, Flecker was not going to fit neatly into the Cambridge scene. He insisted on wearing his Praxiteles blazer (according to the 'Derelict' piece, 'wearing their college blazers in the common street'), which made him stand out in the conventional crowd who wore dowdy Norfolk jackets, as easily as in the days when he wore a sailor-suit and the rest of the pupils wore their more sombre school uniforms.

This flamboyance of dress also revealed his conflict at finding himself on the student-interpreter path at Cambridge. He would surely have succeeded better if he had conformed by donning more conventional attire.

There was an element of snobbery in *The Granta* comments about second-hand clothes. A contemporary, Rupert Brooke, was remembered[688] as saying he found it quite easy to dress on £3. per year. Photographs of Brooke from that time showed that £3 a year for his clothes was extravagance. Three pounds to Flecker was quite a consideration, and for a former student-interpreter, Reader Bullard, also of Queens', whose father earned less than £2 per week, the sum of £3 per year for clothes would be an even greater financial consideration.

Flecker was mindful of the cost of clothes, even if the wearing of his Praxiteles blazer was not entirely an act of economy, but more an act of bravado, which might have won him the admiration of younger men, even if they knew little of the blazer's importance, and that the Praxiteles Club contained only Flecker and Beazley as members. The blazer was a throwback, also, to happier and more secure times, although the mere fact of having been at Oxford would brand him.

The Oxford label continued to be visible; in the next issue of *The Granta*, 6 June1908, it was reported at a Union Debate on the motion in favour of Asquith's Old Age Pension Scheme that 'Mr. G.E. Flecker [sic] (Caius) has the Oxford manner badly, but should persevere. In time he will, with luck, become one of ourselves'.

'Become one of ourselves' Flecker was unlikely to do, so Raglan Spencer, although he wrote poetry himself, may have felt that at that some poets needed taking down a peg or two, because of the attention being paid to them. Cambridge was awash with established poets, in Flecker's first term, because of the Tercentenary of the birth of the prince of poets, John Milton. Not inappropriately, Milton had happier associations with Oxford than Cambridge, from where he had been sent down. But a production of *Comus* was to be staged in which Rupert Brooke was to act to great acclaim. The Poet Laureate Alfred Austin, and Robert Bridges, Edmund Gosse, Thomas Hardy and Laurence Binyon were in attendance at the first performance on 10 July at the New Theatre, Cambridge. One poet not yet as famous, was Frances Darwin,[689] who designed the costumes. It was during the first reading of *Comus* that she began the legend of Rupert Brooke when she saw the light fall on his hair. She called him 'a young Apollo, golden-haired'.[690] Flecker took a more balanced view of people who could be said to resemble Apollo.[691]

The golden hair and good looks of Rupert Brooke attracted men and women of all ages, not only at Cambridge, but even as a child, and childhood friends and schoolfriends remained loyal to him throughout his life.[692] Brooke (unlike Flecker, but like Beazley) not only looked like everyone's idea of a poet, but wrote poetry too. Although, when Flecker first met him, his poetry was unpublished in book form, his poems had won competitions in the *Westminster Gazette*. He read his own poems (some as soon as he had written them) to members of the society, which he and Hugh Dalton[693] had founded and named 'The Carbonari' (The Charcoal Burners), after an Italian Revolutionary Group with whom Byron had been associated. The Carbonari banned politics, and was disbanded in 1907. Members had included Arthur Schloss (later Waley), Gerald Shove,[694] Philip Baker (later Philip Noel-Baker)[695] and Francis Birrell.[696] Francis Birrell is the only member of the Rupert Brooke circle to be mentioned in any great detail in the LIFE.[697]

Gerald Shove and Francis Birrell were said to be mutually attracted, and they displayed their devotion to each other in an ostentatious way.[698] Gerald Shove was a member of the secret society called the Apostles, although Birrell was not a member. The Apostles grew out of a society first founded at Cambridge in 1820. From the turn of the twentieth century, it was said that homosexuality was open, blatant and a creed of the Apostles. Members were chosen by Maynard Keynes and Lytton Strachey for their good looks, and intellectual powers were a secondary feature. Rupert Brooke was a member. The Apostles contained an element of snobbery, and family background was considered to be important.

It is not too hard to see why the Brooke circle, intoxicated by Swinburne's poetry and admiring Chinese and Japanese poetry,[699] attracted Flecker. Brooke was something of a snob where published writers were concerned, and the fact that Flecker had three publications and reviews to his credit served as a valid passport to get him through the frontier and into Brooke territory, even if it was not sufficient to get the people there to like him. Lytton Strachey, a jealous character,[700] for one was not at all impressed with Flecker, in comparison with the impressions made upon him by Beazley, Swithinbank and Brooke.[701]

Douglas Goldring tells of Flecker having lunch with Rupert Brooke in May 1908 in Brooke's rooms in Gibbs' Buildings with two others who are not named.[702] Goldring does not explain if Brooke and he had met previously, but a mutual friend was Albert Rothenstein (1881–1953) whom Flecker had got to know at Oxford, and who was Brooke's guest in College at this time. Rothenstein took over the painting of scenery for the production of *Comus* when Frances Darwin dropped out. Brooke was also acquainted with Ronald Firbank, who had been at Uppingham at the same time as Savery. Firbank portrayed Brooke as Winsome Brookes in his novel *Vainglory*, published in 1915.[703]

Brooke's rooms, with their bright yellow walls covered with Beardsley reproductions, were reminiscent of Albert Rothenstein's last evening in Oxford. On this occasion, two pictures by Beardsley had provoked a discussion about Beardsley's ability to draw, and enabled Flecker to drop into the conversation his reference to being in the studio of Manet,[704] and talking to him. As Manet had died before Flecker was born, it is more likely that, if he had ever talked to any great artist in Paris, it was Monet and not Manet.[705]

Names that Brooke might have chosen to drop into the conversation at this lunch would have been just as impressive but more true to life. Brooke had met Hilaire Belloc and fallen under the influence of his work and anti-Semitism. At the National Liberal club in London he had more recently met H.G. Wells. Brooke was an enthusiastic Fabian Associate and had just (in April 1908) signed the Basis and become a Full Member of the Fabians. Brooke had been persuaded to join the Cambridge University Fabians by 'Ben' Keeling of Trinity,[706] who saw Brooke and Dalton as the best men of their year. It is not surprising Flecker joined the Fabians 'as nearly everyone did who was in or on the fringes of these King's circles'.[707]

The remark about nearly everyone joining the Fabians, was made by a contemporary and quoted by Goldring in his book on Flecker. He also goes on to quote the same source as saying Flecker: 'wasn't much interested in politics. He was inclined to dislike the poor and be bored with them and to regard the large projects of our young hopes as waste of time.'[708]

Goldring goes on to say that for several reasons he ventured to disagree with this statement. He argued: 'No doubt the minutiae of party politics bored him, and the arid intellectual wrangles of the Fabians'. He mentioned Flecker's: 'ardent sympathy with the political idealism of Shelley and of Keats'.[709] Goldring quoted the Cambridge contemporary as saying that: 'At Oxford Flecker had been the [then] conventional high Tory in politics.[710] ... By the time he reached Cambridge, however, his ideas on political matters were rather more "serious". ...Cambridge made him a Liberal, even an enthusiastic Liberal.'[711]

Goldring would have found a more convincing reason for Flecker's dislike of politics in Flecker's play *Don Juan* (Act II, Scene I). Don Juan says to Lady Isabel who wants him in her father's Cabinet:

> Man at the Foreign Office, I suppose. No, but I should
> not fit in to Politics; you've got to hold other people's ideas.
> The Diplomatic now – you needn't have any ideas at all.
> No, I shouldn't fit in. For instance, I don't like the idea of
> war.[712]

Flecker had written to Sedgwick in September 1905: 'To me Motor-Car Acts, Old Age Pensions, the Reform of the Roads seem to be far more important than Protection, Boer Wars, Relations with Morocco, or Home Rule. "One man, one vote" seems to be delirious nonsense. Education seems to me about the most important of all things.'[713]

Least important to Flecker would be a contributory Old Age Pension Scheme, as Norman says in the *King of Alsander*. 'It is the young who want money; Norman had never been able to see the object of saving money with immense toil over against the day when one should become infirm, insane, or dead.'

The Union Debate on the motion in favour of Asquith's Old Age Pension Scheme at the beginning of June 1908 was defeated by 30 votes to 23. Although Flecker's remarks are not recorded, the remarks of others – on the plight of women who had no opportunity for saving, men who needed extraordinary gifts if they were to save any money for their old age, and suggesting that workhouses were not the solution – were recorded if not approved. The cradle to the grave support, which Socialism was said to mean, as well as the statement that it was the inferior brand of citizen who failed to save for his old age, were in print.

Goldring quoted the Cambridge contemporary: 'At one time he seems to have played with the project of throwing up his career in the Consular Service and standing for Parliament'.[714] It is possible that this sort of action (getting into the limelight in order to play a part in Parliament) appealed to the *Boy's Own* side of Flecker's character. In the past there had been the venture to assist the workers in the wine riots, and the tongue-in-cheek references to Flecker at Oxford (recalled by Humbert Wolfe), where he was supposed to discuss the organisation of blanket-makers in Witney. Although it never got off the ground, Flecker was suggested as a participant in the proposed venture.[715]

Flecker was up at Cambridge too late to have participated in the successful strategy to beat the rowdies who wanted to spoil the Keir Hardie visit to Cambridge in February 1907. The Socialists, although greatly outnumbered, managed to get Keir Hardie to speak at the Guildhall. The legend lived on.

But more down-to-earth and personal reasons made Flecker join the Cambridge University Fabian Society, as the Society was one place where lonely or isolated people of both sexes could meet, even if they were not at first greatly interested in politics. The Fabian Society crossed the great wide chasm that yawned between the men's and women's colleges,[716] and this mixing of the sexes was even easier at the Fabian Summer School. Brooke had already planned by May 1908 to take three days to walk to the Fabian Summer School in North Wales and arrive on 27 August.[717] Flecker was prevented from going himself that year as he had to spend the summer on the Continent improving his French, Italian and German.

Fabianism was not the only influence that Flecker got from the Brooke circle; his future writing also owed something to them.[718] The influence of Brooke on Flecker was not as great as the influence Beazley had on his writings and feelings. Brooke and Beazley were not unalike in their good looks. The meeting with Beazley had ended the dullness of Oxford days for Flecker; it could be said that the meeting with Brooke ended the dullness of Cambridge days. Of the two, Beazley was the more stable character with emotions more tightly reined than Brooke's. Brooke, like Beazley, had Scottish connections.[719] Brooke was only a year older than Beazley had been when Flecker first met him, and like both Beazley and Flecker, Brooke was the elder of two sons. His brother Richard had died in 1907, leaving Rupert and his younger brother Alfred. Flecker and Brooke, if not in the same class, were much nearer in class than Beazley and Brooke.

Brooke, the son of a housemaster at Rugby School, had to endure the same double standard as Flecker as he attended the school where his father was on the staff, and his mother, like Flecker's, ran the domestic side of her husband's House. She, too, was a domineering woman.

Brooke and Flecker's rivalry over who could write the better poetry, coupled with Brooke's anti-Semitism (Flecker to him, had a Jewish appearance) made a close friendship unlikely. Arthur Schloss was Jewish, but his contemporaries felt it was the sort of Jewishness they could accept.[720]

Flecker was also a victim of some sort of retrospective jealousy. In a letter dated 5 June 1908, King's College, Cambridge, Lytton Strachey wrote to Bernard Swithinbank: 'Your letter has just come. I am here for a week or so – in delightful rooms in King's, spending my time looking out of the window and writing poetry. Keynes is also here at Harvey Road, and my brother James and several other persons including Flecker (whom we don't much like).'[721]

Thus Brooke did not become Flecker's greatest friend. According to Goldring his greatest friend at King's was Schloss.[722]

Arthur David Schloss (who changed his name in the Great War to his mother's maiden name of Waley) was five years younger (born 19 August 1989), a Jew, son of a barrister and grandson of a German who had made money in cotton broking in Manchester. Schloss had started writing poetry at the age of ten, and he had come, like Brooke, from Rugby School. When Flecker met him he was well on his way to obtaining a classical Tripos. He published two unsigned poems in King's undergraduate magazine, *Basileon*, in June 1909.[723] Schloss's interests lay in the translations of Oriental languages and Eastern studies, under the influence of the shy Don, Goldsworthy Lowes Dickinson.[724]

The friendship of Schloss and Flecker was similar to the friendship of Beazley and Flecker in many respects. In one respect it was more valuable as Schloss did not turn his back on his own poetry as Beazley had done. The personalities and good looks of Beazley and Schloss were so alike that Harold Acton, who knew them both, wrote of them both: 'His silence was the most eloquent I have heard, whether in praise or condemnation. Only Arthur Waley's can compare with it, but that it is eked out with a pipe, whereas Jacky Beazley abstains from nicotine. His silence springs from his depths and envelops all.'[725,726]

Arthur Schloss, like Jack Beazley, was famous for his lack of small talk. He suffered from poor eyesight, ruling out boisterous sports, and affording more time for a mutual love of the East to develop. A reason for the development of this friendship to develop at this time could be a letter Flecker received from Grant Richards dated 1 June 1908, turning down *The King of Alsander*.

J.E. Flecker, Esq.

Dear Mr. Flecker,

Things have come to such a pass now with the publishers of novels that some of them, I judge from what I am told, are thinking of going out of business and refraining from publishing any novels, except those by authors who have already a big public. Booksellers and public alike refuse, in effect, to give any proper attention to a new man. This has influenced me in sending you back *The King of Alsander*. But to be fair, it has not influenced me as much as the fact that I do not feel that the interest and charm of the beginning are carried through the book. It becomes a romance in the manner of *The Prisoner of Zenda* with none of that significance that I am sure you could, and will, put into a novel – a novel which I hope you will give me the chance of publishing in spite of my pessimism in regard to the work of new novelists. This decision of mine is the more disappointing to me because, as you know, I liked the beginning, and here and there throughout the whole are passages showing insight and originality.

Believe me, dear Mr. Flecker,

Sincerely yours,

(Signed) GRANT RICHARDS "[727]

It is as well to try and read between the lines of Richards' letter and realise the difficulties he had faced when considering publishing fiction, in particular the book by James Joyce, *Dubliners*, which had been submitted to Richards in December 1905. It was accepted for publication early the following year and a contract was signed, but when an extra story was added the printer refused to set it up in type. In law, both publisher and printer could be subject to criminal prosecution if material was published that was considered undesirable, and so Joyce reluctantly rewrote some of his material and returned it to Richards.

In the autumn of 1906, Richards finally declined to publish *Dubliners* (although he did eventually publish it in 1914).

It is a fact that 'the interest and charm of the beginning' are not carried through the book. *The King of Alsander* starts in the village of Blaindon ten miles from the sea, and Norman's journey to Alsander and his meeting with Peronella have a certain charm, but by chapter eight Norman has failed to pass the qualifying examination to be King of Alsander and is whipped. At this stage Richards may have wondered whether it was worth risking prosecution, or whether he could get Flecker to make more revisions.

The letter from Richards could have been another reason why Flecker turned away from Ruritania and began writing about the East, where under the cover of scholarship he could indulge his fantasies and get published.

Flecker shared Schloss's interest in Japanese and Chinese poetry. According to Hodgson[728] 'He [Flecker] possessed a volume – which, unlike some of his books, he marked with quaint little signs apparently betokening degrees of appreciation – Adolphe Thalasso's *Anthologie de l'Armour Asiatique*, which had been published in 1907, by the *Mercure de France*. These songs, which he turned into French verse and so published, M. Thalasso picked from all parts and corners of Asia, from Syria to China, from Armenia to India, from Japan to Annam to Circassia.'

Flecker [Hodgson continues] probably valued this book chiefly for those poems he could not read in the original: those, at any rate, are what he marked. One from Beluchistan, '*A Song of the People*', is radiant with his favourite colours, blue, gold, silver. The rest which singled out are from China and Japan: Chi-King's '*At The Western Gate*'; Li-Po's '*On the Bank of the Jo-heh*'[729]; Cha'ng-Sing's '*Song of the Nenuphars*'[730]; and most heavily marked of all, Tin-Tun-Ling's '*The Shadow of the Orange Blossoms*'. Tu-Fu has been described by Captain Cranmer Byng as 'of all the Poets, the first in craftsmanship'. He included four of Tun-Ling's poems in *A Lute of Jade*, which, although it appeared in 1909, possibly did not fall under Flecker's notice.'

It is quite likely that *A Lute of Jade* did come to Flecker's notice, or at least Cranmer Byng's translation of Chinese verse, as shortly *The Nation* published 'The Town Without a Market' in the 8 May 1909 issue, it published the poems 'Calycanthus Flower' and 'Plum Blossom', each from the Chinese, by L. Cranmer Byng. *The Lute of Jade* had come to the notice of the Brooke circle. In a letter to Jacques Raverat dated 3 November 1909, Brooke refers to 'your lute of jade' (this is acknowledged in a footnote as PIH YUH SHE SHOO. Le Livre de Jade; Poésies traduites par Judith Gautier. Paris, 1902).

There seems no doubt that the Brooke circle knew that the lute of jade referred to the male organ, and that the translations from the Chinese conveyed in timeless, delicate and sensitive language the beauty of sexual love.[731] Brooke writes to Raverat: 'What nonsense to pretend I have your lute of jade! I have mislaid even my own lute – and that's but a cheap wood and cat-gut, a tinkly little affair. But yours I have never seen it.' He then goes on to outline a search for 'Some flowery-gowned mandarin with ivory thin pellucid tiny hands and wrists brushing some delicate curved lute,' and ends by writing, 'There is no lute of jade around here.'

Flecker was not Schloss's only friend, as he in turn was a close friend of Noel Compton-Burnett (1887–1916), history scholar at King's and a late developer, who had felt compelled to excel at Cambridge after the death of his elder brother Guy in 1905. He had been helped in this endeavour by Oscar Browning from the day of his entrance examinations. Noel's sister Ivy Compton-Burnett (1884–1969) had already received her degree from Royal Holloway College in 1907, and Schloss, either on his own or with other members of The Carbonari, visited the fatherless Compton-Burnett family in Hove, while Ivy and some of her sisters visited Cambridge.[732]

Rose Macaulay (1881–1958), a family friend of the Brookes since her childhood, was also a visitor to Cambridge (her uncle was Senior Tutor and her father was English tutor to Rupert Brooke), where she continued to be friends with Rupert Brooke. She also embedded in her novels her experiences of mixing in the Rupert Brooke circle, although she was never considered to be part of the 'neo-pagans'.[733]

Ivy Compton-Burnett, Rose Macaulay and Virginia Stephens, who were all writers (Rose Macaulay had been an undergraduate at Somerville for some of the time Flecker had been at Trinity), were not really the women that Flecker was referring to in his *Grecian* piece.

So, to a certain extent, his complaint that a boy did not enter a new life after Oxford or Cambridge and there were no women to help him understand the proportion of things was not entirely true.[734] At Cambridge at least, although no longer a boy straight from school, he came into contact with women, even if they were not admitted to his own College or considered as candidates for student-interpreterships. In fact, *The Caian* predicted that a thousand years would pass before women would be admitted to Caius, a factor that drove him to seek a social life beyond Caius and to join the Fabians.

Another history scholar at King's (1909–12) and a member of The Carbonari and a friend of Schloss, was Francis (Frankie) Birrell (1889–1935). Francis Frederick Lockyer was the elder son of the Liberal

Minister, Augustine Birrell. Francis Birrell was not as physically attractive as Schloss, Raven or Brooke. He was educated at Eton at the same time as Hugh Dalton and he was still a leading light in The Carbonari. Maynard Keynes became a staunch supporter and sexual partner of Birrell and so linked him with both Swithinbank and Beazley.[735]

The relationship with Birrell was at first the same as that between Flecker and Boyce; the admiration of a younger man for someone older and more sophisticated. No evidence exists to show that it was anything deeper. Dean Close could not help but be impressed by Birrell's family connections. Like Boyce, Birrell felt that Oxford was Flecker's true element, although unlike Boyce he had not known him in his Oxford days. Like Savery and Raven, Birrell had great admiration for Flecker's gifts, but he was well aware of his faults. Birrell[736] stated: 'though modest, he had strange arrogancies and wanted half-seriously to bring out an anthology of all the best English poems, with improvements by himself.'[737]

Birrell was more sympathetic to Flecker's preoccupation with the grotesque and bizarre, but makes no reference to having discussed the reason for this preoccupation, or whether he had read Flecker's explanation of his feelings about the grotesqueness in the art of Leonardo da Vinci and Beardsley.[738] Birrell, himself homosexual (his affair with Maynard Keynes was in 1910),[739] may not have fully realised why the grotesque also appealed to him.

Birrell admired Flecker's enthusiasm and energy, whether it was punting a canoe miles from Cambridge, or learning a new language; he felt he learned a lot from Flecker in this respect. Birrell thought that the outbursts of energy were due in part to the fact that Flecker was already suffering from consumption.[740]

Birrell had guessed correctly that Flecker was already tubercular at Cambridge, and Flecker himself suspected it. He hid his fears by a sort of detached hunger for life. He wrote to his mother: 'I amuse myself by punting a canoe to the great envy of all, for Cambridge (with rare exceptions) has not yet learnt to steer its punts. But, becoming hubristic, as the Greeks say, I insisted to-day in taking the lightest canoe in the river and fell into the middle of Camus. (No audience fortunately, as it is a cold day.) Into about a foot and a half of water. Wherefore I praise the Cam that it is not as the Thames ...'[741] He continued: 'I nearly won all sorts of absurd races – sculling, punting, etc., in the Caius Regatta (only a joke it is) yesterday. I coxed a four! The fours are drawn by lot, and as some of the men have never been in a four in their lives, the result is funny. Fours are very wobbly boats. It was the fifth crab that stroke caught that lost us one race.'[742]

He also told her about his playing tennis and fives, and this activity can be seen as a denial of what was troubling him physically, when his energy and enthusiasm were replaced by periods of misery and tiredness.

He had a good relationship with his landlady, Miss Harriet Ransom. When he suffered from illnesses he was able to get over them in his comfortable rooms, so there was no immediate need for Dean Close to worry that his health was neglected or that bad colds could develop into anything more serious. The relationship with the landlady could only have survived on give and take – he put up with her talking too much, and she tolerated his usual clutter of possessions, and the fact that he kept a dog, and hoped to have lots of visitors to stay.

Visitors remembered his library, his dictionaries and a wooden lizard named the 'Demon of All Sloth'. As he had said to the editor of *The Academy* (9 November 1907) 'a love of pleasantly malformed beasts seems most delicately childlike and humorous'. He did not have as many visitors to these rooms as he would have liked and this might not have been entirely due to the laziness of Cambridge people.[743] Or that rooms in College, if he had been able to get them, would have produced a closer contact with Dons, as happened with Brooke and Dalton, because there would be the drawback of the double standard he had already experienced at school.[744]

Opportunities to talk to his Director of Studies on an informal basis were not as frequent as at King's. Flecker dined with Professor Edward Granville (Johnnie) Browne (1862–1926), Fellow of Pembroke, only once a term, but conversation at Browne's table was said to be the best at University; he could not complain of dullness as he had complained about lunch with his tutor.[745]

'Johnnie' Browne,[746] educated at Glenalmond and Eton, Persian scholar (his great work in four volumes on the subject of Persian literature had many Oriental poems in translation), Professor of Arabic and a qualified doctor of medicine (although he never practised as a doctor), loved living languages and was as rooted in the present, and current affairs of the East, as much as some of his fellow dons seemed rooted in the past. A great friend of Browne's, and a visitor to Cambridge, was Wilfred Scawen Blunt (1840–1922), a poet whose literary circle included Francis Thompson, a politician, as well as Suffolk squire and an Arabian Nights figure who had made desert journeys. Browne and his young wife[747] (whom he married on 20 June 1906) had recently visited one of his former student-interpreters, Andrew Ryan, while he was in Constantinople, and been a guest of Ryan's in his bachelor quarters.[748] Flecker could learn at first-hand impressions of Turkey and the life enjoyed by interpreters, and what would be in store for him, if he chose Turkey out of the places available to him. Two places were available for Turkey, two for Morocco (which tempted him) and two for Persia. He wrote to his parents and told them he had chosen Turkey. He also told them in the same letter:[749] 'The triumph of the Constitutionalists will be a great blessing to me: it means a much freer and more comfortable life in Turkey'.

A reason (which would not be readily given to Dean Close) for choosing Turkey at the end of July 1908 would be the possibility of being nearer to Jack Beazley. Beazley's interest in Greek vases took him to Athens,[750] and although Greece was not available, Turkey would provide the opportunity for visits.

There is proof of better relations with Dean Close, at this time as he was asked to adjudicate when the school magazine, *The Decanian* , organized a competition for a prize poem. It was rather late as far as Dean Close was concerned to give him recognition as a poet whose opinions on writing poetry mattered. An essay several pages long by Flecker was published in the August 1908 edition. In it he defended the Prize Poem, and told the competititors that the entries should not be expected to be good poetry. Byron, Tennyson and Matthew Arnold had won prize poems, but their poems could not be described as good poems. The age at which the poem was written and the requirement to write at length on a subject dictated by another, prevented the writing of good poetry. However, he expected the exercise of the same qualities that went into the making of a good copy of a Latin elegiac, and that was mainly invention, command of vocabulary and avoidance of the commonplace.

He felt that the winning poem had the necessary qualities, as well as the great merit, not shared by other competitors, of not taking itself too seriously. He goes on to remark on the subject of blank verse, which one competitor had attempted. He points out that blank verse is the hardest metre to write, and pauses must be made sufficiently subtle to avoid 'the deadliest monotony'. Eight years ago his poetry had been criticised in this very magazine, and now he was in the position of handing out criticism of poetry submitted for prizes.

By the time this criticism and his review of *Poems of Carducci* in *The Academy*[751] came out, he was on the Continent, as he had to spend time there to perfect his French, German and Italian. He had sufficient money left for these travels as the College allowed him to defer paying his bills until October. He was due to return to Cambridge after a visit to Dean Close on 13 October. The journey to the Continent meant that he had rather reluctantly to miss a family holiday in his beloved

Wales, as the Fleckers were going to Radnorshire. But there was some consolation as he would be with Jack on the Continent.

He made no secret, as far as Dean Close was concerned, that he was meeting Jack in Perugia,[752] and postcards home referred to the pleasant weather as he and Jack travelled to Rome via Assisi. To allay any fears that Dean Close might entertain that he was spending extravagantly or being lazy, the cost of his journey out from London to Chiasso was given – the amount was £2.12.3d. (although this sum is attributed to 'a pleasant reminder of pre-war possibilities', rather giving himself credit for being economical).

In case anyone thought that all this austerity brought nothing but gloom, he told them that the extensive journey was pleasant, and his itinerary was outlined. It included San Gemignano, where they walked 25 miles to Volterra, Bologna, where he received a letter from Frank Savery, and Florence, where they stayed at the Pension Scandinavia, 14 Via Nazionale (the same address as the year before) and hoped to pick up mail from home. The journey also included Venice, but this was not referred to in the LIFE.

All this detailed money-saving brought no solution to financial problems. How much of this was known to Dean Close is unclear, but Frank Savery was left in no doubt. 'Finances in ruin', he wrote to Savery on his return,[753] telling him he was sulky to be back. He did not give Savery an itinerary, but explained to him 'we stayed in nearly forty towns', which might have been something of an exaggeration or an effort to show where the money went. Financial ruin might also have been an exaggeration, but he was sincere enough in inviting Savery for the weekend, telling him he has not too many friends 'dans ce monde-ci'.[754]

Evidence in his *Bridge of Fire Copybook* showed that the publication of 'To The World and a Poet a Thousand Years Hence' was on 11 January 1908[755]. He then wrote or rewrote the following poems, which (although not dated) relate to this period in his life: p.78 'Alexis' – from Meleager, p.79 Heliodora' – from Meleager,[756] p.80 'Praxiteles' – from Meleager, p.81 'Love, The Baby'[757,758]

The first lines of 'Alexis' are:

Alexis walked one summer morn,
Through sultry fields of quiet corn

'Praxiteles' first lines are:

> Now love himself has made the art his own,
> And fashioned a divine Praxiteles.

On page 82 is the poem he entitled 'The Londoner'. It is undated and consisted of four verses. It appeared in the *New Age* on 3 October 1908, under the title 'Ballad of the Londoner'.[759] The poem captured in the opening lines, the evening mood of a city in late autumn:

> Evening falls on the smoky walls,
> And the railings drip with rain,

The first lines of the second verse are equally evocative of a feature of London now gone:

> The great and solemn-gliding tram,
> Love's still-mysterious car,

But the remainder of the poem does not live up to its promise, and it would seem better if he had left the poem as he had first written and published it in the *New Age*:

> Deep have I drunk of the joys of life,
> As I would till the sun dips down,
> In love, with the iron towers and walls
> And the people of this town.

> But a rose is blooming beyond the Thames,
> And a wonderful rose it is,
> Oh her hands and her eyes and her delicate hands,[760]
> O dark red star of a kiss!

Beazley appeared to have had a hand in alterations to the poem; he may have favoured the publication of the shorter version. In the second line 'the sun dips down' is altered to 'goes down', a suggestion is made, and there is a brief note (difficult to read) to 'add murky' (or 'smoky'), which appeared not to have been heeded. The last verse reads:

> I found a garden in a street
> That no one ever knew.
> I know[761] a rose beyond the Thames
> Where flowers are pale and few."

Goldring was disappointed in this poem[762] but does not take into account that there were two versions.

The symbol of the rose could have represented the vagina, and this sexual element may have given rise to Flecker's insecurity, resulting in two versions, which in turn gave the poem its unsatisfactory aspect to the poet and reader alike.[763] Rose is the name of the prostitute in the fragment of his play *The Poet's Tragedy*.

This feeling of dissatisfaction with his work continued with three more poems he wrote, revised or translated, after 'The Londoner' (in the *Bridge of Fire Copybook*). One translation was (on page 83) 'Mes Mânes a Clytie a Chénier', the last three lines of which are:

> It is my truant soul has left the sacred shore,
> That still would find thy mouth and know what quiet is;
> Weep, open out thy arms and render back the kiss.

The revising of the next poem 'Vox in Desertis' (on page 84) would bring back memories of past unhappy feelings.[764] It has the verse:

> I am no more the lover that I was,
> No more a lover poet and a lover gay;
> But a dark-girdled monk, bearing a cross
> Through deserts, for the memory of one day.

'The Ballad of the Queen's Bouquet',[765] with annotations by Beazley that tended to damp down the more extravagant words or phrases, is the story of the King whose heart is 'imperilled' by the wife of the Duke. The King tells the Duke:

> My Lord the Duke, not even I
> Possess a wife so splendid:
> Grant her to me: if you comply
> She shall be well attended.

The Duke obeys reluctantly, but one version of the poem ends with a sinister note of revenge:

> The Queen had bidden
> a bunch to be made [ordered to be made]
> of fragrant flower de luces,   [a bunch of] instead of
>   'fragrant'

| And such a heavy scent they had | [perhaps it was the scent they had] |
| That death befell the Duchess. | [the scent that killed the Duchess] |

Poetry writing was not going so well, but he had an opportunity to improve his friendship rating 'dans ce monde-ci' shortly after his return to Cambridge. On the evening of 23 October, he was admitted as a Full Member of the Fabians, alongside six others and three, who were being admitted as Associate Members, in front of an audience of eighty-seven in the hall of the Liberal Club in Downing Street, Cambridge. Hugh Dalton was in the chair, having taken over from Ben Keeling, as president.

An address was given by Reginald Bray of the LCC[766] on the subject of the 'School as a Sorting-House', and a long series of questions followed in which many interesting points were raised.[767]

This meeting, with its emphasis on education, combined with the fact that he was now a Full Member, brought to fruition his scheme on education, which he eventually called '*The Grecians*'. He had outlined it to Sedgwick, in a letter dated 24 September 1904.[768] Flecker's desire to read a paper to the Fabians on the subject of education could be just as strong as his wish to preserve his memories of his times with Jack, as the essay is set in Bologna and Florence.

In that same month of October, Professor Browne began his series of lectures on the history of Persia, which Flecker had attended as part of his course of studies. The lectures were illustrated by photographs, using an epidiascope. In the concluding lecture for the term, on 6 December, Browne introduced a phonograph, so that the audience could hear and follow the intonations of two Arabic poems – one was from the *Romance of Antara*, and the other by Abuyl-Fath-al-Busti was chanted by a modern Muhaddith, or professional storyteller of Cairo.[769]

Just previous to this particular lecture was a crowded and anxious month, in which Frank Savery came on a weekend visit and found his old friend busy with the third draft of *The King of Alsander*.[770] Savery would hear again of the holiday memories and the financial hardship, which combined to produce a poem in the *Bridge of Fire Copybook* dated 20 November 1908, p.88, entitled 'Dulce Lumen, Triste Numen, Suave Lumen Luminium'. It was based on his stay in Venice with Jack (much in the same way as he wrote 'Looking Eastwards' after his stay in Florence the year before).[771]

'Dulce Lumen' was published as 'A God in Venice' in *The Nation* on 27 February 1909. Unlike 'Looking Eastwards', 'A God in Venice' was revised with its original title from *The Bridge of Fire Copybook*, and was published again (but not in anthologies Flecker published during his lifetime).

'Looking Eastwards' and 'God in Venice' reflect feelings about his relationship with Jack at that time, and to some extent, his reaction to Florence and Venice. 'Looking Eastwards' was never reprinted.[772] Flecker's dissatisfaction with 'Looking Eastwards' when he came to consider it for republishing may have been because it was written against a background of a relationship he felt he had to keep hidden from Dean Close. When the impressions of Florence were in his mind, he did not know the outcome of he and Jack being together, so the relationship is not highlighted. In the poem, he writes:

> But I was lonely when the night winds came,
> And feared the ghosts that called me by my name,

'Dulce Lumen, Triste Lumen Luminium' was inspired by his 1908 visit to Venice with Jack; it is much more quietly confident.

Venice he described as:[773] 'The town whose flowers and forests are bright stone', and further on:

> All tall white palaces
> Sway all with dizziness;
> The bells pealed faintly, and the water stirred.

The poem ends:

> Come, friend! We travel on
> (That one brief vision gone)
> Bravely, like men who see beyond the skies.

He did not republish this poem in either of his anthologies, but there is no doubt that Venice delighted him, which may be as much due to his reading of Ruskin's *Stones of Venice*,[774] as to his closeness with Beazley. There is no real evidence that they travelled bravely together after the visionary experience. Visionary experience and sexual experience might have gone together in Venice, a favourite place for homosexuals from England who enjoyed the more permissive background. Sexual relations between men had been legal in Italy since the last decade of the nineteenth century.

Flecker's poem 'To Francis Thompson' has a similar idea, with a feeling that he kept his feet firmly on the ground after the visionary experience. The poem ends:

> Till shadows came and went before my eyes,
> And my raised glance beheld in deep review
> The legionary splendour of the skies.
> Which vision past, singing I went my way
> And tread the dusty roads of Earth to-day.[775]

The remaining part of 1908 was an unhappy time, despite his continued output of poems and his poetry appearing in magazines. '*The Nation* want another carol,' he had written to his parents".[776] Dean Close approved of their son's carols; 'Masque of the Magi' was sung annually by the School in December in preparation for Christmas.[777]

The Nation had published 'A Christmas Carol' in December 1907. (It was revised as 'The Masque of the Magi'). On 19 December 1908, *The Nation* published 'Joseph and Mary, a Christmas Carol in the old Manner' (which was revised as 'Joseph and Mary')[778]. 'Joseph and Mary' was written in the copybook in December 1908. Previously he had written 'Resurrection' on 10 November 1908, 'Dulce Lumen' on 20 November and 'The Lover of Jalalu'ddin' in December 1908. 'Corrumpus' he wrote in January 1909.

'Resurrection', a sonnet, was written as a result of seeing the fresco by Piero degli Franceschi at Borgo in the summer of 1908. Like 'God in Venice' he did not publish it in any of his anthologies. The poem is based on the painting of the risen Christ before the sleeping 'sons of war' who are urged:

> Sleep a little hour;
> Sleep! It were best ye saw not those bright eyes
> Prepared to wreck your world with errant flame,
> And drive strong men to follow mysteries.[779]

He did not appear to have submitted this sonnet to any publication, although he could have had it in mind for *The Nation*, when they had instead wanted a carol.

'The Lover of Jalalu'ddin' is another poem, this time a translation, written in December 1908[780], that he appeared to be dissatisfied with, as he did not publish it in his lifetime. As far as his notebooks show, there is no record of his having submitted it for publication, as he did most of his work at this time. The poem could not offend anyone, but there is a hidden Beazley factor. Although in the notebook there are no crossings out or alterations in Beazley's hand, it might have been that, in order not to embarrass Beazley and anyone who knew them both, he preferred to leave this poem out of the public eye for his lifetime.

The reason why he chose this particular poem,[781] which came through reading *Selected Poems from the Divani Shamsi Trabiz* by R.A. Nicholson (who eventually succeeded Professor Browne in the Chair of Arabic; the book had been published in 1898), to translate may have been the first glance at the lines which he rendered as:

> Over his face
> Flowed truant flames.

As he had written to Sedgwick about Beazley: 'when he lies on the hearthrug, his head almost in the fire'.[782]

But this memory of Beazley itself could be the cause of the dissatisfaction.[783] Gillanders states: 'His is not a literal translation, nor can it be said wholly to capture the mood, of the poem of Jalalu'ddin.'

There is evidence in another copybook, the *Second Book of the Prophet James* (BOD) that he struggled with two versions to achieve something better, such as 'as flames that shone/So shone his face.' (p.111–2)

Gillanders further suggests that Flecker's own phrases let the poem become 'reminiscent of Swinburne'[784] (and equally reminiscent of Beazley). The key to the dissatisfaction in Flecker's mind would be similar to the key Gillanders gives to the understanding of the Sufi poets: 'is that the verse of these poets human affections and earthly pleasures are given a spiritual meaning.'[785]

The human love is beautifully expressed in the part of the poem he translated and may have come more easily to him than the expression of spiritual meaning. The translation was a difficult task, and it is not surprising that the religious ecstasy is missing. He achieved this so much more confidently in 'God in Venice', signifying that the relationship with Beazley reached a peak in Venice, which they never again recaptured, even if they met each other from time to time. The relationship was in decline from the time they left Venice, and the translation of 'Jalalu'ddin', his first attempt from Oriental verse, only brought the fact to the front of his mind.

It is not hard to see why the poem 'Corrumpus', written January 1909, was not published in periodicals or featured in any of his anthologies in the poet's lifetime, or even after he was dead. The poem's subject is men and boys dying of venereal disease, and it contained the lines:

> I had not thought to see the young
> With trembling knees and twitching eyes
> Or a boy's brow with torment wrung,
> As he were old and wise.[786]

Exactly where the inspiration came from for this poem is not easy to discover,[787] nor is it easy to discern whether the men and boys were infected by women or men. The poem has an affinity with one by Beazley:[788]

> I know that many households keep[789]
> One born infirm and wrongly grown,
> A sorry man, a piteous heap
> Of creeping soul and crooked bone.

'Corrumpus' has the verse:

> Though I had met unholy shapes
> And men that should not have been born
> And monstrous things like twisted apes
> Imperfect and forlorn.

The subject matter, the grotesque element, the connections with Beazley's poem and perhaps his own ill-health could have made him too dissatisfied to consider it for publication.

The emotional turmoil and restlessness undermining his poetry composition was matched by physical restlessness and a desire to get away from Cambridge. A sudden journey to Paris in November 1908[790] was triggered off by an offer from the Count de Pimodan, a friend from Oxford days, in the shape of a possible travelling tutorship. There was no time to get permission from Dean Close in advance for this journey. Despite having a lot of work to do and lectures to attend, he went off on what proved to be a wild goose chase, as the people he wanted to see were in the country. After a wasted day he returned tired and miserable to Cambridge and the wrath of his mother.[791]

Another such journey at this time, of which Dean Close was not aware until he got back, was to Oxford to try and write in the Union Library, but this did not give him the stimulus to write swiftly and willingly. He also, at this point, faced disappointment over the publication of his poems and had to seek another publisher.

As if in some way to atone for his trip to Paris and his fruitless attempt to get a tutorship abroad, he took a tutorship at a Crammer's in Woking for the Christmas vacation. He endeavoured to make this work and the pupils he taught as interesting or amusing as he could in letters to his mother, and he emphasised the amount of work he was doing and the money he received, which was £6 for nine days working, counting Sunday.

He had to study Persian at the same time as tutoring and trying to do a few pages of his own writing. He was like a juggler, attempting to keep three parts of his life in the air at the same time, and this conflict could have been at the root of his depression. It is to be hoped that the 500 cigarettes he requested from his father (if they were available from Cyprus) eased the tension from time to time, even if he did not know the harm they would do to his already poor health.

He had a quarrel with his Turkish tutor at this time, which may have been a result of his despair and depression or just another factor to be added to it. He wrote to his parents in a letter[792] telling them that the Turk had abused him for coming in late, although he had sent a message to say he should be late as he was seeing Professor Browne. He swore that he would not be treated like a schoolboy (as he had often told his parents when they did likewise) and left the room. The lecturer was leaving at the end of term.[793] 'Sympathy all on my side'.[794]

The Turkish lecturer had a point. It was important that he attended his lectures regularly and on time, if he was to avoid failing his final examinations and the possible forfeiture of the £500 guaranteed by his father. Regular attendance at lectures would maintain his standard of work, and although the loss of the £500 was not automatic and Professor Browne was not in agreement with this form of penalty, it was still a possibility. Francis Toye, a student-interpreter, had returned his £500 on 15 October 1906, when he decided he did not want to continue the career planned for him.[795] This was the first time this sort of gesture had been made, unasked. Professor Browne, when told of Toye's decision, agreed that Toye was not really suited for embarking on this type of career. Browne himself had not continued with his first choice of career in medicine, so he could understand Toye's feelings on the matter of changing or abandoning his career. Toye instead pursued his interest in music, which had been encouraged while at Cambridge. Flecker did not receive the same sort of encouragement in his literary career. Toye, unlike Flecker, received understanding and consideration from his family, plus the means of deducting the £500 from his inheritance. There was no real alternative but to keep on the student-interpretership path, even more so now the rules had been changed so that failure in examinations could mean the loss of £500, whereas previously the forfeiture had only for those who did not stay in the service for five years from the date of appointment.[796] This change of rules was not an isolated instance. Since 1905, because of financial difficulties and inefficiency, more attempts had been made to reform university affairs. No doubt Toye's cheque caused a mild disturbance at the Foreign Office, and the new rule made the tutors uneasy about Flecker's approach to his studies, which was brilliant, but irregular in performance.[797]

Another complaint about the Turk was that he had been standing 'fizz' to all the second years and the first year had not come in for any.[798] The second year at that time contained Bernard Gilliat-Smith, also at Caius, and referred to by Boyce as a friend of both Flecker and himself. Gilliat-Smith, whose interests were in Romany, was born 20 October 1883 and educated in Bruges. Admitted as student-interpreter on 21 January 1907, he had got a Russian scholarship a year later and went into the Levant Consular Service a year ahead of Flecker. One student-interpreter, Gerald Holgate Selous – son of Edmund Selous and Fanny Maxwell and nephew of the African hunter, Frederick Courtney Selous (1851–1917) – was a friend of both Flecker and Woollcombe-Boyce.

A lecturer with whom he established a better relationship was Emile Audra (born 5 March 1883) in France, and educated at the Sorbonne. A research student and lecturer in French between 1908–11, he started at Caius six months after Flecker came to Cambridge. Boyce[799] tells of evenings with Audra, who was a leading light in the informal Cambridge University French Society, formed in the Michaelmas term 1908 to promote an interest in French literature, language, art and music. On the social side, where half the members were women, Audra gave a talk on modern music in France.

At Caius, Flecker was more successful in relationships with men (some older than he was) of Continental backgrounds and unusual interests, rather than those with more conventional backgrounds who were following a more usual path in life.

The Rupert Brooke circle also contained people who were also of less conventional backgrounds. Jacques Pierre Raverat (1885–1925) was a poet who had destroyed his verse. He was from the Sorbonne, and educated at Bedales, a progressive school, which put the main emphasis on acting, music, literature and the outdoor life. It was co-educational, unlike Dean Close. He was now at Emmanuel. Another ex-pupil of Bedales, and now of Emmanuel was Justin Brooke (1885–1963) (no relation to Rupert) who shared lodgings with Raverat, who due to ill-health had had to give up his studies. Justin Brooke had first interested Rupert Brooke in acting, and was at the heart of the neo-paganism surrounding Brooke. Raverat was in receipt of a letter from

Brooke: 'Cambridge is as ever; but now speciously arrayed in a pretence of heat and light green buds. Really, of course it is a swollen corpse, and we buzz on it like flies.'[800]

If this was so, then the flies were at risk of being caught in the web of Brooke, the attractive young spider. Some people, such as Hugh Dalton and Edward Marsh,[801] became entangled emotionally and were unable to free themselves long after Brooke was dead.

Flecker was not stuck in the emotional web spun, however unintentionally, by Rupert Brooke, either at Cambridge or afterwards. The main attraction of Brooke for Flecker lay in the fact that they both wrote poetry, and there was no doubt in his mind that his own poetry was the better by far.[802] Arthur Schloss was caught in the web; he admitted that he 'adored' Rupert Brooke. He and Brooke took their translations of 'Propertius' to their tutor, who said that Schloss's was better. Brooke was scarlet with rage.[803]

The Brooke/Flecker controversy became common knowledge.[804] Later the reasons for the conflict between them were attributed to the quick rise and decline in Brooke's poetry matched by the fact that Flecker's poetry took off in exactly the reverse order.[805] It is not known exactly which poems the two poets read to each other and discussed.[806]

The pattern of Flecker's working life continued, despite connections with the Brooke circle, in the early months of 1909, as it had done in the last months of the previous year. The work he had to undertake for his student-interpretership was considerable. He had to know something of English law. He had to acquire a thorough knowledge of Turkish, as well as a good understanding of Arabic and Persian. The possibility of conflict with Russia and the Near East meant he had to know a little Russian, the language he was best at and the lectures he attended most regularly. The lack of a Russian/English textbook[807] would not deter him from meeting the challenge of the complex Russian grammar; its nearness to Greek could be part of the reason why he was good at it. He also had a compelling drive to revise his novel, with the idea still in the back of his mind that he needed to earn money over and above what he would get when working for the Levant Consular Service, in Constantinople, when it would be reasonable of him to suppose that handouts from Dean Close would cease.

He was writing more poetry and giving more thoughts to his prose work and his membership of the Fabians. One poem written in February or March 1909, was 'Donde Estan? a Fragment', a translation of an unidentified Spanish poem.[808]

Flecker was unable to attend lectures between 10 February and 27 March because of illness. A medical certificate was sent by Professor

Browne to the Foreign Office,[809] a fact that came to be ignored when the Foreign Office reprimanded him later in the year on his poor attendance at lectures.

It is not surprising that he was depressed and feverish in February 1909. His rise in temperature was due to undiagnosed tuberculosis, triggered off by a crisis in his relationship with Beazley. Sherwood, when referring to this period, states that 'Flecker seems to have felt that Beazley was becoming too absorbed in his Greek vases – or perhaps by Maynard Keynes and his circle'.[810]

Maynard Keynes was back in Cambridge, and was having an affair in 1908 with Duncan Grant (1885–1978), painter and cousin of Lytton Strachey, who was in London, and he was still seeing Swithinbank. Keynes had been elected to a prize Fellowship at King's on 16 March 1909, which enhanced the admiration Beazley had for Keynes's cleverness.

Keynes, after first holidaying in Devon, spent the latter half of the Easter vacation (7–21 April) in Versailles, with Duncan Grant, where he had money to spend due to winning the Adam Smith prize of £60.

Flecker's Easter vacation was in the opposite direction and in stark contrast to the holiday of Keynes and friends. He spent the first part of the vacation alone and ill in Paris with what he thought was 'flu, Beazley and friends joined him after 'a ruinous doctor's bill' had to be paid. Beazley's presence helped him, but not financially, and he had to go back to England with scarcely any money for the fare. Who the other friends were, is not known, but Brooke can be ruled out, as he spent the vacation in England. It is not difficult to see that the Keynes's circle with its better health, more money and academic success attracted Beazley much more than the sick and penniless poet. When Beazley had been ill with a cold, Maynard Keynes had nursed him.

Maynard Keynes used his money to make loans to his friends, including Swithinbank and the Stracheys, until July 1905, when he began to invest his money.[811] Even if he did not lend money directly to Beazley, it is possible that funds lent to Swithinbank helped him also.

As March came in, the sensational disappearance of John Davidson was reported in the newspapers, and on 5 April a parcel was found containing manuscripts that appeared to represent Davidson's last book. On 9 April *The Times* announced evidence of Davidson's suicide. Swinburne died on 9 April 1909. Flecker wrote his 12-line elegy, 'Swinburne', dating it in *The Bridge of Fire Copybook*, April 1909, but he crossed the poem through, as if not satisfied with it. The poem, which could also have been an elegy for Davidson, began:

> At rest beside the waves is he
> Who mastered the wild song the sea,
> Who strung again the Ionian lyre, anew again
> As clear as light, intense as fire,

He struggled with another poem, which he dated 23 April 1909, in *The Bridge of Fire Copybook*. Also on the theme of death, it was 'The Town Without a Market', which he may have begun much earlier as Goldring recalls hearing it read to him by Flecker in the summer of 1907.[812]

'The Town Without a Market' from *The Bridge of Fire Copybook*, p.105, was revised before it was published in *The Nation*. *The Nation* version itself was revised before it was again published.[813] *The Nation* version begins:

> There lies afar behind a western hill
> A town without a market, white and still,[814]
> For six feet long and not a third as high
> Are those dense habitations. There stood I[815]
> Waiting to hear the citizens beneath
> Murmur and sigh and speak through tongueless teeth.

The influence of the East is also in the use of the word 'tongueless' in Eastwick's preface to 'The Gulistan' (p.5), there are two lines:

> If one His praise of me would learn,
> What of the traceless can the tongueless tell?
> Lovers[816] are killed by those they love so well;
> No voices from the slain return.

It was as if, at the start of Flecker's poem, he had stood in the vast cemetery on the outskirts of Cheltenham, on a hot summer's day, just like the ancient anonymous Chinese poet, who wrote 'The Elixir of Life' which began:

> Forth from the eastern gate my steeds I drive,
> And lo! a cemetery meets my view;
> Aspens around in wild luxuriance thrive,
> The road is fringed with fir and pine and yew,
> Beneath my feet lie the forgotten dead,
> Wrapped in a twilight of eternal gloom;
> Down by the Yellow Springs[817] their early bed,
> And everlasting silence is their doom.[818]

Gautier wrote his poem 'Le Comédie de la Mort', which has the setting of a bitter cold winter's day, in a cemetery in Paris, where the dead are not actually 'dead', but live on forgotten by the living.

Each citizen in 'The Town Without a Market' laments the loss of one particular facet of the world they once lived in. For one it is the bright lights and colour, and for another it is making no stir when he or she had enjoyed the violin and the dulcimer.[819]

The poet smiles at the restlessness of the dead:

> I smiled to hear them restless, I who sought
> Peace. For I had not loved, I had not fought
> And books are endless vanities, and strength[820]
> A gathered flower. ....

The poem in *The Nation* version ends on a hopeful note with the words:

> – and I seemed to know
> A timorous man buried long years ago.
> "I long to shape once more the thing that seems:"
> Master of all men, give me back my dreams.
> Give me my world that never failed before,
> The island hills, the dancing on the shore,

In the revised version it is:

> Give me that world that never failed me then,
> The hills I made and peopled with tall men.[821]

The poem in *The Nation* ends:

> If I must lose my fancy, let me live!

The 'Town Without a Market' is in contrast to Christina Rossetti's view of death in her poem 'Song':

> I shall not see the shadows,
> I shall not feel the rain;
> I shall not hear the nightingale
> Sing on, as if in pain:
> And dreaming through the twilight
> That doeth not rise nor set,

Haply I may remember,
And haply may forget.

'The veiled majesty and demure sorrow of Christina Rossetti proclaim her a recluse and a devotee' as Flecker had already written.[822]

Flecker did not, at that time, share John Davidson's desire to die. Flecker appreciated the joy of life and beauty, and the loss of sensations and joys lamented by the dead people in the poem could apply to him as sensations and joys he enjoyed and would hate to relinquish. Despite the pressures to earn a living, he did not appear to share the feelings of the Brooke circle who, before Davidson's body had been found, speculated that Davidson just might have faked his disappearance, so that he could escape the responsibilities of family life, middle age and the failure to earn a reasonable living by his writing. The faked suicide would prevent anyone attempting to find him, and return him to his old life of failure. The Brooke circle thought that Davidson could still be alive and enjoying life; the real motives behind the suicide were much more tragic.[823] The dream of escape from routine was something that fascinated the Brooke circle and they made plans to have a life without the burden of family responsibilities and the tedium of a daily office routine, so that they had a long life of never growing up until they reached the age of seventy, when there was presumably no need to face up to responsibilities and a second childhood could be contemplated.

John Davidson's body was fished out of the sea on Saturday, 18 September 1909. He was buried at sea on Tuesday, 21 September. The date of death on his coffin was 23 March 1909.

There was an unpublished fifth part of 'The Town Without a Market', written later (possibly 1909–1910) with the title 'The Lost Treasure':[824]

I said: 'I am young.' I was old,[825]
I declare 'I rejoice.' I was sad.
My treasure was faded gold
Dead leaves all the treasure I had.

I gather dead leaves still
For the brown will not fade as the green
And the grove that our memories fill
Is the only bright grove serene.

One rose from a tomb and sighed
I am blind, blind miserably,
And some of the men who have died

Began suddenly talking to me.

Davidson's body could have been found by the time Flecker wrote these lines. Later, in December 1909, seven of the Brooke circle went to a fancy-dress ball at the Slade Art School, the theme of the dance was Shelley's 'Ode to the West Wind', and they all went as the wind or leaves.

The Brooke circle, despite their studies, had ample time for these social events. They could also get out into the country. That, no doubt, made the thought of a more humdrum existence in the future, intolerable. They were magnificently unprepared as Frances Darwin said 'for the long littleness of life'.[826]

Flecker did not share the Brooke circle's view that marriage and children were an added burden; he envisaged two servants, in any case, to do the housework in his 'Nonsense Rhyme of Life', in *The Book of Kara James*:

> We'll have John to fetch and carry
> And Elizabeth to cook.

He wanted his future wife and children to accompany him on his journeys abroad, and sixty was the cutting off point, not seventy as in the Brooke circle. Any thoughts that ill-health or physical deterioration might prevent the enjoyment and freedom to live the life they wanted do not occur to Flecker or to the Brooke circle. But John Davidson is incorporated into both Brooke's and Flecker's thoughts for the future, Brooke quotes Davidson's lines:[827]

> Out of time and out of all
> While other sing through sun and rain
> Heel and toe, from dawn to dusk,
> Round the world and home again.[828]

In the 'Nonsense Rhyme of Life' Flecker has the line: 'Round the world and back again.'[829]

He did not go round the world and back again, in the early months of 1909, but as a result of a cross-country journey in April from Paris to Wotton Courtney, Somerset, where his father in the Easter vacation was taking the Sunday services in exchange for the use of the vicarage as a family holiday home, he wrote the poem which was entitled 'A Western Voyage' (p.109 in the *Bridge of Fire Copybook*).[830]

This theme of a journey from East to West and back to the past is one that was to feature in many subsequent poems. The poem also has a more optimistic approach to the fear of death. It begins with what could come to be realised as the Beazley factor, namely a reference to their relationship, which is not readily recognised by the reader as it is suitably disguised:[831]

> My friend the Sun – like all my friends
> Inconstant, lovely, far away,

Of all his friends, Beazley was the 'Sun', and his inconstancy was admitted in his own unpublished verse: 'And left old friends to follow with the newer'.[832]

A poem that contained more than a hint about his relationship with Beazley was 'Invitation' (originally 'The Invitation to Poetry'), and in case there is any mistake under the title are the words:

> 'To a Young but Learned Friend to Abandon Archaeology for the Moment, and play once more with his Neglected Muse."

Flecker abandoned the reference to the 'forlorn and deserted Muse' (and 'play' was originally 'try' in the *Bridge of Fire Copybook*, p.114).[833]

In the middle of the poem he laments:

> Lover of Greece, is this the richest[834] store
> You bring us, – withered leaves and dusty lore,
> And broken vases widowed of their wine.[835]

The poem seems just as much a lament for the fact that Beazley was turning his back on a goal they could share – establishing themselves as poets – as neglecting the friendship they had shared. 'Why are you so silent?' the poet asks his learned friend. As if harking back to Venice, he ends the poem with the lines:

> You who would ever strive to pierce beyond
> Love's ecstasy, Life's vision, is it well
> We should not know the tales you have to tell?

One version of this last line reads: 'That you are mute and have no tales to tell.'

Next to 'Invitation' in the *Bridge of Fire Copybook* is the poem 'Tramps', which Flecker revised in 1909, having written it originally in June 1905 (*Book of Kara James*). It, too, is about the past and happier times with Beazley, and also about travelling from 'sea to sea'. In one version he wrote:

> "Two dusty* tramps are we, *[originally 'bristly']
> Our clothes are torn* well, worn well *[originally 'are
> rent and torn – all]
> We go [Trudge] from sea to sea,
> From Sutherland to Cornwall.
>
> We cross mountains, vallies,
> To Edinburgh city,
> Where palace crowds on palace,
> And children plead for pity.[836]

The next verse is:

> On Skiddaw's height
> Still gleams the sunset fire.
> We turn towards the night
> To visit Lancashire.

[Two songs of Two Wanderers, p.86–7, Book of Kara James.]
This verse is reminiscent of the last lines of the poem 'The Armada' by Macaulay:

> Till Skiddaw saw the fire that burned on Gaunt's
> embattled pile,
> And the red glare on Skiddaw roused the burghers
> of Carlisle.

A poem 'Tramps' was published in a proposed Vol.1 of *The Tramp*, in May 1909. 'Tramps' had eight verses, and formed the main plank in the theme of the magazine, which in its introductory note asked for the support of the principal railway companies of Great Britain. The support was asked for by the 'editors' who hoped that the 'literary tone' and general excellence of production would ensure a long circulation![837]

Flecker's attitude to life at Cambridge was more optimistic after his Somerset holiday which might have made his parents feel that this was due to their influence.

Despite the emphasis on his relationship with Jack, members of the Brooke circle and Dean Close, his poetry reflected that he was working to improve his foreign language skills. On 25 April he wrote[838] 'Lord Arnaldos', a translation of an anonymous Spanish ballad romance 'Del Corde Arnaldos'[839]. It was about 'the strangest of adventures', which happened to Lord Arnaldos on mid-summer's day when he was out hunting. He sees a little ship close to the shore. The person sailing the ship is singing and Lord Arnaldos asks what song it is. The answer is:

> I only tell my song to those
> Who sail away with me.[840]

As well as the poem 'Lord Arnaldos', he was revising in June (according to the *Bridge of Fire Copybook*), a gentle and simple poem, 'Gravis, Dulcis, Immutable' (grave, immutable sweet voice of yours), which he had begun in 1907, as a sonnet entitled 'The Resolve'. 'The Resolve' began:

> My fancy once rode with eagle wings,
> In quest of Fear, and fear I caught and slew:[841]

He also wrote 'The Unyielding Maid' (p.119) and a poem he entitled 'Indifferent and free translation for music of Goethe's "Die Sprode".'

In contrast to the dreamy 'Lord Arnaldos' poem and the wistful 'Gravis, Dulcis', a poem written on 7 June was the rousing 'War Song of the Saracens', which was inspired by his Cambridge course (now much on his mind as he had examinations to take in August). He knew failure was a possibility; success in writing, translating and publishing verse was no safeguard against disappointing examination results, as Brooke could prove to him. Brooke sat for the Classical Tripos, the last exam, on 28 May, and in June took rooms at The Orchard, Grantchester. His rooms consisted of a sitting room, bedroom, use of the river-garden, and all his meals for 30s. a week. Brooke got the results of the Tripos and learned he had been awarded a second class, when he hoped, rather unrealistically, for a First, not fully realising that the second was obtained by the skin of his teeth.

Brooke's disappointing results could have been due to a subconscious wish to fail examinations, so that he could pursue his desire to be a successful poet. In this respect his and Flecker's examination disappointments could be seen to have a parallel.

Brooke had added pressures at that time, unlike Flecker. He had taken over the presidency of the Cambridge University Fabians from Dalton.

Emotionally, Brooke was involved with Noel Olivier (1892–1969), a young schoolgirl who was at Bedales, the daughter of Sir Sydney Olivier, Governor of Jamaica, founder of the London Fabians. Brooke had first met Noel on 10 May 1908, in Ben Keeling's rooms. Brooke was also in a fever at the prospect of meeting the writer Henry James who came to Cambridge on 11 June. The following day Henry James had lunch at Pembroke in Keynes's rooms, and Rupert Brooke was introduced to him. James was bewitched by Brooke, and as a result of this meeting, Brooke continued a friendship with Henry James in London. On Sunday 13 June Henry James had breakfast with Maynard Keynes at King's, which it was said Henry James did not enjoy – the poached egg was cold, the bacon too thick and large and he was bewildered by the conversation going on around him. It is to be hoped that, if this was true, when James got back to 8 Trumpington Street, his host's home, and Rupert Brooke joined him for coffee in the garden, James felt happier. On Monday 14 June, he was poled in a punt by Rupert Brooke in white shirt and white flannels, for more than an hour.[842]

Flecker was not included in these parties and meetings arranged for Henry James, but he was in any case, planning to leave Cambridge on 14 June and stop off in Oxford for a day or two before arriving in Cheltenham on 16 June, and returning to Cambridge early in July. He outlined these plans to his parents, after explaining that he had been busy and Jack had been up for the weekend.[843] He writes in this letter: 'I shall stay with you until I come back here – but don't know how early in July that will be.'[844]

An addition to these plans must have taken place, as he stayed with Birrell at the end of the May term and sent a postcard to his parents dated 1 July from Kensal Rose: 'Have a most lovely bedroom, 6s, for five days with bath. Had a very pleasant time with Birrell; saw their house, which is beautiful.'[845] Flecker was not a house guest at the Birrell home and as usual he gave details of the cost of a room.

A sour note was creeping into Brooke' relationship with Flecker. He told James Strachey, who was going to a job as private secretary to his cousin, the editor and proprietor of *The Spectator* (a publication to which his brother Lytton had contributed many book reviews and essays): 'Lunch with Flecker to-day was simply Hellish – old cold bloaters, sardine paste, and the relics of your gooseberries – oh, and dirty! hairs in the butter! soot in the cream! Why does he creep so!'[846] Brooke was himself not noted for tidiness in his Grantchester rooms.[847]

Brooke, who was living on strawberries and honey in a garden packed with roses, might feel the lunch in Flecker's room in town was something to grumble about consciously, but rather unfairly. As for 'creeping',

Flecker was hardly creeping when he came to visit Brooke, dressed in flannels, with a garland of red flowers on his head, poling a canoe up the river at night, the lanterns on the bow and stern showing him to the way to the Orchard.[848],[849] The reasons for the visit and the lunch could have been in connection with the reading of a paper by Flecker, which he called 'Education, a dialogue' at the first of two meetings of the Fabian Society in King's College, in the Long Vacation. The meetings were not so well attended as they might have been. The minutes[850] were signed by Rupert Brooke, the President. At the second meeting, A. Watkins of St. John's, read a paper on Socialism and Practical Politics. After a beautiful June, July was a very hot month and 'Socialism and Practical Politics' might not have been at the forefront of Brooke's mind in his cool river retreat.

Augustus John, with his large family, encamped in the neighbouring field by the river, while John painted in College a portrait of Jane Harrison, now a fellow of Newnham and who, like John, had an unconventional reputation. Brooke's visitors, who included Gilbert Murray and Edward Marsh, were taken to meet John. Alongside these older people of a Bohemian nature and academic brilliance, Flecker, as a friend of Brooke, might appear almost dull, which may have accounted for some of the sour note, although Brooke's remarks about Flecker could be in some sort of code, and he was to reverse them later.

Donald Robertson (1885–1961) a Fellow of Trinity (1909) (and a future professor of Greek, Cambridge), with Brooke and Dudley Ward (1885–1957), a Fellow of St. John's College (1909), went up the river with the children of Augustus John and entertained them and had tea.[851]

Robertson, with Flecker and W.N. Ewer, a poet, on a return journey by punt from Grantchester, were overtaken by a fierce thunderstorm. Ewer recalled that Flecker waved the pole about and chanted Greek verse.[852]

While Brooke and friends relaxed, Flecker stayed on in Cambridge to study for his examinations, but he still had time to write poems, mainly translations. In July 1909 he wrote his poem 'The Parrot',[853] a rendering from Florida XII of Apuleius which is a witty poem spoken by an old Professor of Zoology. It contains references to:

> .... Like boys they beat at school, [originally
>   'in school']
> Soon learn to recognise a Despot's rule.
>
> Master of all men, give me back my dreams.

A note in the *Bridge of Fire Copybook* on the page on which 'The Parrot' is written reads: 'Too ill to copy this, *Cambridge Review* 1909. Suggested by Ashley Jolly, eh what.' [In Beazley's handwriting]

It is suggested[854] that in writing 'The Parrot' Flecker may have intended to 'hit at' H.E. Butler (a Fellow of New College, Oxford) whose translation of Apuleius' shorter pieces (Oxford 1909) is notably pedestrian. It is understandable that he might feel the need to 'hit at' Oxford life and the security of tenure enjoyed by a Fellow of New College, while he sat in the heat of his Cambridge rooms and studied, uncertain of the outcome and his future.

Another translation from Machiavelli, undertaken in the same month was 'Opportunity' (although the page in the *Bridge of Fire Copybook* on which he wrote a version of 'Opportunity' has been torn out). The poem outlines the swiftness of opportunity and how it is not possible to clutch it, before it is gone beyond recall, especially those who have, 'Busied with thoughts and fancies vainly grand,'.

Another poem written in July 1909 was 'The Ballad of Camden Town', a modern ballad in Davidson style, and similar to 'Ballad of the Londoner'; it had alterations by Beazley.[855] It, too, had elements of regret in it, ending with the lines:

> Once more together we will live,
> For I will find her yet:
> I have so little to forgive;
> So much, I can't forget.

But the room the poet and Maisie share in 'The Ballad of Camden Town' is in stark contrast to Flecker's cluttered room in Cambridge. The room is described as:

> A bed, a chest, a faded mat,
> And broken chairs a few,
> Were all we had to grace our flat
> In Hazel Avenue.

The room in this flat is more like the sickrooms of his experience, or the sanatorium of a school, or the cheap Continental hotel rooms he shared with Beazley. Maisie leaves the poet when he is ill, as Flecker was left alone by his mother as a child, and by Beazley in Paris. Maisie leaves him for good, but the relationship here resembles the relationship between Flecker and Beazley: one in the partnership had to creep away and leave the other not able to explain fully the reason why. The poem contains the line: 'She left the latchkey on its nail'. This latchkey symbol suggests a suspension of sexual relations between the poet and his lover: they could come back together again. There is also the symbol of the broken lily in the ballad, in the fourth line of the eighth verse: 'And clasp the broken lily', which leaves no doubt at this stage, that the poet's lover was female. This seems to show the influence of Chinese poetry, or if the lily is used as a womb-like symbol, then the poet's lover had given birth to a child, or had at least been pregnant at some time.[856]

In the corrected proofs he submitted to the Adelphi Press for his book *Thirty-Six Poems*, Flecker seems to have trouble with the fourth verse, which is scored out and reads:[857]

> ~~hiding~~ dwelling
> "And yet I dream her ~~living~~ still (And yet[858]
> In some dark thoroughfare,
> And often walk to Primrose hill [sic]
> And hope to find her there."[859]

This is crossed out and the following verse inserted:

> I dream she dwells in London still
> And breathes[860] the evening air
> And often walk to Primrose Hill,
> And hope to meet her there.

It seems that there is some uncertainty in the poet's mind when submitting the poem for publication, whether he is writing about a male lover or a female one (the 's' before the 'he' is just a blot – the version in the copybook is very clear what is meant). The poet could be writing about a dead or living love. But he was satisfied with the fourth verse:

> But I could walk to Hampstead heath,
> And crown her head with daisies,
> And watch the streaming world beneath,
> And men with other Maisies.

The reference to 'men with other Maisies' could be a veiled reference to Beazley, as he had written a poem about a 'Maisie'[861] in the notebook copied out in Flecker's hand (now in the Bodleian).

He wrote to Frank Savery, after the publication of *Thirty-Six Poems*: 'In my old style poems – the tourniquets, cinnabar, portcullis, and all the rest of it of Bathrolaire just delight in welding the so absurd words and the sentimental humour of men with other Maisies all one piece – but sentimental humour to be clearly expressed – in the Roman way.'[862]

This reference to sentimental humour could be something of a smokescreen as, although the poems in the Beazley notebook have no precise dates, it is thought they were written around 1905, when Savery, Beazley and Flecker were up at Oxford. As Savery read Flecker's poems and heard him talk about his plans for future poems and as Beazley and Flecker met first in Savery's rooms, he may have had an inkling of the content of the poems Beazley was writing or intended to write.

A verse in 'The Ballad of Camden Town', which remains unpublished and is crossed out in the *Bridge of Fire Copybook* reads:

> Oh Maisie, I am stronger now,
> And cursed with years and old:
> Come back to me and kiss my brow
> Before your lips be cold.

The idea outlined in the unpublished verse comes nearer to the view of Beazley, to the future of the Beazley/Flecker relationship, than that of Flecker. Flecker already knew his time was short. He did not see the point of saving money for some old age that would never come, so he would see even less necessity to save love for old age which would never come. Flecker had made some concession to old age: the opening lines referred to 'long years back' in the sense that these adventures were not part of his life at the time the poem got into print.

Beazley had expressed his feelings about his relationship with someone who had given him love in a poem. He kept his love hidden like a miser, to be taken out when in need or despair. The poem comes closest to letting anyone who reads it know of his real feelings for Flecker, and the outcome:

> Your gift, the ruby Joy-of-Love
> I'll never tell you gave it me,
> But like a miser lock it up
> Deep in my heart where none can see;
> So when I'm old and needing rest
> And tired and full of misery
> I'll wander to the guarded chest,
> And Joy-of-Love shall comfort me.

Love-Happiness, the rose you gave
I shall not wear in vanity,
But earth the roots and water it
And keep it still a living tree:
So when a captive of Despair
Though dead and damp the prison be,
I shall not sicken for the air,
Love-Happiness will solace me.

Your dark red phial. Pride of love
I shall not squander carelessly,
To make a little joy seem great
A little sorrow light to me,
But called to battle, led to death,
Scorning to shrink or bend the knee,
Bury? glory with a little breath;
For Pride – of love shall strengthen me."

Beazley's poem revealed that he did not see Flecker living to a serene old age, but when old age came to Beazley, the love they had once shared would be something to contemplate and ease the isolation of old age. Old age would bring the end of Beazley's youth and beautiful looks, as Flecker wrote in 'Gravis Dulcis Immutabilis':

I dread your perishable gold:
Come near me now; the years are few.
Alas, when you and I are old
I shall not want to look at you;

Flecker was also at this time at work on revising 'The Grecians', which he first entitled 'Phulakes New and Original Dialogue in Education', then he crossed through the words 'Phulakes New and Original' in the first draft, which he wrote in two notebooks (without the preface), both with the address near King's Lynn where he joined his family. He finished the 100 pages of 'The Grecians' and in early August he went to Cambridge to sit his examinations. It is not surprising that he wrote on 9 August from Jesus Lane, to his parents[863] that he was exhausted with overwork. He was honest enough to admit to his parents that it was difficult to try and do during the exam what he ought to have done during the past year. The exam finished on the 10 August. He told his parents he intended to take a good rest before returning to join them, and not return before the weekend unless they especially wanted him.[864]

Flecker travelled by train from King's Lynn in Norfolk, on the east coast, to the Fabian Summer School in North Wales, on the west coast, towards the end of August, and the journey again inspired him to begin to write: [865]

I ride on shining rails
Along the road to Wales[866]

and

The Eastern Sea that was so cold and blue
I saw beneath me from the Norfolk Hill.[867]

The poem he tried to write, like the sun's progress from the east coast of England to the Welsh shore, was much crossed out and rewritten.[868] It reflected conflicting feelings about this period of his life and the journey itself. 'A Western Voyage' (which he had completed earlier and was eventually published), was obviously more satisfactory to him. In 'A Western Voyage' he is going towards the hills he knew and he had hope as he looked forward to his holiday. The journey to the Summer School, although it was to Wales, which he already knew and loved, was not to the Wales of his evangelical summer camps or times with Jack. In fact, he should really have spent six weeks on the Continent that summer and, having failed to do so, faced going there both at Christmas and Easter.

It is not surprising that the surviving part of the poem (inspired by his journey from Norfolk to the Fabian Summer School) is the part that eliminates his Cambridge self, and embodies the vision of the long dead past. He appeared to be satisfied with this, as it was the only part he eventually published.[869]

The basis of this poem is the legend of the drowned lands off Wales and the submerged part of Carnarvon Bay.[870] The remainder of the draft poem (in the Rough Copybook) contains references in more than one version to: 'The Eastern Sea that was so cold and blue'. And in another version: 'I saw the Dawn as cold as steel/Rise from the Norfolk Sea'.

The coldness related to the chill of early morning, and the atmosphere in Norfolk with his family, which at this stage in the writing of the poem was unlikely to be warm. But eventually these particular references are eliminated and a version without any revisions and corrections begins:

I rose from one sea to another sea
I crossed the breadth of England in a day
I saw the dawn upon the Eastern sea
I saw the noon day blaze in Birmingham

And another version about the middle of the journey is:

On Wolverhampton's filth and fire [871,872]
Low hangs this smoky noon[873]

It is unlikely that the train journey from King's Lynn to North Wales gave Flecker the opportunity to breathe the smoke and see the furnace fires of the Midlands, so clearly. This image of the Midlands came from an earlier period at Uppingham, which he had already incorporated in his 'Tramps', which has references to the 'Midland Plain' (in one version) and to 'black gates', 'furnace leaps aflare' where 'We watch the women' who are 'Weary but still fair' (*Bridge of Fire Copybook*, p.117) published in Vol.1 *The Tramp*). It is possible that his journey through the Midlands was with Beazley, and hidden from Dean Close, or that he had made a visit to see Savery in Birmingham while still at Cambridge. Whatever the reason, the Midlands did not have happy associations, and in leaving the 'Midlands' lines out of 'The Welsh Sea', the poem was much more satisfactory.

The last stanza of 'The Welsh Sea' begins:

Listen for like a golden snake,
The ocean ~~moans shines~~ twists and stirs,
And whispers how the dead men wake
And call across the years.[874]

This was eventually changed to:

Listen, for like a slow green snake
The Ocean twists and stirs,[875]

It would seem better if he had left 'moans' in the second line, as this makes more sense after the word 'Listen'; snakes do not moan, nor the ocean for that matter (unless he was thinking of Alfred Lord Tennyson's – '... moaning of the bar'), and at first glance, the motion of the surface of the sea is not exactly similar to the movement of a snake. But, it is said, that during an eclipse of the sun 'the earth's shadow rushing towards you across the land ripples with the reflections of the

254

earth's atmosphere like snakes.'[876] His summer holidays in Wales could have given him the opportunity to see an eclipse, or as the poem is set in late evening ('evening waves or starlit waves' are used in different versions), that Flecker saw the effect of the moonlight on the waves, which reminded him of the skin of a snake.

The poem was begun originally as a result of his holiday in Wales in 1904, when he was rereading *Snake Worship*, 'an interesting book somewhat old now'.[877,878] Also, five years later, when Flecker's knowledge of languages had increased, along with his knowledge of different cultures such as Chinese, Arabic and Hebrew (languages and cultures that interchange the word 'magic' for the word 'snake'), Flecker used snake to describe the sea, instead of a rather over-worked word 'magic'. Snake conveys so much more. He cherished 'a most marvellous enamel snake ring...'.[879]

Magic can have two faces, and so can the memory of being in love. One face is delightful and entertaining, while the other face can bring sadness that it is only illusion, and it will not last. The golden snake can be beautiful, but the slow green snake can have more sinister undertones, associations with slime and jealousy. The snake can slip out of its skin, and leave it behind. The surface of the sea would ever change. Relationships were ever changing, but they would call across the years to him. He would no longer dance 'upon the golden beach/ that once was golden corn' (which he changed to 'yellow beach' and 'yellow corn', and although this was because he thought golden an overworked word in his poetry, yellow is also the colour of extroverts and cowards, and like green is the colour of treachery). In one version of this poem (*Bridge of Fire Copybook*, p.131), he has the line: 'There like a green and golden snake'.

He could no longer himself 'dance upon the yellow beach' like the dead people of long ago (he himself may have never danced, but he had ridden a bicycle along the sands with Beazley during their Welsh holiday).[880] Flecker had removed, under Beazley's, influence the lines: 'The island hills, the dancing on the shore' from 'The Town Without a Market'. Flecker may not have fully realised how much this poem ('The Welsh Sea') concealed and how much it revealed. But as far as Beazley was concerned, it would seem he wanted not only to break away from the relationship, but to deny that certain more light-hearted aspects of it had ever existed.

The Fabian Summer School, even if it was by the Welsh sea, was unknown territory, and he was a latecomer; the Summer School had been open even before the official opening day, 24 July, so popular was it. The earlier opening also fitted in with the Labour Demonstrations at Blaenau Ffestiniog on 23 July.

Pen-yr-Allt, the main house, had been taken for three years and opened first as a Summer School at the end of July 1907. It was a big house, which had once been a school, and was then not completely furnished; the Fabian Committee provided eating utensils and beds. The house could be used at other times in the year by the Fabians, mainly at Christmas, Easter and Whitsun. For those who could not get accommodation in the main building, rooms could be taken in the village, in a stable or farmhouse, or they could camp out at night and listen to the quiet murmur of the river.

There were lectures to attend, which included such subjects as 'Problems of our Eastern Empire and Elementary Socialism' (given by Hugh Dalton), but by the time Flecker arrived, the Rupert Brooke contingent had left (although Frederic 'Ben' Keeling arrived later, for a week, having taken time off from his activities at Walworth Road).[881] It was unlikely that Flecker wanted to settle down to more lectures or study, or had energy left for the Swedish drill or much in common with the crowds of people there; some were suffragettes recently released from prison.

Flecker would more likely have turned to mountains, dense woods, the sea and rivers for enjoyment, even if the rain fell quite often and so prevented as much open air enjoyment as he would have liked. Keeling said 'one or two tramps in the mountains were blessed'.[882]

The bathing was not very safe, and Robert Lorraine (1876–1935), with a close friend, G.B. Shaw, had nearly drowned the year before.

Informal gatherings took place in the evenings, and these included dances. For one dance he borrowed a torch from Jessie Holliday,[883] which he lost and did not return to her. Poetry sessions were also included. He did not shine, as at one of them, W.R. Titterton was judged the better poet.[884]

If Flecker could not find admiration and appreciation as a poet, then he needed to find that he could succeed elsewhere. It was on the grass tennis courts at Pen-Yr-Allt, in bare feet (either because he had forgotten to pack his tennis shoes,[885] or he wanted to emulate Brooke, who played in bare feet to get nearer to Nature) that he attracted the admiration and appreciation of Eleanor Finlayson, who was eighteen months younger and a beauty of the Burne-Jones type, artistic and charming. 'I will spare you all the recital of her virtues and charms', he wrote on September 17, from Llanbedr to his parents in Norfolk, when telling them he was engaged to Eleanor.[886]

The Summer School was a place where engagements were made so that they could be broken the following year. It was an ideal setting in which to shock their elders by: 'stealing out on the moor and the sand, in stable, or under the hayricks without the requisite chaperone to make it look wholly innocent as it really is....conversation is most surprisingly open. "Is dancing sexual?" I found a pretty Cambridge girl graduate discussing with half a dozen men. But mostly talk of economics and political science.'[887]

It was unlikely that Eleanor Finlayson and Flecker talked about economics or political science. Time together was far too short, before each was back in an environment where the sexes did not mix on such an equal footing.

Perhaps he had first seen her, before the tennis encounter, like Peronella in *The King of Alsander*. [888]

'Seated at the window charmingly dressed in white and rose, with the sun on her face and neck and naked arms, with light playing with those said marvellous arms of hers and making all the little downy hairs on them sparkle.'

Or they came together first by something much more mundane – the surnames Flecker and Finlayson were together alphabetically in the lists of members at the Summer School?

It can be concluded that the letter was a bit of a shock, so much so that it is said[889] to have 'miscarried', which may have been a cover-up to explain why there was no immediate response. It must have reached them at some stage as it is printed in full, with proof of its non-arrival in the form of a letter written from Dean Close, but not dated: 'Ten minutes to write in. I suppose you never got my letter! Bother, I wanted you to see her in town. I have to go and see her people, Mother and sisters only. And do ask her here for about the 20th.'[890]

A letter that did not go astray was addressed to Mary Hankinson,[891] at the Fabian Camp. He wrote it from 5 Bramerton Street, Chelsea on 16 September:

5, Bramerton St.,
Chelsea S.W.

Dear Miss Hankinson,

I thought I would like to write you a line to say how sincerely grateful I am to you for all your kindness to us of the Englishman's home at the Fabian Camp. And also I feel how delightful everyone was to – us! I hope this letter will find its way to you: it is a little letter – but it means a lot of gratitude.

Love [?]

Yours very sincerely,
James Elroy Flecker." [892]

1909 September 16

Any comment from his parents on the engagement was sufficiently low key to give no real indication of how they reacted to the news.[893]

The next letter from him, which they quoted, was about the engagement ring which was especially made with a black opal.[894] If the first letter really had gone astray, it could have surfaced at this stage. His parents were aware that Eleanor had £400 a year of her own 'so we need not wait'.[895] Flecker wanted his father to marry them before they went to Constantinople. No doubt there was a sigh of relief in Dean Close when they heard about Eleanor's money; at least they knew they would not have to contribute towards the cost of a wife, salary from the Foreign Office notwithstanding.

There is no doubt what Eleanor's mother thought about the engagement: she said how much she liked Roy, who would make a good and kind husband for her daughter, and she thought they had many interests in common, although she felt he was young for the responsibility he was taking on. 'We all find Roy such good company,' she concluded.[896]

In a letter to Savery, undated but postmarked in Cheltenham on 30 September 1909* Flecker tells him: [897]

I have written a book on education which I can't get published just yet, and sundry poems and tale in the eastern style which is a beauty. I have done nothing exciting this vac. except getting myself engaged to a certain Miss X... whom I met at the Fabian Camp, to the wild delight of my people, and complete satisfaction of myself. We shall not marry unless we find we are still suited to each other in the spring. I think it will be a success. She is eighteen months younger than I, very pale face and blue eyes. As a matter of fact I am damned fond of her; she will make a damned good comrade, is an enthusiast for my writing and never disturbs my work.'

His tale in the eastern style was most probably 'Mansur' and his pride was justified.[898]

It might have been prudent, also, to have got in touch with the Brooke circle, who, although a warmer note had crept into the relationship[899],

258

appeared to be under some misunderstanding about the Flecker/Finlayson engagement. In a letter to Hugh Dalton, from Rugby on 21 September, Brooke wrote:

> 'I remember noting something in your letter about Dodd [900] and Flecker marrying each other. I suppose it is all for the best ....' [901]

The name 'Mansur' may have been taken from the famous Huseyn Mansur-i-Hallaj, who was put to death for advancing the extreme doctrine of the Sufis, a martyr-ecstatic of whom Nesimi was a devout follower.[902]

Flecker's story can be read with enjoyment, even if the reader is not familiar with the Turkish and Arabic studies that inspired the tale. The story tells of Mansur, appointed by the Sultan of Turkey to be Captain of the Escort to go to China with a fairly expensive present for the King. The Sultan says:

> 'Mansur will be pleased with the honour, and cease tormenting my ears with his uninteresting tales of oppression in the provinces.' [903]

Mansur and Flecker had similar attitudes to their destinies, both appeared to accept their missions to leave their native soil without too much question.[904] If their mission succeeded then, as the Sultan said, 'glory will accrue to me', and if not 'peace be on his soul'. Mansur consists of two interwoven stories, the serious with the humorous. The main source for these stories was Gibb's *History of Ottoman Poetry*. But a thread of Flecker's own feelings about leaving Cambridge, and the study of Oriental languages, is worked into the fabric of Mansur.

Mansur, before he leaves on his journey to China, spends very little time saying goodbye to his wife and son. If wife and son can be seen as representing Beazley, Eleanor and his parents, then separation and saying farewell to them would not cause real regret and heartache. He would after all, be seeing them again. Beazley if he was in Athens, and Eleanor might still join him in Turkey. His real regret was in leaving the books and the library and the opportunity to study in Cambridge.

He had the same rights as graduates to borrow books from the University Library. The scholarship at Cambridge was being snatched away from him, and unlike Mansur he knew he would never have the same opportunity to study there again. As Mansur says: 'For these books were in Persian, in Arabic, and in Ottoman, and they were written on fine paper of Samarkand by Beber, and Mustafa the son of Qaf and Ashiq of Baghdad; sumptuous were the tail-pieces and charming the illustrations.'[905]

Mansur wanders about the cool library for an hour wondering which book would be a fit companion for the long journey to China. He selects *Divan of Nesimi* (the story of Nesimi is outlined in Mansur), and later when the *Divan Of Nesimi* is taken away by officials, Mansur sings aloud a song from the lost Divan loved by voyagers, the last two lines of which are:

> My body is the holy glass where eighteen
> thousand aeons pass:
> I talk the language of the stars, I hold
> the secret of the sea.[906]

The time spent by Mansur in the library contrasts with the short time spent bidding farewell to his wife and son. This could be seen as a touch of Flecker humour, but many a true word is spoken in jest. Even if Flecker did not like the town of Cambridge, the library there contained all the magic and wisdom of the East he needed, without having to go there to work for a living, or so he might think at this stage. The disillusionment he was to encounter was already a real possibility to him, and can be seen in some of the poems he wrote, or decided not to publish, before he left for Constantinople. He might see himself, like Mansur, having a chance to go to China from Turkey, but he might know that this was one dream very unlikely to come true, especially if he married Eleanor – a 'Society' woman would not want to travel so adventurously to a place where there could be little 'Society'. Flecker would realise, as Mansur was to find, that the best part of his journey was to be his return, but he was not likely to find his library swept and dusted as Mansur had done. He was even more unlikely to encounter the tall young man, called Joyful Heart, who would magically get him back home. The story reveals Flecker's view of the evils of power and orthodox religion, but in the story the sweetness of life endures and spiritual experience would not be crushed. The library at Cambridge had books on politics, and these might be the 'uninteresting tales of oppression in the Provinces' referred to in Mansur, or, if there had been conflict with Dean Close about his membership of the Fabians, then the knowledge that their son was going to Turkey would mean that Dean Close (or Flecker himself) would be free of tales of the oppressed but he could have heard these tales, already himself. It was still possible for children to die of malnutrition in Cambridge, at that time.

The order in which he imparted the news to Savery in his letter, and what he leaves out, is interesting. His hope of getting his book on education (*The Grecians*) into print was as high on his agenda as the hope of getting married. His pride in the tale of the eastern style was something he wanted to get across to Savery before he broke the news of his engagement. The reference to not marrying unless they were still suited, indicates that the initial excitement of getting engaged and planning a wedding had worn off. This could be due to emotional or practical considerations. A letter from the Foreign Office dated 13 September, drew attention to the fact that his attendance at lectures and his work were not of a sufficiently high standard to make sure his services would be retained.[907] The formal reprimand, coming as it did between the letter to his parents and the letter to Savery, could account for the change of tone between the writing of the two epistles dealing with the engagement and marriage plans. In the letter to his parents 'I am so much in love' becomes 'I am damned fond of her' in Savery's letter, and 'so we need not wait; but hope you will marry us before we go to Constantinople' is changed to 'We shall not marry unless we find we are still suited to each other in the Spring'. He would write differently to Savery about the engagement, but allowing for this, it would seem that the Foreign Office letter did shake him, and he might have thought it prudent to sow the seeds of a possible breakdown of marriage plans or a postponement should he get the chance to sit the exam again in a year's time. It would seem more acceptable to tell the world that two people were not to marry as planned because they no longer suited each other, rather than that the bridegroom had failed to meet the requirement of the Foreign Office through not attending lectures, and was now not in a financial position to suit his prospective bride.

The references to parents' 'wild delight' (in his letter to Savery announcing his engagement) was obviously an exaggeration, although Dean Close could not help but hope that Jack Beazley would be playing a smaller part in their son's emotional future.

For Flecker's deeper feelings about Eleanor herself (as opposed to his feelings about her physical attractiveness, her £400 a year, and the fact that she would alleviate possible loneliness in Turkey), it would be best to read *The King of Alsander*. Some of Peronella's characteristics are near to Eleanor's. Although he began to write the novel before they met, it was revised and rewritten more than once. Eleanor played the violin, Peronella the piano. Both were attractive women, and the letters of Eleanor's name (by accident or design) when mixed up, form the bulk of Peronella's. Peronella had blue eyes like Eleanor.[908] Norman (a name not unlike Herman) tells her:

"How bright your eyes are!"

"Are they? What colour do you think they are?" she asked turning them full on him.

"They are blue. I have never seen such blue eyes in my life before."

"You're quite sure that they are not green?"

Norman was not at all sure that they were not; they seemed to him to change colour like little bright clouds, and shone at that moment like a lustrous emerald.[909]

The mother of Peronella is not treated particularly kindly, and after Norman has given a description of her face, which was: 'wrinkled like an old lemon, or like a raised map of some uncharted country on the invisible side of the moon;'[910] he tones this down slightly and concludes: 'Yet for all her monstrous appearance she walked well, and had regular features, which suggested that neither her intelligence nor her will had disappeared, and had once been wedded to beauty.'[911]

The mistrust of the mother continues: 'Do I look like the sort of man who would misbehave with your daughter?' said Norman stiffly.

The widow is interested in whether Norman is rich and wants to consider marrying her daughter. Norman tells her that he is 'fairly rich' but he has not known her daughter long enough to decide about marriage.[912]

It is interesting to note that, in the romance of Peronella and Norman, it is the mother who brings up the subject of marriage to a reluctant Norman, and it is Peronella who proposes marriage.[913] As Flecker makes Norman contemplate: 'He had fallen into a trap. He was looked upon as a prospective son-in-law by the Widow Prasko – and that was ever so largely his own fault.'[914]

Norman and Peronella had as many problems imposed upon them about their different social classes, as he and Eleanor. It was said, 'He (Flecker) was in no sense a society man; she was essentially a society woman.'[915] This remark did not explain the fact that Eleanor had met her future fiancé at the Fabian Summer School, not an event high on the social calendar, or the fact that Flecker had written to his parents and told them 'Don't talk rot about "mere parson's son"'. 'We're far more important people than the Finlaysons, hang it all.'[916]

He had, after all, mixed with his contemporaries at Oxford who were in all sections of society, but mainly the higher echelons, and managed to hold his own, as he had done at Scoones, the crammers, and also at Cambridge. Some of his contemporaries had disliked him, but not because he was a 'mere parson's son'. He had been admired because of his ability to show off in company but, above all, as a writer. He could adapt to the group he was in, and not absorb his parents' attitude, which was brought about because they did not mix in what they thought of as 'Society'. In the Finlaysons' case, this was mostly money and a superficial desire to be seen in the right places in London. Cheltenham, socially, the Fleckers must have felt was a bit of a backwater.

But Flecker did try to become, in a superficial way, a society man by altering his dress. No doubt the Praxiteles blazer, if he thought of wearing it, would raise a few eyebrows in the drawing rooms of Earl's Court. Douglas Goldring met Flecker shortly after his return from the Fabian Summer School, and described his attire: 'It could NOT have been a bowler hat, a dark grey frock-coat with watered silk facings, trousers to match, a skimpy green-knitted tie, AND yellow boots! But if it wasn't just that, it was a mixture of garments which gave the same impression.' [917,918]

It is surprising that Goldring chose to comment on his dress, as his editor drove about in a hired carriage and wore a magnificent fur coat and a topper. But if that was acceptable in an editor, the poet Ezra Pound was disliked by Goldring because he wore gaudy, blue glass buttons on his coat and he saw him as a stage poet, his inspiration Murger on whom *La Bohème* was based.[919] Goldring may have feared that Flecker would follow the same path. Goldring who was able to see beneath the showy exterior of Pound, realised that he was a kind man, even if he thought that Pound's poetry was pretentious. London's only bright group of poets at that time was The Poets' Club, which was begun in 1908. The Secretary of The Poets' Club was T.E. Hulme, who was back in Cambridge after being sent down in 1904. Frank Flint (1885–1960) did not agree with the way The Poets' Club was run and, in particular, the fact that the poets wore evening dress, which was the 'uniform' of its members.[920] Once again the correct garb for poets was brought into question. A breakaway group from The Poets' Club was formed in March 1909. Frank Flint was a member and Ezra Pound joined the meetings in a Soho restaurant in April 1909. [921]

A restaurant mentioned by Goldring is Beguinot's in Old Compton Street where he had lunch with Flecker, 'the last time I saw him in the flesh',[922] when Knox was present and Goldring heard once more the joint adventures during the wine riots. The Petit Riche is mentioned as a place for lunch with W.N. Ewer, poet and the future diplomatic correspondent of the *Daily Herald*.[923]

Flecker was cultivating a moustache, which may have been an attempt to make him look older; Goldring says he had several during early manhood. Goldring devotes a paragraph to the growing of the

Flecker moustache, which Birrell said grew so fast that he could hear it whistle. He dared not let his fiancée see it until it was fully grown. Goldring thought a moustache certainly suited Flecker, but he draws no conclusions why he had grown one in the first place. At this time Charles Raven was elected Dean of Emmanuel at the age of twenty-four, and he received, anonymously, a moustache-grower; the use of one bottle it was claimed would add ten years to his age.[924]

Flecker's time in October and November 1909 appeared to be taken up with social activities, but this did not mean a neglect of his preparation of tales, sketches and poetry for publication. He was revising poetry for his proposed book of poems (to be named *Thirty-Six Poems*) while still working for his entry into the Levant Consular Service and attending lectures connected with this work.

He wrote a poem under the title 'A Little Poem' on 28 September 1909, which began with the lines: 'Soft as the collied night, and cool.'

He was very angry when Birrell mocked him for taking the phrase 'collied night' out of *A Midsummer Night's Dream* and 'shoving it in to a poem about nenuphars'.[925] It was not a poem about nenuphars,[926] but about Eleanor Finlayson, and Flecker seems to have difficulty in writing about her body. Two versions of this poem exist in the copybook. When it was published in *Thirty-Six Poems* it had the title 'Fountains'. He scores through the lines in the first version where he writes of 'blossom of snow', meaning the shoulders or the breasts of his beloved. He leaves out a whole verse in the second version, which ends:

..... Beneath her dress
Was she not shaped for loveliness?

His anger about criticism of this poem would not be so much because of the line from Shakespeare, but because he could not express in verse his real feelings about Eleanor's physical beauty. He found them easier to express in prose, as he wrote in the *King of Alsander*:[927] 'He set all the snow of her shoulder afire with kisses,'. Gautier, in 'Mlle. de Maupin', wrote about 'her breasts were as cold as snow, the colour of which they shared'.

Poetry publication was much to the fore: four verses of 'The Western Voyage'[928] appeared in *Country Life* on 23 October 1909, 'The Parrot' was published in *The Cambridge Review* of 4 November 1909 and the 'Welsh Sea' in the 20 November edition of *The Nation*.

He did not rest on his laurels but revised 'The Ballad of the Student in the South'[929] in December 1909, adding one verse. 'The Ballad of the Student in the South', five stanzas, had first appeared in *The Bridge of Fire*. It is about a casual encounter, which Sherwood[930] says took place in Grenoble,[931] like Rioupéroux.

It is not entirely clear if the poem is about the love for a man or a woman, unless the reader of the new version is aware that one verse is from the poem 'Dorothy', which had two verses (first published in his book of poems *The Bridge of Fire*). The revised lines of the second verse are:

> Yours is the beauty of the moon,
> The wisdom of the sea,
> Since first you tasted, sweet and soon,
> Of God's forbidden tree.

The second verse he used in *The King of Alsander* to head chapter six, It refers in this instance to Peronella and reads:

> I had read books you had not read,
> Yet I was put to shame
> To hear the simple words you said,
> And see your eyes aflame.

He may have been unsatisfied with the final outcome of 'the Ballad of the Student in the South' because of the alterations, changes in the sequence of the verses, and the concealment of the sex.

Another source of dissatisfaction with this poem could be that he was trying to rid it of the influence of other poems with similar lines.[932] The poem has an affinity with 'Ruth' by Thomas Hood (1798–1843), which begins:

> She stood breast-high amid the corn,
> Clasp'd by the golden light of morn,
> Like the sweetheart of the sun,
> Who many a glowing kiss had won.

The original version of the first verse of 'The Ballad of the Student in the South', published in *The Bridge of Fire*, reads:

> It was no sooner than this morn
> That first I found you there,
> Up to your breast in Southern corn
> As golden as your hair. [933]

He changed this to:

> It was no sooner than this morn
> That first I found you there,
> Deep in a field of southern corn
> As golden as your hair.

The above is the version, which appeared in *Thirty-Six Poems*. This was eventually revised to read:

> It was no sooner than this morn
> That I first found you there,
> Deep in a field of southern corn
> The colour of your hair. [934]

The second last line in the proofs for *Thirty-Six Poems* reads: 'Linger and toil and laugh and die', which was changed to: 'Who live because they fear to die.'

His poem 'The Young Poet', which had first appeared in *The Bridge of Fire* and then in *The Academy* on 2 November 1907 was also revised in December 1909, as 'Dirge' in *The Bridge of Fire Copybook* (p.136), but he did not include it in the anthology which he was preparing.[935] His tales and sketches, which he based on material he was studying for his course, had got into print. The first part of his translation of some of the *Gulistan of Sa'di*[936] appeared in *The Cambridge Review* of 25 November 1909. 'More Gulistan' was printed in the 24 February 1910 edition.

Gulistan in Persian means rose-garden,[937] and the familiar image could not fail to fire his imagination. In his poem 'From Grenoble' he wrote: 'And the rose-garden of my gracious home.'

Sa'di, who died in 1292, wrote: ' "You know" said I, "that the rose will not endure nor is the garden's promise sure; and sages have forbidden us to set our hearts on that which fades and departs." "What then?" said he. I replied, "To furnish the time present with reading merry and pleasant. I can compile the book of the Rose-Garden. Never shall autumn blast scatter its leaves away and the fury of October deform the loveliness of its May".' [938]

Sa'di was known as the 'Nightingale of a thousand songs'.[939] Professor Browne outlined the character of Sa'di in his *Literary History of Persia*. He stated that as far as Sa'di was concerned, 'whatever he touches either in prose or verse, he had the art of making it as agreeable as possible.'[940]

Flecker's translation is agreeable to read, even if, like his translation of 'Mansur', the reader is unfamiliar with the original collection of stories in varying lengths interspersed with verses. The translation is a fine achievement[941] and it is obvious that he had a considerable aptitude for translation over and above the requirements of the Levant course. The standard of his translation and the discipline involved could not have escaped the notice of Professor Browne, who now ignored past lapses and recognised the improvement in his work. The news of Flecker's improved performance in his studies reached the Foreign Office. A letter was sent to him at Christmas congratulating him on the improvement in his attendance at lectures and his work.[942]

The last letter from the Foreign Office informing him of his poor performance does not appear to have been common knowledge, so the second letter telling him of the improvement would also have to be kept to himself. Savery was not told, although Jack is a likely exception.

He was reunited with Jack for a week in Paris and this is noted in the LIFE with the sentence,

'J. may be in Paris for a week, I know one or two students there.' [943]

He did not spend the whole of the Christmas vacation in Paris with Jack, but also went to London for a few days to see Eleanor. He wrote to his father thanking him profusely for a cheque, and telling him he had got paid by *The Nation* (for 'The Welsh Sea'): 'I have had a very pleasant time here, rather whirled about town. Have made some rather hopeful literary arrangements.' [944] But this was not the whole story; he had seen Eleanor in London and she had: 'practically dismissed me' (as he was later to admit).[945]

It is not surprising that he had what was described as influenza on his return to Paris. As a result, he had more 'ruinous doctors' bills'[946] to pay. The illness, in fact, was something much more serious, tuberculous laryngitis, which had flared up again, due to his rejection by Eleanor, and the possible end to marriage plans. A crisis in courtship is known to bring on infection.[947] The crisis itself could have been brought about by his waning sexual attractiveness, brought on by the illness.

The New Year of 1910 brought thanks, in a letter from Paris, for New Year messages from Dean Close, where there must have been illness too, as he is quoted as writing: 'I do hope you are much better and feeling chirpy'.[948] He tells Dean Close that Jack is in the Louvre all day, so he is getting a lot of work done in the fine, large, cheap, warm room they share in the Hotel Jacob. Jack appears to be staying longer than the original week, as the price of the room is given as 32 Fr. 50 for a fortnight. 'Not a large sum to spend on lodgings is it?' he asks, and tells his parents on 4 January that his throat is very much better, but not quite gone. He was working on revising his poetry; 'To An Unknown Friend: Dedication of a Story', first published in *The Nation* on 11 January 1908, was given a new title, 'To The World and a Poet a Thousand Years Hence', and revised in Paris, according to the *Bridge of Fire Copybook*, which dates it January, 1910.[949] He also revised 'The Welsh Sea' in January 1910.

He was back in Paris in the middle of the next term, after a weekend in London with Eleanor. In a letter to his parents from Cambridge, there is a small hint that all had not been well, if they chose to read between the lines. He wrote: 'They are still very nice to me,' and continued, 'Went to Tannhauser, E. and I and did many other pleasant things together. Birrell is very keen on being best man.'[950] Birrell's home in London would make him a suitable best man, and as the son of a famous man of his day, he would be acceptable to both Finlaysons and Fleckers, Beazley or Savery would not have had the same suitability.

He did not appear to consider Douglas Goldring for the role of best man, but he was much in the picture at this time. It was thanks to Goldring, who had started his own magazine *The Tramp* (the Open Air Magazine) in March 1910,[951] that the firm who owned the magazine, The Adelphi Press, 9 Adam Street, Strand, issued a volume of Flecker's poems entitled *Thirty-Six Poems*.[952]

In the volume, fifteen of the poems were new, many of the rest were reprinted in revised forms, or with many alterations, completely rewritten, from periodicals, or from his previous book of poetry, *The Bridge of Fire*. *The Bridge of Fire* had been reprinted with alterations early in 1910, and had been reviewed in *The Cambridge Review* of 27 January 1910, and *The Gownsman* of 10 February, so university periodicals held back from reviewing again, poems in *Thirty-Six Poems*, which they had brought to their readers' attention only a few weeks previously. *The Cambridge Review* had published 'Mansur' in their 20 January 1910 edition, and 'More Gulistan' on 24 February, so their coverage of the work of Flecker could not be found wanting.

The Cambridge Review's review of *The Bridge of Fire* began by describing Flecker as 'though an immigrant from the other University'. The review is unsigned, but it could be from the pen of Rupert Brooke, who had called on the editor of *The Cambridge Review* and offered himself as a reviewer. 'I have undertaken to "do" great slabs of minor poetry for *The Cambridge Review*. I have read volumes of them, all the same, and all exactly the stuff I write. I frequently wonder whether I have not written several of them myself under a pseudonym, and forgotten about it.'[953] Brooke wrote to Geoffrey Keynes on 24 January, the day his father died, that he was writing for the *Review*,[954] so if Flecker suspected that Brooke had written the following review, there was little he could do to question him as he was ill and absent from Cambridge.

'Mr. Flecker's verse is in many respects different from the bulk of poetry produced at the present time: it has less of the vagueness and, if we may say so, eccentricity of expression which appears to be an aim of the modern verse writer, and its author seems always to be striving after a precision of form and expression too much neglected by many of his contemporaries.' The review continued by saying that Flecker did not always achieve his end, then stated: 'when completely successful, his work has certain gem-like Horatian qualities which raise it to a very considerable degree of excellence.' 'Rioupéroux' is quoted in full in the review, and is described as 'of really high poetical merit'.

The review of *The Bridge of Fire* in *The Gownsman* of 10 February is given more space than the one in *The Cambridge Review*. It also mentions the fact that Flecker has been to Oxford and states: 'It is of peculiar interest to Cambridge people, the author having forsaken, though seemingly regretfully, the sister University, and being at present in residence at Cambridge.'

The Gownsman reviewer tells his readers that, 'The author writes in several veins'. In the following poems the reviewer wrote 'he is light and deft' ('Dorothy', 'Narcissus', and 'Golden Head'). The poems described as 'extremely musical' were 'Pervigilium' [955] and 'Ideal'.

The sonnet to Francis Thompson, and the second sonnet of Bathrolaire 'are also of a high order'. The opening lines of *The Bridge of Fire* are quoted which the reviewer says makes 'higher pretentions'.

'The New Year's Carol' and the 'Young Poet' are also picked out for high praise. The 'Old Poet' is not cared for, 'Oxford Canal' is described as a 'poor piece' and the 'dragging in of King Edward' is described as not attractive, even in a ballad. The death of that monarch on 6 May and the obituaries used up space in the newspapers and magazines that might otherwise have been devoted to reviews of Flecker's new work, *Thirty-Six Poems*.

The reviews of both editions of *The Bridge of Fire* had been written mainly by younger men, like Goldring, who knew Flecker personally, or shared the same sort of background. Reviews for *Thirty-Six Poems* would come from a wider and more critical audience.

'Seems I am not going to have any reviews of my new book of poems,'[956] he wrote to Savery in Exeter, in a mood of pessimism. He tells Savery in another letter, written shortly afterwards,[957] news which could not have failed to lift his spirits, namely that Masque 1 was sung in Canterbury Cathedral.[958] He also told Savery: 'No, Franko, it's the one uniting thing that binds my work together, this humour – even the hugeous nonsense of the shadowgraph humour combined with what the gentleman in the *Gloucester Echo*[959] wrote about the Unconventional Poems of a Clergyman's son calls my "yearning sadness".'

It is not surprising that the *Gloucester Echo*, based in Cheltenham, referred to James Elroy Flecker, 'son of the respected principal of Dean Close School', and also headed the piece 'A Young Cheltenham Poet'. The reviewer mentioned Flecker's undoubted gift for writing, and thought some of his verse akin to Poe, de Quincy, Blake and Thompson, and felt (as many reviewers were to feel) that 'Oxford Canal' was a successful imitation of Whitman, but stated that Flecker 'would find solace in the exercise of his promising muse'. He was not going to escape his background, at this stage, but he could feel proud of this review. He concluded the letter by saying: 'Enough of my pig self, must write a rather complete ballad of Iskander Rumi in 50 verses or else betake myself to the tongue of the Turks.'

'Iskander Rumi' was the start of a ballad eventually entitled 'The Ballad of Iskander', which he was to repolish later for publication.[960] He read the story on which he based 'The Ballad of Iskander', according to 'one of his intimate friends'[961] at Cambridge. The friend thought: 'His version was entrancing, and I thought he spoiled it in the poem by the metaphysical colouring he there gave it.'[962] Another friend remembered, 'He used to come and read us his poems as he wrote them – I remember his reading us "Sultan Iskander sat him down", in a cafe on the Boulevards, after the theatre one night; he had just finished it."[963]

'Iskander' is a turning point in Flecker's mastery of the ballad form, and it would seem its theme of death made a better ballad than the previous theme of sexual love in the common speech of the working class of his 'Ballad of the Londoner' and 'The Ballad of Camden Town'. His habit of working in a hidden Beazley factor does not feature in 'The Ballad of Iskander', and the poem seems better for it.

'Iskander' had already been met in 'Mansur' when Flecker wrote: 'he betook himself to his books. He read the "Khosrev and Shirin" of Sheykhi and the tale of Iskander, which Hamedi wrote in a hundred thousand lines, and he became unhappy, and the road of Life was dark before his eyes.'[964]

He has a note under the title of 'The Ballad of Iskander': 'Aflatun and Aristu and King Alsander are Plato, Aristotle, Alexander.' These he had come across in Burton's *The Kasidah*.

'The Ballad of Iskander' is reminiscent of 'Lord Arnaldos' with its mysterious ship, but it also has much more on board; cargoes from the

History of Ottoman Poetry, in which Gibb gives a summary of some of the Iskender-Name, and also the story of the ships appears in the *Shah-Name* or *Book of Kings*, by the Persian poet Firdausi,[965] but the cargoes are kept together by Flecker's humour and twists to the tale, which has echoes of 'The Ancient Mariner' and Sufi philosophy.[966]

'Iskander', like 'Mansur', is about a journey, this time by a ship sent out by Alexander to see if there are any lands still to be conquered. After a year, it meets another ship sent out too by a king whose name is also Alexander, which at first it is thought that:

> Said Aristu to Aflatun –
> 'Surely our King, despondent soon,
> Has sent this second ship to find
> Unconquered tracts of humankind.'

But they are told:

> Theirs is the land (as well I know)
> Where live the Shape of Things Below:
> Theirs is the country where they keep
> The Images men see in Sleep.

Then:

> He spake, and some young Zephyr stirred
> The two ships touched; no sound was heard;
> The Black Ship crumbled into air;
> Only the Phantom Ship was there.

'The Ballad of Iskander' is a step along the way in his maturing process as a poet and master of his technique. He had progressed in his feelings about death, which would bring about the loss of earthly pleasures in 'The Town Without a Market', to the vision of death and what lay beyond. Notwithstanding, his studies for the Levant Consular Service, his possible failure in his examinations, his loss of closeness with Beazley and the postponement of wedding plans, the usual lack of money and conflict with his parents, he continued to be able, even with poor physical health to write his best verse, which he was proud of, although he wondered about the reception his book of poems would have in the world outside. He was already planning his next book and the poems that would enhance it.

This new-found confidence owed something to the fact that Cambridge was accepting him as a poet, more so than Oxford. As Humbert Wolfe said, 'Oxford, on the whole, does not love her poets.'[967] Wolfe also wrote: 'I only saw him once again. I was staying in King's Parade with Morrison, who, like Flecker, had exchanged his University. "Do you ever," I said over our white wine and oysters, "hear anything of that man Flecker?" "I hardly hear of anything else," said Morrison. "Why?" I asked, expecting an epigram or sneer. "Because," said Morrison, "poetry is the fashion here, and they think him a poet." I felt a queer pang in my heart. Was it, could it, be possible that after all he was to cast his shoe over the Front Bench? I remembered his lines. . .' Wolfe then quotes two verses from an early version of 'The Ballad of Hampstead Heath' (published in '*The Bridge of Fire*', p.24.).

He continued: 'Had we misunderstood – Had we been blind? Was it possible that, when he wrote of death, he had written, like Keats and Shelley, in the consciousness of his own immortality? If so, what was I doing with the Bar and politics when I also once had heard, had believed, had conjectured? "Another glass of this admirable Liebfraumilch," some one said in a most accomplished voice. "Rather," I answered, but, as I drank, I sighed.

'Next day I went into "The Bull", at lunchtime to meet a politician or two with all my doubts conquered. As I went in I heard a familiar voice, saying as at the end of a fugue, to three admiring friends, "And that is why I am not a Realist." I saw the brilliant grey eyes for the last time. They looked at me without a flicker of recognition. I went by him to mingle with my politicians.'[968,969]

It was not only in the town of Cambridge but away from the town a contemporary recollected, [970] 'one of the vividest is on a river picnic above Byron's Pool, when we all bathed, and Flecker marched about up to his waist in the river, holding a canoe upside down over his head, entirely hiding it.'[971]

Byron's Pool was near The Old Vicarage and to reach it visitors had to go out of the garden into the lane over the bridge at Grantchester Mill, across the meadow and into the river above the Pool. Brooke bathed naked in the dam above the Pool as he knew it was sufficiently secluded for him to bathe here. His women friends bathed separately, but also nude, and on one occasion it is alleged Virginia Stephens accompanied him, and swam in the nude, as did Rose Macaulay. He felt the cool bathe offered some cleansing of sexual guilt. Brooke wrote about Byron's Pool in his poem 'Grantchester':

> In Grantchester their skins are white;
> They bathe by day, they bathe by night;

and

> And laughs the immortal river still
> Under the mill, under the mill?

Flecker put the same memories into his prose:

> The youths threw off boots and socks, if they were wearing them, and coats, if they possessed them; neither did the girls fear to display their shapely feet; men and maidens entered the stream, the men valiantly, the maids demurely, and then, dipping their hands in the water, they began splashing each other vigorously across the river. When all were soaked with water many of the men swam over, seized a girl and ducked her in the stream; this was held to be a most solemn betrothal. [972,973]

In his letters he used a more sombre picture, as far as swimming was concerned: he tells Savery 'I am drowning love-pangs in work!'[974] This remark is tucked away at the end of a letter, which devoted considerably more space to criticising an article Savery had written about Flecker's poems at his suggestion.

More space is devoted in this letter to a review of his poems appearing in the *Morning Post* of 31 March 1910, which he quotes to Savery:

> Satiety, wantonness, fear of old age and death are characteristic of the joy of life in Mr. Flecker's page. For not only do we feel sure that they are valiant affectations but there is practical evidence in the beauty of some of his rhythms, images and combinations of words that he had adopted them out of fidelity to his time rather than to himself. The fantastic sonnets of Bathrolaire are full of joy, notwithstanding the words describing horror and shame and sickliness. The humour of 'Ballad of Hampstead Heath' is only possible to healthy high spirits.

Flecker found the review 'on the whole is not very encouraging, but it is better than most.'

He wrote to his parents[975] about the *Morning Post* review, calling it 'a fine but not laudatory review', and mentioning 'quite horrid ones in *The Times* and *Scotsman*.'[976]

The reviews were encouraging. Next to a review of Frances Cornford's poems, *The Athenaeum* of 16 April, praised the technique of *Thirty-Six Poems* finding it admirable, and although the reviewer thought that there was a tendency towards gloom, the mysticism was of a kind that 'can transfigure common things'. The striking atmosphere of 'The Town Without a Market' is remarked upon, as well as the quaint and inconclusive humour of 'The Ballad of Hampstead Heath'. *The Caian*, (Easter term, 1910), in a review signed SW, thought that 'Mr. Flecker's development would be interesting to watch as development must be assured.'

The Cambridge Review reviewed *Thirty-Six Poems* in their 5 May 1910 issue, *Isis* on 7 May, the *Birmingham Daily Post* on 17 May and *The Observer* on 24 April, 1910. All these he could read before he left for Constantinople.

The *Birmingham Daily Post*, for Tuesday 17 May 1910, thought that the Adelphi Press, which it said had recently come into the public eye with *The Tramp*, started its career in an 'excellent manner with Mr. Flecker's poems'. The *Birmingham Daily Post* told its readers that *The Bridge of Fire* had 'attracted a good deal of attention....' It dismissed 'The Ballad of Hampstead Heath', as a mere exercise in cleverness and thought the 'Oxford Canal' 'an exercise in Whitman which was both a dangerous and unprofitable occupation in a young poet'. But the paper praised the rest of the poems saying that 'there is abundant proof Mr. Flecker is to be placed among those of his contemporaries who really matter.'

The reviewer found the many moods difficult to reconcile, picking out 'Masque of the Magi' with 'No Coward's Song', but felt that the inconsistency is a sign of vitality rather than weakness. He was thought modern without being blatantly so and that he was generally able to disentangle the essential from the inessential.

It was thought that *Thirty-Six Poems* established Flecker's reputation as one of the most promising of 'our younger men, and his next volume of poetry was looked forward to' – all in all a favourable review, especially as Flecker was thought to feel intimately and vividly and he had quite a fine facility of expression.

Flecker's fears about the success, or failure, of his book of poetry were as real to him as the fear of his success or failure of his marriage plans with Eleanor. As his poems were now out in the world for anyone to see, and comment upon his themes and obsessions, now it had to come out that the marriage was off, and those who knew him in the world at large were free to air their views and comments. He was not having much luck either with his Italian Grammar, he told his parent that Nutt (the publisher) was 'treating with him'. [977]

'Tis definitely off with my Lady at last, for the next year or so,' he tells Savery. In a letter to his parents from the place he went to whenever a crisis loomed in his life – Oxford, he told them briefly: 'I am afraid that marriage is off. We seem hopeless incompatible. I shall be here till Tuesday, then I go to Paris.'[978]

He telegraphed them the next day to say it may be alright. A long letter headed Oxford Union Society, was sent to his parents next day to tell them: 'Somehow I funked coming home as I didn't want to talk about the matter, but to rush abroad at once.' [979]

As usual, he gave the cost of his room at 42 rue Perronet to let them know that, even in the midst of all the emotional turmoil as a result of the broken engagement, he was not being extravagant with the amount spent on living quarters.

He concluded the long letter with as much explanation as he can give of the failure of the relationship between himself and his ex-fiancée: 'Frankly, there were two Es. – one I love and do still, and the other I hate as much it hates me, and when the lovable one writes (as she will) to me, I don't know what I shall do. But it seems to me one dare not marry half a person.'[980]

It could be that Eleanor was two persons to him – the one he had met at the Summer School, where they were free to be close and play tennis in bare feet, whilst back in London her fiancé had to don a frock-coat and yellow boots, and go to the theatre.

Norman and Peronella did not make love, and the reasons outlined in the *King of Alsander* may have some similarities in regard to Flecker's attitude to possible lovemaking with Eleanor. It was not because she was not good enough he says: 'Ah! Peronella as good enough – nay, a prize beyond all dreams! for a Blaindon grocer.'[981]

Norman relates that Peronella's body 'was his for a kiss, for a smile, at the worst for a traitor promise or a roseleaf lie,' but although the thought 'quivered in his mind', he withstood the temptation.

'In no tale since *Tom Jones* have we had an honest Englishman who makes love because it is jolly and because he doesn't care.' [982] Norman wanted legislation so that all offenders against monogamy could be flogged. He knows he would be accused of fear of convention. He would not have blamed Tom Jones for his jolly conduct, but he was not able to make love to a girl whom he was unable to desert. It struck him that Peronella had never yielded to a lover, and his dilemma was that he knew he must marry her or leave her.

He had hinted to his parents already that Eleanor was not used to living on a small income in spartan conditions, when he wrote to them: 'E. is learning how five people can live on 30s. a week, with some Cousins ..... It should prove to her a profitable if painful experience.' [983]

Their son would certainly know about the impossibility of that sort of experience, and although this extract may have been quoted to show Eleanor's good intentions towards becoming a thrifty wife, it does show a tendency to put his own faults on her shoulders, as life in Turkey for Eleanor would hardly be so penny-pinching. They would after all, have her £400 a year and his salary to live on, but as they both were used to subsidies from their homes in the shape of board and lodgings, gifts and financial handouts, the comforts of home and any extras would be missing in Constantinople. It would be as well for Flecker to bear in mind, when considering Eleanor's experience with her cousins, his own unsuccessful effort to live on £1 a week in Wales, when money ran out and he had to borrow from the postman. Neither were only children, Flecker had two sisters and a brother, all younger than him, and their education had to be taken care of, and Eleanor had sisters.

"When will you marry me?" said Peronella, "and will you take me to England? Oh, say you will take me to England, Normano, and when you drive me around in your carriage all the world will say, 'That woman cannot be of our town; she is the most beautiful woman that we have ever seen.'"

But Norman thinks of his life:

> Her pretty words pierced him like little darts of ice, and all the comminations of the sages could not have frightened him more than the maiden's innocent speech.
>
> He saw in his clear-sighted panic that here was an end of all bright dreams save this one; and he knew how soon this dream would fade. He saw Peronella unhappy – a Peronella who could not be afforded a carriage – sulking behind the counter of the Bon Marche, in the rain. He saw how her beauty would fade away in England, swiftly, in a few years; and all in a moment she seemed as she sat there to grow old and tired before him, wasting away beneath the low, dark northern skies.
>
> He judged her character with Minoan rightness. He knew she would always be a child, always be silly, querulous, unfaithful, passionate; he knew, above all, how soon she would kill that spark in him that made him different from other men – that spark the Poet bade him cherish. And he

feared she would bore him at breakfast every morning of his life. [984]

As Norman had thought earlier of Peronella:

> Can beauty be boring? Ah! ye gods, it can, if one has to talk to it, and it is stupid. But was Peronella not romantic? Oh, yes, she was indeed, but romantic with a 'k'. She was romantick like the fair misses of a hundred years ago. But is not the romantick the same as the romantic principle? Oh, yes, indeed, the sentiment is the same; but to be romantic requires intellect, and to be romantick requires none. But was Peronella not educated? Indeed she was, most abominably educated, quite enough to ruin all the fresh roses of her nature. She had not, could not, alas! read Ella Wheeler Wilcox, her poems, but oh! how she would have loved them had she known them! Marie Corelli she did read; you may buy her works in Alsandrian.
>
> But was she incapable of appreciating true literature? Oh, no, she adored Shakespeare and Byron, which she read in translations. You see, her mother had ideas and considered herself a lady. Nevertheless Peronella began to bore Norman; the spell was broken! [985]
>
> If Turkey is substituted for England and Eleanor for Peronella the vision of their life together was an unrealistic one and so was their love.

He had written to Savery,[986] 'Praise God she knows nothing of literature' and, at the outset of their relationship, this might have seemed a bonus, but as they got to know each other better, he would feel this to be a disadvantage: engaged couples have to talk about something. To be fair, they both tried to change superficially to suit the other. Flecker attempted to be the Society man in his dress and in his visits to the theatre. Eleanor bought 'a very fat Mrs. Beeton'. She entertained, however, '.................... no hope of becoming that ideal mistress whose dread perfections were optimistically outlined in the book's preface.'[987] She could not become the sort of hostess who would help her future husband to become an ambassador, or she realised her future husband was not ambassador material.

If Eleanor was indeed the model for Peronella (and reference to her unfaithfulness applied to her), there may have been an older man always in the background, like Cesano, who when Norman first met

Peronella, had already been involved to the point of talking of marriage, and Norman was 'used' to make him jealous.[988]

Eleanor could have been jealous of Jack. A useful guide to his feelings for Jack is the inscription inside Jack's copy of *Thirty-Six Poems*:[989] [990]

> Ti giovani – con lento passo
> si misono   for Jack
> per uno giardino, belle ghirlande di   from James
> Varos fiande faccendasi, et amorasmente
> contando.

In the back of copy he writes lines from his poem 'Pillage',

> No more on the long summer days shall we
> walk in the meadow-sweet ways
> With the teachers of music and phrase, and
> the masters of dance and design.
> No more when the trumpeter calls shall we feast
> in the white-light halls;
> For stayed are the soft footfalls of the
> moonlight bearers of wine .... [991]

Despite the excitement of getting *Thirty-Six Poems* into print and reading the reviews, he had examinations to face. He gave the impression that he was not entirely confident or well-prepared as he indicated to Rupert Brooke. He sent a postcard post-marked 5 May to Rupert Brooke, Esq., at The Orchard, Grantchester:

> Not having heard whether you are going to bring your mythical friend shall order wee meal for you alone tomorrow (Friday) at 7.
> Have got to learn the entire Russian tongue tonight.
> Pray for me.
> Your brother in Poesy,
>
> James Elroy Flecker." [992]

The Cambridge Review published its review of *Thirty-Six Poems* on the day he posted this card, so discussion at the meal would be about this review and not the review that Brooke felt obliged to undertake.

His review stated that Flecker was in the class of poets who can handle metre. Brooke did not consider the few poems that were translations to be very good, feeling that the act of translation robbed a metre of its suppleness, and there were faults he said in grammar, on prosody, and certain general ones, in the original poems. Brooke said a great many readers have since commented on the change of sex in regard to this poem, which they took to have been done in the interest of better rhyme.[993] Brooke was the first to comment on the name of the poem, but he does not say what the moral fault was, in his opinion.[994] Mary Byrd Davis calls it 'an inconspicuous but significant pun into the title'.[995] As in both cases, the actual moral fault or pun is not explained to the reader, there is a possibility that it was the use of the word 'Queen' and that its obscure meaning was obscene.[996]

The review gives the only real picture of Brooke's feelings about Flecker's poetry. Brooke does say that Flecker is 'a quite good poet'. He considers 'The Masque of the Magi' is 'mostly an imitation of Swinburne's, down to the last minutest details; and not good at that.'[997] But he describes the 'Ballads of Camden Town, and Hampstead Heath' as 'quite original, individual and lovely expression of Mr. Flecker's own view of things'. He quoted 'No Coward's Song'.[998]

His piece appeared in the 15 June issue of *The Gownsman*, which Flecker did not see for some time. [999]

The examination papers were all unseen translations and took six hours to complete.[1000] The vivas, he felt, did not go off very well, but his hard work paid off. He passed, 'it is good to be 1st class and 1st,'[1001] he wrote to Savery. Professor Browne was full of praise at the remarkable recovery and told the Foreign Office so, remarking on his unusual ability.[1002]

Flecker was promoted to assistant interpreter on 23 May 23 1910.

Someone else who admired Flecker's abilities, was John Mavrogordato, who was Reader and Literary Adviser (1908–11) at the publishers J.M. Dent's, who signed the letter accepting *The Grecians* for publication. *The Cambridge Review* also must have admired him, as it published Flecker's partly satirical essay 'Pentheus' on 26 May 1910. 'Pentheus' also appeared in *The Academy* on 9 April 1910 (he had sent it to *The Academy* in November, 1907).

His poem 'The Sentimentalist' was published in *The Cambridge Review* on 8 June 1910. A much-corrected version of this poem, a farewell to Jack Beazley,[1003] survives in his Copybook.[1004] In one version he writes:

> I found a photograph of you
> Deep in a box of faded things

In the published version this becomes:

> There lies a photograph of you
> Deep in a box of broken things

The final version makes a more positive statement about the feelings for the person in the photograph. The draft version tends to suggest that the memory is only recalled with the opening of the box, and looking again at the faded things, whilst the broken things present a clear image of the past things destroyed and not mended, but the pieces not thrown away. Or, like a box of broken toys in a child's playbox, although there is no doubt that it is an adult, as one draft line begins:

> To-day I looked my papers through

Then he writes:

> How deep the change since seas were blue
> And you were young five years ago

The 'five years ago' pinpoints the time he is writing about, 1905, the year when his relationship with Beazley was at its highest point, and as the final version states: 'Five years ago, when life had wings;'

In the final version he writes: 'We walked and talked and trailed our gown'.

In the draft version he writes: 'our neglected gown'.

This could be a reference to his own neglect of his Oxford studies, or his being 'progged' after bumping into the Proctor whilst wearing cap and gown and smoking a cigarette.

The finished version of the first line of the next verse reads: 'The precepts that we held I kept;'

In the draft version: 'The precepts that you held I kept'.

The next verse begins: 'Now I go East and you stay West' and was originally: 'Now I must East and you stay West'.

The 'I must East' give the impression that the writer of the poem was being forced to go not entirely of his own free will, which is nearer the truth. The second last line finally read: 'And drank to all that golden day', which originally he wrote as: 'And drank to all that resplendent day'.

It is not likely that Beazley in the photograph (if it was of him) had changed a great deal (in the physical sense) in the last five years as he was well known for his good looks and youthful appearance, but the change would be to the relationship itself, which was not as closely entwined now and which he hoped:

I shall forget what I love best,
Away from lips and hands and eyes.

The poem has a kinship with Baudelaire's 'Spleen' which has the lines:

A chest-of-drawers cluttered with registers,
with poems, letters, songs, certificates,
With heavy locks of hair wrapped in receipts,

Also:

I am a boudoir full of faded flowers,
Littered by fashions of other hours,
Where plaintive pastels, pale Bouchers alone
Breathe scent from bottles opened in days gone.[1005]

It is difficult to see 'The Sentimentalist' as a sentimental poem, or as a farewell to anyone other than Beazley.[1006]

A farewell to Eleanor is contained in the poem 'Pavlova in London' as 'his farewell view of sophisticated metropolitan delights'.[1007] The sophisticated metropolitan delights he enjoyed with Eleanor were *Electra* and *Tannhauser* (it is not known if they sampled the cinema),[1008] but they went together with others to restaurants, and it is likely to a performance by Anna Pavlovna Pavlova when she made her London debut in a Music Hall setting at the Palace Theatre on 11April 1910. [Future Flecker experts explain why to them the poem is not satisfactory.][1009] His relationship with Eleanor was not satisfactory, and although this could be said of his relationship with Beazley at the time he wrote 'The Sentimentalist', the memories went back much further in time, and the deeper feelings he felt at the separation from Beazley made a better poem. He faced physical separation from Eleanor, but emotionally they had become separate.

The beautiful dances performed by Pavlova – the sadness of *Le Cygne*, *Vase de Caprice* with its idyll of love or the passionate dance *L'Automne Bacchanale* from *Les Saisons* – did not any more match the love and passion of his relationship with Eleanor, and would only serve to emphasise how much their feelings differed from what was being expressed on stage. He ends the poem with the lines:

And dreams, the noblest, die as soon as flowers,
And dancers, all the world of them, must fail.[1010]

It was his dream of a lasting love for Eleanor, which he knew in his heart would die; the beauty of the dance would not fail, as he was later to write: 'And swear that Beauty lives though lilies die,'.[1011]

When he wrote 'Pavlovna' he was sitting his final examinations; he was by no means certain he would not fail. 'Pavlovna' did not create a secure anchor in his present sea of uncertainties, and neither did Eleanor Finlayson. He was nowhere near attaining any sort of financial security, and he may have thought that the public interest in the subject would result in payment for immediate publication.[1012]

His novel had not proved a powerful enough vehicle to manoeuvre him out of the Cambridge cul-de-sac, and to the open road of success. His poems would only provide him with brief trips into the fantasy of supporting himself by his writing. He needed to write something much more substantial if he was to break the boundaries imposed by having to earn a living; and a play might provide such a solution. He wrote from London to his mother, in June: 'I am so desperately hard at work doing this play of mine and so forth.'[1013] This reference to his play was contained in a letter explaining why he could not go down to Dean Close for another farewell.[1014]

One reason for this might have been that Eleanor was back in the picture again. She met him at Paddington station on 10 June, and then saw him off on the boat-train at Charing Cross at the start of his journey to Constantinople. (He had originally wanted to go overland via Vienna, instead of Marseilles, to avoid seasickness.) The uniform provided by his parents, a chest of drawers of assorted remedies and his Turkish Dictionary would travel with him.

What his thoughts were, as he travelled through the English countryside, are not hard to guess; he would contemplate all that he had achieved since he first arrived in Cambridge, just over two years before, when he had been lonely, like Norman, in the *King of Alsander*.

> As amid the joyous sunshine of that first morning when he saw Alsander rise up above her meadows, when, afraid of the world's too deadly beauty, he had felt more lonely than ever in his life before, so now when he had achieved this marvellous thing, now that he ruled the ancient, fair and fabled city, he sank into utter desolation of the soul. And this time no golden girl would chase the black phantom of sorrow from his soul.[1015]

'This marvellous thing' that Norman had achieved was to be crowned King of Alsander, even if he was, in fact, an imposter. Flecker might rightly feel already that he was the uncrowned King of the Cambridge poets of his generation, even if he had not, like the rest of his contemporaries, been to Eton or Rugby, or was at Cambridge because his father had been there before him. He might not have obtained the same sort of honours as they had or been a member of the Apostles,[1016] and he might feel like Norman: 'There was no thrill of triumph in his heart for his achievement. His fellow conspirators had taken him into their farce as one might take a spectator from the stalls and dress him up for the role of King.'[1017]

He might think as Norman did: 'His soul and his conscience, his peace of mind, his friends, his love, his youth he flung down as an offering to the city. And like a man, he swore to work.'[1018]

The Schreiner Family. Front Row. Fred Schreiner, with son, Wilfred, and his wife, Emma. Standing behind his sister, Olive, and brother, Will. April 1881 Eastbourne. *Source: William Cullen Library University of the Witwatersrand.*

Holy Trinity Church, Lee 1870 where William Flecker was curate and Herman Elroy Flecker was baptised by the Vicar, November 1884. (Church was destroyed by a flying bomb in 1944) *Source: John Coulter's Collection Lewisham Past and Present.*

9 Gilmore Road, Lewisham (Taken 1979) Birthplace of James Elroy Flecker (This house was no 5. in 1884, since re-numbered) *Source: Lewisham Local Studies Archive*

Dean Close School Buildings 1886 *Source: A History of Dean Close School*

Dean Close School Staff 1887 J. Pritchard C.G. Tugwell J. Harvey The Headmaster. *Source: A History of Dean Close School*

T.M.A. Cooper. *Source: A History of Dean Close School*

Dr. and Mrs. Flecker, Roy, Claire and Joyce. July 1892 *Source: NGJ*

Flecker as a young child. *Source: NGJ*

Dean Close School 1894 or 1895. Flecker in sailor suit *Source: NGJ*

Cheltenham High Street, 1901 *Source: Francis Frith Collection*

Flecker and Beazley. *Source NGJ*

Flecker and Beazley (Two Englishmen enjoying themselves in Germany.) 1907. *Source: JEF*

Undergraduates: Oxford. Flecker with knee on Ridge, Savery sitting, left. *Source NGJ*

Silver Wedding photograph, 1906. Standing from left to right: Claire, James Elroy, Joyce, Oswald in front. *Source NGJ*

Rupert Brooke as
Attendant Spirit
in *Comus* 1908
(Cambridge). *Source:*
King's College Cambridge.

Edward Marsh 1910
(From a drawing by
Violet, Duchess of
Rutland).
Source: King's College
Library.

Leonard Cheesman (left on deckchair) Patrick Campbell on ground who wrote biography (unpublished) of Cheesman. *Source: New College Archives*

John Mavrogordato en route for Salonika 1912. *Source: Peter Mavrogordato*

John Mavrogordato. *Source: Peter Mavrogordato.*

James Elroy Flecker Diplomatic Uniform. *Source: NGJ*

James Elroy Flecker in Arab Dress at Areya on the balcony.
(Photograph taken by T. E. Lawrence). *Source: NGJ/SLA*

James Elroy Flecker in Praxiteles Club Blazer (Photograph taken by Hellé Flecker). *Source: NGJ/SLA*

Hellé Flecker in her
wedding dress. *Source: NGJ*

Hellé Flecker, Beirut
1912. Photograph taken
by James Elroy Flecker.
Source: NGJ/SLA

300

CHAPTER SEVEN

On June 11 1910, Flecker left Marseilles aboard the *Crimée*. Fears about seasickness were soon justified once the cargo boat reached the open sea. But early on the third day it was calm enough for him to go on deck and gaze at the remains of the lovely old city of Messina, recently destroyed in an earthquake. He then began a conversation with a Greek woman of about thirty years old, whom he thought at first 'had the profile of Pallas but full view was flabby'.[1019] She noticed 'a fine black crop of hair blown back by the wind, a clear gaze, and a remarkable Norfolk jacket of greenish homespun. My first impression was that I was talking to an Irishman; he looked so much darker and more intellectually expressive than any Englishman....'[1020]

Neither Flecker nor the Greek woman, whose name was Hellé, was fluent in the other's mother tongue. Linguistically, Peronella and Norman Price had been similarly tongue-tied at their first encounter. Peronella had known some English but had never been to England. Hellé had had an English governess but had never been to England. Norman Price had already acquired some Alsandrian and his first need to practise it had been when he approached Alsandria and conversed with Peronella. Flecker already knew some modern Greek but his first real need to converse in it was before he reached Athens, and he conversed with Hellé. Alsandrian, Norman Price had found, 'is an easy, simple, and sonorous language, and Norman had been learning it and talking it to himself ... yet he was very shy at practising for the first time this newly-acquired tongue'.

"Ah, I thought you were a foreigner," said the girl, speaking with the strained simplicity and slight mispronunciation that we all of us employ for the benefit of strangers and infants.

"What is your country and your home?"

"England."

"England? Why, you are the first Englishman I have ever seen!"[1021]

He was not the first Englishman that Hellé Skiadaressi had seen. Her only brother had been in the Greek Diplomatic Service and she had met diplomats, as well as naval officers, from England. She was returning to Athens from Paris, where she lived with her widowed mother and unmarried brother, who worked in a French bank. She was going to a friend's wedding. Her knowledge of French and France was useful common ground, more so when Hellé mentioned that her favourite poets were Hérédia and D.G. Rossetti.[1022] José Maria de Hérédia (1842-1905), Flecker considered 'utterly remote from private life and turmoil'[1023] and was particularly appropriate to discuss aboard ship.

When the Straits of Messina were passed, Flecker said with a smile that he must go below and make himself beautiful. ('How beautiful you are!')[1024] Flecker was soon back and together they watched the fantastic outline of the Calabrian Coast.

In the evening the magic of a young moon in a green sky brought them closer; and 'the wake of the ship became at night a river of silver in which sirens played'.[1025] Next morning, when the boat crossed the Ionian Sea, Flecker showed Hellé what he described as his latest poem, 'Pillage' (although he had written the first draft in February/April and he had copied a version of it out inside the cover of '*Thirty-Six Poems*', which he had given to Beazley). In handing her 'Pillage', he was giving Hellé an important message. The poem told her about his past emotional life, if she cared to detect the hidden Beazley factor in the second verse. 'Pillage' also had the line:

> And harry with whips and swords till they perish of shame
> or pain[1026]

This line told Hellé about Flecker's attitude to the infliction of pain and suffering. When she told him the poem was extraordinarily good for an amateur, she would, as a poet herself, and of 'extraordinary intelligence and taste and knowing all poetry in the world.'[1027], be referring more to the semi-Oriental theme, the Persian rhyme scheme and rhythm (which was more like 'The War Song of the Saracens') but also owed something to Tennyson and Swinburne.[1028]

'Pillage' also owed much to Flecker's life at Oxford and Cambridge, and his present voyage's purpose, which was to take up a position in the Levant Consular Service. Flecker smiled at her and told her he was not quite an amateur. It was true that he was not an amateur poet; apart from *The Best Man*, *The Bridge of Fire* and *Thirty-Six Poems*, more than twenty of his poems had already appeared in magazines at home or abroad. He was, however, something of an amateur in dealing with a woman with the intellectual power of Hellé. He might deceive himself into thinking that if she were 'a little prettier' then 'she would be ideal – for five years'.[1029] Also at thirty, he felt that Hellé was too old.[1030] Flecker was to complain (to Savery) 'where are there some women like Meredith's [?]'.[1031] The women in Meredith's fiction, the kind he seemed to be seeking, were cold, young and wealthy beauties, like Constantia Durham, from *The Egoist*, whom Eleanor Finlayson resembled. Even if Eleanor failed to marry him, Flecker still thought that Constantia was the ideal for another bride. Yet another of Meredith's women, Laetitia Dale of *The Egoist*, had a great deal in common with Hellé. Both were daughters of doctors (Laetitia looked after her father, Hellé's father was dead but she looked after her demanding mother), both were poets and both were paragons of cleverness. Laetitia and Hellé, as Meredith would have noted, were the modest violets compared to the queenly roses of Eleanor and Constantia. But Laetitia and Hellé had the sort of boldness Meredith attributed to timid people. Flecker still put Meredith's characters on a pedestal, when he wrote to Savery: 'The subtlety of the motives of speech of Meredith's characters makes one feel a coarse common fellow.'[1032] Meredith, he wrote, 'invariably punishes the amorous by describing them as intellectual failures'.[1033] This comparison with his life and Meredith's fiction was a throwback to the first time he had met Beazley, and he was immediately struck by Beazley's physical likeness to Mellot. Beazley had not lived up to the nobleness of Mellot, which might account for Flecker not connecting Hellé with Laetitia Dale. But when he found Beazley, he was someone he felt he had been searching for a long time, whilst he had not been searching for a woman like Hellé, but in this failure he spared Hellé an extra dose of expectations for the future.

The future was not so much under attack as the past. Flecker was under the spell of the Aegean Islands and the proximity of the Greek coastline made him think that the poems he had written about them were 'rotten'.[1034] His poem 'Phaon' about Sicily and Mount Etna, a reality on this voyage, could have evoked similar feelings, and were perhaps easier to admit to himself than having to rethink his narrow views about women; namely that beautiful rich ones were for marrying and plain ones without money were not.

The beauty of the sea, the stars, the sunrise and the aroma of orange blossom and thyme were enough to bring the two together, even if they had scarcely read a line of poetry. Beazley and Flecker had come from different social classes, and Hellé and Flecker from different countries, but Flecker was playing the upright Englishman and was to tell Savery: 'I should have forgotten my English head altogether. As it was we lay for a night on deck without however my attempting ultimate measures...'[1035]

He made the excuse, to Savery, that had Hellé been 'fairer' he would have made love to her, but it was much more likely that he was like Norman, who 'for all that the thought quivered in his mind, withstood, as we say in our canting phrase, temptation.'[1036] He was not going to model himself on Tom Jones, who was 'an honest Englishman who makes love because it is jolly and because he doesn't care.' Because he was bound not to see Hellé again after the voyage he, like Norman, 'was nevertheless unable to make love to a girl whom he intended to desert.'[1037] 'Besides it struck him, that the girl had never yielded to a lover. For him the dilemma was clear; he must marry this girl or leave her'.[1038] Like Norman 'he accepted this dilemma bravely, and fled that very hour from the siren presence, he would have had only a flirtation and a few kisses to store up against the hour of remorse.'[1039] The 'siren' presence, Hellé had stated, was in the silver wake of the boat they were travelling in.

Flecker, like Norman, decided to 'weave a mystery about himself'. Some mystery was already present. He was twenty-five, travelling alone to Turkey to take up a post. Although Hellé would have realised, after reading 'Pillage', that there had been an attachment at Oxford, she may have wondered, although not aloud as Peronella had done:

> "You are not deceiving me, Normano? You do not love an English girl?"
> "No, it is not that."[1040]

He had not told Hellé about Eleanor Finlayson, so he had decided that weaving a mystery about himself, as Norman had done when he found himself in a similar situation, would gain him time.[1041] But only one more evening remained to them and it would need to be memorable, when the time came to part. They might never be as close again, and the mental torture of a life apart was all that could stretch before them. Time was also needed to make certain that each was fluent in the tongue of the other, so that misunderstandings did not arise, although some misunderstandings, as Peronella and Norman found, could prove advantageous.

"My name is Norman."

"Nor-mano, how nice!" said the girl, who seemed to think that this bashful northerner needed encouragement. "Normano. I shall always call you Norman."

"Always?" said Norman, looking up quickly.

The shameless maiden hung her head with a rosy blush as though she had been caught in an indiscretion, – as though the word had slipped from her unawares. But, even at six in the morning, a sane though splendid hour, Norman, that reserved young Englishman, considered such encouragement sufficient ... he embraced this adorable girl from behind and kissed her ravenously. The kiss fell some two inches below her left ear.

She stood very stiff, flushed and angry; but Norman simply maintained his pressure till her whole body unstiffened.'[1042]

Flecker and Hellé watched the splendid sunrise together before returning to their cabins.

The confusion in his feelings after the night of attempted passion on deck with Hellé was reflected in the verse he tried to write about this time of which just a fragment remains:[1043] Part of the first line of the fragment he wrote is 'held you in my arms', but he scored that out and wrote 'By my side', then:

> And watched with you the middle sea
> Driving its sun delighted tide

The next and last line is not clear but he begins the verse again 'Since first with ...'[1044] He found it easier to put his feelings into the mouth of Don Juan:

> Kiss long and deep while guardian overhead
> The noiseless constellations turn and tread.[1045]

Another fragment with which he intended to replace these lines was: 'And every night the heaven we love so well/ Will open all its eyes – but never tell.'[1046]

The attempt to get the memory of that memorable night into his writings of Don Juan could account for his missing the resemblance Hellé had to at least one of Meredith's women.

Hellé was a poet, a breed of women he had not, until then, had much to do with. His distrust of their work had already been expressed in his article on Laurence Hope. In reality Meredith's life had been blighted by a poet. Meredith had married at the age of twenty-one, Mary Ellen Nicholls, who was nearer thirty, the widowed daughter of satirist Thomas Love Peacock. Nicholls, the mother of a child by her first marriage, was a published poet and wit. She was unfaithful to Meredith and eloped to Capri with a painter, by whom she had a child. Meredith refused to let his wife see her first child, until it was obvious that Mary Ellen was dying, and he refused to attend her funeral. Meredith's poem 'Modern Love' was written as a result of the break-up of his first marriage, and gives with some alterations, an autobiographical account of the tragedy of his married life. 'Modern Love' was published in 1862 and much read aloud in the Brooke/Fabian circles at Cambridge.[1047] Flecker could see from Meredith's experience that women poets had minds of their own and freedom in their private lives. Hellé knew about the private lives of English poets such as Byron and Shelley, and she felt that Flecker might follow the same sort of path, simply because he too was a poet. She overlooked the fact that, in character, he was not a Byron or a Shelley, just as Hellé was neither a Laurence Hope or a Mary Meredith. Flecker and Hellé were attracted to each other, but they both had reasons to be wary of complete surrender. It was easier for Flecker to become Don Juan in his imagination than take as role models, characters such as Tom Jones, or those created by Thackeray, Dickens and Thomas Hardy, who were essentially English.[1048]

He had, like Norman Price, been immediately attracted to Hellé.

"I think," said Norman, looking at his watch with a smile, "that it is just twenty minutes since I first saw you and already..."

"Well?"

"I love you very much," He meant only to say "I like you very much," but in southern lands the linguistic distinction does not exist.

The girl seized him by the wrists.

"Don't say things like that, you devil," she cried, "especially if you do not mean it ..."

"I mean it!" said Norman, perforce.

"Say it again!"

"Peronella, I really love you."

Norman could not conceal a little yawn in his voice even at the moment of making this startling declaration; his eyes were heavy with light...'[1049]

Not long after they had seen the dawn together, the *Crimée* came into Pireus Harbour. They disembarked and, together with some of the other passengers, drove up to the Acropolis in two landaus. Despite the heat, Flecker took in the scene with inner delight and pleasure. After lunch, at which he shone with high spirits, they walked the 'dazzling white marble pavements'[1050] before Flecker took the train back to the ship. Hellé went to the wedding, where her peeling sunburned nose caused the smart Athenians to comment, but she ignored them and looked deeply into the burning tapers' light. Hellé knew she had reached an emotional watershed, and although it was hot she felt cold inside. She put her feelings into her letters, using the words to convey her longing for him to write back and reassure her.

Flecker appeared to deal with the dilemma of meeting a woman like Hellé whilst engaged to Eleanor, by putting them both into his play *Don Juan*. Eleanor and Hellé became Lady Isabel and her sister, Anna. Don Juan was engaged to Isabel without the knowledge of Anna, the ugly sister. Engagement to Lady Isabel Framlington, the cold beauty, did not prevent Don Juan kissing Lady Anna, as he had kissed Hellé. The effect on Hellé's life was revealed in the dialogue he wrote between Don Juan and Anna:

> A. Why? say you. Am I not the ugliest girl that ever screamed and broke her looking-glass.[1051]
> [Don Juan had been surprised that Anna was passionate, just as Flecker must have been about Hellé.]
> D.J. (surprised): Anna, you're passionate!
> A. Did you think then
> Because I had read the old books of the world and seemed so dull, I was not passionate?'
> D.J. You're a strange woman.
> A. Oh, I have a mind,
> I've quite a subtle deep intelligence
> God gave it me ....
> D.J. (putting an arm round her waist)
> Anna, don't be so bitter.'

Anna later says:

> Did you but know
> The one brave moment of my life.
> D.J. What was it?
> A. The moment when you stooped to kiss my lips.

With Flecker's kiss (like Anna's from Don Juan), Hellé's love of beauty withered, as Anna told Don Juan:

Not morning and the flames of all her fountains,
Nor evening when she breaks in silver rain,
O not the murmur of those Austrial isles
Poised like red lilies on a sea that smiles.
Not all the chorus of the sons of heaven
Shouting for joy because the stars are fire....[1052]

Hellé recalled the beauty of the night she had spent on board with Flecker, and even if her descriptions were reminiscent of those of Heredia,[1053] her feelings about the beauty of the world were unlikely to be the same again: 'Venus shone to the south, so sparkling and large that it hung like a gem of liquid fire from the sky and threw a long silver trail in the waters. We saw the sunrise – not the gradual emerging of a reddish ball from the morning mists, as in these northern climes, but the God of Light leaping up from the East in full glory and immediately ruling the world – before returning to our cabins.'[1054]

Hellé and Flecker exchanged romantic and lyrical letters and copies of their own poems soon after his arrival in Constantinople on 19 June. An example of Hellé's prose style was: 'Though life is sweet I often feel I should like to lie down on dry earth and die in the sun and become a little cloud of white dust, a vanishing little cloud of white dust in the clear sky.'[1055]

This image influenced by 'parched Athens' was one that Hellé was fond of and she put in one of her poems. Initially, she wrote her verses in Greek with rough translations in English. Flecker sent her a draft of 'Pillage', which he had already read aloud to her when they first met. She acknowledged its receipt on 25 June. It was not until 2 July that he got round to writing to his parents. He could put his private mail in the diplomatic bag at the cost of a penny per letter (as ever a penny meant a lot of things), although he may not have realised that, in saving on postage he was not always guaranteed complete confidentiality.[1056] Complete confidentiality was required of his parents when they were told the startling news that Eleanor had wired (at his request) to tell him that she would marry him in October, but the matter was to be kept secret. Kept secret from Eleanor was the fact that he was now romantically involved with Hellé, who in turn was not told that he planned to get married. A very loving letter enclosing a beautiful new photograph arrived a week later from Eleanor. Exactly why he had arranged his marriage for October, he does not make entirely clear, but the secrecy element pointed to his lack of faith that it would happen as planned. Now that he was firmly on dry land, his telegram to Eleanor bore some affinity to his telegram from Uppingham requesting eggs and jam. In his present environment he was lonely, and a wife would help to end isolation. He was having to behave with more responsibility inside the Levant Consular Service, which operated to the same rules and regulations of society back home. He might have hoped that with a wife who looked the part, he would fare better than with Hellé by his side.

Savery received Flecker's brief initial impression of Constantinople: 'This place, praise God, is not a bit like the Near East Exhibition at Olympia and all mosques are not exactly the same.'[1057] Letters to his parents, as in the past, were filled with news about money matters. In case they thought that money difficulties were his fault, he complained about the loss to him when Turkish coinage was exchanged.

So much letter writing was possible because he had little consular work to do, when he first arrived. He had only to read 'the Turkish papers' every day; this he told his parents kept him 'pretty busy'[1058] He had to make a show of doing some work; there was doubt as to whether he might be sent to Sofia for four months or put into a pretty easy vacant job at Constantinople. Savery got a different view of his daily routine. He was told that he had little to do except translate bits out of the Turkish newspapers and take photographs, while still learning Turkish and law. Someone who knew about the Turkish Press and translating it was Reader Bullard,[1059] a fellow dragoman, who had arrived in Constantinople two years earlier and whom Flecker admired.

Reader Bullard had found that it was difficult to make summaries of important articles, as the key to the meaning in Turkish was in the last word of the sentence. The Turkish Press had been reformed, and unimportant official notices, reports and movements of crowned heads had been eliminated. The journalist could write more freely. 'The complicated high-flown Turkish of the past was inadequate to express the flood of ideas and comments which poured from the Press, and a new, simpler language began to be formed.'[1060]

The life of the Turkish people may have changed since the elections under the Young Turks, after the revolution of 1908. The lives of women, however, had not changed; they still remained veiled, and even the wives of Turkish officials were unlikely to appear at diplomatic gatherings. The working life of British Government officials also remained largely unchanged during Flecker's time. The duties of the junior consular officials consisted of registering documents in the old-fashioned archives, and going to the courts to help British subjects in trouble. 'Have had to settle a dispute to-day between a horrid Maltese and a Greek, and am very exhausted.'[1061] As Bullard explained, 'no British subject could be made to undergo a penalty or discharge a judgment debt unless a representative of his Embassy or Legation had been present throughout the proceedings and had signed the judgment.'[1062] This may have been a more accurate description of Flecker's part in any dispute that had gone to court, when there were British Maltese in Turkey.

It was important to tell his parent about the rigours of consular work, but he also let them know that *Thirty-Six Poems* was being favourably reviewed, and that 'dear old Haines of Uppingham' had written to him to congratulate him on his review in *The Spectator*. 'The oddest provincial journals review me. I really ought to be selling a few. I've had more reviews than any book of poems for many a day, and better ones.'[1063]

The Contemporary Review of July 1910 thought that *Thirty-Six Poems* showed considerable promise and that the poet was 'a young writer with definite ideals', which included 'beauty of sound and form, as well as intensity of thought and feeling'. The two 'Bathrolaire' sonnets, 'The Ballad of Hampstead Heath' and 'A Western Journey' were picked out for special mention. The review ended: 'We look forward to seeing another and more substantial volume from Mr. Flecker shortly'.

The English Review, in its July 1910 edition, also picked out 'The Ballad of Hampstead Heath' – 'Mr. Flecker is indeed an artist'. 'The Ballad of Camden Town' was picked out 'without a hint of a jingle or vulgarity;'. 'The Ballad of the Student in the South' was mentioned as having 'poignant sweetness and a scholarly simplicity'. He was described as 'being an artist, not an amateur', which tied up with what he had already told Hellé. The reader was asked to listen to 'The Queen's Song' and admire incidentally this young man who confronts Time and the relentless hunger of posterity with an exquisite fancy. The Queen's Song was quoted with the second verse omitted.

The *Daily Telegraph* of 4 August 1910 referred to Flecker's three dozen poems as being 'new', which was not entirely correct. The *Telegraph* noted the wide range from grave to gay in mood, and from simple ballad verse to a kind of Walt Whitman prose masquerading as verse. The *Telegraph* was particularly interested in 'The Ballad of the Londoner' also.

As well as a new order in Turkey there was a new Ambassador at the British Embassy in Constantinople. Sir Nicholas O'Conor, who died in March 1908, was reputed to have been one of the diplomats of the old school, a Catholic and very fussy about the conduct of those who worked under him. O'Conor was placed by Sir Gerard A. Lowther, Ambassador from 1908 to 1913. He was a man who had a great deal of money, but was said to lack elasticity.[1064]

Bullard had been happily ensconced for the summer months, as was the custom, in a shared house in the village of Kandilli, on the Asiatic side of the Bosphorus, five miles from the centre of the city. Bullard and Peckham had moved from the winter quarters they shared in Stamboul, where new freedoms in Turkey had meant that the coffee shops, markets and mosques provided a more stimulating atmosphere than Pera, the residential quarter (where Flecker first resided), which was mainly populated by foreigners and where Turkish was rarely heard. Stamboul was nearer their consular work, but by moving to Kandilli, they escaped the heat and continued with their language study. The imam of the mosque visited and chattered and told stories to the 'dragoboys' as the junior dragomans were known.[1065] These informal lessons with the imam meant that their study of Turkish was lacking in discipline. The appointment of lecturers in Turkish, so that the examinations could be passed satisfactorily, was still some time away, as the Foreign Office haggled over how much they were to be paid. Peckham, who had told Flecker about the house before Flecker left England, was transferred to the Consulate in the Dardanelles in 1909, where he was Acting Vice-Consul, and in March 1910 he had been sent to Crete. At the end of July, Flecker moved to join Bullard and others in the wooden house in Kandilli, which had a big fig tree in the garden at the back, under which they ate their meals. The house had been taken unfurnished. The walls were hung, by Flecker, with lots of printed hangings and a 'familiar green dragon of Dardanelles earthenware guarded the window-sill of his sitting-room'.[1066]

This dragon, which 'a celebrated archaeologist declared showed clear traces of Chinese influence,'[1067] was either a replacement or a companion for the 'Demon of All Sloth', displayed on the mantelpiece in Cambridge days. 'The love of pleasantly malformed beasts' continued, but other beasts in the house were not loved; these were the huge bugs that infested the house from time to time. Reference to them broke down the barrier between Bullard the official and Bullard the friend of Flecker.

It was fortunate that, in the absence of Peckham, he and Bullard became friends. As usual, Flecker had not been liked by everyone in the English community. His swarthy complexion gave rise to the usual prejudice, which would not be the case when 'talking to Turks in Stamboul'.[1068] Bullard and Peckham had donned fezes at night in the Turkish quarter in order to escape detection. Flecker shared a sense of fun with Bullard, whose East End of London background, 'dash of Huguenot', religious upbringing and love of Browning made a bond. Although he was not wholly dependent on Bullard for company in sporting pursuits, as Bullard did not care for exercise or games such as cricket.[1069] Kandilli had one of the very few tennis courts by the Bosphorus and Flecker played behind its high walls. He also wrote to his parents about playing one game of cricket, and bathing, although this could not have been at Kandilli, which had very strong currents preventing bathing and boating.

He found that horse-riding was uncomfortable, although he looked forward to it. He had not heeded Peckham's advice about taking his own saddle and bridle, and wrote home asking for them to be sent out to him, because a buckle sticking out of the Turkish saddle had resulted in his being 'nearly clawed to bits...'[1070] Savery took Flecker's interest in riding to mean he was becoming something of an Empire-Builder.[1071] He counteracted the accusation from Savery 'the healthy-minded man'[1072] and promised in the same letter to hang his room round with purple cloth and to take opium, as a remedy. Savery had urged Flecker to be 'decadent', but the nearest he came to following this advice in the open air was when he read 'Theocritus' (slowly translating from the Greek) to Bullard, while they were on a summit of an island in the Sea of Marmora on a beautiful blue day.[1073,1074] Bullard recalled that 'Everything was in keeping, even to a young goatherd with his pipe.'

A poem, which Flecker left unpublished,[1075] resulted from this day, in which the poet described watching 'from the window-seat' a boy playing a flute.[1076] The impression could be gained from the lines of this poem that the poet/speaker still 'hears' the flute playing in his mind back at the house in Kandilli, and that he found the boy attractive. The poem begins:

> A little boy was fluting in the street,
> I own, I watched him from the window-seat.
> His eyes quite bright and brown
> (I like brown eyes)
>
> But spite of fools who dub him bored effete
> God sends the meat still, if we only eat.[1077]

The move to the house at Kandilli, whose steep and cobbled streets were visible from his window, was of immense importance. Not only could he arrange rooms as he wanted, but he was enjoying (as he had the house at Southbourne and the cottages in Wales) an escape from the bustle of the city, He now had a chance to enjoy the view of the Bosphorus from the sitting-room window, which provided inspiration for his drafts of poems about the passing of ships, especially when the lamps swung high on the masts of ships steaming out to Russia through the gloom.[1078]

> Black lie the ships and blacker the men against it.[1079]

But too he wondered at the inside of the mosques:

Now in the Mosques the endless lamps are lighted
The faithful are shouting, the great sun dies
Even as the Faithful turn toward Meccah
I to the Sunset have turned my eager eyes
Sun gone to kiss the silver hills of England
Sun that awakens my lady where she lies.[1080]

Homesickness and thoughts of Eleanor's arrival combined in the lines:

Soon she will come ...
And ride the heathered downs of Asia
Where scent's heavy and the limeflower white...

Another version of this poem had the lines: 'Soon in the Mosques the thousand lamps are lighted.'[1081] (which was used eventually in his poem 'Saadabad') and 'And a thousand swinging steeples shall begin as they began,'.[1082]
And in his notebook:

Come soon to me she with this dream built city
Built in its glory alone for our delight
Come soon, ride the heathered Asian mountains
Only for us.

which eventually Flecker used in his poem 'Areiya', where he described the buildings and the rocks created for lovers alone:

This place was formed divine for love and us to dwell;
This house of brown stone built for us to sleep therein;
Those blossoms haunt the rocks that we should see and
    smell
Those old rocks break the hill that we the heights should
    win.[1083]

The enjoyment of the haven of the Kandilli house, where he could write about the 'outline of the minaret and dome' growing black, was short-lived, as the light burden of work became much heavier. By 2 August he was in sole charge of a vice-consulate, which had an annual budget of £80,000 (of which his share was £8,000), and the accounts and archives. Hellé was amused at his new responsibilities, but Flecker defended himself: 'Accounts you say, for a poet! And why not. Fascinating tidy rows of figures all marvellously balancing and not balancing in the end and the payment of good red gold.'[1084]

Any hint that he had failed to make a tidy job of his own accounts, was unknown to Hellé at this stage, although the irony of the situation did not escape his parents. 'Moreover he was not temperamentally a pastmaster of accounts.'[1085] But he was, he told his parents, grappling with 'the most complicated money system in the world, and the worst.'[1086] His emotional burdens became much heavier at the same time. Hellé was coming to Constantinople in ten days' time, he wrote to Savery 'then there will be a hell of a time'.[1087]

Hellé later stated that 'by a strange coincidence'[1088] she had been invited to stay with friends at Bebek on the opposite shore. Hardly a strange coincidence that she was accepting the invitation. If James Elroy Flecker had not been in Constantinople, she would not have undertaken the journey from Athens to Turkey at that time. It was true that she did not know about Eleanor, and although Flecker had told his parents that he was 'somewhat fed up' with Eleanor (now in Bavaria), whose letters were pleasant enough; he was 'getting sadly callous about the whole affair'.[1089] As usual, he was taking some of the faults that lay on his shoulders and unloading them onto Eleanor's. His treatment of Hellé and Eleanor certainly had an element of callousness in it. A suspicion remains that he rather enjoyed the pain he was inflicting on the women in his life, although they did not suspect it. Hellé complained about feeling pain, when he wrote and told her about Eleanor, although she realised he did not intend to cause pain. He told her that 'human frailty is a little thing under the stars'.[1090] Hellé did not agree and asked him if a star was more than a kiss? (An idea he worked out subsequently in his play *Don Juan*.)[1091]

He had laughed at her 'pretty English' and now to add to her pain she next got a letter telling her of his marriage plans. She replied, telling him that she had liked him, knowing it was only for one night. The letters indicated that she was beginning to get suspicious of his real feelings about his approaching marriage, as he had told her he was 'miserable' about the prospect, and she wondered why this should be so. She questioned the necessity of having a passion for her as well, and she did not think that because he was a poet he had a right to be unfaithful to his wife, she thought this sort of behaviour was simply a bad habit. No prospect, she seemed to be hinting, would be before him of having marriage and Hellé as a mistress in the background. She did not want, as he had suggested, to go through the same experience again with someone else, which she saw as unfair to the other person and not worthy of herself. She next wrote about the devouring force of passion, but she needed this to result in freedom once it was over. She wanted now the role of an affectionate friend. The dream she thought that they had shared, was over.

She was still coming to Bebek, the village on the opposite side of the Bosphorus from Kandilli. Hellé could not cancel her visit at this stage. To have done so, would reveal that she was only making the journey so that she could continue their relationship, and put it on a firmer footing. If marriage had been the sole aim of her visit, then upon the discovery that he had promised himself to another she would have seen it as advisable to cancel it, but in the role of affectionate friend, she would make the visit without losing face.

Hellé also concentrated on the practical aspects of her journey: the prospect of a Greek woman travelling alone, with little knowledge of Turkish, and the help she would need having decided not to give her friends on the European side of the Bosphorus the trouble of meeting her off the boat. (In the past European women had been molested by Turkish soldiers in the streets of Constantinople, if they ventured out without a male escort. They were likely to be pushed into puddles or muddy ground, but kisses were reserved for obese ladies.) Hellé would obviously need to be met by a male escort; it was a hint he could not ignore.

Eleanor got news of a different but still painful kind. She was given the news that he was 'broke'; like Hellé, she was beginning to grow suspicious. She did not understand why he was broke because she knew that he had an extra £100 a year, and no extra expenses, such as buying his fiancée expensive meals, but she was impressed by his new status as vice-consul.

Letting Eleanor know that he was broke (not a piece of news that at this stage he shared with his other correspondents) could be due to his knowing that his lack of finances would irritate her, and even (he might hope) make her consider postponing the marriage to give him a bit of breathing space. He may have been acting like Mr. Rochester in the novel he disliked, *Jane Eyre*, when in an effort to get rid of the rich and beautiful Blanche Ingram, he let her know that he was not as rich as she had thought, so that she would be put off the idea of marriage. Rochester used Blanche to make Jane Eyre jealous, but did not let Blanche know that he was in love with Jane. Flecker sent Eleanor a poem:

LIGHT ARE YOUR EYES

Light are your eyes as the sky before the sunset
Deepening to dark, mysteriously blue;
Pale was your brow as of one who holds a secret,
Honeysweet, meadowsweet, blossom, pale as you
Low was your voice like streams of all the mountains
That pour in the silence their cups of moorland dew.

Love, come to me: and when day goes under
I will tell you tales that only poets know.[1092]

Light were your eyes as the blue before the sunset
Deepening to dark lit mysteriously blue
Pale was your brow as of one who holds a secret
Low was your voice like the streams of all the mountains
That pour in the silence their cups of moorland dew.[1093]

These lines, which are among verses that make reference to 'This song I send' 'for you to read in England' 'maid of England' as well as to 'heathered downs or mountains' of Asia and the 'hills of Wales' where they had first met, were not likely to be appreciated by Eleanor, who would be expected to leave the social delights and comforts of London for what amounted to no more than vague promises of 'tales that only poets know/Sweet tales, old tales/.' He could not have been surprised when she told him that he must know by now that she knew nothing of poetry, she had given him ample proof.

Eleanor had not been given sufficient proof of why he could describe himself now as 'broke'. She did not know about the hiring of landaus and the expeditions around Athens, which her fiancé would have to contribute to if he was to keep Hellé impressed. But Flecker was not the only member of the Consular Service to find himself broke, and his shortage of cash was not due to extravagance. Bullard had found on his arrival that he was still being paid the £200 per year of a student-interpreter instead of the £300 per year of a Consular Assistant. Bullard had had to miss meals because of his shortage of cash, so the habit of scrimping and saving was still with him, although it might not be strictly necessary in his present circumstance. Records show that Flecker was promoted to Consular Assistant on 23 May 1910,[1094] and his lack of cash could be due, in part, to administrative delays, rather than extravagance. Eleanor had pointed out that he had an extra £100 a year to spend and no college fees or books to buy, but the emphasis on being broke (which could have been a temporary problem) was necessary to put Eleanor off the idea of coming to Turkey. In the same way, Bullard put emphasis on his shortage of cash because he wanted to explain his sacrifice in becoming a member of the Levant Consular Service, and he had to pay for his uniform. Flecker's parents had paid for his. Flecker had told part-truths in his letters to Hellé and Eleanor, and this reference to being broke had a similar element of part-truthfulness. Bullard's ability in handling cash and pressing Turkish Departments to pay their debts was one that enabled him to get promotion to Third Dragoman. His financial prospects then improved once the cost of his uniform had been reimbursed. Flecker's parents paying for his outfit or uniform was similar to their payment for him to join the Oxford Union. They quibbled over smaller expenditures and, at Oxford, over what they saw as luxuries and what were considered to be necessities. The uniform was not considered by Peckham to be a necessity, although a frock-coat and top hat were thought to be essential. Peckham told Flecker that he might not be able to attend some interesting functions unless he was wearing his uniform. His parents, who had not thought his wearing a school uniform at Dean Close to be essential, now may have realised that their son would be at a disadvantage if he did not have one. The old idea of not caring what others thought appeared to have died. The undress uniform and cap were made of the same blue cloth. The jacket had a black velvet collar, worn over a buff waistcoat for morning wear and a white one for evenings. Flecker was only able to wear the uniform about ten times, so its cost, about £30, was a bit of an extravagance. He tried to recoup the loss, when Savery also needed a uniform for his vice-consular post as they were both the same size.[1095]

The shortage of money to spend on day-to-day living was not confined to Flecker and Bullard. The revolution had meant a rise in prices in Turkey, which resulted in all Consular Officials clamouring for an increase in salaries to meet the cost of living. In time this was considered seriously by the Foreign Secretary. A shortage of cash coincided, as it had in the past, with a turning to some form of journalism to supplement his income. An article he wrote in July 1910, 'The Bus in Stamboul' did not get published in magazine form, but 'Candilli', another article, was published in the Saturday *Westminster Gazette*, on 15 October 1910. These articles served as a means, too, of expressing his longings for England, and his feelings about his romantic entanglements: 'Thus, like a chime of silver, distant bells, or some sweet poem of a fickle lover who has strung together the names of his mistresses and loves...'[1096]

Political events in Turkey had subsided by the time Flecker arrived in Constantinople; in some ways it was a similar time to his arrival in

Cambridge, when too the excitement had died down. Bullard had experienced the counter-revolution and had encountered , when he crossed the Galeta Bridge (which connected the European town with the Turkish quarter), two groups of Turkish soldiers firing rifles at each other. When Flecker went across the same bridge, in a red motor-bus, he sat down beside a very fat Turk, and the place names Oxford Circus, Marble Arch, Edgware Road and Cricklewood brought back vivid memories, the last in particular. He embodied this incident in 'Bus in Stamboul', writing that if 'brave Cricklewood had you but walls would be found more enlightenment and knowledge, more true learning and humanity than in all this bright imperial city, age-worn, battered, be-jewelled, prostitute of East and West, which you now supply, O wealthy Cricklewood, with your superfluous means of transport.'[1097] The repeated references to Cricklewood and Hampstead reinforce the idea that his poems and prose about that part of London, that his time in London and the poems he wrote about north-west London had deep significance for him, even if in this article he poked fun at the notices still in the bus, warning passengers against putting wet mackintoshes on the seat. He wrote 'Well there was a shower here last month now I come to think of it.' Camden Town's little homes' also featured in *Don Juan* (Act 2, Scene 2 p.90).

He longed for more than the streets of London, whilst he admired the view across the Bosphorus from his window to the 'chivalrous old towers of Roumeli Hissar'.[1098] He longed 'for a slag-heap or a gaswork, or any strong, bold, ugly thing to break the spell of this terrible and malignant beauty that saps body and soul?' This was the theme of his article. 'For here, it seems is the very face of Beauty,' ... But he wondered what he could do with it, and why was it 'part of my foolish daily life': 'A poet might sing of it, and find peace.' He had found the same scenes 'were joyful that day I rode over the Anatolian hills, and the weariness of body banished all sickness from the mind, ...' He was beginning to understand: 'why men of the East will sit by a fountain from noon to night, and let the world roll onward.'[1099]

The trouble was that he was engaged in a humble capacity doing mundane work, not as a poet. He stated (in *The King of Alsander*) that the British Consulate he described was not based on his own experience of consulates. This fictional consulate, with its comical descriptions of the office being difficult to locate, and the caretaker having to be found, the sharing of the office in a building which housed, amongst others, the maker of false teeth, would bear some resemblance to the vice-consulate he did preside over. The vision conjured up of his vice-consular status as far as Eleanor and his family were concerned would be vastly different, as it would be in his own mind, when offered the post. He was not the only member of the service to publish their humorous but fair descriptions of their time in Constantinople. Harold Nicolson in *Some People* wrote about Titty, Head of Chancery at the Embassy. 'If all the Service consisted of Candilli, 'twould be a very pleasant life indeed.'[1100] Flecker had written to his parents in August. Kandilli, too, was useful when expecting guests. Flecker had taken Hellé's not much veiled hint and arranged to meet her off the boat from Athens on 14 August. He had told her to tell her friends in Bebek that she would arrive some time on the Sunday evening, so that they could have 'a whole wicked day together'.[1101]

The feelings they had for each other were strengthened, but Hellé was worried to notice that he was thinner and suffered from a continual sore throat. Despite this apparent ill-health, the lovers were able to meet many times, often alone. Hellé was introduced to Reader Bullard, when they had a picnic together with some other colleagues and charged them for some of the expenses.[1102] Reader Bullard was impressed by Hellé; he did not mention Hellé's friends being at the picnic. If these friends tried to play the role of chaperones, they failed completely; references to 'all the places where we made love to each other' appeared in a letter to Hellé, and referred to this time.[1103]

Flecker's parents eventually knew of Hellé's visit to Constantinople, and they were not unnaturally alarmed at the outcome of the visit from a number of points of view. The fact that Hellé had come on her own was initially covered up, and it was later suggested that their son had met up with more than one Greek friend on the voyage out, and they had all met up together for a series of delightful picnics.[1104] But in mentioning Flecker's poem 'Saadabad' and quoting a few lines, which referred to a secret meeting between lovers, the truth about the meeting of Flecker and Hellé was more honestly revealed:

> Beautiful and broken fountains, keep still your
> Sultan's dream,
> Or remember how his poet took a girl to Saadabad?

These lines 'recalls those long sweet summer days of his early official life'.[1105]

Hellé herself was later reluctant to reveal how much opportunity they had had to meet alone on her visit to Constantinople. But the inclusion of the lines from 'Saadabad' can be seen not only as a sly means of letting the readers know about what went on during Hellé's visit, apart from enjoyable picnics, but the eventual writing of the poem was such an important stage in Flecker's development as a poet, and due dramatically to meeting Hellé on the voyage out. The fact that it initially owed its inspiration to Hellé and Flecker appearing to flout the conventions of their day was neither here nor there. 'Saadabad' was, Flecker was to say, 'the most passionately sincere I have ever written. It was written straight out and not a line revised.'[1106] This approach and feeling about his poem is in contrast to the poem, which he wrote for Eleanor without the same sort of inner satisfaction, and certainly in more than one draft:

> Come with me down back among the centuries
> I will tell you tales that only poets know
> Sweet tales, old tales, tales of Royal lovers
> Whose loves were as our loves in ages long ago.
> Crowns fell and towns fell and dynasties were shattered
> For eyes like starlight and bodies like the snow.[1107]

Verses 1, 3 and 4 of part 1 of 'Saadabad' are translations from the Turkish. Flecker explained to Savery, when telling him about 'the individual passion of Saadabad'.[1108] The Turkish was that of Nedim, a court poet who had lived in the eighteenth century and was a patron of the arts. Nedim had a great reputation in Ottoman poetry, and it was he who said: 'Lie a little to your mother:' and

> Banish then, O Grecian eyes the passion of the
> waiting West!

No doubt remains, that these lines were a reference to Hellé, as Flecker wrote them in the flyleaf of the book of poems (*Forty-Two Poems*) he gave her.

So much of the Hellé/Flecker relationship is at times reflected in the *King of Alsander* that Flecker, as Norman had done, may have invited Hellé to choose a present as some sort of recompense for his behaviour in deceiving her, just as Norman had suggested to Peronella. If he did, it paints a more homely aspect of their relationship, than their passion amongst the ruins of Stamboul. The shop where Norman Price invited Peronella to choose her present had: 'snuff-boxes, shawls, dirty old silver, tattered bits of embroidery, carved walking-sticks, some worm-eaten books, last century oak settees, Turkish zarfs, Hittite cylinders, Chinese saucers full of Greek and Roman coins, real stones, and bits of glass, animals in beaten bronze ware from Damascus, very old leather bottles from England, some forged Egyptian antiquities, some very horrible cameos, some rather pretty intaglios, about three quarters of what had been a fine Persian rug ...'[1109]

Hellé had to return to Athens early in September; she posted a letter at Smyrna where her boat called en route for Athens, and as her love was embodied in Flecker the poet and not Flecker the Consular Official, she read his poem, 'To a Poet a Thousand Years Hence'. She felt sure that one day the world would acknowledge him as a great poet. Her worries lay in the immediate practical consequences of his cold and sore throat, and the more distant prospect when they would be reunited after a long separation or even death.

Added to the emotional impact of Hellé's visit, his poetry writing and consular duties, he had to think of publishing plans once again, this time his prose piece *The Grecians*.

He wrote the preface to *The Grecians*, dating it 'The British Consulate, Constantinople, September 1910'. His chief claim in the preface was to 'the kind attention of my readers', and he told his readers that he had been 'many times and in many places a schoolmaster'. This statement was something of an exaggeration, but he told the readers that he had tried to make the dialogue resemble real conversation, and that he aimed at 'abruptness, vigour and compression rather than at rounded periods and exact arrangement of subjects.' He mentioned this in case any reader was 'offended by a merely artistic violence of language, may imagine it expressive of thoughtlessness or lack of sincerity on the part of the Author.' That bit of work done, Flecker could think of relaxation once again. Shortly after Hellé's departure, he went on a picnic on the shores of the Black Sea and bathed in 'real waves', after which he was taken ill and admitted to hospital with a slight fever, which he thought was due to being overtired. But after coming out of the British Seamen's Hospital his health showed signs of breaking down again. He had been under the care of the doctor from 10 September, and he eventually wrote on 16 September to tell his parents from hospital that 'the doctor has discovered germs of consumption in me'.[1110] He needed to take sick leave at once. The doctor held out hope of a cure, but Flecker made no attempt to hide his deep shock. He needed to borrow the fare home from his parents. Sick leave was granted by the Consular Service, although at this stage they were given no indication as to the nature of Flecker's illness. He wrote to Hellé with the same disastrous news, telling her too of his misery, but that he was not going to die. He hoped to see her in Athens in a few days' time, when his boat called there.

The onset of his consumption was always attributed by his parents to this particular dip in the Black Sea. 'He need not have plunged into an ice-cold sea when he was intolerably hot'[1111] was a comment made by his parents, appearing to be wise after the event. A letter dated 13 September was quoted[1112] in which Flecker mentioned just recovering from a slight fever, before the splendid picnic, but what was not made clear was that this letter was written from hospital, and that the letter to his father dated 16 September, in which Flecker broke the news of his 'germs of consumption', was not the first one written from hospital. It was a fact that Flecker had a fever and sore throat before he plunged into the waves of the Black Sea, and whether this was the sole cause of his admission to hospital would not necessarily be the case; the departure of Hellé could have had an added effect on his health.

Flecker was in the British Seamen's Hospital from the 10 to the 19 September, and Dr. Maclean had found tubercle bacilli in his sputum and signs of early phthisis (consumption) in the right apex of his lung. Dr. Maclean did not pass on these findings to the Foreign Office,[1113] and the Foreign Office did not consider it necessary to find out which doctor Flecker had been under and what the nature of his illness was for another two years.

The British Seamen's Hospital was not entirely for British Seamen but took patients from other walks in life, as well as private patients. It had occurred to the Foreign Office to make enquiries into what went on, from the financial point of view, at the British Seamen's Hospital, in view of the Workers' Compensation Act which meant that the cost of the stay at the Seamen's was offset by the firms that had employed them, through insurance companies. The Foreign Office had been making enquiries about Dr. Maclean's salary and his opportunities for private practice. This financial probing would not endear the Foreign Office to Dr. Maclean, who gave his patient hope of recovery and, as far as was possible, the Foreign Office having taken him on could pay for his upkeep.

The Victorian idea that consumption was avoidable, or a consequence of the sufferer's own actions, prevailed in his parents' minds although the type of TB their son had contracted was of the most lethal form.[1114] They thought that their son could have been 'brought to believe that drastic self-sacrifice and control of immediate desires were absolutely essential to a permanent cure'.[1115] This sort of thinking on their part ignored the fact that there had been something very badly wrong with their son's health, and that this went back at least to the early months of 1908, or even much earlier. Consumption was a common enough disease in Flecker's childhood, when, like most of the population, he would have become infected, but unlike most of the population he would have failed to combat it. Schools have been found to be a source of outbreaks of TB and other diseases.[1116] Uppingham School had suffered an outbreak of typhoid after the boys returned from the summer vacation of 1875, when it was found that the drinking water was contaminated. It was wrongly felt by Thring that his system of separate Houses would make isolation of sick pupils simple, and sending boys home would help to spread the epidemic. Thring did not know the cause of the sickness that the boys suffered from and even the fact that it was typhoid was not known, at first. Thring continued to ride out the storm, even when three boys died, but eventually the school was dismissed in November, only to be recalled in January. In March the school was sent on holiday and then transferred to Borth on the Welsh coast, between May 1876–7. After this enforced exile by the sea, the school did not fully recover its former reputation. Thring's rallying cry, that he did not believe in running from illness, was a legacy that remained, and any sort of repeat epidemic (such as consumption) would certainly not have been welcomed.

Flecker's ideal school, which he outlined at length in *The Grecians* and which can be seen to be based more on his time at Uppingham than Dean Close (his preface refers to having been educated in one public school and that he had lived most of his life in another), discussed the problems of hygiene at schools:

> We must have also a sanatorium under the direct management of a resident doctor. Strange it is, though, that any school which has the impertinence to ask over a hundred pounds a year for training and keeping boys as boarders should be destitute of these advantages.[1117]

Dean Close had a sanatorium where Flecker was said to have written two poems when he was aged 'about fifteen' and he made a 'frenzied protest' against the wallpaper.[1118] His near-contemporary, Ronald Firbank, also had something of a wallpaper phobia, or at least when dying, Firbank did not want his friends to visit him because of the awfulness of the hotel bedroom's wallpaper. Firbank was ill during his time at Uppingham, and could have been incarcerated in a room there, which served as a sickroom. It seems strange, at Dean Close, to put wallpaper on the walls of a school sanatorium, and this illness of Flecker's could have related instead to Uppingham, not Dean Close. Uppingham School, with its poor food, early morning activities, long exhausting country runs and a reputation for beatings, would do nothing to promote the health of the pupils, and if it did not have a resident doctor the onset of illness would not be detected in term time.

The question of why the medical examination before entering the service did not (in Flecker's case and others) detect factors that would indicate that they were unfit medically for the rigours of the service had a simple answer. The medical examination was not strict enough.

The question of making medical examinations stricter had resulted in correspondence and memos between the Levant Consular Service and the Civil Service Commission as far back at 1903, and the matter was not yet resolved. The stumbling-block appeared to be the supposed necessity of changing the existing regulations for the recruitment to the Levant Consular Service, which were designed to attract a large number of candidates.

The Service, it was stated, suffered from those who contracted illness, not long after they joined, which meant that they could only work in 'healthy' posts. Sympathy was not given in these official memos, and a complaint was made about one candidate, whom it was felt that the Foreign Office could have got rid of, but did not. It was also felt by the Foreign Office that it had become a misfortune for Assistants to be of sound disposition, as they had to bear the extra burden of replacing those on sick-leave.

It was not until 1909 that the Foreign Secretary decreed that the medical examinations should be made as stringent as possible. By that time, Flecker had already fallen through the net. How much he would have co-operated with a doctor making the examination, could be seen in the attitude towards doctors adopted by Norman Price. 'The Doctor then rose, came round the table, and seizing hold of the unfortunate, tapped him, pinched him, prodded him, poked him, felt his muscles, sounded his chest, examined his tongue, blew in his ears, slapped his stomach, and tried his pulse. All this to the intense aggravation of his victim.'[1119]

No medical test could be devised to weed out those candidates who would not be considered suitable to withstand the mental stress of the job. Andrew Ryan, a candidate in 1896, chose the Levant Student Interpretership because his health had given rise to anxiety before he made the choice and he thought that it would be a barrier to getting into the Indian Civil Service, particularly as he had not been to Oxford and Cambridge and would be doubly hampered. The fact that his ill-health might prevent him from getting into the Levant Consular Service did not ever seem to strike him, in view of his later breakdown in health. Bullard related that the medical examination 'gave no trouble', which indicated that it was the language examinations, which were the most important hurdle to get over before being accepted as a student-interpreter, the candidate's health was a minor matter.

The chance of a healthy life for dragomen in the Levant Consular Service was never high, even if they avoided the maiming for life or murder, which happened to two of Flecker's intake, in the course of their duties. Bullard had served as Acting Vice-Consul in Beirut in 1909–10, where he got typhoid fever, and was nursed by German nurses of the Order of St. John, a not-too-unpleasant experience he had found, although this period of illness from the end of November 1909 to the middle of January 1910 was one factor that meant he could not be paid an extra allowance for his work as Acting Vice-Consul in Beirut. Diplomatic colleagues were not transferred to provincial posts in this way.[1120] The domino effect of consular staff replacing the sick, the deceased or those going on leave was a continual process. Andrew Ryan[1121] (who had entertained Professor Browne and his wife in Constantinople) had a nervous collapse in 1910, and he, like Flecker, had been ordered home at a moment's notice. Ryan was away from May until October, when he was able, with the aid of strychnine, to carry on through the winter.[1122] The Chief Dragoman in Flecker's time, Gerald H. Fitzmaurice, also a devoted public servant, was to suffer a severe breakdown in health in 1914.

G.H. Simmons, a man of nearly sixty who had been in the Consular Service since starting as a junior clerk at the age of twenty, had been made Vice-Consul in September 1899, and had put in for leave in May 1910, starting August 1910. Simmons had not been on leave since 1907. It was his post that Flecker had filled with no real explanation given as to why, with so little experience, he had been put in this post, except that from Flecker's point of view it was better than being transferred to Sofia and he may have anticipated extra payment. From the consular service's point of view, as Flecker had no specific job, he was the only person free to take on the post. It was not surprising that he made some 'hideous mistakes' and was not 'equal to the job'.[1123]

The Consular Service did not appear to make any connection between Flecker's not being up to the job and his illness at the time the remarks were made about his incompetence. The exact nature of his errors is not outlined, although Bullard tells of two letters, one for London and one for Australia getting into the wrong envelopes but does not rule out Flecker's seriousness in trying to learn the routine of the consulate.[1124] Bullard himself was not above making mistakes. One appeared to be of a more serious kind, when he translated the amended Turkish Constitution, which went unchecked to the Foreign Office, and Bullard received a personal letter of thanks from the Foreign Secretary. But a few months later, a crisis erupted because of two words Bullard had omitted. Bullard was not penalised for this error, but at the time it was discovered he was not asking for sick-leave.[1125]

Flecker's own reaction to his hope of a cure for his illness, and the fact that it was not described at all to his superiors in the first instance, resulted in him not appreciating the seriousness of it in relation to his career. But however he might portray it to others, his illness put his mind back to the first time he had faced such a crisis, which was in 1906, just before his Oxford finals, and this feeling is reflected in his poem:

> I shall never forget that night –
> Mid-April, four years gone – [1126]

This poem, which he dated October 1910, also refers in an unpublished verse to a 'poisoned kiss', which Hellé said referred to a meeting in London with a girl he had known in Oxford who was dying of TB. This poem was called 'Song' and was revised as 'In Memoriam'.

The draft of the poem initially entitled 'Song' contained lines scored through as well as the final but unpublished verse:

> I met you on the ancient bridge
> We met upon

These lines indicate an Oxford meeting rather than London. He also scored through the following lines:

> Was it a poisoned kiss you gave me
> Darling all those years ago

and

> By the river years ago

until he settled for the verse (which he did not publish):

> Dear a poisoned kiss you gave me
> In that silent shining street
> Now they say that none shall save me
> Darling, but the kiss was sweet.

He scored out another line which came after 'none shall save me' which was: 'My feet go where once your feet', the idea of his illness taking him to the same death, now faced.[1127]

'Song' was published in *The Tramp* in December 1910, and revised as 'In Memoriam'. The verse about 'a poisoned kiss' was omitted when published in CP.

The fear at the front of his mind, at Oxford, would not be TB (which had not then been diagnosed) but venereal disease; Baudelaire, under whose influence he had fallen at Oxford, had written in his book *My Heart Laid Bare* that syphilis (from which he eventually died), represented some sort of coming of age: 'The day a young writer corrects his first proofs, he's as proud as a schoolboy who's just caught the pox.'[1128]

Flecker had been correcting the proofs of *The Best Man*, when his finals were looming and he experienced his distress and depression in April 1906. Baudelaire also frequently described his symptoms, which included 'painful constrictions in the throat'[1129] Baudelaire sent a poem to Mme. Sabatier entitled 'To One Who Is Too Gay', which ended with the line that indicated he wanted to inject the woman with his 'blood'; he later replaced 'blood' with 'venom'. The poem was condemned by the criminal court as the last stanzas were 'a possible offence to public morals'. The syphilitic interpretation 'was Baudelaire's.'[1130]

Flecker could have thought that whatever symptoms he had at this time were due to some form of venereal disease, although the only form of the disease he could have caught simply by kissing would be herpes. But the idea of writing a poem four years later when 'a poisoned kiss' was received from a woman (instead of the man injecting the woman) was written by Flecker, when the knowledge that he had TB brought back memories of a time when he also thought he had contracted a fatal illness, and the source was a woman. Hellé stated that the poem 'Song', which Flecker sent to her, was 'the haunting reminiscence of his meeting in London with a young girl he had, I believe, known at Oxford who had been slowly dying of his own complaint.'[1131]

The nature of the relationship with the Oxford shop-girl can be seen in Norman's relationship with Peronella, as Peronella is made up of aspects of Eleanor, Hellé and the unknown Oxford shop-girl. Peronella told Norman 'passionately, 'I love you, and that is enough. What do I care who you are?' '

> "If your love were deep, perhaps you would care who I was."

The saying of this sentence was the worst thing Norman ever did in his life. His conscience haunted him for years and never let him forget those dozen careless words and their cynical hypocrisy.[1132]

In Flecker's play *Don Juan*, the real-life Eleanor, Hellé, and the Oxford shop-girl become Lady Isabella, daughter of Lord Framlington, a Beauty, Lady Anna her ugly sister and Tisbea, a Fisher Lass. Tisbea, aged 19, although she is 'plainly attired' when she comes down the cliff (in Act 1, Scene 2, of *Don Juan*)[1133] and her legs and arms are bare, she is described as tall, strapping and a black-eyed beauty. Tisbea loved Don Juan very much but he abandons her for the reason that he is 'of those who would shape their life into music, and force their solo through the dominants of life.'[1134]

Don Juan does not want the simple vagabond life that might have been his with Tisbea, who admits that she is not a scholar. This is hardly surprising, and the Oxford shop-girl would not have the opportunity for scholarship, but Flecker had written: 'I once heard a shop-girl say that two plays she liked best were *The Silver King* and "that one where the black man gets jealous and kills his girl." She meant *Othello*'. [1135]

Tisbea was left for the reason that Norman abandoned Peronella, namely that she would not allow him to develop as a poet, and just as for Flecker to contemplate marrying a poor girl whilst at Oxford was not among his scheme of things, even if his mother would have accepted a shop-girl as a daughter-in-law. A girl without an income would not have stood in the way of Flecker's poetry writing, but he would have felt the need to get some sort of humdrum toil in order to support his wife and family or perish in the John Davidson mode. Eleanor had her private income, and her social class was acceptable to his mother, the only difficulty was that Mrs. Flecker thought Eleanor's family a bit too high up the social scale. But Flecker had felt that Eleanor's lack of appreciation for his poetry and her reluctance to stay on the same rung of the social ladder on their marriage, put another barrier against a happy marriage and his development as a poet. Eleanor's advantage had been her physical beauty, Flecker had though Hellé plain at first, she did not have as much money as Eleanor, and her Greek nationality (in the eyes of his family and the Levant Consular Service) would be a handicap. She had advantages over the Oxford shop-girl. But the scene in the last act with Tisbea was described as a stroke of genius by George Bernard Shaw, when he read the typescript, and this proves that, at the time of his writing, Flecker's ill-starred love for the Oxford shop-girl was far enough in his past for him to make use of it. The wounds the relationship had inflicted, and the necessity of hiding them, provided convincing prose and drama, and an unpublished poem,

> There is a grey room in my heart
> Where walks my love;

There is a grey shrine in my heart
Where sits my marbled love
And does not move.

I will knock and call at the closed door
To reach my love;
I will cry and cast me down before
The stone face of my love
That she may move.[1136]

A case could be made out for this poem being written with Eleanor in mind, but much as he was attracted to Eleanor at one time, he admitted that 'we have positively never been happy together at all.'[1137] The fact of the poem being written to the unknown shop-girl is more likely.

The poem also could be seen as a way of coping with his old love for Beazley, because it bears some resemblance to his poem 'Oak and Olive', which has the lines: 'And once I touched a broken girl /

And knew that marble bled.' [1138] which has been related to a poem by Beazley.[1139] But as Tisbea's farewell is poignant when she accuses Don Juan:

You just hope
To make a pretty poem out of me.
And when the last line's polished[1140] – off you go,
(Sobbing) And I may swallow blood for all you care.[1141]

it seems to be based on a real experience, unconnected with Eleanor or Beazley.

The drama in Flecker's own immediate life subsided temporarily when his temperature went down, and by 22 September he was aboard the Marseilles packet-boat, which meant he would reach London in about six days' time. He wrote to his parents much in the same way as if to reassure them, as he had done after his arrival in Oxford and was away from home for the first time. He described the boat as 'very fine and comfy'.[1142] His parents were footing the bill for the first-class and speedier travel.

He expected that the boat would call en route at Piraeus, where he would have a brief reunion with Hellé, but due to cholera in Russia, quarantine regulations prevented it, and their letters from being received. Hellé had tried to reassure him that she would do all that was possible to see him. She blamed his illness on over-work, which she thought, if she was by his side on the voyage to Marseilles, would be cured. He wrote describing the few passengers as 'all quite impossible', except for one who was a conjurer. Flecker had been reading 'Theocritus' and novels, in his deckchair, and dreaming of Hellé and himself living together in Stromboli. The creative element of his illness was not something he was slow to recognise, and he was still on full pay.

As the ship went round Cape Spartivento before entering the Straits of Messina, a cargo boat ran into the packet-boat, an event Flecker witnessed. The Commandant manoeuvered, but a large 'dint' was made in the side of the packet-boat, which, Flecker attested in a written document, was all the fault of the other ship, which had gone off 'without so much as whistling its sorrow, on the way to Trieste.'[1143] Flecker realised that he had had a second brush with death, and he told Hellé that he might not have been able to write a letter at all; he would have been washed up on the south Italian coast. *Don Juan*, Flecker's play, opened with the sinking of a steamer and the shipwreck of the crew, but Flecker changed the original from a Naples voyage to the coast of Wales.

On the way from Marseilles to London, Flecker spent some time in the Latin quarter of Paris, which he did not reveal to Hellé at the time. But letters sent frantically as they were both in transit (Hellé was due back in Paris) did not reach their destinations at the right time, giving rise to much unnecessary anxiety, which added to the physical hazards of the journey. The crossing of the English Channel was much the worst he had ever known; it took him, he told his parents, seven hours instead of three and a half, but he was not seasick. The voyage, he felt, had improved his health greatly, but he intended to see a specialist.

Aunt Rachel and her husband, from Sydenham, met him at the station.

CHAPTER EIGHT

Whilst still at Sydenham, Flecker, with his parents, went to consult the Harley Street specialist, who advised three months' stay in a sanatorium. In view of the previous positive test results from Constantinople, the specialist had no other choice. He had to insist on isolation in a sanatorium, despite his patient deciding beforehand that he was feeling far too healthy to enter what he regarded as 'one of those little funnels of infection'.[1144] This prejudice could not have been influenced by advice from Hellé, as at this stage he had not received her letter, which suggested alternative treatment, or by the visit he made with his father to dedicate the chapel of a sanatorium in 1904. It could only have been a less well-appointed establishment, such as one where he had visited his old love when she had been a patient. Flecker had wanted instead, as he had already told his parents in a letter: 'A cottage with a balcony in good air – books – heaps to eat – with a good doctor near to treat me from time to time.'[1145] (When quoting from this letter NGJ p.110, the word 'milk' comes after eat and 'test' is replaced by 'treat'.)

Despite his objections, Flecker found himself in the Cotswold Sanatorium in the village of Cranham, near Stroud, seven miles from Cheltenham, which he had visited with his father in 1904. On 8 October Flecker wrote to Savery, who was starting along a Foreign Office path in Munich. He told Savery that he was suffering from 'incipient and not too serious consumpers'.[1146] He complained about draughts and cold and he wished that there was someone in the sanatorium who was not 'either a tout or else godlessly dull'.[1147] This last complaint was soon to be remedied. His isolation amongst strangers (although he had visitors from outside) ended shortly after his arrival, as it had done at the Fabian camp and on board the boat taking him to Turkey, by meeting a woman. The 'autumn leaves and colours, very lovely,' of the nearby Cranham beechwoods[1148] formed a beautiful background for romantic feelings, and just as powerful as the mountains of Wales or the Greek islands. The woman at the sanatorium was nineteen years old. Her name was Leila Grace Jane Berkeley.[1149] She was not suffering from consumption but she was with her sister Gladys,[1150] who was lying in a bed in the sanatorium surrounded by flowers, and who was described by Flecker as 'wretched ill'.[1151] Both sisters were very beautiful and Flecker thought that Leila was 'the only girl I've seen lovelier than mine'.[1152] This 'mine' could have been a reference to Eleanor, with whom he was still in contact (as he was with Beazley), and not Hellé, whose looks he did not appear to rate as highly, at least not in letters to Savery. But at this stage in his correspondence with Savery, Flecker concentrated on telling Savery that he was going to write what he saw as some horrible poems about consumption. Although Gladys's illness could have been a further source of inspiration, the original inspiration went much further back in his life, to his time at Oxford. Whatever treatment the sanatorium offered Flecker it was not a regime that curtailed his writing activities.

Savery got news about his literary ventures. Flecker had just corrected the final proofs of *The Grecians*; and the publishers, Dent's, were going to suggest some revisions before they considered accepting his novel for publication. As well as some 'horrible' poems, he was going to write a book about poetry. He asked Savery about Galsworthy's *Justice*, which had 'got the prisons reformed', and he asked Savery's opinion of Arnold Bennett's *Old Wives' Tale*, and of Conrad and *Tono-Bungay*. Flecker felt that this was a great school of novelists and that the Victorians 'are outshined'. He told Savery that he was looking forward to the prospect of going to convalesce in Sicily with Hellé. The specialist had advised that after the three months were up, his patient take a further six months' rest in some fresh open country. The opportunity to tell Hellé his plans for them to sojourn together in Italy was delayed due to his not realising, until he eventually re-read her two letters, which had been forwarded from Constantinople, that she had included her Paris address. This seemed a strange oversight, and indicated that he had not read and re-read her letters at every opportunity available to him, but he was in the process of convincing himself that he was not in love with Hellé, and that Leila was his love. 'I like the one who loves me' was how he described his relationship with Hellé, and with Leila he thought that it was the other way round, he was to write to Savery.[1153]

By 15 October, correspondence with Hellé was back on course, despite the risk of a strike of railway workers. Flecker replied to her two 'bitter-sweet' letters in which Hellé had hoped for a meeting in Athens when he was en route for Marseilles. He told her now that he dreamed of Sicily or Corsica or the Lago di Garda, which was soon to be the next destination of Leila and Gladys, but at this stage Hellé was ignorant of the added attractions of the last place.

All these dreams had to be paid for and on 17 October, in a letter to his superiors in Constantinople, he enclosed two accounts, one for expenses for his outward journey from Constantinople and one for half-expenses for his sick-leave home. He also enquired how long he would be on full pay.[1154] It was as well, when financial security was in some doubt, that literary ventures were going fairly well. 'Candilli', his article written in Constantinople, was published in the 15 October edition of the *Saturday Westminster Gazette*.

The *SWG* was an influential literary supplement of the WG and as important as *The Times Literary Supplement*. The Literary Editor of the *SWG* was Naomi Royde-Smith, who was then about the same age as Hellé, equally well-read, knew a literary talent when she saw one, and was prepared to encourage it to grow when she encountered it in its very early stages. Rupert Brooke, whilst still at Rugby School, had his poems published in the *Saturday Westminster Gazette*, as a result of winning competitions, which Royde-Smith had devised.

Whilst Flecker was having his article published in *SWG*, Royde-Smith was publishing many articles by another poet, Walter de la Mare (1873–1956), a poet whom Flecker very much admired 'to take an English example, that fine poet Mr. De la Mare.'[1155] He also quoted de la Mare in his novel and referred to him in his letters. De la Mare was aged 37 and married to a woman (fifteen years older than Royde-Smith) by whom he had children. It had been Royde-Smith's influence also that was of financial help to Rupert Brooke, enabling him to travel the world at the *Gazette*'s expense, and Royde-Smith's influence that made her such an important figure in the periodical field. It seemed strange that Flecker did not benefit more in the professional sense at this time, from publication in SWG. De la Mare, like Brooke, whom de la Mare later befriended, had gone in for the literary competitions and in winning them had come to the attention of Royde-Smith. In putting some of his manuscripts at this time in the way of Goldring and *The Tramp*, Flecker did not put his literary career in the best of hands as far as his long-term and financial future was concerned. But acceptance of a little known writer's work is often a matter of chance, and an editor a writer has met and known over a period of time is often seen to be a safer bet than those publications where the editor was unknown to the contributor. Flecker was to write for the SWG in the future[1156] Goldring, an aspiring poet and editor, was later vague on this period and gave the following not very convincing explanation:

'After Flecker's departure for the East I heard little news of him until the beginning of 1913, when I became

associated with the new publishing firm of Max Goschen...
Whether we corresponded at all during the interval, I
cannot remember. I suppose we must have done, since I
knew his address. But, unfortunately I have not kept any of
the early letters.'[1157]

The Tramp, which had published 'War Song of the Saracens' in its
first issue in March 1910, now published 'Pillage' in its 10 October
issue. Flecker had sent Goldring a story of Savery's entitled 'Heart of
the Rock', which he eventually published in the 11 January issue, but
irritated Flecker by not acknowledging receipt of the manuscript.

The Tramp was owned by The Adelphi Press, publishers of Thirty-
Six Poems, and although The Tramp was an offshoot of the company,
it appeared to be under Goldring's sole command because he was
responsible for its production and advertisements. Goldring, at the
age of twenty-three, had had no chance to gain experience in these
responsibilities and he was to lose hundreds of pounds of his own
money. Some contributors also lost money. The strain on Goldring's
nervous health, as a result, was considerable, and could be one reason
why his memory of his correspondence with Flecker was vague about
that period.

The Tramp had included in its pages, before it folded after twelve
issues, translated short stories of Chekhov whom, Goldring stated, was
then unknown to English readers. The Cherry Orchard was produced at
the Aldwych Theatre on 28 May 1911. Besides Chekhov, Goldring had
published work by Edward Thomas, Arnold Bennett, W.H. Davies, Jack
London and F.S. Flint, as well as the work of his own friends, Flecker,
Beazley, Savery and illustrations by Trelawney Dayrell-Reed.

Goldring always maintained that the idea of The Tramp was his alone
and reference was not made in his writings to sheets that survive[1158] of a
proposed publication also called The Tramp, dated May 1909, in which
a poem of eight verses called 'Tramps' by Flecker formed the main
contribution and, as has been seen, where support and help was asked
for from the principal railway companies and hopes expressed that the
literary tone and general excellence would ensure a long circulation.
Goldring stated, when he described in the 1910 launch of The Tramp:
'The literary distinction of The English Review was to be happily blended
– such was the ingenuous idea – with the commercial success of Country
Life! As The Open Road was not available as a title, another had to be
found, and in an uninspired moment I hit on The Tramp. I had a certain
amount of backing though not nearly enough.....'[1159]

The lack of sufficient financial backing was an important factor in the eventual demise of *The Tramp*, as was the bankruptcy of The Adelphi Press. Some of *The Tramp*'s failure to survive was rooted in the character of Goldring. His character was interesting enough to make an author, Alec Waugh (1898–1981) put him later in one of his novels. Alec Waugh was under the impression that Goldring had been left a 'legacy', which had enabled him to lead the life of a man about town, after a year at Oxford. This was not the whole truth about Goldring, who had never been an undergraduate and who had not enjoyed a legacy. Goldring was not good at handling money, and like Flecker he ran up debts. In aiming to model *The Tramp* on *The English Review* and *Country Life*, Goldring was at the same time aiming to produce something better than these two publications, although he might not express his aspirations in that way. Whatever the real aspirations, he was like Flecker in some respects with his *Don Juan* play, too impatient to make his mark in life. Unlike Flecker, whose impatient literary aims were influenced by his illness, Goldring's unrealistic aims were part of being given at a young age an entry into the magazine world without an apprenticeship in the commercial expertise so necessary if a magazine is to succeed.

Goldring who had run up debts, like Flecker, would never have had the ability even in working for other publications, to develop that side of an editor's role in running a magazine. Like Grant Richards, Goldring had been apt to live in a fantasy of what he could have achieved had he had the advantages of the university education and inherited financial advantages of the class he came to despise. Goldring seemed to think that if he could have been given a second chance he would have learned from the mistakes of his editorship of *The Tramp* and made a success of another magazine. The opportunity never came his way. Goldring despised the class of people who sold advertisements and he though that they were among the 'least noble of God's created creatures.'[1160]

While Savery was getting news of Flecker's past literary efforts now appearing in print, Hellé, in the letter written to her on 15 October, got news of his writing 'new and splendid works',[1161] which she would be glad to hear as a lover of his work, but she would not be pleased to hear later, in the same letter, about his opportunity to laugh at mealtime 'with a pretty and extraordinarily odd and stupid maiden'.[1162] Flecker told Hellé that he had put this information in to make her jealous because she had said she never was, although when considering jealous feelings neither took account of jealousy on the purely physical level as opposed to jealousy of other more important attributes. The reference to Leila was also a means of blackmailing Hellé to come south with him in mid-November, otherwise he would stay in the sanatorium 'and watch the leaves fall and sprout again'.

Hellé (who by this time must have realised that Eleanor was no serious rival for the heart and mind of Flecker the poet, even if Eleanor had more suitable qualifications for a future wife of a Consular Official, which she might be jealous of at times) was not pleased at the mention of yet another woman in Flecker's life whom she was soon to learn (on 21 October) that he had thought of marrying. This was just a jest, he was soon to reassure her, and he counteracted her anger by showing his resentment that she thought he would show her letters to another woman. Englishmen did not do that kind of thing. Hellé could have been forgiven for wondering exactly what the Englishman's code of conduct was when dealing with women in his life, as more than one sweetheart was acceptable, as long as each was unaware, at the start, of the existence of the others. Flecker made the excuse to Hellé that he was the weakest of men and cursed by amiability. He could not help but be fascinated by people, and he told Hellé that no one had fascinated him as much except for 'a wonderful boy poet' who was now a professor. Flecker promised never to make her jealous again, even as a joke.

Hellé wrote back and told him she was no longer angry, only because she never remained angry for long. But Hellé's anger and suspicion were not entirely without foundation and she was right to feel alarmed that Flecker might show her letters to this other girl because her letters contained scarcely veiled references to the fact that their lovemaking ,at times, consisted of their beating each other for mutual enjoyment.[1163] These references would be hard to explain away to another lover, unless this new lover had the same sort of tastes in lovemaking, and that might be a real source of jealousy.[1164]

Hellé would be relieved when she learned that her letters were for his eyes only but she wanted the truth about his message that she was not to think badly of him if she suddenly heard that he had married 'a little fluffy English girl'. This description would hardly lead her to believe that he was referring to Eleanor as she was not 'fluffy' in view of her Burne-Jones type beauty, was never referred to as little in height, and Hellé had known about the engagement. But he had already described Leila (although not by name) as 'a pretty and extraordinarily odd and stupid maiden' to Hellé, which would have aroused her suspicion. Leila was not just pretty he had told Savery, Leila was 'lovelier than Helen of Troy', which was a description that Hellé remembered and used to describe Leila.[1165] 'Extraordinarily odd' may at first reading have seemed to indicate that this was not an attractive quality, but he may have used 'odd' because Leila puzzled him, as she had let him exchange kisses with her, which he may have found odd in the circumstances as she did not return his feelings in the same way, which was something he did not tell Hellé. He may have thought it odd that Leila was so devoted to her sister Gladys when she might have been devoting her time more to the social round, like Eleanor. Leila's background had more in common with Eleanor's than Hellé's; class was something that Hellé' would not be able to fathom very readily. Leila he had described to Savery as 'good Gloucestershire & descended from our old friend the idealist'[1166] Leila had an advantage over Eleanor, but not Hellé, because of her devotion to her sister Gladys, which could be transferred to a future husband who was suffering from the same disease, although not yet in the dying phase. Leila's devotion might be seen as such (in Flecker's mind) that she could bring about a respite or even a hope of some sort of cure to the patient she would come to love if she were not so stupid. In this caring aspect Hellé did not compete with youth and beauty when he thought of Leila or Eleanor. But Leila was not stupid in relation to Flecker's poetry because he let her read and comment upon the poetry he had written in the sanatorium, and Leila did not display the lack of interest in his work that he had got from Eleanor. So Leila, if she had remained long enough with her sister Gladys in the sanatorium, was a reason to cause Hellé anxiety, more so than Eleanor about whom he felt fascinated and repelled on alternate days.[1167]

Hellé was also anxious to know about the winter weather in Sicily and she thought that he should go to Switzerland instead. Leila Berkeley and her sister had departed for Switzerland at the end of October, where Leila had already written to Flecker about the beauty of Lago di Garda, the place he had told Hellé he was dreaming about but she, unaware of Leila's intention to go there, seemed to have thought that the dream was inspired by the better climate. Savery eventually got more detailed news of Leila Berkeley who had written again and sent a photograph. If Flecker was dreaming of going to Switzerland to be with Leila, with Hellé somehow in tow, this was a bit unrealistic. Hellé, he still thought, was too old at thirty, even if she was, he had written to Savery, 'a great woman'.[1168] She would indeed be a great woman if she took him to Switzerland to see another woman, while he was still engaged to yet another.

Flecker's correspondence from the sanatorium was not all concerned with his health, literary efforts and romantic hopes. Financial matters also played their part. On receipt of his letter of 17 October, his superiors, on 27 October, thought it was extraordinary that Flecker should have contracted a pulmonary illness (as Flecker's illness was described in the official memo) in so short a time (19 June–22 September). He was therefore granted only six months 'sick-leave, one month from the date of his arrival in England on full pay, and thereafter on half-pay. 'The pigs' at the Foreign Office had put him on half-pay, he wrote to his parents.[1169] The financial horizon was stark; if he wanted to get back on full pay, he had to be on board a boat bound for Constantinople by 22 March 1911. If he furnished another medical certificate after the first one expired, he would face yet another financial crisis, and would need to rely on his parents even more heavily for financial support. If he decided to leave the Consular Service, at this stage, his parents would also face a financial crisis, because they risked having to repay the £500, due to his leaving the service before the five years were up. The Harley Street specialist had written out Flecker's medical certificate on 29 October 1910, stating that Flecker was suffering from a pulmonary disease contracted in Constantinople. This was the evidence to support his parents' belief that he had first contracted the illness in Constantinople. The specialist had also stated that treatment had to be continued until May. The certificate was forwarded to the Foreign Office on 30 October.

In a forlorn effort to get some money from the Consular Service after the half-pay decision, Flecker wrote from the sanatorium on 2 November and asked if he could claim an acting allowance for the time he was Vice-Consul, which would have been for a month had he stayed. A letter was soon sent in reply from his superiors on 16 May, telling him he was not entitled to an acting-allowance. This was the stage when reference was made, unknown to Flecker, to 'some hideous mistakes' made by him whilst Vice-Consul, although as Bullard had found out when in a similar position, the acting-allowance would not be paid, however well he had performed his duties. No extra money was paid unless it was a case of filling a vacant post, which was not applicable in Flecker's case, as he was filling in for Simmons who had gone on leave.

This tendency of Flecker's superiors to make judgments about their junior staff without thinking of the consequences to the welfare of the junior staff member concerned, was not unusual. Peckham had failed his final examinations for Assistant, at this time, and Mr. Marling[1170] thought that Peckham should not be allowed to regain his seniority. No evidence exists (in official memos) to show that Marling talked the matter over with Peckham, but Marling was reputed to have a very biting and sarcastic tongue.[1171] Sympathetic contact of some sort might have revealed that Peckham suffered from 'incipient deafness'[1172] which, although it was not made known to the Consular Service until Peckham went on leave later on in the next year, still could have been worrying Peckham, as a large nasal obstruction was the cause of his deafness;

an operation was needed to remove it. This was not confirmed until Peckham returned to England; his posting to Crete would make the diagnosis of such a medical problem difficult. A more stringent medical examination before entry could have discovered Peckham's problems, but like Flecker he fell through the net. If the superiors in the Consular Service had dealt with the work problems or examination failures and health difficulties with more insight than simply applying the rules or over-ruling those who thought otherwise, then a better relationship with junior staff might have resulted.

Bullard had passed his examinations with distinction, at the same time as Peckham had failed, but he was not immune from the pettiness of his superiors. Bullard's father took ill the following year. Bullard had hastened home, but he arrived just too late to see his father before he died. Bullard did not know before he left Constantinople that, during the time he sorted out the affairs of his widowed mother, who had little means of support, he would be put on half-pay. Care was taken that Bullard was not made aware of the half-rule being applied to him, before his leave was granted. Bullard's return to duty was motivated more by shortage of money than loyalty to the service over and above his family duties. Flecker found that his need for a quick recovery from his illness was under more pressure than ever before, now that any hopes of further money from the Consular Service had ceased. The pressure to get better meant that he was more eager than ever to convince Hellé of his need for her in Sicily, and he wanted her to follow him, even if it meant taking her family along. Hellé wished that she could follow him, even if it meant taking her family too, but that did not make the prospect any easier. All Hellé still hoped for was that he would be able to see her when he passed through Paris on his way south.

A subject that kept the correspondence flowing when references to another woman in his life caused difficulties was a request for information about a collection of Greek folk songs by Fauriel and Legrand, which Flecker wanted to get hold of. This was sent, as well as material Hellé had got published, although under her brother's initials. Flecker made an adaptation of one, called it 'The Ballad of Zacho', and sent it to Hellé, who thought that he had made 'a fine thing with the simply told tale of the brave who went to the underground world.'[1173] Hellé had shuddered at the last line about Charon and his tent, which she thought 'unwholesome'. Flecker had written:

My tent is fast and fair:
The pegs are dead men's stout right arms,
The cords their golden hair.[1174]

Hellé took the opportunity, after she had received the draft of 'The Ballad of Zacho', to outline at length the story of Zachos, with particular reference to the poorly clad youth who sang a song so fair the roses bloomed all around and the downcast King's daughter was spellbound and saw no more her suitors including Zachos. A message from Hellé to the man she loved seemed to be in this story of Zachos, although the sexes would need to be reversed, so that (Zachos–Eleanor/Leila) was turned away from and the downcast king's daughter/Flecker would only have eyes for the poorly clad poet/Hellé, whose 'dear poems' Flecker had wanted her so much to send him once more. Flecker sent a copy of 'Zacho' to Leila, and she too would receive a message about a poor poet; no need for sex reversal for her. Leila was greatly impressed with 'Zacho'.

Later, Hellé was to recall that, although she had sent a rough translation of the story of Zachos among a collection of Greek folk songs, she thought that Flecker's was not a very close translation of the original Greek.[1175] 'The Ballad of Zacho' appeared from the drafts in his notebook[1176] and in the published form (it was destined to be published in *The Oxford Magazine* on 1 December 1910 and for inclusion, after small alterations, in his *Forty-Two Poems*) not to follow the romantic story she outlined to him in a letter after receiving her copy of 'The Ballad of Zacho'.[1177]

His 'Ballad of Zacho', although sub-titled 'A Greek Legend' (in his *Oxford Magazine* version, it is subtitled 'A Greek Story'), told the story of Zachos riding to find the gate/door of Hell where the dead surge round him and tell him how unwise he is, but Zachos believes he can ride out again from Hell, once he has greeted his fallen comrades. The dead are proved to be right and Charon shows Zachos the gruesome tent. In 'Zacho', Hellé was getting yet again the message about his fascination with cruelty and death. Her comments were plain and she told him she thought that death was a bad subject because it was 'so easily pathetic'.[1178]

'Don Juan from the Shadows' (which he was later to revise as 'Don Juan Declaims') was mentioned in a letter to Hellé on 24 November[1179] in which he told her that his Don Juan 'is the modern idealist.' He was sick of writing pretty lyrics and he wanted to write a 'gorgeous play' on Don Juan. He had read nothing on Don Juan except a column in his little encyclopedia. He had not seen Mozart[1180] and he had not read Molière[1181]. He had to get hold of all the literature, all he knew was Baudelaire's 'fine sonnet'. This was 'Don Juan aux Enfers' which Flecker had translated and which was to be published in his *Forty-Two Poems* under the title 'Don Juan in Hell'. Flecker wrote to Hellé a few days later to say he had received from his bookseller 'a splendid book,' *La Légende de Don Juan* by Gendarme de Bevotte, and he found it contained all he wanted on the subject.

Flecker also enclosed in a letter to Savery at the end of November a version of his poem 'Don Juan from the Shadows'[1182]. In the letter he told Savery that he would see that it was his 'masterpiece' and explained to him that it was a result of his being involved with three women at once – a reference to his love triangle with Eleanor, Hellé and Leila. He did not indicate to Savery that he had already let the women concerned see versions of the poem (although Eleanor might be a possible exception). Flecker lamented the fact that Leila had been gone three weeks already and told Savery that his proposed life's work would be his play, which he hoped would rival in aim *Faust* and *Peer Gynt* (which would seem more a sideswipe at William Archer than Ibsen), that Don Juan would be a modern concept and he would portray him as a man seeking refuge from sickly and decadent despair, questioning religion until he become 'an utter sadist'. Some of these characteristics would seem to refer to the author himself. Then he would introduce the miracle of the statue. He was tired of writing 'little pretty lyrics' and he was miserable when he compared his own writing with Browning's. He told Savery, as he had told Hellé, that he had written 'Don Juan' 'without knowing anything whatever about him; never having so much as read Molière. Now I have read his marvellous play *Don Juan ou le Festin de Pierre*.' He was reading all about 'the legend in a French monograph of enormous length'. He did not tell Savery that it was Hellé who had supplied him with details of other versions of the Don Juan legend, and she was impatient to know about the progress of his work.

Savery was able to reply by 3 December and he did not agree that the poem was Flecker's masterpiece; he thought it too long and he was not convinced by the women, especially Elvira. Savery liked the beginning and the end and he was glad that Flecker was for Browning, as he had thought that he was against him. In contrast, Hellé was overwhelming in praise for 'Don Juan Declaims' but she had reservations about Elvira because by comparison, she felt 'uncomfortable, virtuous and shabby; makes me feel the earth in me.'[1183] Leila wrote on 11 December; she appreciated an altered version of 'Don Juan Declaims' but complained that there were some bits of the poem that she rather missed'.[1184] Flecker had originally based 'Don Juan from the Shadows' on Don Juan's relationship with Elvira, Lenore and Raymonda, but in the final and published version which he put into his play *Don Juan*, references to the woman have been removed. The part removed was the separation of Elvira and Don Juan, which took place after one night together, because

Elvira says it is better to part and to 'burn to quenchless memory' than to live together until love turns to 'loathing'[1185]. This philosophy was one that Flecker was to use supposedly about the lack of need to marry Hellé, and in sending her this version of the poem she was getting another message about the future.

Hellé would not necessarily appreciate the way their time together had been incorporated and used in *Don Juan*, and how she was portrayed as ugly. At this stage Flecker was convincing himself that, if only Hellé had been younger and better looking, she would be ideal for a shared life; as it was the idea made good theatre.

Flecker was engaged in a lot of outgoing correspondence at this time, but worry about one item of incoming correspondence was ended when Goldring sent Flecker a copy of his book of poems *The Country Boy*, published by The Adelphi Press, for his birthday on 5 November. Goldring is vague about the fact that it was *The Country Boy*, when he later wrote:

> And when, a year or two later [after his review of Flecker's *Bridge of Fire* in *The Academy* in October 1907] I gathered up my own stray verses from the periodicals which had printed them and issued my first book, he [Flecker] took the trouble to review it in a Cambridge paper in characteristically generous terms.[1186]

The sending of the book to Flecker was a shrewd move, even if Goldring described himself as being devoid of any publicity sense.[1187] Flecker's review of Goldring's book appeared in *The Cambridge Review* of 9 March, 1911, which also contained Flecker's review of the *Life of Benjamin Disraeli* by W.F. Monypenny.

In his review of Goldring's book, Flecker turned the tables on the reviewer of *The Bridge of Fire*, because he used it as an opportunity to write on modern verse when he outlined the falsity of the notion that Modern Poetry 'is chaos lit by a thousand minor lights, all wandering and none more brilliant than the others.' He stated that 'Modern Poetry is a curious distinct and delightful phase of English literature.'[1188]

The Cambridge Review of 24 November 1910, contained Flecker's poem 'Pavlovna', which he later revised as 'Pavlovna in London'. By coincidence, Rupert Brooke was involved with *The Cambridge Review* and two articles of his were waiting publication in *The Cambridge Review* of 19 January and 23 February 1911.[1189] Flecker wrote to Brooke in November:[1190]

The Cotswold Sanatorium,
Near Stroud, Glos.
Sunday. Nov. 1910

My dear Rupert,

Verily I could tell you many things, but my pen is idle.
What I desire to know is this. Are you still at the Orchard?
If you are, could you put me up for a few days in about a
fortnight's time? I should not be allowed to live in Cambridge
itself, and with you I should be able to live an open air life
and yet see my friends. You observe that the proposal has
many advantages from my point of view. Whether it has
any from yours I don't know. But perhaps you are in town
buying rubber shares. God is great.

Yours sick of an old passion,
(sgd.) JAMES ELROY FLECKER.

Brooke, must have received Flecker's letter, as he wrote a postcard
to Hugh Dalton, King's College, Cambridge, dated 8 November and
although Flecker referred to the need for isolation and that he was
writing from a sanatorium, his reference to being 'sick of an old
passion'[1191] may have made Brooke unsure of exactly what ailed his old
rival in poetry, as Brooke's postcard revealed:[1192]

W. HOSKIN[1193]
Ale, wine and spirit merchant
George Hotel, CHATTERIS, Cambs.
postmarked 8.30 a.m. 8 November 1910
CHATTERIS, Cambs.
Hugh Dalton,
King's College.

You'd better come to tea (or supper) on Thursday am
booked for lunch that day. Flecker has written to me. He is
dying in a sanatorium for ventrical [? venereal[1194]] diseases
in Gloucestershire. I hope you show my friend and school
fellow Steel-Maitland (ne Steel)

AB
my pseudonym

Brooke did not reply straight away, and Flecker wrote for a second time:

> (Postcard. Postmark: Stroud 6.45 p.m. 15 Nov. 1910)[1195]
>
> Glos.
>
> Addressed: R. Brooke, Esq.,
> King's College,
> Cambridge.
>
> The Cotswold Sanatorium,
> Nr. Stroud, Glos.
>
> Tuesday.
>
> My dear Rupert,
> Wrote a long letter to you to the Orchard: as I have had no reply I presume you are there no longer. Write and tell me where you are, however, as I want to see you again if may be.
> Presume a joyously amusing Review of me in *The Gownsman* was by your pen.
> Yah, Wordsworth. I'm much more famous than you. I have written a splendid poem on Don Juan.
> Thine,
>
> (sgd.) JAMES ELROY FLECKER[1196]

Flecker gave the reason for his stay in Cambridge as simply the desire to see friends, but in contacting Brooke in particular he may have seen him as a possible source of a review for *The Grecians*. Also, the reference to the splendid poem on Don Juan meant that he would like Brooke's opinion on the poem.

'Don Juan Declaims' was a poem Flecker wanted to show to a lot of people. This sort of exposure would not necessarily help him achieve the perfection he craved, and it would have been better if he had regarded it as an exercise in concentration for himself alone, at this stage. One of the copies he prepared was sent to the poet John Masefield to whom he also proposed a brotherhood of poets. The use of the word 'brotherhood' indicated that the poets would be male. Masefield, although he appeared interested in the idea, felt that as the poets of the day were too scattered, the opportunity to meet would be too rare.[1197] This idea, if it had succeeded, would have had to include Brooke and could have been put to him when Flecker and Brooke met for lunch.

A glance at some of Brooke's activities after, and even before, getting back to Cambridge in October, give some indication why it appeared that he was only available for lunch with Flecker. Brooke had entertained lots of visitors at the Orchard, these including Edward Thomas, Dudley Ward with two beautiful German ladies and E.M. Forster, who stayed for two days. Brooke recommended Forster's latest novel *Howard's End* to his mother. Brooke went to stay with Edward Thomas again. After this visit Brooke took three weeks off to concentrate solely on writing his own poetry. Brooke was also preparing an address on a long-neglected subject, 'Socialism and the Arts', and made one trip in to Cambridge on 9 November to have dinner with the essayist, A.C. Benson (1862–1925), who advised Brooke against taking a lectureship in English at Newcastle and concentrate on working for a Fellowship at King's. Brooke had to submit work for that end. Brooke was also writing a critique of the *Cambridge History of English Literature*. Brooke gave his lecture on 'Democracy and the Arts' on 24 November, in his capacity as President of the Fabians. Brooke advocated that a panel of thirty members should administer a fund and award thirty creative artists an allowance of £250 a year each. The idea that a creative artist should earn his living at something else during the day and work on his masterpieces in the evening would result, Brooke said, in a 'culture of amiable amateurs'.[1198]

So Flecker's visit to Cambridge early in December, and a meeting with Brooke, would be fruitful from many angles, not least Brooke's help in eventually bringing Flecker's work to the attention of Edward Marsh. The old rivalry of the two poets remained, and Brooke as yet had not brought out a volume of his own poetry. Flecker's 'Pavlovna' was published in *The Cambridge Review*'s 24 November edition. But Brooke's views on the artist in Society and the lack of money for individual artists meant they had much in common.

Yet Flecker's time in Cambridge was not entirely taken up with visits to old friends, as he wrote to Hellé from Cambridge telling her that, despite his progress, the doctors wanted him to remain at the sanatorium for yet another month, after which he wanted to be in Italy with her.[1199] He wrote and told her, once he had returned to the sanatorium, that he could not just pass through Paris and go on to sunnier climates without her. Hellé was tempted and urged him to concentrate on getting better with a sensible diet and rest. Flecker wrote and told her he was tempted to marry an English girl he was only fond of and who was only fond of him if Hellé would not go with him to the south.[1200] At this stage it was his fear of being alone, which was always with him, as much as wanting still to make Hellé jealous, that prompted these statements. The new wife, whether she was Eleanor or some other girl, would have to go with him to the warm south. He soft-pedalled any threats of marriage in his next letter. He did not intend to go to Italy until the end of January. In this sort of situation, where neither was prepared to alter their stance, some sort of compromise had to be reached, especially as they were again in different countries.

Flecker decided to make a short stay in Paris after Christmas, which greatly cheered Hellé. She had to endure the mental stress of being apart from him, added to the hardship of the intense cold of a northern winter. The plan to go to Paris and not return after Christmas to the sanatorium was not greeted with similar pleasure by his parents with whom he was spending a depressing Christmas. At one stage he felt sufficiently hysterical to reach the point of packing his bags and fleeing to Paris. Exactly what had triggered off this particular row, he appeared not to tell Hellé, but he let her know when thanking her for her Christmas gift, a Mona Lisa (the expression on the face of which, Hellé had once told Flecker reminded her of his), that it was the only pretty thing he had to look at in 'this vast ugly house where I live'. He told Hellé that she did not know what it was like 'to live with rigid Evangelical puritans'.[1201]

This reference to 'puritans' pointed to knowledge about Hellé's possible role as a companion during his six months' convalescence after the three months (now extended to four) and thus would have been some cause of rows with his parents had the fact been added to by a possible abandonment of the sanatorium regime as well. His parents thought that he was rebelling against the restrictions of life in the sanatorium, but the sanatorium appeared not to restrict his writing activities. He hated the sanatorium now that Leila had gone; she had made the place bearable for him and helped in his feelings of well-being, which could be restored now by Hellé's presence. But in case anyone thought that they grudged the idea of their son going off on a long convalescence, his parents had made plans for him to go on a travelling holiday in Norway with a cousin of Wilson the Explorer. The cousin was a young man described as having had a similar attack to Flecker's. The explorer, Edward Wilson of Cheltenham, (who had joined Captain Scott's expedition to the Antarctic in 1901) had also suffered from TB and went to Norway to recuperate (where he did not regard himself as an invalid: 'He ran wild on the woods and fells;'),[1202] before going to a sanatorium at Davos in Switzerland. In 1910 Wilson joined Scott on what was to prove the Last Expedition. The plan was that after Norway, Flecker was also to go to Switzerland, but Flecker would have none of that plan even if the proposed travelling companion was said to be related to the editor of *The Athenaeum*. Leila and her sister Gladys had gone to Switzerland, and Flecker's parents could not have failed to know something about them, when they visited the sanatorium at Cranham, because they had complained that their son 'persisted in sitting with other patients if they chanced to interest him, no matter how advanced was the stage of their illness.'[1203]

His parents also knew about the relationship with Hellé, and if they were told that she was in their son's mind as a possible travelling and holiday companion, with or without her mother in attendance, this could have been an understandable cause for rows. Not only was Hellé unmarried, but they saw other possible daughters-in-law already on the horizon who were, unlike Hellé, English. Hellé was also not a member of the Church of England. They would have to help finance this journey and sojourn south, which (although it might be the sort of cure the specialist had ordered and would also give the opportunity for literary pursuits) would not further Flecker's career in the Consular Service. The reference to the editor of *The Athenaeum* indicated that the opposition to his literary pursuits could be altered when it was prudent to do so. Even if the opposition was not running along the same lines, now he was on sick-leave, although they could argue that the time could be better spent on language study for examinations, there was conflict and a battle running on different lines when *The Grecians* appeared in print. His mother was enraged to read a passage from *The Grecians* in which he described at great length, in unflattering terms, a congregation of schoolmasters and clergymen at an unnamed public school. His mother knew that the gathering referred to a special service held at Cheltenham at which Flecker had been a guest. It was this fact of his having been a guest which his mother felt was her real source of anger, although it was difficult to see how he could have written a full and honest account without being present, or if he had sneaked in at the back door of some public school chapel of which he knew nothing, the accusation of 'questionable taste' could still be brought if he had written unfavourably about what went on there. Flecker felt real disappointment that at the time his parents had refused to discuss *The Grecians* and saw it as 'nothing but a jeer'[1204]. When the offending passage was reprinted in full,[1205] although his mother stuck to her 'questionable taste' accusation, the realisation that [*The Grecians*] said a great deal about 'some of the defects of our English system'[1206] was made clear, if not by his parents themselves, the statements were not, as many others had been, eradicated.

The idea that praise was bad for him had to undergo some modification now that praise for *The Grecians* was appearing in print.

The January 1911 edition of *The English Review* (which was available in December) went so far as to state that *The Grecians* should be in the hands of every headmaster. As the review pointed out that *The Grecians* was not concerned with the legislative problems of free education, the headmasters in question must be those of fee-paying schools. The review also stated that a headmaster would be stimulated by Flecker's enthusiasm and charmed by his intelligence. One headmaster at least certainly was not charmed and the atmosphere not enlivened by discussion of the aims to change a system that Dr. Flecker had supported for so long. Even if the passage to which his parents took great exception had been overlooked or if Flecker had left it out altogether, it is doubtful that his parents would have been prepared to admit that the book was a remarkable achievement for someone who, despite what he had written in the preface about having been 'many times and to many places a schoolmaster', had spent so little time in the classroom teaching. The book would prove to be right in so many aspects for future changes in education, slow as they might be to come about.[1207]

Criticism from Hellé pointed to a weakness: she felt that *The Grecians* did not need much help, in the first place.[1208] Hellé sympathised with him over the family rows, she also had experienced them, but thought that it was worse for 'you north people'.[1209] This could indicate that she knew of Mrs. Flecker's refusal even to discuss the offending passage in *The Grecians*, as Hellé wrote of 'no emotional reaction following', but it also indicated that her family were reacting against the direction the relationship between herself and Flecker was going.

The publication of his poem 'Song' in the 10 December issue of *The Tramp* could have given rise to conflict of a different sort; not only with his parents who could have concluded wrongly, but with Hellé who would have concluded rightly, that it was about Eleanor. His poem 'An Old Story', which appeared in *The Nation*'s 24 December edition (as once again that magazine had asked for a Christmas poem), would not have the result of stirring up conflict of the same sort. It is a poem with dialogue between Mary, Her little Maid, and The Archangel Gabriel.[1210]

The conflict over *The Grecians* was not one that could have taken the elder Fleckers entirely by surprise as proposing reform of the educational system was not a new idea. William Archer had published a short volume called *Let Youth But Know* in 1905, which had advocated educational reform. Archer had published his book under a nom de plume, Kappa, which was an idea the elder Fleckers would have welcomed for their son's volume. Much of the conflict over *The Grecians* was due to his parents having to face the fact that their son was ahead of them in his views on education. It was also due to their son appearing now to be under an influence more powerful than theirs in the emotional dominance battle. It was an influence stronger than that exercised by Beazley, namely the emotional power of Hellé in Paris. Hellé was Greek and the other sort of tension was Flecker's Englishness, his love of England and his growing love of Greece, which was embodied in his later poem 'Oak and Olive'.[1211] Flecker later explained away 'Oak and Olive' as 'a jest after all in the good old manner'.[1212] He had explained his attempt to make Hellé jealous as a jest and although 'Oak and Olive' can be seen as the poet's explanation of how he dreamed of Greece when in England and when in Greece he dreamed of England, it could hide more: Beazley had been in Athens in winter, and had written a similar sort of poem[1213], so that too could have been part of the jest. The reference in the poem to 'a hall in Bloomsbury/ No more I dare to tread,/ For all the stone men shout at me,/ And swear they are not dead;/' could be his past attachments to Oxford men and Beazley in particular when he was at the British Museum (as has been seen).[1214] The next two lines 'And once I touched a broken girl/ And knew that marble bled./' This 'broken girl' could be his old Oxford love, or the 'marble' a reference to Eleanor's coldness and the bleeding a hidden reference to the result of something more than a touch. Flecker had gone for walks while at Cranham and he had kissed Leila Berkeley; did he kiss her on walks together? It would seem that 'And Autumn leaves like blood and gold/ That strew a Gloucester lane./' would be more romantic than the sanatorium where Gladys lay so ill. The eighth verse of 'Oak and Olive' could mean that Leila was in his fantasy a 'nymph':

> Have I not chased the fluting Pan
> Through Cranham's sober trees?
> Have I not sat on Painswick Hill[1215]
> With a nymph upon my knees,
> And she as rosy as the dawn,
> And naked as the breeze?

His line 'Oh well I know sweet Hellas now,' in the last verse and the whole theme of the poem can be seen as embodying his love for Hellé. But the use of Pan and a nymph were fashions of the era.[1216] In 'The Public as Art Critic',[1217] Flecker wrote: 'The word "tree" for him as for the poet must signify a thing that was once worshipped, where still maybe hides a nut-brown Dryad, and where falling leaves symbolize the end of all our dreaming.'

Flecker arrived in Paris on 7 January 1911. This flight from Dean Close resembled his to Oxford in January 1907 to continue his literary pursuits, and to be with Jack Beazley. The desire then, as four years later, was to be with the object of his affections, which outweighed any immediate considerations about his health and paid occupation. Only Hellé was later to state that his journey to Paris was just to be a stopping place en route for Switzerland, and while in Paris he changed his mind about going there.[1218] This idea of Hellé's indicated that she was still not fully in the picture about the presence of Gladys and Leila Berkeley in Switzerland. Even at this stage, Flecker's parents referred to Hellé's being in Paris, and that their son had met her on the boat going to Constantinople, and it was this acceptance of the unvarnished truth that reinforced the view that it was Hellé's presence in Paris and Flecker's desire to go there, over and above his leaving the sanatorium's care, which was at the basis of the rows over Christmas. His parents also thought that Flecker went back to England in March, but he was to stay in Paris until February, coming back to London for a break, before going back again to Paris. No opportunity appeared to be offered to stay at the Skiadaressi home because Flecker stayed in hotel rooms close to the Étoile, where he could work at a big table in a small sitting-room, which could have been like one Norman Price booked into for a month.

'She showed him a small bedroom, almost entirely filled by an enormous curtained bed. It was a pretty room, papered in pale blue, ornamented with cuttings from French illustrated papers, a statuette of a nakedish lady apparently eight feet high, called Mignon, an oleograph representing a romantic northern castle surrounded by impossible waterfalls, and a clock which had been for many years too tired to work. Peronella it was who drew up the sunblinds and let in the pure air, for which the room thirsted.....

Norman expressed himself delighted. He settled the terms, and paid in advance for a month. He arranged to have meals with the family; he did not want to be lonely, and wanted to learn Alsandrian. All this obviously pleased the old lady, and Norman too tired even to walk about in the city, shut himself up and slept, to the disgust of Peronella, till late afternoon.[1219]

From the hotel Flecker went for long walks round about and in the Bois, but his isolation was alleviated at the same time each day when he waited 'for the hat with the lilies at the Friedland tram'.[1220]

Hellé and Flecker went together to Versailles and she remembered him striding among the fountains and statues, and telling her he would one day like to emulate the political career of Disraeli. Flecker had been working on a review for *The Cambridge Review*, which was to appear in the 9 March 1911 edition, of *The Life of Benjamin Disraeli* by W.F. Monypenny, Vol.1, published by John Murray. This was the first volume of Disraeli's life, as Flecker pointed out in his review. It took the reader to Disraeli's first election to parliament. The book did not deal with the serious politician: it dealt with, according to Flecker, 'the dazzlingly handsome, witty and charming young dandy and author'. The book, Flecker observed, had been received unfavourably 'by modern reviewers and politicians, Tory as well as Whig'. Flecker defended Disraeli against his detractors. Disraeli was a devoted friend, and although he was careless of money, he was 'stainlessly honourable'. Disraeli, Flecker admitted, was 'desperately conceited' but this was 'joyous and boyish,' and he was not pompous and he was 'as enthusiastic for his friends as for himself.' Flecker seemed to be defending Disraeli as much as himself. He went on to compare the brilliance of wit of Disraeli with 'Byron and Congreve'. Flecker concluded that there were not enough 'great writers of this age to write the biographies of great men of the last'.

Flecker seemed to see in the life of Disraeli the ideal of being able to have a worthwhile political career alongside that of a writer. Flecker's political aspirations were channelled into prose and verse. He drafted out his article 'Liberalism and the Young' in his notebook.[1221]

This article was not published and nor was another, which was not as long, entitled 'Liberalism and Youth' and typewritten.[1222] His poem in another notebook[1223] was not published until it appeared in *NGJ*.[1224] This poem contains the lines 'Young Liberals, our day is all but won,/ Out with your arms and flash them in the sun,'. Non-publication of this political material, at this time, could have been a help to his consular career, although not to his career as a writer. His articles were along general lines and did not make particular references to the politics of Turkey. It was suggested by the Foreign Office that this was to be discouraged because there would be a great danger of politics creeping in. The writing of such articles would need to be first referred to the Foreign Office.[1225] The failure of Flecker to do this would not have endeared him to his superiors and writing under a nom de plume would not give him the public acknowledgement that was essential to future politician and author alike.

Flecker had written in 'Liberalism and the Young' that 'we young liberals' were not ashamed of its name and 'glorious traditions'; the young liberals had forgotten the 'faddist and the cranks' (this looked like a sideswipe at the Fabians). He went on to assert that they saw 'Englishmen starving at our doors are not going to listen to the woes of

Armenians, or black men, or the dogs of Constantinople. We have work to do near home. We are men of the tradition.' The tradition he thought went back not only to men of the eighteenth century but to Byron, Shelley and Swinburne. The Centre Party, Flecker felt was the 'finest of all positions'. The Tory Party, he felt was 'Capital allied with Religion, Privilege, Militarism.' On the other side there were 'the terrible dark forces of Labour which were eager to clutch the Squirearchy by the throat'.

The strikes and the industrial unrest, the proposed strike of railwaymen, which had put his correspondence with Hellé in jeopardy whilst at Cranham, had not enhanced the socialist within him. The Foreign Office's attitude to his sick-pay had not made him happier with traditional elements. The fact that MPs were, in 1911, going to get paid, plus the reduced powers proposed for the House of Lords, made a career in politics look attractive to Flecker from the centre ground.

The Athenaeum of 21 January 1911, under a heading 'Books for Students', reviewed *The Grecians*. The anonymous reviewer thought that the author was a 'bright and attractive writer'. Smith was described as 'a somewhat cocksure Socrates' who 'airily disposes of the opinions of his two friends, who are working schoolmasters'. After reinforcing this statement, the reviewer acknowledged that 'there are many sound criticisms and quotable remarks', and that Flecker was 'bold enough to dissent from many crusted or popular institutions.' The reviewer remarked on his lack of sympathy for Cecil Rhodes. The reviewer concluded that 'the book may be read with profit by all grades of Secondary School teachers'. As he had after reading Goldring's review of *The Bridge of Fire*, Flecker wrote back and a letter was published in the 28 January 281911 edition of *The Athenaeum*, headed 1 rue Brey Paris.

THE GRECIANS

1, rue Brey, Paris

Your reviewer, though complimentary, has done me some injustice in his review of my book. He says that my Socrates 'works himself up to make lurid and far-fetched contrasts. "Do you not know," he asks, "how the monotonous hours are only varied by epidemics, whether of chicken-pox, religion, silkworm-keeping, or Sandow exercises?" '

Far be it from any Socrates of mine to use such untrammelled violence. It is Hofman, purposely represented as a rather outrageous and Nietzschean personality, who uses the words which are meant to be in keeping with his character. 'There is too much of this kind of smartness,' says your reviewer. I thank him for the compliment. I was drawing the portrait of a smart man; I seem to have succeeded. There is usually too much of him.

JAMES ELROY FLECKER

Flecker's writing during the few weeks in Paris consisted mainly of working on *Don Juan*, and the poem 'Epithalamion', which he was later to include in *Don Juan*, and *'The Golden Journey to Samarkand'*. He also revised 'Ballad of Iskander' and wrote 'The Princess', a happy poem about a princess who was also a pirate, which was based on a Greek folk song. 'The Princess' was later set to music.[1226] The poem had some connection to his own life, although the roles were reversed. The pirate princess captured a prince in a conflict at sea and the pirate boat anchored in 'the gulf of Istamboul', where the pirate and the captive have the promise of surrender to each other. 'The Princess' was first published in *Country Life* on 4 February 1911. 'The Ballad of Iskander' was published in *The English Review* of March 1911, paying a much-needed nine guineas. Iskander was to be added to *Thirty-Six Poems* for publication in *Forty-Two Poems*.

'Epithalamion' was the most beautiful and mature work produced in this period, at first in the published versions; the only simile has reference to 'white as the summer snow,' which at first reading is puzzling, as snow in summer would be a shock and it would melt quickly. But in one of the typescripts of *Don Juan*, Flecker had written originally:

> Stay and smile then, hand in hand
> Children of sunbeams, white as snow
> As Peleus King of the Grecian land
> Smiled pon Thetis, long ago[1227]

When published this verse read:

> Smile then, children, hand in hand,
> Bright and white as the summer snow,
> Or that young King of the Grecian land,
> Who smiled on Thetis, long ago,[1228]

Flecker put this speech about a wedding into Anna's mouth. No wedding plans were formulated at the time of the writing of this poem. The relationship appeared to be going along the same lines as it had done in Turkey, that is day to day growing closeness, but still an uncertain future. The weather now might be cold instead of hot but the emotional climate remained the same as before although this time it was Flecker who had made the extra effort and crossed the sea.

Flecker had borrowed money from Hellé, so she would have some inkling of his ready cash situation and attitude to money. In the recent past he had been reasonably secure financially, which meant he could play for time and keep his emotional options open. But these sorts of options had gone, although payments made for his published poetry were greater than the few pounds of paid sick-leave allowed by the Foreign Office. Payment for his literary efforts could not be looked upon as a form of security, long term. London was the place where his work was being accepted and reviewed and early in February, Flecker returned to England. 'I have been to Paris, Oxford, Cambridge, London, Paris since January 7th.'[1229] This itinerary did not include Cheltenham. The Oxford part of the trip was to see Beazley and get his opinion on the work done on Don Juan. Beazley was well established in Oxford life. Since he had obtained his BA in 1907, he was a Lecturer in classics at Christ Church and a Student and Tutor there since 1908 and would be awarded MA in 1911. He was not in a much better position to give Flecker emotional support than he had been in the winter of 1907. Beazley had not entirely turned his back on his poetry, he was to publish three poems in *The English Review* of April 1911.

Evidence of the shortness of the Oxford visit could be proved by the fact that he was back in his old rooms at 10 Jesus Lane, Cambridge, and writing a letter dated 17 February 1911 to the Foreign Office informing them that he was ready to return to Constantinople as his health was quite restored. On 27 February his superiors were made known of his intention to return and take up his duties.

The February edition of *The English Review* published Flecker's 'Two Critics of Poetry'.[1230] He reviewed *History of English Poetry* by W.J. Courthope, Vol.VI, London, Macmillan and Co. 10s. net, and *The Romantic Movement in English Poetry* by Arthur Symons, London, Constable and Co. 7s.6d. net. These reviews, if he got prompt payment, would have given him an extra source of cash.

From Cambridge, Flecker repaid the money he had borrowed from Hellé, whether Beazley had been the source of this cash is not clear. Beazley, like Eleanor, now became a background figure in Flecker's life, because although at one point in both the lives of Eleanor and Beazley, Flecker had played a close part, they both had futures in which

Flecker could not realistically play the same part, as he became closer to Hellé. Beazley, due to his background with little financial support, and Eleanor, because she lived in the sphere that could be described as 'Society Woman', however much Flecker denied this, had nothing to gain by taking on a penniless and sick poet. The Oxford scholar's niche and the London Society circuit were not ones that Flecker could enjoy and continue to be a published poet as a means of making his living.

The main source of help during the ten days spent in London was Mavrogordato, who was reader and literary adviser to the publishers, Dent's, and he had been behind the publication of *The Grecians.* Mavrogordato arranged for the transferring of unbound sheets of *Thirty-Six Poems* with the addition of six more of Flecker's poems to form *Forty-Two Poems* to be published by Dent's. Flecker had given up hope of getting a publisher for *The King of Alsander,* but on sending the manuscript to Mavrogordato, he was advised to send it to Martin Secker, the publisher who accepted it for publication in January 1912. Mavrogordato also read all the manuscripts sent to *The English Review* and Flecker advised Savery to send in his contributions because the publication liked Savery's work. This suggestion compensated for *The Tramp*'s failure to pay Savery for his past contributions, as it had 'gone bust'.

Flecker got his play *Don Juan* revised and typed in a matter of days and sent it on 3 March to Bernard Shaw at 10 Adelphi Terrace. Shaw had returned from Jamaica, where he and his wife had been staying with the Fabian, Sydney Olivier. Shaw had finished his *Fanny's First Play* on 5 March 1911. In choosing Shaw to read *Don Juan,* Flecker was contacting someone who had written on the same subject. Shaw had written a story 'Don Giovanni Explains', fifteen years before the production at the Royal Court Theatre of his play *Man and Superman* in 1905. *Man and Superman* was Shaw's modern Don Juan play and he had also written *Don Juan in Hell,* which was staged in 1907. As when he was choosing Archer, and now Shaw, who were older and successful men in the theatre world, Flecker failed to see that he was running the risk of not getting their full support, just as he had failed to get his father's approval when submitting *The Grecians* to him after publication. The chances of Dr. Flecker being able to step outside his own world of education and praise his son's work, were remote. Archer and Shaw could not either step outside their own world and praise and encourage him in the way he really needed – that was that he was already one step ahead of them, and however unsteady that step, he needed their helping hand for a while. Both Shaw and Archer had criticised Davidson's plays, even those enthusiastically received by others. Flecker had been better received by Davidson, when Davidson had been down on his luck and neglected. Hellé praised and encouraged him because she genuinely felt that his work was better than her own.

Shaw's letter to Flecker was dated 6 March 1911 from Ayot St. Lawrence, Welwyn Garden City.[1231] It said that he was 'a genius if inexperienced'.[1232] Shaw's attitude towards Flecker and his play's future was reminiscent of the Uppingham headmaster's reaction to Flecker's ability to get a scholarship to Oxford. Dr. Selwyn had stated beforehand that only a genius could get one at his age. Shaw also used the words 'stroke of genius' when referring to scenes with Tisbea in the last act of *Don Juan.* The singling out of the scene with Tisbea pointed to the fact that the character of Tisbea was one that he had given sufficient time to in his own mind to enable him to create a convincing character. Shaw had complained about the lack of credibility of some of the other characters, in particular the labour leader, who was one type of person that Flecker had not had a close acquaintance with. Shaw remarked on some carelessness of the work, much in the way of Flecker's schoolmasters. Some of *Don Juan,* Shaw felt, was 'too fantastic' and he was unsure that *Don Juan* was not an 'astonishingly fine' flash in the pan that could not be repeated. Shaw warned Flecker that there were plenty of geniuses about, and Shaw saw the difficulty in finding 'writers who were sober, honest, and industrious and have been for many years in their last situation.' He wanted Flecker to make a fool of himself for ten years or so, which suggested that Shaw had been given no idea of Flecker's consumption in the same way as Shaw had no idea of the state of Davidson's mental health, when even if Davidson had been sober, honest and industrious, that had not meant that his plays were performed. So, had Flecker survived for another ten years and come to Shaw, help would still not have been forthcoming. But any offer to give Flecker money at this juncture so that Flecker could work on perfecting the play, was not suggested, although sufficient money to buy time would not necessarily have been a solution as far as *Don Juan* was concerned as it was a play written by a poet and the real worth of the play at this time was the beauty of the poetry. Flecker thought the production of the play, even if he might not admit it to himself, would be a quick way to get himself out of his present financial and career predicament, to say nothing of having a reason to stay in a healthier climate than Turkey in the height of its summer. The tragic result of the offer and payment of money to John Davidson to write a play was not one that Shaw was likely to repeat, although he had told Flecker that *Don Juan* was 'in bits too lacking in trade finish and conventional presentability for a regular commercial production.' Shaw followed this with a piece of useful advice, which was that Flecker should write for the Little Theatre. A piece of advice that Flecker was to reject at this point.[1233]

Gertrude Kingston's Little Theatre, Shaw knew, was looking for a play because the Little Theatre had decided that Shaw's *Fanny's First Play* was not long enough. Shaw then added an Induction and an Epilogue and his play was accepted by the Little Theatre, where it opened on 19 April 1911, and on 1 January 1912 was transferred to the Kingsway Theatre and ran for 622 performances.[1234]

Flecker was given an introduction by Shaw to Herbert Trench, Artistic Director and Lessee of the Haymarket Theatre, where Flecker took his play for Trench to read. It is unclear why Shaw, having recommended the Little Theatre, enclosed a letter for the opinion of someone in the commercial theatre, unless Shaw and Flecker met at some point, or another letter was exchanged during this time, when Shaw was made aware of Flecker's refusal to consider the Little Theatre.[1235]

Trench's verdict on the play was much the same as Shaw's and he would not commission it, telling Flecker that it was too décousu (unsewed, unconnected), although he admitted that the play contained some beautiful poetry. If Flecker could have had the chance to see the play in rehearsal it would have helped him to pull it together. If he could have considered writing the whole play as a verse drama, some of the play's problems could have been resolved because the best parts of the play are in verse form, but some of the difficulties such as, for example, the realism and fantasy, may not have been able to be reconciled however much he rewrote the play.[1236] Time at this juncture was not on his side. Herbert Trench was preparing for a celebration at His Majesty's Theatre of the coronation of George V and he had composed a 'Paean of Dawn in May' to be sung by six famous actresses. Trench's song was published in *The English Review*, July 1911 edition.

Flecker went back to Paris on Thursday, 9 March, the same day as he had received what he saw as flattering and hopeful advice from Trench. Flecker had decided to give one copy of *Don Juan* to Savery in the hope that he would be able to offer advice and help in pulling the manuscript together. Shaw and Trench's criticisms appeared to have been heeded.

Flecker spent two weeks in Paris once more at the Hotel Bon Sejour, 1 Rue Brey, to be with Hellé, whom he had missed very much while in London, despite his tight schedule of visits to people he hoped would help his literary career. He continued with these aims in Paris by writing to James Strachey, as well as Savery. On a postcard postmarked 11 March,[1237] he wrote:

Hotel Bon Sejour
1, rue Brey,
Paris

James Strachey, Esq.,
Spectator Office,
1, Wellington Street,
Strand,
London, W.C.

Dear Strachey,

Could your people review my book '*The Grecians*' (Dent 2/-) part of which I sent to you on a now forgotten occasion. 'Twould be a great favour. I have had very good reviews (*Athenaeum* eg) but very few send me a p.c. if you haven't got a copy (or send a p.c. to Dent's, Bedford Street., WC) and one will be sent. Do forgive a post-card as I am too poor to afford 2d. I have a novel coming out in January.

Off to British Embassy Constantinople on the 20th.

Ever yours.
James E. Flecker.

The Grecians had already been reviewed in *The Times Literary Supplement* on 17 November 1910, and *The Oxford Magazine* of 9 March 1911.

The short review in the *T.L.S.* stated that 'Mr. Flecker has the advantages of much experience as a schoolmaster and of a literary gift which refuses to be pedantic and his conversation between three Englishmen who meet in Bologna is a welcome addition to educational literature of the moment'. The review of *The Grecians* in *The Oxford Magazine* was considerably longer and was headed 'The Amateur on Education'. The review began:

'The subject of education is the playground of the amateur. Every one is convinced that the painful and laborious process which made him the learned man he is has taught him how not to have his own sons educated, just as every one is assured that from observance of the maladjustments of his own home he is familiar with that most difficult of arts – l'art d'etre père. The author of this attractive little book is no exception; he is an amateur, and amateurs are always cheerful and light-hearted company; he writes well, and his subject is that eternal cleavage between special training and education which, we are told, was disputed upon by Amphion and Zethus many years ago.'

The review went on to quote extensively from *The Grecians* and the reviewer in his last paragraph concluded:

'It is a fact too little dwelt upon that the views of the average undergraduate are those held in pre-Reformation times or even earlier. And this (gentle reader) is an attack on Pass Moderations.'

Flecker's departure for Paris at the time this edition of *The Oxford Magazine* came out could have meant that he failed to know about the review.

Mavrogordato got a postcard from Paris with a picture of Cranham village on it and the same excuse that he did not have 2d. [postage on a letter] until a fiver from his bank arrived. He told Mavrogordato that he had sent his three Don Juan poems ['Epithalamion', 'Don Juan Declaims', 'The Dying Patriot'] to [Austin] Harrison [the editor of *The English Review*] and that Secker had sent him an agreement form and that he would dedicate his novel to Mavrogordato. He asked him to consider some prose from Savery at *The English Review*, which Flecker recommended as being suitable for that magazine.

Flecker wrote to Savery about his literary plans and also about his relationship with Hellé. Flecker then described his emotional state to Savery, and told him he was 'more or less living' with Hellé and he described her as the finest woman who had ever lived, and he was very happy except that he would have to leave her, but he wrote 'we cannot afford to marry' and he added, as he had in a previous letter to Savery, that Hellé was too old at thirty. He told Savery that he was as much in love with Hellé as he could be with a woman. Flecker also made a reference to his English girl, 'who has worried me for so long now wants to marry me which is awkward'. This English girl must have been Eleanor, although she is not named in the letter. Flecker felt he could not now marry her because 'we have positively never been happy together at all.'[1238] The appearance in *The Tramp* in the March 1911 issue of the poem Flecker had sent to Eleanor from Constantinople 'Light Are Your Eyes' may have attracted Eleanor back into his life again, although she had tended to drift in and out of his life throughout their engagement. Eleanor had, when she had first received that poem, told him she knew nothing about poetry. But she now knew enough of the poet and his being back in the country, and two more poems had appeared in March, 'The Ballad of Iskander' and 'Don Juan in Hell' (which had been published in *The Nation* on 18 March), and may have impressed her. If Eleanor had wanted to break off the engagement, to be seen doing so to a sick man would have put her in a bad light, even if the engagement had been in trouble before the nature of the illness was known.

The important phrase in Flecker's letter to Savery, in relation to Hellé, was not being able to afford to marry, even if more romantic notions were later used as explanations as to why an agreement to marry was not reached at this time in Paris. Money was the real cause of the lack of decision, whereas the engagement to Eleanor and thoughts of Leila had been barriers to a marriage proposal in the past. But it must have been at this time that a firmer understanding about marriage with Hellé was reached and he knew that if he proposed a time and place, she would not turn him down. He must have become aware that Hellé had some money of her own, which although not the same sort of money that had been Eleanor's, would be enough to make marriage a possibility sooner or later.

Flecker was depressed and miserable when the time came on the 21 March for he and Hellé to be parted. Their feelings had deepened but the future was still uncertain. The letter he wrote to Hellé from Marseilles, just before he boarded the boat, bore nothing more positive than a hint at the possibility of marriage and sharing a house full of books. He would never forget her and would do everything possible to see her again as soon as possible.[1239] He also wrote from Marseilles and reminded Mavrogordato that he was keen to review Norman Douglas's book, which he had promised to send him. Hellé wrote back to him to tell him she was with him in spirit but well aware that he would be susceptible to the charm of another woman who would hear his 'most enthralling voice' asking her if she had read the last number of *The English Review*[1240], a reference to the March edition of the magazine containing 'The Ballad of Iskander'. Hellé had protested in the past that she did not have a jealous nature, but her insecurity was understandable, as she did not appear to know about Eleanor's willingness still to get married. She did eventually acknowledge that the engagement to Eleanor was broken off by mutual consent, but how mutual was the breaking off is difficult to prove. One means of breaking it off would have been to let Eleanor know that he wanted to ask someone else to marry him.

Hellé's insecurity had reckoned without the powerful memory that haunted her lover, as the boat went round the Cape of Malea, where they had first been physically close and remained to watch the sunrise.[1241] It was passing again this important emotional turning point for both of them, that enabled Flecker to write a long letter to Hellé telling her that, after all, he could not leave her for fifteen months and he could not look on the sea, the mountains or stars without yearning for her. He wanted them to be married as soon as it could be arranged. In case Hellé thought that he was simply intoxicated with yearning for her and that this was influenced by the sea and the scenery and his boyhood love of Greece, he wrote to her of listening all night to an Armenian being seasick. Hellé had written to him about the rolling of the sea and the smell of cooking in her dream of longing for him. Their love was coming down to earth, giving it a grounding in reality, as Anna told Don Juan: 'No more dreams'[1242] Like Anna, Hellé knew:

> I know your eyes are worth all poetry,
> Your speech the whole of music faint and far,

Hellé had been given little time to think over the marriage proposal and she had to be prepared to wire her answer to Constantinople and leave for Athens at once, if the answer was yes. This last instruction indicated that Flecker felt that she would not hesitate to agree to marriage, and that Hellé had money of her own to finance the trip. His proposal put up emotional as well as practical barriers against immediate acceptance. Later Hellé was to state that she had felt that marriage was not what he had wanted, because he was fond of quoting the lines to her:

> Time turns the old days to derision,
> Our loves into corpses or wives. [1243]

She did not mention money as a barrier. The emotional barrier was the health of Hellé's mother, which had meant that she needed to be looked after by her daughter. But she had an unmarried son, Spiro, who was prepared to fill the position in the family previously held by his sister.

Flecker arrived in Constantinople on 28 March and found suggestions from Savery about improving the *Don Juan* manuscript awaited him. He told Savery that he would probably adopt almost all the suggestions but not until he had reached Smyrna, and he would certainly send Savery the revised manuscript. Savery had suggested omitting the Owen-Jones–Don Pedro scene, which Flecker agreed with. It is important to realise that Flecker's apparent handing over to Savery of the rewriting of *Don Juan* was not a tribute to Savery's ability as a writer, but more because of another rewriting task that awaited Flecker's arrival, which he saw as yet another 'dreadful trial' as he had to rewrite his novel to make it acceptable for publication; another task that was given to Savery. In some ways rewriting *The King of Alsander* with a publication in view would be a rewarding task, more so than rewriting *Don Juan*, which even Flecker could now see was not going to be, as he had intended, 'his life's work', which would rival *Faust* and *Peer Gynt*. He had read Molière's play *Don Juan ou le Festin de Pierre*, and may have hoped that his modern version would rival the old. In this he was not so successful as he had been in the translations of the works of past poets, and plays of his own had remained fragments, never to be completed. Flecker had used the hidden factor to less advantage in *Don Juan*. The hidden Beazley factor had been in some ways to protect Beazley and involved one love for one person, while trying to handle the love of three women was awkward and difficult and he saw the solution to be the dramatic killing of his real love, Anna (based on Hellé). Flecker realised that he was picking Savery's brains and he would write his own article about J.C. Snaith. This letter although it was dated 'April, 1911' was written very soon after Flecker's return to Constantinople, as marriage is only seen as a possibility, 'If I marry you must come and see us' ......[1244]

A letter from his mother also awaited him in Constantinople and he protested about the lack of news in it and the extent of the lecture it contained. He replied to his mother's letter on 31 March, the day before Hellé's telegram arrived, accepting the proposal of marriage.

He told his mother he was grown up now and would never change. He also told his mother that he was in splendid health,[1245] which was not entirely true; he had been suffering from a cold, which had started in Marseilles. He also explained in the same letter that he had no consular work to do, but he had written to Savery that he had been set to work on accounts.[1246] The reason behind letting his mother think that he was in better health than he was could be due to his not wanting her to be proved right about his decision to return to work, and he backed that up with letting her know that he had no consular work to do in any case, and that was not entirely true. The uncertainty about his consular work, was that his period of sick-leave really did not end until 5 April (six months from the day he had arrived back in England, and not six months from the day he had left Constantinople). The sick-leave ended on 28 March instead and the appointment to Smyrna was from 10 April.

Flecker would not be Acting Vice-Consul until June. He told his mother that he would be free in the meantime to see 'numerous friends' in Constantinople and to get on with his own writing, of which he had 'a perfectly terrific amount of work to do in that line'. He also put in a request for tins of tobacco because he could only get 'the most horrible 'Navy-cut'.' All this facade of normality would help to lighten the load he would have to drop on his parents' shoulders when he had to let them know of the possibility of marriage to Hellé. One real objection they could not raise (and he would anticipate many) was that he was not well enough or too burdened with consular work to consider marriage plans.

On 7 April, Flecker received Hellé's letter in response to his written on the boat, and despite what she saw as the unexpectedness of the news his letter had brought, she was determined to promise to come to him and hoped for a meeting in Athens in May. The real element of her surprise lay in the haste at which she was expected to prepare for the wedding, because she had already telegraphed her agreement to get married. But Flecker had followed up his letter of proposal with a second, urging her to 'be ever so quick'. Hellé had been warned of her future husband's lack of money but this penury, which he hoped would be relieved now and again by the payment for a poem, was not a reason to postpone the wedding for a long time.

Flecker now added a note of caution about the prospect of 'grave doctors' advising postponing the wedding for another month or two. This was a little strange in view of his 'splendid health' and his knowledge that Hellé had always held the restrictions of doctors in contempt. Hellé placed much more importance on her own loving care. But the delay of a month or two would mean his getting some money together while he worked on his novel, the rewriting of which he had not known about when he had proposed marriage.

Hellé, in the middle of plans to transport herself, her mother and brother to Athens, brushed the caution aside. She was prepared to look after him and love was a great physician.[1247] Hellé already realised that she was under the spell of her love for the man she was going to marry and knew she had burned her emotional boats and weakened the bridge back to family duties. A delay in wedding plans at this stage could result in a delay for a very long time, if not forever. If his health again broke down and he was in hospital, it would mean a long postponement, even more so if he was again sent back to England. Marriage and looking after him would be a dream that would quickly fade. Hellé had been against sanatoria in the past, so she would not be depriving him of skilled care, and she knew that a sanatorium would not bring about a cure, even if his stay had appeared to bring about an improvement in his health; the change in climate and rest and the opportunity to get on with his literary works had helped in the process. Hellé knew she could not bring about a lasting cure, what time remained would be spent together. When she got the proposal of marriage he had told her that God had 'made us for each other' and in the next letter it would be worth it if they were happy for a year. If she did not get married her alternative was to spend her thirtieth birthday still a spinster, and looking after another invalid, her mother, or to be a married woman for a short period if that was what God had in store.

The separation from Hellé, even with marriage plans going forward, would take a toll on Flecker's health, as well as the amount of his own work and consular work he had been doing. But he was also, once he reached Smyrna, coughing and feeling depressed. The fear that he might be ill in his lungs again was not as damaging as the ultimate knowledge that he was indeed ill in his lungs. One of his 'gloomy tasks' was to make an inventory of the effects of William Edward Collins (1867–1911), Bishop of Gibraltar, a widower, in poor health, who had died aboard the boat taking him from Constantinople to Smyrna. One reason for Collins to have visited Constantinople was to confirm the Ambassador's wife, Lady Lowther. He was a close friend of both and much loved by his flock.

The funeral took place on 27 March, attended by the Consul-General and his staff in uniform. The list of mourners gave some indication of the extent of the foreign population in Smyrna, the influence of the church and the sadness in the air on Flecker's arrival at Smyrna's Consul and at Constantinople when he was there. Three English churches in the area supplied the clergy, the Greek Archbishop was joined in the church near the British Seaman's Hospital, by the Armenian Bishop and the French and German protestant Pastors and members of the American Mission and College.[1248] But Flecker was not entirely despairing in his spirit, as his article on J.C. Snaith revealed.

Flecker, in his article for *The English Review*, stated that Snaith was the fifth greatest novelist of the age. The four novelists ahead of Snaith, Flecker put as Wells, Conrad, Bennett and Galsworthy. John Collis Snaith (1876–1931) born in Nottingham, the son of the owner of a small wholesale paper business. Snaith's first book, *Mistress Dorothy Marvin* was a historical novel published first in 1895.

Snaith's novel *Broke of Covenden*, the novel that Flecker had asked Savery's opinion on, he thought showed the influence of Meredith, who he saw as 'a more rigid, more passionate, stupider Sir Willoughby Patterne.' When Flecker came to compare, in his review, Snaith's novels *Henry Northcote* and *William Jordan, Junior*, something of Flecker's own inner conflict and the reason why he had become less interested in working on *Don Juan* the play and his novel is revealed. *Henry Northcote*,

William Jordan Junior and *Broke of Covenden,* all published in 1906–8 by Constable, Flecker saw as resembling 'nothing but each other'. He saw 'William Jordan Junior' as depicting 'the soul of genius battling to keep its purity untainted in the material world.' 'Henry Northcote', the advocate and central character of Snaith's novel, Flecker saw as a failure as a man. Northcote was, at the start of the novel, a man of thirty who, after six years at the bar, was poor and without friends and was facing starvation, but by the end of the last chapter he is likely to be made a judge. Northcote's fictional career had something akin to Beazley's real life career. Northcote's mother, after the death of his father, had made great sacrifices to educate her son so that he could go to a public school and university. His mother had impressed upon her husband before his death, and also to her son, not to write books but to concentrate on a career. So writing took second place to his success in his chosen profession. '*William Jordan*', in contrast, Flecker saw as a success, despite his imprisonment, poverty, sickness and ridicule. Flecker wrote that Snaith was perhaps the only writer of prose who had understood the poetic character. William Jordan did not die until he had written the poem that it was 'his mission on earth to write. There is nothing in literature like this story of a sublime spirit imprisoned in a wasting frame.' Jordan living, as Flecker saw it, in a world of poetry and dreams, was something that Flecker could fully understand. His (and Jordan's) physical deterioration had released their poetical imagination. He did not see Beazley, who was getting to the top of his profession at Oxford, and who was in the best of health, and having turned his back on his poetry, as a success, even if he too had risen in the world from a home where money was never in great supply. *William Jordan, Junior* Flecker thought a masterpiece although 'all but unknown'. Flecker was not prepared to be an unknown, at this juncture.

Just before he left Constantinople, Flecker had written to Mavrogordato to get him to make sure his Snaith article got into the May edition of *The English Review.* The Snaith review appeared in the July 1911 edition of *The English Review,* unsigned. Flecker wanted a copy of Beazley's poems, if they had appeared in the April edition of the *Review.* Flecker now appeared to reverse his decision not to send *Don Juan* to the Little Theatre, because he asked Mavrogordato to take 'it to the Little Theatre to see if they wanted to see the revised version. He told Mavrogordato that he hoped to be married in a month's time. On 20 April, Flecker wrote to Mavrogordato again and told him the marriage was arranged for the 10 May. He enclosed an amusing review for, he hoped, publication in *The English Review.*

Indications that arrangements for the wedding were not going smoothly were illustrated by the fact that on 21 April he wrote to Savery from Smyrna and gave a formal announcement of his marriage, which was now to be on 15 May. Hellé was still in Paris and this, he told Savery, made it difficult to send him a formal invitation. He told Savery that he had not been quite so well recently but he was getting better.

His feelings of getting better could only have been of a temporary nature. While he was looking for a house to rent for his future matrimonial home, he became very exhausted. The fact that he had little money to spare could have meant that the searching had to be extensive until he found somewhere he could reasonably afford. The searching he described as 'been looking all over the place for a wee house',[1249] which he eventually found.

Flecker used the searching for a house as an excuse for the fact that the letter to his parents in the middle of April containing the news that he was going to marry Hellé, was overdue. He told his parents that it was a decision reached after the reflection of many months. The fact of his having reached the decision en route to Constantinople was not revealed; this would be an obvious source of complaint if he had, and another he counteracted before it was delivered was that he could not help that she was Greek. He told his parents that Hellé had none of the Greek ways and that she spoke perfect English. He told his parents that her late father had been a doctor and that she was a member of the best family and a great friend of Dragoumis, the ex-Premier. He told them of Hellé's cleverness, and that she had a little money.

Hellé was wise enough to realise (and told her future husband) that however much he sang her praises, if her prospective in-laws saw her they would not think her 'such a monster'.[1250] Flecker did not appear to have learned any real lessons from his past efforts to get someone he loved accepted by his parents. It was obviously prudent to let his parents realise that there would be no working-class elements to contend with in Hellé's past. But in elevating her to a social class above their own in a sense, he risked the same problem he had encountered when engaged to Eleanor, namely that his parents would think of Hellé as a Society Woman. It was not a good move to over-emphasise Hellé's cleverness, an attribute that had never endeared his parents to Jack Beazley. He omitted to mention what would be a source of real objection, which was Hellé's Greek Orthodox faith and her insistence that the wedding took place with the blessing of her own faith; Hellé's adherence to her faith would raise alarms at Dean Close almost as loud as Jack Beazley's lack of religious belief. It would make a convenient peg on which to hang their prejudice against the woman they had never had the opportunity to meet. The real advantage in marrying Hellé, which was her willingness to nurse her future husband, and so do away with the need for more care in a sanatorium, which would have to be paid for, was also not mentioned. If he had done so, it would be to admit that the splendid health he had boasted about was far from the truth.

Hellé, like Jack Beazley, was not prepared to compromise on the question of religious belief. Flecker had wanted the wedding to take place in Smyrna without a religious ceremony, and in the Consulate. A marriage between a British subject and a Greek subject, one a Protestant and one a member of the Greek Orthodox Church, would not have been a straightforward matter.[1251]

Flecker wanted a honeymoon in Turkey, but Hellé held the purse strings at this stage. As when this had been the case with his parents in the past, Flecker had little choice but to curb his plans. No hope could be entertained that any of the Flecker family would be able to attend the Athens wedding. Apart from the fact that it was still term-time, Naomi Claire Flecker, his twenty-three year old sister (whose engagement had been announced about the same time as her brother's to Eleanor Finlayson) was to marry her fiancé, the Rev. Edward Charles Sherwood, aged thirty-eight, on 20 July in St. Mark's Church, Cheltenham. Not only was the bride's father a clergyman, but the groom's father was also. The planning for the event looked likely to be marred by the much more chaotic set of arrangements for her brother's wedding, which were stretching between two countries, had been arranged in haste and to which the parents of the groom appeared not to have been invited.[1252] However much his parents were upset by his decision to marry and the unconventional wedding plans, this was nothing compared to the next piece of news they received from their son, in a letter written from the Consulate, dated 1 May, in which he told them even more distressing facts: 'All my life is utterly ruined; I've broken down with consumption again – can't get away – no money – mustn't marry, but am going to see Hellé at Athens – simply don't know what to do.'[1253]

The disease was in the same place, the apex of the left lung. In order to calm their fears, he told his parents that the disease did not confine him to bed, he was in no immediate danger, and the condition was curable, but he asked 'in how many years?' His parents' first reaction to the tragic news was to blame the flouting of the specialist's advice and not having the six months' rest, which had been prescribed. The fact that later, his parents omitted (from publication) the news that their son was complaining of having no money, meant they did not acknowledge to themselves that the reason he had flouted the specialist's advice was not a wilful failure of his judgment of the situation, but a flaw in his parents' financial judgment. The financing of the six months' further rest would have been made by his parents if he had made it with a companion of their choosing, rather than the companion he had wanted, which was Hellé. The underlying conflict between the Flecker parents and their elder son had always been governed by money and the idea that they knew what was best for him. Hellé, they thought, would not be good for him at this stage, any more than she had been in the past.

The prospect of expecting the elder Fleckers to help pay for convalescence, in the south, of their son and an unmarried woman, but with her mother around, was unrealistic, even if these considerations could be set aside in favour of an improvement in his health. If it is unfair to blame the elder Fleckers for not digging into their pockets at this stage, it is just as unfair of them to blame their son entirely for his later breakdown in health due to his early return to duties in Turkey. The Foreign Office Rules about sick-leave were an important factor in his decision to leave the care of the sanatorium, a rational consideration to be put alongside the emotional void left by Leila's departure and the emotional pull of Hellé on the other side of the Channel. A frantic pursuit of literary endeavours was governed, too, by the need for money, which he could achieve better outside the sanatorium. The part played by the Foreign Office Rules was still an influence on decisions that Flecker made now, as the fact that he had just returned from sick-leave on 28 March and his application for more sick-leave arrived in Constantinople on 3 May (with the medical certificate not enclosed) was not going to go unnoticed by those in charge. His sick-leave was eventually sanctioned (from 29 May until 29, August) but this was not finalised until 8 June, the delayed medical certificate turned up on 7 May. Flecker appeared to have made more than one visit to the Consulate doctor in Smyrna: the first on 20 April to have tests taken, and the second visit at the end of April, which was the most decisive one, as after his one month's period of local leave, his three months' sick-leave began, on 29 May.[1254] Flecker went off to get married with the matter of his sick-leave unresolved.

Flecker arrived in Athens a week after Hellé's arrival. She thought he looked well enough, except for a hoarseness which came on every evening. Hellé advised him to stay in Cephissia, the Athens summer resort. Hellé was later to embellish this pre-wedding period with the heavenly smell of flowers, pines and light air her future husband could inhale, and the memory of that time was recalled in his poem 'Ode to Hellas', when he wrote later of the recollection of a sunset my 'My Cephassian window high and cool'.[1255] The reality of that pre-wedding period is better summed up when he wrote to his parents much later, when the realisation dawned on him that if he was constantly covering up his real problems, then the help and sympathy that might come from Dean Close would be nil. His parents could not be expected to read between the lines of his letters but they could not fail to get the message when he at last wrote to them of his time in Athens. 'I was so ill in Athens'.[1256] He eventually told his parents that he had to marry 'under frightful difficulties' and he complained about doctors and consul-generals he had encountered during that time and how Hellé had paid all their expenses.[1257]

Flecker made a visit to a specialist in Athens, and although Hellé had suggested he visit a doctor in Smyrna to ascertain what regime he could follow, the illness in Athens needed a visit to a doctor. He visited the Athens doctor in the middle of May and, although he had already been let off consular work, sailed in the Gulf of Aegina and been reunited with Hellé, all of which could have contributed to a temporary improvement in health, either before or after the illness, these were not sufficient reasons for the extraordinary change in the medical opinion about the state of his health. Flecker and Hellé were persuaded that the grave news he had been given had been greatly exaggerated, and the three months' sick-leave application was unnecessary. He wrote to his parents and told them that the 'whole business could have been stopped with two pennyworth of iodine and some terebinth inhalation.'[1258]

This new verdict was either a case of the Athens doctor being incompetent (which was unlikely) or astute enough to realise that the only medicine he could offer his patient was a mixture of hope, marriage and nursing by Hellé. The Athens doctor was not employed (like the doctors he had recently seen) by the Consular Service, and Flecker's immediate ability to carry out his Consular duties was a prime consideration in their prognoses. Flecker had not dared tell the doctor in Smyrna that he was getting married.

The new verdict could also be the result of both Hellé and Flecker realising that he would be better off financially if his pay was not reduced to the usual pittance that represented the amount the Foreign Office would be prepared to sanction once the decision was made known. Hellé was using her own money for expenses, she had hoped that she could raise money on a house she owned in Athens but that was proving difficult. Her mother and brother had come to Athens not only for the wedding, but to pursue a lawsuit; money could not be forthcoming from that source. Flecker himself had scarcely the fare to get himself to Athens; if the sick-pay could be cancelled, finances would improve.

The new verdict was also useful to convey to his anxious parents, although they did not get the news until after the wedding had taken place. His mother had lectured him on the folly of his defiance of previous medical advice, and he wrote to his mother and told her of what he described as a 'little relapse' as a 'natural sequence of his illness'. He had no temperature, he was putting on weight and he had got over what he described as 'beastly bronchitis', which the doctor had not been able to tell him was a symptom or a cause of his disease.

This subterfuge was not really necessary: by the time he thought his parents had been convinced that there was no longer any danger to his health in getting married, he had spent his last bachelor days. Nothing more could be done by his parents or anyone else to stop the wedding taking place.

CHAPTER NINE

Hellé's first reaction to the prospect of marrying in May was to tell her future husband that it was a month for love and happiness when the myrtle bushes[1259] were in bloom. She later recalled that, according to an old Greek belief, it was considered to be unlucky to marry in May.

The date of the wedding, 25 May, was the only detail that Hellé published in her reminiscences. She did not state where the ceremony took place, but it would be safe to conclude that it was not on the same scale as the society wedding she had attended in Athens the year before. Her wedding would have little of the joyful beauty of 'Epithalamion', written for her in Paris and incorporated in *Don Juan*. If a formal reception was held afterwards, Hellé does not describe it, nor does she give any details about the health of her bridegroom. The nearest to a description of the wedding ceremony would be gleaned by comparing Norman Price's coronation in the Cathedral:

> 'It proved to be an elaborate function, invented by an old-time Bishop with a passion for symbolism and an eye for the scenic effect. It consisted of appropriate ritual minutiae, as, for instance, the re-annointing and replacing of the crown – which it would be tedious to describe in detail.'[1260]

The coronation of George V on 22 June 1911 also could be an influence on these lines. The dreadful things the bridegroom had predicted would happen during the wedding ceremony, such as having a wreath tied on his head (akin to the re-annointing and replacing of the crown) and the giving away by a Ministress of Public Instruction cannot be fully verified, nor the bridegroom's reaction to them. But later, when Flecker reviewed a book[1261] where the author described in detail attending Greek weddings and the attire of the brides, he did not comment on the accuracy (or otherwise) of the descriptions of the weddings,[1262] as he did on other aspects that he had also experienced. Flecker had not always shied away from writing about intimate and more private matters between himself and Hellé, either in letters to

371

friends or thinly disguised in poetry or prose. But his wedding and the reception were exceptions, pointing to a not truly joyful occasion.

The fact of the bridegroom having been ill in Athens was a reason later given to his parents as to why the couple could not have their photographs taken. Studio portraits would be expensive and the newly-weds' opinion of professional photographers could have been similar to Norman Price's when he encountered one who 'exhibited the terrifying results of his art'.[1263]

In the past, Eleanor and Leila had not hesitated to have their photographs taken, but Hellé was more self-conscious and thought that she did not take a good photograph. Her in-laws for that reason did not receive a photograph of their daughter-in-law (and no photograph of Hellé appeared in the LIFE). Her husband did take his 'splendid' camera on honeymoon, but problems arose with it; any photographs of Hellé as a bride would have to wait until later. A photograph of Hellé, in what could be her wedding dress, has survived to be published.[1264] This picture was taken by her husband, and the dress she is wearing is long, formal, square-necked and with a tasselled cord round the waist. Hellé is not wearing jewellery, and in other portraits she appears not do so, except for a small brooch or a simple comb in her thick dark hair. In this respect she shared something with her mother-in-law who did not deck herself in jewellery when photographed.

If the question of what the bride looked like on her wedding day could be postponed for her in-laws, the question of her age needed a more immediate answer. Both bride and groom gave their ages as twenty-seven, although Hellé would be thirty on 14 July 1911, and Flecker twenty-seven on 5 November 1911. This younger age was one that Hellé continued to maintain[1265]

His parents had suggested that his bride might be as old as forty, but he eventually told them that Hellé could be taken for no more than twenty-five (which would have been Eleanor's age, had he married her instead of Hellé). Bullard had met Hellé and he was to describe her as 'the girl he [Flecker] afterwards married'[1266] and did not recollect the fact that she looked older than Flecker. Thus, what Flecker now said to his parents had a truthful ring.

The first two weeks of the honeymoon were spent in a hotel in Old Phaleron, a pleasant seaside suburb, a few miles from the centre of Athens. The weather was cool, still springlike and windy enough to blow the long bedroom curtains (across the four tall French windows, which opened out onto the sea-front balcony) which, Hellé recalled, 'beat us out of our beds'.[1267] The indication that they slept in separate beds and the use of the word 'beat' were some of the underlying messages in Hellé's descriptions of the honeymoon. The premarital lovemaking referred to in Flecker's letters to her from Turkey had the taste of forbidden fruit. But now their method of lovemaking would be considered more a part of the wifely duties than those of an unmarried woman; when opportunities were not always limited to a few snatched moments, the flavour would not always be so sweet. Hellé's declared distaste for the crueller aspects of her husband's 'The Ballad of Zacho' was some proof of a conflict of feeling. But from the moment she had heard her future husband's poem 'Pillage', she would have some sort of inkling of what she referred to as an 'affinity with him'. She had had an English governess, which could have been the source of her own problems. Hellé had experienced the emotional cruelty her husband had put her through during their courtship, when he had told her of his intentions towards younger and more beautiful English women. Hellé may have hoped that now they were married no reason remained to have her devotion tested so severely.

Whatever problems may have arisen or may have been solved, now they could enjoy lovemaking without the same fear of discovery, another problem may have been added due to the fact that the bridegroom was slowly recovering from an illness.

Their conflicting attitudes towards money, unlike lovemaking, need not be hidden completely from view. Hellé explained her husband's attitude towards spending money while on holiday as: 'A dearly cherished principle that one ought never to return from a trip with more than a penny in one's pocket.'[1268] This remark hid the fact that her bridegroom had started off married life with little, if any, money to spend. In his past, some sort of financial security in the shape of his scholarship or salary, awaited him on his return from trips abroad, or board and lodging at Dean Close. Hellé's remark indicated that, until she had agreed to get married, she was not fully in the picture about her husband's attitude to ready cash, except for her view that money management for a poet was bound to be difficult. She could have then realised that having a poet for a husband would be difficult, not only in the emotional sense, but in the management of household bills. This latter sort of difficulty could be lessened if the man she married was also in the diplomatic service and in receipt of a regular salary, which would not be reduced so regularly when the poet/husband was ill.

When Hellé had voiced her doubts about a poet's ability to handle money, she had no inkling that his health would so quickly fail. When Hellé had gone to Turkey and met Flecker again and knew also of his engagement, she may not have known, or not have attached much importance to the fact, that Flecker asked Bullard and the others to contribute towards the cost of the picnic when they all met up. Flecker may not have told her, but it does pose the question of the reasons behind the asking of money, which Bullard concluded indicated that Flecker on this occasion 'showed the business instinct once'.[1269] Hellé's conclusion about her husband's attitude to spending money while on holiday indicated that she was also regarding him as a child. She did not see herself as taking over the management of the finances of the marriage and doling out pocket-money as her in-laws had done in the past. When, as it turned out, it was Hellé's money that was being spent and the problem was not confined to holidays, she may have realised that her husband's problems with money were too deep-rooted.

For Hellé to make the effort to take control, or to encourage him to be more responsible financially, would create more problems than it would solve on an income that was liable to be cut without much warning. Hellé had to be the stronger partner, but she only achieved this by appearing at first to be the dutiful and submissive wife. Also Hellé's long-term health prospects were the better, while she now realised that her husband's life was going to be short, however much she might try and reassure him that this was not the case. Her husband, even before the doctor's verdict had been given him, had never seen the necessity of saving for some old age (at least not for himself) that would never come. The thought that he may have to try and provide for Hellé's early widowhood could be dismissed (if it ever crossed his mind), with the notion that her own family could provide the very fragile safety-net, which his family had grudgingly in the past provided for himself, or the Consular Service could provide.[1270]

The honeymooners were not extravagant; hotel accommodation and meals were cheap; it was not yet the high season. They went for leisurely walks along the shore. Sailing trips from Piraeus were made occasionally in the direction of Aegina and Salamis. Flecker planned the trip by steamer, which went through the Straits of Euboea; the cost was only a few drachmas to sit aboard, amongst the crowds of passengers, produce and livestock. The view of the Euboean mountains on the way to Chalcis, the capital of the island of Euboea, was thought by Flecker 'one of the finest things'.[1271] Flecker thought Chalcis, where they stayed for two days, was 'a dreary place',[1272] but Hellé thought that the strong current running in and out of the narrow Straits of Euripos between Euboea and the mainland made Chalcis more lively.

Hellé, at this stage in her reminiscences about the honeymoon, brought in the story, which she had translated from the colloquial style (spoken by a fisherman) that her husband could not follow. The fisherman's tale was about a moneylender who had told the teller of the tale that, if he wanted to stop being short of money, he should give up smoking. The moneylender came to a sticky end and the fisherman went on smoking. Whether Hellé had ever suggested that her husband could give up smoking so that they could save a little money, is not known, but the telling of this tale, and the mention of borrowing money (had they thought of borrowing money against the house that Hellé owned?) makes it a course of action that she, too, could have favoured.

The next memorable sight was the beautiful sunset behind the mountains of Thermopylae, where they listened to a nightingale, and a boatman (from Stylis) was remarked upon because he recommended wife-beating. Despite the nightingale and the flower scents, the honeymoon couple spent a very uncomfortable night in Stylis. They were eaten by mosquitoes, which were thought to be the culprits when Hellé was feverish. She dosed herself with quinine; malaria was still a health hazard in the Greek islands.

Hellé described Livadia, which they visited next, as a 'quaint little town at the foot of the Helicon'[1273] but to her husband it was 'one of the most wonderful and fascinating villages in the world. By rail from Athens, (see Baedecker). Quite unknown and off the track. Marvellous springs, Venetian Castle ....'[1274] Flecker did admit that the inns of Livadia were filthy.

Next morning they had breakfast of black coffee and bread in a taverna, on its wooden balcony, which jutted out over a deep gorge. Later, when out walking, they encountered an amateur archaeologist who alleged that he had found the underground sanctuary of Trophius, the oracle. Any idea that the man would be given sympathy because of his interest in archaeology, which was Jack Beazley's profession, was not sustained, at least by Hellé, who described the man's story as 'pathetic'.

It would have been a good opportunity whilst at Livadia to have visited the oracle of Delphi, but it became obvious that lack of ready cash prevented this visit: 'They say Delphi is one of the great sights.'[1275]

The following morning they faced yet another precarious situation (which also had in it the element of a pathetic story) which arose when Flecker (who had been in charge of a budget of thousands in Turkish money while Acting Vice-Consul) mistook a ten drachma note for a hundred. They were forced to travel back to Athens without train tickets, but some cigarettes bought with their one remaining drachma placated the railway officials. The splendid camera had to be left as security on arrival at Athens station.

The couple stayed again at the hotel in Old Phaleron, where a telegram and letter awaited, from Mavrogordato. Flecker replied to his letter on a postcard with news of decisions he was taking on the revision of his play *Don Juan*. He had altered the manuscript a lot in parts, but due to different criticisms he had decided to leave the play as it was. Flecker wanted to know what G. Barker thought (Harley Granville Barker (1877–1946), actor, author, producer) and on hearing Barker's views he would send him 'the new edition'.[1276] Flecker went on, in this letter, to make uncomplimentary remarks about A.C. Benson and the re-organisation of *The English Review*, which must have been outlined in Mavrogordato's letter.

At this stage in her recollections of the honeymoon, Hellé did not give any details of trips made to other Greek islands. She gave the impression that these trips were all made when they first stayed at Old Phaleron. Hellé did not make any mention of trips made in the period when they were back at Old Phaleron, which could initially have been due to lack of ready cash, although finances must have shown signs of possible improvement as Flecker was shortly to write again to Mavrogordato and thank him for the promise of a cheque.[1277] But until that was known about, further trips would have to be curtailed, before they left to spend the second part of the honeymoon in Corfu.

One Greek island Hellé does not mention was Santorini, which her husband later wrote that he had visited although he did not give a date, but he mentions it after describing Chalcis and other places visited on his honeymoon. 'One of the most glorious out of the way trips is to <u>Santorin</u> (Thera) the volcanic island.[1278] Santorini inspired Flecker to write his poem 'Santorin (A Legend of the Aegean)'. The legend of Santorin is much less stark than the one on which he based his Zacho poem. The Santorin legend was the story of the Sea Lady who rose from the sea around the Isles of Greece and who was asked by the captain of a British ship: 'Why drops the moonlight through my heart,'. The great engines of the boat have gone quiet and the Lady of the Sea asks about her lover, Alexander, and is told he died many years ago.

The island of Santorini, one of 'those cave-eared Cyclades', from Flecker's poem 'A Fragment', is indeed glorious and out of the way and the images of Santorin fired the inspiration for more than one Flecker poem, as did all the isles of Greece. Santorin has the reputation of being part of the lost isle of Atlantis, destroyed by a great eruption in times long past. The island is in the shape of a crescent, or sickle moon, and could be 'A crescent ship without a sail', referred to in the last line of Flecker's poem 'A Ship, an Isle, a Sickle Moon.' The ship in this poem 'appears as an actual ship, as a star, as the moon, and as an island.'[1279] The island (without having to name it) in the poem could appear to the poet as a ship without a sail because of its shape, and also an island is motionless, so it can resemble a ship at anchor or a ship in the doldrums. The island can appear as a moon because of its shape, as in the case of Santorin, and the moon too can resemble a ship without a sail drifting with the tide. Guidebooks on the subject of the Greek islands describe some islands (such as Salamis) as resembling ships afloat. A ship at anchor lit up at night can be compared to many things, a star and an island among them. The images and the comparisons made are not unusual, but they are clear and simple, which made it likely that for Flecker they hid a more complicated feeling. The limericks and nonsense rhymes of Lear and Japanese and Chinese poetry can also indicate more by the simplicity of the words.

'A Ship, an Isle' has been compared to 'Oak and Olive'.[1280] It is possible to see a connection with the latter's underlying theme, where it relates to Flecker's relationships with Eleanor, Hellé and Leila and the places where he had been close to them. In the second verse of 'Oak and Olive' he wrote:

> And when I stand by Charing Cross
> I can forget to hear
> The crash of all those smoking wheels,
> When those cold flutes and clear
> Pipe with such fury down the street,
> My hands grow moist with fear.[1281]

Eleanor had seen him off on his journey to Constantinople from Charing Cross station, an event she put only in brackets when telling her future in-laws that she would like to come and explain everything to them. Her coldness when saying goodbye, if that is implied, could have turned what might have been an emotional time into something of a shock, because in other poems Flecker liked to hear the flute, now it made his hands moist with fear when he realised that he could face being alone in Turkey.

If the connection between 'Oak and Olive' and 'A Ship, an Isle' can be established, then the writing of the latter can be seen as partly inspired by his first night aboard the *Crimée* with Hellé. When he recalled to Savery how he and Hellé had lain on deck 'for a night without my attempting ultimate measures'. Flecker had tried to write a poem about his first encounter with Hellé and failed to complete it. He could not write, except in a letter to Savery, about his experiences with Hellé. He could not write a poem with the truth and hope for immediate acceptance and publication. 'A Ship, an Isle' was to be published in his *Golden Journey*. In the poem there is the certainty of his feelings for Hellé and the uncertainty of their future, and at the same time any coming together of two people aboard can make them both feel that they have, for a while, willingly lost their separate identities. Flecker's ultimate feeling of merging with the soul of Hellé was always more powerful than any attempted merging with the soul of Eleanor or Leila. His love for Hellé had begun on first meeting her and it was not based on physical attraction alone, but the sharing of minds. He had attempted to deny his initial feelings for Hellé for many reasons. The poetry he wrote once he had met her and he matured was much more satisfactory to him than the poetry he had tried to write about his longings for Eleanor and her physical presence. His draft poem with the lines 'Soon she will come ...' also contained feelings of homesickness,[1282] unlike 'A Ship, an Isle', although it could be said to embody a longing for a happy though uncertain time recently experienced but now more securely anchored in the present.

Flecker seemed to have the capacity to write eventually, poems on themes he had already worked on but had not been able to develop to his satisfaction, often because at the time his feelings were confused. He did not publish 'Soon she will come...' but he did publish 'Light are your eyes', which can be described as an Eleanor poem, but he did not republish it in his anthologies, which is one means of assessing his dissatisfaction with it.

Parts of 'Oak and Olive' can be seen as based on his feelings for Eleanor, and the other parts on Leila and Hellé, but there is no obvious spiritual element, and Flecker described it as 'very slight' and a 'Jest after all in the good old manner'. It was also written about a time when his feelings were confused about the three women.

'A Ship, an Isle' has more in common with his poem 'The Welsh Sea', which was first inspired by his holiday with Jack Beazley in 1904 when, as on honeymoon, the place and the loved one came together. Two poems that he had written about longings for Jack Beazley, although using a pseudonym and changing the sex of the person the poem is addressed to, 'Song' and 'The Little Song of her Sorrow' do not have the same power as 'The Welsh Sea'. The twinning of 'The Welsh Sea' and 'A Ship, an Isle' could be due to the fact that both appear to show the influence of Japanese poetry, 'A Ship, an Isle' more markedly in its merging of images. In 'The Welsh Sea', where Flecker altered the line 'Beneath the starlit waves,' to 'Beneath the evening waves' in January 1910, Flecker seems to be using 'evening waves' in the same way as evening waves are used in the Japanese Noh Drama *Sumida-gawa* (the Sumida River), when the Woman says to the Ferryman:

...... No, for evening waves
wash back to times past...... [1283]

Flecker in 'The Welsh Sea' writes:

Far out across Carnarvon bay,
Beneath the evening waves,
The ancient dead begin their day
And stream among the graves.

The use of 'evening' in Japanese makes use of a pun, which is common in Japanese poetry, the word evening (*yu*) and say (*iu*) so *yu* can mean both 'evening' and 'say'. Also it was used in 'Eguchi' when the chorus sings:

Why say I do, when evening waves
come not again, nor the old days,
for now, O you who scorn the world,
set not your heart on worldly tales![1284]

The fusing of all the images in 'A Ship, an Isle' makes the poem more mysterious, and the introduction of the 'star-ship' and the absence of a legend with no direct reference to the poet himself, reflected the inner feelings of Flecker as he journeyed round the isles of Greece, where he could assume the role of poet and shed the more restricting role of Consular official.

Flecker's feelings for the sea, not only the seas around the Greek islands, entered poems he wrote about the city and the rain. In his unpublished poem about rowing on the river with the unknown Oxford shop-girl, the lines are weaker than the poem he wrote about her memory, when the nature of his disease had been made known to him. He could not have fully realised what despair the girl had gone through, until he had to face a similar fate. Then he wrote the poem he first called 'Song' and revised as 'In Memoriam', which in a sense seemed to be his trying to unite with the soul of the dead girl. When it came to publication he left out the verse that suggested he had been infected by her, despite the sweetness of the kiss. Flecker describes the girl's inability to speak to him when she was dying 'Save in a low and whispered note/ As through a shell the sea'. Flecker did tell Savery that 'A Ship, an Isle' was a very subtle poem, and when Savery read Henri de Régnier 'you will find some more'.[1285]

Flecker warned his readers in the preface to *The Golden Journey* that those who are for ever seeking profundity of inspiration are welcome to burrow in my verse and extract something, if they will ... '. Flecker went on to say that his attitude to life expressed 'in these pages, in the Poet's appreciation of the transient world, the flowers and the men and the mountains that decorate it so superbly, they will probably find but little edification'.[1286] Flecker does not include the sea and the sky in that declaration. The meaning and the message behind 'A Ship, an Isle' have eluded many who have studied it, and even the reference to de Régnier given by Flecker does not solve the whole mystery.[1287]

The kinship with de Régnier's poetry is much more obvious in some of the poems Flecker was to write besides 'A Ship, an Isle.' The life and marriage of de Régnier and the life and marriage of Flecker show certain similarities, but these are not numerous because de Régnier lived so much longer and in much more affluent circumstances. De Régnier was a successful novelist, as well as a poet, and he had a play performed in 1908.

Henri de Régnier was born in Honfleur, Brittany, where he lived until he was seven years old, when his family moved to Paris, where his father held a variety of government posts. De Régnier graduated in 1883, studied law and passed an examination into the diplomatic service, but his diplomatic career (unlike Flecker's) went no further. De Régnier was able to spend his time writing poetry and reading; he came from a long line of aristocrats with some literary connections. He first got his verse into print in two small volumes, and in 1885 began to attend the weekly salon of the poet and schoolmaster Stephane Mallarmé (1842–98). Mallarmé had a long history of ill-health, and his battles with the school authorities to get adequate sick-leave resembled Flecker's with the Foreign Office (although Mallarmé did not have TB). Mallarmé's work as a schoolmaster (he had revolted against the idea of a career in the civil service) did not impress his superiors, which was similar to Flecker's superiors' complaints about his consular work. It is true that Flecker's short spell as a schoolmaster had impressed those who employed him, but if he had chosen schoolmastering as a career, he might have found, as Mallarmé had done, that his pupils' parents would have objected to his publishing poems in avant-garde publications. The drudgery of teaching would only have been eliminated for Flecker (had he lived long enough) when, like Mallarmé, he had the opportunity to retire after thirty years in the classroom. Mallarmé had, also like Flecker, married a foreigner when away from his native land. In Mallarmé's case, it was a German woman, when in London in 1863. This union did not have the approval of Mallarmé's family, who were not present at the first wedding. Family responsibilities and the birth of children only increased Mallarmé's financial problems. These events give some sort of view of 'what might have been' had Flecker been granted a longer life, or if his illness had been one that he could have conquered for a longer period. The choice of a bride in de Régnier's case also bears some similarity to Flecker's choice. In 1888 de Régnier met Jose-Maria de Hérédia, who had three daughters, all lovers of poetry. In 1896 de Régnier married one of the daughters, who was herself a poet who published under a male non de plume. Flecker was to be intrigued by 'a sweet skit by La Jeunesse on Heredia's horror on hearing an odelette by his son-in-law which actually dared to contain an idea'.[1288]

Flecker was to discuss in his preface to *The Golden Journey*, the poets of the Symbolist movement and the Parnassians – two movements that de Régnier could have been said to have inhabited. An important factor in Flecker's admiration and identification with de Régnier's work was that Hellé had introduced that particular poet to him.[1289] But it is also possible that Flecker had encountered de Régnier at Cambridge, as at least one of his Cambridge contemporaries, Ronald Firbank, was well-read in French poets and novelists such as de Régnier and was prepared to introduce de Régnier to those he met.[1290] Hellé had stated 'that de Régnier was little known in England even to those who read French verse'.[1291] Edmund Gosse (in a letter to Flecker) had called de Régnier 'a cloudy genius', but Flecker told Savery 'by God it is genius and a damn fine cloud...'[1292] Henri de Régnier did not face lack of recognition during his lifetime. In 1911 he was elected to the French Academy. Hellé stated in her article that this was in opposition to Zola and that it redeemed the unfortunate rejection of Gautier and Baudelaire.

Flecker's admiration of poets such as Baudelaire and Gautier went back to his Oxford days, although Flecker's debt to Mallarmé appears not to be as obvious and as deep as his debt to de Régnier; (Flecker made one reference to Mallarmé and Parisian culture).[1293] In the Parisian culture of Mallarmé is found the literary people that Flecker also admired. Mallarmé greatly admired Baudelaire, Gautier and Leconte de Lisle, the last he had met as well as de Hérédia in Paris. Mallarmé had formed a friendship in 1873 with the painter Manet. (It was Manet whom Flecker was supposed to have spoken to in his studio, despite Manet having died just before Flecker was born.) It was Flecker's references to Manet and his interest in two more of Mallarmé's connections, Huysmans and Verlaine, that link him to Mallarmé, apart from Flecker's own visits to France and the men he had met with French connections, such as Paul Morand, whose father was a painter and playwright, Eugene Morand. Flecker had known the de Pimodan brothers and many others with close

French ties, so his interest in de Régnier was not unusual. De Régnier was still alive, while Mallarmé had been dead for a number of years. The poems of de Régnier have a similar sort of sadness and his choice of Greek and mythological subjects are similar to Flecker's choice of themes. But it was Hellé's influence in bringing her own enthusiasm for de Régnier, whom she regarded as 'the French supreme poet of their age.', which first attracted Flecker to his works, and then he found the affinity that enabled him to write poems on similar themes. But it was an affinity that, unbeknown to Flecker, he was seeking. Hellé knew him well enough to know that he could embrace de Régnier's works, or revive an interest that had started at Cambridge.

Flecker, in calling 'A Ship, an Isle' a subtle poem in the same sentence when he told Savery to read de Régnier, did not necessarily mean that the poem's inspiration owed everything to de Régnier. If the ship 'appears to symbolise Flecker's attempts to recreate his romantic visions',[1294] then it could be, depending on the interpretation of the word 'romantic', that it was also recreating the moment when Flecker and Hellé had lain side by side, like the ship and isle, aboard the *Crimee* and he had argued later that 'human frailty is a little thing under the stars. Is a star more than a kiss?' Their love had, like the poem's star-ship, sailed on, regardless of the lovers' separate circumstances. But in the poem, which he entitled 'Santorin', Flecker ends it with the Sea Lady sinking into the moonlight, 'And the sea was only sea.'

Another poem of Flecker's, 'Hyali', is also about a Greek island, and the image of an island appearing as a ship to the poet, is in the first lines:

> Island in blue of summer floating on,
> Little brave sister of the Sporades,

The brevity of the experience of passing Hyali is illustrated by the lines:

> Hail and farewell! I pass, and thou art gone,
> So fast in fire the great boat beats the seas.

Flecker also wrote in 'Hyali', 'thy naked boys/ Like burning arrows shower upon the sea.'

Flecker mentioned too, in this poem, 'the old Greek chapel' and 'A thousand poppies.' The poet of 'Hyali' is poor and unknown, as Flecker could contrive to be, if he chose this role whilst sailing around the Greek islands. Hellé could converse with the local people, translate when necessary for her husband and tell them he was a poet. Flecker seemed happier in his role of simply being a poet. In Greece, much of this happiness was also due to the sea air, the improvement in his health, the absence of consular work and above all the companionship of marriage. The role of poor and wandering poet, alone, had never been acceptable at Dean Close or anywhere else. His present environment and Hellé allowed him to adopt the role with confidence and to write about his surroundings with joy. When he had been writing about the view from his window in Kandilli, while he was still working as a Consular Official and parted from Hellé, he had written 'Sick at heart with so much loveliness was I'.[1295] He then longed for 'a slag-heap or a gaswork, or any strong, bold, ugly thing to break the spell....'.[1296] He did not confess to similar longings when he was in Greece. He was able to shed the role of Consular Official (much more easily than in Turkey), feel in contact with the Greek legends and be inwardly conscious of his Britishness. It was unlikely that Flecker would be able to blend in easily with the crowds; he had never been able to do that anywhere. Hellé had recalled that foreigners in Greece were 'a rare species' which she had concluded was a factor for the successful conclusion of the episode when they had had to travel on the train to Athens without money to pay the fares. Hellé had stated that her husband's 'best Greek' and his being a foreigner were enough for the Greek Railway officials and 'generally inspired confidence and respect.' This type of respect in awkward circumstances would be an asset, even if it could result in those the foreigner came up against concluding that he was more important in the Consular Service than he actually was at the time. Hellé did not say that as a Greek wife of a foreigner she commanded respect or that she took control of the situation, which would have rendered her husband's 'best Greek' unnecessary. It was nearer the truth to say about foreigners in Greece, as Flecker wrote about them in fictional Alsander: 'The Grand Tour Englishman of fabulous wealth and high distinction remained traditional in Alsander, since the Polytechnic Englishman, neither wealthy, nor distinguished, nor fabulous, had not yet arrived'.[1297] If some of the local people had overheard him speak and asked him, as in his poem 'Santorin', where he was from: 'And where may Britain be?'

Flecker could answer like the bold sailor: 'Oh it lies north, dear lady;/ It is a small country.' This statement could be seen as having a degree of Imperial pride,[1298] but also in the mind of the enquirers, England was more readily identifiable than Britain.

They planned to spend the next part of their honeymoon on the island of Corfu, one of the seven Ionian islands off the western coast of Greece. Another of the Ionian islands is Zante, which had been recommended as a possible convalescent stay, by the doctor in Smyrna, to bring about a cure and accompanied by the Skiadaressi family. Lesbos, an island under Turkish rule until 1913, had been favoured by Flecker because it would have been convenient to reach after the wedding if that had taken place in Smyrna, which he had wanted. But Hellé was doubtful about finding a place to stay in the capital of Lesbos, Myteleni, where they had no relations.[1299]

Flecker had addressed Hellé as 'Ionian Maid' and 'O Lady of the Ionian Sea',[1300] but this could have been a reference to the fact that he had first met her on board the ship while it crossed the Ionian Sea. Hellé's brother was named Spiro, all first-born sons on Corfu are given this name, after the patron saint of Corfu; the island may also have been her birth place. In her reminiscences, Hellé does not mention where in Greece she was born. If she had been born in Lesbos, under Turkish rule, she would not, as a Greek, want to make a particular point of the fact.

En route to Corfu, via the Corinth Canal, while admiring the sunset when the boat reached Patras, a new red leather belt, in which Flecker held most of their money, was found to have gone. Nobody on board seemed sympathetic, except a young woman with beautiful eyes who thought that poets were inclined to be careless with their possessions. Her comment was enough to restore Flecker's spirits. Thus, the sight of Fortress Rock, 'which makes the approach to Corfu a memorable event in the life of every aesthetic traveller',[1301] was marred by their not having any ready cash except for Hellé's, which was in one of five trunks they had brought with them and still in the hold. The porter from the St. George's Hotel turned up in time to pay for the food and drink taken on the voyage. The honeymooners stayed at the St. George's Hotel, where for the first two days after their arrival Flecker had to rest because he was so ill.

The name St. George's was a reminder that the Ionian islands had been under British Protection until 1864, and that Corfu Town had been a garrison town during the Crimean War, when many of the Corfiotes had been in the employ of British families. One aesthetic traveller to Corfu, on more than one occasion before 1864, had been Edward Lear (1812–88) whose limericks and nonsense verse had been imitated in *The Best Man*. Humbert Wolfe was to edit a volume of Lear's verse.[1302] Granville Hamilton, with whom Flecker had been much taken at Oxford, was to print a cartoon of Lear's.[1303] Hamilton changed his name to Proby. John Joshua Proby (1823–58)[1304] was a close friend and travelling companion of Lear's. Lear's landscape paintings of the island had been published in 1863; the beauty of Corfu was not entirely unknown to foreign visitors. Lear's paintings and his published records about the life of the Corfiotes and the British people who had resided in Corfu can help to show the kind of background Hellé's parents' generation would have known. Hellé's affinity with the British, which she said she had acquired in Athens, can be seen as having also been absorbed from the Ionian islands and her parents. Flecker had described Hellé to his parents as having none of the Greek ways. Ghosts of the British Protection lay in wait for both Lear and Flecker, and Hellé too. Not only ghosts but something more solid, a picture postcard of the British Fleet at anchor in a black and white panoramic view of Corfu, which Flecker bought to send to Mavrogordato. Edward Lear had also stayed at the five-storeyed St. George's Hotel, which overlooked the harbour, but he had moved out because of the noise from his fellow guests. For the Fleckers, their reason for moving must have been the necessity to find a cheaper way of living; until their lost money was replaced, some sort of economy was essential.

They were fortunate to rent what was described as a cottage, not too far away, on the Canoni Road, the name yet another reminder of the British past. Their new abode, Casa Bogdanos, had four rooms and a large garden with a low wall at one end, which overlooked olive groves. Nearby was a headland and a lagoon, near where, it was said, Odysseus was cast ashore.

The day they moved in the beautiful view was obliterated by a torrential rainstorm, which turned the garden into a quagmire and their first evening into a miserable one. The wind yowled as they huddled inside the dining-room by the light of two candles because the local shop could not provide fuel for the lamps. Next day, the weather cleared up dramatically, a breeze brought in myriad scents from the garden and the birds sang again. This storm's unexpectedness and the memory of it can be seen as symbolic of their stay in Corfu. It was unlucky to get such heavy rain so early in the summer and the storm swept away for a short while the prospect of a period of serenity, which the break would have been expected to bring them. (Corfu was liable to have earthquakes, and Lear had experienced one while he was there, so thanks could be given that the rainstorm was the worst natural event they experienced.) The storm may have brought memories of an English summer but no longer did Flecker strut about in the rain, as it was said he had done when returning by punt from Grantchester.

The hope of some sort of financial security, with the prospect of three months on full pay, was obliterated with the same suddenness as the rainstorm, with the arrival of a letter from his superiors, in answer to a letter written from the cottage on 14 June to ask how long he would be 'wholly or partially on full pay'. He signed his letter 'Your obedient humble servant, H.E. Flecker'. The reply, dated 24 June, told him that from the 28 June he would be on half-pay. This lack of full pay and the financial hardship that followed on from the loss of cash on the boat journey appeared to be the cause of the only real admitted drawback (except for the lesser ones of heat and flies) to this otherwise idyllic time. Flecker's health seemed to improve and he could get on with his own work. The fact of his having written to his superiors indicated that he could not have been entirely sure that he was going to be able to count on full pay. The use of the word 'partially' meant that some sort of cut in salary was to be expected, but he did not expect it to be so soon and to be so drastic. He wrote to Mavrogordato, 'Am on half pay which is damnable'.[1305] Hellé was later to maintain that the three months were 'generously' granted by the Foreign Office, but 'generously' really meant with time and not money. The length of time was recommended by the doctor in Smyrna and not due to any generosity on the part of the Foreign Office officials who could not easily overturn the medical opinion. The doctor who had given the verdict on Flecker's health was based at the British Seamen's Hospital at Smyrna. The lack of communication between the Foreign Office and the British Seamen's Hospital, which existed when Flecker was a patient, still existed. The Foreign Office was thus still not aware that Flecker's illness was TB. If Hellé chose not to record that the Foreign Office had again put her husband on half-pay, it was not because she had forgotten, because her parents-in-law revealed the facts and feelings in the LIFE, which was published before Hellé's reminiscences. Flecker's parents told of their son's surprised disgust at being put on half-pay while he was on sick-leave.[1306] But this was counter-balanced by their stating that he 'was still full of cheeriness:' and they went on to mention his tasting marmalade, which he and Hellé had made themselves from the one tree in the garden amongst the sweet oranges that bore bitter fruit. This marmalade-making venture (which Hellé also mentioned in a letter to her in-laws)[1307] seemed to be more a symbolic act related to financial savings and the need to impress the elder Fleckers that they were doing some practical work, than to demonstrate some hitherto undiscovered culinary skills. Hellé made sure that her in-laws knew that bitter orange marmalade could not be found in the local shops, so it was a necessity, not an unnecessary occupation. Eleanor had told her then future mother-in-law that she had bought 'a very fat Mrs. Beeton', which would let her know that she was not just a society beauty, she was trying to be a perfect housewife. Hellé was letting her mother-in-law know that she had some home-making skills and was not just an intellectual aide to her husband. If Hellé had followed the advice of Mrs. Beeton on marmalade-making, it was a process that Mrs. Beeton had stated took four days. Hellé emphasised how much the marmalade was enjoyed by her husband and herself, thus also indicating that she was looking after her man. The marmalade was a reminder of home, just as it had been when the schoolboy Flecker had sent for jam when away from home for the first time. The honeymoon couple could not expect the elder Fleckers to send out supplies of marmalade to Corfu. It was the sort of reminder of home that Flecker had always needed. Lear had been credited with the introduction of bread-and-butter pudding to the Corfiotes. Cricket played on gravel and ginger beer were also lasting legacies of the British in Corfu. Flecker sat in an old armchair in the garden, which Hellé thought was a relic of the British occupation. At the same time as news of the marmalade-making was given in letters to Dean Close by Flecker and Hellé, the parents were told also that both were studying Turkish, he for his Consular examinations, and Hellé in case they were to be posted to a remote part of Turkey. This piece of news let Hellé's in-laws know that she was not as clever at languages as they may have thought, even if she was fluent in English. She needed to be taught Turkish. Having to be taught by her husband would certainly not involve extra cost and indicated that he was cleverer than she was in that respect. It also let Dean Close know that they were not just relaxing and enjoying themselves in this paradise island.

Dean Close were told that Hellé would not be able to sell the house she owned, to release capital, until next year. This news let them know that finances could be tight, but that if the in-laws had any thoughts of advancing money, some hope of getting it back existed. Flecker chided his parents, when telling them of this financial set-back, for not offering money (which he would not ask for). He suggested that his parents might intend to disown him, but he also let them know that he and Hellé could live cheaply and still be very happy. It was at this stage that Flecker revealed to his parents the extent of his illness (prior to the wedding), in Athens, and the difficulties he had encountered. His entire family, caught up in plans for Claire's wedding, seemed to have had no time to get in touch with him, a fact that he complained about bitterly in his letters to them.

It was possible to live fairly cheaply in Corfu, if the visitor did not hanker for a more varied diet or look to the local shops for all their supplies. The Fleckers' meals consisted mainly of lamb chops, or fish and lobsters delivered to the door by fishermen. Fresh butter was provided by a gentleman (introduced by friends of Hellé) who had a model farm on Corfu and who had taken them round the island in his car. The cottage boasted a landlady and a maid, which meant that (apart from the marmalade-making) Hellé was not tied to the kitchen stove.

Plans to go to Italy (Siena) were said to be the result of Flecker's restlessness, but when the mood subsided all thoughts of going there were given up. Lack of money could have played its part in this proposed change of plan, just as much as Flecker's supposed moodiness. He had to concentrate on his literary plans and more travelling would undo the improvement in his health and take more time away from his work.

First, he had his play *Don Juan* to consider and he sent a revised version to Mavrogordato, enquiring about the possible publication of his Don Juan poems in *The English Review*. He also asked Mavrogordato about the publication of his *Italian Grammar* by David Nutt whom, Flecker said, had refused to communicate with him on the matter. Flecker had already been discontented with Nutt around the time of his broken marriage plans with Eleanor, but he had failed to appreciate that, since that time he had travelled so much that Nutt had found it impossible to keep in touch with him to try and discuss problems. Flecker's *Forty-Two Poems* was being published by Dent's and he needed to know if he had been granted permission for republishing his poem 'Ballad of Iskander'.

Mavrogordato was told (in case he had not got the message) that Flecker was hard up, so much so that he was writing on his last scrap of paper. But Flecker let Mavrogordato know that his health was improving and that he was grateful for his help and kindness.

Flecker sent off a reply on 22 June to Mavrogordato and asked him to forgive a postcard. Flecker had learned that Mavrogordato had interviewed Mrs. Nutt. Flecker now had the proofs of his *Italian Grammar* and he had found that 'a whole damned appendix on Dante' had been added and that Mrs. Nutt had cut his preface and also added to it. Flecker told Mavrogordato that he had written to the reviser, Mr. T. Okey 'who is presumably a scholar and a gentleman (You know him, I expect, he is Dent-ist and a Dante-ite) expounding my sorrows to him [1308] the Nutt woman is hopeless but I shall try to get more money out of her if possible'.

Flecker told Mavrogordato that they still might go to Italy and he complained about the heat, but amongst this chat crammed onto the postcard, a much more important message was conveyed, namely that he had 'started off' his new Arabian Nights' play' which he stated 'will be more marvellously unsaleable and unstageable than anything ever written'.[1309] It appeared that the lack of immediate success for *Don Juan* had not deterred him from embarking upon the draft of yet another possible masterpiece. He gave the impression that he had not learned any lessons from the reception of *Don Juan* in London, but this was not the case. By describing his new play in such uncharacteristically modest terms to Mavrogordato, Flecker appeared to be curbing the show-off side of his nature. But it was really the other side of the same coin, because Mavrogordato could not help but be intrigued when he eventually read the manuscript. He would be impressed by the changes that had taken place since the writing of *Don Juan*. But Flecker's forecast about his play being 'more marvellously unsaleable and unstageable than anything ever written' could also mean that *Don Juan* was unsaleable and unstageable and 'anything ever written' could refer to 'anything I have written', and also that 'unsaleable and unstageable' did not mean that the play itself was a bad one, but only that it was beyond the powers of those in the theatre world to stage it, but he still had a vision. The idea of his new play was overwhelming him and whether it made money or ever got performed were not the most important factors. 'He was caught up on the wind of his own genius and carried so far that he could not descend to earth on the selected spot.'[1310]

However high Flecker's vision had soared when he was writing his play, the material he incorporated into it was still deeply rooted in the popular imagination of his present day and consequently his hoped for audience. If it could be staged and managed, there was a market for it. The lure of Central Asia and the magic of the Silk Road (one stop -over point was Samarkand) had been brought to life in Flecker's time by Mark Aurel Stein (1862–1943), Orientalist, traveller and scholar, who had followed in the footsteps of Marco Polo.[1311] Stein had visited the fabulous Caves of a Thousand Buddhas in Chinese Turkistan between 1906 and 1908. His photographs of these caves had appeared in the *Illustrated London News* of 12 June 1909. One photograph was of a large fresco painting in one of the cave-temples, where the scene depicted was of a Buddha surrounded by lesser beings, in heavenly residence, which resembled:

> White on a throne or guarded in a cave
> There lives a prophet who can understand
> Why men were born:[1312]

Some of Stein's finds were exhibited at the Festival of Empire in 1911, he had published accounts of his expeditions, and his exploits had been widely reported in *The Times*. Stein had visited the British Museum to lecture between 1909 and 1911 and stayed at Merton

College, Oxford. Stein's book *Ruins of Desert Cathay* was not published until 1912, but either through Waley or Beazley or his own personal observation, Flecker must have been aware of the expeditions of Stein and others. A hoard of manuscripts had been found in the caves and brought on the first stage of their journey to England by camel, a fact again echoed in Flecker's work:

> The Principal Jew:

> And we have manuscripts in peacock styles [1313]

The method whereby Stein took the manuscripts from the caves and deposited them in the British Museum was not one that resulted in a great debate. Waley was an exception to the general rule that it was thought better to have such precious items carefully stored than left to possible neglect in the desert or more careful storage in the country of origin. Few foresaw the day when the countries of origin might decide, although usually in vain, that they wanted these and other treasures returned to them. The romantic view of such travels and items acquired was paramount and the general public did not want any other sort of view thrust upon them. But another message was carefully hidden in Flecker's verse about Samarkand and if nearly all his generation of lovers of the Silk Road did not discover it for themselves, Flecker's unique view of travellers to Central Asia would be debated by future generations. [1314]

Stein was a Hungarian Jew who had become a British subject in 1904. The Master of the Caravan says:

> 'But you are nothing but a lot of Jews.

> The Principal Jew:

> Sir, even dogs have daylight, and we pay.

Now Flecker had seen for himself (unlike Beazley or Waley and many others) that 'praise God, is not a bit like the Near East Exhibition at Olympia and all mosques are not the same', which was what he had written to Savery, when first arriving at Constantinople. He was entitled to poke fun privately at that sort of view and also at the archaeologists' view. Flecker had already, in his poem 'Invitation', stated that he wanted his young but learned friend to abandon archaeology for the moment, and he had written about:

And those things that come not to view
Of slippered dons who read a codex through.' [1315]

Since writing that poem he had been able to view the security enjoyed by archaeologists and if he was ever to enjoy the same sort of security he needed to sell his work to an appreciative market.

Flecker still needed to get his literary wares onto the London marketplace and his contacts with Mavrogordato and influential people in the London theatre world were even more important than the American market. It was important to let Mavrogordato know that his health was improving (without letting him know of any temporary setbacks) so that Mavrogordato would not have to worry about publishing deadlines failing to be met. The reference to lack of paper conveyed an image of poverty of a sort, although not greatly exaggerated. It was enough to convey to Mavrogordato that Flecker needed immediate payment and not just an enhanced literary reputation. Mavrogordato appeared to have replaced Savery as a regular correspondent on literary matters because he could be invaluable in helping to get Flecker's work to the right people for future performance on stage or for future publication. The case of a Greek in London helping an Englishman travelling around Greece was one that tended to make Mavrogordato dream in his London office of sailing around the seas of Greece, and Flecker to dream of running a magazine in London.

The output of literary work, correspondence and study accomplished during the honeymoon period was tremendous, even if Flecker tended to convey to his parents that he did almost nothing all day. In some ways this was to let them know that he was resting and not over-tiring himself. Flecker continued, in the heat of Corfu, to write letters to other friends, such as Leonard Cheesman and Mr. Cooper, and to publishers to correct proofs. He was also writing poetry and in June he wrote the poem that was to be the 'Prologue' to *The Golden Journey* which he first entitled 'A Divan of the West' and the 'Epilogue' to *The Golden Journey to Samarkand* in July, when he also wrote his poems 'In Phaeacia', 'Bryan of Brittany', 'Yasmin', 'The Hamman Name' and 'Saadabad'. He also made translations of Mistral's 'Le Contigo', which he gave the title 'Denis and Antonia. From the Provencal'.[1316] Flecker had left the manuscript of *The King of Alsander* at Smyrna or he would have worked on that as well.

The fact of Flecker having written the first draft of *The Story of Hassan of Bagdad and how he came to make the Golden Journey to Samarkand* in the notebooks he used for his studies in Turkish civil, criminal and commercial law (he also had to have a knowledge of Turkish history) bears out the shortage of paper statement, although it is hard to understand why, with five trunks, none contained enough writing paper. Flecker may have genuinely not realised how much of his own work he would be able to accomplish on honeymoon. A postcard was cheaper to send and Flecker was adept at cramming as much onto a postcard as he did in a letter. The fact that his examiner's verdict[1317] was soon to conclude that in Ottoman law there was in Flecker's case, a revelation of insufficient study of the subject, meant that in Corfu the urge to concentrate on his studies of Ottoman law was not nearly as strong as his urge to write *Hassan*.

The dullness of his studies for consular examinations could have been livened up by reading Turkish farcical plays, one of which Hellé said was to form the basis for the opening scene of *Hassan*. In the opening scene Hassan is seen to be a fat, ugly (except for his forehead, it later transpires) forty-five year old confectioner, whose father and grandfather had followed the same trade. In Flecker's time Hadji Bekir's 'Turkish Delight Factory' was familiar to all in Constantinople. Bekir's 'Turkish Delight Factory' consisted, as did Hassan's in Flecker's play, of one room 'behind the shop' where huge copper pans were kept filled with sugar-syrup.[1318] Bekir's ability to make Turkish Delight for all to see was the main attraction for passers-by and customers[1319] It was Bekir's skill in making 'boiled sweets in many colours',[1320] which Flecker made use of so lyrically in the plot of *Hassan*.

Hassan's 'behind the shop premises' were not inspired solely by Bekir's in Constantinople. Flecker, had in a sense, lived 'behind the shop' at Dean Close and dramas in school life were re-enacted in home life. Flecker knew all about the back premises of The Shelley Bookshop, Gloucester Street, Oxford, where H.V. Storey, the manager, had let him work when they became friendly in 1906. In that year Flecker had written 'The Evening Tale' and in it Dick Hamilton had started a small sweet shop in Lewisham and a description was given of the back parlour of the shop. Hassan's room 'behind the shop' had 'some Persian hangings', which had 'geometrical designs, with crude animals and some verses from the Koran hand-painted on linen'. This description is reminiscent of the 'many printed hangings' on the walls of Flecker's rooms at Kandilli, which Hellé described.[1321] Hassan's room had little furniture 'beyond a carpet, old but unexpectedly choice,' which has particular significance for Hassan. He had expensive tastes but because he was poor he had to be content with this one carpet. Hassan soon emerges as a Flecker-figure and in drawing attention to the choice carpet of Hassan, Flecker now seemed to be defending himself over the expenses he incurred when furnishing his rooms in Kandilli, a reason at the time to describe himself as 'broke' without giving the precise reason to Eleanor who was baffled by his confessed lack of cash. In Kandilli, the need had no longer arisen for Flecker to submit accounts to his parents and an interval existed before he needed to submit accounts to a soon-to-be-wedded wife, so he went overboard on furnishings, which would, as it turned out, impress Hellé.

Flecker needed to impress Mavrogordato and keep his interest and he wrote to him on 25 July 25 and told him: 'I am bust on an "Arabian Nights" farce, entirely popular, to run ten thousand nights (or at least 1001)'.[1322]

The 'Arabian Nights' stories provided Flecker not only with some of their stock situations, but also with some of the rest of the characters, for 'Hassan'. He used the personalities of Haroun (The Caliph), Ishak (The Caliph's minstrel), Jafar (The Caliph's Vizier) and Masrur (The Caliph's Executioner).

Flecker finished the sentence about 'The Arabian Nights' by telling Mavrogordato about Hassan's contents:

> 'love, intrigue, ghosts, pageants, everything in Arabian-English prose.'[1323] The use of the Arabic-English prose style (he also incorporated other styles) was to be central to the ultimate success and enjoyment of Hassan when it was staged.[1324]

The Arabic-English prose used by Flecker in Hassan can be seen to add obvious dramatic, poetic and comic advantages. The less obvious advantage is that the Caliph can be seen as representing God. Hassan addresses the Caliph as 'Ruler of the World'. Also as 'O Serene Splendour, thy servant is a man of humble origin and limited desires.'[1325] Flecker made a note on the manuscript of one version of Hassan that he had deliberately reversed the usual usage of 'thou' and 'you' in French and German, when 'thou' is used to familiars and 'you' to strangers and superiors. It is this use of 'thou' and 'thy' by Hassan to the Caliph (and study of the manuscript shows that he had difficulty in remembering to make the change) that also puts the reader or audience's mind in touch with the Authorised Version of the Bible. Flecker then can make known his feelings about the Almighty in an effective and sincere way.

Ishak says to Hassan, who has been extolling the generosity of the Caliph's friendship:

> Have you not seen the designer of carpets, O Hassan
> of Bagdad, put here the blue and here the gold, here the

orange and here the green? So have I seen the Caliph take
the life of some helpless man – who was contented in his
little house and garden, enjoying the blue of happy days
– .....[1326]

But Hassan protests, saying:

He has been so generous. Do not say he is a tyrant!
Do not say he delights in the agony of men!

What Flecker seems to be making Ishak state is that God had been
generous in letting him (Flecker) have the happiness of marriage
and the enjoyment of the beauty of Corfu and the sanctuary of the
cottage and the garden. The Caliph tells Hassan: 'This is your little
house, good Hassan, where you shall find a shelter from the wind you
so much dislike and all other blasts that harm or chill.' and 'Here in
this remote corner of the garden you will hear no noise of street or
palace, but enjoy complete repose.'[1327] But all the happiness with 'here
the orange and here the green' of his Corfu garden was taken away, on
the surface, by the Foreign Office and the need to work. It was the fact
of having contracted TB that was cruel and made him helpless in the
face of this knowledge, that he would die before his time. The loving
God could be very cruel or so it appeared, and so did the Caliph appear
to Hassan. Flecker was on ground he knew very well, when he wrote
about the plight of the poetic soul (Hassan denies frequently that he is
a poet, as Flecker might feel that he was not accepted as a poet where
he was not earning his living as one) who was a tradesman (Flecker was
a tradesman in a sense in the Consular Service, compared to the more
privileged Foreign Office staff).

In *Don Juan*, he was not on ground he knew so well, when he had
introduced modern preoccupation with contemporary social upheaval,
and this had not proved as successful as he might have thought when
caught up in the play's creation. In the creation of *The King of Alsander*,
Flecker had also described beforehand his intention to make it an
Arabian Nights' story, but the novel owed more to the *Golden Ass of
Apuleius* and, because it was written with the hope of money and
popularity, also something to *The Prisoner of Zenda* by Anthony Hope.[1328]
Neither *Don Juan* or *The King of Alsander* had the prose style of *Hassan*,
which would have helped to make them more successful.

If Flecker had worked on the manuscript of his novel whilst in Corfu
and it had not been left in Smyrna, he might have saved it from its
sense of failure. But Arabic-English would not automatically make it

a successful novel, and the style was better employed in poetic drama such as *Hassan*. Ronald Firbank was to publish a novel in Arabic-English, which he called *Santal* and which came out in 1921, but it was not considered an instant success, like *Hassan*. Both Flecker's and Firbank's lives had close connections and it is possible to see this in their respective works. In both *Hassan* and *Santal* can be seen the influence of Edward Fitzgerald's *Omar Khayyam* and the Koran. Both Flecker and Firbank had lived in the Mohammedan culture but not been part of it; they had mixed in the rich bustle of the bazaars and heard the faithful called to prayer in the mosques, and they used these experiences in their two works. Firbank, like Flecker, could be seen to be an exotic.[1329]

Firbank had visited Egypt as a little child, where it was said he was badly affected by sunstroke. Firbank's early first-hand encounter with an Arabic culture was not one that Flecker shared. It is something that sets them apart, as did Firbank's conversion to Catholicism and his ability with languages, which was not equal to Flecker's, and Firbank's publications were mainly in novel writing and not poetry. Firbank was to live longer and have more money than Flecker, and he did not marry, and had no desire to do so. The conception of *Santal* was said to have been in the autumn of 1920. Firbank could not have read *Hassan* until it was published first in 1922, unless he had an opportunity to read it in manuscript. *The Golden Journey to Samarkand* was published in 1913 and could have put a similar idea in Firbank's mind and also been a factor in Firbank later stating that *Santal* was boring to write. This was similar to Flecker's dissatisfaction later when he was in the same frame of mind with his unconscious imitation of W.B. Yeats' poem; simply because it was an imitation. Firbank and Flecker, when in their imaginations they were attempting to use another writer's work as a stepping-stone to a work of their own, were also excited about their future and much more successful work. In Flecker's case it was to be *Hassan* and in Firbank's his novel *The Flower Beneath the Foot*. The hero of *Santal*, Cherif, undertakes a pilgrimage. Both *Hassan* and *Santal* were written within four or five years of their respective authors' own deaths and the vision of a pilgrimage came to both at a time when they faced the realisation of the brevity of their lives.

Another literary influence common to both Firbank and Flecker was the playwright Congreve. The Literary Society, which Flecker was said by Charles Raven to have founded, included Brooke. Firbank was not mentioned by name, by Raven, as a member of these Societies, but he would be seen by him to have fitted in as one of the 'mere poseurs, bundles of rather nasty affectation', which had upset Raven in those days, at the Societies. Or, 'the affected frivolity' also mentioned in that connection.[1330] Time would produce a more understanding view of Firbank and his works by his contemporaries.[1331]

The plays of Shaw, Ibsen, Wycherly and Congreve were read at these Societies. Another dramatist from the period of Wycherly and Congreve was John Webster (c.1580–1634) who was chosen by Brooke as the subject for his dissertation. Brooke's *John Webster and the Elizabethan Dramatists* was published in 1916. In the future productions of *Hassan* and *The Duchess of Malfi* were to be compared.[1332] Firbank's works have influences and borrowings from Webster. It was the plot of *The Duchess of Malfi*, as summarised by Brooke, that Waley was to read to the Japan Society in 1919 to illustrate how the theme of *The Duchess of Malfi* would have been treated by a Noh writer.[1333] A lesser influence on the work of both Flecker and Firbank, and if not absorbed at Cambridge, then absorbed by both when they spent time in London before going up to Cambridge, was Japan. Then there had been the Japanese Prints exhibition, the Kabuki Theatre of Japan[1334] its and its performances and Flecker's wearing of a kimono.

One of the Noh plays *The Damask Drum* was attributed to the dramatist Seami (1363–1443) and it is possible to see that it was the sort of work that would influence Flecker. *The Damask Drum* is outstanding in its lack of compassion, a characteristic that the first draft of *Hassan* also shared. Seami set *The Damask Drum* in a remote realm and *Hassan* took place in what was a remote realm for Flecker: eighth-century Baghdad. In *The Damask Drum* the Gardener falls in love with the Princess, who cruelly pours scorn on the love of the old Gardener, in the same way as Yasmin despises the love of Hassan. Both *The Damask Drum* and *Hassan* portray love between unequals, although the Princess says: 'Love's equal realm knows no divisions.' This had been the case, in a sense, with all Flecker's loves, particularly with the Oxford shop-girl, and his love for Beazley and Eleanor had been of an unequal intensity. It is Hassan who is in trade and Yasmin who is unobtainable. 'She must be the princess! ... The unobtainable ideal!'[1335]

The Princess in *The Damask Drum* hangs the drum on the branches of the laurel tree beside the pond . She wants the old man to beat the false drum and when she 'hears' it she will see him. The drum in the play represents the moon, the laurel tree is the one tree that grows there. The Gardener, not realising that the drum is made of cloth and that the Princess will never hear the drumbeat, goes ahead and beats it. When the Gardener discovers he has been deceived, he drowns himself in the pond and after death haunts the Princess. The Princess is in torment and the Gardener remains in Hell.

In his poem 'Stillness' Flecker wrote:

When from the clock's last chime to the next chime
Silence beats his drum. [1336]

The old Gardener in *The Damask Drum* says:

To the tolling of the evening bell
I shall add the drumbeat of the days,

'Why do you not say that beauty is as hollow as a drum?' Hassan asks Ishak in Act 2, Scene 4.

In *Hassan* Flecker makes dramatic use of deceptions, which go badly wrong, as in *The Damask Drum*. Hassan dreams of making fabulous sweets for Yasmin, which are 'like globes of crystal, like cubes of jade, like polygons of ruby'. Hassan will make the sweets to smell and taste of flowers.[1337] Firbank, in *The Artificial Princess*, describes sweets that resemble crystallized flowers, Orchid and Wild Rose. When making the sweets, Hassan has put in a drop of a very expensive 'magic' philtre, which his friend Selim has persuaded him to buy, because he thinks it will make Yasmin fall in love with him. Hassan does not know that Yasmin is already aware of the 'magic' philtre when sent the sweets. Hassan serenades beneath Yasmin's window. She opens the shutters and pretends to like the ghazel, which she has heard him intone (like the songs Flecker had heard recorded by Professor Browne at Cambridge) to the accompaniment of the lute. Yasmin also pretends to like the sound of the ghazel better than the taste of the sweets. She leads Hassan on to think that she returns his passion. All Hassan's joy is turned to misery when Selim pokes his head out of Yasmin's window. Yasmin pours water over Hassan in order to get rid of him, and her rejection turns his love to hatred and thoughts of revenge. Yasmin afterwards spurns the love of Selim and she returns briefly to Hassan when he becomes rich and famous, but when he falls into disfavour she will again leave him.

Yasmin is something of an Eleanor figure, although her type of character had appeared in works by other writers. Yasmin is very beautiful and it is her eyes that attract Hassan, like Eleanor's when Flecker first met her. Yasmin had visited his shop veiled. She had at first let Hassan know that she liked his serenade. At their first meetings, Eleanor had been enthusiastic about his writing. Later, when Eleanor was sent a poem from Turkey, she was much less enthusiastic, as Yasmin was, after a time, unenthusiastic about Hassan's ghazel. It was Eleanor's rejection of him as a poet that had made him realise that he could not spend what remained of his life with her. There had seemed to be some sort of change of heart by Eleanor when Flecker had returned to England. His prospects then briefly would have looked better than Eleanor may have hoped. Yasmin, in the same way, spurned the love of Hassan, but returned briefly to him when he became rich and famous. When Hassan falls into disfavour, Yasmin will again leave him. It was Yasmin's telling Hassan, after she had pretended to like his serenade: 'Go home, and cook sweets!' that had made Hassan realise that, despite her beauty, she could be 'so brutal' and his deep love turned to deeper loathing. Yasmin's husband had been executed the year before, which could account, in some small measure, for her apparent brutality. In one version of *Hassan* Flecker made Yasmin a prostitute. Yasmin became a secondary character in his play, as Eleanor was when he started to write *Hassan*. The saintly Pervaneh is the central character. Yet when Hassan is faced with Yasmin for the last time, he says her name with 'infinite tenderness'. Flecker used in his ghazel 'Yasmin' the image of dead flowers:

> ..... For one night or the other night
> Will come the Gardener in white, and gathered flowers
>   are dead, Yasmin. [1338]

It is possible, with this image, to see something of Leila and Gladys too in the character of Yasmin; Flecker had seen Gladys so ill amid all the gathered lilies in her room at Cranham. The memory of her beauty lived on, even if the lilies were long dead and Gladys herself faced, in the time he knew her, a similar fate. The lilies were not flowers used in Japanese poetry or plays; in these works the brief passing of the cherry blossom would be used instead. Flecker uses the Gardener for his own effect in his poem. The lines about lilies and whiteness are used in a way that could be taken by Firbank to refer to him.[1339] Firbank's *Birth of Venus* by Botticelli was a feature of his room at Cambridge and he used *Birth of Venus* in his novel *The Flower Beneath the Foot*. The lilies in Botticelli's painting are stiff, which the lilies in Gladys's room would be: lilies bought in a shop. Firbank, if he had visited Flecker at Cranham, would have seen the flowers or he could have been told about them.

Firbank was to write in his novel *Inclinations* about Miss Dawkins who takes the novel *Three lilies and a Moustache* to read on the train.[1340] If Flecker can be taken as 'Moustache', the three lilies can be taken to be Hellé, Eleanor and Leila.

Flecker's attraction for Leila had not ceased when she left the sanatorium. Her name appears amongst a list in his notebook which he used in 1910–11.[1341] The list also included GBS, Masefield and Hellé. This indicated that he could have had Leila in mind as someone to contact before he joined Hellé in Paris and he had been trying to interest managements in *Don Juan*. His earliest version of *Hassan* contains a slave-girl Leila who later is taken out of the play, but Leila remains as a name when Hassan tell Selim:

> ... she on whom my heart is bent is not less fair than
>   Leila [1342]

This is reminiscent of Flecker writing about Leila: 'the only girl I've ever seen lovelier than mine...'[1343]

Great contrast is evident between his earlier attempts to write about the body of Eleanor in his unpublished verses[1344] before he left Cambridge and the comparison Hassan used to describe (to Selim) Yasmin's hips, which he said were:

> large and round, like water-melons in the season
> of water-melons. [1345]
> Later, he makes Yasmin ask: 'Is not my bosom burning for
>   kisses?'[1346]

This is in contrast also to the 'blossoms of snow' he used to describe Eleanor:

> ..... Beneath her dress
> Was she not shaped for loveliness?

Yasmin also says to Hassan: 'Yet there is little of love's language that I do not know. When the bird of night sings on the bough of the tree that rustles outside your window, and the shadows creep away from the moon across the floor, I could have sung you a song and shown you a whiteness whiter than the moon.'[1347]

This speech of Yasmin's contains an element of 'what might have been', which can also be seen in the memory he had of Leila. If Leila had not had to leave the sanatorium, or if she had left under different circumstances, who knows how the relationship would have progressed? Yasmin has aspects of Leila in her character; Yasmin tries to seduce Hassan and was this a possibility with Leila and Flecker, or only a fantasy? Lovemaking against the cool of the English autumnal landscape, even if a fantasy, or now only a memory, could be an enjoyable contrast with the attempts at closeness in the heat and discomfort of the honeymoon in Greece. Flecker could have backed off at the last moment when the opportunity came to get closer to Leila and he may have had time to regret it. Now he was married and he had every opportunity to get physically closer to Hellé; the song of the nightingale would only go a small way towards softening the atmosphere of their rough sleeping quarters. He used moonlight to illuminate Yasmin's tempting of Hassan, and in using the full moon, he implies an ending of a relationship, one that has passed its peak. In using the crescent moon in 'A Ship, an Isle', Flecker signifies the start of a relationship and the possibility of a full flowering. In this he shares something with Japanese poetry[1348] In reality, as far as Leila and Eleanor were concerned, the honest conclusion, when it came to resisting temptation, lies in Hassan saying to Ishak: 'All men are brutes, you and he and I. I thought I was kinder than other men – but I was only more afraid.' [1349]

Eleanor's mother had been sure that Flecker would make 'a good and kind husband' for her daughter.[1350] The fear of the consequences of his sexual advances towards women, especially when he had met Hellé, was greater than his desire to put them into practice.

He also had to contend with the fact that Eleanor had interests in other men, which threatened his future. He had told Savery, at the time of his engagement, that Eleanor was a flirt and had a passion for handsome men. In that respect she and Yasmin had a lot in common.

In *The King of Alsander* he had planned to introduce a bride out of *The Arabian Nights* because at that time he knew no woman intimately enough to do anything else convincingly. When it came to writing *Hassan* he was much closer to the women in his life and he had used both cruelty and lust to effect. He was able to explore 'a dark, unexplored connection between outward and inward loveliness?', which he outlined in his Laurence Hope article. He thought he knew about the passivity that 'accompanies' women's passions, but by the time he came to write *Hassan* this sort of passivity was attributed more to the main female character, Pervaneh, than to Yasmin. Laurence Hope thought that it was the woman's role to be passive at times in the face of cruelty. The elements of love and shame, which Flecker had quoted from Laurence Hope's verses about the woman's lover pricking out his name on her breast with a shell, were similar to the lines in *Hassan* which Pervaneh speaks when she voices her fear of the sword pricking its steel on her breast.[1351] Flecker had introduced a flogging scene in *The King of Alsander*, but when he came to write *Hassan* he eventually took out a similar sort of scene. The fact that Flecker used his own experiences of life and travels and loves resulted in his characters appearing to be characters from a bygone age with contemporary problems.[1352]

Hassan's problems in eighth-century Baghdad were similar to Flecker's. Both Hassan and Flecker were without private means and they had to work in order to earn their bread and butter. In Hassan's age there was a genuine Islamic division between the art of the upper classes and the people.[1353] The division for Flecker was that between the popular poets of the day, such as Stephen Phillips and Ella Wheeler Wilcox, whom he did not admire, and poets like Davidson who had been out of favour and lived in poverty. This was a theme that Flecker repeated again and again in his prose. Flecker makes Hassan tell Selim:

> 'Oh, cruel destiny, thou hast made me a common man with a common trade. My friends are fellows from the market, and all my worthless family is dead. Had I been rich, ah me! how deep had been my delight in matters of the soul, in poetry and music and pictures, and companions who do not jeer and grin, and above all, in the colours of rich carpets and expensive silks.'[1354]

In making Hassan a Flecker figure and in writing about what was a deeply held view about the necessity for someone who wanted to be a poet and appreciate beautiful objects of art to earn his living at something else, Flecker is writing about what he knew to his cost. 'Most of them have to add up figures or something equally absurd; and the rest are almost starving.'[1355]

Hassan tells the Caliph that for him 'poetry is a princely diversion but for me it is a deliverance from Hell. Allah made poetry a cheap thing to buy and a simple thing to understand. He gave men dreams by night that they might learn to dream by day. Men who work have special need of dreams.'[1356]

The beautiful serenade to Yasmin, sung by Hassan, could mean that it is almost one of the 'dreams by night', and this one perfect poem of passion and perfection was the dream that Flecker would hope to write himself. *Hassan* contains more poems by Flecker, 'The War Song of the Saracens' and 'Epilogue' from *The Golden Journey to Samarkand*. It is in 'Yasmin', and not the other poems, that Hassan can be seen not only as 'the type of poet Flecker believed himself to be',[1357] but it would be nearer to the truth that he was the sort of poet Flecker actually was.[1358] Hassan has the poetic soul[1359] of Flecker and in loving Yasmin, his 'one love, but unattained....'[1360] for a brief spell before his love turns sour, he is able to transcend the restrictions of his previously mundane life. Even after he is disillusioned with Yasmin, Hassan goes on to experience a life of a quite different order. Flecker's marriage, after the disillusionment and breaking-up of his previous close relationships, had brought him a private life of quite a different order. If he had married an English bride with some money of her own, she would not have been prepared to take a back seat and let him, during their honeymoon, lead the life of a full-time writer. Flecker had previously written a great deal when he was alone and unhappy, but his work had reflected his sad feelings and the landscape had been distorted in his mind by his despair. Flecker's family, unlike Hassan's were not dead, but their ignoring of him since his marriage was as much a result of his marrying a Greek bride and honeymooning in Greece as anything else, and if he had made a conventional marriage in England, the isolation would not have been as great but the opportunity to get down to his writing would have been very much less.

If similarities can be seen between Hassan and Flecker, there is one very great difference; Hassan did not suffer from TB or any similar fatal illness. Hassan had been fat and complacent before he set eyes on Yasmin. Flecker's disease, like Hassan's love for Yasmin, freed his spirit in Corfu to write such poems as 'A Ship, an Isle' and 'Yasmin' and to express feelings about the transitory nature of his happiness. The discipline of daily writing helped him to make what sense he could of his future and to make use of past relationships and see them for what they were, now they never could be resumed in the same way. The beauty of his surroundings, with their British ghosts, and with Hellé, were more satisfying for a while than being at home again. Marriage had brought the opportunity to continue to enjoy with Hellé the infliction of pain for mutual enjoyment, either as foreplay or as a substitute for the sexual act. This was not an important influence on his work, as might have been supposed. The depiction of cruelty, which Flecker put into the first draft of *Hassan* was later taken out or played down. Lear, too, had produced a similar outpouring of work, and he too had been ill on Corfu, with epilepsy, which he concealed. He had repressed his homosexual feelings and had nearly broken down on Corfu.

While her husband was embarking on his first draft of *Hassan*, Hellé had her thirtieth birthday on 14 July. An event in itself that could have contributed to the depression she much later confessed to feeling in Corfu. She afterwards stated that she should have realised that the depression (which she blamed entirely on herself) should have been faced 'with the spirit of the ephemera, dancing away their short hour in a ray of sunlight.'[136] Hellé would find this difficult to do, even if she set aside the practical considerations of having little money to spend and the discomforts of travel. She was not a good sailor and the sun made her face peel. She was more used to living in cities, although Corfu could not be regarded as a social backwater. Corfu had associations as a holiday residence for the late Empress of Austria, Kaiser William II and the Greek royal family. Corfu was a more fashionable place than the rest of the Greek islands, and in a sense it was similar as a holiday place to the Isle of Wight, which had its associations with Queen Victoria.

Hellé always got a present of a poem written by her husband for her birthday. The poem written for her in Corfu was 'In Phaeacia', which was to be included in *The Golden Journey*. Flecker was later to tell Savery that he thought 'In Phaeacia' a 'rotten poem'. He also included his poem 'Sacred Incident' (revised as 'The Old Story') in this category and he described both poems as 'harmless rather than offensive'.[1362]

The essence of 'In Phaeacia' is his love for Hellé. Flecker was also to tell Savery, after it was published, that 'In Phaeacia' was 'an unconscious imitation of Yeats and Jack Beazley'.[1363] The use of the word unconscious and even imitation, indicates a confirmation to Savery of the word 'rotten' to describe the poem. The poem of Beazley's to which he referred was 'If I knew',[1364] which had been one of three published in *The English Review* of April 1911. Flecker had read and then copied them out in the book he kept of Beazley's poems. The poems of Yeats ,which he had referred to (but not named), were 'Aedh wishes for the Cloths of Heaven', and 'The Wind in the Reeds'.[1365] Flecker's poem 'Oak and Olive' can also be seen as akin to one of Beazley's.[1366] The 'rottenness' was also a result of comparing himself to poets like Robert Browning. He was to confess to Hellé of 'weeping' when he read Browning, when pressures of work prevented him from getting down to write his poetry. The weeping was for his own rottenness. In Corfu he felt rotten because his own poetry did not reach the popularity of Yeats ,or even achieve the desire of Beazley to leave most of his work unpublished. 'Oak and Olive' and 'In Phaeacia' contain just enough of the hidden Beazley factor, but no more, now Beazley could no longer have a hand in altering lines, which he thought too obvious in their reference to his relationship with Flecker. The poems contained mixed feelings about the poet's past and present feelings, not yet fully worked out, as was his homesickness, and he could not find it in his heart to jettison them from *The Golden Journey*, as he had done to some of his other poems.

This part imitation of Yeats and Beazley resulted in the show-off element (imitating another poet) appearing to be tolerated more than similar behaviour in the non-writing part of his life had been by his parents. A reference to 'In Phaeacia' (although only the first line is quoted , compared to thirteen lines of 'Epithalamion') is used to illustrate that it is among a group of poems where 'time and the loved one altogether' were portrayed against the background of 'this Phaeacian Island'. So the poem served as a reminder for his parents and the rest of his family, who were at the time of writing the poem, tending to ignore his marriage and the happy life he was leading. They could not in the future deny the facts unless they were prepared to ignore the poem. The fact of the poem having links with Beazley would not be known, unless they read the April edition of *The English Review*[1367] and put two and two together, but the influence of a poet of Yeats's stature would be recognised by Hodgson, if not his parents. 'In Phaeacia' was also influenced by other well-known poets.[1368]

Phaeacia is thought to be the island, which Homer called Scheria, the land of the Phaeacians where Odysseus was cast ashore. The poem reflects Flecker's love of the olive trees on Corfu (which had also meant so much to Lear) and above all the garden where he spent so much time:

> And bind it with the silver light
> That wavers in the olive tree.
>
> Had I the gold that like a river
> Pours through our garden, eve by eve,
> Our garden that goes on for ever
> Out of this world, as we believe; [1369]

Another poem he was to write for Hellé's birthday, two years later, was to be his first version of his poem 'The Old Ships'. It also had Phaeacia as its theme when he wrote:

> Who knows. In that old ship – but in that same
> (Fished up beyond Phaeacia, patched as new and
> painted brighter blue)
> With patient comrades sweating at the oar
> That talkative, unskilful seaman came
> From Troy's fire-crimson shore
> And with loud lies about his Wooden Horse,
> Wrapped in eloquence, forgot his course. [1370]

'In Phaeacia' can be seen too as 'a rotten poem' in Flecker's estimation because, as with his poem 'The Old Story', it was also written with the idea of making money (it was written in response to a request for a Christmas poem). 'In Phaeacia' was eventually published in *Everyman* magazine, in the 27 June 1913 edition. This poem had not been given sufficient time to mature first in his mind, like more successful poems written about his love for Hellé, such as 'Sadaabad', also written in

Corfu, and 'Epithalamium', written in anticipation of marriage. The underlying message of 'In Phaeacia' was that Hellé should be content with the beauty of Corfu and what he felt was 'the time and the place and the loved one together.'[1371] The message was not one that Hellé would find easy to appreciate now she had ample time to ponder on her own future, the uncertainty of her acceptance by her in-laws and her suitability as a daughter-in-law. But one side of Hellé's nature, her poetic side, could have been pleased with 'In Phaeacia', even if her husband was not. They differed about another poem written during this time on Corfu, 'Bryan of Brittany', which he later told Savery that he hated 'or rather find it cold. But the story (a Greek story again), is jolly enough'.[1372] Hellé liked 'Bryan'; she had told her husband the story and he had written the ballad afterwards and compared it, he wrote to Cheesman. Flecker told Cheesman in a letter that it was not a translation but on the same theme as the Βρυκδλακας (Theros p.106: Jack has the book)'.[1373] The title, from a collection of folk ballads by the modern Greek poet Agis Theros, given by him is 'The Vampire'. Flecker had mentioned 'where vampires roam' in his poem 'South East and North' written in 1904, when he was separated from Beazley, at Oxford.

Flecker's description of the beauty of Bryan is contained in the lines:

> Her glorious hair was spread in the sun
> And her feet were dewed in the grass.

These lines are reminiscent of Flecker's first meeting with Eleanor when they had played tennis barefoot at the Fabian Summer Camp. Also in the poem, when Bryan has reluctantly entered into a marriage of convenience in a foreign country, she asks peevishly: 'What shall I do in Babylon/A crownèd king to keep?'

This is similar to Eleanor's dislike of having to live in Turkey with Elroy – 'le Roi' to help support.

The story of Bryan of Brittany, in thirty verses, traced the story of 'the loveliest girl alive', who 'Home she came with the West in her eyes,'. This image was used previously by another poet, Mary Coleridge, in her poem, 'Unwelcome'.[1374] Bryan has to leave her heartbroken old mother and her seven brothers to marry the King of Babylon. The seven brothers all die and the ghost of one brother, John, goes to bring back his sister, who, not realising he is already dead, follows him back to Brittany. This poem with some traces of an old love, Eleanor, and some affinity to Hellé having to leave her elderly mother to marry and the 'borrowed' line may have added to Flecker's dislike of it.[1375] He was also dismayed when *The English Review* offered him £4 payment for such a long poem. As in his poem, 'Santorin', he had created a story that was not as harsh a version as the original legend. Flecker could have felt that, in writing about cruelty in other poems and also in his first version of *Hassan*, he was getting nearer to the truth of his own feelings for Eleanor and the hurt they had inflicted on each other which was initially to see each other as suitable life partners. One other reason for his future discontent with some of the poems written during this period could simply be because the number he was writing gave him less time to revise them all.

The amount of work sent out was embodied in the reasons he gave to Mavrogordato 'Am sending many things to America in the hope of raising money.'[1376] Flecker's notebook,[1377] which contained jottings for the Corfu period, bears this out:

[Title of Poem]	[Destination]

'Don Juan Speaks'   *English Review*
[Published as 'Don Juan Declaims' in the ER September, 1911]

'Epithalamium'   *English Review*
[Published in *The Nation*, 7 December, 1911]

'Fairy Story'[1378] Nash   [*Nash's Magazine*]

'Phaician'   *Nation*
['In Phaeacia' published in *Everyman*, 27 June 1913]

'Queen's Bouquet' ['The Ballad of the Queen's Bouquet'][1379]

'Dream Afloat'   *Spectator*

'Journey to Samarkand'[1380]
[Published as *The Golden Journey to Samarkand, Poetry and Drama*, No.1 March 1913]

'Contigo *USA Independent*[1381]

'Mansur' [Published in *The Cambridge Review*, 20 January 1910]

'Gulistan'   *USA Atlantic Monthly*
[Published in *The Cambridge Review* 25 November 1909]

'Xmas 3 Blind Men'[1382]   *USA Atlantic Monthly*

Despite Flecker's records of where he had sent his work, tracing whether it had appeared in publications was also a task, as a postcard,[1383] which he wrote to James Strachey at the Spectator Offices revealed:

Casa Bogdanos, Stratia, Corfu, Greece.

My dear Strachey, – Forgive the postcard of pressure and be kind to me. Has the *Spectator* published (a month or more ago) a poem of mine and if so, which one? I do not think it probable, but someone said it had and if so it must be a poem. I want to send somewhere else if it wasn't published, and you'd better send this sentence to *Punch*, because it's involved.

I am living in a cottage, married.

Thine,
J.E. Flecker

Flecker's publishing horizons, as the list shows, were not all set on new poems getting published in London magazines. His prose article 'From the Rose-Garden of Sadi' (which had already been published in *The Cambridge Review*'s 25 November 1909) was sent to the *Atlantic Monthly* in the USA from Casa Bogdanos with instructions to send any cheques to Flecker's bank in Cambridge and any correspondence before 10 August to Corfu, after which he would be spending eight days in Greece and hence to the British Consulate in Smyrna, where he would be permanently.[1384]

Some of the poems he had noted in his notebook, he sent (enclosed in a letter dated 28 July) to Mavrogordato with queries about where to send them. One he suggested should be sent to the *Nation* 'cutting out the naughty verse about the humanist!'. The reference to 'the humanist' meant that the poem was a deleted stanza from his 'Diwan of the West' which read:

The Chief Humanist

And we have boys and girls of special kinds,
White, brown and black, fragile or fair or strong:

Their bosoms shame the roses: their behinds
Impel the astonished nightingales to song[1385]

Flecker cursed the fate that had inspired him to write long poems.[1386]

Many of the poems were destined for publication in *The Golden Journey to Samarkand,* as well as appearing in magazines. 'The Hamman Name' (from a poem by a Turkish Lady) was written in Corfu and included in *The Golden Journey to Samarkand* published by Max Goschen in 1913, but did not appear in a magazine. This is the poem about 'Winsome Torment', based on Ronald Firbank.[1387] Flecker was to say, when the poem appeared in print: 'Of course the "Turkish Lady" won't wash. The poem is a pretty close translation in the book.'[1388] Hamman in Turkish means Turkish Bath and the poem begins:

Winsome Torment rose from slumber, rubbed his eyes,
    and went his way
Down the street towards the Hamman. Goodness gracious!
    people say,
What a handsome countenance! The Sun has risen twice
    to-day! [1389]

Flecker's *The Hamman Name* is a translation of a Turkish poem, *Book of the Bath* by the eighteenth-century Ottoman poet, Mehemmed Emin Beligh of Larissa,[1390] who had much in common with Nedim, the poet whose *Saadabad* Flecker had also translated in this period. *The Hamman Name* 'reads like an original poem'.[1391] Flecker introduced his own words, as well as the character Winsome Torment, when he wrote of 'a yellow towel growing yellower in fright'. This does not disturb the balance of the original comic poem because it is not a literal translation such as Gibb's in his *History of Ottoman Poetry*. Flecker quoted from 'the Eastern poet,' in *The King of Alsander*, when Norman Price was told by the doctor to take off his clothes, 'and Norman, with growing reluctance, shed garment upon garment till, in the words of the Eastern poet, 'the shining almond came out of his dusky shell,' and 'the petals of the rose lay strewn upon the ground.' '[1392]

In *The Hamman Name* Flecker wrote: 'All the growing heap of garments, buds and blossoms like a rose', and 'How the shell came off the almond, how the lily showed its face'. Firbank, in his novel *The Flower Beneath the Foot* describes one of his characters, the Hon. 'Eddy' Monteith, deciding to have a bath and after he had asked his manservant to pass him a favourite Flecker leisure garment, a kimono, he undressed and the garments drop away. 'Eddy' lies amid the dissolving bath crystals in a similar dreamy state to that of Winsome Torment, and he sees through the open window 'the blue air of evening'. ('Eddy', it seemed, had a habit of bathing before an open window, as Flecker had boasted of doing at Oxford, although 'Eddy' is thought to be based on someone else.[1393] A former school friend, Lionel Limpness, now enters and before Limpness can persuade 'Eddy' to let him chastise him, they are interrupted.

This scene seems to be based on a real life situation between Firbank and Flecker as 'Eddy's' appearance is described as having: 'light, liver-tinted hair, grey narrow eyes, hollow cheeks, and pale mouth like a broken moon.'

This description bears a closer resemblance to Flecker than to the photograph published of Evan Montague, although 'Eddy' is also assured that he had a profile of 'Rameses', which was something that Firbank attributed to Montague. 'Eddy' was not based on Firbank's looks as he has been described as having 'a pink and white clean-shaven skin and small mouth'.[1394] Lionel Limpness's appearance ('Eddy's' former school chum, a possible candidate for 'Vice-Consul at Sodom') is not described in such detail, but the threat of chastisement and the use of Winsome Torment in 'The Hamman Name' point to a Firbank/Flecker incident.

Flecker's depiction of cruelty in his writing was more often the cruelty of men towards women set against a background of the beauty of nature. Examples of extreme cruelty occur in *The Last Generation*, Flecker's unpublished one-act play *The Dead People*. His (also unpublished) story 'Boy and Girl', which differed from his other writings, about a savage death (but not in this case by another person) contained elements of tenderness and love, which Flecker went on to develop more fully in *Hassan*. In *Hassan*, unlike *Don Juan*, it is the hero who is more in love, and who is tortured for a time because the object of his love, Yasmin, is more involved with another. Flecker had experienced these feelings himself with Beazley and Eleanor, and although it is less clear with Leila, she was devoted to her sister who was dying. It would appear from Firbank's writings, where he depicted so vividly the despair of the spurned lover, that he had deep feelings for Flecker ,which were not returned in the same way or with such intensity. Flecker saw Firbank as Winsome Torment because it was possible that they had indulged in mutual chastisement. 'Arnie' Firbank, as he was known, is also portrayed as Arnolfo in *The King of Alsander* whom Norman Price saw 'as shallow as you are clever'.[1395] He turns out to be the Princess Ianthe in disguise, which Norman bitterly regrets.[1396]

Flecker had tried to inflict mental pain on Hellé before marriage by making her think he was involved seriously with someone else. The residue of this mental pain could still stir Hellé, in spite of herself, as her husband dredged up and put in his writing the memories of recent loves. Her husband's absorption in his writing and studies (she had tried to share the study) could shut her out for most of the day. But in the 'Epilogue' to *The Golden Journey to Samarkand*, which he was to incorporate in *Hassan*, Flecker mentioned some of the more homely touches that being with Hellé in Athens and Corfu had brought him:

The Chief Grocer

'We have rose-candy, we have spikenard,
Mastic and terebinth and oil and spice,
And such sweet jams meticulously jarred
As God's own Prophet eats in Paradise.' [1397]

Their time in Corfu was not taken up entirely with writing and study, or remedies for the treatment of illness and putting marmalade in jars. A particularly lengthy, delightful drive was made to the monastery of Palaeokastrika. The beauty and quiet of this place had also enchanted Lear, although he was not as interested in the simple white-washed monastery as the Fleckers, who were shown round by the prior. A terrace screened by a vine gave shade and a view towards the Italian coast. 'Had I that glory on the vine'.[1398] Words in such a beautiful place usually take second place to the visual arts. The giant rocks rising steeply from the calm sea at Palaeokastrika were painted by Lear over and over again. For the Fleckers, the visual art had no place – the photographs they took did not come out because of problems with the locally bought plates. Flecker's enjoyment of the monastery and his interest in the lonely life of the monks, to whom they gave a newspaper, is akin to his love for the homely atmosphere of the Arlesford churches. His interest, too, was growing in the Greek Orthodox Church. Another expedition they made was to Pantocrator, which gave them an opportunity to see the marvellous views over the sea, and to picnic under the pines. This expedition was made possible by the generosity of the Corfiote man who had been introduced to the Fleckers by some friends of Hellé's from Athens. This was the man who owned a candle and nail factory and a model farm, which provided good fresh butter for the Fleckers' breakfast and tea. But they found this decent, kind man dull, and because they were exhausted they stopped any more attempts to integrate into the society of Corfu. It seems a pity when money was so short, they had no transport of their own and the Corfiote man had his own car. Could he have served as a model on which to base some aspects of the character of Hassan?

Another expedition was made by horse-carriage to the village of Péléka in the mountains. This was marred by contact with the village children, who were warned off by the coachman. One young boy persisted in mocking them; Flecker chased him with his stick until he ran back into the woods for a while. Lear had been annoyed by picnic parties destroying the peace. Visitors, such as the Fleckers were at the time, may have felt that the peace of the island somehow belonged to them. The Corfiotes may have tired of being invaded by outsiders. In her book about Corfu, Sophie Anderson had written that letting outsiders know about the paradise island would in time render it no longer an island of calm and quiet and unspoiled places. For once, Flecker's vision of the future did not share this accurate view, but he did say that the question of 'whether it is better to be beautiful and dead or ugly and alive' was avoided by Miss Atkinson 'in Corfu of all places the problem presses.' The beauty of the, as yet, unspoiled surroundings was not the only influence on his work, nor did it have a calming effect on his spirits. His bursts of irritability could be due to fatigue and the exhaustion of travelling in the heat. He had previously found in Turkey that the local people were amusing and a contact with the past, as he mentioned them resembling satyrs and herding goats. In Greece, where he had closer contact with officials and a landlady, he could have been less appreciative of their quaintness.

Sea-bathing would have been a source of enjoyment, but even that was spoiled by the loss of a ring Flecker had been given that had belonged to Hellé's grandfather. The ring was described as 'an old Greek intaglio with a figure of Demeter holding a pomegranate cut in red cornelian'.[1399] A loss that Hellé was to recall later in a line of her poem 'Echo of a Greek Folk-Song'. 'If I send down a pomegranate it sinks and will not float'.[1400] The ring disappeared in a bed of seaweed and a long search did not produce it.

They also sailed in a little white cutter, which took five hours to get them to the shore, just before sunset. Hellé had felt badly seasick during the hot and airless day. She was assured by her husband that there

411

was nothing like rowing to cure seasickness. So they each took one of the heavy oars and Hellé became like one of those 'patient comrades sweating at the oar'.[1401] She endured this very difficult task because:

> And all these ships were old,
> Painted the mid-sea blue or deep sea green,
> And patterned with the vine and grapes in gold. [1402]

Next time they went out in the same boat they were with a boatman who was more experienced in the ways of the sea than they were. But he must have been the same boatman who nearly capsized the boat. Although they were in no real danger, they had a lot of money on them as they had just been to the bank.[1403]

By the middle of August they were due to leave, with great regret, the island where, despite practical difficulties, they had enjoyed so much happiness. Flecker's health had improved and he had been able to do so much of his own work. Flecker in Corfu had endured similar problems to Lear and other travellers, such as bad weather, being robbed and not always finding the peace to work and concentrate on reading. But Lear and Flecker, while pursuing their creative activities on Corfu, appear to have been reassured by the ghostly elements of the immediate past. No such reassurance existed for the Fleckers in their immediate present. Despite cash drawn from the bank, only a few pennies remained once expenses had been met. They had to refuse to pay even for damaged saucepans (those used in the marmalade-making?) belonging to the irate landlady. The carriage ordered to take them to the pier was delayed. They had to hail one that was passing and then saw that the driver was a dying man but eager to help. A large trunk containing their most valued belongings was left behind and had to be retrieved, despite the landlady sitting determinedly upon it. The boat due to take them out to the Athens steamer was held up as the boatmen were not the regular boatmen for the trip. Because they arrived on board at the last minute, the Fleckers had to pass a nightmarish time on deck sleeping on uncomfortable sofas in what passed for a smoking-room.

On arrival in Athens the temperature was over 110ª in the shade. A letter from Savery and a welcome postcard from Jack Beazley awaited; Beazley's past failure to comment on the marriage had caused upset. Flecker replied to Savery's letter[1404] and told him of his good health, which he hoped would last. He went on to mention that he had finished the first Act of *Hassan*, which he described as 'a marvel!', and that all his 'copies of *Don Juan* were with Managers.' He told Savery that he had written 'many poems' and that he was off soon to the British Consulate in Beirut. He urged Savery to drop him a line 'and make that pig Jack write'. The exact reasons why Jack Beazley chose not to comment on the Flecker marriage or write regularly are not easy to fathom, although one reason could be similar to that of most other correspondents, who found it difficult to keep track of Flecker's frequent changing of addresses.

Yet another unexpected change of address was evident when the Fleckers realised that they were not now en route for Smyrna, as they had supposed while still in Corfu. A telegram had been given to Flecker when he called to collect his passport from the Legation. He had to report to Beirut (then in Syria) to be Acting Vice-Consul at the Consulate there.

Jack Beazley's lack of communication could only be partly due to postal delays and preoccupation with his own concerns. The suddenness of Flecker's marriage plans must have given Beazley (for a number of reasons) a severe emotional jolt. One reason was the fact that Flecker had TB. Any power Beazley had felt he still had over his old friend, would now need to be shared; Hellé would have the greater share of power. Beazley had always hidden his deeper feelings, and immersed himself in scholarship. It is difficult to fathom exactly what his feelings were at the time of the Flecker marriage. The assumption that the feelings were stronger on Flecker's side, and that Beazley took on the feminine role in the relationship, was not always possible to maintain, after the Flecker marriage. The marriage may have tipped the balance so that Beazley felt more isolated, if he had planned to meet Flecker abroad, while Flecker saw the possibilities of a threesome, overlooking the resentment that both Jack and Hellé might feel about such a prospect.

Clues as to how the Flecker/Beazley and Flecker/Firbank relationship were affected by Flecker's marriage can be gleaned from another reference in the fiction of Ronald Firbank, which describes the desolation of characters who discover that their beloved has married overseas. Firbank also depicts the atmosphere back home and the reception of characters resembling Flecker who have got their work into print, ahead of someone like Firbank who, before he began to write his adult novels, had not been nearly as prolific or as successful. It would seem that Firbank began to write his best fiction after the pain and rejection he would have felt around the time of the Flecker marriage, when he was alone, whilst Flecker's writing blossomed even more profusely when he was happily married and had a companion.

Firbank published, after his novel *Vainglory*, another novel *Inclinations*, which he had begun to write in London in 1914, before he was driven by bombing to escape to Oxford, where he stayed for nearly four years and continued to write. In this period Firbank had the opportunity to look back on the years since Flecker had been abroad, and he could realise that Flecker and others around him, such as Jack Beazley, were not now as they had once seemed. They were able to make relationships successfully with the opposite sex, while Firbank was unable to do so or want to do so. Firbank was again in the position of having to pay Grant Richards before he agreed to publish *Inclinations*, which first came out in 1916. The dust jacket was illustrated by Albert Rotherstein, who had by then changed his name to the less German-sounding, Rutherston. After a dispute about the use of the name, he and Firbank became close friends. It was Rutherston who had been mentioned in connection with Flecker (while both were in Oxford) when he was boasting about his personal knowledge of Manet in Paris.[1405] Thus, Flecker could be part model for Mrs. Calvally in *Vainglory*, who was 'one of those destined to get mixed over Monet and Manet all their lives.' Another female character of Firbank's who seems almost wholly modelled on Flecker, was Mabel Collins who is the heroine of *Inclinations*. She is a character who is not entirely what she seems. Mabel Collins is already engaged when the novel starts but she has not made the fact known to her travelling companion, Geraldine (always known as Gerald) O'Brookomore, when they leave England for Athens. Mabel's fiancé, Napier Fairmile, like Flecker's, remains at home. Napier Fairmile's name has Edinburgh connections; Firbank had been in Edinburgh and his name Ronald, like Eleanor's surname, was Scottish. Napier did not kiss Mabel when he said good-bye to her, he just crushed her to his heart. This lack of a kiss points to Napier Fairmile and Eleanor Finlayson, at this stage, being the same sort of person, rather than representing Firbank, who was in Siena in Italy when Flecker left England for Constantinople in June 1910. Mabel Collins travels by the same route as Flecker to Athens, leaving by boat from Marseilles. Gerald O'Brookomore, 'The Biographer' as she is known, is more of a Beazley figure at this stage than a Firbankian one. The Irish surname and her devotion to her work of digging up the past is reminiscent of Beazley, but Gerald's love for Mabel, which is never openly declared, seems to be more Firbank than Beazley. Aboard the boat, just as Flecker did, Mabel meets the love of her life and her future husband, Count Pastorelli, an Italian who speaks excellent English and who has money. He follows Mabel to Athens, and subsequently all over Greece. Mabel is not keen to spend time in the royal gardens because, as she explains, gardening in the rain was one of our punishments at home. When told that the palace has few flowers, Mabel replies that the very sight of a wheelbarrow upsets her. Firbank, who had gardeners in his childhood, liked the idea of being a gardener and the hero of his early story, 'Lady Appledore's Mésalliance', preferred to work incognito as a gardener when he needed to start a new life. So Mabel's dislike of gardening reflected the dislike that Flecke and his sisters had of working in their mother's rose garden, much as the roses might be a source of Flecker's admiration and longing.

When they reached Athens, Mabel, Miss O'Brookomore and the Count encounter, amongst other foreigners, Professor Cowsend and his wife. It had been Mrs. Cowsend who suggested the morning in the royal gardens to Mabel. Professor Cowsend is always gathering notes for lectures in the Museum on the subject of vases and he holds classes in the Vase Room there. Cowsend seems an obvious Beazley figure, whose speciality was also Greek vases. At the time Firbank was writing, Beazley had met a married woman (at a party at All Souls in 1913) whom he would eventually marry in 1919 when she was a war widow. Her name was Marie Ezra (née Bloomfield – a name that would appeal to Firbank who had invented the character Olga Blumenghast). Then Miss O'Brookomore turns into a Firbankian/Flecker figure when she says that to visit Greece with Professor Cowsend would be her idea of happiness. Like Beazley's future wife, Mrs. Cowsend does not share her husband's life interest. The foreign contingent embark on an expedition in open carriages to the Acropolis (as Flecker and Hellé did). The Count, on account of his corns, does not go. In order to allay Miss O'Brookomore's suspicions that Mabel is falling in love with the Count, Mabel tells her that she likes the Count 'dreadfully'. This statement is similar to Flecker writing to Savery (and he may also have written to Firbank) and telling him 'I like the one who loves me'. Mabel, like Flecker, does not write to Napier to break the engagement. Napier becomes more of a Firbankian figure when Mabel tells of rouge in his room, and a Savery figure when he is described by Mabel as a Yorkshire pudding.

The news that Mabel and the Count have got married is given by Mabel in a brief note to Gerald, telling her that she had wanted to be married in the Cathedral but the ceremony had taken place in a registry in the presence of a priest. Mabina Pastorelli (as she now signs herself) and her new husband are to leave next day for a honeymoon in Corfu. The reaction to this startling news is starkly stated in a simple lament by Miss O'Brookomore. She repeats eight times 'Mabel!'. The chapter consists of nothing else.

The response of Miss O'Brookomore to Mabel's elopement can seem exaggerated, but Firbank was known to break off relationships with his friends [not named] without explanation or apologising, when they got married.[1406] The early months of the Pastorelli marriage are not described (nor is the honeymoon in Corfu), but that does not indicate that the marriage was unhappy. Part 1 of *Inclinations* ends with the brief letter to Miss O'Brookomore about the wedding and Part II begins two years later with Mabel back in England with her adored baby, Bianca. The Count is to join her later.

Firbank's novel is not just an attempt to use Flecker's real-life experience to parody romantic novels of his day, some of the antics of the English abroad and the prejudices against marrying a foreigner, especially when one of them is apart from their spouse. Some prejudices are understandable, some less so, such as 'In Italy have they Brussel sprouts like we have?' Mabel is asked on her return.

Firbank, in order to make the love between Mabel and the Count believable, has to make it real love. The attraction Hellé had first for Flecker was as much a physical attraction as a meeting of minds. The Count kisses Mabel's charming hands and she is intrigued. Hellé wrote about 'those fingers taper-fine' in her poem 'Envoy'.[1407] Both Mabel and Hellé are attracted by the hair of their men. In the brief chapter when Mabel realises she cannot resist the Count, she tells herself that she could not be more in love, in the same way as letters from Hellé, which he received at Cranham had revealed her love to him. Both Mabel/Flecker had appreciated that they were loved when the person who loved them was prepared to pursue them from their own country to another. Spice was added when their more conventional fiancé/fiancée had remained at home in ignorance of what was going on. The person in their lives, Firbank/O'Brookomore, who was unable to get their love returned, suffered the deepest pain.

Firbank had worked on the novel he first entitled Salome, Or *'Tis A Pity That She Would* (which he later re-titled *The Artificial Princess*) during 1906 at Cambridge, and he put it aside unfinished in May 1911, which by coincidence was the month that Flecker had married. He later wrote 500 extra words to *The Artificial Princess*, which was published in 1934, eight years after Firbank's death. A character in *The Artificial Princess* is asked at the end of the book if he had ever been to Greece, and Sir Oliver's dry reply is that he had married there, a Demitraki, who was a lesbian. This could be a reference to the Flecker marriage, and one reason why it remained unpublished in Firbank's lifetime. Flecker, in *The King of Alsander*, portrays his character Arnolfo as a sort of 'Artificial Princess' in reverse. Arnolfo (Firbank was known as 'Arnie' to his family and friends) had a father like Firbank's who was a railway pioneer, about whom Flecker wrote, if he 'got a chance, he'd run a funicular up the mountains...'. As has been seen by other slighting references to Firbank's origins and his inability to learn German, Flecker, in his writing, at least, did not admire Firbank as a person in the way that he admired Beazley and was prepared to make his feelings public. When Arnolfo finally reveals that he is the Princess Ianthe in disguise, Norman looks at her 'with a rather inscrutable smile' which was a Flecker characteristic and one that Firbank used in his fiction, and tells him that he bitterly regretted the loss of Arnolfo.[1408]

If hidden references in Flecker's poetry, prose and plays to his relationship with Firbank can be used as some sort of guide as to how he regarded him, then on Flecker's part it was their mutual interest in chastisement that he tended to make use of to most effect. It would seem to indicate that, at that level, it was, for Flecker, where the relationship remained in his mind. The name Winsome Torment was used to disguise the Firbank connection and Firbank had to use similar means to disguise the Flecker name and also his sex, but not his type of poetry or plays. Mabel Collins's name seems to have been taken directly from William Collins who was born in 1725 and who in 1742 published his *Persian Eclogues* of which the Second was entitled 'Hassan; or, the Camel-Driver'. When Mabel Collins meets Count Pastorelli, Miss O'Brookomore tells her that he is not as pastoral as he sounds. This could be a reference to Flecker's work; Firbank could conclude that was the message of Flecker's 'Oak and Olive'; although he was 'bred in Gloucestershire' he 'walked in Hellas years ago'.

Firbank uses another pastoral name for another Flecker figure, the poet Claud Harvester, in his novel *Vainglory*. *Vainglory* was published by Grant Richards, at Firbank's expense on 15 April 1915.[1409] In *Vainglory*, Claude Harvester, the young poet, playwright and novelist, arrives at the Sappho party without his wife Cleopatra, much to the relief of the hostess. Harvester can be seen to be a Firbankian character, but also because he has a wife with the name Cleopatra (which does not call to mind a typical English rose)[1410] to be more of a Flecker-type writer. Harvester's book of poetry *Vaindreams!* is described later as calling to mind 'a frieze with figures of varying heights trotting all the same way'. Flecker's book of poems *The Bridge of Fire* had as its central theme a frieze of gods.[1411] Firbank did not publish a book of poems and some of the poems in *Vaindreams!* are described as 'too classic' and 'He's too cold', which is how Firbank may have originally found some of the poems in *The Bridge of Fire*. Criticisms given in the same passage to Harvester's style would just as likely apply to Firbank's own style – 'odd spelling, brilliant and vicious'. Firbank had not published plays by the time *Vainglory* came out, but Harvester, it was said, had begun to suspect all along that what he had been seeking was the theatre, and he had discovered the truth in writing plays. Flecker, it could be said, in writing his plays, had discovered the truth about his own life, more so than when writing his early poetry. *Vainglory* was Firbank's first published adult novel (previously he had published two stories in pamphlet form), and he could not describe himself as 'almost successful' as a novelist. Flecker's *The King of Alsander* was published in 1914 and could have been described, by reading reviews, as 'almost successful'.

Harvester, like Firbank and Flecker, had travelled around Greece and visited Cairo. In Greece, Harvester said he had stayed in 'a funny little broken-down hotel upon the seashore', which was more the type of accommodation that Flecker had to endure, when travelling, than Firbank. Harvester's hotel was in Mytilene, which had been the proposed destination for an ideal honeymoon by Flecker, had he married in Smyrna as he had wanted. Firbank had other possible connections with Mytilene, but there the accommodation was a villa, not a broken-down hotel.[1412]

Whether the chief guest at the gathering to honour Sappho in *Vainglory* is married is not immediately revealed, but his discovery of a single line from the 'Ode to Sappho' is the main purpose of the gathering. Professor Inglepin, who appears to be held in much higher regard than Claud Harvester, arrives exhausted from his day at the British Museum. The divine 'Ode to Aphrodite' is declaimed but the Professor is unmoved because of the 'old pagan in him', which makes the Professor something of a Beazley figure. (The news of Beazley's professorship was given in a letter to Hellé, written from the sanatorium at Cranham.) In one of her replies to him at Cranham, when sending him a print of the Mona Lisa, Hellé refers to Flecker's 'queerly sly expression, it makes you look something like a faun who knows everything about life but won't tell, and something like the Gioconda, who is a she-faun under her black veil'.[1413] This is similar to the impression Miss Compestella has of Harvester when she looks at him. 'She admired terrifically his charming little leer; it was like a crack, she thought, across the face of an idol. Otherwise, she was afraid, his features were cut too clearly to make any lasting appeal....' Unless Firbank had a habit of leering at himself in the mirror, this 'charming little leer' could only have been observed on someone else, such as Flecker, whose features he had closely studied. At the time, Flecker was recuperating in Cranham. Firbank's father had died on 7 October and was buried on 10 October 1910. Flecker and Firbank could have been in contact and when Hellé accused Flecker of showing her letters to another woman, there was the opportunity at least to show or mention some of the contents to another man, Firbank. Firbank was based in London after coming down from Cambridge in 1909.

Firbank travelled around Italy from his mother's London home between the time he left Cambridge and the Flecker marriage. Firbank portrays another unconventional marriage, which takes place abroad and which disturbs the happiness of the woman left behind in England who had hoped she would be the bride. Thetis Tooke loves Dick Thoroughfare and in Jackdaw Woods she recalls how he had explained to her the origins of her Greek name and how he had kissed her. Dick's marriage ceremony has doubts cast on its legality, even more so than the Pastorelli marriage. The Flecker's marriage ceremony, as far as the Catholic Firbank was concerned, may have had similar doubts cast upon its legality. Dick Thoroughfare's bride is a negress and she appears in the novel, ahead of her bridegroom, when bride and baby daughter are christened in a double ceremony. Thetis is prevented from committing suicide by drowning herself, in despair at her rejection by Dick. If Thetis Tooke and Geraldine O'Brookomore's despair at the marriage abroad of their beloveds can be seen to have been written from Firbank's first-hand experiences, then something can be understood about Firbank's, and some of Flecker's other male friends' reaction to Flecker as a married man. Firbank's novels trace the development of the feelings he had about the Flecker marriage. In *Vainglory* he denies that there is such a person as Harvester's wife; by the end of the novel, Harvester is treated as if he was unmarried. In *Valmouth* there is the despair when the bride appears and the rejected lover is driven to suicide but saved from the act. In *The Flower Beneath the Foot* the heroine, who becomes St. Laura de Nazianzi, and is also driven to despair by the marriage of her lover to another, is a Firbankian figure, although her nickname, 'Rara' is akin to Kara James. Laura's lover, Prince Yousef, who is a Flecker figure and is less than saintly, is reluctant at first to wed the Princess Elsie. Laura has to listen in her convent, where she is sent, to the clamour of her beloved's wedding outside. Firbank appears in *The Flower Beneath the Foot* to be showing how he had been barred from Flecker's life by marriage. (He even may have felt excluded by the appearance on the scene of Eleanor Finlayson, as Laura and Yousef have just parted in the garden when they are aware of being watched by Olga Blumenghast.) Desperate as he might feel at the circumstances that drove them apart, no realistic means existed whereby he and Flecker could have lived together. If Firbank but knew the truth of the events that followed the Flecker honeymoon, they were stranger than the fiction. The events after the honeymoon did not, as a critic described the development of the *Inclinations* story, lead to 'flatness and banality'.[1414]

The Fleckers sailed on a Greek boat to Egypt. It was so hot that their meals were served on deck, but Flecker, despite the heat, appeared to be cheerful as they bid farewell to the Acropolis. On the second night they must have passed close to Santorin before they saw the lights of Cairo's southern coastline and reached Egypt.

At Alexandria, while getting their passports stamped at the Consulate, they met the Vice-Consul whom Flecker already knew. Once again, while speeding by carriage to catch the Cairo train, Flecker discovered that he had left something valuable behind. This time it was his wallet and the carriage had to turn back, but fortunately they met the rider who was bringing it to them and thus enabled them to catch the train, just in time. The journey was not long but they were both exhausted in the rising inland heat of the Delta plain where canals cut through the reeds and boats glided, their sails in the shape of butterflies.

The lofty-ceilinged hotel room was cool in the noon-day heat, where they rested until sunset; then they ventured out to visit the Sphinx. Flecker took pictures of his wife on a camel with the camel-driver and their bodyguards, and the pyramids and Sphinx in the background. They left on the third day for Port Said to board the Beirut boat and from the dining-car they saw what they thought was a town with minarets and domes and even a few palm trees, only to be told (by an Anglo-Egyptian) that it was a mirage.

When they arrived at Beirut, after calling at Jaffa [now Tel Aviv], a quarrel broke out between the Turkish customs' officials and the Consulate *cawass* [official] Flecker had fetched from the consulate. Diplomatic conventions were being breached as the Fleckers' luggage could not be landed without it being searched for tobacco. Flecker managed to separate the two men, one of whom, like Hassan's rival in his play, was named Selim. It was Hellé's French that finally resolved a tense situation. Hellé again came to the rescue when her husband made the mistake of calling what he thought was the guard on the now full train 'a dirty Turk who wanted Bakshish',[1415] when he asked him to put on a first-class carriage. The man, in fact, was the station-master and a Christian. In a rage he threatened to complain to the Consulate. Hellé had to explain that there had been a misunderstanding due to language difficulties. The dispute was settled, and the guard ordered a first-class carriage to be added for their destination, the town of Aley, where Consulate staff retreated in order to escape the intense summer heat of Beirut.

CHAPTER TEN

Misery did not end on arrival in Aley, where they found their hotel's accommodation so depressing that they both broke down in tears. Flecker soon found a much better hotel in which they were to stay for two months. From the back of that hotel they could watch the marvellous sunsets over the sea, the pinewoods and the misty valleys.

It was as well that the weeks in Corfu had brought about an improvement in Flecker's health. Good health was much more important than cleverness to Consul-General Cumberbatch who, since his arrival in Beirut (after eleven years in Smyrna), had endured eight changes in the post of Vice-Consul. In the interval between the departure of the last Vice-Consul and Flecker's arrival, the vacancy had been filled by the Pro-Consul, who had been paid a full salary. No decision could therefore be entertained about getting Flecker's recently depleted salary restored to him. Cumberbatch was not likely to be sympathetic to any requests for extra money or the restoration of money already deducted. Cumberbatch had not been on home leave since 1897, and he had to take on the burden of teaching new Assistants the thousand small daily routines.[1416] If there was to be extra cash available, Cumberbatch should be the recipient, although he did not blame the Assistants for their ill-health, or the system of recruiting staff who would prove to be less than fit into the Levant Consular Service.

Flecker did not become officially Mr. Acting Vice-Consul Flecker until 15 September, 1911, although his sick-leave had ended on 29 August. A period of settling in was essential. The heat in Beirut was stifling all summer with no coolness in the evenings. It was not only the climate that sapped health; the filthy streets were insanitary and the winters brought no respite when it was very wet and cold. The winter of 1910–11 was the worst for nearly a century with deep snow in the mountains. The custom was for Consular staff to spend September and October, when the heat was most intense in Beirut, in Aley, a village above sea-level. There they had 'the pleasure of sleeping on the cool spurs of the Lebanon.'[1417] They then would descend on certain days when work demanded. Then they had 'the anguish of being hoisted up and down at a walking pace in the rack and pinion railway'.[1418]

The Lebanon, Flecker was to decide, 'is a privileged land with a Christian Governor; while Beyrout is a sort of island of pure Turkey'.[1419] He also commented that the Lebanon was 'rather splendid', in a letter at the end of September, written to his old schoolmaster Mr. Cooper, thanking him for the beautiful piece of china sent as a wedding present. He told Cooper that they had found 'a very good place by the sea' and that he was busy with his Consular work and study for examinations. Thoughts about poetry and publication (his *Forty-Two Poems* and *Scholar's Italian Book* were due to come out later in the year) had to give way to more immediate consular duties when the rumblings of the Italo-Turkish War echoed in Beirut on 29 September 1911. Turkey had objected to the Italian policy in Tripoli. Beirut was then in Syria and was part of the Ottoman Empire. The risk of an Italian Force landing in Beirut resulted in Flecker, who was up in Brumana when the news came, striding down the stone-strewn paths with Hellé to catch the train to Beirut. Hellé was heartened by her husband's ability to make the three-hour descent and later wrote to her in-laws about this to prove to them how much her husband's health had improved. Flecker's long legs would help him too, like Norman Price's in *The King of Alsander* ('No wonder they go far. I have never seen such long legs, except on a grasshopper.')[1420] At the Consulate, Flecker found that the Turkish naval attachment was inefficient and the involvement (where he thought that he might be needed) did not materialise. The Christian Syrians had been on the Italian side and much against the sovereign power of Turkey. The immediate risk of an Italian force landing at Beirut proved to be unfounded, but the war continued elsewhere.

After this sudden burst of activity, life appeared to go along more peaceful lines. The only conflicts that broke out were those between Flecker and his parents, who, because they had not yet received photographs of Hellé, had concluded that this was part of a plot to conceal evidence of her age and looks. They did not understand that Hellé disliked having her photograph taken and thought that any that had been taken were unsatisfactory.

If some doubts remained about Hellé's suitability as a wife, in the mind of her in-laws, no such prejudice was evident in the mind of Consul-General Cumberbatch and his wife, who invited the Fleckers to stay with them at Areiya, the village near Aley, on two separate weekends in October.

Another change of scene was enjoyed when the Fleckers went on a ten-mile train journey along the coast to Dog River, on a Sunday at the end of October. There, as Norman Price had found in Alsander 'grass was sprinkled with cyclamen, asphodel, red anemones, and with the wild remnants of old cultivation.'[1421] Assyrian figures carved out of the rock were visible at Dog River, alongside banana and pomegranate trees. The date palms were heavy with fruit, which they enjoyed eating, Flecker told his parents. Also, he told them, they were going to try and grow a cyclamen in a pot. Expeditions along the beautiful river valleys could not be too numerous; Flecker still had to work for his consular examinations, which he was due to sit at the beginning of November. He was not now mixing locally with as many Turkish-speaking people as he had been while working in Constantinople and Smyrna. He was not getting any lectures on the subjects needed to pass his examinations satisfactorily. As a result he was put in a position of weakness and (to add to this) he also wanted to get on with his literary ambitions.

By 23 October, correspondence with Mavrogordato was back on course. The period of creativity, which had resulted in an output of literary work on Corfu, had no room to expand, as it was pushed to one side by other activities. The 'great slaving' as he referred to it in his letter to Mavro, had only gained him £10 to £15 in a year. Contact with 'this literary business' had to be re-established. Flecker told Mavro that he was accepting that *Don Juan* would never be played. Whether this was what he really believed, or whether it was a ploy to make Mavrogordato more active on behalf of *Don Juan* was not clear, as he was telling him in the letter that he had not heard from the person who Mavro had sent *Don Juan*, although Flecker had written. *Hassan of Baghdad*, Act I, was already in the hands of George Alexander, who had acknowledged it, and he had been asked to return it to Mavro. Flecker also wanted to know if *The English Review* had an interest in his ballad 'Bryan of Brittany', a copy of which he had sent to Mavro. Flecker went on to say that he thought that 'four pound was a little cheap for three crowded pages of verse.' He hoped that the *ER* weren't annoyed. The cheapness could be taken to refer to the payment for 'Don Juan Declaims' and 'The Dying Patriot', published in the September edition of *The English Review*. He also wanted to know if the '*English Review*' would consider his 'Samarkand' dialogue poem. A typewritten copy of 'Yasmin' remains with this letter (although it is not referred to in the letter. Letter now in the BOD). The survival of this copy of 'Yasmin', which the ER did not publish, may provide a clue as to how poems sent through Mavro eventually went missing.

Flecker must have got his manuscript back from Smyrna of *The King of Alsander*. He told Mavro that he was rewriting it in preparation for letting Martin Secker have it by January. If Mavro saw Secker, he was to let him know that Flecker had not forgotten him. Flecker also wanted the October issue of the *ER*; he would have found it more rewarding to get a copy of *The Nation*, where his poem 'Epithalamion' had appeared in the 7 October issue. He wanted a copy of *An Artist in Corfu* to review, and Norman Douglas's book on Capri, which he had asked Mavro to send him in March but had never received. Flecker did give Mavro some impressions of Beirut and not just confine his letter to a list of his literary wants and instructions, which he admitted was selfish. Beirut he described as 'filthy' although he thought the country otherwise pleasant. He mentioned the missionaries and his impression was similar to that voiced by an old man in *The King of Alsander*, who said about American Missionaries that they were those 'Who believe in Noah's Ark and the historical existence of Methusalem....'[1422]

By the end of October 1911, the Fleckers were back living in Beirut, where they took rooms in the annexe of the German Hotel. These rooms they furnished with draperies and embroideries to hide the German furniture and, as was usual, the room was stuffed with untidy heaps of books. The hotel on the east side of the harbour had not yet got its own electric light, it was clean and the guests were mainly members of different consulates who ate together in the dining-hall, pervaded with the after-smell of cooked vegetables. All this was in stark contrast to the side room of the British Consulate where Flecker worked, which had a desk, a wooden chair and a cane chair for visitors and framed photographs of Greek temples on the walls. The side room in the Consulate would not have the same view as the Fleckers' sitting-room at the German Hotel, which looked out on the sea front where they could watch the sights. One sight was that of an old man who sifted the sand for gold. Another sight was that of a camel brought to the sea for a bath. On the Damascus road one day, Flecker had seen a camel insane with anger, jigging about as it shook off its load of oil drums before the eyes of its badly scared driver. This interest in the camel Flecker could relate to lines in his translation of 'From the Rose-Garden of Sadi'[1423]

> Then I remarked that the camel which that surly eremite
> bestrode began to prance and dance till it flung that holy
> man and disappeared into the desert. Said I 'Sir, your camel
> has run away in an ecstasy: can you remain unmoved'?
> 'Before the dark began to pale, I heard the little
> nightingale: O base and brutish heart, he cried, if love is

never to prevail. Hearing that sweet Arabian lad, your camel
rose and danced like mad:

    If you don't care you ought to wear a snout in front,
behind, a tail!'

Flecker's abilities as a translator were needed again when he sat
his intermediate examinations at the beginning of November. A brief
respite from consular work was possible by 18 November, when he and
Hellé went north to the village of Mamettain. There, he told his parents,
were 'a beach, waves, and a little hotel'.[1424] At other beaches in the
Lebanon they had enjoyed horse-riding (SLA p.60 has a photograph of
'A little hotel in the Lebanon'). At Mamettain, Flecker bathed without
repeating any of the consequences that were blamed on the dip in the
Black Sea.

By 23 November, back at the Consulate, Flecker was writing a long
letter to his former Dean Close schoolmaster, Mr. Cooper.[1425] This letter
to Cooper was mainly taken up with answering his questions about the
metre of 'The Dying Patriot', a version of which had been published in
the September issue of *The English Review.* Cooper, the mathematician,
scholar and authority on music had been interested in an explanation
of the metre and meaning of 'The Dying Patriot'. Flecker told him he
had never thought of the metre and how could he explain it? Flecker
did not put in the letter that 'The Dying Patriot' had its roots in much
earlier work, both published and unpublished. 'The Welsh Sea',
'Western Voyage' and his unpublished poem 'Cross Country' were all
forerunners of 'The Dying Patriot'.

Flecker's long working out of the theme of a journey in England
from East to West and the legend of the drowned lands of Wales had
made the actual rhythm of less importance in the final construction of
the poem, but without realising the connection to past work, Cooper
would focus on the metre and meaning. Flecker told him that the whole
question of rhythms was a hard one and Saintsbury[1426] alone could
explain them properly. Flecker referred to Tennyson and Swinburne
in support of his arguments. He thought that the basis of 'The Dying
Patriot' was trochaic. He was surprised (he told Cooper) that the *ER*
took 'The Dying Patriot' instead of 'other poems from the 'Don Juan'
play'. He also wrote that he had 'not got it here unfortunately', which
must have meant his own manuscript copy and not the September
edition of *The English Review* because 'Don Juan Declaims' was in the
same edition. The only other 'Don Juan' poem that Flecker recorded
as having been sent to *The English Review* was 'Epithalamium', which was
to be published in *The Nation* in its 7 October edition.

In outlining the meaning of 'The Dying Patriot' to Cooper, Flecker wrote: 'The patriot has been shot: and as he dies, very mistily he thinks of England from East to West – Dover suggests Augustine to him – its most important connexion with English History. Oxford is in the middle of England, and he mixes it madly with the sun voyaging over England...'. 'Floral air', he explained was inspired by the smell of the 'Lime Walk of Trinity Quad any spring day'. 'Feet of snow' he had forgotten but it was 'just symbolic of the purity of Augustine's fervour – and mind you he was probably barefoot.' (It would have been more appropriate to have written 'feet of ice'; the feet would be covered in mud.) Flecker's previous descriptions in his work had been of female feet. The first time he was fascinated with feet of snow could have been when he and Eleanor played tennis barefoot in Wales. 'The slender feet' of the women bathing in the 'K of A' is remarked upon but not the men's feet. He used 'blossoms of snow' and 'breasts cold as snow, the colour of which they shared' also in his unpublished poetry and in 'K of A' as already seen.[1427] It is strange that he should have forgotten entirely why he used 'feet of snow' in this context, although once the thoughts had been released from his imagination and put into words he may have been facing the difficulty of explaining precisely enough, so that Cooper could have understood completely. He would not have wanted to go into explanations about Eleanor to Cooper. He told Cooper that Augustine was 'probably barefoot', which is not precise either. Another explanation for 'feet of snow' lies in a letter to Savery from Paris in April 1910, when he wrote:

> b. 'Criticise the masques as poetry if you like. But they are not void of the true spirit of me which is hugeous humour. Masque I. was sung in Canterbury Cathedral: when I imagine some good voiced pork-chopper singing about
>
> My children who are very wise
> stand by a tree with shutten eyes
> and seem to meditate or pray
>
> I rejoice in my heart. Surely it is a jolly well-written verse exercise. And those splendid asses trailing along their robes in the snow. O for a picture by Aubrey! I think it a vivid scene for so wee a drama.' [1428]

If this is part of the explanation, then it too would not be something he would want to discuss with Cooper. Flecker told Cooper of the legend of the drowned lands off Wales, and that the poem was 'dramatic and not lyrical'.

The version of 'The Dying Patriot' in *The English Review* is not the only one Flecker wrote, but it is not clear whether he made changes as a direct result of the questions raised by Cooper.[1429]

Cooper's writing to Flecker to ask for an explanation about 'The Dying Patriot' has a parallel with Flecker's 'The Dying Century', published in the school magazine in August 1900, unsigned, which failed to gain a prize. The critic (also unsigned) who published his opinion of 'The Dying Century' was revealed in print forty years later to be Cooper.[1430] Cooper selected two other poems in the competition for detailed criticism and judged another poem to be superior to Flecker's, this other schoolboy poet never fulfilled his early promise. The only factor that may have made Cooper select this young poet's work over Flecker's was that he was 'striving after a form which several well-known poets have essayed without complete success.'[1431] Cooper, who knew the identity of the poets in the competition, may not have selected Flecker simply because he was the son of the headmaster, or else he genuinely thought of form as the important feature of a prize poem. Cooper still wanted to demonstrate to himself that although he had not chosen the best poet of promise in 1900, he still found fault with Flecker, who had published more than one book of poetry as well as many poems in magazines, in an effort to prove that he had a point, in 1900 as well as in 1911. Flecker's approach to metre could be said to be instinctive[1432] and thus hard to explain to someone such as Cooper who attached so much importance to it. Cooper could have attached just as much importance to grammar, both English and in learning a foreign language.

Flecker told Cooper that what he described as his 'new Italian Anthology (Nutt's 3s.6d.)' was out, but that he had quarrelled with the publisher and had no copy to send him.

Alfred Nutt had taken over from his father David, but while driving with his invalid son in Paris in May 1910, the carriage had slipped into the Seine. The invalid son had been saved but Alfred Nutt drowned. The publishing firm had been carried on under the firm rule of Alfred's widow. M.L. Nutt was a strong-minded French woman, her late husband's former secretary and a future novelist. It was not uncommon for her writers to quarrel with her over the publication of their works.

It was Mrs. Nutt Flecker had been angry about in his letter to Mavro written from Corfu on 22 June 1911. Mavro was given a thousand thanks for interviewing Mrs. Nutt when Flecker was determined to get more money out of her. But getting spare copies out of her to send to friends was not a task he appeared to have faced.

Flecker had to wait in order to see his idea of his *Italian Grammar* get into print and this may have added to his anger with the publishers. Woollcombe-Boyce had first seen the manuscript in Flecker's room at Jesus Lane in Cambridge. It was at this time that Flecker was writing less poetry and he had come up against the lack of suitable textbooks for the advanced study of modern languages. Scholars had to avail themselves of a Russian textbook for German scholars. Neville Forbes, from Oxford days, had eventually published his own Russian textbook for English scholars.

The Scholar's Italian Book was an offshoot of some of the ideas that had first taken root in *The Grecians*. In *The Grecians* Flecker had attempted to change the approach to educational methods in public schools. *The Scholar's Italian Book* attempted to change the neglected study of Italian and its literature in public schools. Flecker stated that Italian was easy to learn and could be mastered in a fortnight, provided the intelligent scholar already knew some Latin and French.

This was an idea already outlined in *The Grecians*.[1433] The book contained what was described as a 'skeleton' grammar not to be learned by heart, and without exercises. Flecker stated that in order to learn a language thoroughly the scholar needed 'teachers, experience, travel'; these were indispensable. The experience Flecker had already gone through in trying to acquire a working knowledge of languages, especially Turkish, underlies this statement.

The Scholar's Italian Book did receive mention (just a few lines) in the LIFE, but not his parents' personal opinion of it. It was referred to as 'this so-called 'grammar', which recalled the mediaeval meaning of the word.'[1434] Headmasters (in particular his father) were unlikely to buy the book, either for themselves or their pupils, especially if they read the following: '.... Headmasters may find this book useful recreation for a sixth form exhausted by successful labours in scholarship hunting:'

This statement seemed to poke a little fun at the work of headmasters. This is not to say that *The Scholar's Italian Book* was unworthy of serious attention, even the LIFE described it as an important part of Flecker's literary work and that it was 'important in itself and as yet another instance of Flecker's manifold interests'. *The Scholar's Italian Book* reflected Flecker's ability to pass on his own enthusiasm for learning more of a subject for its own sake. This ability had made him a well-liked, if short-lived schoolmaster. Some of his more personal feelings could also be buried in the preface to the book. Flecker argued in it that commercial German had banished the study of 'this beautiful tongue'. Flecker's resentment of his eventual rejection by Eleanor, the bilingual (German/English) love, and his acceptance briefly by Leila before she went to join her sister in Italy underlies this statement. This reference enhanced the preface but the element of jest would not.

An element of jest had been incorporated into a lot of Flecker's past work. The success of this type of jest was mainly due to the failure of the object of the jest to appreciate the fact. Humour, Flecker had told Savery, was the one uniting thing that 'binds my work'.[1435] Humour was not necessarily the thing to bind a textbook. In *The Scholar's Italian Book* it was still obvious against whom the joke was aimed; it was not the scholars. In doing this, Flecker may have alienated the sort of people who would have helped in the financial success of the book although he had sold the copyright.[1436] Flecker, in his references to headmasters in *The Scholar's Italian Book*, may have been recalling the favourable review in the January edition of *The English Review*, which had stated that '*The Grecians* should be in the hands of every Headmaster, who would be stimulated by the Author's enthusiasm and charmed by his Intelligence'. 'Every Headmaster' would not be stimulated or charmed, as the reviewer could well have realised, and he too could have been jesting in a way that was not helpful as far as sales of *The Grecians* were concerned. But in the case of *The Scholar's Italian Book*, the preface had been 'cut about and added to'[1437] by Mrs. Nutt, which may not have helped to convey Flecker's exact intention.

In Flecker's 'The Ballad of Hampstead Heath' he appears in some of the lines to make a comic figure out of a Dean Close master, William Judson:

> Sir Moses came with eyes of flame,
> Judd, who is like a bloater,
>
> ....
>
> He spake in Greek, which Britons speak
> Seldom and circumspectly;
> But Mr. Judd, that man of mud,
> Translated it correctly.
>
> A wistful Echo stayed behind
> To join the mortal dances,
> But Mr. Judd, with words unkind,
> Rejected her advances. [1438]

William Judson came to Dean Close as a master in 1890 and, until his retirement in 1934, was very successful in getting pupils through their examinations in Latin and English. Judson was a shy man who was well known for inviting small groups of his pupils to partake in very lavish afternoon teas. If the teas were a feature of the Fleckers' reign, their son may not have been invited. It was said that Flecker tended to eat rather better than the average Dean Close boarder. The general public who read 'The Ballad of Hampstead Heath' did not know who 'Judd' was supposed to be. Those of Judson's pupils who had read the poem did not like the reference to Judson, but they read the poem just the same.[1439] In his 'Hamman' Name' 'Winsome Torment' would not complain; Ronald Firbank used the same sort of disguises in his prose works and if he had cut off his friendship with Flecker on his marriage, he would not then have an opportunity to see the poem until it was published in Flecker's *Collected Poems*, after Flecker's death. An unpublished tale[1440] of Flecker's, which had a Firbankian character with a name more easily recognisable than 'Winsome Torment', had an Italian background. If published, this tale would have had a wider readership than *The Scholar's Italian Book*. This story concerns Arthur Mowbray, a name that could be linked to Firbank who was christened Arthur and 'Mow' can be associated with the fact that Firbank thought he had a conspicuous mouth. 'Bray', or brae, is a steep bank. Arthur Mowbray, it was said in the story, 'loved to wander alone by unfrequented ways viewing the small but wonderful galleries in the little Tuscan and Umbrian towns, and hoping, ever hoping, to find in some poor shop or inn parlour a priceless and forgotten picture that should be his not only by right of purchase but by right of discovery.'[1441] The fact of Arthur Mowbray wandering alone points more to the character being based on Firbank than Flecker himself (as suggested by Mary Byrd Davis, p.104). Flecker, unlike Firbank, had never had enough spending money to think of buying priceless pictures. Arthur Mowbray is a rich American, Firbank was neither American nor very rich, but like Arthur Mowbray (and Flecker too) there are financial problems connected with his father; in Mowbray's case the father was long dead.

In another tale,[1442] Flecker translated 'The Tale of Grasso', which was a condensed form of the *Novella del Grasso Legnaiuolo*. In this translation Flecker gives a picture of Renaissance Florence. Flecker put 'The Tale of Grasso' in full in *The Scholar's Italian Book*.

Also in *The Scholar's Italian Book* was the only verse translation by Flecker. This was his translation of Machiavelli's 'L'Occasione', which he had first translated at Cambridge and which he subsequently published (his translation only) with the title 'Opportunity' in his *Thirty-Six Poems* and *Forty-Two Poems*.

A similar spirit exists in *The Scholar's Italian Book* to the spirit which had made him tell his parents that he wanted to teach his friends to swim, to ride a bicycle and be healthy. He wanted the reader of *The*

Scholar's Italian Book to enjoy what he had enjoyed, the literature and language of Italy. In the same spirit, he had wanted Beazley to give up archaeology and share his enthusiasm for writing verse. This desire was behind Flecker's poem 'Invitation' (which he had originally given the title 'The Invitation to Poetry'). This poem was later to cause a case of mistaken identity with T.E. Lawrence whom he was soon to meet in Beirut. Lawrence wrote to a friend:[1443] 'Got a letter asking if I was Flecker's archaeologist. He wrote the poem about ten years ago about one Beazley a don at Ch.Ch.'

Flecker had told Mavrogordato in a letter written from the Consulate and dated 10 December1911, that he was living in clear sunshine among damned fools. He must have composed this letter just before he met Mr. R. [Raff] Fontana and T.E. [Ned] Lawrence. Fontana, British Consul at Aleppo since 1909, was to be described by Flecker as 'a glorious specimen of high worn out aesthetic Genoese aristocracy'.[1444] Fontana was in Beirut on 9 December (just before his forty-sixth birthday) in order to be reunited with T.E. Lawrence. Lawrence was returning to the archaeological dig at Carchemish in Syria, not far from Aleppo. Lawrence's boat from England was due on the same day that Flecker had to go and arrest two deserters on a British boat, which was 10 December.

When Lawrence had to visit the British Consulate in Beirut, this was his first opportunity to meet Flecker and to talk.[1445] Lawrence's appearance on the Beirut scene, when Flecker's feelings about his surroundings were at a low ebb, was similar in its timing to Beazley's appearance on the Oxford scene. A new relationship enabled Flecker for a while to accept the drawbacks of his daily life. In Beirut the streets ran with green slime and his thoughts had turned to the idea of leaving the service in two years' time. He was also dreaming of spending a golden holiday in Damascus and Baalbeck, the great temple ruins 56 miles from Beirut.

In this encounter with Lawrence, Flecker could recapture the memory of past involvements with men whose minds and appearance had intrigued him. Now he had Hellé's companionship he did not depend on Lawrence nearly so much or react badly to his absences. Lawrence's giggle 'with which he often punctuated his conversation'[1446] was reminiscent of Firbank's giggle, and Lawrence's interest in literature, like Firbank's, was important in the Lawrence/Flecker relationship. Lawrence was interested in the fact that Flecker was a poet and writer, and just as Lawrence was mistaken for Beazley, in time Lawrence was to have the same opinion of Beazley's poetry as Flecker.[1447]

The important point of Flecker and Lawrence's initial meeting was not only that Lawrence was a gifted archaeologist like Beazley, but that both Lawrence and Flecker had been up at Oxford. Their respective times there had been very different. Not least was the fact that Lawrence had been based at home and he had obtained a first-class degree. Lawrence had chosen a subject that interested him, which was history, and then used that subject as a stepping-stone towards archaeology. That step enabled him to get enough money to travel away from his parents and their desire that he adopt a steady profession at home. Another important advantage that Lawrence had was his 'adoption' by David George Hogarth (1862–1927). Like Norman Price in *The King of Alsander*, Lawrence's singularity 'was much more likely due to this curious and close intimacy with a gentleman'.[1448]

Although Flecker had Raleigh to support and guide him for a time while he was at Oxford, Lawrence's relationship with Hogarth was of a much more important and far-reaching kind than any sort of relationship Flecker had been able to form with older men at Oxford. Hogarth's life and Beazley's had similarities, and if Beazley had been in his forties when he and Flecker had first met, the Beazley influence on Flecker would have been more important and Flecker too might have been attracted to the archaeologist's life. Hogarth was a linguist, archaeologist, author and Keeper of the Ashmolean, who had interested Lawrence, while he was still a schoolboy, in collecting pottery fragments.

Hogarth had married at the age of thirty-two (as Beazley was to do) to a woman who did not share his interest in his work (unlike Beazley's wife who supported him in his work). Hogarth and his wife had a son, thus the need to be a substitute father to Lawrence did not arise out of a lack of a son of his own. In his turn, although he had no children of his own (he had step-children), Beazley eventually 'adopted' A.L. Rowse. These 'adoptions' enabled the 'adopted son' to have a better start in life. Like Beazley, Hogarth was a brilliant classical scholar but he too lacked financial means. It was William Martin Ramsey's acceptance of Hogarth as an apprentice that resulted in his being able to get a foothold in the subject.

Beazley's success along the path of scholarship could not have been due solely to help from his father or entirely due to his winning of scholarships. Beazley's father was not a rich man and Lawrence's father was not a poor man but it was said that he never opened a book, which is something that could possibly be said about Beazley's father. If Flecker's father had not been an educated man, but one who begrudged the spending of money, then his son may have felt the need to be taken under the wing of a man like Hogarth. Or if, like Brooke, Flecker's father had died while he was still at university, he could have been 'adopted' as Brooke was, by someone of similar standing to Edward Marsh. Not all aspects of these 'adoptions' were always along academic lines. It was Hogarth who saw the qualities in Lawrence that would make him into an unofficial spy for his country. Lawrence was to see in Flecker, if not all the qualities, at least the qualifications to be an unofficial spy for his country. Lawrence always saw people as part of a wider plan. Flecker, in his literary spying out of opportunities, also had to have people in his plans.

On 10 December 1911, Flecker wrote from the Consulate to the poet Harold Monro (1879–1932). Flecker began his letter in a humble fashion, enquiring whether Monro knew him or not and explaining his fear of being snubbed. But also he told Monro of his having an established reputation among a small circle. Flecker told Monro also that if he had been in London he would have been to see him. If Flecker had been in London he would have learned that not only did Monro know of him, Monro liked 'some of his poems extremely'. When Monro gave lectures on Modern Poetry he always read 'The Ballad of Camden Town', which he considered 'an example of some of the best work being done'.[1449] Flecker had contacted Monro because Monro was planning his new magazine *The Poetry Review*, the first edition of which was due out in January 1912. Flecker enclosed his ballad 'Bryan of Brittany' with three new verses added. This poem, he told Monro, was one of his best and he presumed *The Poetry Review* would pay the same as *The English Review*.[1450] This ploy of appearing to play off one publication against another was risky and it seemed to result in neither publication for a while agreeing to publish any of Flecker's poems. Monro, at the time Flecker wrote, was not in a position to help and advise. He was in the process of searching for premises, printers and a publisher and collecting material in the middle of a very dismal winter. Monro was also not in a position to answer in detail such queries of Flecker's, such as whether Monro wanted shorter poems or poems already published, or whether the magazine was for poets or critics and whether he should join the Society. Monro had been asked by the Poetry Society to edit their journal. The Poetry Society had been founded in 1909 by Galloway Kyle, a man who was still in his thirties, to foster an interest in poets, poetry and the reading of verse. The supporters of the Poetry Society were the more traditionally minded poets. Monro was not a supporter and when he was asked to take over the Poetry Society's publication, *The Poetry Gazette*, he refused. He offered instead to start his own monthly independent magazine, which would incorporate *The Poetry Gazette*. Monro wanted to bring younger poets into his *Poetry*

Review. The Poetry Review could not hope, at first, to pay the same rates as *The English Review,* which had been established since 1908. Flecker had already sent 'Bryan of Brittany', without the three new verses, to Mavro before he sent it to Monro.

Flecker told Monro that if he rejected 'B of B' he hoped that the *ER* would accept it. But as the *ER* was considering another poem of his ('Golden Journey to Samarkand'), he did not think that the 'B of B' would come out for some months. The result of all this trading, when he appeared to want to try and auction his work to the highest bidder, did not bring about the desired results, or had little influence on the eventual publication. His anxiety to get work into print but not choosing the right marketing news from the London literary scene was an obvious result of his being based in Beirut. If he had been able to talk to Monro face to face, the placing of his work would have been more straightforward. Monro would not have taken Flecker under his wing and befriended him in a useful way as Monro was only five years older than Flecker and he would have needed someone younger for this type of arrangement. Monro had, however, taken under his wing Arundel del Re, who was in his late teens when they met abroad. Monro was married with a son, but was separated from his wife. Monro was deeply attracted to del Re and brought him to London, where he became Assistant Editor on the '*Poetry Review*'. This was not a very satisfactory arrangement as del Re was at times moody and difficult and needed the distractions of London life. The fact that he and Monro lodged together may have put a strain on their relationship.

Lawrence seemed to have a need to be adopted into the Fleckers' marriage for a brief while. This could be due to the fact that his own parents had kept him at a distance from the secret of their own unmarried state. Lawrence had to stay on an extra day in Beirut due to the closure of the post office. He was appreciative of Hellé's mothering qualities and he was also to become appreciative of the same qualities in Mrs. Fontana. It is to be hoped that the elder Fleckers appreciated Hellé's looks. A batch of photographs taken by Flecker were sent to Dean Close on 14 December.

At this time a tragic event took place that was to profoundly affect Flecker, although at the time he was not immediately aware of it. Richard Barham Middleton killed himself in Brussels on 1 December 1911. Richard Middleton was born in England in 1882. On his mother's side he was a distant relative of the Rev. Richard Barham (1788–1845) who wrote *The Ingoldsby Legends* under the pen name of Thomas Ingoldsby. The three volumes of *The Ingoldsby Legends* were published between

1840–7. They consisted of verse stories of the supernatural kind, which were very popular due to their sense of humour.

After Middleton left school he was employed as an office clerk for five years, a life he described as 'hell', and he sympathised with John Davidson who had also endured life as an office clerk. As John Davidson had done, Middleton escaped the dull office routine by writing in his spare time. In 1905 he was awarded a five guinea prize for his short story by the *Morning Leader*. Middleton also went to the theatre as often as he could and read widely. Also in 1905, as a result of seeing an advertisement in *The Academy*, Middleton joined the New Bohemians, a society that devoted itself to encouraging intelligent conversation amongst journalists, critics, artists, etc. The New Bohemians' motto was 'Talk for talk's sake'. Members read their own verse, sketches were drawn and views expressed about new books and plays.

Middleton left his parents' home in 1906 for two rooms in Blackfriars Road. He got his first poem published in the *Gentleman's Magazine* and his articles and book reviews appeared in *The Academy*. The acceptance of his work was largely a result of Middleton's friendship with the editor of *The Academy*, Lord Alfred Douglas, whom he had met at the New Bohemians alongside Arthur Machen. Middleton also wrote for *The English Review* and the magazine *Vanity Fair*. Middleton was helped in his journalistic ambitions by Harrison, when he was editor of '*Vanity Fair*' and the writer Frank Harris (1856–1931). Harris in his time was also editor of the *Fortnightly Review, Saturday Review* and the *Evening News*. Despite the payments Middleton received for his work, the money was irregular and he often went without food for days and suffered from neuralgia and sleeplessness. He decided to go and live in Brussels in order to live more cheaply. It was possible that the Belgian canals gave Middleton the inspirations for his fantastic tale 'The Ghost Ship'. The story was not published until after Middleton's death but it received great praise from many sources. It was at first rejected by a magazine in England but accepted by a New York magazine which cabled the payment of £25 a week after Middleton had died penniless.

Middleton's working relationship with the editor of the *ER* (especially when Middleton was ill and finding it difficult to concentrate on writing) is interesting when comparison is made with the unsatisfactory working relationship Flecker is said to have had with the editor of the *ER* after Middleton's death. The editor, Austin Harrison, had published everything that Middleton had sent to him. When Middleton had grumbled about the payment of eighteen guineas he had sent him in payment for his stories: 'Harrison bunged me another tenner with a charming note.....'[1451] Flecker had written to Mavro telling him that he had complained to the *ER* about the four pounds he had been paid for his poetry. There is no evidence that Harrison responded by paying Flecker more money. Middleton and Flecker were in similar situations. Both were not happy in their exiled lands and both complained about the lack of decent English company and the problems of getting work accepted promptly or rejected promptly (Middleton submitted his work to other publications besides the *ER*). But Harrison could not favour Middleton's work because he was ill, hard up and living overseas; if that was a reason, Flecker was in similar circumstances. The accusations made long afterwards about Harrison's treatment of Flecker are unlikely to be entirely true. The blame heaped on Harrison could be shared amongst others. The motive for Middleton's suicide cannot be said to be entirely his failure to make a living as a writer; although payments were not regular he did continue to get money but he always spent it. Money was spent on drink, which did nothing to help his physical or mental health.

Middleton was the subject of articles after his death[1452] and a series of 'Poetical Tributes', amongst them one from W.R. Titterton. Henry Savage stated that what was the 'last straw' for Middleton will probably never be known. Middleton himself was sufficiently affected by the suicide of John Davidson to write about it. But he could not understand the motive and this may offer a clue, because (like Henry Savage) when commenting on Middleton's suicide he did not know everything about his friend's early life and that might have been a contributory factor to Middleton taking his own life. The fact that Middleton suffered extreme pain rather than visit the dentist, even when he had cash to spare, could have been the result of a childhood experience he could never talk about to adult friends. Middleton equated the poet Chatterton's suicide[1453] to Davidson's, which he said was due to 'stricken vanity'. Middleton thought that the immediate cause of Davidson's suicide was lack of money. Davidson thought that Middleton was 'one of those unfortunate people who believe they have a message to convey to the world; forgetting it is impossible to convey a message to a stomach. The bitterness of the unhonoured prophet is cumulative, and in the end his message smashed John Davidson....'[1454] When, in the September 1912 edition of *The Poetry Review,* John Drinkwater reviewed Middleton's *Poems and Songs,* Drinkwater described Middleton's poems as among 'the eternally sad things of beauty'. Drinkwater stated that the 'poet's temperament is, normally, but one-half of his poetry, which needs external life for its fulfilment, ...' Drinkwater concluded 'But the poet [Middleton] had become an emotional specialist, and specialisation is the thing above all others that precludes a poet from the company of great ones'. Drinkwater appeared to be concluding,, as Middleton had concluded about Davidson, that a failure to get away from the necessity of leaving a message in his poetry had 'smashed' him. Drinkwater had concluded that 'emotional specialisation' had 'smashed' Middleton. Shortly before his death Middleton had written about the hopelessness of the feeling of not being able to write again and the truth of his having 'had a sort of nervous breakdown' which he described in a letter to a friend, '(? a neurasthenic rag-time)'.[1455] All that contributed to the tragedy of the last months of his life.

The character of Snaith's, '*William Jordan*' (about whom Flecker had written in the book notices of *The English Review* of July 1911) had faced poverty and sickness, as had Middleton, but nevertheless did not die 'till he has written the poem it was his mission on earth to write', due to what Flecker had stated to be his 'gifted with dauntless resolution'. It may be truer to say, as Firbank has said, that one's best work is never written and it is not safe to put some blame on what is afterwards perceived as an in-built flaw in the poet's work on the poet's suicide. But for poets like Middleton and Davidson, the 'dauntless resolution' may have for a time failed. For Middleton 'the last straw' could have been his landlady who had 'just collared the petty cash for sundry trifles I had forgotten'. For Flecker, when moments of despair threatened to overcome him, his resolution to write had not completely failed. Flecker and Davidson had both had strict religious upbringings but Flecker had not been sent out at an early age to work for a living like Davidson and Middleton. Nor had Flecker, like Davidson and Middleton, lived in London trying to make a living by his own writing and contributing, when asked, to magazines and enjoying the social life that London offered. If Flecker had been (and he had tried it for a short time in Oxford and suffered hardship but had Beazley for companionship) in London without his studies for the Levant Consular Service, he could have experienced many of the problems suffered by Middleton and the warnings that Flecker's parents had received from his friends at Oxford against letting their son adrift in London to make his living in journalism, in the light of Middleton's fate, seem justified.

Flecker was to introduce Lawrence to the works of Middleton and Lawrence was much impressed.[1456] But at the time of Middleton's death, when Flecker had not yet learned of it, his mind was on future travel plans; thoughts of obtaining extra cash were always present.

The three days spent over Christmas in a hotel in Damascus were very wet and Flecker busied himself rewriting his 'accursed' novel. The rain did not keep him indoors the entire time. A fellow hotel guest (Hellé identified him only as 'Mr. P.') who was a student of Arabic, whom Flecker, she said, remembered from Uppingham days and Beirut, was also staying there with his wife. These two, both Anglo-Indians and expert linguists, and the Fleckers went to visit the British Consul and his wife who were also both already known to the Fleckers. Mr. and Mrs. Devey had been fellow-passengers aboard the boat en route for Athens where Hellé had first met her future husband. The Deveys had also been among the party that had made the landau trip to Athens and the Acropolis. George Pollard Devey was a man of nearly fifty. According to Hellé, he was much disliked by the British community for his strangeness and lack of decorum. He married his Italian wife, who spoke no English, during his time (nearly twenty years) as Vice-Consul in Jeddah. Mrs. Devey (although no direct reference is made to her behaviour or presence aboard the *Crimee*) could have been the inspiration for Firbank's mysterious character from *Inclinations*, who was also a passenger aboard the boat taking Miss Collins and Miss O'Brookomore to Athens. She is described as: 'There's on person on board, someone perhaps should speak to her, who sits all day staring at the sea beneath a very violet veil. And when the waves break over her she never even moves...'[1457]

'The poor veiled thing', as she is referred to, turns out to be Miss Arne – the actress (Mrs. Devey was described by Hellé as 'a singer' and Miss Arne accompanies Gerald and Mabel in the carriages to the Acropolis). Miss Arne is also known as Mary Arne and Mary Anne and Marianne. Miss Arne, who was shot dead during the stay in Greece, is recalled in a chapter (which Firbank rewrote many years afterwards) in the hearing of Miss Dawkins, the Australian (who could be based on Knox): 'With the Member for Bovon on her right, her tongue tripped heedlessly from Mussolini to Miss Anne'.[1458] This reference to 'Miss Anne' (which could be a misprint), makes an Italian connection, like the name Count Pastorelli.

The Deveys, like the Fleckers, were very fond of animals. The cats and dogs, which the Deveys kept at the Consulate, could be substitutes for children (like the cats and dogs the Fleckers kept from time to time). It would be harder to see the owls, crows, parrots, the ostrich, which stuck its head out of the unused porter's lodge, or even the gazelle as substitutes for a family. The stench from this Noah's Ark was overwhelming but the Deveys must have become used to it and neither the menagerie nor his wife was an obstacle to progress in his Consular career.

Another Consular official met at this time was the French Consul who, like Devey, had spent long years in the Levant. He was newly arrived in the same hotel and had booked into an opulently furnished room.

He sat in his black frock-coat playing a game of cards with the daughter of the Greek owner of the hotel. It was in this man that Hellé saw what she described as the detrimental effect of long years of dull Consular duties while living on a poor salary. Hellé dwelt at some length on the dismal aspects of this man's official life, which had resulted in his not going back to his native land for many years because there he would feel he was a foreigner. If you were a female foreigner and married to, or a companion to, another foreigner, it would be advisable to speak fluently your husband's or companion's native tongue, was the message that Hellé seemed to put in print. Foreign women should not draw attention to themselves, either by their dress or lack of intellectual qualities (which was a weakness of the Greek daughter of the hotel owner). The French Consul was not dressed flamboyantly and at least in the eyes of the local people he conformed to what a Consular official should look like. Hellé did not prefer him to the British Consul Devey, who was eccentric and roamed, a battered hat on his head, around his ramshackle house. If his Italian wife had been more of a conventional creature she might have balanced the outward appearances of the couple a little better. In bringing all this information, Hellé seemed to be saying that, despite views that might have been expressed to the contrary by her in-laws or by comparison with Eleanor Finlayson, she was a good Consular wife. Hellé might have felt at some disadvantage with Mrs. Devey, because Flecker spoke fluent Italian and Hellé did not. Hellé also seemed to be saying that, even if a longer life had been granted to her husband, he was not amiss in his longing to get out of the Consular Service.

The mental and physical strain on Consular staff continued to make the service a professional graveyard for many and in the light of her hints on the subject, this could be the reason why Hellé went straight on, after references to the French Consul during their time in Damascus, to describe the 'rows and rows of thickly set tombs of pilgrims who had fallen on the way, behind them the immensity of the desert...'.[1459] This was a remembrance of a late afternoon during that time, when the rain had stopped and they had driven out to the old pilgrims' road. The sight of stone turbans and fezes on the graves along the road had made them shudder.

It was not all gloom during their stay in Damascus. They were woken up by the beautiful singing voice coming from the nearby minaret, where the singer was 'warbling like a nightingale'. The singer was a devout neighbourhood cobbler and was said[1460] to become the bird-voiced 'Singing man' of Flecker's poem 'Gates of Damascus'. The timing of this allusion to the bird-voiced 'singing man' gives the impression to the reader that part of the inspiration for this poem (which Flecker thought of as his best) was the Christmas visit to Damascus. Hellé does not make clear (as she was the person who was supposed to have introduced, later in 1913, de Régnier to her husband) if he had de Régnier's 'Inscriptions pour les treize portes de la Ville' in 'Les Jeux et divins' prior to his stay in Damascus. The comparison with this work of de Régnier's could point to two poets separately inspired by the same theme. In its turn, 'Gates of Damascus' was compared to 'The Waste Land' of T.S. Eliot. But also it could mean that Flecker was first inspired by de Régnier's work through being introduced to his work at Cambridge by Firbank. The 'singing-man' intrigued him because it was a reminder of something he had already encountered in print. This was a similar experience to his interest in the antics of a male camel on the Damascus Road. 'Gates of Damascus' is not a translation and it has more of a spiritual element than the poem of de Régnier's, which Flecker did eventually translate in April 1913 – 'The Gate of the Armies'. The writing of poetry while in Damascus was not only a spiritual exercise, but hard work to make money to cover the expenses of goods purchased in the bazaars.

Hellé had given her husband what Flecker described to his parents as 'a beautiful camel-hair burnouse' and he told them he bought Hellé 'some old Bedawin necklaces and things'. These also seemed to be more to his taste, as he was photographed wearing what looked like a necklace with Arab dress.[1461] They had also bought, he told his parents, 'embroidered saddlebags, a pair of bellows, a silk scarf, coffee cups of the true Eastern kind – they fit into sockets like eggs into eggcups.' He was working hard 'with a poem or two' to cover these expenses.[1462] Flecker wore the burnouse on the train journey back to Beirut, which 'risked a scandal',[1463,1464] although the outfit (if he wore the camel driver's heavy black merino head-knot and the camel-hair coat) could provide warmth in the wet, icy-cold winter weather. It was around this time (at the end of 1911) that Flecker made an arrangement to pay off the last of his Oxford debts. Having done that he could have felt he could afford to spend money over Christmas. But financial matters were far from easy now that Hellé had used up her money and paid so many expenses. She had also not been able to sell the house she owned in Athens.

The brief spell of escape and relaxation was abruptly ended when Flecker got news of his results in the intermediate assistants' examinations. His results were described as unsatisfactory but the fact that he had been ill (although no reference was made to the type of illness) was taken as some excuse.[1465] He had a total of 158 marks out of a possible 450.

His translations of Turkish into English showed 'a fair elementary knowledge of the language'.[1466] His highest mark was 44 out of 100 for his translations from Turkish into English without the use of a dictionary. This mark showed his strength in translating in his own style because when he used a dictionary he got a lower mark of 35 out of 100. The weakness was said to show clearly when he had to struggle with the 'more difficult official style'.[1467] It was here that the poet-translator clashed with the poet-consular official. In some respects the results were not so poor when consideration is also given to the nature of his illness, travels, marriage and honeymoon whilst he was preparing for these examinations. Also the FO considered linguistical ability was not the most important quality in their Assistants; social and personal qualities mattered more.[1468] The badness of his Turkish spelling (Lawrence had difficulty with the spelling of Turkish) and his handwriting in Turkish were remarked upon, as was his failure in Ottoman Law, which the examiners said showed insufficient study. Flecker had used his Ottoman Law notebook for his first draft of *Hassan*, which indicated that the examiners could have had a point; his mind was not entirely on the subject. But the Foreign Office was not without fault. It had stipulated that two lectures a week for six months were necessary if Consular Assistants were to gain sufficient knowledge to pass the Ottoman Law examinations. No agreement had been reached whereby the Foreign Office was prepared to grant the £72 per annum necessary to pay the lecturers if they were to be employed in the task of instructing Assistants. The decision to pass or fail candidates rested with Ryan in Constantinople. Ryan had been prepared, in another candidate's final examination, to pass him at 45 marks out of 100 for his translations. If all these factors were taken into consideration, the poor results at this stage need not ruffle the surface of life too much. Flecker still had the prospect of being able to do better in the finals he had to take in June.

One outcome of the visit to Damascus was the realisation that while the Fleckers were there his replacement had appeared and immediately gone on leave. His replacement was to be Henry Charles Hony, who was a few months older than Flecker and had joined the service a year before and had gone to Marlborough. Hony may have been confused in Lawrence's mind with Flecker. Lawrence described Flecker as 'longing for the Marlborough Downs'.[1469] When writing to his parents to tell them the news about his successor, he also told them that in all probability they would be staying on at the hotel for another four months for which he was glad, as they were 'comfy' and the hotel had installed electric light.[1470] Despite being better lit, the hotel did not appear to be 'comfy' for long. January 1912 found Flecker trying to keep warm by placing an oil-heater under the table while he continued to work on 'Gates of Damascus', *Hassan* and *King of Alsander*. He was also writing on 10 January to Savery to let him know that he was going to receive his copy of *Forty-Two Poems*. Flecker tended to play down the importance of the publication of *Forty-Two Poems* by indicating to Savery that it was 'the old 36 with 6 new ones'.[1471] This apparent lack of confidence in the reception of *Forty-Two Poems* was another example of the disadvantages of being so far away from the London literary scene. He would not get news of a favourable review of *Forty-Two Poems*, which had appeared in the 30 December 1911 edition of the *Athenaeum* until February 1912. In this review the reader was told: 'Those who deplore the buoyant profusion and the attenuated poetic quality of our modern output of verse should extend no niggardly welcome to Mr. James Elroy Flecker's *Forty-Two Poems* (Dent & Sons).'

The reviewer was glad to see that 'The Masque of the Magi', a pearl plucked, as it were, from some mediaeval argosy, has been included.' The reviewer went on to discuss 'Mr. Flecker's craftsmanship, the exquisite way in which he fashions the receptacle to contain his thought and his feeling, is perhaps in this volume seen at its best. He pours the metal of his inspiration into a wide variety of metrical forms, creating by unswerving taste and felicity of touch an entity which is as balanced as it is loyal to the emotion that gave it birth.' The reviewer then went on to discuss possible influences on Flecker's work: 'He owes something of the texture of his thought to the French decadents, particularly Baudelaire, whom, as in his apprentice period, he is still inclined to echo. But though steeped in their wan melodies, he has shaken himself free of their frequent pose of jaded amorousness and pseudo-ferocity.' The reviewer then praised the six ballads, and Flecker's 'ready fund of imagery, his subtle power over rhythm.' The reviewer finished by saying: 'Mr. Flecker has assimilated something of the true poet's magic – that of conveying and suggesting a richer meaning than the actual words imply.'

Several more, mostly favourable reviews of *Forty-Two Poems* were to follow, but as Flecker could not anticipate these, the general note of pessimism continued to be evident in his letter to Savery, who was then told of the slow rewriting of *The King of Alsander*. Also Savery was informed about the prospect of leave at the end of the year, when he would be looking seriously for 'a decent post', which meant either a lectureship in English Literature or working for a newspaper. He felt that the life he was leading was 'good for the soul' and told Savery he would give anything to cross the desert.

The rest of January 1912, was not entirely devoid of hope for literary aims. 'Yasmin' was published in the 6 January 1912 edition of *Country Life*, 'The Dying Patriot' in the *Living Age* of the same date, and 'Sadaabad' in the *Nation* of 20 January, 1912. Time had to elapse before Flecker had proof of publication of these poems, which had not all appeared in the editions promised, and he had to wait for copies to be sent to him. It was the same with reviews of *Forty-Two Poems*.

The *Aberdeen Journal* of 25 January 1912 published a shorter and less favourable review of *Forty-Two Poems* than the review that had appeared in *The Athenaeum*. The *Aberdeen Journal*'s reviewer remarked upon the poet's 'considerable thinking power' and 'a lyrical faculty much beyond that of contemporary versifiers'. The atmosphere of decadence, the reviewer felt, left a bad taste in the mouth, although he thought that Flecker was always clever and frequently daring. The only quotation was from 'The Translator and The Children', from where the couplet about the children was taken:

> Their witless chatter is more dread
> Than voices in a madman's head:

It was also stated that these lines had 'occurred to us time and again, as we read through this book, only we applied it in a larger and wider sense than the author had done'.

In February, Flecker was able to tell his parents of the favourable reviews and poetry publication. He also told them that he had received a letter from *Century Magazine* (America) asking him for details of his 'Life'.[1472]

A favourable review of *Forty-Two Poems* was to appear in the March 1912 edition of *The Poetry Review*, which bore out the editor's admiration for 'The Ballad of Camden Town'.

This book deserves careful reviewing. It is, that is to say, near a border-line. It is hard to say whether it is just very good magazine poetry, or whether it is something more.

It is pleasant to read, it is companionable to know that someone else has read Machiavelli's 'L'Occasione'. The remaining question is, why should we read Mr. Flecker's poems in preference to those of some other two, or two dozen modern poets of the same order? He regards his art and its standards, as he knows them. This is good. Yet one is not sure that these standards have been subjected by him to any very searching analysis. The effect of cultured technique does not exceed that produced by, let us say, Sutton-Pichart in 'Ariadne and Biainomine', or Lady Margaret Sackville in 'A Hymn to Dionyssus' (the volume).

Mr. Flecker's work is good conventional work. There is strength in his intention to write poetry. I wish I could say that there was that saving grace of individuality, that grain of leaven which should be Mr. Flecker himself and no one else; that something which we could find only in his verses.

He has to his own mind considered life; one cannot feel that life has hammered from him the clichés to which he was born. He has not the élan of Bromley. Yet a man who has written 'The Ballad of Camden Town' need not be greatly troubled by a friendly censoriousness on the part of his reviewers: *meliora speramus*. Z.

Flecker's literary work was interrupted by the social round, which may have helped to lift his spirits for a while. He and Hellé gave dinner parties and attended dinners and dances, all in the line of consular duties. At one dinner, they met someone who was described as 'a clerical colleague of Dr. Flecker's' who reported back favourably on Hellé's suitability as a wife.[1473,1474] Hellé's acceptance amongst her husband's colleagues and T.E. Lawrence as a suitable wife appeared not to be in doubt.

Flecker, in a letter to his parents from Oxford when he was an undergraduate, tells them 'I shall hear Winnington-Ingram; he will interest me, being an orator.'[1475]

Lawrence in a letter sent to Flecker, which was written on 18 February 1912 from Aleppo,[1476] sent Mrs. Flecker kind regards. Lawrence had returned from Egypt ten days before and met up again with the Fleckers in Beirut. In the letter he referred to delivering a fish to the Deveys in Damascus, which was a gift from the Fleckers for which Devey had been grateful. Whilst in Damascus, Lawrence had bought Hittite seals at bargain prices. In Aleppo, Lawrence had continued to see Fontana who he said was 'up to the ears in Greek Anthology: Erotica of course'.[1477] Among all the general news about mutual friends, Lawrence's letter contained two important indications as to how Flecker's friendship influenced him and also the support of the idea that 'all his letters were adapted to the person he was addressing and wanted to influence. Everything he did was consciously and deliberately planned and willed, except when fate or accident tripped him up, at least so he would have us believe. But in this conscious adaptation in letter-writing he was after all only exaggerating what everyone does more or less unconsciously; and in any case, the process is not very obvious in his early letters.'[1478]

Lawrence's description of Aleppo in his letter to Flecker showed the influence of 'The Golden Journey to Samarkand', when Lawrence wrote:

'Aleppo is all compact of colour, and sense of line: you inhale Orient in lungloads, and glut your appetite with silks and dyed fantasies of clothes.[1479] To-day there came through the busiest vault in the bazaar a long caravan of 100 mules of Baghdad, marching in line rhythmically to the boom of two huge iron bells swinging under the belly of the foremost. Bells nearly two feet high, with wooden clappers introducing 100 mule-loads of the woven shawls and wine-coloured carpets[1480] of Bokhara! such wealth is intoxicating: and intoxicated I went and bought the bells. 'You hear them', said the mukari, 'a half-hour before the sight.' And I marched in triumph home, making the sound of a caravan from Baghdad: "Oah, Oah", and the crowd parted the ways before me......'

From the *Letters of T.E. Lawrence,* Selected and Edited by Malcolm Brown, 1988. Dent. p.45–6

Lawrence also wrote in this letter: 'Woolley thinks he knew your son at Oxford, and that you may be useful: wherefore be warned and don't lean towards altruism. Expect him about March 5th...' (The reference to 'your son' is not clear, although it could mean Beazley, and 'you may be useful' could refer to unofficial espionage.)

C. Leonard Woolley (1880–1960) (later Sir Leonard Woolley), formerly Assistant Keeper at the Ashmolean Museum, was due to be in overall charge at the dig at Carchemish from the end of February 1912. The money from the British Museum arrived shortly after Lawrence's writing to Flecker from Aleppo and Lawrence went to Carchemish on 24 February. Lawrence faced delay in his plans to build a house and excavate the site and while he waited he made contact with the railway engineers from Germany who were working on the Berlin-Baghdad railway. This railway was possibly going to cross the exact place at Carchemish where the British excavations had been taking place. The building of a railway from Berlin to the Bosphorous was seen as a long-term threat in the event of a war in Europe. The immediate political importance of this railway was evident and hence the usefulness of someone like Flecker to pass on information. A bridge was being built across the Euphrates at Carchemish that could be blown up in the event of war. Friendship with the German railway-workers had a purpose.

While Lawrence was involved in his open-air work, he was eventually attempting to get his own way, aided by Woolley, using methods against the Turkish authorities that were undiplomatic, such as flourishing revolvers and threatening the arrival of gunboats in Beirut harbour, Flecker was experiencing the real thing. The Italo-Turkish War, after the false start in the autumn of the previous year, had continued elsewhere. The war came back when the presence of a Turkish gunboat and a torpedo-boat in Beirut harbour on 24 February brought a dawn presence of Italian warships. The Turkish sailors were given the opportunity to surrender or have their boats destroyed. When no reply was received by the 9 a.m. deadline, the Italians acted and by 9.20 the Turkish boats were sinking. Beirut was not protected by land-based weapons of sufficiently long range to defend itself. Beirut harbour was French-built and a virtual amphitheatre. The Italians must have realised that their shelling was bound to cause civilian casualties and damage to buildings. Fifty sailors were said to be missing and between 100 and 200 people killed on the quay. The main casualty during the whole incident was the truth about what precisely happened on that day. From the British point of view, the most notable casualty was nearly Mr. Acting Vice-Consul Flecker.

Flecker was confronted by an armed and hostile mob of Moslem men who were intent on revenge and mistook him for the Italian Consul. He had been woken up by the noise of what he described as 'a shot' and he had driven to the Consulate, which was in the Christian quarter, just as the Italian warships opened fire on the Turkish boats. He was already aware that seven people of European appearance had been murdered in the streets in the mistaken belief that they were Italians. Flecker, deeply hurt that Cumberbatch had not sent a *cavass* for him, found the Consulate empty and unguarded except for 'the old boy', who was taking photographs upstairs. Flecker, despite his protests, was sent away immediately by Cumberbatch, who wanted him to look after Hellé and bring her back to the Consulate. It was on his way back to the hotel to pick up Hellé, this time in a carriage with a *cavass* and the Russian Consul of Hama, that the mob with arms and ammunition looted from the nearby barracks stopped their carriage. It was only the intervention of two armed soldiers, who got into the carriage and turned and faced the mob, that eventually enabled the party to get safely back to the hotel.

Flecker was badly scared by the incident, which brought back memories of the time he and Knox had been threatened with hanging by the mob during the French wine riots. Flecker came to appreciate that he had looked upon that particular incident with something of a feeling of enjoyment despite his terrible nervousness. This time, in Beirut, Flecker had been armed with a revolver and had been resolved to shoot 'a horrid fat man', but it was his knowledge of Turkish, which hitherto had not been considered by the Foreign Office to be of a high enough standard, which enabled him to repeat 'England' and prevent further action by the mob who did not, in the hostile atmosphere, make the connection that he was Christian. It was the fear of what had happened to Moslems at the hands of the Italians in Tripoli that was also behind the hatred. In time, his sense of humour enabled him to get the entire incident into better perspective. He realised how little the bombardment had meant to the average person back home. 24 February was a Saturday and the earliest the account could have been read about in England was in *The Times* of 26 February, which did devote space to the bombardment and also wrote about it in a leader. His parents were mystified to receive a telegram informing them that he was safe and well. He wrote a long letter on 27 February[1481] and started by telling them that all the details would be in the papers. *The Manchester Guardian* of 26 February 1912 had covered the conflict in Beirut with headlines that read 'Unrest in the Lebanon', 'Italian Warships at Beirut', 'Turkish Vessels Sunk in Harbour', 'Spectators Killed', 'All Italians to be expelled from Syria', but no mention was made of the threat to the life of Acting Vice-Consul Flecker, so although his parents may have read about the conflict they could not have known just how much personal risk their son had faced. The same newspaper in the same edition, 26 February 1912, contained a review of *Forty-Two Poems*[1482] but no connection could be made, as the threat to Flecker's life was not reported, nor that the poet was caught up in the conflict. The Miners' Strike, which was going on at the same time, was more likely to absorb the newspaper readers' attention than conflict in the Lebanon. No photographs were published, but Flecker intended to send his parents photographs of the damage done by the bombardment. If these were the photographs that Cumberbatch had taken from the Consulate on the day, he does not say so. Flecker explained to his parents that the danger was 'only momentary however'. He had to end the letter because of the arrival of tourists wanting to know if they were safe, but not before he thanks his parents for 'exquisite sardines'.

In Flecker's much later account of events 'Forgotten Warfare',[1483] he brought in an encounter he had with a Young Turk; although not named, this Young Turk was Nazim Bey, who had taught Flecker Turkish at Cambridge. Nazim Bey had played an important part in the Young Turk Revolution and was now Turkish Governor-General in Beirut. Cumberbatch, in his dispatch to Lowther, took the view that it was Nazim Bey who was responsible for preventing greater harm coming to foreigners and Christians. Flecker also, in his letter, told them 'The Vali [Governor-General] has done splendidly'. Cumberbatch, after seeing the Bey, went round reassuring families and British Institutes and recommending people to stay indoors. Strong military guards were placed on hotels and banks.

In the official report, Cumberbatch does not make it clear why he took on so much responsibility and left Flecker with just the task of looking after Hellé. Hellé, in any case, was 'as cool as a cucumber' about the whole incident and ready to kill a Turk (this was the opinion of her husband, but that piece of information was left out of the LIFE). Hellé was in little immediate danger: the hotels were flying their national flags.

In the official memo about events, Cumberbatch tells his superiors that Flecker had left the Consulate 'about 9 a.m.', which gives the impression that he left just before the bombardment began, but it must have been nearer 10 a.m. when Cumberbatch and Flecker left the Consulate, because by that time the mob was already active. Cumberbatch appeared to take on the entire burden of responsibility during the conflict.

Cumberbatch (born 1858) had started his career in 1876 with the consular service in Constantinople, Bucharest, Salonika and Smyrna. In 1895 he had been present at the Consulate in Kurdestan when Armenian demonstrations had resulted in the deaths of 50,000 Armenians. He may have felt that he had no time or no real need to take his Assistant with him. When in the past so many of Cumberbatch's Assistants had been too ill or absent when needed, he may have been so used to taking sole responsibility that he continued to do so when not strictly necessary. He could have been genuinely surprised when Flecker turned up at the Consulate, knowing that danger was out in the streets. Unless he already knew of Flecker's past association with Nazim Bey, and realised that it was not wise, in view of Flecker's opinion of Nazim Bey, to let them meet under prevailing circumstances. Or he preferred not to let the Foreign Office know of the Bey/Flecker connection, at this stage.

By Sunday 25 February, when the Cavalry Regiment from Damascus arrived, martial law was proclaimed and the mobs were controlled. Cumberbatch thought that Nazim Bey was the hero of the whole situation. Flecker described Nazim Bey as a 'Mahommedan friend of mine'. The Bey, who had been exiled to Paris, had a knowledge of its culture and had read Mallarmé. He had felt that a massacre of Christians was 'a mere measure of natural justice'.[1484] Flecker did not share 'the ancestral fanaticism which blazed in the Bey's eyes.' Flecker did come to realise that the incident was 'a paltry affair of a few hours',[1485] but while it had lasted it had seemed to him like the end of the world. He had heard the thunder of guns shake the golden blue of the sky and sea and 'not a breath stirred the palm trees, not a cloud moved on the swan-like snows of the Lebanon'.[1486] In the midst of mortal danger the poet had appreciated the beauty of his surroundings. Much later, Flecker was able to reassure himself that at least he had done his duty, even if he had been 'nervous as a dog'.[1487] A few days after the incident, Flecker went to the barracks to thank the soldiers who had protected him. Further proof of the lack of real understanding of the incident appeared in a letter from Rupert Brooke written in April 1912, from the home of the Oliviers, Limpsfield in Surrey.[1488] Brooke's letter was in response to a request from Flecker for a copy of Brooke's *Poems 1911*. This was Brooke's first published book of poems (and the only one published in his lifetime). *Poems 1911* was published by Sidgwick and Jackson in December 1911, at a cost to Brooke himself, with money provided by his mother. Despite Brooke having said that he had read of the Beirut bombardment in *The Times*, he asked Flecker why the Italians shot at him? Brooke told Flecker that he was not going to send him a copy of *Poems 1911* because he was too poor to do so. Brooke dwelt at length on his nervous breakdown, which he seemed to be suggesting was of much more importance to him than any physical dangers Flecker had recently faced. This reaction was understandable, but not likely to console the recipient of his letter, who was already having to come to terms with the indifference back home to the consequences to him of the Italo-Turkish War in Beirut. The old rivalry lingered between the lines of Brooke's letter. He lamented the fact that Flecker would never let him teach him how to write poetry. He called Flecker 'my swarthy friend', 'my golden tongued and lax-metered Orpheus'. Brooke did admit that it did not matter now and he thought Flecker a fine fellow. He implied that they would both be dead soon. Brooke was still recovering from his breakdown, and vulnerable after the publication of his long-planned book of poems and sensitive to the reviews that were coming out throughout the year. Some reviews praised but others criticised some of his poetry strongly. Brooke had reviewed Flecker's work in the past and criticised it. Flecker could do the same as soon as he got a copy. The plea of poverty was only one reason. Brooke may have been temporarily short of ready cash during April when he needed to borrow money to travel to Germany. A more important reason for denying Flecker a copy was more likely to be Brooke's insecurity about Flecker's reaction; delaying tactics were a safeguard against an adverse reaction to his book. In another letter written on 15 April 1912[1489] to Mr. Harrison, editor of *The English Review*, Flecker began:

Dear Mr. Harrison,

Please let me know – as a great favour, for here one is so horribly cut off from the world – whether you received my recent review of *Artist in Corfu* and will publish same and also whether you have accepted my poem 'The Divan of the West.'

He also thanked Harrison for sending all the back numbers, except January, of the *ER*.

The English Review had published in its February edition an article about Brooke and a review of *Poems 1911* and this may have been the first realisation by Flecker, when he received his copy of the *ER*, that he and Brooke were each having a book of poems published. The letter of Flecker's to Brooke in reply in April has not survived and it is not possible to know with any certainty whether or not Flecker wrote to Brooke in a light-hearted way about his feelings of homesickness, as he had written to Savery while he was in Damascus about longing to be in Chipping Candover. While he was in Germany, Brooke sat down at a cafe and wrote the poem, which he was first going to give the title 'The Sentimental Exile' before he called it 'The Old Vicarage, Grantchester'. This now famous poem deals with nostalgia in a light-hearted way, but by no means unfeeling manner. Whether Brooke caught the idea for the theme of the poem from Flecker, either consciously or unconsciously, it is not possible to say. The poem was based on Brooke's longings for Ka Cox, whom he was awaiting to join him in Germany. Brooke's feelings about Ka Cox, whom he felt he was no longer in love with, now she was with him, were confused, as he was about marriage. Even without knowing exactly what was in Flecker's letter to Brooke, but knowing how Flecker broke the news of his marriage to most of his friends (in a brief and light-hearted manner), it is safe to conclude that he announced the fact of his marriage in a similar manner in his letter to Brooke. Further proof is seen in the manner in which Brooke responded to Flecker's marriage. Brooke mentioned the marriage only after he had outlined in detail his agonising nervous breakdown. He asked Flecker why he had married, and in a postscript he urged Flecker to beat his wife 'less worse befall'.

Another conflict that broke out at this time and got considerably more space devoted to it (in Hellé's *Reminiscences*) than the incident in which Flecker was nearly killed, was the private feud that arose between the Fleckers and the other occupants of the hotel annexe they shared. The elderly Russian Military Attache, whom Hellé described as having a fondness for beer, and his equally elderly wife had erected three screens across the common hall which nearly cut off the access to the Fleckers' sitting-room. Flecker, as he emerged from the bedroom just having woken from his mid-day siesta, gave one of the screens a mighty kick which toppled them all over. The scene that followed included the manager, who was a German, and to Hellé's annoyance, Flecker, whom she had already pushed back into the bedroom. The upshot of this exchange of words (although in which language is not revealed) was that the Fleckers and the Russians were no longer on speaking terms.

The Fleckers decided shortly afterwards to leave the hotel for good, in favour of staying at an English pension. This appeared unfair, if Hellé's published version of events many years later can be completely relied upon. She knew that her husband had a clear conscience and the reasons why the screens had been at the root of the problem were that the Russian wife had already taken up too much room in the common hall. Another version of events tells of Flecker fighting and knocking someone, who was described as 'the German', to the floor; 'almost a scandal' had resulted.[1490] The real truth would be somewhere between the two versions, and Flecker considered it prudent to move out. It is not exactly clear if the Russian Official was the same Official who had shared a carriage with Flecker when he had nearly been killed. Hellé remembered him as the Russian Military Attaché. Flecker described him as the Russian Vice-Consul. Cumberbatch described him in the official report about the shooting incident when faced by the mob, as the Russian Consul of Hama. Whether there was one Russian Consular Official or more than one playing their part in these dramas, he (or they) would be older and further up the career ladder than Flecker was at this stage. The rights and wrongs of the petty incident would not be sorted out in Flecker's favour, if it was to be decided by an outside body in the same way as the rewarding of the saviour of the Russian Consul of Hama. The Russian Government paid £50 as a reward, the British Embassy gave Flecker's saviour a silver cigarette case.[1491]

The Fleckers had no more rows with fellow guests while living in the two rooms at the English pension, but the move brought them little peace. The mosquitoes were worse, the food was uneatable and the nightly noise of the fighting street dogs kept them awake until they had to get up and deal with the nuisance by throwing down water when other methods failed, just as Yasmin had done when trying to get rid of Hassan from underneath her window. If they got rid of the dogs, then the chorus of frogs from the nearby pond prevented any further attempts to sleep.

The only solution was to move once again to their own separate summer quarters. They found a cottage in a Lebanese village near Aley, and although Hellé was ill with fever and her wrist was sprained, the Fleckers moved up to Areiya in May. Noise, this time of the human variety, still bothered them in their new abode. They found that they could not sit out peaceably in the garden; it was shared with noisy neighbours, children, and hung with washing. But tranquil moments sometimes existed. Flecker was able to sit out under the pomegranate tree when it was in bloom in June 1912 and write an 'Open Letter' to the poets of England.[1492] This was a draft (which was to remain unfinished and consequently unpublished) in which he praised the beauty of his surroundings, but as ever he longed for the rain and pavements of the Strand. (*The English Review*'s offices were in Tavistock Street, just off the Strand, and it was thought that the 'Open Letter' was aimed at publication in *The English Review*.) The 'Open Letter' had something of the tone and theme of 'Candilli' and 'The 'Bus in Stamboul', when the intense heat made him long for the damp cool of England. Flecker, in his 'Open Letter', told the poets to come out and live in 'Turkey proper' and learn not to take their own civilisation for granted.

'My thrice blessed brother authors' were told: 'Seek for the magic of the Arabian Nights and you will learn that the East changes – all that belonged to a civilisation dead long years ago.' And also they were told 'at least do not beat your gossamer wings on the hard blue cover of the minority report...'. This last seemed to be aimed at 'thrice blessed brother authors' of the Firbank/Brooke sort. Firbank was compared to a butterfly by those who knew and read his work [1493] (although he could not be described as a poet of England, Flecker could see Firbank as a butterfly too); Rupert Brooke had campaigned and lectured about the Minority report of the Poor Law Commission in 1910. If the 'Open Letter' had been published, then Flecker could also be accused of combining poetry with present-day problems in his play *Don Juan* and failing to make it a successful play. Flecker had not himself shown any liking for the Bohemian life. He told the poets of England to 'appreciate a metalled road, an express train, or sweet and sanded oyster bar...'. In the Lebanon he had suffered from streets running with green slime and the distress of travelling in slow trains in stifling heat.

Mavrogordato could also be one of those to whom the 'Open Letter' was addressed, as he was again dreaming of being an artist in the Lebanon and he told Flecker that he would do his best for his poems but 'they are sure to be crowded out by articles on syndicalism or some Masefieldian petulance'.[1494] Flecker did not want the poets of England to 'allay the pain of poverty and fight the injustice of the rich'. He told the poets that their business was 'to write stories and songs, to fill

England with merriment and laughter and make the hearts of people young'.[1495]

Merriment and laughter from the Fleckers' home was not filling their neighbours' hearts. Two of the occupants of the Flecker home were guilty of making a din that was loud enough to be long remembered by those living close by. But this noise was not a result, as the neighbours thought, of Hellé and her husband having rows.[1496] The voices overheard were loud and argumentative, male and female, English and Greek. The voices were those of Flecker and the Greek cook, Angela. Angela was hot-tempered and although no precise reason was given, she and Flecker did not get on. Angela had formerly worked in the kitchen of the British Consul-General and she may have felt that she had come down now in the domestic servant world. Also she was not the Fleckers' landlady, but she must have felt she deserved respect for her culinary skills. The Fleckers respected their landlord, unlike their landlady in Corfu. Angela was the Fleckers' first domestic employee and this sort of relationship was one he found hard to handle. He had already clashed with the foreign 'servants' of the railways. But it was not a case of Angela's foreignness being at the heart of the problem (although she was also devout, like the landlord) but more likely Flecker's inexperience caused the trouble, and also he could not pose as a well-off Englishman and command respect.

Flecker's only previous experience of temperamental cooks would have come from seeing his mother handle the domestic regime at Dean Close. His mother had to balance her books. Could the Fleckers really afford Angela? Finances for the Fleckers were 'not brilliant' during this period.[1497] If the rows with Angela are seen alongside the rows he had had recently with other people, such as the Russian Consular Official, then these could all be seen as an indication of recurrent ill-health, which had to be added to financial worries and anxiety about his Turkish studies and the examinations due to be taken in June, as well as literary hopes, which were unfulfilled. The work that he had sent for possible publication in America had been returned to him. It was not a case of his work in general not being known or appreciated in America. *The Evening Post* in New York on 1June 1912, in its Literary News and Reviews section, favourably reviewed *Forty-Two Poems*, commenting on the influence of Lecompte de Lisle and Baudelaire on Flecker's work and quoting lines from 'No Coward's Song'. But the knowledge of this favourable review would not be known to him at this time so his despair continued.

He was continuing to be under a strain in June 1912, after he had sat his examinations, for his illness was supposed to be due to eating raw fruit. Or so his parents chose to state, that 'the sharp attack of illness with fever' was to be blamed on the eating of raw fruit.[1498] Outbreaks of cholera and smallpox were reported from Aleppo in June 1912. If his parents knew of the extent of these outbreaks, the risk did not appear to be so high in their minds as the knowledge of the folly of eating raw and unwashed fruit in a hot climate. His parents long afterwards seemed to want to maintain that the bout of illness could not be related to a recurrence of consumption. Flecker, on his part, could have blamed his bout of ill-health on the eating of raw fruit because he did not want to face up to thoughts of any recurrence of consumption. The temptation to eat raw fruit in a land where it was grown in abundance did not enter into the argument. As in past disagreements, an element of real understanding on both sides would have eliminated the need for an aftermath of blame and cover-up.

July 1912 (judged on two letters written from the Consulate; to Mavro on 11 July and to Frank Savery on 26 July) brought no more news about ill-health. 'Santorin' was to be published in the September edition of *The English Review*, which appeared to have temporarily lost its copy of 'The Golden Journey to Samarkand'. Flecker complained to Mavro that he had heard nothing for six months and he wanted the *ER* to publish 'The Golden Journey to Samarkand' with 'Santorin' if possible. If not wanted, he suggested that it was sent to *The Poetry Review* where he was already going to withdraw 'Santorin'. Norman Douglas, who had replaced Douglas Goldring as sub-editor at *The English Review* in 1909, blamed *The English Review*'s editor, Austin Harrison, for temporarily losing Flecker's poem. Harrison's delays and indecision over the acceptance of Flecker's work were always a cause of resentment. Douglas was greatly taken with the island of Santorin when he visited it, but he did not record (a quarter of a century later), whether or not he had tried to get any particular poem of Flecker's into the *ER* as he said he had done with other writers' work. Douglas knew that Flecker was a consumptive and not well off.[1499] He was in a position to see that a chance to be paid for a review of his own book would have helped Flecker's income. Douglas, in his own account of his time at the *ER*, does not mention Mavrogordato, but he does give his version of the working practices of the editor of the *ER.*, Austin Harrison. Harrison (according to Douglas) was in the habit of keeping manuscripts that had been submitted to him, even those which were topical, until they lost their point and value. Writers came and collected their manuscripts themselves from the *ER* office. Many of the complaints about Harrison's attitude to the manuscripts and comments made were not at all unusual and still exist in offices of magazines, where a great deal of mail, enclosing contributions, is received. The letter that Flecker had sent to Harrison on 15 April 1912, with a poem enclosed (as has been seen), could never have reached Harrison and that was why he was not able to reply. Harrison was said (by Douglas) to be obdurate, which Douglas had to admit was Harrison's prerogative. Harrison had replaced one of the great literary editors, Ford Maddox Ford, who had at the *ER* published D.H. Lawrence, Pound, James, Wells and Hardy. But the *ER* had lost money and, although Ford would have liked the magazine to be purchased by someone who would keep him on as editor, the new owner sacked Ford and appointed Harrison instead. Ford was last involved with the *ER* in February 1910, but continued to choose material for the *ER*. Harrison was not in an easy position because he had to make the *ER* pay, or he was out of a job.

Added to all these worries, Hellé's health gave cause for alarm. One night she took a sudden turn for the worse; she was seriously ill and thought that she was about to die. Nursing help in this crisis was not provided by her husband or even Angela. It was a Consular Official whom they had first met in Damascus who arrived by chance and saved the situation. He suggested Flecker write to a Danish lady who was a good nurse and she came at once and looked after Hellé. This nurse also brought much needed civilised conversation to mealtimes. Flecker told Mavro on 5 June that except for Hogarth and two fellow archaeologists who called to and from Carchemish, they never saw 'a civilised soul'.

The house Flecker described to Mavro as idyllic. Whatever their pressing problems, even if they could not sit out in the garden because of the noisy neighbours, they could sit out on the balcony and look down on the sea and up to the mountain snows. The porch as a place to sit out was disturbed only by the whirring of dragonflies' wings (as they looked at the several pomegranate trees). The garden had a pergola, which must have afforded some shade and privacy, if it did not shut off the noise completely. The jasmine in full bloom provided shade. Roses in June in the garden added to its colour and on the mountains fiery red anemones 'gave way to broom'.[1500] The red anemone was as visible in his poetry as in his prose, when he wrote in his poem 'Santorin':

> His father was Adonis
> Who lives away in Lebanon,
> In stony Lebanon, where blooms
> His red anemone.

The whole essence of the stay at Areiya is distilled into Flecker's poem 'Areiya' which begins with the lines:

'This place was formed divine for love and us to dwell;
This house of brown stone built for us to sleep therein;'[1501]

This first draft of 'Areiya'[1502] is not dated, but both the content and the fact that it was 'wrote in minutes', as he states in the second last line (in a letter to Savery he was more precise and said it was written in three minutes), points to the likelihood of the poem being written for Hellé's birthday in July 1912. Flecker put 'Areiya' alongside 'Sadaabad' in his estimation and described it as 'the only poem of individual passion I have ever written'.

In the year of marriage and honeymoon, whatever else had happened that was not a cause for celebration, the love he had for Hellé and the beauty of the surroundings had been captured in 'Areiya'. The search for a matrimonial home had always been in Flecker's mind and after abandoning the search for a house in Smyrna, the cottage in Corfu had been a fortunate find. Areiya, they must have felt, was their only real chance of some sort of permanence while in the Consular service. Flecker had to go down to Beirut three times a week but he came back after an uncomfortable two-hour train journey. Hellé waiting for him in Areiya gave him a sense of homecoming, which he had never quite experienced in the past. Hellé's homemaking made a great improvement in the living quarters, not present in the bug-infested bachelor quarters in Candilli, where she had been a visitor.

'Areiya' was not only the result of the place and the beloved coming together but the fusion of an idea and a memory, conscious or unconscious, of Baudelaire's. All these ingredients made 'Arieya' much more satisfying to Flecker than 'In Phaecia', although in that poem the place and the beloved came together as well as an idea and a memory from Yeats. The attempt to imitate Yeats' work had more of an element of jest in it. Flecker may have, like Firbank, been bored with 'The Lake Isle of Innisfree' or, like John Davidson, had some resentment towards Yeats because he felt equal or superior to him as a poet, but shared little of his success. 'In Phaecia' was a means of expressing his feelings about Yeats' work. 'In Phaecia' reflected Flecker's feelings about the beauty of Corfu and also that, although he was happy there and wrote so much of his best work, Hellé was depressed and unsure of her immediate future. In the Lebanon she had been able to establish herself in the role of Consular Official's wife and got some acceptance as a daughter-in-law.

Another element of the contentment whilst at Areiya, which was not present in Corfu, was the civilised company (although not nearly enough for Flecker). The company was provided by the visits of Hogarth, Lawrence and another who was not named in letters home, but who would be Woolley. The Carchemish dig closed down in June for the summer. For their part, the archaeologists would find the Fleckers more agreeable than the average dinner-party guests or the social round elsewhere in the region. Hogarth had found himself introduced as 'a digger in the Levant' by a 'vague hostess' and although women in general were intrigued by archaeology, the woman Hogarth encountered had no idea of the hardship and disappointment of such work. At the archaeological dig, the women belonging to the local people did not participate in any sort of social gathering. If Lawrence had any idea of getting married (which might have stifled some of the gossip from the local men that he was homosexual) he would not have been allowed to bring his wife out to Carchemish. One of Hogarth's assistants had married and when told he could not bring his wife out to Carchemish, he decided not to come at all. Gertrude Bell (1868–1926).

The Fleckers would present a good balance between Gertrude Bell's knowledge and the lack of understanding of archaeological digs present in other households. Flecker, through his friendship with Beazley, knew something of the subject and both he and Hellé had made local trips and discovered signs of previous civilisations, of which Lawrence was aware. The Oxford connection with Hogarth, Woolley and Lawrence was also an important factor, in appreciating these visitors. For their friendships with women, men like Lawrence had to make friends with the wives of the Consular Officials such as Mrs. Winifred Fontana and Hellé.

One morning, Lawrence turned up at the house at Areiya early enough to surprise Flecker. He had arrived by train the night before, but so as not to disturb his hosts had slept on the floor at the station (much to the disturbance of the station master). The precise date of this particular visit or length of stay is not recorded, but Lawrence had written in a letter[1503] to one of his brothers from Jerablus [July 1912] and informed him of his intention of going to Aleppo and then journeying to a place in the hills or in the Lebanon to visit a number of people, which included 'the Beyrout Consul', which could refer to Flecker or to Cumberbatch, who also had a house near Aley, not far from Areiya. Lawrence told his brother that he did not intend to stay with 'these people'; he was going to take rooms in a house nearby because 'these people' were not alone. This could indicate that in the case of the Flecker household the Danish nurse was still in residence. One reason behind Lawrence's reluctance to stay at Areiya with the Fleckers and to arrive unannounced was the fact that Lawrence himself was not alone. He was travelling with his servant. A photograph exists of a handsome, fair-skinned boy in his early teens, taken in the garden of the Fleckers' cottage.[1504] The boy is not named and is only described as Lawrence's servant. Lawrence, in his letters, had given the impression that the boy, whose nickname was Dahoum 'the dark one' (his real name was Ahmed) was just his servant and that he had hired him because he was cheaper than local labour. Dahoum had first been a donkey boy and then a cook who could wait at table. Dahoum came to mean more to Lawrence than an ordinary servant. Dahoum was more an adopted brother than a servant and because of this, if he had been introduced to the Flecker household without prior warning late at night, problems could have arisen over sleeping arrangements. Or in the morning, with meal preparations by Angela in the kitchen. Dahoum was not the only one to have his photograph taken by Lawrence during this stay. Lawrence was responsible for the Carchemish expedition's photographs. He took photographs of Flecker standing and squatting in front of the three-arched balcony of the house at Areiya. On one photograph is written 'Royal Arab dress'. Flecker is wearing what could be the camel-hair burnouse that Hellé had bought him for Christmas, and over his head he is wearing what could be the silk scarf also bought at Christmas in Damascus. He was like Mrs. Thoroughfare in Firbank's *Valmouth*: 'swathed, quasi-biblically, in a striped Damascus shawl that looked Byzantine...'. The taking of these photographs, if he used the expedition's camera, was not merely to provide portraits for the Flecker family photograph album: Flecker also took a photograph of Lawrence in European clothes, at Areiya.[1505]

These photographs must have fulfilled some other purpose for Lawrence, who preferred to take photographs to illustrate his plans rather than write paragraphs about them. But plans of the kind Lawrence had in mind required more than photographs and practical considerations. In drawing Flecker into any future plans there had to be some sort of mutual admiration. Woolley[1506] had found Lawrence in his work as an archaeologist to be 'curiously erratic'. Woolley stated that it all depended on how far he was interested in archaeology or it appealed to his sense of values. Lawrence could look at a small piece of Hittite inscription and remark upon where it fitted on an equally small piece found a year ago. All this approach to work and the reaction of Woolley was similar to the reactions of Flecker's teachers and others who had been in charge of him in the Levant Consular Service and elsewhere. Woolley later admitted that he had not got the insight to see the genius within Lawrence and to realise that Lawrence was unusually gifted. But no such lack of real understanding could have existed between Lawrence and Flecker as to whether genius lurked as yet unrecognised within each other. Flecker was to remain doubtful of the authenticity of the Hittite seals given to him, but Lawrence's vision of the desert was transmitted to Flecker and Flecker's belief in himself as a poet transmitted itself to Lawrence. Lawrence's opportunities for poetry writing were limited and Flecker's opportunity for adventures equally limited, but a chance to partake in some sort of adventure planned by Lawrence was not completely out of the question.

Lawrence was fully aware that because of his fair complexion he would never be able to 'take on the Arab skin'[1507] even on his travels dressed in Arab clothes. Flecker's dark moustache and eyebrows were remarked upon by Lawrence as well as Flecker's skin, which Lawrence described as 'sun-coloured'.[1508] Flecker in Arab dress did not face the obvious drawback that Lawrence faced when dressed in Arab clothes, when he wanted to blend into the background for the purpose of unofficial spying or buying Hittite seals; Lawrence's fair skin never tanned. Lawrence described Flecker as 'an Arab looking gentleman in a cloak',[1509] but also pointed out that in the photograph Flecker had 'one bare forearm thrust forward to show woman's beaten silver old Damascus bangle on wrist.'[1510] Lawrence's looks may not have been those that made him able to pass as an Arab, but his ability to speak Arabic was good.

Flecker could be useful if he could be persuaded to join Hogarth's unofficial intelligence service in an acting unpaid capacity. Lawrence's recollections of Flecker in print did not refer to Flecker's possible involvement in these extra-consular activities. In print, Lawrence described instead Flecker and himself carelessly flung beneath a tree talking of women, slippers and of whippings. Of reviving *Hassan* and Viola Tree.[1511] The mention of what could be taken as a mutual interest in sexual masochism diverts attention from what would be a more important discussion, which would need to take place out of doors. Lawrence was aware of Flecker's brush with death at the hands of the armed mob (who had looted over a thousand weapons). Another incident that took place in August 1912 was not as serious but was also experienced by Flecker. While he waited on the crowded platform at Aley station, he witnessed fugitives who were fleeing in large numbers on the train going up towards the mountains and he realised that once again Italian warships were in Beirut harbour. Flecker did not hesitate to go down to the Consulate, despite the threat to his life last time there had been trouble in Beirut. He found this time that no crowds were demonstrating on the quays and he had no duties to carry out. When he returned to the cottage he found what he described as 'a little squadron of Lebanese cavalry prancing before the door'.[1512] Inside, he met two American lady missionaries from Abadieh who were taking refuge with Hellé.

Eventually Cumberbatch, with Flecker, drove together by moonlight and saw the Druse elder whose wounding had been the cause of the disturbance. While Cumberbatch tried reconciliation, Flecker had to deal with what he described as 'lesser notables'. Flecker's account of the incident in 'Forgotten Warfare' (he also wrote to his parents about it,[1513] like his accounts of the two other encounters with disturbances and conflict during the course of duties as Acting Vice-Consul) was enhanced with descriptions of his surroundings.[1514] He wrote of moonlight 'streaming in the enormous rocky gorge of the Beyrout river' and the few Lebanese gendarmes's strange costumes, 'so fantastic in the moonlight that the whole scene seemed to stiffen into cardboard, and one waited to hear music of some absurd Oriental opera by Herold or Rossini'. He went on to describe the 'little fortress-like houses, on the runic carvings of an old Druse tomb, mysterious beneath a splendid chestnut tree,'. This tomb could have been the one in the cottage garden that is featured in a photograph in SLA (facing p.66) or the one that was said to be a favourite place of Flecker's and where he wrote some of his verse.[1515] Flecker gave Cumberbatch due credit for defusing a difficult confrontation between Druse and Maronite.

It was these sorts of volatile situations and unrest, when British Consular Officials and Consulates were vulnerable to attack, that Lawrence aimed to prevent in the future by supplying more arms to those who would need them. Lawrence needed to initiate illegal gun-running from the sea, with the support of Cumberbatch, Flecker, Fontana and others. The small number of guns had to be stored somewhere until needed and Lawrence was to suggest 'a sea-side house in the vicinity of where he was said to compose his verse, Beyrout belonging to friends of his'.[1516] By the time this notion of a seaside house was put forward, the Fleckers were no longer living in Areiya but the idea of help from Flecker could have already been in Lawrence's mind when he visited that summer and the object of the visit could have been to sound Flecker out about the plan. It was revealed in the letter to Lowther that the venture was discussed with Cumberbatch between November 1912 and February 1913. The event, when it took place, did not directly involve Flecker and was undertaken by Lawrence and naval personnel. But Flecker was not such an unlikely candidate in the mind of anyone who did not know the true nature and extent of his illness. He had some training for intelligence gathering, if not the actual taking part in ventures that Lawrence had in mind. Under a plan put forward by the FO in 1909, student-interpreters, once they had passed their final exams and before going to Turkey, would have to call on the Directorate of Military Operations so that they could at least learn the difference between a battalion and a regiment. As a result, any reports of movements of troops not given by the Military Attache but by the civilian Vice-Consuls would not be too misleading.[1517]

Another visitor at this time was the officer from Damascus with whom Flecker went to the mountains to see the cedars while Hellé was still too ill to go with them. By September, Hellé's health was better and she and Flecker, despite the heat, went for brief walks and drives. Literary hopes too were better, *The English Review* had published 'Santorin' in its September edition. He had withdrawn 'Santorin' from *The Poetry Review* and he still hoped that *The English Review* would publish his poem 'The Golden Journey to Samarkand'.

By 19 September, any brief upturn in fortunes was dispelled with the news of failure to pass the examinations retaken in June. If he did not pass in nine months time he would have to resign and forfeit the £500 bond.[1518] On 9 October, Flecker applied for leave of absence so that he could accompany Hellé to Paris for the benefit of her health, despite his failure in examinations.[1519] This was not a sudden idea, it had been outlined in a letter to Savery in July. Then it was Hellé who had to go to Paris to visit her mother and her husband who was considering going with her because he did not 'look forward even to a temporary spell of celibacy: even Oxford would bore me, alone'.[1520] In July, Hellé's illness was thought to be over, but now her 'Mediterranean low fever' had flared up again and the pleasant summer days in the Lebanon when he could dream under pine trees or play the piano to accompany Hellé's violin, only to be interrupted by thrice weekly visits to Beirut, were coming to an end: home beckoned.

Hogarth had been consulted in July about the possibility of a job at Oxford. Flecker had wanted the post in England, which would pay at least £350 a year; he would not live on less. Cumberbatch did not wish to raise objections to the granting of one month's leave from 9 November, despite the examination failure. Cumberbatch wanted to apply for accumulated leave starting in the following June. The underlying message to the FO seemed to be that if Flecker got his home leave out of the way he would then not be eligible for any more during the time that Cumberbatch was out of the country, thus not depleting the Consulate of any more staff, although Flecker would not be in sole charge of the Consulate during that time. One important message which Cumberbatch spelled out to the FO was that if, through unforeseen circumstances, Flecker's leave exceeded one month, he begged leave that he may be replaced; an inexperienced Assistant would be of no use. Once again, the Pro-Consul would fill in for Flecker while he was away.[1521]

Flecker was not singled out for this reluctance to grant him leave; by coincidence, Devey, it was stated in the official memos, had been 'induced' to postpone the leave that he had applied for on 19 October. It was in the same quarter of the year that Bullard was to discover (after he hastened back to England in a vain effort to see his father before he died that he would be on half-pay, and he had to hasten back because of a shortage of cash.)[1522] Flecker was given the month's leave, not knowing that there would be no question of his being able to extend it. Cumberbatch must have known that rather than arrange for an inexperienced Assistant to be sent out to replace Flecker while he was on leave, he would be ordered back. Flecker must have realised that if he had asked for an extension before he left, it would not have been agreed to, especially if Cumberbatch knew it was for the reason of seeking another post outside the Consular Service. Cumberbatch was not an unreasonable man, or one who stood on his dignity. His family had the reputation in their younger days in Constantinople, in the very cold weather, of sliding on a toboggan down a public road, which was disastrous to pedestrians.[1523]

Once the question of a month's leave had been set officially in motion (it was not finally sanctioned until 17 October), Flecker could look forward to his plans for making influential literary contacts in London. On 12 October, he wrote from the Consulate to Edward Marsh to tell him that he hoped to be in London in December, when perhaps they could meet. Marsh had written to Flecker to ask him if he would agree to have some of his poems appear in a proposed anthology. Flecker told Marsh that he would be very glad to appear in the company of his old friend, Rupert Brooke. The suggestion from Brooke to include Flecker came while Brooke was making his London home with Marsh. The idea of publishing an anthology to represent the existing poetic renaissance, had first arisen in Marsh's chambers. Brooke had first put forward the idea of writing a hoax book of poetry. He would use a dozen different false names and pass the book off as genuine. This was less realistic than an idea of Flecker's when he had wanted to bring out an anthology with improvements written (genuinely) by himself, or his suggestion made to Masefield for a brotherhood of poets. Marsh was sufficiently shrewd to realise that it would be more profitable to issue an anthology of twelve of the best (in his view) of the new poets. This anthology would whet the appetite of the general public for more of this type of anthology. However promising the chosen poets might be individually, the public would not go out and buy quantities of their twelve separate books of verse. The poets were not always the best judges of which of their own poems fitted into the anthology and Marsh chose to guide them. Flecker, in his letter to Marsh about which of the poems to include, advised against Marsh's choice of 'Joseph and Mary' and he suggested he choose instead from 'Rioperoux', 'Tenebris interlucentem', 'The Saracens' (or, instead of 'The Saracens', 'Pillage') as these were shorter, or 'The Ballad of Hampstead Heath' if Marsh 'care[d] for the less lyrical style'. Marsh still chose 'Joseph and Mary' and 'The Queen's Song' to represent Flecker in the anthology. Both poems came from *Thirty-Six Poems* and *Forty-Two Poems*. 'The Queen's Song' seems to have been chosen, despite Brooke having referred to it as having 'a serious moral fault' when he had reviewed *Thirty-Six Poems*. 'Joseph and Mary' was appropriate in an anthology due to be sold in December. Also *The Morning Post* of 15 July 1912, when reviewing *Forty-Two Poems* had picked out 'Joseph and Mary' as amongst some of the best and had described 'Masque of the Magi' as like 'an old Miracle Play'. 'No Coward's Song', 'The Ballad of the Student in the South' and 'The Ballad of the Londoner' were picked out also as amongst the best. The reviewer in *The Morning Post*, like the reviewer of *Thirty-Six Poems* in the same newspaper in its 3 March 1910 edition, was 'not at all at home' with 'Ballad of Hampstead Heath'. In the same sort of manner as past reviewers of *Thirty-Six Poems* and 'The B of F' such as those in *The Times, Gloucester Echo* and *The Birmingham Daily Post* when commenting on 'Oxford Canal', *The Morning Post* described the poem as a parody of Walt Whitman.

Reviews of *Forty-Two Poems* could have influenced Marsh's choice of verse for inclusion in his anthology. Later reviews of *Forty-Two Poems* such as the one in the *Daily News* of 18 November, which was favourable, would bear out Marsh's correct choice of Flecker for inclusion in *Georgian Poetry*.

This letter of Flecker's to Marsh was similar to letters he also received (or some cases visits made) from poets such as Ezra Pound, W.H. Davies and others. For a variety of reasons the poets disagreed with Marsh's choice, sometimes because the chosen poems were already due to go into their own anthologies. Marsh and Pound could not agree on which of Pound's poems to select and a great deal of dislike grew up between the two men. So not having face to face contact with Marsh at the time the selection of Flecker's poems were in some disagreement, was an advantage in case hostility had broken out between Marsh and Flecker, which would result in neither poem going into any anthology of Marsh's. It was not all bad feeling between Marsh and would-be contributors;

some poets showed generosity of spirit towards their fellows. They also put forward suggestions about other poets whose work they liked. De la Mare, in his letter to Marsh, included specimens from Flecker's *Thirty-Six Poems* and *Forty-Two Poems* ('what an odd fashion in nomenclature').[1524] T. Sturge Moore (1870–1944), who had already published volumes of his own poetry, also suggested Flecker's poetry to Marsh for inclusion in the anthology. Flecker did not have a high regard for Sturge Moore's work.[1525] Once again, if Flecker had mentioned this dislike to Marsh in person it would not have endeared him to Marsh. Marsh did not automatically consider poems from poets who had been recommended to him. Robert Frost (1874–1963), despite recommendations from fellow poets, was not included. Frost's poetry collection, *A Boy's Will*, was in the process of publication by Mrs. Nutt, not without the same sort of difficulties as Flecker experienced. *A Boy's Will* was published in Nutt's *Series of Modern Poets* in April 1913. Monro, whom Frost disliked, mainly because of the failure to get included in the anthology, was a Flecker admirer. Monro was editor of *The Poetry Review* and had been asked to publish the anthology under his Poetry Bookshop imprint. Monro, his assistant editor and contributor to *The Poetry Review*, Arundel del Re, Brooke, Wilfrid Gibson (1878–1962) a published poet who had featured in *The Poetry Review* of January 1912, John Drinkwater (1882–1937) and Lascelles Abercrombie (1881–1938) also published poets, were present at a lunch party on 20 September, the day after the idea had first been discussed. Monro was already known to Marsh, although at first Marsh had not got a high opinion of *The Poetry Review*. Marsh had written an article and appreciation of Brooke's *Poems 1911* for the April 1912 edition of *The Poetry Review*, when *Poems 1911* had been chosen as 'Book of the Month'.

The proposed anthology had to have a title and, not without some dissent, the title *Georgian Poetry* was decided upon. The use of the term 'Georgian Poetry' has been credited first of all to Monro, when he decided that the title aptly described himself and A.K. Sabin (1879–1959) in June 1911.[1526] A.K. Sabin was on the staff of the Victoria and Albert Museum. Marsh took on the job of editor of *Georgian Poets 1911/12*, although Monro would have preferred to have had that job himself. Monro, instead, had to take on the more practical task of making the volume pay its way. Marsh had guaranteed against financial loss. The decision was taken to publish five hundred copies, at 3s.6d. each, in time for Christmas. Monro, at this stage, was cautious about sales. Monro was to get half the royalties, with Marsh dividing the remaining half equally between all contributors. *Georgian Poetry* in all its editions was to be a fantastic success.[1527]

By the time of Flecker's twenty-eighth birthday on 5 November, the proofs had arrived and Marsh sat up until the early hours to correct them. One error not corrected was Marsh's statement in the preface that two years ago some of the represented writers had published nothing. This was not strictly true if poems published in magazines were taken into consideration. In Flecker's case, Marsh may not have known about *The Bridge of Fire* published in 1907. Rupert Brooke's *Poems 1911* was just out, but his poetry had already appeared in magazines. Another contributor, Edmund Beale Sargant, also published his volume of verse in 1911, but other contributors had got their work into the public domain before 1911. Seventeen poets were featured in *Georgian Poetry 1911/12.* These were: Lascelles Abercrombie, Gordon Bottomley, Rupert Brooke, Gilbert Chesterton, W.H. Davies, Walter de la Mare, John Drinkwater, James Elroy Flecker, W.W. Gibson, D.H. Lawrence, John Masefield, Harold Monro, T. Sturge Moore, Ronald Ross, Edmund Beale Sargant, James Stephens and R.C. Trevelyan.

The task of researching the lives and published works of all seventeen poets was a task that Marsh could not do successfully in the time available. Monro was also busy and in November 1912, he told readers of *The Poetry Review* that he would be opening on 1 January 1913 a 'Poetry Shop'. The Poetry Bookshop at 35 Devonshire Street (renamed Boswell Street in 1938), off Theobalds Road near the British Museum, was in operation before the opening performed by Henry Newbolt on 8 January.

Monro told his readers that he had leased the whole of an eighteenth-century house, where, besides his Bookshop, the offices of *The Poetry Review* would be housed, lectures would be held, rooms would be let cheaply to sympathisers and a sort of informal Guild would be established. Monro felt that the old-fashioned bookseller had almost disappeared to be replaced by the 'Universal Provider in literature and the Newsagent'. Monro thought that secondhand booksellers alone remained as a relic.

The November issue of *The Poetry Review* also contained six poems by Rupert Brooke, which included 'The Old Vicarage, Grantchester' (Café des Westens, Berlin, May 1912), criticism by Lascelles Abercrombie, stretching to two pages, of a book of poetry by 'Q' and a review of *History of English Prose Rhythm* by George Saintsbury. The Correspondence section printed a long letter, taking up two pages, from Rupert Brooke in which a footnote to an article by Ezra Pound on 'A Selection from *The Tempers*' by William Carlos Williams was discussed. The footnote, Brooke felt, was suggesting that the poetry of Lascelles Abercrombie was 'worthless'. Brooke defended Abercrombie, describing him amongst other things as having signs of 'a high and rare genius'. Brooke quoted over forty lines of Abercrombie's work.

The December issue of *The Poetry Review,* which was entirely devoted to the publication of poems, included Flecker's poem 'Art' (which he later revised as 'The Painter's Mistress').[1528]

On 30 October, Flecker had written to Mavro telling him that he was to leave 'this cursed place' on 10 November, and giving him the address of his mother-in-law in Paris where Mavro was to send the proofs of 'Gates of Damascus'. Flecker hoped to see Mavro on 1 December.

Flecker's birthday (so soon after writing about 'this cursed place') was a day that Mavro would envy. Angela had prepared a delicious lunch of wild duck, cooked in the Greek manner with green olives and tomatoes. Jasmine and roses were in bloom under a clear sky and at such a time some regret was expressed that they had opted for the cold and damp of an English winter. However many times Flecker had cursed the East, he had also had adventures, which he hoped would impress his grandchildren. He felt that the East had 'unearthly beauty' and was not only merely pretty, as a man may find Naples or Palermo, 'but deeper violet, the splendour and desolation of the Levant waters, is something that drives into the soul'.[1529]

On 10 November 1912, the Fleckers loaded up their numerous pieces of baggage and drove down from Areiya to Beirut harbour to board the slow steamer for Alexandria. En route, the vessel put in at Jaffa, where they went ashore to enjoy a pleasant lunch on a terrace overlooking the wide expanse of orange groves. This location was in contrast to the quays where Hellé recalled that the stench from numerous camels was only just made bearable by the scent of blossom.

CHAPTER ELEVEN

At Port Said, the stewards on board got news that the Greek army had taken Salonika from the Turks. The captain of their steamer was English but the stewards were mainly Greek and the Greek stewards rushed up to Hellé to tell her the joyful news. The Italo-Turkish War was over but the First Balkan War had broken out.

The late arrival of their steamer at Alexandria resulted in a rush to join the P & O cargo boat just as it was about to leave. The Fleckers were also travelling with two chameleons and only one of these showed any sign of life by the time they had disembarked at Marseilles and travelled to the Hotel du Forum at Arles. The remaining animal (who was suffering from the cold) did not revive sufficiently when they lit a fire. This one died the morning after they arrived in Paris, the 20 November. The stay in France had been prolonged to include a visit to Les Baux and a view of Avignon. Also, on the day after their arrival, chez Mme. Skiadaressi at 10 rue Marche, Neuilly, Flecker wrote to Mavro to remind him that he would be in London on Thursday 28 November. He had already written from Beirut to Mavro to ask him to send on to Paris the proofs of 'Gates of Damascus'. In the PS to his Paris letter[1530] Flecker told Mavro: 'Make *ER* publish 'Gates of Damascus' after a journey from Beirut to Paris state of finances appalling.'

It was a disappointment to find that Mavro had already left *The English Review*, although some comfort might have been found (at least by Hellé) that Mavro's absence was due to the fact that he was reporting inside Salonika, for the *Westminster Gazette*, the Greek Army's triumph. Flecker had previously told Mavro that he was 'the only person who seems to take an interest in this unfortunate poet.'[1531]

On the 28 November, when he had hoped to see Mavro at *The English Review*, he saw instead Norman Douglas. Douglas decided that he liked Flecker much better than he did Brooke, who was also a visitor to the ER. Douglas (as has already been seen) said that he knew that Flecker was consumptive and not well off, but whether he was told these facts by Flecker himself when they met at *The English Review* offices is not clear. Douglas does not say whether or not he also knew Flecker had been a

467

pupil at Uppingham, as was Douglas (although at different times). 'The Gates of Damascus' was not published by *The English Review* but (as has also been seen) Douglas blamed Harrison for keeping manuscripts for 'an unreasonable length of time'.

Flecker could not have spent much time with Douglas at *The English Review* because he spent a short time that same morning seeing Lord Dufferin about a transfer to the General Service. The Secretary of State for Foreign Affairs gave Flecker the impression that he could apply to be transferred without undergoing any more examinations. But transfer to the General Service could mean transfer to Russia or Morocco. This was almost all that Lord Dufferin could decide without first finding out what his administrators would say further down the chain of command.

On the same day, 28 November, Flecker wrote from the hotel he was staying in (Brown's Private Hotel, Craven Street, Charing Cross), giving his permanent address for his leave as Dean Close School. The purpose of his letter was to find out whether or not his period of leave could be counted from 20 November, allowing for one day travelling from Paris to London, which was the day of his arrival in Paris, and not 10 November, the day of his leaving Beirut.[1532] The timing and wording of this letter was useful. The FO at first did not see his application as an extension of his period of leave.

Next day (29 November) Flecker went to the Admiralty to see Edward Marsh. He had two purposes in mind, one was to get Marsh to use his influence to get him a post outside the Consular Service. A.C. Benson, who was on the Cambridge Appointments Board, was the person to target. The second purpose was to interest Marsh in *Hassan*, which he did successfully and Marsh offered to let Granville Barker see it when the ms. was typed.[1533] Even in this short meeting, Flecker was up against unfavourable comparison with Brooke. Marsh wrote to Brooke on the same day, 29 November, and described his encounter with Flecker.[1534] He told Brooke that Syria bored Flecker 'stiff' and also: 'There is much to be said against his exterior, but I hope to see him more at length when he comes back, and to get over it....'. Marsh went on to tell Brooke that the night before, he had been to see Masefield get the Polignac Prize, in the company of Gosse, de la Mare, Newbolt and Sturge Moore, amongst other poets. Flecker left the Admiralty to have lunch with Monro of *The Poetry Review*. It may have been Monro who was instrumental in letting him have 'a little general reviewing work'. This was how he described it in a letter to Hellé (the sentence follows the one where he mentioned lunching with Monro). In comparison with the meetings with Marsh, Flecker may not have been able to see how equally, if not more so, Monro would be useful in conjunction with the Poetry Bookshop in publishing Flecker's works.[1535] Flecker must have also met Arundel del Re. Re described James Elroy Flecker as 'a mysterious, impassible, eastern-looking figure with a smouldering flame in his dark eyes'.[1536]

His letter to Hellé was full of descriptions of his isolation and loneliness because he had received no letter from her.[1537] He had sent her a loving message on the evening of his arrival in London and written the next day to tell her of his unhappiness and how he cried in the cinema but clapped his hands at the film on the Greek army. All this emotional blackmail was leading up to telling Hellé that he was going to stay with Beazley in Oxford. The mention of Beazley was enough to arouse Hellé's jealousy, as was the news that he had left London earlier than had been decided upon. Hellé was not well enough to travel to London and she would have preferred that he came back instead to Paris. She was going to come to London as soon as she had got over her cold. She urged him not to be too pessimistic about his failure to get a firm offer of a suitable post.

If Hellé was aware of the sentiment expressed in his letter to Savery from Beirut a few months before, in which he wrote that 'even Oxford would bore me, alone',[1538] she would realise that this visit to Oxford would not help to raise his spirits. She had no real reason to feel jealous of Beazley any more. Flecker found Beazley in an even more pessimistic frame of mind than his own. Despite the fact that Beazley's quality of life was much better at this time than his own, Flecker felt obliged to give his old friend a little toy woodpecker (to keep his pecker up?). The underlying cause of Beazley's pessimism was not explained but Beazley could have shared the conclusion of A.C. Benson, although he was writing about Cambridge and not Oxford:

> I feel now that the mistake I have made in coming up to Cambridge was to feel that people here lived in an intellectual atmosphere. They do not – they live in affairs and gossip. They hate their work, I often think, and have few other interests. I believe my own intellectual temperature is higher than the average here.'[1539]

It was around this time that Beazley fell in love with his future wife, but the prospect of marriage seemed impossible as the woman concerned was already married. The fact of Flecker having got married (and even if Hellé was not with him and he did not enjoy the period of temporary celibacy) still put up a barrier between himself and Beazley, who could in the circumstances look forward to a period of permanent celibacy. The question of Flecker now being a married man could also put a barrier between himself and Leonard Cheesman, who was at Christ Church for a year after winning the Arnold Prize in 1911, and whom Flecker now also met. Cheesman was unsure whether he himself would ever marry. Oxford was the centre of Cheesman's universe and accounts of Flecker's adventures abroad would seem to be very remote from his Oxford surroundings. The main cause of disagreement with Cheesman was about the First Balkan War. Cheesman was on the side of the Bulgarians and he did not share Flecker's enthusiasm for the Greek cause.[1540] It was said that Cheesman knew more about the drill of a Roman legion than a modern British platoon. Flecker's first-hand experiences of conflict in the Levant and his support for the Greek side, reinforced by his marriage to Hellé, set him apart from Cheesman even before any heated discussion had begun. The fervour Flecker felt for the Greek cause was evident in his poem 'For Christmas 1912', which he later revised as 'A Sacred Dialogue'.[1541]

This poem was found among Cheesman's possessions but not included in a letter, which indicates that it was given to Cheesman during Flecker's visit to Oxford.[1542]

'For Christmas 1912' could have been written for *The Nation*, which had asked for and published a Christmas poem of Flecker's more than once. 'For Christmas 1912' is written in dialogue between Christ and the Bishop of Bethlehem and the poem's war references could have rendered it unacceptable for publication at that time. The poem contains the lines:

Christ:

'Peace and good-will the world may sing:
But we shall talk of war!

How fare the armies of the North?'

The Bishop:

'They wait, victorious peace.
All the high forts of Macedon
Fly the proud flags of Greece.' [1543]

When the revised version of 'For Christmas 1912' was published in *Collected Poems* in 1916 it was given the new title 'A Sacred Dialogue' (Christmas 1912) and a Note by the author added.[1544]

Conflict of a more personal kind broke out when Hellé received a telegram on Monday, 2 December, informing her he was on his way to Dean Close. Hellé was amazed; the arrangement was for them to go together to Cheltenham with future plans agreed upon. She wrote and told her husband so, and wanted to know what had brought about the change of plan because she had hoped that he would have returned to London first. She guessed that because he had decided to go to Cheltenham without her, it meant that neither Oxford nor London visits had resulted in the promises of a reasonably alternative well-paid post. She saw no reason for her to come over to London at this stage.

One reason why he had no firm offer of alternative work was that he might not have seen Professor Raleigh (now Sir Walter Raleigh: he was knighted in 1911). Flecker may have been referred through Raleigh to other people. A letter from Raleigh dated 9-12-1912, to H.H. Turner, states: 'Very many thanks for your kindness to Flecker. I hope Lindsay understands him. His appearance and impression disaffects all disciplinarians. But he's all right, in the wide world.' [1545]

As a result of this visit to Oxford, a lectureship at Nottingham University College had been considered but the salary of £210 was thought by Flecker to be too low. Marsh had already told Brooke that Flecker was 'off to see Raleigh and try to get a Professorship of Literature out of him'.[1546] This sort of hope would be much too unrealistic from the point of view of the seniority of the post. The salary of a professor at Nottingham University College would be £400, attractive, but not within Raleigh's gift. Another drawback to the consideration of the Nottingham post was the fact that it did not become available until September 1913. Even if he reconsidered the Nottingham post, the salary would not compensate him for the repressive lingering Victorian atmosphere of Nottingham University College. The cramped quarters of the College would be reminiscent of Uppingham.[1547]

Flecker was in no position to pick and choose, and his stipulation that he would not live on £350 a year in England stated in a letter to Savery,[1548] dated 26 July 1912, prevented his accepting a lower salary and limited his choice of suitable posts.

Hellé would have preferred that her husband first returned to Paris. She still felt too ill to travel and she knew that unless they arrived together at Cheltenham and presented a united front, then winning any arguments against the elder Fleckers would be difficult. The precise reasons why he went to Cheltenham at this juncture are not made clear.

But this trip to Europe was proving to be very expensive and tiring. The pain of separation from Hellé and his dislike of being on his own would be eased a little at Dean Close. He arrived at Cheltenham exhausted and spent some of his time resting. *Hassan* was still on his mind and he wrote to Marsh[1549] explaining that he had stupidly left some dull papers in the waiting-room at the Admiralty. He was having the Second Act of *Hassan* typed and he was going to send Marsh the First and Second Act in the course of the week with a synopsis of the Third. He suggested that 'if you yourself think they are worth bothering Barker about, you might do so'. He also suggested sending his appointment application through Marsh to A.C. Benson. Flecker also requested a copy of *Georgian Verse* [sic] from Marsh.

Flecker had never liked coming to stay at Dean Close in term-time. Even if the fact that it was term-time did not upset him too much he would find that Dean Close was not a warm and cheerful place. When the *Gloucestershire Echo* reviewed his *Thirty-Six Poems* in May 1910, the paper had commented: 'Despite its spiritual and educational advantages... Cheltenham must at times be a rather sad place to the young – that is, if they possess any imagination'. Flecker's nephew, John Sherwood, wrote: 'I remember the famous rose garden only in its winter aspect, weak and inhospitable.'[1550]

Flecker's poem, written in July 1905,[1551] which he gave the title 'A Garden Where Love Died', (although not for the season when the roses would be blooming, and his love for Hellé had not died) illustrates Flecker's unhappy feelings against the background of the Dean Close garden. In the third verse of 'A Garden Where Love Died', the first line reads: 'Stir, stir your listless wings, sweet naked boy!'

In a photograph of the Dean Close rose-garden[1552] there is a statue, which could be the one Flecker refers to in this line. Flecker's thoughts at being home again could resemble those of Mabina Pastorelli (née Mabel Collins, the character Firbank based on Flecker, in his novel *Inclinations*) when, after her marriage in Athens and her life in Italy, she returns alone to her old home and she sees 'the fine old carpet stained with tulips, and the familiar text upon the lightly figured walls, ... and the medicine chest above the rocking chair... 'It's a joy to have no mosquitoes!'

And later:

> The Yew-tree walk, the cause of so much gloom, ran ring-
> like about the house, to meet again before the drawing-
> room windows above the main road, where a marble nymph

with a worn flat face dispensed water, rather meanly, out of a cornucopia into a trough full of green scum.' [1553]

'It's pretty peaceful here anyway,' Miss Dawkins said, with a sigh, her eyes riveted upon the cornucopia of the niggardly nymph.

'Is it iron?' she enquired.

'What, the water? It's always rather brown...'

Miss Dawkins pressed a hand to her hip.

'It looks like a stream of brandy,' she said, going off into a laugh. [1554]

One practical reason for returning to Dean Close at this particular time was to see if the FO had granted him an extension of his leave.

Time to brood on his life during the brief respite at Dean Close was cut short by his departure to meet Hellé and be reunited on her arrival from Paris, in London on 7 December. He must have spent time in London, because a letter from Flecker from Brown's Hotel, dated 'Thursday', could refer to 5 December. In it, Flecker tells Marsh that he will try and come round tomorrow evening at 11. If he did not get there by 11.30, Marsh was not to expect him. He told Marsh he would be in Oxford on Sunday.[1555]

On Saturday 7 December, he and Hellé went first to Oxford and stayed in his former lodgings, 170 Walton Street, where his landlady was a good cook. From this address he wrote to Marsh at All Souls' College, Oxford, telling him that 'We shall be in at six o'clock and hope to see you'.

Marsh and the Fleckers must have met up in Oxford. In a letter to Brooke, who was home from Berlin by 8 December, Marsh told him about the problems with the printers handling *Georgian Poetry*, who were not fulfilling their promise to deliver 500 copies by 1 December thereby delaying the publication date, and so giving *The Oxford Book of Victorian Verse* the opportunity to upstage *Georgian Poetry*. Marsh told Brooke that he had been seeing Flecker, 'whom I like, and his wife is a nice pretty woman'. [1556]

Besides seeing Marsh, the Fleckers went round Trinity and saw his old rooms. Hellé later stated that her husband was delighted to be back in Oxford 'again'. This gives the impression (because she did not add 'so soon') that he had not been back in Oxford in the week that they had been apart. Hellé went on to say that her husband was in high spirits, which would send a hidden message to anyone who was aware of the true sequence of events, that being in Oxford with her was a much happier experience compared to his recent reunion with his male friends. If this was a message and not just a lapse of memory, it was in keeping with the spirit that lay between the lines of her published account of her life with her husband. Hellé was always discreet and not openly disloyal in print to her husband's close friends and family. Many reasons, both practical and emotional, compelled her to adopt this line, not least was the fact that by the time her book was published most of the people she was writing about were still alive. They would not be in total agreement with the views expressed if these were of a very personal nature. It is with this in mind, that it is as well to note the one sentence that Hellé devoted to the next part of the journey from Oxford to stay at Dean Close and compare it with the many sentences and paragraphs devoted to other less significant journeys. She wrote briefly: 'We went to stay with his parents at Cheltenham for a few days, and then returned to London.' [1557]

Thus Hellé's first-hand impressions of her in-laws, Dean Close and Cheltenham are not in her book. The little space devoted to what must have been an important time in her married life, gets little mention, perhaps for the same reason that her wedding day gets little mention, simply because it did not live up to her dreams and expectations, even those she had before her husband went first to visit Dean Close, leaving her in Paris. Hellé could not have had many illusions about the atmosphere of life at Dean Close, even for a short period, and even if 10 December, when they were at Dean Close, was Dr. Flecker's birthday. The purpose of the visit, besides the obvious one of welcoming Hellé into the bosom of the Flecker family (beforehand Hellé was told 'You will find as much of a loving father and mother as you will permit'[1558]), was also to be the question of sorting out her husband's future so that he did not need to return to the Levant.

On 10 December, Flecker was writing his letter to the Secretary of State for Foreign Affairs, Lord Dufferin, in which he applied for transfer to the general service. This neatly written and well thought out gives the reader the impression that it was written with Hellé looking over his shoulder. The letter was headed Dean Close School, Cheltenham, and he began by begging 'to observe with the deepest respect' that it was 'the first time to the best of his knowledge, that the warning after a first failure in a final exam had been issued'. [This was the warning that if he did not pass the exam when taken again in May, he would have to leave the service.] He pointed out that in a country where Turkish lessons were difficult to obtain and where only Arabic was spoken, he was at a disadvantage in acquiring sufficient knowledge of the language. He also made the point that, with the capture of Tripoli and the possible partition of Macedonia, fewer consular officials with a knowledge of

Turkish would be required. He hoped that if he had failed as a Turkish scholar, he had not failed in his duties as Acting Vice-Consul at Beirut, either generally or on special occasions of difficulty and danger.

On the question of his health, Flecker alleged that it had been 'permanently enfeebled at Constantinople', although at present his health was excellent. He wanted consideration given to his financial position and stated that he would not be able to go back to Beirut without an allowance for an outfit and travelling expenses. He declared himself 'seriously unfitted by temperament for life in the East.' He asked for his leave to be extended from 20 December to 3 January, to enable 'my wife to have a chance of recovering her health'.[1559] Flecker, at the time of writing this letter, had not yet received confirmation that he could extend his leave to include his travelling time, as requested in the letter written from Brown's Hotel on 28 November. Time had to be allowed for telegrams to go to and be replied to from Beirut. Flecker did not know at this stage that Cumberbatch would not change his mind about not wanting to let him extend his period of leave, a fact which Cumberbatch had already made known to the FO on 17 September. It was these bureaucratic trip-wires across his path (in his attempt to try and change direction in the Consular Service or leave it altogether) that made the discussions, which were said to have taken place at this time at Dean Close, rather pointless. He had to return to Beirut and the best he could gain from letters to his superiors was a brief respite in which he could try to alter the course of his life. But short of resigning from the Levant Consular Service and risking the loss of the £500 bond, he had to return to Beirut. Even if Dr. Flecker was prepared to concede the loss of the £500, the problem remained of how he could support himself and Hellé until alternative paid work could be found. Flecker's parents had their own long-term future to consider, as well as the short-term future of their elder son. Unless Dr. Flecker thought he could stay on at Dean Close indefinitely, he had to face retirement, which would mean he and his wife finding a home and some sort of extra income not dependent on his pension. James Elroy was not the only child whose health was poor. Claire, now aged twenty-five, had never been in good health and she was pregnant. She and her clergyman husband were now, in 1913, waiting for the birth of the first of their three children. After she left Cheltenham Ladies' College, Claire took a BA degree at London University. Her husband started a theological college after resigning his headmastership. Claire took a London diploma in Theology and she lectured in the college started by her husband. The next sister, Joyce, also went to Cheltenham Ladies' College; she was five years younger than her sister and went there when she was twelve. She obtained a Class 1 in the external London Pass BSc, which was something that her mother thought that she should not be congratulated upon.[1560] The younger son, Oswald, was still a pupil at Dean Close; he was sixteen and not destined for Uppingham like his elder brother. The other Flecker brother and sisters were still at a stage in their lives when they could be expected to involve their parents in the day to day concerns of their lives.

The amount of space devoted (in the LIFE) to this short stay at Dean Close reflects the importance attached to the decisions that were said to have been made at the time. The conclusion (made with hindsight) was that Flecker should not have been advised to return to the Levant. One sentence stands on its own in the book: in the chapter dealing with Flecker and his wife's brief return to Dean Close: 'A small income, with no conditions whatever attached, was Flecker's real need.' [1561]

The income would need to be large if it was to keep both Flecker and his wife in some degree of comfort for an unspecified time. If the income came from the elder Fleckers' purse, it would need to have some conditions attached, unless they could break the long-standing arguments over what was, in their eyes, a necessity and what was a luxury. It was stated, after the sentence about the small income, that 'his parents proposed to provide him with a small home and income – Brighton was suggested'. But it was next stated, 'It was thought that with such basal security he might be able to earn what he needed beyond it'. Then it is stated 'Various circumstances made the acceptance of this offer just then not feasible'. The 'various circumstances' are not explained in the text.

The true facts about a firm offer of a home and income was that the offer was made, not in December 1912, four months later. This offer was supposed to have been rejected also in December 1912, it was said 'under the influence of his money-grabbing Paris relatives'.[1562] But Flecker's mother was persuaded not to publish these references to her son's in-laws because of the contradiction to the written evidence.

Also in the pages devoted (in the LIFE), reference is made to a place at a Teachers' Training College, which is not named, but because Nottingham University College was also a Teachers' Training College the place referred to could have been for teaching and not training. The opinion then given was that, although Flecker was always 'eager to serve youth', an elementary Training College would not be the right place for Flecker. He had been a success as a schoolteacher, although the time spent in that profession was brief. In *The Grecians* he described the modern schoolmaster as social outcast or a social failure.

The masters Flecker envisaged for La Giocosa would not be treated as subordinates, but as honourable friends of the headmaster. They were to have every chance of visiting London and many more privileges. If Dr. Flecker had offered as a solution to the problem, the post of master at Dean Close along the lines of the posts offered to the masters in *The Grecians*, then problems of Flecker also being the headmaster's son would be fraught with even more double standards than during his time as the pupil and son of the headmaster. The prospect of Hellé sharing the Flecker living quarters and domestic duties with her mother-in-law would not work out satisfactorily. The idea of Hellé helping the Dean Close schoolboys with Greek lessons, along the lines of her mother-in-law's Hebrew lessons, would throw up similar difficulties.

However, at one time, Flecker had suggested to his father that he came to Dean Close as an assistant master. The published part of the letter[1563] does not give dates but merely states that this was 'at one time'. What is interesting is that Flecker did not propose to model himself along the lines of the schoolmasters of his ideal vision in *The Grecians*. Instead, he stated to his father that he would get on 'smoothly' with other masters and be unobtrusive in his views and manners. He only wants 'some small form'. To this suggestion, the author of the book where the letter was printed makes the comment: 'This would obviously have been quite impossible.' This discussion about being taken on as an assistant master (on probation) could have taken place before the positive diagnosis of consumption and before Flecker's marriage. The same sort of discussion could not have been taken seriously in December 1912, because to introduce a master who was suffering from consumption into Dean Close would have been disastrous from the point of view of the health of the other pupils. The elder Fleckers had not faced up to the fact of their son's 'grave illness', as it is described when referring to this period.[1564] It is stated in the LIFE[1565] that 'the deadly severity of his illness was not realised for so long, practically by some not until the end came, it is clear that he must have suffered great physical misery, while he actually said very little about it.' If 'some' referred to those outside his immediate family, then it was not surprising that they did not realise how ill Flecker was 'until the end came'. But those in his immediate family must have had some realisation of the 'severity' of his illness, however much they denied it to themselves at the time. Otherwise, the 'small income, with no conditions attached', would not be so important: the income was needed not so much because it would help what the LIFE described as 'the prime business of artistic achievement', but because he was too ill to do any work that would have brought in a reasonable salary.

Hellé, when in discussion about their joint financial future, could not be wholly on her husband's side. In relation to her husband's attitude to spending money, she could not help but sympathise with her in-laws; namely that they were not prepared to hold out a safety-net when he faced financial difficulties, his state of health notwithstanding. Hellé had herself already provided her husband with a share of her own money, and that provision had to be curtailed simply because (like her in-laws) she did not have a bottomless pit of money. The elder Fleckers had married under similar burdens of ill-health and lack of cash as had their son and daughter-in-law. Flecker's father, if he had looked back and made comparisons, would have realised that he had been more persistent than his son when it came to getting a schoolmaster's post and he also took on private pupils. The parents of the elder Fleckers were reluctant to give their consent to the marriage of William and Sarah Flecker. William had gone back to early morning school the morning after his wedding. No honeymoon in Greece or anywhere else beckoned the new Mrs. Flecker. She had coached her young sister-in-law and she took a post as a daily governess. She and her husband had found difficulty in paying the rent and had looked for a smaller house. This unspoken criticism (that her son and his wife should have taken more trouble to curb their expenditure) would be difficult to point out, now some of the money spent was Hellé's own. It was much more likely that a remark of the 'Do you have Brussels sprouts in Greece?' Firbankian variety would cause more friction that any suggestions about how money should be spent.[1566] The money question hinged on the expenditure necessary on leaving the Levant and establishing themselves back again permanently in England. It is stated[1567] that after Hellé joined her husband at Dean Close (no mention of visits to Oxford) 'he did not at once discuss his wish to come home permanently to England'. Also he was quoted as writing that he was 'horrified at the prospect of endless years at Beyrouth,' and 'Nottingham is a deadly prospect too.' This reference was explained as a 'possible lectureship at Nottingham University College'.[1568] Flecker was torn between the advantages and disadvantages of living in Beirut. This was the sort of dilemma he had outlined in his poem 'Oak and Olive'. One disadvantage of moving back to England permanently was the influence of his parents. His coming home again would awake memories of past gloom and sadness that the family home evoked in him. Hellé, too, already knew what life at Dean Close could be before she married into the family. She had received two years before an account of his stay when he had felt driven 'into sheer hysteria' by 'family strife' and 'rigid Evangelism'. The cold of a northern winter in Paris had previously broken her serenity. She did not understand how such a climate could make anyone 'proper' and she thought that the climate was only good for 'hardworking brutes'.[1569] It was still term-time during Hellé's visit and although they could not be described as 'brutes' the masters at Dean Close were still working hard and headed by Dr. Flecker, in gown and mortar board, carrying out his responsibilities for teaching religion in the school while his wife was still controlling the domestic side. The long-serving masters on the teaching staff, such as Hellér Nicholls and T.M.A. Cooper, were also still teaching but may have had time to speak to the new Mrs. Flecker. Hellé at least knew something about them already. Judson of the 'Ballad of Hampstead Heath' was still there also. Meeting the rest of the teaching staff at Dean Close could have been an enjoyable part of Hellé's visit. The fact that in the account of her stay at Dean Close (although much space was devoted in the LIFE to the number of discussions that were supposed to have gone on about her husband's future), the amount of space devoted to Hellé is almost as short as the amount of space devoted to this visit published in her account. It was stated in the LIFE: 'His wife crossed from France and joined him, thus, at last, meeting his family. Their stay was very short....'[1570]

Hellé would leave Dean Close with few regrets, not least that she had not brought her mother with her as had been suggested. The period between leaving England for Paris on Christmas Eve and their departure from Cheltenham was spent at 12 Dorset Square, London. Flecker's most important day in this period was his accepting Marsh's 'kind invitation' to lunch and going round to the 'Golden Ship' with his dramatic works under his arm. He was so flustered at this luncheon that he left with the copy of his dramatic work still in his pocket.

Marsh soon received Acts I and II and the synopsis of *Hassan* with a letter telling him that he had got fixed up to review 'your book [*Georgian Poetry*] for the *E. Review*.' In the next letter to Marsh he made apologies and asked him to send back Act II and not bother to register it. Marsh at this time was very busy getting *Georgian Poetry* from the printers. By the 16 December, only 250 of the promised 500 copies had arrived. Orders were flowing in and all but 50 copies sold or sent for review. Despite his involvement with *Georgian Poetry* and the fact that Flecker had previously written to Marsh to say that he had not got time to go and see Rupert Brooke, Marsh's apartment was the place for a reunion with Brooke. After dinner, Flecker copied out 'Yasmin' into Marsh's book of manuscript poems by poets of the day.

Marsh had got Granville Barker interested in *Hassan* and the Fleckers went to see Barker's production of *Twelfth Night*. It was while watching the production that tears rolled down Flecker's cheeks; the only time

Hellé had seen him so moved by a theatrical production.[1571] She did not say why this particular production caused such an emotional reaction. Barker's productions of the plays of Shakespeare (he had previously produced at the same theatre a production of *The Winter's Tale*) were not in the mould of the popular traditional productions of Sir Herbert Beerbohm Tree. The only published reference to this production of *Twelfth Night* made by Flecker was in a letter to Marsh when he wrote that he and Hellé 'were quite overwhelmed by its excellence'.[1572] An explanation of Flecker's emotional reaction to Barker's production of Shakespeare could be found in Firbank's novel *Vainglory,* when the narrator gives the experience of the poet Claud Harvester who had seen a matinee of *The Winter's Tale.* This experience of Harvester was said to have been linked to Firbank's seeing Barker's 1912 production.[1573]

Firbank wrote of his Flecker-type Claud Harvester: '... he had been into Arcadia, even, a place where artificial temperaments so seldom get – their nearest approach being, perhaps, a matinee of *The Winter's Tale.* Many, indeed, thought him interesting. He had groped so... In the end he began to suspect that what he had been seeking for all along was the theatre. He had discovered the truth in writing plays.' [1574]

Claud Harvester was, like Flecker, both poet, an 'almost successful novelist, author of one play'. The truth can be seen: Flecker also discovered at this stage of his involvement with *Hassan* that the staging of *Hassan* could become a reality. But Flecker's reactions could be mixed; he wanted *Hassan* to run for ten thousand nights but he knew his efforts so far had failed to get any prospect of it running at all, even for one night. He needed to stay in England if he wanted to succeed with *Hassan.* Even if he could manage to stay in England, he needed to get work, which would then prevent him from working even harder on his play. He needed to stay there if he was to have a real chance to get the acclaim for *Hassan,* which he felt it deserved.

Flecker was not the only poet overwhelmed by Barker's production. John Masefield, after he saw the productions of *Twelfth Night* and *The Winter's Tale* because he greatly admired Barker's style and the encouragement given by Barker to his own playwriting, then decided that he must adopt a similar presentation for the play he started writing in 1913. The influence of Barker on Masefield, whose play was based on a legend in the history of Japan, was the sort of practical and emotional influence Barker had on Flecker's *Hassan.*

Flecker's mind was not wholly on *Hassan* during this part of his stay in England. Journalism as an option, in order to supplement his income, was said to have been discussed at Dean Close. One article he wrote with the address given as Dean Close School (which was cancelled out and

12 Dorset Square substituted) was entitled 'The New French Spirit' and another, giving his mother-in-law's address as the one where cheques were to be sent, was entitled 'What Insecurity in Turkey means with some general reflections on the impending Armenian question'.[1575]

It was important, after the Fleckers in a depressed state left England, to write to Marsh from Paris and let him know how well they thought of Barker's production of *Twelfth Night* because Marsh had what Flecker described as 'The hope of my life, ... in your hands'. He was longing to hear what Marsh thought of it, as well as Henry Ainley (the actor in both *The Winter's Tale* and *Twelfth Night*) and Barker. It was prudent to make sure that Barker knew that Flecker was a great admirer of his work and had seen it in performance. In this letter, Flecker told Marsh that the FO had given him what he described as 'an extension of leave for a fortnight'.

When, on 11 December, his letter arrived at the FO asking for transfer to the general consular service, importance was attached to the period at the end of Flecker's first year at Cambridge when he had been informed that unless there was some improvement in his work, it would not be possible to retain his services. No reference was made to the information the FO received on 16 March 1909,[1576] where it was stated that all the students' work was satisfactory except Mr. Flecker's, whose absences from work had been due to illness. Another student-interpreter, it was also stated, had also been ill but this student-interpreter, it was stated, 'is certainly backward'. It was noted by the official considering Flecker's application for transfer that Flecker's work had 'improved greatly', that Flecker was 'undoubtedly very clever' and he had 'really exerted himself'. The reason why the FO had dug back into Flecker's past history without first considering the rights and wrongs of arguments he had put forward in his letter about his disadvantages in learning Turkish in a country where only Arabic was spoken, is not entirely clear. The FO was still dragging its feet on the question of paying a reasonable salary to those who would lecture in Turkish; the FO was not in a position to contradict him on this point. Also Flecker had stated that fewer consular officials would be required in future, and the FO did not contradict this statement, which was to prove to be accurate – consular officials of Flecker's sort would eventually disappear altogether. The question of his health being 'permanently enfeebled in Constantinople' was not the main consideration, any more than consideration was given to the fact that it was his health breakdown at Cambridge that had affected his work. No curiosity was shown by the FO as to the nature of this illness.

Without realising that a letter had already been sent from another department (as a result of Flecker's letter from Brown's hotel on 28

November, requesting an extension of leave) informing him that he would have to return to Beirut at the end of his month's leave, the FO granted an extension of Flecker's leave until 3 January. Some disagreement was recorded on FO memos as to whether this was an extension or just a disregard of the time spent travelling from Beirut to London.

This was the only part of his letter that appeared to have gained him some small advantage. The fact that it was Hellé's health, he had stated, and not his own that needed the extra amount of leave seemed to have turned the tables in his favour, for the moment.

Once in Paris, their moods changed and they spent what Hellé described as a merry Christmas. Jack Beazley was also in Paris and Hellé afterwards wrote that her husband was glad to see him again. She went on to recollect that her husband 'lived once more in his company the old life of a student in the Latin quarter, and in the then still existing Cafe Vachette'.[1577] Hellé does not mention whether she accompanied them, or if duty to her family compelled her to stay at home, or if Beazley was welcome chez Skiadaressi or if, under Beazley's influence, she took her husband to see a doctor in Paris. This doctor, Hellé reported to her in-laws, had said nothing fresh but advised Flecker that he needed special treatment for his larynx. Flecker preferred to wait and see the specialist he knew in Beirut.[1578] Shortly after Christmas on 27 December, Flecker wrote to Monro about publishing the Prologue and Epilogue to the *Golden Journey to Samarkand*. He told Monro that it was no good his saying that he did not like it 'because every one says it's the best poem I (or perhaps anyone else – I borrow this hearty egoism from old John Davidson.....) has ever written'.[1579] He explained to Monro that the Epilogue was written 'as a poem in itself' but that he would turn it into the final scene of my 'Eastern play', of which Marsh now had the first two acts. Flecker wanted Monro to send him three or four little volumes of John Davidson's works so that he could get on with the article on Davidson that Monro had asked him to write. Monro must have also written in favour of the Turks, which judging from Flecker's reply did not go down well. The only consolation Flecker found in returning to the East was the prospect of having 'heaps of time to write'.[1580]

Meanwhile Hellé was keeping up an exchange of correspondence with Dean Close. She now addressed her mother-in-law as 'Dear Mother' instead of 'Dear Mrs. Flecker'.[1581] This change did not prevent further disagreement arising between them. This was due to Hellé's doctor advising her to stay away from the Levant for a period and not return to Beirut at the same time as her husband. But Flecker had been advised by his doctor to go back to Beirut for the sake of his health. Hellé's health problems went back to the time of her honeymoon during the summer of 1911, when mosquito bites she suffered gave rise to what appeared to be relapses of malaria in Beirut less than a year later and in Paris several months after that. The elder Fleckers could argue about where Hellé's wifely duties came in the order of events and whether or not her health problems came second to her husband's needs. But in line with A.C. Benson's views, the elder Fleckers felt that the fact of Hellé being Greek made the FO 'badly disposed' towards their son.[1582] Hellé was able to put them right in a letter she wrote at this time. She stated that if she had known of opposition to their marriage she would not have gone against it'.[1583] No basis existed for the elder Fleckers' side of the argument because those in the FO (who had power over his future progress but did not know Flecker personally) knew that he was married not the fact that his wife was Greek. A posting to Athens, if it had come about, would have been helped by having a Greek wife. It was Flecker's failure to do well in the examinations that eventually made the FO 'badly disposed' towards him, as well as the fact that his health was poor. It was not recognised in time by the FO that the illness was TB.

Whether it was as a result of his receiving the Foreign Office's decision (taken on 20 December) that Flecker's 'request for a transfer to the General Service cannot be entertained,' but Flecker wrote with bitterness to his father on 30 December 30th: 'I am so disheartened. It is my tragedy. I have got to go back to Beirut alone, possibly to die. No one will do anything for me.' [1584]

He told his father in this letter also: 'If you had the slightest idea of the difficulties of living in the East, as we have tried,[1585] part of the time on £150[1586] a year, with no fixed home, with a most serious illness, with four weeks' nursing at £2.10[1587] a week and druggist's bill (paid) of £8, with £4 to pay in tips twice a year, with £10 to pay for a season ticket on the rail, and on top of that the awful expense of coming to Europe and now going back you would not think of making such unkind and unfortunate unjust reproaches.'

This was the sort of letter he should have written to the FO, if he had dared, but he must have known it would do more harm than good. Instead, it appeared he took his anger out on his father who may have sent the letter on to Paris from Dean Close, having had permission to open it.

It was true that the elder Fleckers could have 'no idea' of the financial difficulties faced by their son and daughter-in-law, but the difficulties were not of the elder Fleckers' making. The 'no fixed home' was partly as a result of the incident at the German Hotel (which, if not a 'fixed home', was a place to settle in the winter months). If the FO had not suddenly switched Flecker's posting to Beirut, a 'fixed home' (if that could ever be achieved in the Levant Consular Service) might have been more easily available. The expenses of illness listed in the letter to his father could be partly or entirely due to Hellé's recurring bouts of fever. The decision to get married and bring Hellé to the Levant was not something the elder Fleckers had encouraged at the time or had fully accepted; a period of waiting would have been preferable in their eyes. The reference to 'a most serious illness' could have brought about some sort of agreement, although even in this letter the word consumption is not mentioned. It was 'most serious' but, unlike other illnesses, hope of a complete recovery could not now be hoped for and that was at the root of 'the unfortunate unjust reproaches', if only both sides could have fully recognised the facts. But, as in the case of past conflicts between father and son, the letter from his father is missing. This time there is no reference to Flecker having destroyed it.

Flecker must have been in a more hopeful frame of mind when he had got rid of his misery and resentment in this letter to his father, and then wrote to Marsh.[1588] Or, he realised it would not be prudent to draw Marsh into his bitterness against the FO's decision. It was in this letter that Flecker told Marsh about the excellence of Barker's *Twelfth Night*. He also told Marsh that he was 'definitely going to be an Usher in Nottingham next September unless' as he hoped 'something more cheerful turns up.' More importantly, this was the letter in which he told Marsh: 'The hope of my life, which is *Hassan*, is in your hands, my dear Marsh'.

He was 'longing to hear what Ainley thinks of it, still more to hear what Barker hears of it, and no less to hear what you think of it. Do not scruple to tell me bad news and bad opinions.' Flecker sent best love to Rupert and gave Marsh many thanks 'for your great kindness to one as unfortunate as Ovid'. This reference to the Roman poet, whose works included poems on love and exile and mythology and who was banished to the shores of the Black Sea where he died, gave Marsh the message that time was not on Flecker's side. In the letter, Flecker also says that he will write to Benson, which meant that at this stage Benson had not been able to convey any news of a post in England.

Marsh was too busy getting advanced copies out of *Georgian Poetry* to give a lot of consideration to *Hassan*. It was alleged[1589] that *Hassan* gave Marsh more work than any other literary work 'he ever touched'. Marsh's criticisms of *Hassan*, which he sent to Flecker, were the ones with which he told Marsh he honestly agreed with and 'without being merely amiable'.

Flecker told Marsh that he wanted to make the scenes 'more exalted' by making Hassan himself 'more exalted'. He told Marsh that he wanted 'to have plenty of buffoonery – but it should be universal'. He hoped that Marsh would tell anyone he sent *Hassan* to that they were not to despair until 'he reads past Act I, Scene II.' He promised to have the Third Act ready in a month. He was going to leave out 'the further magic scene' that he had planned 'and try and give the beggars a better show'.

The letter that Marsh wrote to Flecker about *Hassan* is not in print but Sherwood states[1590] that Marsh 'had evidently expressed concern about the low comedy tone of the opening scenes'. Also Sherwood states[1591] that the 'incomplete typescript' of the first two Acts must be the one that Flecker left with Marsh in London in December, 1912.[1592] Comparison can be made with the version Marsh first read because some of it is in the Introduction to *Hassan* published in 1922 by J.C. Squire.[1593] The typescript is headed:

The Story of Hassan of Bagdad
And how he came to make the Golden Journey to
Samarkand
A Farce

'And he laughed so, he fell back upon his bottom.'
(Arabian Nights).
'He was seized with inextinguishable laughter.'
(English translation of the same.)

These lines are not in the final published version of the play and they could have been, in part, the 'low comedy' element that Marsh objected to, just as in a letter to Mavrogordato, dated 28 July 1911, he agreed to Mavro 'cutting out the naughty verse about the humanist!' This stanza had the reference to 'their behinds/Impel the astonished nightingales to song.' *Hassan* was subject to a great deal of revision during its creation and whether Flecker did the revision at this time to please Marsh (or Marsh's criticisms tied up in his mind with his own feelings about the way he wanted *Hassan* to change) would be difficult to prove. Or, whether, after seeing Barker's production of *Twelfth Night*, Flecker was spurred on to improve *Hassan* would also be hard to decide but at this stage drastic revisions were made to *Hassan*.

In the first typed draft sent to Marsh there is a list of characters, some of whom finally disappear when Flecker revised this part of the original text. One of the characters who disappeared was the stubbly bearded Yakub, a friend and contemporary of Hassan, dressed in a similar costume. Selim, also described as 'a friend', comes in later and in the final version all Yakub's lines are spoken by the younger Selim. The characters Hassan and Yakub were so similar that this would obviously be confusing to the audience. Also Zachariah, the Jew, appears in the first typed draft but does not appear in person in the published version, although his exploits are recounted by Selim. In the published version Zachariah 'lately arrived from Aleppo' was said by Selim to have caused a stone flung at him to be suspended in mid-air, and the man who had flung the stone 'walked all round Bokhara over the heads of the passers by.' Zac took the dome off the Great Mosque, turned it round, had a bath in it, and put it back again. He turned the whole population into apes for half an hour. In the original version[1594] a demonstration was staged by the plotters in order to persuade Hassan to pay an immense sum for the magic potion that will make Yasmin fall in love with him. Zachariah's powers are shown by Yakub crashing down into the room on a winged donkey. The omission of this visible feat from the final version of *Hassan* could be due to what was to be a future criticism that 'Hassan's' production on stage would not be a commercial proposition.

Also, in the version that Marsh first read, Hassan cannot pay the twenty pieces of gold for the brew of black magic 'that shall bring her running to thy bed: and thereupon thou shalt know the three delights of Paradise, which are, Approach, Fulfilment and Renewal.'

Selim ('in scorn') tells Hassan that twenty dinars is 'The price of a small cow for the love of Leila.' Leila does not appear in the cast list and in this version it is said: [1595] 'there had been a bare mention of a slave-girl Leila who had been stolen from the King of Beggars for the Caliph's harem. Flecker's imagination fastened on this girl, and this episode, no doubt lightly invented in the beginning: and there came into being all the story of Rafi and Pervaneh, and in that story an image of the immense cruelty and courage and beauty of life, a tragic vision that demanded and indeed compelled all the deepest sincerity of the poet's nature for its embodiment.' It would seem that, in the first version, Leila was Hassan's mistress (like the real life Leila Berkely?) but she was not in love with him (also like the real life Leila?). The potion would be tried out on Leila and she is referred to in the final version when Hassan says: 'for assuredly she on whom my heart is bent is not less fair than Leila.'

In the later version of *Hassan* (where Zachariah does not appear in person) the potion is only intended to 'draw her love' when referring to Yasmin. No reference is made to 'running to thy bed'. Thus an obvious reference to Yasmin's sexual passion is left out in favour of a much less crude use of language, but the ghazel, which Hassan intones on his lute to Yasmin, it nevertheless contains the lines: 'And some to Meccah turn to pray, and I toward thy bed, Yasmin,'

At this stage, Flecker did not want to lose the support that Marsh was prepared to give to his revising of *Hassan*. This was evident in the wording of the letters he wrote to Marsh and it was to be hoped that Marsh's suggestions kept pace with what was already going on in Flecker's mind. Marsh's attitude to the phrases used to describe the sexual attraction between men and women was bound to be different from Flecker's. Marsh's attraction was to his own sex.

Flecker took *Hassan* with him when he left Paris, without Hellé, to join the Messageries boat due to leave Marseilles on 9 January. He did not reach Marseilles: deeply depressed, he got off at the first available station and, after an overnight stay, returned to Paris. Hellé, at this point, nearly made up her mind to go back with him despite the risk to her health. If this had happened she would not have been well enough to be able to help her husband. But what Hellé described as good spirits returned and Flecker again set off for Marseilles a week later.

The sea voyage helped what he described to Hellé as 'my beastly larynx'. He also told her that if it had not been for her he would 'have stayed at Naples and lived on macaroni'.[1596] This reference to living cheaply in Naples was hardly a serious consideration when previous efforts to live cheaply in Italy when he was with Beazley had failed.

He was miserable to be back in Greece without Hellé and soon he was forced to leave. He intended, he told Hellé, to finish his novel and work on *Hassan* in Beirut, which would take him to the middle of February. If he was well enough he would get on with his Turkish, if there was no alternative. He wanted her to come by the first boat in March. Another reason for his loneliness in Athens could be due to his failure to meet up with Mavro. He had written to Mavro from Paris on 3 January, suggesting that Mavro, if he could, meet him off the boat. After the boat left Constantinople and headed for Smyrna, Flecker heard what he described as 'the distant rumble of the battle of Lemnos – the one effort made by the Turks to secure mastery of the Aegean'.[1597] He had that morning seen the Turkish fleet ready for battle and lining the entrance to the Dardanelles. But amid the atmosphere of war he described beautifully the surroundings: 'It was one of those indescribable winter days on the Aegean, with a hot sun and a piping breeze: the water was all laced blue and silver, and the windmills of Tenedos whirled fit to break.' [1598]

He wrote poetically that it was near Mytilene when we heard the guns. 'Thrilling enough it was to me – fired with the glory that is Greece – this fight against the Unspeakable for that Greek and Christian sea.' [1599]

He described a trio of American ladies on board 'on their devout way from Athens to Jerusalem'. He hoped to awaken their interest by telling them that men were killing each other, but one of the American women put up her eyeglass 'at me' and said 'Nonsense!' and walked down to lunch.

After that, the boat glided through the beautiful Strait of Mytilene and 'passed the little town buried in olive groves, with its mediaeval castle all on a green lawn, a great Greek flag waved proudly over the scene, its colours blending with the blue and white waves so finely that it was impossible to imagine the Turkish scarlet in its place.' The boat slowed down as it reached the harbour and 'a lot of rough-looking pirates' rowed out and 'shouted to an old Greek priest on board for news'. The old priest told them that he had only heard the noise and seen the smoke. The pirates, hailing a glorious victory, let off their revolvers 'into the windy void'.[1600] However well he could afterwards describe the battle of Lemnos, at the time he told Hellé in a letter it was 'the inevitable naval battle which follows me everywhere had come again'.[1601]

By the time the boat reached the Gulf of Smyrna, depression had overtaken him. He wrote in despair to his father and begged him not to forget him and told him that it should not be too difficult to get him a suitable post. He could not face the future years in Beirut and also what he described as 'the prospect of starvation'. He saw Nottingham as a 'deadly prospect too'.[1602] In a footnote this statement is explained as 'A possible lectureship at Nottingham University College.' He told his father he would do as much Turkish as 'his health would stand'. He asked him to send on the Turkish books, which he had packed and sent to Dean Close when he was determined never to return to Beirut.

His mood appeared to change again when the boat passed Rhodes and he began work on his poem 'Hyali', which Hellé stated[1603] was the island that he saw on this part of his voyage back to Beirut. But Flecker wrote to Savery when the poem was published[1604] [July 1913] telling him that he was glad that Savery liked 'Hyali', but that he had never seen the island but passed it at night. This poem (as has been seen)[1605] is written as if the poet had seen it during daylight hours but according to Flecker, Hellé also in the same sentence states that Flecker began 'A Ship, an Isle, a Sickle Moon' at this stage in the voyage.

Flecker arrived back in Beirut on 22 January, two and a half months after leaving on what was supposed to be a month's leave. He had not reported his departure date from Paris and telegrams were exchanged on 16 January with the FO to try and establish his whereabouts. The FO was not over-helpful in their response: 'I hope he has turned up by now'.[1606] In view of the confusion about the granting of an extension of leave and the fact that the First Balkan War disrupted the mail, it appears that Flecker's late arrival back in Beirut did not reflect badly upon him. If there was a backlog of work awaiting him, it did not prevent Flecker writing from the Consulate on 22 January in reply to a letter from Douglas Goldring, which must have been waiting for him.[1607] Flecker had not been able to contact Goldring in London, although Goldring was now working for Max Goschen, the publishers. He told Goldring that he had asked after him in London, but 'no one seemed to know where you were'. The despair, which he had outlined in his letter to his father, continued in his letter to Goldring and he supposed, he told Goldring, that he would 'have to live in this bloody country all my life'. He lamented also in his letter, that 'I never get paid a penny for anything and my book [Forty-Two Poems] has not yet sold 200 copies'. He also told Goldring that he was trying to place a play. All this information was a useful way of letting Goldring know that, once again, Flecker needed money and not just an enhanced literary reputation. Goldring, in his letter, had requested some of Flecker's work to use in an anthology. Flecker told Goldring that Victorian Verse had got 'Saracens', 'Rioupéroux' and 'my friend Marsh has got' 'The Queen's Song' and 'Joseph and Mary', which Goldring could not take, but left him to choose anything else he liked. He told Goldring that he had much to thank him for and said that he [Flecker] was fairly well known now, at least about as well known as Ezra Pound or T. Sturge Moore.

Letters from Hellé followed in which she let him know of the distress she shared about their enforced separation and the amount of money needed for the fare if she was to be able to join him in the near future. Hellé sent books and magazines to cheer him up, encouraged him in his writing for the stage and passed on Jack's remarks about his faith in Flecker being 'a good dramatic poet'.[1608] Flecker was staying temporarily at the pension they had moved to from the German Hotel a year ago. Hellé had disliked the pension so much then that they had moved to Areiya. With this in mind, Flecker began to look for alternative accommodation for them both. He spent his morning revising for two to three hours his Turkish language studies. In the afternoon he worked on his own writing, which consisted of his novel, poems and an article on the suicide of John Davidson. Consular duties at this stage did not appear to be his priority or to be too arduous. He also found a little furnished house, suitable for himself and Hellé, to rent from a professor of the Syrian Protestant College.[1609]

On 27 January, he wrote to J.M. Dent, Esq., in London, requesting news of two articles he had sent, and stressing that the articles should not be signed and that he would like to do more for *Everyman.*

At the end of January, due to pressure put on him by Hellé, he saw a specialist about his throat. He was told that there was nothing wrong with his larynx whatever. It was a little red. He was told not to smoke.'[1610]

Flecker, after he heard the specialist's optimistic verdict, reported to Hellé that his throat was cured, he felt very well indeed and 'his frogs diminished to two a day'.[1611] As if to confirm this view of his well-being, Flecker was able to revisit on foot the beautiful places he and Hellé had previously enjoyed together when they first arrived in the Lebanon. He picked cyclamen flowers 'because the orchids and anemones weren't out'.[1612] He also wrote a poem about his solitary expedition on 1 February, which expressed his longing for Hellé's return. The poem contained the lines:

> Wait for the girl who
> Lay in the shadow
> With the sea in her eyes
> And her breast as the spray
> Then you shall blossom,
> All red and blue flowers:
> Then, little hyacinths
> Brighten the way.[1613]

The reference to blossoming 'All red and blue flowers' echoes the promise Hellé gave, writing from Paris, of giving him 'the finest whippings he's ever had in his life to keep him cheerful'.[1614] Her husband told her 'I'm going to give you such a sweet time when you come to Beyrouth, you'll think you're on your honeymoon again!'[1615]

When Hellé eventually published her husband's poem in her chapter headed 'Reminiscences 1913',[1616] the lines are revised to make the signs which point to whippings less obvious:

> Wait for the girl who
> Sat in our shadow
> With the sea in her eyes
> And her breast as the spray,

Then we will order
All red and blue flowers
To break into blossom
And sing on her way.

Flecker's more open approach to the writing of his feelings about lovemaking with his wife is in contrast to the steps he was prepared to make to tone down his verse to suit the reader when the verse would be published. The day before he set off up the Beirut river valley (31 January) he wrote to Monro confirming that he would write the John Davidson article for the June number of *The Poetry Review*. He had agreed while he was in Paris to making alterations to *Hassan* because he had said that he honestly agreed with Marsh and was not being 'amiable'. He agreed to Monro's taking out a verse from the poem that was to be entitled 'The Golden Journey to Samarkand' due to be published in Monro's *Poetry and Drama* in March. This was the same verse that he had already referred to in his letter to Mavro, written from Corfu on 28 July 1911, telling him to cut out 'the naughty verse about the humanist'. At the time of writing to Mavro, the poem was entitled 'Diwan of the West' and Mavro was told to send it to the *Nation*. Flecker wrote in his letter of 31 January to Monro that he could 'Leave out the whole verse about behinds if you like. It was meant to make you laugh. How difficult some people are: is there no such thing as high poetic humour?'[1617] This was not the first time a critic had failed to appreciate the different aspects of humour in his verse. In April 1910, he had written to Savery to tell him that 'it's the one uniting thing that binds my work together, this humour'.[1618] A certain humour existed in his poem 'Hyali', which he was writing at this time, if the reader could realise that the poet had not seen the island in daylight.

In a letter to Marsh written on 11 February from the Consulate, he mentioned he had 'also written a few poems'. These were 'When Viewless Roses', 'Oak and Olive', and 'A Ship, an Isle, a Sickle Moon'. When replying to this long expected letter from Marsh, which he welcomed although it contained disappointing news, he hid his dismay: *Hassan* had been regarded by the actor Henry Ainley as being 'not commercial'.[1619] It would obviously not be produced in its present form. Flecker agreed with Marsh to cut out the farce and he intended to rewrite the Third Act after his exam. In the meantime, Flecker wanted Marsh to show it to Mr. John Drinkwater. He told Marsh also that he [Flecker] had 'adopted a cavilling air in my review [of *Georgian Poetry*] to the *E.R.*,' which he did not know if they had or would publish. He told Marsh that he had praised him as an anthologist and also praised Davies, Brooke and de la Mare, but cursed Mr. Gibson and the particular poem of Masefield's that Marsh had put in. He thought it better not to be 'too rhapsodical, so as to avoid all appearance of insincerity'.

He told Marsh that he had hopes of the 'C.U. Appointments people. I should think I ought to get a secretaryship'. That was the summit of his ambition. He could not 'learn enough about the stage here in Beirut in order to become a dramatist – even if there were no other reasons'. [1620]

Marsh may not have wanted at this stage, in view of the disappointing news about *Hassan*, to have added yet another disappointment. Flecker's appointment prospects courtesy of the CU Appointments Board were equally disappointing, although Flecker had written 'I have hopes of the C.U. Appointments people'. Benson told Marsh (at one stage after he was approached to help Flecker), that he had once met Flecker 'an interesting creature, with a sort of curious and rather attractive wildness about him. To speak plainly, a man who writes fine poetry, has married a Greek wife, and wants to throw up a consular post, is difficult to place .... the same sort [of difficulty] as there would have been in placing Shelley'.[1621] The precise date of Benson's first meeting with Flecker is not given (Flecker, in a letter to Marsh writes: 'But I don't know Benson'), but it could have been during Flecker's brief visit to Cambridge in early December 1910 when Flecker left the sanatorium. Or Flecker forgot the meeting or Benson mistook someone else for Flecker. It was during November 1910 that Benson had advised Brooke against taking a lectureship in English at Newcastle University and to concentrate instead on working for a Fellowship at King's. Benson, at that time, thought that some of Brooke's poems were very charming and some very ugly. Flecker's involvement with Brooke in December 1910 could have coincided with Benson's involvement with Brooke. Benson would not be in a position to appreciate fully Flecker's lack of finance. Benson, at that time, had an income of £3,600 of which he spent £2,100, he invested about £700 and gave about £800 towards decorating his College in various ways. Benson felt he had made a mistake in coming up to Cambridge, thinking that he was going to inhabit an intellectual atmosphere. He found instead that people there 'live in affairs and gossip'. This statement of Benson's could also be a part of the reason for Beazley's despondency and why he did not appear to want to help Flecker get back into the Oxford or Cambridge scheme of things.

If Benson had been able, at some stage, to promise Flecker the sort of income he needed with no strings attached, then this would have been the sort of temporary solution needed. But this was never likely to happen any more than Flecker's parents would be able to offer the financial solution to their son's problems. Benson may have genuinely felt from what he knew, that Flecker would have been saved by his not getting a CU post through his influence, from the dullness and ultimate disappointment of life at Cambridge. Benson did not realise (any more than anyone else) how short a life at Cambridge it would be, even if Flecker had been able to take advantage of it. Benson was not sympathetic to Flecker's marriage because of Hellé's nationality. Benson himself was not married. Although he had fallen in love, he had decided against marriage because he was over forty. However much Flecker had fallen in love, Benson would consider that Flecker could have realised that, in some eyes, marriage to Hellé would not help his career. He shared the elder Fleckers' views on marriage to a Greek woman. Flecker finished his letter to Marsh by telling him about the ten consecutive days of brilliant sunshine in Beirut in February and that for three weeks the countryside had been ablaze with flowers. He also told Marsh that Hellé was due to come out to Beirut the following month and that he had written to 'about 100 people' about getting work in England.

But no news came to him about firm offers of work in England and he had no news from Hellé; he was hoping she would write telling him that she was booked to sail from Genoa on 3 March. If she was not on the boat he was threatening to return because he did not want to die alone in Syria.[1622] On 20 February, he told his father, who had also not written, that he was a fool to come back. 'I have missed all my chances'.[1623]

He did hear from his father and told him that under no circumstances would he yield to his father's advice and stay in the service another year.[1624]

Hellé, too, when she eventually wrote, did nothing to help his peace of mind, because in her letter she told him she was tired of borrowing money and did not feel the need to follow him out to Beirut.[1625]

In order to cope with his misery, Flecker worked on and finished his novel *The King of Alsander* on 23 February. It was fortunate, in view of all the depressing news coming out from England, that at this stage the mail brought out better news from Goldring. Goldring had soon dropped the idea of using some of Flecker's work in an anthology of modern verse and instead was determined to try and get Max Goschen to bring out a volume of Flecker's poetry. Goldring offered to take on the financial risk of the new book of Flecker's verse himself. The reasons Goldring later gave[1626] was that 'By this time my belief in him was unshakable and I knew that sooner or later he was bound to come into his own.'[1627] It was also possible that Goldring was influenced in his decision by the favourable reviews of *Georgian Poetry* and the opening of 'The Poetry Bookshop' officially on 8 January 1913. Goldring and others were reported as saying that 33 Devonshire Street, where 'The Poetry Bookshop' was sited, was 'a slum',[1628] but as an outlet for the sale of poetry books in the centre of London it was undoubtedly an asset for anyone who wanted to market a book of poetry and make a profit from it.

Georgian Poetry 1911–12 appeared almost at the same time as Quiller-Couch's anthology *Oxford Book of Victorian Verse* and in some publications the books were reviewed in the same editions. This was the case for the *Manchester Guardian* of 8 January 1913, where the reviewer, Abercrombie, was on the side of *Georgian Poetry.* On 14 January, Edward Thomas reviewed *Georgian Poetry* in the *Daily Chronicle* and emphasised that 'much beauty, strength, and mystery, and some magic – much aspiration, less defiance, no revolt – and it brings out with great clearness many sides of the modern love of the simple and primitive, as seen in children, peasants, savages, early man, animals, and Nature in general.'

The *Cambridge Magazine* on the 18 January 1913, published a review of *Georgian Poetry.* Benson, too, saw no sign of revolt in *Georgian Poetry* and liked Brooke's 'The Fish'. Benson suggested a series.

The *Morning Post* carried a review by Edmund Gosse called 'Knocking at the Door' on 27 January and compared it to the first *Book of the Rhymers' Club* of 1892. Gosse thought that the seniors, Chesterton and Sturge Moore, should not have been included. Gosse concluded that the *Georgian Poets* exchanged 'the romantic, the sentimental, the fictive conceptions of literature, for an ingenuousness, sometimes a violence, almost a rawness in the approach to life itself'. This 'violence' and 'rawness' were later confirmed by Flecker's *Hassan* and Brooke's play *Lithuania.*[1629]

On 1 March (on headed notepaper of the British Consulate General, Beirut) Flecker wrote to Messrs. Max Goschen and accepted their generous offer to publish his volume of poems to be entitled *The Golden Journey to Samarkand.* Flecker confirmed their offer of the advance of £10, which was to be made on account of a royalty of 10% of the published price, that the American profits, if any, would be equally divided between author and publisher and that he £10 would be paid on receipt of the ms.

He went on to tell the publishers that this volume would be longer than 'my former volume' as most of the poems were of 'considerable length'. Only one of the poems had appeared in book form before. [This was the poem 'Bridge of Fire'.] The press notices of *Thirty-Six Poems,* he told the publishers, were with Mr. Goldring and Mr. Dent had the press notices of *Forty-Two Poems.* Flecker thought that the extracts printed on the cover of his *Forty-Two Poems* had been badly chosen. He pointed out that three weeks were needed to get a reply from Beirut. He reckoned to return the corrected proofs within a month, and wanted to have the usual dozen free copies.[1630]

Also on 1 March, Flecker wrote again to J.M. Dent asking for news of his articles.[1631]

Despite the future publication of his book of poems appearing to be a positive feature of his life, his health broke down; due he thought to getting a house ready for Hellé, who was to leave from Marseilles on 23 March. On 14 March he was writing to his mother informing her that he was in hospital with fever and a cold. The weather was blamed as contributing to his breakdown in health; he told his mother of 'awful siroccos and days of heat and dust, alternating with blinding rain and hail'.[1632] He told her of his despair of ever seeing England again. He did not think that even Hellé's coming to Beirut would help 'for she poor girl hates this horrible country worse than I do'.[1633] Hellé first received news of her husband's illness in a letter written in pencil, when her boat [1634] reached Alexandria. He appeared to make light of the fact that he was in hospital and he would 'die of joy to see you again – unless that horrid letter you sent me means that you don't love me any more'.[1635] Before the boat left Alexandria for Beirut, Hellé spent a very anxious day and night. She had no precise details about her husband's condition. In Beirut, the official view was that after the two weeks in hospital Flecker 'did not derive much benefit' and that he had been 'laid up ever since'. The Foreign Office knew that Flecker's health was what they described as 'indifferent' and that he had remained away from the Consulate 'occasionally' in February.[1636]

But he had been able to do what he described in a letter to his parents as 'a good deal of work'[1637] while in hospital. One piece of work was his poem, originally entitled 'Hospital'[1638] (and revised as 'In Hospital'), which he dated March 1913. The poem begins:

> Would I might lie like this, without the pain,
> For seven years – as one with long white[1639] hair,
> Who in the high tower dreams his dying reign

The next verse of 'In Hospital' is:

> Lie here and watch the walls – how grey and bare,
> The metal bed-post, the uncoloured screen,
> The mat, the jug, the cupboard, and the chair;

There is a kinship with the third verse of 'The Ballad of Camden Town': in that poem he wrote:

495

> A bed, a chest, a faded mat,
> And broken chairs a few,
> Were all we had to grace our flat
> In Hazel Avenue.

Lying in hospital in Beirut could have brought back memories of a period of illness in Camden Town. 'The Ballad of Camden Town', in its fifth verse, begins 'When I was ill ...'.

Flecker had lost his voice, so that the care he received was necessarily silent, as outlined in the next verse:

> And served by an old woman, calm and clean,
> Her misted face familiar, yet unknown,
> Who comes in silence, and departs unseen,

Flecker's feelings of isolation and distress in hospital (which even his parents were prepared to record in the LIFE[1640], stating 'he was so distressed that he said he hardly knew how to live through the nine days necessarily intervening.') was evident in the next verse:

> And with no other visit, lie alone,
> Nor stir, except I had my food to find
> In that dull bowl Diogenes might own.

The weather he had complained about to his mother is described in the fifth verse:

> And down my window I would draw the blind,
> And never look without, but, waiting hear
> A noise for [1641] rain, a rustle[1642] of the wind.

'In Hospital' also shares kinship with a poem translated by Arthur Waley from the Chinese, although the poem is entitled 'Being visited by a Friend During Illness'. This poem begins:

> I have been ill so long that I do not count the days;
> At the southern window, evening – and again evening.
> Sadly chirping in the grasses under my eaves
> The winter sparrows morning and evening sing.[1643]

The fear that he should die in Beirut would be even more in his mind as he lay in hospital. In the poem a vision takes over the last four verses of the poem while he lies and dreams:

> Noon-dreams should enter, softly, one by one,
> And throng about the floor, and float and play
> And flicker on the screen, while slowly[1644] run

The poet then writes:

> And only know that flame-foot Spring is near
> By trilling birds, or by the patch of sun
> Crouching behind my curtains. Then[1645] in fear,

'Flame-foot Spring' could refer to the swiftness of the arrival of spring in the Lebanon.

In view of the rainy season being part of spring in the Lebanon, the reference to 'flame-foot spring' does not seem to point to Flecker's time in hospital in the Lebanon but more likely to 'flame-foot' autumn days when he was in the sanatorium at Cranham. But the lines where the poet lies ill, knowing only of the world outside by the 'trilling of the birds', is also reminiscent of the poet in Arthur Waley's translation from the Chinese 'Being visited by a Friend During Illness' with its reference to sparrows 'sadly chirping'.

In another poem translated from the Chinese by Arthur Waley, 'Last Poem', begins with the lines:

> They have put my bed beside the unpainted screen:
> They have shifted my stove in front of the blue curtain.[1646]

This poem, like Flecker's, emphasises the importance of the sickroom's surroundings, 'the uncoloured screen' and the curtains. These surroundings, stark as they seem, allow the poet's mind to create his verse. In 'Last Poem' the poet has a line: 'With rapid pencil I answer the poems of friends,'

Once out of the hospital, Flecker had his joyful reunion with Hellé to look forward to, but that was to be delayed on account of the five days' quarantine Hellé would have to endure on board due to an outbreak of cholera in Egypt. She would not be allowed to land immediately at Beirut but would have to go up to Tripoli before returning. So as not to be parted for another few days, Flecker came aboard her boat, the *Lotus*, and spent the quarantine period with her before the boat returned to Beirut.

Once inside the single-storeyed rented house, Flecker, exhausted, had to rest for most of the day. The heat was intolerable and on doctor's advice in April, Hellé took her husband up to Brumana on Mt. Lebanon in the hope that the cool mountain air would aid his recovery. They moved into a 'cheerless barn' of a hotel, where they were the only visitors. On the terrace, where the acacias were in bloom and with no consular work to do – he had abandoned his Turkish studies, Flecker was able to concentrate on finishing poetry and translating new work. He finished 'In Hospital',[1647] 'Brumana', 'Taoping',[1648] 'Hyali' and 'Doris'.[1649] The translations were from Jean Moréas' *Stances*, the first verse of which has lines that are reminiscent of his feelings about his mother's rose-garden:

> The garden rose I paid no honour to,
> So humbly poised and fashioned on its spray,
> Has now by wind unkissed, undrenched by dew,
> Lived captive in her vase beyond a day. [1650]

The translation by Flecker 'captures the mood of gentle melancholy of the French poet.'[1651] He also translated Albert Samain's 'Pannyre Aux Talons d'Or', a dramatic poem about which it is said that in reducing the poem from 20 to 18 lines there is 'a certain loss'.[1652] The dance of Pannyra, however, is caught dramatically with the ending: 'Pannyra naked in a flash divine!'[1653]

Flecker also translated during his time at Brumana 'The Gate of the Armies' from Henri de Régnier's *Inscriptions pour les Treize Portes de la Ville*.[1654] Also 'Philomel' (from the French of Paul Fort). Some of the unsatisfactory nature of these two translations[1655] could be explained by the shortage of time available and the amount of work attempted.

Flecker also wrote the preface to *The Golden Journey to Samarkand*, which is dated April 1913 in the published version. He ended the preface with a paragraph which began: 'To this volume, written with the single intention of creating beauty, now the Moslem East, now Greece and her islands has a furnished setting.'

Flecker wrote to Goschens on 20 April in reply to their letter of 3 April enclosing his preface, which he hoped that 'they would find it sufficiently controversial.' He wanted the publishers to omit from publication the following poems:

(1) The Bridge of Fire which is a re-hash

(2) The poem beginning with the line 'When viewless roses' which I consider too personal to be published and insert the poems

Brumana ⎫
Doris   ⎬ In the space of the Bridge of Fire

In Hospital / in space 'When Viewless Roses '

He enclosed what he described as three fresh poems. He hoped that the printers would not be too angry. He thought that the improvements to the volume would be very considerable 'as 'Brumana' will be perhaps the best poem in the book'.

He continued:

'(3) With regard to the advertisement paragraph in the 'Poetry Review', I suggest something of this sort:

'The Golden Journey to Samarcand'

This volume consists entirely of original poems here published for the first time in book form. The poems are proceeded by a most polemical preface of which the concluding paragraph runs thus:- [not included in letter]
But this is only a suggestion. If you think it advisable to make the advertisement more of a 'puff' please do so.'

He tried to discuss the question of the press cuttings, for unfortunately he had none with him. He thought it would be best to repeat those on the paper cover of *Forty-Two Poems*. He wanted omitted what he described as 'the silly quotation from *The Times*'. He wanted extracts added from the *Daily News* and the *Athenaeum*. He thought that it would be 'absurd to publish the rather worthless criticisms in full'. He was 'very eager that the criticisms should appear on the cap [cover] of the book only, and not spoil by their hideous English the interior'.

He thanked them for the cheque and he went on to say 'I have been very ill, have as I think you will acknowledge on reading the Preface and additional poems' and he had 'spared no pains even at the 11th hour to improve my book'. He told the publishers that he was afraid that he had not got 'quite the physical energy to send an exhaustive list of subscribers. Nevertheless I send a few names as they come into my head

499

and will send more subsequently'. He enclosed 'a list of some of the less known periodicals where nevertheless my work is assured of a good review'. He also sent a list of special bookshops. The list included all the Oxford and Cambridge papers (*Isis, Review,* magazines etc., etc.,), The *Caius College Magazine,* the *Gloucestershire Echo,* the *Cheltenham Looker On* and the *Blue Review.* He also gave the address of *Mercure de France* and *Tanathencia* in Athens, as well as a list of bookshops.

The letter to the publishers was, of necessity, full of practical matters concerning the publication of his book and except for the reference to the lack of physical energy, his real feelings about the poetry he was sending them was bound to be absent. But in a letter[1656] sent to Frank Savery he told him of the haste he had been put under to get a volume of poetry together for the publisher. He described this to Savery as a 'weird collection of stuff to make up a volume including a revision of the poem 'The Bridge of Fire'.' He then described that, after he got the proofs, he managed 'to hoof out all sorts of godless rot'. He also told Savery that he had suddenly, at the last minute, rewritten and enlarged 'The Gates of Damascus'.

He told Savery that 'The Preface' was written, like all the later poems, when he was 'pretty ill'. 'The Preface' was not quite sincere. He wanted to say what he thought was wanted 'to shake up the critics'. He did not want 'to expound the essence of poetry which would take 500 pages'.

The poem 'Doris', he explained to Savery, was very short and he did not find it easy to say how sincere it was and it might have come out of the Greek anthology. He meant by the Ship, the Ship of Dreams. The poem is short:

DORIS
My ship had spread her phantom sail,
And now the Warden of the West
Blew from his horn a rosy gale,
And Doris breathed upon my breast.[1657]

Flecker did not doubt the sincerity of his poem 'Brumana' (in his letter to Savery) despite by that time what he described as 'a horrible misprint'[1658] had appeared in the lines:

And all around the snowy mountain[1659] swim
Like mighty swans afloat in Heaven's pool. [1660,1661]

'Brumana' first lines are:

Oh shall I never be home again?
Meadows of England shining in the rain
Spread wide your daisied lawns: your ramparts green
With briar fortify, with blossom screen

Flecker, in this poem, was echoing the lament for England outlined in
his letters to his parents, Hellé and friends. This feeling was heightened
by the sight of pines near the place where he was staying temporarily in
Brumana. He told Savery that the poem was 'sincere enough', and he
was thinking of the Bournemouth pines. He wrote of the pines in the
first lines of the second verse:

O traitor pines, you sang what life has found
The falsest of fair tales.

While under the pines he tells of:

Hearing you sing, O trees,
Hearing you murmur, There are older[1662] seas,
That beat[1663] on vaster sands,
He ends 'Brumana' with the lines:

Half to forget the wandering and [1664]pain,
Half to remember the days that have gone by,
And dream and dream that I am home again!

Flecker, in taking out 'sweet pain' appeared to be removing again
something 'too personal'. He explains to Savery that 'lavandon', which
he used in the poem, is the Greek name for cytisus, a rock rose, which
made 'the woods lovely in Syria. It has a queer little scent.' Arthur Waley
translated from the Chinese the poem by PO CHU-I (772–846) 'The
Pine Trees in the Courtyard' (821), which presents a different and
more loving relationship with the pine trees. This relationship is more
akin to Flecker's early version of 'Brumana'.[1665]

Flecker sent his John Davidson article to Monro on 20 April and
told him of the difficulties it had been written under due to his illness
of several weeks, but that he was now better. He thanked Monro for
sending him *The Poetry Review* and printing 'The Golden Journey'. ['*The
Golden Journey to Samarcand*' was published in Monro's *Poetry and Drama*,
March 1913.]

Monro had fallen out, at the end of 1912, with the Poetry Society and
was dismissed from the editorship of *The Poetry Review*, to be replaced by

Stephen Phillips. Monro instead started *Poetry and Drama*, which came out quarterly between March 1913 and December 1914. On the front cover of *Poetry and Drama* was an engraving of the exterior of the Poetry Bookshop.

Flecker raised in his letter, a challenge to Flint, the poet and Imagist friend and backer of Monro, on the question of Paul Claudel (1868–1955), a French poet, dramatist and ardent Catholic, influenced by the Symbolists. He had published in 1910 his 'Five Great Odes' and his play 'Brought to Mary' in 1912. The challenge to Flint was to 'quote a single line of Paul Claudel that has the slightest merit whatever. It is certainly not the little thoughts on God that are going to impress anybody. He is the French Ella Wheeler Wilcox, only far more poisonously pretentious, and much duller.' He told Monro about his new anthology and 'with a passionate preface against fools and all who do not admire the Parnassian theory of verse'.[1666]

On 26 April, Flecker acknowledged receipt of the contract for his book in a letter to the publishers and signed it with what he described as the 'unvariable nom de plume J.E. Flecker.' He explained that his first initial was 'H' but that this in no way invalidated the contract.

He wanted his new volume to match in binding paper his *Forty-Two Poems* and also a deluxe version with a cover design of 'good solid buckram.' [This had been done in the production of his first book of poems The Bridge of Fire.] He realised that an extra edition would be expensive.

He also told Goschens that his last volume was proposed for the £100 Academy Prize. He had hopes that his new volume would win it because it was far more advanced.

In a PS he told the publishers that he was anxious that the circular sent to possible buyers would not in any way reveal that their names had been given by the author of the book.[1667]

The month up in Brumana had not strengthened him; he arrived back in Beirut in a very weak condition, according to the FO report. He had experienced more fever and a sore throat. Flecker responded to his parents' offer of a cottage by asking instead that they helped to get him through the illness.[1668] The only solution, he told his parents, was to get to Switzerland somehow, despite the enormous cost of getting there. Hellé wrote to Cumberbatch requesting sick leave in Switzerland for her husband. A medical certificate was signed on 14 May, which stated that there 'appears to be a very serious lung trouble'. The doctor recommended that his patient went to Switzerland for three months without delay. Flecker's leave was officially granted by telegram from Constantinople on 19 May. A medical certificate and a full report on his health had to be forwarded. On the same page as the copy of the telegram, Mr. Flecker was described as a 'crock' and the writer 'would not be surprised if ill-health compels his resignation: His unsatisfactory record had already nearly led to his enforced retirement. (See Minutes 52930/12.)'[1669] It was noted that Flecker's leave had been almost continuous since November 1912. It was recommended that he went before a board to see whether he should be made to retire. This was not entirely unexpected. Flecker had on 5 April, in a letter from Beirut to his parents before Hellé had arrived, written: 'I am not yet well, and haven't been to the Consulate for a month. The Foreign Office will certainly turn me out of this goes on.' [1670]

The Fleckers boarded the first available boat, which was an Italian ship, to take them to Genoa. The ship was due to stop for two full days at Alexandria, where the stifling heat of the cabin and the din of the cranes overhead unloading the cargo made it necessary for the Fleckers to get out and go to a hotel. There, a young English doctor was needed to come and see Flecker. Despite another visit of an unwelcome kind, when an intruder came into the Fleckers' room in the middle of the night having mistaken their room for his own, Flecker was able to get back on board. The heat on board was no less suffocating but when they were out on the open sea, Flecker was able to get up on deck and recline on a deck chair. On arrival at Naples they went ashore to have a delicious lunch.

Two days after leaving Naples, with a stop at Leghorn, they at last reached Genoa en route for Aigle in Switzerland. It was necessary, so that Flecker could rest, for an overnight stop to be made at Arona where, by the lake, they had a good meal. Another overnight stop had to be made at Aigle because the funicular, which ran up to Leysin, had by that time stopped running. At Aigle, Hellé wrote a postcard (dated 29 May)[1671] telling the publishers, Max Goschen, that her husband had been 'seriously ill lately and was not able to write to you'. Hellé gave their address as Post Restante, Aigle, Switzerland, 'where all further proofs' of her husband's poems were to be sent. She posted the card on 30 May on the way up to Leysin. Five days before, on a journey she described as 'rather like a nightmare', they had reached their second wedding anniversary.

Chapter Twelve

> 'Selim: Do you believe in magic, Hassan?
>
> Hassan: Men who think themselves wise believe nothing till the proof. Men who are wise believe anything till the disproof.
>
> Selim: What do we know if magic be a lie or not? But, since it is certain that only magic can avail you, you may as well put it to the test.'
>
> Act, 1, Scene 1

'Really this place is like magic', Flecker wrote to his mother on 4 June 1913, a week after his arrival in Leysin.[1673] The magic of Leysin for consumptives was similar to the magic that Hassan was asked if he believed in. Like the magic philtre and the sweetmeats, which were supposed to make Yasmin fall in love with him, it was the promise of the people who sold the idea that made Hassan, in his desperation, pay the money. In the absence of any other sort of cure, consumptives were sold the idea that the air of the Alps would prove beneficial.

The reputation Swiss villages enjoyed as places where consumptives could find improvements in their health went back to 1862 as a result, initially, not of magic but a scientific paper. It was noticed that consumption was absent amongst inhabitants of one high Alpine village. Villages may be something of a misnomer because the inhabitants lived in farmhouses some distance from their neighbours. When these inhabitants left the villages for foreign parts, usually to do military service or live in crowded cities, and then contracted consumption, the condition gradually improved when they returned to their native valleys. In the absence of any other sort of hope, this was the magic that invalids had to believe in, whether or not they had realistic prospects of recovery.

Money was not available by magic for the Fleckers; one of Hellé's first tasks on reaching Leysin was to try and cash a cheque. She had only been able to travel from Paris to Beirut because of a loan of £21 sent to her by her in-laws. Much as she deplored borrowing from her husband's family, she was not in a position to return it or even repay it.[1674]

Hellé's initial view of Leysin was far from a 'magic' one. She was not sharing her husband's pleasant room, opening out to a small arcade, at the Hotel Belvédère, as the sanatorium was euphemistically named. Instead, she had to find a room in a small pension at the other end of the village. She described her living quarters in anything but magic terms: 'I shall never forget that dismal place or the unfortunate creatures that fought for life in it. Its description could have furnished Dante with another circle for his Inferno.' [1675]

Leysin was indeed a place of 'unfortunate creatures', many of them children. Flecker, in his euphoric mood on arrival, despite his feelings of weakness and coughing, did not identify himself at first with the hosts of other consumptives. In distancing himself, he coped with the realisation that he was at this stage no nearer a prospect of a complete cure than he had been in Beirut. Much of the magic was in the absence of Consular duties and Turkish studies and the prospect of making contact again with publishers and magazine editors and continuing with his literary work. After the heat and stench of Beirut, Leysin was indeed magic for a while. The Hotel Bélvèdere was very different, in many ways, from the Cotswold Sanatorium because at the Belvédère it was thought that he was given 'perfect liberty'. Hellé stated that her husband was only 'visited daily by a very courteous but not particularly interested doctor.' [1676] Hellé went on to observe that the patients 'were otherwise left to take care of themselves'. Hellé's observations are borne out by the description of treatment for consumptives at another Alpine resort in 1878, which also indicates that the treatment had not varied much in the intervening years:

> The method of cure is very simple. After a minute personal examination of the ordinary kind, your physician tells you to give up medicines, and to sit warmly clothed in the sun as long as it is shining, to eat as much as possible, to drink a fair quantity of Valtelline wine, and not take much exercise. He comes at first to see you every day, and soon forms more definite opinion of your capacity and constitution. Then little by little he allows you to walk; at first upon the level, next up-hill, until the daily walks begin to occupy from four to five hours. The one thing relied upon is air. To inhale the maximum quantity of the pure air, and to imbibe the maximum quantity of the keen mountain sunlight, is the sine qua non. [1677]

Hellé, recalling that patients were taking care of themselves, overlooked the fact that she was never able to see for herself what went on at the Cotswold Sanatorium where the romance with Leila Berkeley was able to flourish. Flecker's parents had complained of his mixing with other patients 'no matter how advanced was the state of their illness' at the Cotswold Sanatorium. Flecker wrote to his parents about the Belvédère:

> Why give little digs at the dear old Cotswold San.? It cured me very quickly, and it was an infinitely better place than this, air and a certain hotelly comfort apart. What do you mean by 'letting me do as I liked at Etlinger's? Here, I can do anything I like, walk seven miles, order quarts of champagne and all the poisonous liqueurs on earth, read till 2 in the morning, take no real rest hour. Here there is no discipline at all, while there it was extremely strict. [1678]

The elder Fleckers' 'digs' at the Cotswold Sanatorium treatment were later added to digs at the doctors their son had seen before his arrival at Leysin.

> 'The deplorable fact remains that it seems clear that if the doctors who had attended him in the previous nine months had taken the most grave view and ordered sanatorium treatment then, there might have been a chance of cure. As the disease developed, one of them, apparently forgetting his former optimism, said steps should have been taken six months before.'[1679]

This was the nearest the elder Fleckers came to admitting in print that their son should not have gone back to the East. Flecker did not have much choice in the matter, but when the immediate risk of forfeiting the £500 bond put up by Dr. Flecker had receded, it was safe to blame the doctors. Exactly which doctor was to blame is not stated, but it appears that before a decision was made by Flecker's parents to pay the sanatorium expenses, they had taken medical advice. The only doctor mentioned was the one Flecker consulted in Paris and whose verdict Hellé passed on to her in-laws. Whether or not the decision Flecker's parents took to pay the sanatorium fees was based on the fact that it would bring about a cure or that they could at least make his last year or two comfortable is uncertain; it was more likely to be the latter.

In order to sort out more of his financial future, he wrote to the Foreign Office on 3 June, giving Hotel Belvédère as his 'permanent address' and asking whether 'leave has been granted.' Sick-leave had been officially granted by telegram from Constantinople on 19 May, but there may not have been time for the telegram to be forwarded to the departing Fleckers. As usual, the FO could not overrule the doctor's advice but the real need was to know how long the sick leave was to last. He needed a long period of sick leave to recover from the weakness and coughing, which persisted even if he was feeling, as he told his mother, 'immensely better'. [1680]

He needed to resume correspondence with the publishers Goschens and he wrote to them on 5 June:

Sanatorium Belvédère[1681]
Leysin-sur-Aigle
5th June [1913]

Dear Sir,

I herewith enclose the complete proofs of the entire book. The corrections are fairly heavy in places: I have rewritten 'The Gates of Damascus' and 'Taoping' and I have thought it advisable to erase the first page of the Preface. But no further alteration of any importance is to be feared on my part so please send me the revised proofs.

Please see the order of the poems is kept as I have indicated as it was wrong in the paginated proofs sent me. Please acknowledge receipt.

The above is my permanent address. I am fortunately much better and shall be able to attend to the revise proofs promptly.

Yours faithfully
J.E. Flecker
I enclose a note for Mr. Goldring

Next, on a picture postcard of Arona-Porto e Piazza Garibaldi, where he and Hellé had broken their journey to Leysin to have a memorable meal, Flecker wrote to Goldring:[1682]

'Sunday
Hotel Bélvèdere
Leysin
Switzerland

Dear Goldring,

Unfortunately am not so well to day and can't reply at length to your very kind and careful letter.

I would much rather Goschen published the novel than anybody. They have certainly the first right to my work. But of course the novel may be a bloody failure and of course neither you nor Goschen's may take it. However I'm sending it to you. Its gay and fantastic and a little bit improper[1683] and adventurous and perhaps utterly poor as pure literature. That won't spoil its chances of success however. Don't be frightened to tell me truths about it.

Yours rather feebly
J E Flecker

You'd get these proofs back. Send notices of the edition de luxe <u>to the addresses I gave you.</u>

Written in the margin of the letter is the sentence: 'Am sending proofs to day Monday with some slight but important corrections.'
He wrote again, next day, to Goldring:

Hotel Bélvèdere,
Leysin
Monday

Dear Goldring,

I suppose you will swear bitterly – but would you be so kind as to get the following little alterations done in the poem Taoping.

Explanation: I wanted to send you off the proofs without a moment's delay and I discovered I hadn't got a single copy of my revised version of Taoping. So I botched it up from memory. Now a copy has turned up. The alterations are very slight. The lines about the middle should run

By these grim civil trophies undismayed
In lacquered panoplies the chiefs parade.
Behind, the plain's floor rocks: the armies come:
The rose-round lips blow battle-horns: the drum
Booms oriental measure. Earth exults.

508

And still behind, the tottering catapults
Pulled by slow slaves, grey backs with crimson lined [1684]
Roll resolutely west. And still behind
Down the canal's etc. ...

The first 4 lines of the last part should run

Now with swift slide and flaming shadeless red
The sun's large circle dips toward the dead.
At once the old night-hunted flags are furled:
The armies halt and round them halts the world.
A phantom wind etc.,

These alterations are very slight but had better not wait
the revise. All this nuisance simply because I'm hurrying
with all my might. Please forgive me. It is the last!

J.E. Flecker [1685]

In *The Golden Journey to Samarkand,* the version of 'Taoping' reads:

Now level on the land and cloudless red
The sun's slow circle dips toward the dead.
Night-hunted, all the monstrous flags are furled:
The Armies halt, and round them halts the World.

This version of 'Taoping' published in *The Golden Journey* (and also
in CP) is proof that the alterations Flecker wanted were never made.
The fact that the letter containing the alterations is now in the letters
of Goschens at Houghton and not in the letters Goldring published, is
further indication that Goldring was not able to act upon the instructions
or did not receive them. The production card for *The Golden Journey to
Samarkand* shows that instructions to the printers, Arden Press, were
given as early as 1 April 1913 and instructions to bind copies on 20
June.[1686] 'The slight but important alterations' appear to have been
ignored due to lack of time and cost, or Flecker did not mark the proofs
of 'Taoping'. He preferred to write to Goldring instead.

A letter from Flecker, which Goldring must have received, is dated 5
June,[1687] in which Flecker told him 'Thank the Lord this place is curing
me. The journey nearly killed me. There is nothing terribly wrong – but
I shall take a month or two to recover, and always have to live with
precaution.'

509

He tells Goldring to look over the revision of 'Taoping' 'in its new version, [or it] will come out in a hash'. This indicates again that the letter with the suggested alterations of 'Taoping' may not have been received by Goldring (it is marked 'file').

Flecker went on to tell Goldring in this letter that he had left out the first page of the preface [to *The Golden Journey*] 'as being rather babyish'. He wanted Goldring to know what he thought of the book (*The Golden Journey*) especially his alterations to 'Gates of Damascus'. He told Goldring that he was 'immensely proud of it. I've turfed out all the rot.'[1688]

He thought that *The Golden Journey* was 'to be miles ahead of *The Forty-Two*'. He thought that Goschens, in order to advertise the book, could safely say 'that the Oriental Poems are unique in English'. He complained about 'the dearth of de Luxe copies', those 'on fine paper and with fine binding!'. This was done in France. He complained that he had lost money by not having time to get 'all the poems into mags'. This necessary concentration on correspondence with his publishers about the forthcoming publication of *The Golden Journey to Samarkand* took time away from earning money by submitting poems to magazines.

He wrote to Monro, also on 5 June,[1689] and told him he had sent off 'this auspicious day corrected proofs of my new volume *The Golden Journey to Samarkand*. I have put all my power up to the last moment in making the book absolutely major poetry from beginning to end (tho' it does contain 'Bryan of Brittany'), and I'm immensely proud of it, and of course it will fail.'

He began the letter by telling Monro:

> 'Severe illness, which was already coming on, when I somewhat feverishly wrote you "John Davidson", has driven me here. This place, however, is rapidly curing me – but an end to the purple East! Henceforward, infinite poverty – a cottage, and a pen! Shere [sic] ill health has driven me to the literary career.
>
> I suppose you disliked "John Davidson" – for I hoped greatly for a line of receipt from you and never got one. If you didn't dislike it and printed it, please send me a copy of *Poetry and Drama* (why didn't you call it, "Serres & Drama",) also an infinite cheque for it and the *Golden Journey*, to buy a Cottage Piano with.'

The article referred to was the one he sent Monro on 20 April when writing from the British Consulate in Beirut. In that letter he thanked

Monro for printing *The Golden Journey,* as well as for the books on John Davidson that Monro had sent. Flecker was sending the books back but wanted to keep the 'Selections'. This was Flecker's second article on Davidson. The first was 'John Davidson: Realist', first published in *The Monthly Review* in July 1905. This second John Davidson article remained unpublished in magazine form but is published alongside 'John Davidson: Realist' in Collected Prose. One reason why Monro did not publish the article on Davidson could be because Davidson's reputation was not high at this time. [1690] Flecker concluded the article with a message: '... cannot a few thousands be collected to publish the books, if not to prolong the lives, of those who, like John Davidson, write not for ten thousand to read in ten days, but for ten more wise men to read for ever?' [1691]

A letter written to Savery also on 5 June, told him almost the same sort of news about his health as told to Goldring and Monro; now he had recovered from his near-death experience on the voyage his temperature was down to normal after 104ª. He wrote that there was nothing seriously wrong '(only the old spot touched up again by an influenza)'. He hoped to be well in a few months. He told Savery that his parents wanted him to live in a cottage and write. He boasted that *The Golden Journey* challenged 'any volume of verse published since *Atalanta in Calydon* – yea, even *The Shropshire Lad* and *The Wind Among the Reeds.*' He supposed it would sell '70 copies'.

When he wrote on the same day to Marsh (in reply to a 'kind' letter forwarded on from Beirut), the number of copies he hoped would sell had gone up to 75. He told Marsh that he had, that day, sent off the corrected proofs of *The Golden Journey to Samarkand* and he was 'immensely proud of the volume', which he thought 'is about twice as good as the 42 poems, and I feel it ought to redeem me from the stigma of minor poetry for ever'.[1692] He wanted Marsh to send on the typescript of *Hassan* with Drinkwater's remarks. He might feel well enough to work on the revision and finish the third Act. The 'marvellous air of this very horrid place has set me well on the way to convalescence'. Marsh was also filled in with details of the breakdown in health in Beirut and the near-death experience on the voyage out. But despite all that, he was 'going to live in a very small cottage and write – it's nearly the only thing I'm fit to do; though I may perhaps get an appointment on the '*Near East*'.'

Marsh, if he cared to read between the lines, seemed to be receiving the message that Flecker would be able to stick with completing *Hassan*. He continued to have an interest in the literary world back home. On the question of the next poet laureate, he hoped that it would be Rudyard

Kipling. 'I have a horror of their giving it to that fellow Watson, [William Watson] who has exactly the amount of initiative melody and second-rate imagination that captivates the Stock Exchange or Parliament.'[1693]

Next day, Flecker changed his mind about *Hassan* and he wrote again to Marsh asking him to 'rescue for me the ms of *Hassan*' because he could not find Act I. He was determined to finish *Hassan*. He told Marsh that he was 'going to cut the farce clean out – or modify it greatly, and be less heavy with the oriental expressions'. He was not going to 'worry over much about the requisites of the Stage. A lot of rot is talked about the literary plays not succeeding'. He thought that it usually meant that 'plays which are written in lifeless blank verse on Boadicea or Savonarola, and which are infinitely boring to read, are not good stage plays'. He was only going to try and keep '*Hassan* interesting;' and he intended to revise *Don Juan*.[1694]

On 11 June, Flecker wrote a long letter to Goldring,[1695] which began by telling him he was 'most frightfully glad about the Edition de Luxe'. He supposed he would be allowed 'one or two copies' for himself. 'But what about sending round notices of it?' He continued with practical matters concerning the publication of *The Golden Journey*. He offered to pay for the printer's note, he would 'pay[ing] anything in reason' – but he did not consider himself 'liable for additions or omissions of complete poems. Against the omissions can be put my writing the Preface specially to please the publishers.'

He agreed that he was liable to pay for:

> Alteration to 'Gates of Damascus',
> One verse altered in 'Hyali'
> ½ do. do. 'Oak and Olive',
> About six lines altered at beginning of Preface,
> Alteration of 'Taoping',

A copy of the alterations wanted for 'Oak and Olive' are published in JEF facing page 138. The alterations are slight but in the fifth verse do not seem to have been made; in the fourth line the alteration is:

> How Byron like his heroes fell
> Fighting this country free,'
> But the line remains
> 'Fighting a country free, [1696]

And from the next verse:

And while our poets chanted Pan
Back to his pipe and power,

But the line remains:

And while our poets chanted Pan
Back to his pipes and power, [1697]

He blamed the 'apparently extensive minor alterations in the first few pages of the proofs' on the 'gross carelessness of the printers'. He thought that the last few pages 'were 20 times better done', but that 'a dirty joke' had been played on him which he did not think funny. (The printer put 'tips' instead of 'lips' in four separate places. He thought this had been done on purpose.) His letter was not all complaints; he told Goldring that the advertisement was excellent and went on to outline his plans for future publications. He had a long held scheme for an anthology of French verse. This would be from 'after' Hugo and Musset [1810–57] who would not be included. A short notice would head each poet. He told Goldring that his proposed anthology would 'thus resemble Walch's great three-volume work – but in no other way.'

He wanted this anthology to be 'a large and very different choice of the more important people and none of the pages of dreary rot by the great unknown'.

Criticism would be 'original and not borrowed'. The whole book would not be more than one volume. He realised that such a book would mean 'a lot of toil, but very pleasant toil,' but he wondered if the enterprise would pay. If a sale could be arranged in France, then it might. He would need 'three or four pounds for buying books to cut up, typing, copying, and other exes.' His next topic of discussion in the letter to Goldring was his conflict with Martin Secker,[1698] who had made him 'revise it [K of A] twice, the last time in December (1912).' He told Goldring that he had 'half-killed myself to get it finished this January...'. After three months he told Goldring: 'the inconceivable person' returned the ms of the novel, saying 'after all this time' he had lost interest in it. Secker would not answer the letter Flecker sent in reply. He had his contract 'somewhere', possibly 'at Cheltenham'. He wanted to take legal action and claim about £200 damages. He went on 'I had to put in altogether 4 mortal months' work on the novel. [But perhaps you would like to help me or find someone who will – on a fat commission – get me good compensation.]'[1699]

Flecker thought that *K of A* 'originally a very poor production, is now a very jolly and fantastic work'. He did not think that there was a publisher in the world who could say whether or not it would sell. He was going to send Goldring a copy of the ms of *K of A* but realised that Goschen 'may well fight shy of a book which another publisher has broken his contract to evade publishing'. He suggested that Goldring might care to go round to Secker[1700] and tell him that Flecker was going to claim £200 from him immediately. He wanted the 'address of a solicitor who is a friend of literary men'. Goldring, not surprisingly, advised Flecker that he stood little chance of receiving damages from Secker.

The manuscript of *The King of Alsander* was sent for consideration to Goschens. When Goldring read the manuscript he recalled that 'my heart sank a little, in spite of all the pleasant memories which the opening chapters revived'. Goldring had heard the first two chapters read to him in Flecker's Bloomsbury rooms. These were the chapters (plus a third) that Flecker remembered (when he wrote back to Goldring on 21 June) that he had lost on the way to Paris at the time of the wine riots. When he was accompanied by '..... and ..... of your acquaintance'. These names are omitted from the published letter[1701] but one would be Knox and other most likely to be Firbank.

Thoughts of the possible publication of *K of A* were temporarily put aside by his receiving *Hassan* safely and 'the very encouraging letter from Birmingham [John Drinkwater, Birmingham Repertory Theatre son of A.E. Drinkwater].' This news was relayed to Marsh on a postcard dated 17 June.[1702] The letter he told Marsh 'has set me to work at once on revising and completing the play. The farce with the Jew has gone clean out at once.' [1703]

In a PS to the postcard, he tells Marsh: 'I favour Kipling, as you may have seen.'

It is not clear whether or not this is a reference to his paragraph to Marsh of 5 June, when he hoped that Kipling would be the sensible option, or to the fact that a letter entitled 'The Laureateship' by Flecker was published in *The Daily News and Leader* (p.6) on 14 June, which repeated his opinion as told to Marsh that William Watson was not in the running. He stated also that Hardy 'is not a poet. He has written about a dozen good poems – but these are accidents of his genius and read as such.' It was not a post that should go the best living poet, otherwise 'we should have to give it to Mr. Yeats without hesitation. It is a post for a good poet who is willing to be a Court poet... Think of Tennyson's 'Ode on the Funeral of Wellington'. Kipling he described as 'one poet who can sing of England and the Empire with conviction'. He went on to write about Kipling's proposed appointment that he was 'the poet who seems to have been veritably born for the position'. The King did not appoint Kipling to the post of poet laureate: Robert Bridges (1844–1930) was appointed instead.

Revision of *Hassan* had to be carried on alongside preparations for the publication of *The Golden Journey to Samarkand*. On the same day as he sent a postcard to Marsh (17 June) he wrote to Goschens:

> Goschens & Co.
> Publishers
> 20 Gt. Russell St.
> London WC

> On the other side a small supplementary list of names to which to send prospectus of book. I send it to you so that you can send announcement of 7/6 Edition also.

> J.E. Flecker

The list consisted of nine names, ranging from consular colleagues in Beirut and Jerusalem to masters at Dean Close School and Uppingham and also John Drinkwater of The Birmingham Rep. The last name was: 'Monsieur Paul Morand, École des Arts Décoratifs, Rue de l'École de Medecine, Paris.'

Paul Morand (1888–1976) was the son of Eugene Morand (who was born in Russia), painter, playwright, excellent English scholar, translator of *Hamlet*, director between 1908–28 of the important 'École des Arts Décoratifs', which was the address used by Flecker to write to Paul Morand. Paul Morand spent summers in England in order to learn the language and, in 1908, on the advice of Lord Alfred Douglas, Morand's father agreed to let his son spend a full year at Oxford. During 1908–9, Morand met Jack Beazley at Oxford, and although this was during Flecker's time at Cambridge, he also met Flecker. These meetings with Flecker and Beazley, although not authenticated by surviving correspondence, are evident in Morand's novel *Les Extravagants*. This novel, which was left unpublished and was assumed to have been destroyed, came up for sale in 1977 and was acquired by the Beinecke Rare Book and Manuscript Library, Yale University Library. It was edited by Vincent Giroud, Curator of Modern Books and Manuscripts and published by Gallimard in 1986.[1704] Morand, on his return from Oxford, decided on a career after his military service. He entered the

French Diplomatic Service and after, a short stay at the Department of Protocole, he first went to England as an attaché at the French Embassy, where he stayed for nearly four years between 1913 and 1916. Morand, much later, published more novels, short stories and essays. Flecker could not have had the opportunity to read *Les Extravagants*, which was written two years after Morand left Oxford, but in suggesting that the prospectus be sent to Morand he exhibited an ability to make sure his book would be noticed by someone who would be interested enough to buy it.

On 21 June 21, Flecker's revision of *Hassan* and his plans to circulate details to friends of his forthcoming *Golden Journey*, were interrupted by his answering a prompt reply from Goldring to tell him he had written to Goschens accepting their offer to publish *King of Alsander*.

Hotel Bélvèdere
Leysin
Switzerland
June 21 13

Dear Sir,

    Thank you very much for your kind letter.

    I will accept your terms for the novel (10% royalty) which I suppose will include the usual stipulation about American prices.[1705] I hope that despite its defects its gaiety may carry it through.

    I am looking forward to seeing the *Golden Journey* in book form. Could I have four copies of the 7/6 edition? I will then ask for only 2 of the 2/6.

    I think I should like to have the proofs of *Alsander* fairly soon. Correcting proofs is rather convenient work for an invalid. But in any case I want to have good leisure for them.

Yours sincerely,
J.E. Flecker [1706]

Flecker agreed with Goldring that the novel 'is a most patchy affair'.[1707] He was not a novelist 'because I don't really think novels worth writing – at the bottom of my heart'. He went on: 'A drama is a thing, now, that is worth writing'. He told of 'most encouraging letters' from Drinkwater, but he hoped that 'Granville Barker and no other will take up *Hassan*, my Oriental play'. He told of Yasmin being out of 'my play – was written for it – and also *The Golden Journey to Samarkand* is nothing but the final scene. I admit a little verse into my play here and there.' He urged Goldring to read the poem 'The Golden Journey' and in the poem consider the 'pilgrim with the beautiful voice' to be Hassan, the hero of the whole drama, and think what it would sound like actually on the stage, with Granville Barker scenery – moonlight.'

In the first of three PSs he told Goldring that he should much like to read his novel. He did not know that Goldring had written one. [1708]

In the second PS he wrote: 'What do you think – if by chance *The Golden Journey* gets known – of having the Oriental poems (plus 'Saracens' and 'Ballad of Iskander' from 42) illustrated by Syme [Sidney Sime, acclaimed Fantasy Artist – illustrator of Machen's *The Hill of Dreams*] for a Christmas volume.'

The next letter to Goldring was written on 30 June and is published in part. [1709] The part that is omitted appears to concern a misunderstanding on the part of Goldring as to whether or not Flecker had sought permission to republish some poems. [1710] In the published part of the letter, Flecker tells Goldring that 'In Phaecia' which he described as 'the rottenest poem in the book', would appear in *Everyman* and 'Taoping' in *The Spectator* '(eh, what? the citadel of respectability stormed!) this week.'

He asked if Goldring had seen 'Solomon Eagle's extremely amusing jibe at me in *The New Statesman*? 'Who is he?' Flecker asked. The 'jibe' was a result of advance publicity *The New Statesman* received about the forthcoming publication of *The Golden Journey to Samarkand*.

The Solomon Eagle Column of 21 June 1913, told its readers that Mr. Max Goschen would be shortly issuing a new volume of verse by James Elroy Flecker entitled *The Golden Journey to Samarkand*. Mr. Flecker, Solomon Eagle went on, had 'other claims to distinction than the fact that his second volume was substantially his first volume with a little added, and his third volume substantially his second volume with a little added'. Solomon Eagle considered that Flecker had written 'one or two fine poems, notably 'The War Song of the Saracens' .... has astonishing individuality and vigour'. The new title, it was said, will contain what was described as 'an essay of highly controversial nature on the present state of English criticism. There is plenty of room for such an essay and it might at once be controversial and quite irrefutable.'

Solomon Eagle knew so much about Flecker's works because his real name was Jack Squire.

Flecker also told Goldring that he was 'getting fatter and stronger' and hoped to be in England in the autumn 'producing my play'. He lamented the fact that nobody translated 'great French books like Jules

Renard's *Lanterne Sourde* or Claude Farrère's marvellous *Bataille?*' It was *Bataille* that had inspired Flecker's poem 'Art', first published in *The Poetry Review*, December 1912, and revised as 'The Painter's Mistress' when published in *The Golden Journey to Samarkand*.

On 5 June, in a PS to Marsh, Flecker had asked him to send a copy of *Rhythm* or *Blue Review* via the editor. *The Blue Review*, in its June edition, had published 'Yasmin, a Ghazel' (a slightly revised version of 'Yasmin' published in *Country Life* (6 January 1912)) and it is not clear whether or not Flecker wanted a copy because of this or the review by D.H. Lawrence of *Georgian Poetry* in *Rhythm*. In June 1913, *Rhythm* was tottering towards its last number under the new name *Blue Review*.[1711] In his March review of *Georgian Poetry* in *Rhythm*, D.H. Lawrence referred to 'The Nihilists, Ibsen, Flaubert, Thomas Hardy' as intellectually hopeless people who represented the 'dream we are waking from.' Lawrence described the Georgian poets as 'not poets of passions, perhaps, they are essentially passionate poets. The time to be impersonal has gone. We start from the joy we have in ourselves, and everything must take colour from that joy.'

Lawrence was a 'Georgian Poet' (he contributed to *Georgian Poetry*). On 14 January 1913, Edward Thomas in the *Daily Chronicle* described 'Messrs. Brooke, Lawrence and Sargant, are, as it were, the core of the group'. Of the volume itself, Thomas wrote: 'It shows much beauty, strength, and mystery, and some magic – much aspiration, less defiance, no revolt – and it brings out with great clearness many sides of the modern love of the simple and primitive, as seen in children, peasants, savages, early man, animals, and Nature in general.'

Lascelles Abercrombie, also a 'Georgian Poet', wrote an article in the *Manchester Guardian* on 8 January 1913, and attacked Quiller-Couch's *Oxford Book of Victorian Verse*. He thought that the Georgians had broken away completely from Victorianism. He wrote of 'poetry's determination to undertake new duties in the old style'. Ellis Roberts, in the *Daily News* two days later, wrote again about the Georgian Poets breaking with the late Victorians and 'veering away from ornate diction'.

A.C. Benson, in the *Cambridge Magazine* on the 18 January, wrote of 'No sense of revolt'. He praised Abercrombie and Sturge Moore and thought that Brooke's 'The Fish' was one of the best contributions. Edmund Gosse, in his review of *Georgian Poets*, which was called 'Knocking at the Door' in the '*Morning Post*' of 27 January, thought that the volume would have been better without Chesterton and Sturge Moore. Gosse wrote of exchanging 'the romantic, the sentimental, the fictive conceptions of literature, for an ingenuousness, sometimes a violence, almost a rawness in the approach to life itself'.[1712] [1713]

The reviews of *Georgian Poetry 1911–12* were no sooner dying embers then the reviews of *The Golden Journey to Samarkand* burst into flame, after its publication at the beginning of July. Flecker was first alerted by a telegram from Savery of the fact that his book was out and he wrote to him on 5 July to thank him for it.

On 7 July, he wrote to Goschens:

> I have heard from a friend that my book is out. If by any chance you happen to have sent me my copies per parcel post instead of by book post; please send me some more copies by book post. I have known parcel post take ten days. I will return the surplus of volumes. Forgive my troubling you.

> J.E. Flecker[1714]

His anxiety grew about the fate of his book and he wrote again to Goschens:

> Wednesday Evening
> Hotel Bélvèdere
> Leysin in Switzerland

> Please let me know when if at all you sent me any copies of my book. I have not received one though it has apparently been out nearly a week. I am in a great hurry to have the copies for certain personal reasons.

> Yours faithfully,
> J.E. Flecker [1715]

The 'certain personal reasons' would be Hellé's birthday on 14 July. He wrote again on the 10 July: [1716]

> Hotel Bélvèdere
> Leysin
> 10th

> I have got your letter of the 8th. The books have not yet come and will probably not arrive till the 18th.

Please send another lot. Please send me 2 extra copies of the de luxe [1717] edition, for which I will pay (4 in all).

Yours H.E. Flecker

Once he received his copies he wrote back: [1718]

Hotel Bélvèdere: Leysin 12th

I've received 2/6 copies of Samarkand, am delighted with get up: will write when I get luxe copies. There is only one misprint, due to my carelessness or illness. p.42 L 14 should read mountains not mountain. Will pay up to 5/- for an erratum slip which I think it would be worthwhile sticking at least in luxe copies – especially if nicely worded thus

Please correct mountain into mountains on p.42 1 14

I note 2 copies of Samarkand luxe are being sent by parcel post. Please send as per my request 2 more copies by book post. There is no danger of the most delicate binding being damaged if the book is wrapped in cardboard wrappers projecting well over the sides left open. At any rate; I take the risk.

J.E. Flecker.

Flecker did not comment on the fact that his alterations to poems such as 'Taoping' had not been made, which suggests that at this time, for financial considerations, or because he had left the alterations too late, he had decided to let the original versions stand. Likewise there is no erratum slip and the line in 'Brumana' remained: 'And all around the snowy mountain swim'. The line remains the same in *Collected Poems*, first published in 1916.

On the final receipt of all the copies he wanted, he wrote to Goschens again:[1719]

Hotel Bélvèdere
Leysin
Switzerland
July 15th

Just a line to thank you heartily for the charming get up of my book and especially the luxe Edition. Both binding and paper are excellent.

I have now all the copies I asked for.

One can never hope that poetry will be a commercial success – but the Edition is sure to trickle out in time – if nothing else. I have had the most enthusiastic letters, but seen no criticisms as yet.

With best wishes for the book and to the firm.

I am,

Yours sincerely,
J.E. Flecker

One 'most enthusiastic' letter came from Walter Raleigh and another, enclosing a note from Gosse, came from Marsh. Flecker replied to Marsh on 15 July sending him a deluxe edition.

The extent of Marsh's enthusiasm for *The Golden Journey to Samarkand* is evident in a letter he wrote to Brooke on 13 July.[1720] Marsh told Brooke he had read the book 'in floods of tears, on the way to the Admiralty!' He told Brooke 'I do think he has been and gone and done it! He has set out to make beauty, and has made it – a rare achievement, usually it only comes on the way to other things.' Marsh quoted eight lines from 'The Gates of Damascus', starting with: 'The dragon-green, the luminous, the dark, the serpent-haunted sea.'

He told Brooke that 'Wilfrid [Scawen Blunt] has read the book and thinks it beautiful but doesn't like it for that reason. He first said the beauty was merely 'an ornament', but I drove him from that position by proving that in each case the beauty was the poem, not something stuck on – he then said he preferred people to find beauty in places where it wasn't, rather than where it was – on which I remarked with asperity that I supposed he would like the 'Ode to the Nightingale' better if it were 'Ode to the Crow' – to which nice knock-down argument he found no answer. Tho' I fear he is not convinced.'

As well as comments on the poems, Marsh gave Brooke news of being in a position to pay the contributors £3 each and, because the book was selling well, more money was to come. Marsh was not only enthusiastic about Flecker's poems in his letter to Brooke. He read them aloud at meals in his apartment to an audience made up of the actresses Mrs. Patrick Campbell and Cathleen Nesbitt (who, having recently broken a relationship with Henry Ainley, was now having a love affair with Rupert Brooke), and the painter Mark Gertler (1891–1939), then a student at the Slade to whom Marsh was attracted both by his beautiful appearance and his paintings. Brooke, still abroad, would not share Marsh's enthusiasm for Flecker's poetry. In a letter to Marsh from Canada, Brooke wrote: 'I don't think I should value Flecker's poems so highly as you seem to ... I expect I'd find him too fluid.'[1721]

Marsh was not overwhelmingly enthusiastic; he though that 'Phaeacia' and 'The Sacred Incident' were far below the rest of Flecker's poems in the book and told him so.[1722] Flecker replied that he would not have inserted 'Phaeacia' or 'The Sacred Incident' if he had had time to revise the book thoroughly or write more poems.'[1723]

Another criticism of Marsh's was the use of 'Diarbekir' in 'Gates of Damascus':

> Postern of Fate, the Desert Gate, Disaster's Cavern, Fort of
>   Fear,
> The Portal of Bagdad am I, the Doorway of Diarbekir.

Flecker agreed with Marsh, telling him: 'Of course "Diarbekir" should have a note. It is known as the "black city" throughout the East on account of the dark stone of its walls.' [1724]

'Diarbekir' was pounced on by others for different reasons. In the review of *The Golden Journey* in *The New Statesman* of 2 August 1913, it was stated: 'The 'Gates of Damascus' has good passages, though it is hard to understand how Mr. Flecker, who apparently knows both Damascus and the Arabic tongue can have rhymed "Diarbekr" to "Fear," when the word is pronounced "Diarbekr." But let that pass.'

Flecker was not prepared to let it pass and he wrote to Squire about the pronunciation of 'Diarbekir'. Squire appears not to have replied. Flecker reminded Squire, when writing to him on 26 December, 1913: 'Diarbekir is the regular Turkish pronunciation – and all Europeans follow it. Darbekr is Arabic.' [1725]

Reader Bullard, in his memoirs, did not let it pass either, when he wrote: 'There is a line in 'Gates of Damascus' which shows that Flecker never penetrated very far to the east. He says [he quotes the line] .... but it is that Diarbekir rhymes with Flecker, and thus provides a nucleus of a limerick which Flecker could have completed with great skill.' [1726]

Bullard journeyed to Diarbekir and whether or not Flecker was wrong or right in Bullard's estimation over the pronunciation of the name of the town, Flecker was right about 'the dark stone of its walls'. Bullard described Diarbekir as: 'a town on a hill, completely surrounded by a high wall of black basalt and looking like one of those castles in the background of Italian pictures'.[1727]

Bullard continued in his belief that Flecker was misled by the name Haji Bekir, the maker of Turkish Delight in Constantinople, and did not appear to have read Flecker's side of the argument in his published letter to Squire.[1728]

Extra work of a different sort, more time-consuming and irritating than the use of Diabekir, was revealed by Flecker in a postcard to Goschens posted 7 July 7:[1729]

> Mrs. Graham, British Consulate, Paris writes to me to say that she has asked your permission to insert 3 poems out of *Samarkand* and that you have not answered and that her book is being held up in consequence and would I write to you, etc., etc.,
>
> It is of course entirely your affair – but I have no objection and it would only do good You might force the lady to take a few copies in payment but in heaven's name don't say it was my suggestion.
>
> (I am a little cross because she wanted a <u>free</u> copy of the 42 to pillage for her anthology, but be nice to her as she is a Consuless.)

James Elroy Flecker

Mrs. A.C.W. Graham, whose address was given as Fordfield, Cambridge, was on the list that included Paul Morand, sent in June by Flecker to his publishers in order that they would receive a prospectus of *The Golden Journey*. Flecker must have met Mrs. Graham's husband, Constantine, who had also studied to enter the Consular Service, at Cambridge. Graham was transferred to Paris as HM Vice-Consul in 1913.

Mrs. Graham's anthology was *Cambridge Poets (1900–1913)*, chosen by Aelfrida Tillyard. Introduction by Arthur Quiller-Couch, Cambridge 1913, W. Heffer and Sons Ltd. The poems included in *Cambridge Poets* by Flecker:

'To a Poet a Thousand Years Hence'   – (*Forty-Two Poems*)

'Tenebris Interlucentem'   – (*Bridge of Fire* and *Forty-Two Poems*)

'The Ballad of Camden Town'   – (*Forty-Two Poems*)

'Mary Magdalen'   – (*Bridge of Fire* and *Forty-Two Poems*)

'I Rose from Dreamless Hours'   – (*Bridge of Fire* and *Forty-Two Poems*)

'Yasmin, A Ghazel'	– (*The Golden Journey to Samarkand*)
'The Golden Journey to Samarkand'	– (*The Golden Journey to Samarkand*)
'Oak and Olive'	– (*The Golden Journey to Samarkand*)

The Golden Journey to Samarcand was first published in *Poetry and Drama*, March 1913. (Revised as *The Golden Journey to Samarkand*.) *Poetry and Drama* was the new name of *Poetry Review*.

The new name for *Rhythm* (formerly *The Blue Review*) did not help the magazine to survive the problems of unpaid printers' bills, balanced against having Rupert Brooke and others on the Board.

'Yasmin, a Ghazel' was published in the June edition (the last of three) of *The Blue Review* and as a result, a much more extensive criticism and irritation appeared in *The New Age* of 10 July 1913 in the form of a letter to the editor. The writer of the letter was Beatrice Hastings, who was on the staff of *The New Age* when Flecker's 'The Last Generation' was published in May/June 1908, but the letter contained no mention of his previous work.

Mr. Flecker's Ghazal

To the Editor of THE NEW AGE.

Sir, – With regard to my poem 'Yasmin' in the *Blue Review* your critic writes:

It is probably rather incompetence than tame impertinence that allows Mr. James E. Flecker to call his verses a 'ghazal'. But, in fact, a few conceits and the mere mention of Mecca will not make a ghazal.'

'How splendid in the morning glows the lily: with what
   grace he throws
His supplication to the rose: do roses nod the head,
   Yasmin?'
'Thy silver locks, once auburn bright,
Are still more lovely in my sight
Than golden beams of Orient light,
My Mary.' (*Cowper*)

... Mr. Flecker is one with those ignorant contemporaries of ours,' etc., etc.

In reply, I beg to point out:

(1) The poem is an absolutely perfect ghazal of the *strictest possible* Oriental type. If your critic cannot read Persian, he may refer to Gibbs' *Ottoman Poetry* for confirmation. The word 'head' before 'Yasmin' rhymes completely through the ten verses. This is the chief mark of Ghazal. I do not suppose your critic is so fantastic as to expect me to reproduce a 'failatun' metre, or the mute izafat.

(2) The lines from Cowper no more resemble 'Yasmin' in metre than Tennyson's 'Boedicea.' Where are rhymes to 'Mary' or to 'my'?

(3) Has your critic (or the obscure person called Mrs. Hastings, whom he quotes) lived in the East? I have. Has he been forced, like myself, to study Turkish, Arabic and Persian? Has he even such acquaintance with their literatures as English books can give?

(4) Ignorance? Incompetence? Perhaps, at least, *tamed* impertinence.

J.E. Flecker.

[Our Reviewer writes: Am I to conclude that Mr. Flecker has tried and found me guilty of impertinence towards himself – so famous a self, too, as he implies – and that he has inflicted upon me the punishment of a snub? If *tu quoque* might settle our quarrel, I might be disposed to run away impressed to annihilation by this opponent who has been obliged to possess three Oriental languages. But the question is not very important whether I have been impertinent to Mr. Flecker's linguistical accomplishments, whereas I do find this important – whether Mr. Flecker's excursion into an imitation of Oriental poetry is justified by his poetical powers. It is a poor reply for him to make that his obligatory studies of Turkish, Arabic, and Persian, together with his sojourn in the East place his verses, written in English, beyond English criticism. The point is that these verses give an impression of being manufactured: for while Mr. Flecker adopts, as well as the form of the ghazal, some well-worn local colouring and certain quite as threadbare expressions of Eastern verse-writers, he utilises these adjuncts with the least credible skill. I quote his verses in full, and, with your permission, will consider them at, I hope, satisfactory length.

YASMIN A GHAZAL

'How splendid in the morning glows the lily: with what
  grace he throws
His supplication to the rose: do roses nod the head,
  Yasmin?
'But when the silver dove descends I find the little flower
  of friends
Whose very name that sweetly ends I say when I have said
  Yasmin.

'The morning light is clear, cold: I dare not in that light
  behold
A white light, a deeper gold, a glory too far shed, Yasmin.
'But when the deep red eye of day is level with the lone
  highway,
And some to Mecca turn to pray, and I toward thy bed,
  Yasmin,

'Or when the wind beneath the moon is drifting like a
  soul aswoon,
And harping planet talk love's tune with milky wings
  outspread, Yasmin,

'Shower down thy love, O burning bright! For one night
  or the other night
Will come the Gardener in white; and gathered flowers
  are are dead, Yasmin.'

My last conclusion about these verses is my first – namely, that there is not line of poetry among them, not one single inspired phrase. It was upon this conclusion that I gave my opinion of Mr. Flecker's ignorance and incompetence. He thinks that he has made a poem. But rhythm, thoughts, and words are all hammered. It is nonsense for Mr. Flecker to claim even strictness of form, for his very first phrase is faulty, being decasyllabic, and, withal, adorned with a feminine ending! If he can produce me a ghazal by any acknowledged Eastern poet which exhibits a similar licence, he will be at liberty to claim a model, though still not one in strict form. The stifling piffle about the lily, a male, one supposes, supplicating a presumably female rose, were best left further unexamined. But to seek for coherence and sense in these verses is to seek almost vainly. The name that 'sweetly ends' must not be taken to begin unsweetly, distinction being made here only for the sake of the rhyme. I find no necessary contrast between the first and second stanzas, yet a contrast is implied by the 'but.' In the third stanza the uxorious lily turns out to have been glowing splendidly in a 'clear, cold light.' This stanza puzzles me, in spite of the familiar Tennysonian comparatives; and the glory 'too far shed' has to my ear a comic tone of pigeon English. At the fourth, I merely pause to wonder wherever Mr. Flecker can have observed the 'deep red eye of day' in the East. This deep red is a Northern phenomenon, and, even so, a winter one, which would indeed time very well with clear, cold mornings, but not with the glowing lilies and roses, let alone the stupendous wheeling sun of the Orient, as at least, I have seen it. The fifth stanza completes my bafflement. Harping planets .... that *talk* love's *toon*.... with milky wings, Yasmin! Nor finally, can I conjecture how 'the other night' the Gardener will, in the future, come, even in white. Feebleness is the character of Mr. Flecker's verses; he has acquired the three tongues in vain for making poetry.

'How, his; but whose; the, a; but, and; or, and; shower, will' note how miserably he opens his lines. In charity we will suppose that he give us by his *deep* red and a *deeper* gold, a Gardener in *white* and a *whiter* light, and *light* thrice in three consecutive lines, that subtle play upon words which we are accustomed to in Oriental verse. Our poet appears to expect poetical form through compulsory studies of Oriental languages, and a stay in the East. Should he, then, be able to neigh if he had lived in a stable? Truly, he is one with those versifiers I mentioned, who string us off so many curious 'sapphics' and 'Anacreontics,' Alcaics, and what you will, on the strength of a knowledge of Greek. Shakespeare in all his diversity, Keats of 'The Grecian Urn,' were not equipped like one of these. But so much is only proof that poetical genius has for its perfect attribute universality of comprehension.

I propose now to quote the ghazal by Mrs. Hastings, since I have been so unlucky as to provoke Mr. Flecker's frown against her. This ghazal, I understand, was modelled upon Jami's 'Ringlet' poem, with the substitution of a second rhyme, 'day-may,' for the customary weighty effect of introducing the poet's name in the final phrase of Oriental songs. The first few and the last lines of Jami's poem may be given:-

'Ay dil' í man sayd' i dám i zulf' i tó
Dám i dilhá gashta nám i zulf i to
Banda shud dar zulf i tó dilhá tamám
Dám u band ámad tamám í zulf i to
Dád i tashríf' í ghulám' í-bandará
Zulf í tó ay man ghulám' í zulf i tó
. . . .
Bnda-Jámi-rá zi shám' i zulf i tó.'

'GHAZAL'

'Guide, thou laughing fairy, home where laughter dwells,
    Him from whom thy ever-bubbling colour wells.
Wing! From me, with wishing wings, now wings emerge;
Weaves he high in cloudland, his enwreathing spells;
Or, in million spirals, hath he million homes,
Voicing low from rhythm-haunted ocean shells:
Clings his ruddy form on buoyant mountain peaks:

Greenly, makes he heaven in enfolded dells,
Copses where creative music ripples through;
Is't his laughing voice among the woodland bells
Flatters these to flourish forth their shielded buds?
Lead me, lead me where the god his story tells!
Yet, fay, wouldst thou still thy secret, secret keep,
Tell not me: for I to larks and philomels
Word will send – that these by night, and those by day,
Wing the path to Laughter may that Care dispels.

BEATRICE HASTINGS

I leave it to readers whether by merit of poetical rhythm, subject, imagery, and diction the writer of 'Yasmin' has the claim to judge of Mrs. Hastings' composition. In mere craftsmanship the latter is incontestably superior, there being nine rhymes on a single sound as against Mr. Flecker's six. I may point out, not being so ignorant of my subject as Mr. Flecker would like to believe, the deliberate repetition of significant words; the excellent play of the third line, where the thought, though still upon the subject, is cast completely in the Eastern world; the variety of word and image; the typically Oriental pun on 'secret'; and finally the sound instinctive taste in avoiding all those garish colourings and senseless conceits which seem to be thought inseparable from exotic imitations. There are several faults in this ghazal, but I challenge Mr. Flecker to point them out.]

Flecker was able to defend himself from this onslaught in a letter headed 'Yasmin: A Reply' published in *The New Age* of 24 Jul 1913:

YASMIN: A REPLY

Dear Critic, Had I but seen Mrs. Hastings' ghazal, before I wrote my former reply, I would have lifted the hat of admiration from the head of shame. I cannot accept your challenge to criticise this fine poem. I am no critic, and, in any case, I would not like to criticise a lady. And what could I say but praise? And praise is always such dull reading. Is there not, by the way, a misprint in the last line:

'Wing the path to laughter may *that* Care dispels'?

Should it not run:

'Wing the path to Laughter, May! *That* Care dispels'?
Or even:
    'Wing the path to! Laughter may *that*. Care dispels'?

It is then, dear critic, with humility that I accept your most ferocious strictures. True, I never defended my poetic skill against you, but merely my knowledge of the East: and you must forgive my saying that to call an author *personally*

529

ignorant and impudent, as you virtually did in your original remarks, is a breach of etiquette, of a kind which, among our hot-headed neighbours, might have exposed you to a nasty sword-cut from the victim of the outrage. But of my poetry say what you will: you have the absolute right. I never have and never will write a line in praise of my own work. What, indeed, could I write? Though I pronounce 'tune' <u>tyoon</u> and not <u>toon</u>, as you do, I suppose we poets must leave off our old, old habit now you tell me by implication it must not rhyme with moon. As for the red eye of Day, I regret to state that I saw several red sunsets in the desert, but perhaps I should not have mentioned it. I am sorry 'glory too far shed' is pigeon English, as I have never been to China. I wish I could work a jolly phrase of yours, 'stifling piffle,' into my next poem. I am *beastly* sorry the gardener in white may not come one night or other: at any rate, that will keep him out of Clapham.

Finally, please accept my apologies for having written so feeble and occidental a lyric. I quite realise my remarks about the correctness of the metre of Yasmin were not worth answering. And you have done justly, if cruelly, in exposing my verses by the side of what I may perhaps call 'Mrs. Hastings' Greenly Ghazal.'

JAMES ELROY FLECKER

[Our reviewer writes: Mr. Flecker's letter is like Swift's lady who prided herself upon her haughty looks, which, however, nobody quite understood and everybody completely disregarded.]

'Yasmin' was referred to in a long letter to Savery[1730] in which he thanked him for criticism received about *The Golden Journey*. Flecker told him (in a note No.4 of 16):' "Yasmin" is an anthology piece. It is part of *Hassan* – written for it and should sound well in its place. '

Hellé agreed with Savery 'practically in everything.' Flecker did too. He thought that Savery underrated Santorin, which was 'much admired by Dunsany'. [Edward, 18th Baron Dunsany 1878–1957, Irish writer.[1731]] 'Lord Arnaldos', he told Savery, 'was after all a translation.' ('Lord Arnaldos' was not republished in *The Golden Journey*.) He also told Savery of his last-minute rewriting of 'Gates of Damascus' and enlarging it. 'Gates of Damascus' he considered his best poem, as Savery agreed. It was inspired by Damascus where he had spent all his time 'dreaming of Oxford. Yet it seems – even to hardened Orientalists – that I understand'. 'Taoping', he told Savery, he had sweated over when very ill and 'turned it from rot into a good poem of workmanship'. He did not refer to his original version of part of the poem not being incorporated into the final version. 'Taoping', he explained, was suggested 'by a strange amazing book by one Daguerches *Consolata fille du Soleil....*' He then goes on to ask Savery: 'Do you really shudder at a Japanese print?' 'Taoping' can be compared to a Japanese/Chinese print and that was why Flecker responded with this reference.[1732] Also in the description of 'the old Mandarin' in Taoping:

Down the canal's hibiscus-shaded marge
The glossy mules draw on the cedar barge,
Railed silver, blue-silk-curtained, which within
Bears the Commander, the old Mandarin. [1733]

This must have provoked Savery's criticism because in the letter Flecker writes:

Concerning the Chinese. Frank, I almost accuse you of insincerity.... Do you really believe in the 'inhuman oriental' myth? Or do you think you ought to believe in the myth?

Don't you think that the healthy honest way for a European to look at a Chinaman or a nigger is to laugh at him? Don't you think they are there for the joy of the picturesque – as I portray them in 'Taoping'?

Returning in his letter to 'Santorin', Flecker asked Savery if he did not think that the *Legend*, at least, was one of the loveliest in the world? 'I wonder if you weird Catholics realize that the Middle Age is still in flower in the Aegean. "That man married a Syren" said a peasant once to my wife – and showed the man!'

Savery liked 'Hyali' but did not mention 'A Ship, an Isle'. Whether or not it was because of Savery's reaction to his poems of the Aegean or that his present situation was similar in some ways to his time in Corfu, but Flecker wrote his first new poem since he had sent off 'Brumana' from the Lebanon to be included in '*The Golden Journey*'. This new poem was a version of the poem that was to be revised as 'The Old Ships' and some of its lines are taken out to

appear in a separate poem 'Fragment' in the collected Poems. In SLA the first draft of the poem appears thus:[1734]
'FOR Hellé

Written on a Happy Day – July 13th, 1913'

Why he was reminded of his time in the Aegean could be because in Corfu and in Switzerland, Hellé had to shoulder the day-to-day living problems while her husband was free to get on with his literary endeavours. Corfu and Switzerland harboured British ghosts in beautiful, if very different, surroundings. Flecker's health was much worse than two years ago in Greece, although reaction to the ghosts was also very different.

Hellé's birthday was not the only reason for celebration around the middle of July: favourable reviews were coming out in newspapers and magazines for *The Golden Journey to Samarkand*. All in all over twenty reviews were to appear.[1735]

One of the earliest reviews of *The Golden Journey to Samarkand* was published in *The Globe* of 18 July 1913, and was one Flecker approved of because of its interesting criticism and its quotable content.[1736] *The Globe* critic thought Flecker 'a better poet than a critic'.[1737] This last was a reference to the preface. The critic writing in *The Aberdeen Journal* of 22 July 1913, also focuses on the preface to *The Golden Journey* and began by quoting at length from it. The comment was: 'Brave words! but does Mr. Flecker practise what he here preaches?' The critic also quoted some lines from 'The Hamman Name' and asked if this poem 'with its ultra "conceits" is superior to the poetry that Mr. Flecker runs down?' After quoting lines from 'The Hamman Name' the critic asked: 'Will such poetry make any soul worth saving?' This was a reference to the quote from the preface in which Flecker states: 'It is not the poet's business to save man's soul, but to make it worth saving'.

The critic balanced his criticism with praise and thought that Flecker 'has a fine poetic imagination, and a great power of melodious rhythm and beautiful diction; of which he gives choice examples here. We like him best when, leaving the burning Orient, he sings under the inspiration of his native land, as in the lyric ending: .....'.

The critic quoted the last verse of 'Oak and Olive' (which was, the critic failed to note, also written under the influence of Greece), but if the critic realised that Flecker's love of 'his native land' meant his poems of beauty were linked to the theme of homesickness, then he had a valid point to make. 'The burning Orient' served to create for Flecker the longing for his native land that the critic appreciated. The critic did not appear to see that 'Oak and Olive' was as Flecker described it to Savery[1738], 'A jest after all in the good old manner. No, I wouldn't have left it out of the volume though of course, it's very slight'. Flecker had written to Savery in the same letter: 'Of course the "Turkish Lady" won't wash'. This reference to 'The Hamman Name' echoed what appeared to be in the mind of the critic in *The Aberdeen Journal* who saw 'The Hamman Name' as some sort of jest and 'Oak and Olive', which Flecker intended as a jest, as something beautiful. In *The Golden Journey to Samarkand*, 'The Hamman Name' is subtitled ('From a poem by a Turkish lady') and it was as Flecker had written to Savery :'The poem is a pretty close translation in the book.' It was (as has been seen) a translation of a Turkish poem 'Book of the Bath' by the eighteenth-century Ottoman poet, Mehemmed Emin Beligh of Larissa, who, as has also been seen, had much in common with Nedim, the poet whose 'Saadabad' Flecker also translated and included in *The Golden Journey to Samarkand*. Flecker's gifts as a translator were not appreciated by the critic in *The Aberdeen Journal*. 'The Hamman Name' had the hidden Firbank element (which Savery might have guessed at because he was at Uppingham at the same time as Firbank), which the critic might just have felt was a homosexual reference carefully disguised.

The critic writing in *The Athenaeum* of 26 July 1913, also focuses on the preface to *The Golden Journey to Samarkand*, stating: 'Mr. Flecker's poetical ideals are high, and his theory of poetry, as expressed in a brilliantly written Preface, worthy of consideration. But he is an enthusiast, and his horizon is limited by enthusiasm.'

He then went on:

> Mr. Flecker is a poet, and, had he chosen to be didactic, would have performed his task worthily. *The Golden Journey to Samarkand* is a haunting piece of verse, rich in the glamour of Syria, and without a superfluous line. The remaining lyrics derive their inspiration from various sources, Oriental and Hellénic, but all are faultless in form and in no sense imitative. We quote the following from 'Oak and Olive:

The first two verses are quoted.

The critic ends his review by stating: 'We look forward with interest to the author's next venture, but the use of such a phrase as "amoral sentiments"[1739] (Preface pii) is surely to be deprecated.'

The critic's comment about Flecker's verse being 'in no sense imitative' missed, as other critics did too, what Flecker described when referring to 'Phaeacia' as 'one of two rotten poems in the book and also as an unconscious imitation of Yeats...'[1740] In 'Oak and Olive', which got a good deal of attention from the critics, the 'no sense imitative' did not apply either because of its 'A Gloucestershire Lad' theme resembling A.E. Housman's *A Shropshire Lad.*

The Glasgow Herald of 31 July 1913, reviewed *The Golden Journey* and Flecker found it satisfactory.[1741]

The review in *The New Statesman* of *The Golden Journey*, which was published in the 2 August 1913 edition, was more astringent in view of what that publication had already said about the book – that his second volume was only the first with a little added and the third, his second volume with a little added. The critic in *The New Statesman* was quick to point out that 'there is nothing in the new book to equal the two outstanding lyrics in the old one.' The critic explained that *The Golden Journey* was 'divided into three sections: the first Oriental in subject and form, the second inspired by Greece; the last miscellaneous.' The critic stated: 'The latter two sections are the worst'. The critic continued, 'It is the Orient that moves him to his best work'. This is in contrast to the opinion of the critic of the *Aberdeen Journal. The New Statesman* critic thought that the best thing in the book 'is *The Golden Journey* itself. Apes, ivory and peacocks have terrible "fake" associations in these days, yet Mr. Flecker really makes us believe in his caravan, and there is a wonderful dexterity in the way in which, with scarcely a word of description, he makes us (by means of conversation between the watchman, the merchants, and the woman) see very vividly the assemblage and gradual departure from Bagdad of this company setting out for its great journey.'

He then quotes from 'The Merchants (in chorus)'.

> The critic thought it was 'a little stagey but effective. In its way 'Ghazel" Yasmin is equally good; it shows Mr. Flecker at his best as a rhythmical craftsman. 'The Gates of Damascus' also has good passages......'. Then the critic went on to complain about the rhyming of 'Diarbekir' to 'fear'. It was as if, like the critic in *The Athenaeum* with the complaint about 'amoral sentiments', they could not resist a sting in the tail of their reviews of *The Golden Journey to Samarkand.*

Flecker's interest in reviews of *The Golden Journey* nearer his former home was displayed in a letter to his parents on 24 July. He asked them to send a cutting from the *Gloucestershire Echo.* On 2 August, a review of *The Golden Journey* appeared in *The Cheltenham Looker-On* coupled with a review of a book of poems by Maud Tymms entitled *The Cotswold Queen*. The pairing was explained by the statement that both were 'natives of Cheltenham, but Mr. Flecker seeks his inspiration mainly in the sensuous East, while Miss Tymms apparently derives her's from the "hills and fields" of the local Cotswolds.'

The fact that he was 'the son of Rev. Dr. Flecker, of Dean Close School' was one reason why *The Golden Journey* was reviewed in *The Cheltenham Looker-On* in the first place. The critic mentions that: 'Mr. Flecker confesses to the "single intention of creating beauty." He has no wish to preach. "If we have preaching to do," he says, "in heaven's name let us call it a sermon and write it in prose."'

The reference to 'sermon' seems to be made in connection with the poet being the son of Rev. Dr. Flecker. The critic, like many others who reviewed *The Golden Journey* was intrigued with the preface. But unlike most of the others, this critic thought that Flecker seemed 'safest' when writing 'from the standpoint of *Arabian Nights* or *Omar Khayyam*.' But that Flecker was weakest 'when he takes his Muse to Gloucestershire and dallies with her in Cranham Woods and Painswick Hill; and we think that he – though 'one bred in Gloucestershire, one of the Englishmen' – would prefer lying in 'Grecian fields, smothered in asphodel,' to endeavouring to discover the 'autumn leaves like blood and gold that strew a Gloucester lane'. His jest, 'Oak and Olive' appeared to have been discovered by this critic.

The opportunity to learn more of the reactions of the critics to *The Golden Journey* had to be missed when the longing to move out of Leysin became a reality. The weather during the last weeks of July was dull with heavy rain. Whether or not as a result of his not being able to go out for walks because of the weather, throughout July he had requested Dean Close to send out his books. These long lists of books were to be housed, when received, in his little bookcase with the red dragons, if it could be sent out in sections to him. The last request was for the three large volumes of *Arabian Nights*; he wanted the pictures for the costumes for *Hassan*.

He had also written to Mr. Cooper in July and suggested to him that he read Paul Fort as part of his proposed tour in France. Flecker extolled the 'rhythmical, rhyming prose of extraordinary beauty, about the little towns of the 'Ile de France,' Nemours, Senlis, Velizy, and it would be a most joyful thing to follow some of his footsteps.'[1742]

It is unlikely that one of the reasons for choosing the new location, Montreux on the shores of Lake Geneva, was for Flecker to follow in some of the footsteps of Lord Byron or Shelley. The reasons for the move were many, not least the fact that Flecker was tired of the place. He even wrote to his father from Leysin in July:

'The Church of this place is vile beyond belief.'[1743]

It could be that 'this place' referred to Switzerland in general but it was obvious that the euphoria of the first weeks of settling into life at Leysin had quickly worn off. The necessity of remaining there until the business of proofreading and awaiting reviews was completed, was not, in July, so pressing. But the fact that he was allowed to leave with his doctor's permission only underlined the fact that he was not improving steadily enough to be a good advertisement for staying on at the Hotel Belvedere. His parents, when they heard of the proposed move, wrote (quite rightly, as it turned out) that Montreux would prove to be much more expensive.[1744] The fact that their son argued that it would be cheaper and as healthy as Leysin pointed to his worries about money and health. His health did not improve; 'a little trip on the lake' was to bring on a day's temperature.

Flecker wrote to Marsh from the Pension Alexandra, Montreux, with a request for the address of Barker's reader, A.E. Drinkwater, who, he complained, had kept *Hassam* for two months. He asked Marsh if he knew of a 'boy or young man vaguely at or formerly at Cambridge?' [Nottingham?] who had written to Flecker a letter of appreciation after reading *The Golden Journey*.[1745]

The writer of the letter could have been Cecil Roberts (1892–1976) who had also, in July 1913, published by subsidy a book of poems, which had received some good reviews. Amongst the well-known people to whom he had sent a copy was A.C. Benson. Roberts was later to meet Marsh and visit Marsh's apartment in Gray's Inn. Roberts had ,by chance, picked up a copy of *The Nation* and read and then memorised the whole of the poem that was later revised as 'Brumana'. (The date of the publication of 'The Pines', revised as 'Brumana' was said by Roberts to be a year before he read, in 1913, *The Golden Journey*.) So started a life-long admiration of Flecker, which resulted in correspondence with the Flecker parents and an invitation to Dean Close and also the publication of Roberts's poem entitled 'James Elroy Flecker. In Memoriam'.

In Flecker's next letter to Marsh from the Pension Villa Alexandra, he told him that Montreux 'was divine after the Mountains'. He enclosed for Marsh his new version of 'God Save the King', which he could not make up his mind about, telling Marsh:'… if it's rather good or a joke or both. It wants a final verse on the Mother Country.'[1746]

Divine as Montreux seemed to Flecker, there were more down-to-earth matters to consider; it was not much cheaper than Leysin, as he had argued with his parents, and cost could be another reason why, by 14 August, the Fleckers had moved out of the Pension Alexandra to the Hotel de Glion, Glion-sur-Montreux. He wrote to Savery from Glion, telling him he had been 'ordered to this lower summer and incomparably more delightful place'. *Hassan* had been sent off to the typist. He was sending a copy of *The Grecians* to Savery via the publishers Dents.

The reason why there was a reawakening of interest in *The Grecians* was its inclusion in *The Golden Journey* under 'By the same Author' heading *Forty-Two Poems* and *The Grecians* (but left out *Thirty-Six Poems* and *The Bridge of Fire*). The reference to *The Grecians* must have also interested Marsh because Flecker arranged for a copy to be sent to him too. (A copy must have also reached Flecker's parents, as the LIFE gives December 1913 as the date of conflict with his mother, in particular, over passages in *The Grecians*.) Flecker described *The Grecians* to Marsh (in a letter dated 18 August from Hotel de Glion): 'It was a little book a little bit vulgar but full of profundities. Nobody has ever taken the slightest notice of it: and the publishers took no trouble with it at all.' [1747] He also added, later in the letter: 'Meanwhile you can criticise the 'Grecians' as severely as you like!' He again emphasised to Marsh the vast improvement Glion was on Leysin.

Glion was the inspiration for Flecker's poems 'Glion – Noon' and 'Glion – Evening', which he wrote during his stay on his own in Lausanne in 1904 in the same month – August. In 'Glion – Noon' he wrote:

> The Dent du Midi now uprears
> His proud tiara through the mist, [1748]

He wrote to Savery on 14 August 1913, from Glion: 'One can see France and it sort of hallows the surrounding Helvetic air.'

His brief stay in Glion in August 1913 did not contain the inner loneliness of his visit to Glion in 1904, when he was separated from Beazley; although his physical health was better, it was his career future that was in doubt in 1904. In 1913 he was not alone and the publishing horizon of his work was much more widespread and optimistic, he could appreciate the beauty of the place and it was not distorted by his inner miseries although his physical health was not improving.

He also wrote to Messrs. Goschens on 14 August:[1749]

Hotel de Glion

Glion-sur-Montreux

14th August Switzerland

Dear Sir,

I write to give you my new address, which will be permanent for a month or two. I have received excellent notices of Samarkand from *Globe, Telegraph* and *Morning Post* – but unfortunately I know that good reviews don't mean a good sale. My friends are working hard for me. I have secured a promise of a further notice in the *Times* – beyond the miserable two lines they gave me.

My play being finished, I am quite ready to receive proofs of the *King of Alsander*.

Please if you see Mr. Goldring tell him that I am about to write and thank him for his kind letter of congratulation.

Yours faithfully

James Elroy Flecker

Marsh also, on 18 August, got notification of the Hotel de Glion address. He was thanked for persuading *The Times* to review his book. (*The Times Literary Supplement* published a review of *The Golden Journey* on 28 August 1913.) Marsh was also thanked for sending on a postcard from Gosse, which Flecker found 'most inspiring'. It read: 'I marked one or two poems for special praise, and then found I was marking more than half the book. This is certainly a most authentic poet that you have so cleverly discovered.'[1750]

Gosse later described Flecker's work in more favourable terms than the work of Brooke, when he wrote:

'... Flecker, whose touch was the most magical of all, surpassing in actual thrill of witchcraft that of the beloved Rupert Brooke.'[1751]

More praise of a different sort for Flecker's work must have been contained in Marsh's letter because Flecker replied:

I wish I had been at the luncheon party and heard Ainley spout the 'Gates of Damascus'. It would be still a greater joy to hear him in the part of Ishak [Ainley later played Hassan on stage] on the stage (despite his justifiable aversion to my first draught of *Hassan*).[1752]

(Mrs. Patrick Campbell also read out Flecker's poems at this dinner party.) The statement made on the 14 August to Goschens that the Hotel Glion 'will be permanent for a month or two' proved to be wrong. On 24 August he was writing to his parents of his settling in to the Sanatorium Stephani, Montana-sur-Sierre. It appeared that his health and the Hotel de Glion were not satisfactory.

He did not enjoy, after Glion, being back among the black fir trees and the horrid snowy mountains.[1753] He was very tired after his journey, which could partly account for this unhappy description of his new surroundings. The tiredness he felt after the journey from Glion to Montana would also be behind the writing of the letter he wrote to the Foreign Office on 30 August, telling them that he was not yet in a fit state to make the journey to England and undergo the medical examination. He needed a full winter to recover and he would send a medical certificate. He wanted his full travelling expenses from Beirut to be paid.[1754]

He was complaining of tiredness when he wrote to Savery on the 28 August, sending him *Hassan* and asking him to pencil anything he liked on it and return the manuscript at his leisure. Marsh, on the same day, also got a copy of *Hassan* sent to him for his opinion and a suggestion he show it to Barker. The response from Savery was quick and positive. Flecker wrote to him and told him to show it to his friend and get it translated with a view to its being taken by a German Theatre. Savery's criticisms of *Hassan* followed shortly afterwards. Whatever remarks Savery made about *Hassan*, he told him: 'I am pleased with myself, my dear Frank, as usual. *Hassan* is, I think, supremely stageable and written with a certain consistency and polish....'[1755]

He thanked Savery for all the trouble he was taking because Savery's friend was still considering *Hassan*. He wanted the friend to get *Hassan* acted because he stated that plays were hardly ever published before they are acted. He wanted Savery to come to Montana for Christmas; a plum pudding from home was guaranteed.

On 31 August, from the Sanatorium Stephani, he apologised to Goldring for 'a most shameful time' he had taken in answering Goldring's 'delightful and enthusiastic letter of congratulation'. He told Goldring that he thought the reviews 'especially *The Times* and the *Morning Post* – have been good enough for Shakespeare'. He did hope that the reviews 'will even be enough to sell a few copies of the book; I should hate Goschens to be badly had by the transaction'.

He told Goldring of the difficulties he had lately experienced in finding a new place to live. (These difficulties indicated that the state of his health prevented him from getting a room at hotels that were not sanatoria. 'None of the other hotels accept any lungs' was how he described his getting into Hotel Stephani to Savery.[1756]) He was 'pretty sick of life'. His play, he told Goldring, was finished, 'but I don't suppose it will ever be played'.

In this frame of mind – despair about the future of *Hassan* – he went on to ask Goldring how he could 'make a little gold by writing (and drawing)' (by Hellé) advertisements for Pears' soap. He also wanted Goldring's opinion on his idea of 'making a Xmas illustrated book out of my Eastern poems. Trelawney could do it very well'. He was going to write a book 'one day on "How to spend money in a jolly way," for men of moderate income (£500–£1,500 a year)'. He hoped the book would sell 'by the hundred thousand million on the railways' bookstalls.'[1757] The need to try and make money from sources other than his plays and poetry was bolstered by the insecurity caused by his uncertain future whereby he could be prevented from earning money as a consular official.

On 31 August, when he was writing to Goldring, Flecker had not yet had an answer to his letter of 30 August informing the Foreign Office that he was not fit enough to make the journey to England. He must have feared that the Foreign Office's answer was that he would have to resign.

On 1 September, Dr. Flecker wrote to the Foreign Office, emphasising the fact that his son had entered the service in perfect health and contracted pneumonia while in Constantinople and that a whole winter in Switzerland would effect a cure. If his son was forced to resign and be entirely dependent on his father, Dr. Flecker feared the effect on his spirits and the retarding of his recovery. It would be a serious matter for Dr. Flecker personally.[1758]

How much of this Dr. Flecker really believed to be the truth and how much was angled to help prolong his son's stay in Switzerland is not hard to decide. (Sherwood states that a sentence in one of Flecker's letters home suggested that this line of approach was dictated by his father.[1759]) It could not have escaped Dr. Flecker that his son was almost entirely dependent on him already. He must also have known that the consumption had been established before his son entered the service, but it was prudent to make sure the FO accepted the blame for the disease appearing to manifest itself first in Constantinople. The facts were that his son could not stay at Dean Close; he would need to be nursed elsewhere and by Hellé. Both son and daughter-in-law would need financial support. The longer his son remained in the Consular Service, the easier it would be for his parents. The 'cure' would at best only mean a period of remission, in which he could get back into the service for a short time and then it would be hoped he could apply for more sick-leave when the period of remission came to an end. This was unrealistic, but his parents put in print their view that 'it must always be a satisfaction to remember that his official service was sufficiently valued for the Government to give him every possible chance and consideration.'[1760] The Foreign Office's opinion of Flecker was that 'he's not a satisfactory officer, although clever'.[1761] This was the problem; 'clever' appeared not to be an attribute that was valued. He had not been 'clever' enough to pass examinations the FO required; they wanted candidates with sufficient marks to satisfy their examiners. The key to all this lay hidden in the remarks about Flecker and his progress at Cambridge, namely that it was his health that held him back, not his ability. It was in the FO's interests, however, to give him the opportunity to recover his health. On 4 September, sick-leave was granted to enable him to stay in Switzerland until the end of February/March.

This was the news he was waiting for because he still had to wait for information on the progress of *Hassan*, which was at a crucial stage on its path to acceptance. The payment of travelling expenses was not settled, it was pointed out that he had already been paid half his travelling expenses. For health reasons and his literary aspirations, it was more satisfactory for him to remain where he was than to consider a return to England. His contacts at home, such as Marsh, were more likely to be working on his behalf simply because he was bedridden and in exile. If he were back in England and appearing to enjoy any sort of recovery, however brief, it would mean that he would have to fend for himself in the literary world. He got on with his correspondence. One aspect of the FO's consideration of Flecker as a suitable Consular Official, which appeared not known to them, was his literary aspirations.

He wrote to Goschens on 7 September,[1762] exhibiting a degree of business acumen and knowledge of his market:

> Hotel Stephani
> Montana-sur-Sierre
> Switzerland

Dear Sir,

I am a little troubled at receiving no communication from you with regard to the *King of Alsander* or other matters mentioned in my last postcards. I hope the book is 'moving' a little since the *Times*'s Review. Have the *Times* bookclub taken it up: they ought to.

1. Would you please do this – send a dozen copies per parcel/book post (there is a British post office: it is quite safe) to Sarrafian Bros. Booksellers, Beyrouth, Syria, with a communication in the following sense

'Mr. Flecker has suggested that you might be able to take a few copies of this book as it contains poems on Brumana and the Lebanon. Please return the books at our expense if you cannot take them.'

They will be sure to take the books as I have many friends in Beyrouth and you can rely on them to pay you.

Please let me know if you are doing this. I could also write to other booksellers I know, but you don't seem to think it worthwhile. At the beginning of Oxford and Cambridge term it can do a lot for you – if you back it up.

2. Please send me three copies of my book which I am going to use for <u>review purposes</u> strictly – I want to write personally to the Editor of *Vers et Prose* (Paul Fort) and a big Athenian[1763] review. <u>Did you send a volume to Davray of the Mercure de France?</u> If not, I will send him one.

Did you send a review copy to the *Evening Post*, New York City, which gave me an excellent review last time?

It would be well to type a few copies of the *Times* and *Morning Post* review to the Booksellers. Poetry will never sell itself, one must push like Sisyphus.

Yours faithfully,
James Elroy Flecker.

The numerous reviews of *The Golden Journey* appeared not to have caught the attention of the FO and connected in their minds that the author and Herman Elroy Flecker, the Consular Official, were one and the same person.

The review in *The Times Literary Supplement* of 28 August, was extensive and the critic praised the poem 'The Golden Journey' for its spirit and beauty, which the critic was attracted 'to read it again and again'. 'Brumana' and 'The Painter's Mistress' were picked out for special mention. 'Oak and Olive' was quoted at length, as well as 'Epithalamium' and 'Taoping'; the latter was described as 'a poem merely decorative without inspiration', 'Oak and Olive' as 'charming perversity of the imagination'. This critic stated that Flecker's purpose 'is to achieve beauty, and he achieves it, but not because that is his purpose'. He had every reason to feel pleased with the review in the *TLS* but a review in the *Saturday Westminster Gazette* did not please him. He wrote to Goldring: 'The *Westminster* review is a mad muddle it seems to think I'm a plot. How reviewers love prefaces – it's astonishing.[1764] The critic in the *Westminster* on 16 August did find the preface of interest. *The Golden Journey* headed the *Westminster*'s list of nine books of poetry and it was pointed out that 'Among these writers of these most recent books Mr. Flecker alone has been bold enough to proclaim his poetical'. The critic thought that Parnassian Poetry 'had utterly failed him'. The critic continued to point out what he saw as the weaknesses in the poems of *The Golden Journey* rather than focus upon what other critics had seen as its strengths. 'Doris' was quoted in full with the comment that it was typical of the volume and that: 'Presumably convinced of its poetic excellence devotes a page to a four-line poem entitled 'Doris'.

This critic did not think that Flecker had created beauty, but 'has done no more than describe beautiful things'. The critic continued 'beauty cannot be inherited; it must be rediscovered by each generation of individuals'. This critic appeared to be unfamiliar with Flecker's previous anthologies or he would have read 'To a Poet a Thousand Years Hence', which deals with the inheritance of future poets.

The criticism was not all adverse in the *Westminster*. Flecker's technical excellence was acknowledged, but he thought that it was 'conventionally beautiful without a trace of individuality or emotion'. This critic was at odds with other critics who thought that Flecker had mastered his emotions and that his was an individual talent; he was not one of a group.[1765] The conclusion drawn by the critic in the *Westminster* about Flecker was:

> 'Among minor poets none is more excellent than Mr. Flecker. Among excellent poets none is more certainly minor.'

Flecker wrote to Marsh on 8 September, thanking him for *The Times* review and the trouble taken over commenting on *Hassan*. He thought that Marsh's criticism was just, but Marsh must have criticised the scene with the Fountain Ghost, Ghost of Pervaneh and Ghost of Rafi, because he told him ' but I love my ghosts!'[1766] Savery must also have criticised the ghosts because he was told: 'I love my ghosts – I suppose because my poetic soul loves the picturesque in the play above everything.'[1767,1768]

Flecker's time was not entirely taken up with hopes of acceptance for the stage production of *Hassan*. On the same day as he wrote to Marsh, he sent a postcard[1769] to the editor of *Everyman* at 21 Royal Terrace, Edinburgh. He complained that the publication owed him money for 'In Phaeacia', which he wrote and was published 'several months ago' [the published date in *Everyman* was 27 June, 1913]. He also complained about two articles ['What Insecurity in Turkey means with some general reflections on the impending Armenian Question.' And signed:- 'A Resident in Turkey', the proofs to be sent chez Madam Skiadaressi, Paris. Also 'The New French Spirit' which was not published with a signature, which he sent from Dorset Square, London, W.1.]; he did not know whether or not they were to be published or returned. He thought that the policy of *Everyman* was never to answer letters. The fact that he had started the correspondence with *Everyman* about publication of his work, in Beirut, and he had moved from there to London via Paris and then back to the Lebanon and was now in Switzerland, appeared not to enter into the argument about answering letters with *Everyman*, who were also instructed to send any payments to his bank in Cambridge. *Everyman* itself had not been first written to at its address in Edinburgh. The remark made in the LIFE about his refusing to comply with arrangements made to go to Switzerland with his family in 1904 had some truth:

> it puts him definitely in that small company, of all times
> and places, who expect things to come right, however few
> or whatever contrary plans they themselves make. Flecker
> always tended to expect 'things' to right themselves, even to
> suit any complete and abrupt change he might make.[1770]

One person whose own changes of addresses, coupled with his old friend's changes of addresses, did not prevent the flow of correspondence, was Savery. His policy was to answer letters promptly. Flecker also wrote to him on 8 September. He wanted Savery's friend, Ernst Freissler, to begin translating *Hassan*. He enclosed a sole right of translating *Hassan* into German. He would be 'hellish glad of twenty quid and will have to restrain myself from writing once a week to Herr Freissler to urge him to buck up and get it done'.[1771]

By 24 September, struggling with his German, he had written to Herr Freissler and he realised, he wrote to Savery, that he may have muddled him. The joy of having *Hassan* 'played in any language' seemed very remote. He was more optimistic about the acceptance of his other work. He told Savery that he was bored, but this had been alleviated by a letter from the Greek minister in London thanking him for his Hellénic letters to the papers. This was a reference to his letter on the Balkan atrocities in *The Nation*, 23 August 1913, and 'In Defence of Greece' in *The Near East* on 12 September 1913.[1772] This success could be another reason why he wanted his articles published by *Everyman*.

His optimism about his future literary aims changed when he wrote to Marsh on 3 October. Letters not answered again were the source of despair. He had got no reply from Granville Barker or Drinkwater. 'Hope this silence of Death will be dispelled by your magic wand.'[1773] He complained that since 'the good day' of *The Times* review, he had had nothing 'but spasmodic insults from the papers re. the "Golden Journey," especially from the periodicals where I have published such poems as *Nation* & *Poetry and Drama*. Middleton Murry had been asked for a review when written to c/o the *Daily News* but he had had no answer. A review of *The Golden Journey* appeared in the *Daily News and Leader* on the day he was writing to Marsh, 3 October 1913. He complained to Marsh about making about fifty attempts to get a prose article published without any success. As 'a last hope' he was sending his ms to an agent. He told Marsh: 'It's all very well to be burning with a saeva indignatio but if you can't get into print it's rather useless.'[1774]

This did not mean that despite his poor health and lack of success he was going to give up writing. He wrote to his father also in October: 'I don't suppose there is any chance of a real cure, or of my ever being able to do anything but a little writing.'[1775]

In an effort to help with suggestions to relieve symptoms, also in October, he wrote to his mother:

> You talk of respirators: there ain't much novelty about 'em. I imagine Noah tried it for a cough he caught in the Ark. I even had one and flung it away. They're mostly ugly and awkward. There's a very good one invented by an Italian sanatorium doctor: but I should be very glad if you would inquire about Sir Hiram Maxim's Pipe of Peace, which he invented for himself, and is said to be <u>far</u> the best of all inhalers.
>
> But nothing would induce me to sniff hideous drugs with a deforming mask on my face eight hours a day except the certainty that it was a speedy and miraculous cure. The worthy doctor (according to the article you sent) says it takes the patient's mind off his illness. I should think it would

> never allow him to forget the hideousness and imminence
> of his disease. [1776]

On 6 October, Flecker's disagreeable mood was also transmitted to Savery. He complained of 'most bleeding reviews'. He planned a holiday whereby he and Savery could be reunited. By 17 October Flecker was more optimistic, having received a copy from Paul Fort of his new *Choix* and was plodding through its 600 pages. This news he conveyed to Savery from yet another change of address, back at Pension Alexandra, Montreux, where they hoped to stay until the 15 November. A month before receiving a copy of *Choix* from Paul Fort (on 13 September), he had written from the Hotel Stephani to Goschens asking them to send a 2/6d copy of *The Golden Journey to Samarkand* to Paul Fort. That letter to Goschens contained thanks for 'good news for 'Samarkand'. He also wanted 'some idea' about the publication date of *The King of Alsander*. He wanted a 7/6d copy of *The Golden Journey* sent to his mother (although the copy would be for himself.)

He continued to advise Goschens on publicity for *The Golden Journey*, urging them to print a 'single sheet puff' for display in Varsity windows. He just wanted *The Times* and *Morning Post* reviews reprinted and also *The Globe* review, printed. He wanted to know if he could, 'Pay the bill for 'corrections' at the end of the quarter. I returned it as it was taxed by the post 'by mistake)'. [1777]

Flecker had written to Savery of 'plodding through' the work of Paul Fort, which may have given Savery the impression that reading Fort was something of a task and somewhat tedious. But 'plodding' could also mean Fort's work needed a good deal of effort and concentration. He wrote to T.E. Lawrence and recommended to him Fort's *Choix de Poèmes*: Figuiere 6 frs.' also Henri de Régnier's *Arethuse*, and Albert Samain (*Jardin de l'infante* & *Flancs du Vase*). Lawrence wrote to Mrs. Reider on 26 December, asking her to order the recommended books.[1778] This sort of recommendation, which he also made to Savery, indicated that despite the 'plodding' required, Fort's works and others were well worth reading. The sunshine improved Flecker's spirits and he was beginning to love the countryside. He was able to get about on steamboats but, as was usual after this sort of outdoor activity, he caught a chill and was again in despondent mood and complaining about not hearing from Freissler or Barker. He was 'quite mad for the want of a bit of civilised society'. 'I'm rather cheerless', he told Savery and he had composed an anti-Catholic song to irritate him when they met.[1779]

On 22 October, he wrote to Goschens about the publication of *The King of Alsander*. He told the publishers that the reason why he was anxious about his novel was because his 'oriental play' was under consideration in London. He had received £15 from the German publisher. He offered Goschens the first refusal of publishing the play, which he hoped would be a work of permanent literary value and should sell well. But he wanted *The King of Alsander* to come out first.[1780] Four days later, he wrote to Goschens again, telling them that he would prefer *Alsander* to come out as soon as possible 'but of course I am in your hands.'

The reasons behind the eagerness to get *Alsander* published is revealed in the rest of the letter, when he went on:

> 'I said at the end of December quarter for the account but if you are in a hurry will pay at once. Why not get *Alsander* out and see if it will come out of the royalties.
>
> I suppose you will send me account of the *Golden Journey* at Xmas.'[1781]

Further clarification of this arrangement with his publishers is revealed in a letter written to his parents:

> I am very busy with proofs of my novel. I have had to make a great many alterations in the proofs which is a plague. But the alterations are unfortunately very important indeed.
>
> I have to pay my publishers £3 for alterations made in my poems.[1782]

The King of Alsander, as this part of his letter to his parents and also to his publishers indicates, was extensively revised but it was always seen as a possible source of cash, which would also help subsidise the promotion of his poetry.

The bad weather had influenced Flecker's moods that year and yet another aspect of the weather delayed his hopes and aims for literary success. On 9 October, the train journeying to Locarno reached a railway bridge that had been undermined by recent heavy downpours. The bridge collapsed under the weight of the train, and although there were no deaths amongst the passengers, the mail van was lost. This Melun train disaster featured in a PS in answer to a letter to Marsh, telling him of his isolation, dated 6 November: 'P.S. Your letter happily escaped the Melun disaster in which much correspondence addressed to me perished.'[1783]

On 10 November, Flecker received from Goschens the first part of *Alsander* in proof, which had been held up by the Melun train disaster.

He told Goschens that it was much better than he thought it was and looked excellent 'in print'. He thought that if Goschens helped it like they helped *Samarkand*, it should be a great success. The fourth impression of *Samarkand* was being advertised, he noted.[1784] This letter also contained discussion about the fact that the secretary at Goschens had to pay 4d. on mail sent. Flecker promised to send a cheque at the end of November. Goschens were also informed that after 14 November, his address would be Hotel Stephani, Montana, where he would be for the rest of the winter. This date was not kept and he had to write to Goschens on 24 November, still at the Pension Alexandra: 'I have been forced by illness to remain here longer than expected. Page 67 of the Galley proofs has become detached and lost.'

He wanted a replacement for the missing page and told Goschens he would send back the corrected proofs at the end of the week.[1785] By 26 November, he had arrived at the Hotel Stephani and was writing to Marsh from what he described as 'this horrible hole'. It was the only place that took invalids. Healthy men came for the winter sport and the lakes. He told Marsh of a letter of his that should appear in the 'next *Near East*' (a previous letter of Flecker's was 'In Defence of Greece' which appeared in the *Near East* of 12 September 1913). He thought the letter would amuse Marsh and 'pulverize' some named apologists for the Turks.[1786]

On 1 December, in his next letter to Marsh,[1787] he enclosed 'The Old Ships', which he had written 'some months ago'. Marsh had suggested Flecker send him some poems for Jack Squire. He explained to Marsh that he was trying to make his novel 'a little less crude at the last moment, and really I have polished it fine'. He trembled to think of the printer's bill for altered proofs.

He told Marsh 'the snow is not yet fixed or thick enough for winter sport', but the mountain winter had begun. He had to admit that the effect of 'the sunset, sunrise and moonlight on the snows, and the sea of cloud beneath one give amazing stage effects'. He was 'fairly well' but had to remain in bed. But he was occupied with his novel and finishing an article on Paul Fort. He told Marsh of someone 'suggesting' to Monro that *Forty-Two Poems* was eligible for the Academy's £100 prize. He did not think that the *Golden Journey* had the slightest chance but he wanted to know, nevertheless, the procedure for entering the competition.

He had had a tooth pulled out, he told Savery in his next letter. The good news was that *Samarkand* had sold four hundred copies.

Flecker sent off the proofs of *The King of Alsander* on 8 December with a long letter to Goschens.[1788] He enclosed a cheque also for £3 for the proof alterations to *The Golden Journey*.

He told Goschens that he felt 'absolutely forced' to alter the second half of his novel. He had added four complete scenes and he found that the structure of the novel would be 'vastly improved by the transposition to the end of the fantastic chapter about the Poet's return to Blaindon'. To this chapter, he said he had added 'a Fairy incident', an addition which pleased him greatly, but it could not be called necessary. He went on 'But all the other alterations and additions were an absolute necessity to ensure the success of the book.' The passages that he omitted he thought 'were abominably crude', those that were added 'were my very best work. I have worked very hard and very quickly at this, and I very much hope that you will give a glance at what I have done and seeing how necessary a work I have done, forgive me for disturbing the proofs.'

He excused his last-minute alterations by telling the publishers that this worried him, but he had fully intended to revise the ms and had delayed because he thought that the novel was not going to be published until the spring. The proofs had come suddenly down upon his head. Flecker appeared to overlook the fact that he had put pressure upon the publishers (in more than one letter to them) that he wanted his novel to come out without delay. He told his publishers that as there were eighty-one galley proofs, he realised that it would land him in considerable expense, which he could not face. 'But I am sure I can trust to your courtesy to make some equitable arrangement.' This suggestion, however politely put, was unfair to his publishers. He admitted to them that although he had omitted the equivalent of eight proof pages, twelve such pages (12,000 words) had been added. Flecker, in his letter, told the publishers that the burden falling on the publishers was 'very fair' and that his alterations gave the possibility of doubling the novel's sale. If the publishers did not agree with him, then they could return the ms. and he would let it stand as it was. This sort of blackmail, which was reminiscent of his arguments in the past over getting money from his parents, did pay off. Goldring relates:

> 'Flecker, despite much illness, seems to have been fairly active during his stay in Montana. I had another very long and complicated business letter from him, sent from the Hotel Stephani, chiefly about the cost of the corrections to *The King of Alsander*. I am very glad to gather from it that the firm let him off lightly and raised his royalties.' [1789]

He further put forward his claim for special consideration by explaining to the publishers in the letter that he did not understand the question of royalties and the cost of printer's alterations. His exile, he wrote, had 'kept me in ignorance'. He did not understand how he had run up a bill for £3 plus 10 per cent of total cost for the *Golden Journey*. He supposed it was the result of adding several poems. But the added poems had helped the book towards success. He added: 'I may mention that most of Mr. Goldring's criticisms of the book have been answered by the alterations.'

Flecker knew that he had no control over the binding of *The King of Alsander* but he did not want 'the horrible modern fashion of binding a book in blue and colouring the top blue to match, so much loved by Secker,'. He finished his letter to Goschens with another plea for increased royalties.

By 10 December, Flecker wrote to Marsh to tell him that after three weeks' hard work he had finished correcting the proofs of his novel. This word 'finished' appeared to bear out his hope that the ms. would be returned to him with his alterations ignored. Something not accepted was his letter to the *Near East*, which he told Marsh was refused 'in terror' because of his 'anti-pro-Turk' content. He was furious, and in despair sent it to G.K. Chesterton. This disappointment was small compared to hopes that Marsh had raised about the production of *Hassan*. Marsh had passed *Hassan* on to Tree, who in turn passed it to his daughter on 13 December.

Also, on 10 December, Flecker wrote to Savery[1790] thanking him for books, sending him stamps and 'a little poem I wrote t'other day'. [1791]

The 'little poem' is not given a name, but Flecker wrote 'Stillness' between November and December 1913. This is the poem where the second verse begins:

> When from the clock's last chime to the next chime
> Silence beats his drum,

Then the poet describes how he is:

> ... emptied of all my dreams;
> I only hear Earth turning, only see
> Ether's long bankless streams,
> And only know I should drown if you laid not your
> hand on me.

The comfort of Hellé's hand in 'Stillness' is proof of the comfort her presence brought to him during his illness. The feeling is in contrast to 'In Hospital' where he writes instead:

> And served by an old woman, calm and clean,

Her misted face familiar, yet unknown,
Who comes in silence, and departs unseen,

The uncertainty of 'Stillness', when Flecker felt that he was losing his grip on the real world from which he is saved by the touch of a human hand, but not a kiss, is repeated in Hellé's poem 'Envoy',[1792] which begins with the lines:

When I have crossed the guarded border-line
And passed alone out of the world of sight
Will you be there, close by the Gate of Night
And in the dark will your hand reach for mine?

Shall I feel pressed those fingers taper-fine
That round all things of earth closed e'er so light.

Hellé is uncertain in her hopes that she will again hold her husband's hand in the next life. But she hopes, it appears, to live again with him the days of happiness they had together in Corfu, Constantinople and Beirut; the beauty of those places transcending all the earthly discomforts. 'Stillness' is also thought to be influenced by Paul Fort and by Albert Samain's 'Silence' and a poem in Beazley's notebook.[1793] Beazley's poem contains the lines:

Lost friends, lost friends
Come near and touch my hands... [1794]

'Stillness' is also seen as owing some of its influence to Virgil's Book Six of the *Aeneid*, whose blank verse translation Flecker was undertaking.[1795]

Flecker went on to tell Savery: 'There's just a gleam about *Hassan*. Viola Tree and Alfred Parsons are hugely enthusiastic and want to play it. But of course it will come to nothing.'

Proof of the enthusiasm of Viola Tree, eldest actress daughter of Sir Herbert, and her husband, civil servant and critic Alfred Parsons, is given by Basil Dean who, in the introduction to *Hassan*, describes a bulky package deposited on his desk at His Majesty's Theatre. One of Basil Dean's duties when he joined the staff of Tree, was to report on new plays.

The package containing the ms of *Hassan* was accompanied by a hastily scribbled note, which read: 'Please give this wonderful play special attention; I can't get Daddy to read it as he says it's too long.'[1796]

Basil Dean (1888–1978) was born at Croydon. He was encouraged by his parents from an early age to act. Encouragement that continued when he went to Whitgift School. (Old Whitgiftians were Leon Quartermain, Charles Quartermain and Harcourt Williams.) No encouragement was given to the adolescent Basil Dean by his parents to consider acting as a career. His father was not able to afford to keep his son at university, even if he had won a scholarship. After leaving school, Dean went to work in a city office. In the evenings, he continued acting in amateur dramatics and attended plays. Despite an offer of a doubling of his salary, he left the City office to go on the stage. His first paid stage job started in September 1906. His writing ambitions were recognised when Dean's play, *Marriages Are Made in Heaven,* brought together Sybil Thorndike acting with Lewis Casson for the first time. Dean's play was well received and remained in the repertoire of the Horniman Company, which employed him between 1907–10. Another short play of Dean's, which was sent to the Stage Society, was well received by Dr. Gilbert Murray, but not by Shaw. A letter from Sir Herbert Beerbohm Tree, offering him employment at His Majesty's Theatre, brought Dean to London from the Liverpool Playhouse. Dean worked for Tree as an 'assistant producer'. Dean had already met Marsh before he started work with Tree. He went with Marsh to the first night of Barker's *A Midsummer Night's Dream* at the Savoy Theatre. Dean also went to Marsh's rooms where he met some of the Georgian Poets. He also went to Harold Monro's Poetry Bookshop and read *The English Review* and the *Blue Review* and met Jack Squire. Dean could therefore have had the opportunity to come across Flecker's previous works. Tree, despite an enthusiastic report on *Hassan,* continued to complain about its length. But Dean recognised: 'Even in draft form, the play was clearly of major importance.' [1797]

But why precisely Dean was drawn to *Hassan* he does not make clear in any detail or state what made it important. But during the period when Dean was deciding upon his future, he longed to join his elder brother who was in India. Dean had also been taken to the Oriental Club in London to meet the nephew of a retired District Manager of the Niger Company. The life of a British official overseas fascinated him and, coupled with Dean's romantic longings for India and his own experience in the acting and playwrighting world, could have helped him to be especially attracted to *Hassan.*

All this enthusiasm for the future of *Hassan* Flecker could not know about first hand; he knew of it only as a 'gleam'. It was not surprising that writing at the beginning of December for his father's birthday, Flecker wrote a 'cross letter' telling him 'I am in considerable despair'. He complained to his father 'I can't get a line published anywhere'. His novel he thought would be a failure. 'I have got so much to say to the world, and no one will let me say it'.[1798] It was understandable that on 10 December he wrote to Savery of the joy he would feel if Savery were able to undertake the long and costly journey to visit him.

His mood of despair would have been lifted had he known, at the time, of the article that appeared in the *Englishwoman* of December 1913, written by his future biographer, Geraldine Hodgson, entitled 'An English Parnassian'. Later he told his father:- 'you will find an extremely sensible and well-written article on *Samarkand,* by a lady critic who is quite unknown to me.'[1799]

To Goldring he described it as 'an excellent and sensible article'.[1800] Marsh and Savery also got news of the excellent and good article by Hodgson. Flecker asked Marsh if he knew Hodgson, which could indicate that he had a suspicion that Marsh was behind the article's publication because Marsh was behind other projects of this kind.

On 15 December, Flecker wrote a long letter to Hodgson.[1801] In this letter, he thanked Hodgson for writing such an appreciative article, which was always flattering to the vanity of poets, who were the vainest of all mankind, but specially for writing such an extremely intelligent article. He told Hodgson that it was: 'no good just writing poetry and flinging it at the public's head – especially if your poetry isn't all of one piece, but rather apt to vary with moods.'

He told her: 'the message nowadays is usually an "immoral one", a revolutionary one. It is the art of Ibsen, of Shaw, of Galsworthy, the whole modern drama at its best; it is Swinburne, Shelley, Browning at their worst who have been ruined. It is not so simple to say what I mean. The message gives the enthusiasm: the enthusiasm is a glorious thing: Shelley is a greater poet than Leconte de Lisle or Hérédia because his enthusiasm for a lot of very dull doctrines of Godwin's. No Parnassian ever rose to the height of 'Hellas'. No Parnassian ever fell as low as 'Peter Bell'. Shelley's enthusiasms made a flame of his poetry: Swinburne's obsessed him till they burnt up his genius by killing his sense of proportion. He forgot to interest himself in words, or new impressions: as long as there was liberty, and the sea, and the big metre, and a few of his old stock epithets, he though he could go on renewing for ever the inspiration of "Dolores".'

Flecker then went on to say that Masefield 'whose genius I once admired' had no message whatever. He told Hodgson also: 'It is Paul Fort who can show us what it is to be a Poet, it simply means an enthusiasm for the world in every detail.' He explained to Hodgson about his 'rather lunatic novel' coming out and that his 'hopes are centred in an Oriental play...'.

He also explained to Hodgson that his poem 'The Sacred Incident' was 'piffle', which was 'like most of my other sacred poems'. He though that they 'degrade religion with a decorative motive, and are very popular!' (In a footnote, Hodgson, when she published the letter in the LIFE, stated 'This was Flecker's deliberate view. She quoted from Flecker's essay on Paul Fort to support her statement.) Flecker was sorry Hodgson admired William Watson. When writing to Hodgson about *Hassan* he had told her that it was 'now doing a long and weary tour of the managers'. He told Savery in a letter that he received on 16 November: 'I hear from Marsh that Tree's slumbers are ruined, because he can't tell whether to play *Hassan* or no. Meanwhile everybody's frightfully full of alterations for *Hassan!*' [1802]

Flecker was worried about the reasons for his main characters not being able to commit suicide during their 'day of love' and that these were not strong enough. He thought of writing an extra scene but the play was considered too long already. Savery knew a dramatist (Flecker though it might be Maugham) to whom Flecker could write for advice about the contract. He told Savery that although it was obviously good news that *Hassan* was going to be produced, he had the frustration of not being in England to discuss the matters arising.

He told Savery of a publisher wanting to know if he would write on the 'Future of Poetry'. Flecker's comment was 'What a bore!'. Despite his frustrations about not being in England, he had to tell Marsh, when writing to him on 16 December[1803] 'Of course, I leave everything in your hands and Dean's.' Flecker was not content to leave his dispute with Jack Squire of *The New Statesman* in Marsh's hands. Writing to Squire on Christmas Eve, he told him that he hoped that there was nothing in his postcard to suggest that he was disparaging the verse column of *The New Statesman*: 'All I imply is that with the best contributors in the world one can't get one good or even fairly good poem to publish every week.'

He went on: 'I told Marsh I had written about this matter to you, the 'New Statesman', and he was, I think, a little unreasonably vexed with me. Please don't tell him I mentioned this.'

Squire had though that Flecker was demanding an extra guinea. He explained to Squire about the *Nation* rejecting his best work from time to time, including 'Old Ships' (which *The New Statesman* published on 13 December). He described to Squire the reception of his 'last book', which he told him 'was given an insolent ten line review with a batch of nincompoops – after I had been working with the paper for years.' These insults and snubs (as he described them) were 'sufficient to make me desire never to write another line for the *Nation*....' If *The New Statesman* would treat him better, then they would get his 'best work....'.

He had a more humble approach when writing to Monro (despite telling Savery he 'gave me a bleeding review') on Christmas Day.[1804] He wanted to continue his subscription to *Poetry and Drama*. He praised the last number of Monro's publication, as well as Monro's poem. He was equally humble in his offer of poems to Monro: 'If you would care for some poems let me know. At present I am translating Vergil; Aeneid V1. into blank verse. What ill the Futurists say?' [1805]

In his next communication with Savery, written on Boxing Day, he asked him to come and help him finish the '6th Aeneid'. He thanked Savery for his Christmas present of Claudel. Paul Claudel (1868–1955), poet and dramatist, a Catholic under the influence of the Symbolists, was a writer he had never cared for 'in my desultory dippings till I read the first play – the Chinese one – the first act of which is very grand and Dantesque indeed. The 2nd act which I am half way through is a wee bit stiff and tiring.' Flecker, when he had written to Monro on Christmas Day, had told him to tell 'Flint (if he cares to know) that I am converted to Claudel by *Le Repos du Septième jour*. He told Savery 'A Traditionalist like Claudel ought to use verse but he can't his verses are no good. So he uses prose'. [1806]

Less literary matters were discussed in letters to his mother. In December he wrote to her: 'Lozenges! I've just paid 10s. to get a cupboard never to see a medicine except when I take them. I have to buy and eat these foul lozenges. And if anyone dares to send me lozenges again as a present, I'll send a tooth-brush for their Christmas.[1807]

The dawn of the new year saw Flecker still confined to bed having, he told Savery, 'upset my stomach on Christmas Day'. He had 'a horrible fever', which left him for a few hours only in the morning. He was 'rather despairful'. He had wanted to send Savery 'some quantitative hexameters', which he had written under the influence of Stone's essay on Milton. [W.J. Stone's 'Classical Metres in English Verse']

A letter to Monro written on 12 January 1914, gives similar news to that contained in the letter to Savery.

Hotel Stephani,
Montana sur Sierre
Switzerland

My Dear Monro,

I have been since Xmas too bloody ill to write a line, confined to bed with fever, and precious miserable. Have managed to gather strength to send you an extremely sincere and passionate poem in quantitative hexameters which sounds like a contradiction in terms. A note was necessary: must have it to the taste of *Poetry and Drama* readers (if you accept it) to see that the poem is not a pedantic exercise.

Of course just when one's helpless in bed and not a poem in one's wallet one gets requests from everywhere, and many of the best poems in Samarcand never got printed!

If you accept this send me *proofs* and if you don't please return at once. I plan some pentameters which will send if in time: also will review Spanish poems if I possibly can if not in summer. I'm no good at Portuguese.

The *Sphere* has asked me for two poems and you mustn't be cross if you see some there as they've offered special terms. You couldn't have anything better than the hexameters which nevertheless would probably puzzle some of the amicable readers of the *Sphere*.

Write as letters are very cheering these days.

Ever Yours
James Elroy Flecker [1808]

The poem referred to as 'the hexameters' was 'A Prayer to the Brightness of Day' which Monro 'first liked, then disliked, then liked'[1809] and published in *Poetry and Drama* No.5, March 1914. The same edition as Flecker's 'The National Anthem' to which Monro objected 'to God being brought in and to the Imperialism of it'.[1810]

A version of 'A Prayer to the Brightness of Day' was first sent to Cheesman as early at 1904–5. This version was typewritten, which helps to try and place it among Flecker's earlier work. Flecker sent a letter with the poem to Cheesman explaining the effect of having written quantitatively, ending the note with: 'to write Quantitative verse is to set sail on a very strange and charming ocean.'[1811]

'A Prayer to the Brightness of Day', in the version sent to Cheesman, has the last line: 'Break the ebon soldiers, restore his realm for a dreamer.' In the published version, Flecker wrote: 'Break the ebon soldiers, restore his realm to the dreamer.' This is also the line that remained when the poem was revised as 'Hexameters' in Flecker's Collected Poems.

'O Lord, restore his realm to the dreamer' was chosen by Hellé for the inscription on her husband's gravestone, a grey granite cross. Hellé was involved in the revised version of this poem, inasmuch as she was writing the words down from her husband's dictation. She was, in a sense, particularly close to the lines and that was one reason perhaps why she chose them. The translations of Virgil, which he was undertaking in November were shared with his parents. On the 19 November he was going to post the *Aeneid* translation to his father but this was not yet typed and it was further delayed by the seriousness of his illness, which had detained him in Montreux and made Hellé write to his parents, telling them of their son's painful throat and broken spirit.[1812] The elder Fleckers made the journey to Montana early in January and stayed for four days. Hellé, in her *Reminiscences*, makes no reference to her in-laws' visit but she is referred to in the LIFE as during this visit she played the violin to her mother-in-law's piano accompaniment. This was described as 'frequent recreation'. This pleasant family picture is a little at odds with the fact that Flecker was confined to bed, because his room surely did not contain a piano?[1813] The elder Fleckers are described as being 'considerably distressed at the smallness of his room, littered, as it was with medicines, apparatus for writing, and his usual collection of curios and odds and ends.'[1814] Part of the clutter was due to the contents of the Beirut packing cases which had just been unpacked. In view of the long running battle with their son over his extravagance, the elder Fleckers could have rejoiced that their money was not being spent on a too large room or perhaps it was that, for the money they were supplying, the room should have been larger? It was said that Flecker wanted his father constantly with him and that they 'eagerly discussed *Hassan*, problems of education, and the to-be-epoch-making translation of Virgil, which was simmering in his over-busy brain'.[1815] It could have been that, as the room was too small for four people, Hellé and his mother played their music elsewhere in the sanatorium but the father and son could hear the strains as they worked together. Whatever the exact arrangements were, Hellé could have been grateful for the break in her sick-room duties.

Whether or not the elder Fleckers wanted to ease the burden on Hellé is not clear, but on their return home they arranged for an 'excellent' nurse, whom their son had known since childhood, to go out to nurse him. How much Hellé or her husband agreed to this is not stated and how much Hellé wanted a nurse is not known. At one time, they had suggested that Helle return to her mother in Paris for a while, in an effort to save money, and they maintained that they 'took a hopeful view of his case and still looked for a tolerable if not complete recovery.'

It was also maintained that Flecker's health had improved. There was something in this remark, which was coupled with the engaging of the nurse, that suggested that Hellé's nursing had somehow contributed to their son's decline in health. The fact that she had more than likely, with her care and devotion, prevented his complete decline in health was, at this stage, not something Flecker's parents would admit to themselves. They were bound to have noticed a great change in his appearance since they had urged him to return to Beirut, a year ago. By coincidence, Dr. and Mrs. Flecker 'met in the train at a station called Sion on their way back that scoundrel Jack Beazley of all people and made him write to me. He's back from Greece – lucky beast.'[1816]

Cheesman visited Flecker at the Hotel Stephani, Montana,[1817] and this could be a reason why Flecker revised 'A Prayer to the Brightness of Day' at this time. On 17 January he wrote to Savery because he was concerned at not having heard from him.

Flecker was still in bed and he told him that his parents' visit had tired him and then went on to tell Savery of their encounter with Beazley. After writing to Savery, Flecker, in January 1914,[1818] answered a welcome letter from Marsh, which contained a cheque for royalties on Flecker's contributions to *Georgian Poetry*. (This was the second cheque for *Georgian Poetry* royalties. When he had thanked Marsh for the generosity of the final cheque, received in July 1913, Flecker had told him he would use it to get *Hassan* typed.[1819])[1820] The most important paragraph in this letter to Marsh was Flecker's statement that, if he had not been in exile and ill, he would have thought and thought again before accepting the terms offered for the production of *Hassan*. Flecker had, in this letter, accepted as unreservedly as possible proposals by Basil Dean who was going to undertake alteration work on *Hassan* with the prospect of getting *Hassan* accepted by Tree or someone else whom Dean also knew.[1821] Flecker told Marsh that he was 'nervous of the mania for alteration theatrical people have'.[1822] He wanted Dean to write to him as soon as possible.

Less pressing matters dealt with in this letter to Marsh included a completed 'God Save the King' with an extra verse added at Marsh's suggestion. He thought of sending 'God Save the King' to the *Sphere* and to King George V, via Robert Bridges. He told Marsh that the article he had read in *Poetry and Drama* had set him off on the path to writing 'God Save the King'. He told Marsh of his longing to revise *Don Juan*; it was less exotic than *Hassan*. He told, too, of his learning to write fine blank verse and practising on the *Aeneid* VI. translation. He was waiting to hear what Monro thought of 'some quantitive hexameters'. The *King of Alsander* was to be out soon. He had been invited to send poems for a Chicago poetry publication. The *Fortnightly* had rejected 'Paul Fort'. He sent his love to Rupert Brooke.

No sooner had Flecker posted that letter to Marsh, as a result of feeling better, he wrote again. He wanted to know more of Dean's intentions and he wanted 'a free hand in negotiation'. Dean, according to Flecker's letter, wanted 'a very heavy percentage and he wants his name to the play'. He told Marsh that if 'Dean comes to you and says I'm a bloody bargaining Jew, you won't be cross with me.' Echoes come across here of his past battles with his parents, when in the past he had told them: 'You are turning me into the most avaricious Jew. I begin to shape my life with a view to getting money. This does not agree with my aesthetic taste.'[1823]

He told Marsh that he would still have liked 'one last shot at Granville Barker. And if Dean isn't going to get me free I imagine J. Drinkwater, to judge from his enthusiastic letter about a very muddled draft of Acts I and II might accept it without wanting to hash it all up.'[1824]

The truth behind all Flecker's insecurity, was that the time spent bargaining in exile for a better deal for the production of *Hassan* would only delay its acceptance. His health was such that, knowing his time was running out, he could only, at this stage, make his views known and then agree to what Dean offered him. By 18 January, he wrote to Marsh and told him to definitely let Dean co-operate as he wishes.' The second letter he had written had to be cancelled. Flecker made the excuse that he had a fever of about 102ª, when 'one's apt to be vague about business principle'.[1825] He was thankful indeed for Marsh having got *Hassan* to this stage. It is hoped that Marsh was made a little happier by the thanks because Marsh found Flecker 'really a most difficult person to be agent for!'[1826]

Marsh must have also taken issue with lines in Flecker's poem 'Stillness':

> And Space with gaunt grey eyes and her brother Time
> Wheeling and whispering come,
> She with the mould of form and he with the loom of
>   rhyme:

because Flecker wrote to Marsh: 'I think the line about Mould of Form is alright: but can't explain it in words. The connection between Space and Form should present no difficulty: form of rhyme (the weft and woof of alternate rhyming verse) is a good phrase, and surely the connection of time and rhyme – for rhyme is the marking of time, nothing more or less – is right.'[1827]

It is not clear exactly what Marsh wrote about these lines, but there is agreement that the last line quoted above is 'an unnecessary ornamentation to the central idea of the poem'.[1828] Flecker emphasised to Marsh that his second letter was cancelled and told him of the 'lovely Zither' bought with his 'Georgian' royalty money. Marsh had sent him *Sons and Lovers*, which Flecker found to be 'as unreal as a dream'.

'Unreal as a dream' was the sort of comment T.E. Lawrence made, when it was published, about *The King of Alsander*. Marsh was also told that in *Sons and Lovers* 'the characters don't seem to hang together a bit'. Although this was also a comment D.H. Lawrence could have made about Flecker's novel, the question of Lawrence's characters in his novels and their hanging together was to be raised by others.[1829]

Flecker concluded his remarks about *Sons and Lovers* with a statement that was not entirely borne out by the facts and somehow revealed that he was not being honest with himself over his reactions to the novel: 'But there. I'm no judge of novels!' Later, when writing to Savery,[1830] he continued to judge *Sons and Lovers*. He made the comment: 'Coal miners etc. Negatively written – nothing vulgar. No characters no passion – a sort of unreal haze of dreariness'. Exactly what Flecker meant by 'dreariness' is not clear when the term is used about a novel that has many descriptions of the landscape that are far from dreary. Flecker admired the work of John Davidson whose work could be said to contain some working-class dreariness, although it was mainly Scottish 'dreariness' of the sort that Beazley was also familiar with in his youth. Flecker had no long-term experience of the 'dreariness' of the Midlands and Nottingham (where Flecker had not wanted to be 'an Usher ... unless something more cheerful turns up'[1831]) and he was not able to appreciate Lawrence's depiction of it. One reason could be that Flecker had given up his attempt to incorporate his lines about the Midlands when he wrote about journeying to the Fabian Summer School in Wales.

He also did not put into print his poem 'Ennui', which depicted the dreariness of a dull provincial town, but the reason may not have been so much the dreariness as the disguised sexual content. The sexual content was not something that Flecker could put into his work in the way that Lawrence was able to do. When Flecker ventured into working-class territory and love, he tended to take a more romantic view:

> And I will change these gentle clothes for clog and
>   corduroy,
> And work with the mill-hands of black Rioupéroux,

And walk with you, and talk with you, like any other
    boy.[1832]

Flecker, when he briefly depicts the dreariness of the room in 'The Ballad of Camden Town', soon escapes by walking over Hampstead Heath and Primrose Hill.

Flecker could easily identify with such fictional lovers as Don Juan, Sir Willoughby Pattern and Tom Jones, but he did not appear to have an opinion on Paul Morel, whose relationship with his strong-minded mother, and other women, could be seen as close to Flecker's own family relationships and those with other women in his life. Could the criticism on Flecker's part be somewhat tinged with envy? Lawrence had concentrated on his novel while Flecker had concentrated on his poems and plays to the neglect of *The King of Alsander*. In so doing did he now realise that he would never be like Lawrence, a poet-novelist? He already knew that he had earned the anger of his parents over what he had published, in the *Grecians*, about a small part of their life. He knew that Beazley and Hellé would not want some of the poems that had references to them published, and he had not published prose that contained disguised references to Firbank. Firbank was able to write and publish his novels with the Flecker element, after Flecker was dead. Lawrence's mother was dead by the time *Sons and Lovers* was published and her son could not hurt her, although he hurt others depicted in his book. If Flecker was not prepared to see any merit in what would be considered Lawrence's greatest novel, Lawrence was not prepared to see any merit in what would be considered Flecker's greatest poem. Lawrence did not share Marsh's admiration for *The Golden Journey to Samarkand*. This was not surprising, because Marsh had held up *The Golden Journey to Samarkand* as a correct use of rhythm and told Lawrence 'to pay more attention to poetic form'.[1833]

Lawrence defended his use of poetic form, which he thought Marsh might have described as 'rag-time'. Lawrence poured his subject and the emotion into his poetic form. He blamed Marsh's ear for not appreciating the rhythm of his lines and preferring Flecker's subject and poetic form.[1834] Lawrence referred to 'Flecker-rhythm' and told Marsh that *The Golden Journey to Samarkand* only took place on paper.[1835]

Lawrence published his first book of poems entitled *Love Poems and Others* in February 1913, and he had had poems published in periodicals, but he felt because of his disagreements on rhythm, his poetry was not appreciated. *Sons and Lovers* and *The Golden Journey to Samarkand* were two important literary events of 1913. It was ironic that the respective authors disliked each other's work. In the case of Lawrence, his criticism of Flecker's use of poetic form was not entirely personal. Lawrence was credited with adopting a similar stance towards purveyors of metrical poetry and their choice of subject, such as Keats and Shelley.[1836]

Some critics have sought to find similarities between Flecker and Lawrence because both writers suffered from TB. The toxins of the disease, it was said, produce similarities in the writing, such as sensitivity, colour and brightness.[1837] It is difficult to prove beyond reasonable doubt that there is a positive connection between the onset of TB and any remarkable change in Flecker's work or Lawrence's.

The onset of TB has been linked to bereavement and rejection, both experiences more likely than the toxins to produce powerful work. The 'exile' that disease brings to the sufferer so that he or she is thrown back into space and time for writing, is another connection between the output and the choice of subject. The need to make money when paid employment is not possible is another influence more pressing than the disease itself. The nearness to death has been cited as a spur to more creative work, but when the writer is in denial, that does not apply. It was Flecker's play *Hassan*, unlike his novel, that he wanted to be well enough to see performed on stage. But the desire to make money could override the desire for literary fame. In order to make money, it was important for Flecker to try not to break from the tradition and craftsmanship of the past.

Flecker's lack of money is evident in the request made to J.C. Squire on 31 January for a free copy of *The New Statesman*. This was a legitimate request because two poems, 'The Old Ships' on 13 December 1913, and 'Stillness' on 10 January 1914, had been published in that publication. But Flecker added that he had not seen his poems in print, and he wished he could afford *N.S.* every week, but hoped that if he became 'a diligent contributor', he would. He wanted Squire to let him review Chesterton's '*The Flying Inn*', which he thought 'magnificent' and a 'masterpiece'.

He enclosed with his letter to Squire two translations, which he described as his best work and offered the choice of one or both of them. These translations are not named but *The New Statesman* published 'Pannyra of the Golden Heel' on 14 March 1914. He was still 'too ill to do much and quite incapable of writing poetry.'[1838]

A similar message about his state of health and how it affected his ability to write poetry is also evident when he wrote to Clement Shorter (1857–1926), editor of *The Sphere*.

Feb.10 14 Hotel Stephani
Montana-sur-Sierre

Switzerland

Dear Sir,

Thank you for your kind invitation to send you some poems of June 13th ult. Severe illness has prevented me from answering till now. I enclose one poem: must I wait till I have two ready? It may be a long time in my present state of health before I write again.

Yours truly

J.E. Flecker

To Clement Shorter [1839]

The poem enclosed, although it is not named, was 'The Blue Noon', which was published in *The Sphere* on 7 March 1914. Flecker wrote to Marsh on 4 March, telling him that he was sending him 'a print of a poem'.[1840] which he explained either has or will be published in the *Sphere*. This showed that Shorter must have decided to publish 'The Blue Noon' without any hesitation. Marsh was told in the same letter about the proposed date of the publication of *The King of Alsander*, which was to be 10 March.

The manuscript of 'The Blue Noon' is in Hellé's handwriting[1841] with Flecker's signature and the Hotel Stephani address. 'The Blue Noon' is not written from the perspective of the sickroom. The poet is lying under the summer sky 'vestured in silken blue'. The influence behind this poem is Paul Fort.[1842] The reason for the poem being first set down on paper may have come in October 1913, at the Pension Alexandra. Flecker wrote to Savery[1843] when he was working on the Paul Fort article[1844] and enjoying '20 days consecutive brilliant sunshine' and that he was beginning 'to love the country round Montreux'. He was smoking 'a delicious cheap cigar on a bed of dry leaves on Mount Pelerin with a glorious view and feeling quite happy'. This happiness is reflected in 'The Blue Noon' when the poet looks up:

... when nothing earthly stirs or sings
You hear them wave their wings,

The 'them ' refers to 'large blue butterflies'.
The poet continues to describe them as:

The tardy butterflies
Who dive in hosts toward the diving sphere
That holds the light's frontier,

563

And the poor vanquished, turning as they glide,
Show their gold underside.

Flecker described 'The Blue Noon' to Marsh[1845] as 'rather a Herrick poem'. Robert Herrick (1591–1674) wrote such poems as 'Corinna's going a-Maying', which begins with the lines:

.... the blooming morn
Upon her wings presents the god unshorn.
and: 'To the Virgins, to make much of Time', which begins with the line:

Gather ye rosebuds while ye may,

and 'To Daffodils'. This poem begins:

Fair daffodils, we weep to see
You haste away so soon;

Herrick's poems about the short life of flowers seem more in keeping with the theme of Flecker's poem 'Yasmin' than 'Blue Noon', where the poet lets himself dissolve into the blue sky, which to him resembles butterflies. He imagines the approach of evening as a conflict between the sunlight and the butterflies and the encroaching shadows.

Another poem, which Flecker referred to as the 'Spartan Flower' ('Oak and Olive'), he told Marsh in a letter dated 18 February, he was sorry not to say 'means something specially recondite'. The poem, he explained, was 'quite general in meaning'.[1846]

He told Marsh that his novel was being advertised at last[1847] and that he had written to *The Oxford Magazine* to explain how he came to be featured as a Cambridge poet. *The Oxford Magazine* published Flecker's letter under the heading 'A Disclaimer' on 26 February 1914.

He was not encouraged, he told Marsh, by the news that Dean was terribly busy, not well and planning to get married and thus could not get on with *Hassan*. Flecker realised that this was not satisfactory but it was all he had to hope for at this stage. In his next letters to Marsh he enclosed the scenario of *Hassan*,[1848] which he had done in haste because of restrictions on his working hours. This indicated that the nurse, whom his parents had arranged, had arrived and was imposing her regime. Although Miss Schor, the nurse, tolerated her patient's playing of the zither, she curtailed his writing and reading in an effort to curb the activity of his brain. Although, at the same time, she realised that in trying to do so, this only upset his nervous system.[1849] Hellé, too, tried to prevent his writing for more than a very short time, just over an hour every day, because of the resulting tiredness, but this was a prevention that hurt him. She did not fully understand how necessary it was for him to write for much longer. The amount of correspondence that her husband despatched from his sick-bed was an indication of the help that Hellé gave him in writing the letters to his dictation. Much of the content of his letters to Marsh, Monro and Savery was repeated when it referred to health, writing progress and the desire for at least one, if not all, three to try and visit him. The object of a visit from Marsh would be to thank him profusely for all his help. Flecker hoped he would be able to come to London in April to see *Hassan* performed. He imposed again on the kindness of Marsh to ask him about the article on Paul Fort which was under consideration by the *Fortnightly*. Gosse knew of this article because Flecker had written to him about it. He wanted Marsh to mention the fact to Gosse, whose interest might then tip the balance towards publication.

When Flecker wrote to Savery on 7 March, he was able to send him a copy of *The King of Alsander*.[1850] He was also hoping, he told Savery, to be taken to Locarno. Flecker's health was improving and if the weather had been better he would have been able to get up. Flecker had sent Savery a typed copy of 'Virgil little proof of a new poem.'[1851] On 15 March, Flecker wrote to Gilbert Murray, telling him that he was delighted to have his 'letter about Virgil'. Flecker modestly protested to Murray that he was 'no scholar', as he had told Cheesman, who had passed the translation on to Murray.[1852]

In his next letter, Savery did not appear to have given his opinion of Virgil but he had given it on 'the *King of Alsander*', which Flecker found to be 'rather ferocious'.[1853] But Flecker's vanity was pleased by Savery picking out for special praise the passages that the author had written while in Montana, which were the last hundred pages. He thought that Savery was expecting too much from 'a very light and fantastic piece of writing'. A few reviews, Flecker went on, had indicated that already it was going to be the popular success. which was the object of writing it. His novel had been compared to Stevenson and others. Gilbert Murray had written 'a warm encomium' of his Virgil translation: Flecker told Savery that he was beginning to feel alive again and had been for a drive. This news, by coincidence, came at a time when Savery himself had been ill. The renewed health of Flecker had resulted in his being able to consider revising *Don Juan*. He wanted to revise the last Act but found that some of the earlier passages he could not better. He hoped to arrive in Locarno on 28 March. Dean was due to visit him there on 13

May. Dean was not going to cut out the Ghosts, which reassured Flecker 'vastly'.

The Ghosts appeared in Act III of *Hassan*, when the Ghost of Rafi is welcomed by the Fountain Ghost and reunited with the Ghost of Pervaneh, until the Fountain Ghost vanishes and the wind sweeps the ghosts out of the garden. The Fountain Ghost has already told them: 'You will forget, when the great wind blows you asunder and you are born with ten million others like drops on a wave of air.'

Flecker's use of the supernatural entered his new work. In his next letter to Monro dated 22/3/14[1854] he told him he was 'now writing a magnificent ode on the New Greece in which there is something like a real newness of Form – a broken Lycidas metre with unrhymed lines, very long lines, and all sorts of weird effects.'[1855] The ghosts in this unfinished poem, which he called 'Ode to the Glory of Greece', are those of Byron and Shelley. The inspiration came, as he told Monro, 'not as with the futurists from an exterior formlessness which is damned easy to achieve (I do futurists at from 5/0 to 10/6d the page according to length of line).'[1856] He believed, he also told Monro, 'in building on tradition', and the background of the poem is based on Flecker's love of Greece, interest in the Balkan War and the involvements of poets in the founding of a Greek tradition. The use of what Marsh might have seen as a 'rag-time' element in 'Ode to Greece' (A Fragment), is not the most usual choice for a poem on a rousing theme when the first line is: 'HELLAS victorious!'

But the 'newness of Form' showed that Flecker was prepared to experiment and triumph over the 'exterior formlessness', which he deplored in letters and in his preface to *The Golden Journey to Samarkand*. This 'newness of Form' would also lead to an acceptance for publication and success, unlike his version of 'God Save the King', which he told Monro in the same letter he thought 'a failure' and he was thinking of writing 'a new one in the metre of my "Saracens".' Monro published Flecker's 'The National Anthem' in *Poetry and Drama* No.5 in March 1914. Flecker agreed with the criticism of the *Daily Mirror* of his revised Anthem.[1857]

The next letter to Monro, dated 27 March, gave him the change of address to Pension Rheingold, Villa Primrose, Locarno, while still snowbound at Montana. Marsh also got the change of address in a reply to a letter of his, written a day later, with news that the reviews of *Alsander* had been, so far, rather excellent. He emphasised, too, that he had never put the same value on his novel as he had on his poems or *Hassan*. He gave Marsh (as he had also Monro) details of how to get to Locarno. If Monro or Marsh were planning to come they would find that Flecker was longing, on 29 March 1914, for a visit from Savery also, and looking forward to Italy and the spring.[1858] While sorting out old papers, he had come across Savery's original critical letter about *Don Juan* and hoped that they could work together on revising it. Savery was told also that J.N. Raphael proposed to turn *Alsander* into a popular play with twenty-five per cent royalties for the author. Whether or not this piece of news was intended as an added incentive, because it was something else they could get involved in, is unclear. But in the last letter Flecker wrote between 22–28 March, from Montana to Goldring,[1859] he gives the impression that the matter of turning *Alsander* into a popular play was far from settled. But if it came about, Flecker was resigned to letting Goldring act as go-between (as he did with Marsh and *Hassan*) and Raphael would take a major share in the project (as Dean appeared to do with *Hassan*). Flecker's present state of health and absence from England, prevented any other settlement.

He wrote to Goldring: 'Re. *King of Alsander*. Dramatic Rights. I know the signature of J.N. Raphael under many an inadequate verse translation from the French and some fairly adequate Paris gossip. Of course make a bargain for the stage rights... I will write formally on this subject if you like. But I would like to work the play in collaboration with JNR if possible – a collaboration in which I should take the minor part.[1860]

What may have inspired the confidence to see *Alsander* as a popular play beyond the aim to make some money, could have been the excellent review in the *Spectator*. This periodical went up in Flecker's estimation, as a letter addressed to Mr. Masters, whose thanks Flecker gave him in a letter that has survived:[1861]

The letter [April 1914] tells Masters that his letter arrived just as Flecker was about to write to him and give him the new address. He very much appreciated the *Spectator* and the way it had reviewed his book so well. He told Masters that he was allowed to drive out a bit, and he was able to get away 'from those horrid fir trees down to this charming lake'. Masters was also told of Flecker's 'decent quiet slow-curing-but-still curing consumption I consider to be rather a boon to a literary man'. But following on from that statement was the next, which illustrated that the 'slow-curing' had its setbacks, when he wrote: 'I wrote a play which is my best effort and will be played next season: but horrid attacks like this are no good for anything – and even now I'm too weak for anything but an occasional scratch of the pen.'

Flecker also wrote that he had thought of sending him *Alsander* but decided that Masters would probably dislike it. Flecker's next statement ('I don't take myself very seriously as a novelist – poetry and the drama are my real work') was similar to remarks made to other people about *Alsander*. Despite the good reviews, his tendency to see *Alsander* in third place after his poetry and drama does not explain why he embarked upon the writing of *Alsander* in the first place. It would have pleased him to be a poet, dramatist and novelist, all of the highest order. Flecker finished the letter to Masters with an offer to send a copy of his poem.

The title of the poem to be sent to Masters is not given but in his letter to Goldring (the last he sent from Montana) he told him that 'As for poems I've only written 4 since *Samarkand* and they be small ones. Clement Shorter offered me three guineas, and I've only been able to send one, whereas he asked for two.'[1862]

He went on to give many thanks to Goldring for introducing him to Goschens. 'They are certainly advertising excellently. I shall not only be disappointed but astonished if the *K. of A.* don't move. The *Evening Standard* review and *Globe* are better quoting than *The Times.*

A review such as the one in the *Westminster Gazette*, that was not as glowing as he would have wished did not deter Flecker from asking Goldring to continue to send out review copies of both *The Golden Road* and *Alsander*. On a card posted 18 April 1914 from Locarno, Flecker asked Goldring to send a copy of *Alsander* to 'L.P. Dole c/o Boston Herald'[1863] 'He is a worthy fellow who offers to puff me illimitably in America: he offers to pay for the books – but I hope you can send him a free copy as he is full of youthful enthusiasms and promised to review the book in some rag or other.'[1864]

Someone else who received a communication from Locarno was Donald Robertson from Cambridge days. In it, Flecker gave instructions on 8 April, how to reach him from S. Remo.[1865] Flecker also lamented to Robertson: 'What a pest! Are you going to make me regret having quitted the fir trees, snows and thaws of that infernal Montana?' The lament of needing to have someone to talk to was repeated on a postcard sent to Marsh on 13 April[1866] also thanking him for a cheque.

'We are absolutely alone in a dreary German pension, whose inmates we never see, and are slowly going mad. I wish the deuce we had a Villa at Monti for the summer and I wish you would re-visit your ancient haunts. We had a mauve blancmange for lunch to-day. We suffer.'

Savery got a similar dismal picture from a depressed Flecker, who had been in bed for fifteen days except for an hour's drive. He wanted Savery to visit him, to come as soon as he could. They both regarded Savery as a sort of 'Messiah'.

In late April and early May, Flecker was reunited with Savery for two weeks – the first time they had been together since Cambridge days. Savery realised that his old friend was very ill as he listened to him coughing continually. He was unable to venture out during the two weeks of Savery's visit.

Flecker was thus a prisoner unable to leave his room. 'The Pensive Prisoner' was an appropriate subject to discuss when the opportunity arose to consider Flecker's literary work. 'The Pensive Prisoner' was written by Flecker at Locarno in April 1914, but Savery did not find his old friend to be pensive; instead, as Savery recalled: 'He was very cheerful that spring at Locarno – cheerful, not extravagantly optimistic, as is the way of consumptives. I think he hardly ever mentioned his illness to me, and there was certainly at that time nothing querulous about him.' [1867]

The following line from 'The Pensive Prisoner' did not seem to apply to the time of Savery's visit: '... my Body's Chain and all the Dragons born of Pain.'

Savery took the opportunity, when he recalled his visit, to remark on Flecker having stated that he liked his work as Consul and that he was proud of being a good business-like official. Savery concluded:

> .... thereby disposing, in his case at any rate, the time-honoured conception of the poet as an unpractical dreamer. He was certainly no mere dreamer at any period of his life; he appreciated beauty with extraordinary keenness, but, like a true poet, he was never contented with mere appreciation. He was determined to make his vision as clear to others as it was to himself.[1868]

Savery also commented (at the same time as he made these remarks, gathered at the Locarno meeting) on Flecker's religious beliefs: 'He confessed that he had not greatly liked the East – always excepting of course Greece – and that his intercourse with Mohammedans had led him to find more good in Christianity than he had previously expected.'[1869]

Savery's vested interest as a Catholic convert would prevent him from exploring more deeply in print Flecker's Protestant convictions, and his turning away from his evangelical roots and the leaning towards the Greek Orthodox Church. Savery would also feel inhibited on the subject of his old friend's religious beliefs by the knowledge that any suggestion that their son was interested in any other branch of Christianity was unacceptable to Flecker's parents. Savery was to find that out to his cost much later.[1870] Flecker's parents' statement left no doubt that it was their son's illness that precipitated his return to religion and not the influence of anything else: 'What, however, cannot be doubted is, that as his illness increased Flecker craved more and more for the real inward consolations of religion'. [1871]

'Religion', in this context, meant the Anglican Church of his childhood. Any other interest in religion was due to his intellectual curiosity, as his parents also stated: 'It was impossible that a man who had wandered widely and met many varieties of people should fail to grasp the world-wide significance of the Latin Church.'[1872]

And when referring to their son's interest in other religions during Savery's Locarno visit, an historical aspect was added when they quoted: 'He liked to picture the Patriarch of Constantinople still wearing the imperial eagle of Byzantium on his vestments.' [1873]

Savery was a Consular Official in Munich when he visited Flecker in April/May 1914, and subsequently in Berne, Switzerland, when they met again. At the time of the first publication of his meeting with Flecker (in 1916 in the *Collected Poems*), Savery was a long way off retirement in 1949, the award of the CBE and death in 1965. But it would be as imprudent in 1916 to make any mention of Flecker's conflicts with the FO as it would be to comment fully on Flecker's conflicts over religion with his parents. Strictly speaking, having resigned, Flecker was no longer a Consular Official by May, 1914, any more than he had returned to the religion of his early years by that date. The reference to 'business-like' official and the mention of Flecker not being an 'unpractical dreamer' was something Savery could do to redress the balance in his old friend's favour. Savery might never have known that the FO knew nothing of Flecker's literary endeavours, during his service. Even the FO admitted that Flecker was 'clever',[1874] but this was not the quality that the FO valued. Good health was the main strength, although the healthy officers carried the burdens put down by their less fit colleagues. The kind of conclusion made sixty years later about Flecker's work as a Consular Official has to be weighed against Savery's remark about a business-like official: 'The consular service is not the place for dreamers, particularly those who dream continually of home'.[1875] Many writers have to combine their Consular or other types of post alongside literary hopes. But it would be nearer the truth in Flecker's case to say that the Consular service is no place for consumptives.

At the end of May, the Fleckers moved from Locarno to Davos, in the high Alps. In his first communication written to Marsh from the sanatorium, Hotel Buol, Davos Platz on 21 May 1914, Flecker referred to the fact that John Addington Symonds had 'lived for some years in this hotel and bequeathed all the rubbish in his library to it'.[1876] John Addington Symonds (1840–93) Renaissance Scholar and author, gave a picture of what life was like for consumptives in Davos between 1877–8:

'It is generally conceded by doctors that to stay in Davos after the second week in April is unadvisable. The great mass of winter snow is then melting, the roads are almost impassable by walkers, and the sun has acquired great power. Chills, almost unknown in winter or the summer may now be taken and the irksomeness of the protracted residence in one place is beginning to tell on the nerves and spirits. Therefore the colony breaks up.'[1877]

It would seem from Symonds's statement that the Fleckers were arriving at Davos at a time when the resident patients were leaving, which might be helpful in finding suitable and cheaper accommodation but not in helping with the ever-present desire of the Fleckers to meet like-minded people. Another statement of Symonds would give more hope: 'The verdict of the Davos physicians as to the probability of a cure may, I am confident, be trusted. They are extremely averse from encouraging patients to stay who would not be likely to thrive and do credit to the place.' [1878]

This statement may go some way in explaining why Flecker was encouraged first to leave Leysin, then Montreux and lastly Locarno. Not only was Flecker restless but his progress was poor and he was not a good advertisement for the establishment chosen. Lastly, Symonds stated: 'it is well to be provided with some mental occupation; for, though my own experience is that one suffers less ennui'. [1879]

Symonds was fortunate that he was able to enjoy conversations with Robert Louis Stevenson, at another sanatorium, the Hotel Belvédère at Davos. Their joint discussions, which ranged over both English and French literature and the two years from 1880–2, when Stevenson was in Davos, Symonds described as the best of his life.

The emphasis that Flecker put on his need for civilised company was real enough, but he could not hope to be as fortunate as Symonds, who not only found such good company but also an improvement in his health. Symonds (who was married) became the lover of Christian Buol and he refers in his book to the pedigree of the family Buol 'who now own a large hotel at Davos'.[1880] This association with the family Buol was another reason why, in his book, Symonds was able to write so much about the history of Davos, and the Hotel Buol in particular. The fact of Stevenson having stayed at Davos many years before was said to have been an influence on Flecker's desire also (as Stevenson had done) to install a hand-press to print his own poems. Further evidence came from W.G. Lockett, British Consul at Davos, to whom Flecker wrote to ask where he could find an amateur printing-press.[1881]

A more up-to-date version of life for TB patients was provided by the author, Thomas Mann (1875–1955) who, while on a visit to his wife who was a TB patient, at the same time of year, May (but a year earlier than the Fleckers) found that Davos engendered the magic of inspiration. Mann felt able to consider a novel, which eventually he called *The Magic Mountain*. Mann first intended that *The Magic Mountain* would be a counterpart to his novel *Death in Venice*, published in 1913. '*The Magic Mountain*' (published in 1924, won the Nobel Prize in 1929) portrayed from Mann's and his wife's point of view, the enclosed world of sick and dying patients at Davos. Mann was mistakenly diagnosed for a time as having TB. But because of the delay between the inspiration and the writing of *The Magic Mountain*, the enclosed but not lonely world of the Davos TB patients was more likely to be Davos of the 1920s. So if Flecker had entered the enclosed world, if it even existed in a slightly later era, the civilised company they sought would not have been so hard to find. Symonds had written of the break-up of the Davos 'colony' by May, and this, added to Flecker's long stays in bed, resulted in a longing for company from outside. He was not able to mix with the patients around him. Magic that Mann attributed to the mountains around Davos was not similar to the magic Flecker had felt when he first arrived at Leysin. At Leysin he was released from the stifling heat of Beirut. But by the time he reached Davos he was depressed by the inner knowledge that no magic cure was in the air.

Flecker told Marsh of his depression and despondency, which were not due entirely to his physical state. He could not get on with his creative work, but his ability to get on with his correspondence continued. Flecker had had to leave Locarno before he could meet Dean, who was planning to spend part of his honeymoon at Leysin. Dean, on arrival at Leysin, found only a note begging him to meet the Fleckers at Davos. But Dean decided not to do this, which he later regretted. Flecker, when telling Marsh about having missed Dean, only described it as a 'nuisance'; Flecker was finding it hard to take an interest in *Hassan* and he wished that Dean would do all the work. This could be due to the fact that there was 'some chance' of *Hassan* being acted at the Court Theatre, Norwich.[1882]

Flecker wrote to Savery, on the same day, to thank him for a parcel of books and to discuss, amongst others, those by George Moore, Dickens and Wilkie Collins, which he was reading all day to keep himself 'from groaning and moaning'.

He also told Savery: 'I have just a hope that they'll be able to give me a pneumo-thorax – which is a certain cure. But you must have the other lung alright to stand it, and it's a bit doubtful.' Pneumo-thorax was a process of invasive surgery, whereby the lung is collapsed so that the bacilli are deprived of oxygen and die, or fail to spread. This procedure was to become more widespread among patients with TB in the 1920s than in Flecker's day, although it had been known about for a long time. Pneumo-thorax was obviously not without risk for sick patients and could be seen as a treatment alongside care in the sanatorium rather than offering 'a certain cure'.

Only in a PS to his letter to Savery did Flecker make a reference to Hellé and her burden of 'tending a rather dismal invalid like me if you have no distractions whatsoever'. Hellé had 'found a jabbersome but pleasant Scotchwoman to walk with. I am very glad.'[1883] Hellé, herself, in her reminiscences when describing this period at Davos, does not dwell on the tediousness or the anxiety of caring for her husband. In the same way as her parents-in-law attributed their son's return to organised religion to his illness, Hellé did not take any credit for the maturing of her husband's literary gifts. She maintained that the illness 'matured him'.[1884] Hellé's influence may have been behind Goldring asking Flecker to write a book on Greece – a descriptive tour. On 1 June, Flecker's reply was: 'I can only preserve the rotten remnants of my life by lying in bed here for years – in the ugliest hole God ever created.'[1885]

Despite this refusal to comply with Goldring's suggestion, Flecker sought assurance that Goschens would accept 'his great ode to Greece', which was to be published 'separately with a forty-page preface of a most violent kind, full of abuse and invective of pro-Turks, pro-Bulgars, the Liberal Press, with history of the Eastern question.' He realised that 'it might create a bit of a stir', The realisation that his preface to *The Golden Journey* had caused more than 'a bit of a stir' had not put him off attempting an even more stirring preface. He finished the letter on an even more unrealistic note: 'I'd give all my poems to be a healthy navvy.'

In another letter[1886] to Goldring, there were more practical matters concerning the publicity and advertising of *The King of Alsander*, which appeared not to be satisfactory in the author's eyes, when he wrote: 'What sells a book is an advertisement with about ten extracts underneath it. A book got a column review in the *Spectator* about a week before mine: the next week it was advertised in the *Spectator* itself with a large chunk of review and has multiplied its editions. Also one doesn't see Goschen's lists with the other lists in the *Spectator*.'

He had seen an advance notice of *The King of Alsander* in the *Daily News* and he wanted that publication to review his novel because he felt that the *Daily News* was very important and, if necessary, another copy should be sent. He wanted *Punch* also to be gently reminded of the author's hopes of a review. He wanted to know if review copies had been sent to America. The criticisms of the handling of review copies of his novel were obviously due to lack of royalties. He finished his letter by asking: 'Send me along the half-crown or whatever it is *Alsander* has earned.'

But before that, in case he had gone too far, Flecker reassured Goldring that *The Golden Journey* was splendidly pushed and he was not ungrateful.

He apologised to Goldring in his next letter to him for writing a 'crusty letter' but he was 'so damned ill I'm almost in despair'. He had lost the Polignac prize,[1887] although Murray and Yeats had voted for him. This letter, despite the despair, contained a photograph of Flecker and the promise to send twelve more 'for most important customers'. Biographical details were also enclosed for Goldring to work upon to send to enquirers. ('One can't do these things oneself: it's so grotesque.') Money was still the underlying problem. Flecker asked about the £10 advance by Goschens for the 'Virgil'. He wanted Goldring to see about an American Press Agency for him.[1888]

In his next letter to Savery (2.6.14.) he told him of revising his own version of *Hassan* for the German stage. This shortened copy would be Flecker's exclusive version, whatever Dean did to the manuscript afterwards. He hoped that this would not incur the wrath of Freissler, but Savery would get to see the corrections beforehand. In the next letter to Savery, which he dictated to Hellé on 11 June, he appeared to have climbed down. He wrote: 'I don't mind a bit *Hassan* appearing in its old version in German and shan't ask Freissler to make any changes'. Flecker had cut about forty pages out of one hundred and eighty and he thought he had improved it a great deal for the stage.

'I cannot help thinking it is so immensely improved that it will require very little alteration;' Flecker wrote to Basil Dean on 18 June. He did not want to be blamed for wanting to improve 'my work', which sent the message to Dean that *Hassan* was Flecker's work, however much Dean might want to alter the text. He told Dean that he did not want to institute 'a sort of Literature v. Drama quarrel!'... every correction,' he told Dean 'makes the play better literature. The play I send you now is the play I shall publish.'[1889]

Flecker still wanted *Hassan* shown to Tree on the grounds of Tree's ability to make a great financial success of *Hassan* (if Tree were to agree to take it), which would be diminished by Flecker's request to have real camels in the final scene. Flecker's desire to come to London for the performance of *Hassan* would diminish profits further. He told Dean of his being 'so hopelessly ill', but there was an operation that would bring about 'a real cure'. The prospect of 'a real cure' could let Dean think that he was not dealing with a dying poet. He would not realise that time was already running out for their partnership.

The next (undated) letter to Dean followed the familiar pattern of Flecker taking a stance about alterations and then backing down: 'I shall be very careful to carry out your suggestions'. This was one sentence in the letter, but he also wrote to Dean: 'You will very likely want to preserve some passages I have omitted'.[1890] Dean's own acting edition of *Hassan*, in which he incorporated Flecker's later last-minute revisions, is not available for comparison with the final acting version of *Hassan*. So it cannot be seen how much difference to *Hassan* revisions by Dean would mean in the end. As well as Dean's alterations to *Hassan*, Flecker had to chase up the manuscript with his own corrections, which he had previously sent to Savery. He did this by writing to Savery on 22 June, telling him that he agreed to alterations that Freissler might be keen to make.[1891] Flecker wrote to Savery a week later to press for his critique of *Hassan*. He also thanked him for sending him two volumes of John Dryden's plays. Flecker continued to complain of a sore throat and temperature and being 'in the very lowest depths'.[1892] Marsh also got information about Flecker's health which he explained was 'about as rotten as possible'.[1893] The date of this letter is given as June(?) but it must have been written in reply to a letter from Marsh written after 11 July; Flecker's reply refers to Rupert Brooke's 'new Fish', which Flecker did not like. The letter also contains reference to Dean and the new Georgian Poetry.

11 June was an important day in Marsh's calendar. It was the day that Brooke, on his return from the South Seas arrived in London to have lunch with Marsh. After dinner they went to the first performance of *Papillons* at Covent Garden. After that a late-night party began at Marsh's apartment with many guests, including Granville Barker, John Drinkwater, Harold Monro and Henry Ainley. After the party on 11 June, Marsh gathered material for the next edition of *Georgian Poetry*, which it was hoped would be titled *Georgian Poetry 1913/4*. It was due out in December 1914, but it was postponed and eventually appeared as *Georgian Poetry 1913/5* in November 1915. The edition of *Georgian Poetry 1913/5* contained the following poems of Flecker's:

'The Old Ships'

'A Fragment'	(from his anthology *The Old Ships*)
'Santorin'	(from *The Golden Journey to Samarkand*)
'Yasmin'	(from *The Golden Journey to Samarkand*)
'Gates of Damascus'	(from *The Golden Journey to Samarkand*)
'The Dying Patriot'	(from *The Golden Journey to Samarkand*)

Flecker's view of Marsh's proposed choice of his work was not without its differences, as is shown in the letter: 'No. <u>Don't</u> have the Epilogue, [*The Golden Journey to Samarkand*] and I would rather not 'Yasmin', as both are in 'Hassan' and I don't want 'em too well known. (But do have anything if you want it – I only give my ideas.) <u>Please</u> include 'Taoping'. What about the all blue butterflies poem? Or 'Saadabad'? Or 'Brumana'?'

Flecker, in this letter, also drew Marsh into his differences with Dean over the alterations to the ms of *Hassan*. Dean had sent Flecker the manuscript of *Hassan* for him to make his own alterations and Flecker 'with great skill cut and altered the whole play'. Dean, in the meantime, wrote to Flecker and told him he had been altering the old version. Added to the annoyance this lack of communication (and crossing in the post of the manuscript) produced, Dean was rehearsing a play and had no time to look at the alterations made by Flecker. He ended the letter to Marsh with a PS lamenting the fact that nobody commented on his poem 'Don Juan Declaims' and sending:

Impromptu Poem in the style of 'Poetry and Drama'

'I'm ill
Bloody ill,
Damned ill
If I were not so ill
I'd get up
And knock the Doctor down.

While differences of opinion on *Hassan* were circulating, Flecker had to contend with the contrasting reception by critics of *The Golden Journey to Samarkand* and *The King of Alsander*.

On 26 December 1913, T.E. Lawrence had written a request to F.A. Fontana, the British Consul at Aleppo, for a copy of *The King of Alsander* to be sent to him. Lawrence wrote in June 1914 to Flecker, telling him about 'the little fuss at Carchemish' and illustrating the letter with a map. (The inclusion of the map of the battlefield could indicate that the Fleckers never visited Carchemish.) Lawrence also told Flecker what he thought about The King of Alsander and *The Golden Journey to Samarkand*.[1894]

'The little fuss at Carchemish' had taken place on 22 March 1914. The incident was sparked off by a dispute over wages and resulted in the death of a Kurd and the eventual involvement of two hundred and fifty troops. Lawrence had already written from Aleppo to Flecker about the derision he felt about the incident. But the Fleckers move from Pension Rheingold in April resulted in the first letter not being received. The incident was reported in *The Times* on 25 March under the heading 'Riot on the Bagdad Railway', which could have first caught Flecker's interest and he had written to Lawrence. Lawrence included the criticisms of Woolley and Hogarth after he had described the battle at Carchemish:

> However I'm very sorry, for Woolley Hogarth and I were all reading Alsander together with mutual jealousies. I have forgotten Hogarth's remarks. They included a desire to know who William Jordan Junior was... [a reference to 'William Jordan, Junior, greatest of unread modern books' which is referred to on p.10 of *The King of Alsander.*] Woolley was cut to the quick over the sad fate of Arnolfo... he regarded it as apostasy on your part of the worst, and a deplorable tragedy, which blinded for him the book. [Arnolfo turns out to be the Princess Ianthe in disguise when she reveals herself to Norman Price.] I think myself it is exceedingly annoying as a book: if it had been three it would have been streets more satisfactory... all your characters seem so much more capable and interesting than they have room to show. It is more of a dream or a chapter of dreams than a novel. No doubt you meant it so, but I'm a pedestrian, and I don't like to see glorious things for a hundredth part of a second only. That's why I prefer Samarcand as more satisfactory, though I quite agree that parts of Alsander are as good as anything going. By the way you can write better than Snaith.... the battle in Alsander, and the description of the disordered garden, and the crossing of the hills are very wonderful. As for the description of the girl with the pails ... well you know, it struck me as falling between the two pails: a little too exuberant to be solemn, and not as fat as a show fat-lady should be. You won't be able to make any sense of that as 'art criticism'.

Two or three things of Ernest Dowson have pleased me lately. Alas I suppose you have read everything like that.

[Ernest Dowson, the poet (1867–1900) to whom Lawrence also referred in a letter to C.F. Shaw, 17 May 1928 MB p.374 BL Add MS.45904. Lawrence wrote: 'I am very grateful: for poor Dowson who wrote ten lovely poems, and died.' Wilson p.827 and to David Garnett from Miranshah 14 June 1928, 'Somebody said that Dowson wasn't a great poet; or Flecker. God almighty! Must everyone be as seven leagued as Milton and Byron and Hardy!'[1895] Had Lawrence been rereading 'lately' the poems of Ernest Dowson in the following edition – *The Poems of Ernest Dowson* (described by Rupert Brooke as 'bound in pale sorrowful green.')?[1896]

The memoir by Arthur Symons (dated 1900) describes most movingly the dying Dowson: 'He did not realise that he was going to die and was full of projects for the future.....'[1897] Symons then goes on to relate Dowson's hopes of money from the sale of property and his starting to read Dickens. From Symons' picture of Dowson dying from consumption at the age of 32 (not much older than Flecker and born at Lee, a stone's throw from Flecker's birthplace) Lawrence would have been helped to picture the dying Flecker and his ultimate death almost too clearly.

Lawrence does not name the 'two or three things' that pleased him. Dowson's masterpiece is the poem 'I have been faithful to thee, Cynara! in my fashion,' lines that have passed into the language:

> I have forgot much, Cynara! gone with the wind,
> Flung roses, roses riotously with the throng,
> Dancing, to put thy pale, lost lilies out of mind;
> But I was desolate and sick of an old passion,
> Yea, all the time, because the dance was long:
> I have been faithful to thee, Cynara! in my fashion.

Jad Adams states: 'It [Cynara'] is full of iconography of decadence with the writer trading, like Swinburne, the 'lilies and languors of virtue/ For the raptures and roses of vice'.[1898]

In Flecker's poem 'Yasmin', the opening lines echo those of 'Cynara!':

> How splendid in the morning glows the lily: with what
>   grace he throws
> His supplication to the rose: do roses nod the head,
>   Yasmin?]

> I have never read a book of yours called the Grecians.
> Do you approve of it?

[Lawrence states that he had never read the *Grecians*. In the *Grecians*, Harold Smith, the stranger of aesthetic appearance, is based on Dowson, according to Edgar Jones. La Giocosa: James Elroy Flecker's Aesthetic Academy. Part 2. Durham University Journal.]

Did you know that in January and Feb. Woolley and I explored the desert of the exodus, looking for the footpath of the children of Israel. [This expedition was a cover for spying.] And now have to write the next annual of the Palestine Exploration Fund to describe our non-success. The Fund inform us that the tone of the annual is usually slightly devotional. So prepare yourself for something hotter than Alsander.

I expect to be about another two or three weeks yet in England, and thereafter Eastward ... I'm afraid it is not very easy to come to Davos!

Am exceeding sorry to hear of your being so bad. To be in bed for six months must be a ghastly trial ... unless you really are ill, when it would no doubt seem natural. Write to me here once more if it does not weary you. After writing you three sheets I deserve many things: However one doesn't get them usually.

Yrs.
E.L.

While Lawrence stayed with Flecker at Areiya, he recalled 'talking of women, slippers, and of whippings. Of reviving *Hassan.*' It was more likely that the discussion was about *The King of Alsander* and not *Hassan.* Even if Lawrence was reading *The King of Alsander* for the first time without pre-knowledge, it was strange that in his letter he made no reference to whippings in *The King of Alsander.* In Chapter VIII Norman Price failed to pass a qualifying examination for the post of King of Alsander and was whipped. When part of the examination consisted of a command to Norman Price to climb, naked, along a rope that hung from the ceiling, he refused with anger. The youthful President told him to dress and leave the room immediately. Norman demanded an apology first. The President pressed a bell, four guards appeared and Norman is whipped severely and then allowed to walk free. Norman tried to get help and revenge from the British Consulate in Alsander. He was at a disadvantage because he did not have a passport. After Norman had told his tale to the British Consul, he was met with official apathy. Norman, in desperation, threatened to write to *The Times.* But the Consul smiled because his brother edited the letters columns and he would be prevailed upon to print alongside Price's letter a note to say that he was treated 'with all civility' even if he had no passport and no letter of introduction and was telling 'half-truths'. At that point the handsome young President appeared and was none other than Signor Arnolfo, who in turn revealed 'himself' as Princess Ianthe.

This fictional account of the whipping of Norman Price bears a resemblance to an experience that Lawrence said he had in November 1917. But. if it ever did take place, the likelihood would have been at another time and place – 1912, and could have been told to Flecker.[1899]

The experience that much later Lawrence published an account of in his *Seven Pillars of Wisdom* in 1922 (and he also discussed in letters and conversations) took place, Lawrence said, in the Syrian town of Deraa. Lawrence, by then a British officer, entered the town disguised as one of the local Arabs, with the intention of spying. He was stopped by Turkish soldiers, imprisoned and then told he was wanted by the Bey.

The Bey was said by Lawrence to have made homosexual overtures, which Lawrence repulsed. No doubt as angrily as Norman Price when the test was put to him by the President of Alsander. As a result of his refusal, Lawrence was hit with slippers, then severely beaten by guards, and sexually abused. Lawrence eventually escaped because a door was conveniently left unlocked. Norman Price escaped from his ordeal by the same method. Lawrence did not say anything about this episode for eighteen months and Norman Price kept quiet about the ordeal he was put through in Alsander. If Lawrence had thought of complaining to the British Consul at the time, he would have had visions similar to Norman Price's:

> Visions of Britain's might awake to protect her humblest subject rolled across his mind; of Dreadnoughts blackening the horizon, of a ten minutes' bombardment, of being hauled from prison by merry bluejackets pouring brandy down his throat, of shaking hands with a clean-shaven Admiral, of a protectorate over Alsander, and the immediate repaving of the roads and reconstruction of the sewers.[1900]

Lawrence would have found the sort of British Consul described by Flecker, who must have been based on Fontana and others whom Lawrence also encountered in Syria and Lebanon.

'Art criticism' may have been more important than their mutual interest in real or imagined incidents of floggings. 'Art criticism' was a subject that Lawrence was to devote time to in the future.[1901] Unlike Flecker, Lawrence appreciated *Sons and Lovers*. Lawrence's references to Flecker's sickness indicated that he was aware of the severity of it and that he would not want to add to the distress by making cruel comments about *Alsander*. He praised parts of it but the real admiration for Flecker's work, for Lawrence lay in the poetry.

Later it was said that the 'chief influence on his [Lawrence's] determination to be a writer was James Elroy Flecker, the poet.'[1902] Flecker's poem 'The Pensive Prisoner' appeared to be so much of an influence that it crept into a passage in Lawrence's 'The Mint'.[1903]

'At ten-fifteen lights out; and upon their dying flash every sound ceased. Silence and fear came back to me. Through the white windows streaked white diagnols from conflicting arc-lamps without. Within there ruled the stupor of first sleep, as of embryons in that natal caul. My observing spirit slowly and deliberately hoisted itself from place to prowl across this striped upper air, leisurely examining the forms stretched out so mummy-still in the strait beds. Our first lesson in the Depot had been our apartness from life. This second vision was of our sameness, body by body. How many souls gibbered that night in the roof-beams, seeing it? Once more mine panicked, suddenly, and fled back to its coffin-body. Any cover was better than bareness.'[1904]

The resemblance to Flecker's poem has been pointed out[1905] when an anthology of Lawrence's favourite poems was published posthumously. Flecker's poems 'Yasmin' and 'Stillness' and the Prologue to 'The Golden Journey to Samarkand' were selected as well as 'The Pensive Prisoner', the lines of which can be compared with the lines in 'The Mint'.

THE PENSIVE PRISONER

My thoughts came drifting down the Prison where I lay –
Through the Windows of their Wings the stars were
    shining –
The wings bore me away – the russet Wings and grey
With feathers like the moon-bleached Flowers – I was a
    God reclining:
Beneath me lay my Body's Chain and all the Dragons born
    of Pain
As I burned through the Prison Roof to walk on Pavement
    Shining.

The Wild Wind of Liberty swept through my Hair and
    sang beyond:
I heard the Souls of men asleep chattering in the Eaves

And rode on topmost Boughs of Heaven's single-moon-
   fruited Silver Wand,
Night's unifying Tree whereof the central Stars be leaves –
O Thoughts, Thoughts, Thoughts, – Fire-angel-birds
   relentless –
Will you not brood in God's Star-tree and leave Red Heart
   tormentless!

'The Mint', was also published posthumously and was compiled from notes made by Lawrence at the RAF Depot, where he enlisted in the ranks under the name of John Hume Ross, in 1922.

Flecker and Lawrence were influences on each other. An influence from which they both could have drawn ideas was Arthur Machen's novel *The Hill of Dreams*, published in 1907. Machen's novel tells of the woman who bought a beautiful slave-boy in the market of an Asian city and took him to her house and tempted him for three years. Then: '... fighting in agony against his green and crude immaturity, I devoted him to the theatre, where he amused the people by the splendour of his death.'[1906]

This part of *The Hill of Dreams* bears a resemblance to the story of Pervaneh, the beautiful girl taken from the slave-market to the Caliph's palace and her eventual death, in Flecker's *Hassan*. In the same part of *The Hill of Dreams* is a description of the girls (belonging to the woman who has fallen in love with the slave-boy) undressing him, bathing him and also tempting him. The slave-boy is dumbfounded and abashed in much the same way as Lawrence himself was said to be when he encountered a group of young Kurdish women in Syria, who were drawing water. He was alone and asked for a drink of water. The Kurdish women were said by Lawrence to have been intrigued by his white body, which did not burn in the sun and they stripped him and then allowed him to escape. Lawrence said nothing for a time when he got back to Carchemish. This incident, like others in Lawrence's life, could be fantasy or taken from literature. Machen's *The Hill of Dreams* was in Lawrence's library.[1907]

In late July, Flecker replied briefly to Lawrence's long letter: 'I'm sorry if you really can't come and see me as – well I won't be macabre. Should like to see you again so much. I am miserable. Many thanks for your jovial account of the Row. You promised me some toys from Carchemish – you horror and never have sent none. Too weary for more.'[1908]

Another 'Row' of much greater magnitude was brewing, which would not need a 'jovial account' from Lawrence. Storm clouds already threatened the world horizon. War would break out in August. But before this happened 'some toys' of a different kind were also on his mind. The writing of a special poem for Hellé's birthday on 14 July appeared to be a task Flecker was too weary to accomplish. Instead he wrote to Savery with the following suggestions for the purchase of an alternative present for Hellé: 'It might be a quaint umbrella handle or something Japanese or a bit of Jap silk for a blouse or a Russian toy or a parasol or anything depicting animals especially tigers or cats or a bracelet or kimono.'[1909]

Savery chose Russian dolls, which amused Flecker. He sent in repayment a cheque, which indicated that there was not an immediate lack of funds. News of future lack of funds was relayed to Marsh when Flecker told him of severe money losses of 'my unfortunate father'. Later he explained to Marsh that these losses were from capital but his father still retained 'a largish income'. The precise cause of Dr. Flecker's losses is not explained, but a contributory factor could be the approach of war, when investments he made in Austrian Bonds were rendered useless.[1910]

Flecker hinted to Marsh that he 'may have to look around for a Civil List pension'. He thought, he told Marsh, that he would stand no chance because of his age and 'have done so little' and the fact that his illness prevented his writing. He hoped that *Hassan* would 'take me out of the "Puree" – but who knows?' In case Marsh had not got the message that his help was needed in the matter of a Civil List Pension, Flecker added a PS 'Give me your opinion about the Civil List.'[1911] It was unfortunate for Flecker that Marsh did not become Secretary in Charge of Civil List Pensions for another year. But Marsh endeavoured to help Flecker, despite the approaching war and the plight of other writers, such as D.H. Lawrence, Lascelles Abercrombie and Gordon Bottomley. Marsh consulted Edward Thomas 'who knew vaguely of some relief fund for men of letters'.[1912] Marsh passed on the information about the Royal Literary Fund (founded in 1790 as a charity to help writers facing hardship). Flecker replied that he was 'very glad to know about the Literary Fund as I may be on the rocks any day'.[1913] 'Any day' had not yet arrived, because, as he told Marsh, Dr. Flecker had written to tell him that he would continue to support him. But Flecker could apply for a pension, when he could rightly point out that his father could no longer support him. He would also then apply for an emergency loan from the Literary Fund. But in case Marsh thought that there would now be an end to the emotional pressure put on him, Flecker wrote: 'Honestly I don't expect to trouble the face of the earth much longer – and as long as *Hassan* comes off I shall expire happily'.

Despite this gloomy view of his future, Flecker thanked Marsh for books sent and asked him about the choice of his poems for 'the new Georgians'. The 'new Georgians' referred to the proposed *Georgian Poetry 1913–1914*, which had to be cancelled. Harold Monro was relieved; he deemed it absurd to bring out the second volume of *Georgian Poetry* when, as soon as war had been declared ,there were scarcely any customers in the Poetry Bookshop.

A postcard to Mavrogordato, at 52 Queen's Gardens, London, once again encapsulated Flecker's despair:

> Hotel Buol,
> Davos Platz
> Switz.
> [August, 1914]

Dear Mavro,

Damn Austria. Also damn Austin Harrison. Will you please be so monstrous kind as to rescue my Paul Fort MS. I can't get a *word* out of him.

I am horribly ill – can hardly write. Hope some day to finish ode on Greece. The savage bitterness of its preface would relieve me. Do let me have your *Westminster Gazette* letters. Why don't the league protest against the vile Balkan league and Bryce's [James, 1st Viscount Bryce (1838–1922), Liberal politician. He entered parliament 1880] pompous ineptitudes. Do write me a letter yourself.

All I can do is a few lines of translation of Virgil.

Do write.

Ever yours and very feeble.
James Elroy Flecker.[1914]

The outbreak of war in August was responsible for another possible small setback against the much hoped-for German production of *Hassan*. When escaping from the Consulate in Munich, Savery had to leave his copy of *Hassan* behind. Flecker told him that 'there's another corrected copy safe with my collaborator'. But he also told Savery: 'Alas, alas. *Hassan* is stached. And the famous Embankment scene in *Don Juan* is stached forever.'

And another piece of news was: 'My old Mother-in-law is here, poor old dear, and I'm helpless so my wife has to do everything for me'.[1915]

Flecker was disappointed that Savery, who was now in Berne, did not come to Davos, despite a telegram having been sent with the suggestion. News of the problems at the Hotel Buol would not encourage Savery to visit; although there would be plenty of spare room. Only a handful of guests remained, including the Fleckers, and the hotel was due to close. The Fleckers had to live on credit because, due to the war, cheques could not be cashed. They were starved of news of the war and Flecker longed for an English newspaper. The financial situation eased when Flecker told Savery of managing to get £20 by wire.

By 24 August, he was still awaiting a visit from Savery and urging him to bring cash as the Consul would not be able to cash cheques. On 4 September, he wrote to Savery of his horrible disappointment at Savery's non-arrrival. But English newspapers must have reached him, as he gave his views to Savery about 'the hellish news'.

On 11 September, he gave Savery the address of Maison Baratelli, the flat that they were moving into in a few days' time. It appeared that Savery had sent the Fleckers money. Savery was told that he would need to pay the Fleckers five francs a day to stay with them because 'I have no money of my own in the world'. Despite the emphasis on money matters, Flecker sent Savery a list of late Victorian novelists divided into Class I, Class II and no class.

In his next communication to Savery, written on 17 September, Flecker congratulated him on his promotion and the possibility that he would be promoted again to Vice-Consul in Berne. Some doubt existed that Savery had received the news of the Flecker's change of address. Flecker described the pine-panelled sitting-room of the new flat. He told Savery of a system he had of writing his opinion of books, etc., and putting them in a bag. He thought *Jane Eyre* was 'surely the worst book that ever appeared. Classic! What tosh. I admired *Villette.*'[1916]

When he wrote to Savery on 29 September, he wondered if a lack of a long reply to the 'Great Screed' had resulted in Savery not being prepared to write any more. Despite his unhappiness and a discussion of war issues, he managed to write 'a pome in which the Germans are not called:

> shamble breathing sharks
> bloodsteeped assassins
> spike booted baby tramplers
> sons of Hell and Death.

In another communication with Savery, written on 21 September, in answer to the 'great letter' and telegram, Flecker outlined his experiences in Beirut when he was nearly killed by the mob. The reason for doing this could be a response to Savery's experience in having to burn cyphers after the Declaration of War, in Munich. Savery had thought he was in danger from officials, but Flecker thought that the danger, in Savery's case, came from the mob. Flecker was also able to profit from his experience of danger when his article 'Forgotten Warfare' was published in *The New Statesman* in the 24 October 1914 edition.

On 2 October, Flecker enclosed in a communication to Marsh what he described as 'a War Poem' (this was revised as 'The Burial in England'). He had intended 'to send it to the *Sphere*, the only journal which I know will take it'. He wanted it to appear in what he described as 'some better place – best of all *Times*.' He wanted Marsh to have a word with the Literary Editor of *The Times*. The poem was eventually published as 'The Burial of England' in the *Sphere*, 27 February 1915.

'The Burial in England' begins with the lines:

> These then we honour: these in fragrant earth
> Of their own country in great peace forget
> Death's lion-roar and gust of nostril flame
> Breathing souls across to the Evening Shore.
> Soon over these the flowers of our hill-sides
> Shall wake and wave and nod beneath the bee
> And whisper love to Zephyr year on year,
> Till the red war gleam like a dim red rose
> Lost in the garden of the Sons of Time.
> But ah what thousands no such friendly doom
> Awaits, – whom silent comrades in full night
> Gazing right and left shall bury swiftly
> By the cold flicker of an alien moon. [1917]

This poem contrasts the burial of the dead in England with the quick much less friendly doom that awaited the soldiers killed in France, in the early stages of the war.

The poem's theme is similar to that of Rupert Brooke's 'The Soldier', which is a much shorter poem that begins:

> If I should die, think only this of me:
> That there's some corner of a foreign field
> That is for ever England. There shall be
> In that rich earth a richer dust concealed;
> A dust whom England bore, shaped, made aware,

> Gave, once, her flowers to love, her ways to roam,
> A body of England's, breathing English air,
> Washed by the rivers, blest by suns of home.

Brooke's 'The Soldier' was first called 'The Recruit' and Flecker's first version of 'The Burial in England' was entitled 'The Speech of the Grand Recruiter'.[1918] The inspiration for Brooke's 'The Old Vicarage, Grantchester' was said to be Hilaire Belloc's 'The Four Men', the first verse of which is:

> He does not die that can bequeath
> Some influence to the land he knows,
> Or dares, persistent, interwreath
> Love permanent with the wild hedgerows;
> He does not die, but still remains
> Substantiate with his darling plains. [1919]

But 'The Four Men' can also be seen as an influence on both 'The Soldier' and 'The Burial in England'.

Flecker sent his poem to Marsh on 2 October but it was not until 29 November that Marsh wrote back giving Flecker his opinion of it. Marsh did explain that he had been too busy to 'disturb his private correspondence' but he gave his opinion on 'The Burial in England' as 'too literary, too effective, too ornate, too metrical, too poetical!! to fit in with my feelings ...'[1920] Marsh also added: 'When one is looking on at a great war from the hub, one's point of view gets completely changed – one wants the arts to divorce the Graces, and to walk in only the most naked majesty.'

Had Brooke read 'The Burial in England' (with Marsh's approval) prior to his writing 'The Soldier'? Brooke had ample opportunity to disturb Marsh's private correspondence, which contained 'The Burial in England'. On 27 September Brooke had been seen off from Charing Cross station by Marsh to join the 2nd Naval Brigade in Kent and on 4 October the Brigade marched to Dover in order to cross the Channel. The destination was Antwerp, where they marched through the streets. It was not long before the Brigade was forced to march back again under the pressure of the German attack. (The scenes they encountered were described by Brooke as 'Hell'.) It was not until the troops reached Bruges that they had some respite. By 12 October Brooke was back in Dover. He went straight to the Admiralty, where he saw Marsh and was granted a week's leave. While spending it at Marsh's apartment, he had the opportunity to read 'The Burial in England'.[1921] Brooke's attitude to the war after these experiences was to beat the Germans and, after his leave, he worked on his war sonnets of which 'The Soldier' was one. Brooke also had a change of mood towards those who could not share his view of participating so wholeheartedly in the war. When he was asked to contribute to a fund to aid a friend spend the winter in California to help with a cure for consumption, Brooke replied that it was not the time to be wintering abroad. The money should be spent on the Belgian refugees instead. Brooke told E.J. Dent, who had written to him for the money, that he knew of a girl whose doctor had told her that she would probably die if she did not spent the winter in a sanatorium. She was instead doing work in a Belgian refugee organisation.[1922] From this evidence can be seen Brooke's lack of real sympathy for Flecker's situation in Switzerland. The poets had always seen themselves as rivals. It was inevitable that now Brooke had experienced some of the horrors of war while Flecker lay in a sanatorium writing poems about war, their differences would continue. Flecker had criticised what some would see as Brooke's best poem 'Heaven' and Brooke had criticised Flecker's *Golden Journey to Samarkand*. It was ironical that Brooke's 'The Soldier' was about the burial of an English soldier in a foreign field, which was to be the fate of Brooke. Flecker's poem was about burial in England, which was to be his fate. But whatever differences existed, both Brooke and Flecker would agree with what Hassan told the Caliph:

> 'poetry is a princely diversion but for us it is a deliverance
> from Hell.'[1923]

Poetry apart, Brooke did not share the money problems experienced by Flecker and other poets. De la Mare was one poet whose plight Brooke was aware of through Marsh's offer to help with money.[1924] Marsh made a similar offer to Flecker, so Brooke was not unaware of the health and financial problems that beset his fellow poets. If Brooke had experienced these himself he might have shown more understanding.

Brooke would not have appreciated the rare reference to Switzerland in 'The Burial in England':

> ... as in the sunny Alpine morn
> The jodeler awakes the frosty slopes
> To thunderous replies, – soon fading far,
> Among the vales like songs of dead children.

Flecker enclosed twelve lines of a new version of 'The Burial in England' for Marsh, whom Flecker supposed was 'still working like hell' when he wrote on 6 October. The twelve lines were to be 'pinned onto the MS. because I have just found the old don't make sense, and the metaphors were badly mixed'.[1925] Two days later, he sent 'The Burial in England' to Savery with the remark: 'It's very good according to my wife'.

The death in battle of the poet Charles Peguy (1873–1914) was relayed to Savery: 'Charles Peguy, *'Mystère de la Charité de Jeanne d'Arc.* Know you this astounding mystic work deformed by hideous echolalia? After your heart, Franco. He's just dead in battle.'[1926] Peguy's death was also of concern to Brooke, who wanted the death in battle of an English poet 'lest England be shamed'.[1927]

Flecker complained of stale news being sent to him by Savery and looked forward to having a copy of the *Daily Mirror* and news of 'my pome' ['God Save the King']. He also wanted to see a 'copy of English paper with your question in the Commons'. An answer to a question less important to Savery but most important to Flecker was the question of whether or not Savery would buy his Consular uniform from him:

> If you are a man of vast pride you will insist on spending
> £30 on a brand new vice-consular uniform. If you are a man
> of wisdom you will purchase from James your ancient [?]
> at low figure if not the uniform itself at least the extremely
> expensive yokes [?] like cuffs collar buttons sword hat
> (the only thing that may not fit). The uniform itself could
> probably as we are much of the same build as made to fit
> you lovely. Of course this must wait until communications
> are easier: the thing's in England. Uniform worn perhaps
> 10 times. [1928]

Savery was not the only contact of Flecker's to be displaced by the outbreak of war. Basil Dean got a letter dated 12 October from Flecker when Dean was at an army training camp. Flecker had sent him the second revision of *Hassan* and Dean felt that Flecker 'longed for some message of hope about the possibility of production to encourage him to improve the work still more. I could not give it to him.'[1929] Flecker, in his letter to Dean, understood the situation and wrote: 'I suppose you intend not to think again of *Hassan* till after the War.' But as was usual in Flecker's letters, he could be realistic and unrealistic in his hopes. He also told Dean: 'Alas, if I could only get well enough in a year's time to see it played, I wouldn't mind the delay.' Not only did he see some return to health for himself, but he did not think the war would last longer than a year.

The postponement of the production of *Hassan* until after the war (whenever that might be) would be a sufficient reason for depresssion and despair on the part of the author. But when Flecker described to Savery[1930] that he had experienced a two-day period of depression when he had 'shed tears of sheer desolation for hours' he did not blame the postponement of any *Hassan* production. Instead he told Savery (who received the information on 23 October) that the cause was 'the Froehn wind and lack of circulation... '. In another communication Savery received in the same month,[1931] Flecker complained of never leaving his bed and of the torment of a cough, which lasted sometimes from ten o'clock at night until midnight. At the end of October, Flecker told Savery[1932] that he was prescribed a sleeping draught by a 'damn fool of a doctor'. Flecker had only agreed to take the medicine because he was told: 'it didn't affect brain and give dreams, it didn't affect stomach.'

But as it turned out: 'Perceive in my handwriting the remaining effects. It drove me nearly mad and split my brain in half, dissociating my personality in a beastly way. (..........) As for my turn it made me horrid sick.'

Flecker apologised for writing at length and explained that he was recovering from the drug. He asked Savery to send a male Persian kitten by post. Not surprisingly, subsequent letters received from Savery contained arguments and protests about political matters (mainly concerned with their differing views on the Bulgars). Flecker's instructions to Savery on how to deal with consular matters were not appreciated by Savery. No kitten was sent. Flecker realised that his old friend's unfriendliness was unintentional and anything Flecker had written was to let Savery know how concerned he was about his state of health due to overwork. The next news Savery received, on 1 November, described to him: 'Horrible pleurisy last night; wife up all night with me: nearly died of pain – and then of anti-pain drugs.'[1933]

Also on 1 November he wrote to Jack Squire and thanked him for publishing 'Forgotten Warfare' and acknowledged the receipt of a letter and a copy of *The New Statesman*. He also gave Squire 'this very carefully written article on Italy', which he wanted Squire to publish. If Squire did not want it, Flecker wanted it sent on to the *New Witness*. He also enclosed 'a little poem for you, topical indeed, but of the Season not of the War'. ['November', revised as 'November Eves'.] Flecker wanted to know if Squire had seen Marsh lately. He told him: 'I wrote so sumptuous a war poem that I had the indiscretion (tho' knowing he was frightfully busy) of sending it to him to send to *The Times*, and have not heard since.'[1934] Flecker emphasised that he was very ill and not able to write much and that the Italian article 'had exhausted me horribly'.

The New Statesman supported the Government's aims in the war and was not supporting pacifism. Flecker's war poems stood a better chance of publication by Squire in *The New Statesman* than some other publications. Squire was exempt from war service on account of his poor eyesight; unlike 'Ben' Keeling, who had attained the position of assistant editor with *The New Statesman* at the outbreak of war. Keeling volunteered right away for the army. He refused a commission and when killed in action in 1916, he was a company sergeant-major.

In November, Flecker wrote to Clement Shorter, editor of *The Sphere*:

Maison Baratelli
Davos Platz
Switzerland

Dear Sir,

I send you a poem more or less a war poem, but in any case about the best poem I have ever written.

I am very much afraid that I could not let you have it for 3 guineas – not that I try to sell poems by their merit, but that poem is 50 lines long and has exhausted me so terribly to write in the present desperate state of health that I must get some reward for the very physical fatigue it has caused me. I consider it worth 10 guineas myself but will take any reasonable offer. I have no desire whatever to bluff you who have made me almost the only generous offer I have ever received in my life but my [?] [word missing] is not much above *Review* prices and I've had plenty of poems in the *Review*. I am pretty sure I would get it into the *Times* – but I've just sent them another War Poem.

I enclose a photo as I believe you once asked for one but I don't suppose it's a time to publish photos of Poets (but lean Poets?). Details of my biography (for which I think you also asked but may be perfectly mistaken) will be sent by Messrs. Goschen on application.

May I say I have written several little poems and preferred to send you them eg. to the *New Statesman* where I get a guinea rather than to you who have promised me 3 for my next because they weren't good enough for you? Also that I am preparing you a poem suitable for the three guineas on the [word unclear] turning their eyes on the Calais dunes which seems to me to be a great subject.

Yours faithfully
James Elroy Flecker[1935]

P.S. An illustration by Syme would be superb on a full page.[1936]

Clement Shorter
Editor
The Sphere

Cheques to be sent to JE Flecker account Capital and Counties Bank, Cambridge

post card informing me of amt and copy of paper

The poem referred to in the letter to Shorter as 'more or less a war poem, was 'The Old Warship Ablaze' which *The Sphere* published in its 26 December 1914 edition. The 'several little poems' included 'November' published in the 14 November edition of *The New Statesman* and later revised as 'November Eves'. Flecker had written to his father about this poem: '*New Statesman* Nov. 14th has a quiet little poem about the view from Nursery Window.' [1937]

However much Flecker might want to convince himself and his father that 'November' was 'a quiet little poem', it can now be seen as a more powerful poem than the longer war poems. It is also unique because, alone of his mature work, in 'November' the poet goes back into his earliest childhood. 'November' begins:

November Evenings! Damp and still
They used to cloak Leckhampton hill,
And lie down close on the grey plain,
And dim the dripping window-pane,
And send queer winds like Harlequins
that seized our elms for violins
And struck a note so sharp and low
Even a child could feel the woe. [1938]

'Our elms' were visible from the Dean Close Nursery.[1939] As well as recreating the atmosphere of the Dean Close Nursery in 'November',

Flecker had tried to recreate it in his sick-room at Davos: 'like the nursery used to be got up – with pictures without frames, beautiful 1720 maps (I had picked up in Paris for a penny years ago), photos, pictures out of the old "Studio", etc.' [1940]

'November', however much it would please Flecker's parents, was not just a nostalgic poem like 'From Grenoble' where, in the last line, the poet wants to see again 'the rose-garden of my gracious home'. The line in 'November' 'That seized our elms for violins' is similar to the line from John Davidson's 'A Ballad in Blank Verse': 'A trembling lyre for every wind to sound.' (302). Davidson's poem, in which the poet lets all moods pass through him, is a rejection of the father's church and Christian values.[1941] The 'woe' that Flecker felt, the subsequent 'gloom' of the interior of the nursery and even the use of 'violins', which he played in childhood, are all reflections of childhood misery. The 'choking memories' and the moods that pass to the child from the winds outside are painful.

Flecker wrote to Squire about 'November': 'I also send a little poem for you, topical indeed, but of the Season not of the War. I have exhausted myself writing heroic great war poems and intend to write several like this. I will send you some more if you like them.'[1942]

The New Statesman did not see the poem as 'not of the War'. Directly above Flecker's 'November' which ended with the lines: 'Is it the mist or the dead leaves,/Or the dead men – November eves?' was the conclusion of an article by Robert Lynd in which he stated:

> In a world of dead leaves – dead leaves that since Homer have symbolised the succession of countless families of men – one walks with a peculiar sense of tragedy: one cannot forget dead bodies that are being heaped like the leaves into little heaps and like them burned in a fire.
>
> And, if one turns to literature at all for understanding, it is, perhaps, to Meredith rather than to Dickens that one turns, and that only for one poem:

> A wind sways the pines
> And below
> Not a breath of wild air;
> Still as the mosses that glow
> On the flooring and over the lines
> Of the roots here and there.
> The pine-tree drops its dead; [1943]

They are quiet, as under the sea.
Overhead, overhead
Rushes life in a race,
As the clouds the clouds chase;
And we go,
And we drop like fruits of the tree,
Even we,
Even so.[1944]

It seems that in placing 'November' underneath the piece by Robert Lynd, it was seen at the time it was received as a poem about the war, even if that was not Flecker's intention.

While *The New Statesman* saw 'November' as indeed having some relevance to the war and the poet himself saw it as only one of 'several little poems', in the post-war years 'November Eves' and 'Stillness' would be seen as more important than the 'great war poems' that had exhausted him:

'.... Flecker was turning to new pastures: he was beginning, at an age when many poets are ceasing to do so, to be interested in himself, and by that time he had forged a weapon which, 'Toledo-wrought neither to break or bend' was ready to raise him into the front rank of English poets.'[1945]

The final couplet of 'November' about the 'dead leaves' and 'dead men' can be seen as:

> 'gathers the whole together, and rounds it off with a nervous vigour that it as appropriate as it is un-expected.'[1946]

Another of the 'little poems' was 'Narcissus', published in *The New Statesman* in the 15 January 1915 edition. This is another version of the poem first published in *The Bridge of Fire*. This was the poem that Wolfe remembered Flecker reciting to him in Flecker's cluttered Oxford rooms. One line common to both versions is: 'Than any watery moon!'

Wolfe had asked: 'Why watery?'

'Because,' he said 'it was.'

'How do you mean it was?'

'Hylas',' he returned impatiently. 'It's all a water-colour. Don't you understand that you take your brush, hardly dip it in the water, feather a paint of two, and then with the lightest possible fingers mix the tones.'[1947]

The second version could not have any connections with watercolours and it is a farewell to a homosexual love, which could be Beazley.[1948] Flecker writes of: 'O broken Lilies, strewn!'

This is reminiscent of 'The Ballad of Camden Town':

> And waits to catch the fallen rose
> And clasp the broken lily.'

Flecker continues in 'Narcissus': 'Golden lily – oh, golden hair!'[1949]

This version of 'Narcissus' seems to have changed into a farewell to Beazley – almost the last hidden Beazley factor in a Flecker poem. The reason for a farewell at this time was not only that Flecker's own death would separate him from Beazley, but that Beazley himself was in danger of death, due to his war service in the Navy. Lines in 'Narcissus' refer to what could be naval battles:

> Afloat with night, still trembling
> With captured mysteries:
> But sulphured wracks, assembling,
> Redarkened the bright skies.[1950]

If news had already reached Flecker via letters from Cheesman or from Beazley himself, of Beazley's falling in love, then these lines could reflect Flecker's reaction:

> Ah, thou at least are lying
> Safe at the white nymph's feet,
> Listless, while I, slow-dying,
> Twist my gaunt limbs for heat! [1951]

The lilies added to the first verse of 'Narcissus' could mean that the poem was intended also as a farewell to Ronald Firbank.

Flecker's writing of these several small poems would be less exhausting than the long poems written in an effort to extract more money from editors because of the poems' length and topicality. The effort to get more money was temporarily lessened by Flecker's receiving a gratuity of £125 from the Foreign Office. He wrote to his father with news of the gratuity: 'I am sure I don't deserve it as a Consul, tho' what England owes me as a Poet is a different story. Tell me your wishes about it ....'.[1952]

He realised that this news would cheer his father who was still supporting him financially. His father had sent him an extra cheque for his birthday on 5 November. Flecker thanked him: 'If that's a birthday present, it's a most handsome one.'[1953] He aimed to buy 'a little toy type-writer', with the money and also to get ' doz. vols. of yellow French books (poetry) bound which are falling to pieces.'

Exhaustion was not the only problem. The depression he also felt was transmitted in letters to his parents about the ethical problems of the war. The old arguments about Christianity came back again. He wrote at the end of September in part of a long letter to his mother:

> About Christianity, do read a little Chesterton ('Orthodoxy', for instance) and the life of S. Francis or something – to see what it can mean to other people – and to me. For me that's what it means. Really there are higher forms of it than your Welsh revivalist. I am not a good Christian, and hours of bed make me impatient. I am worried with a sore tooth.[1954]

Later, he wrote to his father, telling him: 'Tell Mother she should be glad I had spirit enough to reply to her little jabs. Usually, I don't care what anybody does, thinks, says, or is: I'm too tired ...'.[1955]

But as was usual with Flecker's stances (which he took against views put up against him from outside) he could be prepared to soften. He later wrote to his mother: 'How touched I am by the constant way you write to me. It's you who really love me, dear Mother – and I am afraid I wasn't cheerful at Montana – but you were so nervous...'[1956]

And also: 'My dear old mother the more I think of things the more I see that you only care. Of all my friends only Frank has stuck close ... Father's half sheet of paper made me cry bitterly. I do want a bit of affection and he is just too callous. I've no doubt he'll warm up when he hears I've some money.'[1957]

Dr. Flecker, too, was capable of climbing down and softening his approach and so was his son when he wrote thanking him for a telegram that cheered him immensely. Flecker sent his father *The New Statesman* article on the war by Bernard Shaw for his father's opinion and suggested that the Dean Close boys write an essay on it.[1958] Flecker's enthusiasm for this article was also relayed to Squire: 'Let me know by return if you like the idea of a jolly bang at the Cambridge Local examination (timed for sitting Dec. 10-20) with a whack in it at B. Shaw (what a grand article of his on the War, I've had the luck to hook with my copy of the paper)...'[1959]

He told Squire that his father would, if he acted on his suggestion, get fifty copies of *The New Statesman* on loan. Flecker thanked Squire in that same letter for speaking to Chesterton about his Italian article. This article, which he titled 'The Italian Attitude', remained unpublished.[1960]

It was a pity that 'The Italian Attitude' was not published because Flecker carefully forecast that Italy was a danger with designs on Greek territory. One of the chief dangers was within Italy, Flecker estimated, and this was the influences of the Futurists.

The Italian Futurists in 1909 issued the Futurist Manifesto in which 'there must be no past, no museums etc'. Flecker must have realised that he had over-emphasised the Futurists in this type of essay. The Futurists, he thought, had developed 'Nietzschean doctrine' and he suggested to Squire: 'Couldn't I do up the purely Futurist bit for you as a literary article and leave out the politics (except as illustration). There's good literary stuff in that part.'[1961]

Chesterton's opinion of 'The Italian Attitude' is not known but the fact that Flecker suggested Squire try 'anywhere you think of' to get 'The Italian Article' published, indicated that Chesterton (and Squire also) had not held out any hopes or given practical suggestions of where it might be published. Flecker's own suggestion to Squire that he might try the *New Age* (despite problems in the past with that publication) and also the *Westminster Gazette* (a publication that had not been wholly appreciative of *The Golden Journey*) also showed a lack of confidence on the author's part that 'The Italian Attitude' would get immediate acceptance.

Undeterred by this possible setback for 'The Italian Attitude', Flecker told Squire: 'Have sent purely literary and amusing article (Philanthropists) to *New Witness*. Write to-day to tell them to hand it to you if they're full. I sent it to them because you had Italy; it's just the thing for you.'

Flecker's game of pass-the-parcel, which he had played before with various publications, appeared not to pay off. 'Philanthropists' was not accepted for publication in his lifetime. It was published in *Collected Prose*.

'Philanthropists' was certainly amusing: its opening paragraph set the tone:

> My heart goes black with fury and horror when I read their Wills. The only consolidation one has is that there is another of them dead. Ten thousand pounds to the Wigan Home for Cats, five thousand to the Society for the Suppression of Sunday Amusements, a thousand for the Syrian Lunatic Asylum on Mount Lebanon, and fifty pounds a year (altered by a pencil-stroke to twenty-five) for their old and faithful clerk, Mr. Jinks.

Despite the tongue-in-cheek content of 'Philanthropists' and the author's own self-interest, the article was topical and reflected the view expressed by Shaw in his supplement to *The New Statesman*. Flecker wanted £10,000 spent on the publication of 'jolly or sound poetry:' and also 'a travelling fund to take promising young authors on a holiday to Corfu'. He wanted money to preserve the countryside from pollution, modern architecture and vandalism: a little closer to home was the hope that the philanthropists would have helped someone not unlike Flecker: 'He might have helped some poor devil of a struggling author to publish his works, or backed some play a little too good for the British stage.'

Flecker stated, 'War is a great eye-opener all round.' He also stated: 'Here again the War is making us think. It is obviously right for the women to knit socks. It's obviously right for Lord Roberts to ask me to give my saddle if I have one – because I can have the real pleasure of thinking of the gallant soldier who gets it, blessing its excellence after a hard ride in France.'

Flecker had sent his own saddle, which he realised he would never need again, in respect to Lord Roberts' appeal.[1962] Flecker emphasised that he 'was not talking socialism'. He made the statement that illustrated his grasp of the future, which must have come to him as he realised the expenditure needed to keep him alive in the Swiss sanatorium: 'But the vast burden of supporting our indispensable London hospitals should be, if not undertaken, at least organized and controlled by the State.'

Despite telling Squire that the writing of 'The Italian Attitude' had exhausted him 'horribly', Flecker continued with his correspondence. On 18 November, he apologised to Marsh for bothering him with poetry. Marsh must have also been exhausted, but for different reasons; due to the war he was working from 8 a.m. to 2 a.m. Flecker considered himself to be free 'to hawk the poem [new version of 'The Burial in England'] from 1 December.' But Flecker held out hopes that Marsh would not fail him:

> 'If you have been quixotic enough to start any negotia-
> tions a postcard or (perhaps less trouble for you) a wire
> (cut this out for the slave) Flecker Baratelli Davos Platz
> Stop.'[1963]

Flecker told Marsh not to bother to answer.
Flecker also resumed correspondence with Clement Shorter:

To Clement Shorter post-marked 25-XI-14

Davos Platz Maison Baratelli
Davos Platz
24th November, 1914

Dear Sir,

Am perfectly satisfied for your offer and thank you heartily for making the arrangements.

I return proofs with light corrections as they may arrive in time (2 important slips).

I beg a copy of the paper be sent here.

As writing tires me, may I mention that I am probably sending you in a week's time a 80 line blank verse poem called 'The Burial in England', more directly patriotic and I think better in a good as this which I also offer you if I send it for £5 only begging you to arrange the American rights if possible for that also.

I will send you the ms. without comment please keep this pc for reference.

Please send copy of *Sphere* to above address but cheques to Cambridge (see ms.)

Yours faithfully,
JEF[1964]

Flecker wrote again to Shorter the next day. This letter although undated, can be assumed to have been written on 25 November due to the reference in the letter to the writing of the poem ['The True Paradise'] which he gave the date 25 November, and signed 'James Elroy Flecker. Between 5.45 and 6.15 am.' [1965]

Dear Sir,

I send you not my war poem yet but my second 3 guineas poem. A quaint and jolly effort which suddenly came into my head at 5.45 am this morning was finished at 6.45 and apart from the [? word unclear] of 6 lines was hardly altered since. I hope you'll like it. It reads like Donne or somebody. I think a spirit work it for me.

Yours sincerely,
James Elroy Flecker [1966]
Await publication of Battleship and my copy of *Sphere* with expectation.

Clement Shorter
Editor Sphere

The reference in this letter to 'not my war poem yet' was to his poem 'The Burial in England'. His 'second 3 guineas poem' was 'The True Paradise' and 'Battleship' was a reference to 'The Old Warship Ablaze', which *The Sphere* published in its 26 December edition.

The description of how he came to write 'The True Paradise' is borne out by Hellé:

> Then on another November night he woke up before daybreak and sat up writing with a blue drawing pencil on a sheet of drawing paper (at the time I had to prevent him from writing more than about an hour a day for it exhausted him, so he had neither pen nor paper near him but some coloured pencils with which he amused himself, drawing imaginary landscapes. I did not know the end was so near or I should have let him do as he liked and not have vexed him with an interdiction that caused much painful discussion and was cruelly felt by him). When I went near he gave me to read the 'True Paradise', and then asked me to write it down clearly there and then.[1967]

Flecker had recorded in the past his ability to write poems in a short space of time. 'Areiya' was one poem in which the poet said that he '... sat and wrote in minutes soft and few/ This worst and best of songs, one who loves it, and you.' This capacity to write work very quickly and be satisfied with the result could be due to the effect on his mind of the pain-killing drugs that had to be administered to ease the symptoms of consumption. But the vision of Heaven in 'The True Paradise' owed much to what Hellé stated that she did not know: 'that the end was so near'. And also the swiftness of the writing could be a result of the breaking of the dam that had been put in place by Hellé's 'interdiction', so that the ideas were already well formed before they reached the page.

On the same day, 25 November, as he had written 'The True Paradise', he dictated to Hellé a letter for his parents which contained important news: 'It will please you to know that I intend to take communion this Christmas. Please write nothing but just mention your pleasure in your next letter.'[1968,1969]

Sherwood explains that a fortnight earlier Flecker had written to his mother 'It was nice of you to stop those little sermons in your letters, to please me'. So the plea to 'write nothing' was to his mother asking her not to resume her 'sermons' with their perhaps 'I told you so' message.

He told his parents in the letter that he had not been 'suddenly converted or anything like that. It is partly that B., though a very nice man, was rather feeble, and this extremely nice old saint from China has turned up'.

The 'nice old saint' was a bearded missionary and the new chaplain to replace 'B'.

How much the old missionary had influenced Flecker's decision to take communion is not entirely clear because he had written to his parents about 'a charming talk on China' that had taken place between himself and the missionary. Flecker had been scathing in the past about missionaries, but the China missionary's presence could have been a reminder of Oxford days and visits to the Christian Union with Stanley McKelvie, who was now a missionary. Flecker also had memories of Arthur Waley and their translating Chinese Poetry. The China missionary would not be unaware that his parishioner was a poet isolated from his home by his illness and the war. The writing of 'The True Paradise' and Flecker's decision to take communion were not unconnected, but whether the missionary or Flecker's parents knew that 'the end was so near' and that Flecker needed the comforting presence of the missionary as well as the need to write about it, is uncertain. But Flecker did tell his parents:'... partly that I feel the attraction of the English Church Service and Bible, and the Englishness of it all too keenly to turn to foreign creeds however much attractive.'[1970]

The war as inspiration was proving to be attractive, as the two other poems mentioned in the letter to Clement Shorter indicated. 'The Burial in England' and 'The Old Warship Ablaze' were also on his mind on 25 November 1914. In a postcard to Monro[1971] he shows how he considered them in relation to patriotism:

Dear Monro

Have you forgotten me? Here I am stuck to bed and haven't had my *Poetry and Drama.* War poem of mine 'The Battleship' has appeared in *Sphere* another more directly patriotic yet better (80 lines) will appear in December probably in same paper. I much want these poems published in broadsheet soon after their appearing in the magazine. Goschens has gone to war and shut up. If you care to undertake the job will be delighted and hereby give you full authority to negotiate with *Sphere* etc., Postage to Switzerland is perfectly safe but takes 7 days.

Yours sincerely,
J.E. Flecker
(dictated) [by Hellé]

The poem referred to as 'more directly patriotic' was 'The Burial in England' which was not published in *The Sphere* until 27 February 1915.

In May 1905, Flecker had written his poem 'On Turner's Polyphemus' and a version of this poem is in *The Book of Kara James* p.68. 'On Turner's Polyphemus' was published in *The Bridge of Fire* but not republished in *Thirty-Six Poems* or *Forty-Two Poems.* But it is in Flecker's *Collected Poems.* Turner's painting *The Fighting Temeraire* and Ruskin's account of the painting influenced the writing of 'The Old Warship Ablaze'.[1972] It begins with the lines:

Founder, old battleship; thy fight is done!
Yonder ablaze like thee now sinks the sun,
Shooting the last grand broadside of his beams
Over thy blackened plates and writhing seams.[1973]

Some lines in the poem about the sinking of the old battleship can be related to Flecker's watching the battles in Beirut harbour during the Italo-Turkish War in the autumn of 1911. These battles were not as glorious as 'thy fight' in his poem. But the Lebanon is brought into 'The Old Warship Ablaze' when he wrote:

But eastward and still east the World is thrown
Like a mad hunter seeking dawns unknown
Who plunges deep in sparkless woods of gloom.
Lebanon long hath turned into night's womb
And through her stèlled casements pass new dreams:[1974]

The precise date of Flecker writing 'The Old Warship Ablaze' is not known in the same way as the writing of 'The True Paradise'. But when writing to Savery on 21 September 1914, Flecker relived for him, his feelings during the Italo-Turkish War. This was in response to Savery's recounting his experiences of getting out of Germany and across the Swiss frontier at the outbreak of the war. 'The Old Warship Ablaze' is not only a reconstruction of Flecker's experiences of war in the Lebanon brought back into his mind by the war in Europe. The poem is made up of several layers, one of which is the ship's past life. In 'The Old Warship Ablaze' Flecker recollects its past as he had done in 'The Old Ships'. Flecker had attended a dance on a British warship early in 1913, when separated from Hellé when she had remained in Paris.[1975]

Flecker, in 'The Old Warship Ablaze' wrote:

> 'Or moonlight scattered like a shower of leaves
> Dost thou recall? – Or how on this same deck,
> Whose flaming planks blood-boultered tilt to wreck,
> The dance went round to music, and how shone
> For English grey, black eyes of Lebanon? [1976]

The opening lines of this part of 'The Old Warship Ablaze' recall the lines of 'The Old Ships'

> It was so old a ship – who knows, who knows?
> – And yet so beautiful, I watched in vain
> To see the mast burst open with a rose,
> And the whole deck put on its leaves again.' [1977]

The last two lines suggest that the grey eyes of Flecker met a Lebanese male or female who momentarily intrigued him.

But he also wrote in 'The Old Warship Ablaze' the lines:

> .... 'Alone O ship, O flower
> O flame, thou sailest for a moth-weak hour!

The 'moth-weak hour!' symbolises the brief battle of the Turkish gunboats and the poet's life when:

> ... Thou nevermore
> Shalt glide to channel port or Syrian town;

But in 'The Old Warship Ablaze', as in the writing of his prose work 'Forgotten Warfare', the poet appreciated the beauty of the surroundings even when in mortal danger. He wrote:

In that curv'd bay where once the film of morn
Brake azure to thy bugles, skilled to bring
The Afric breeze, who, prompt on honied wing
Silvered the waves and then the olive trees,
And shook like sceptres those stiff companies
The columned palms, – ....

Now his own life was sinking, he knew the tragedy of a war that, as he had already written, in the last line of the first verse of 'The Old Warship Ablaze':

Have left so many dead – won such proud names.

The war not only brought the inspiration for grand poems but also presented communication difficulties for Flecker. On 29 November, he sent a postcard to Dean asking him to send him the manuscript of *Hassan*. Dean was reassured that he could send the manuscript safely through the post, despite the war. 'I haven't lost a parcel, sample, letter or newspaper since the outbreak of war and that with a biggish correspondence.' He assured Dean (rather optimistically) that he had another corrected copy of *Hassan*, which was at Munich but 'quite safe'. The war will 'be over in six months – mark me.' He enquired whether or not Dean would come out to Davos for winter sport.[1978]

Books sent by Marsh early in December got through, despite the war, 'with a letter as unreserved in its encouragement as his note to [DH] Lawrence of about three months before. Flecker's reply of the 12 marked the end of a correspondence that had lasted for two years. Flecker, now gravely ill, was obviously much moved. 'The last sentence of your letter is the sort of thing a fellow doesn't forget – or write about on a postcard. Oh why didn't poor Middleton have such luck as mine?'[1979]

The reference to Flecker being 'now gravely ill' was not exaggeration on Marsh's part, although exactly what news of Flecker's health was given to him was not revealed in the second last published letter from Flecker to Marsh.[1980] But Savery was left in no doubt of his old friend's state of mind: 'Nearly sent for the priest t'other day. Would prefer you. Very miserable and bad tempered and all hate me. Refuge in Bible and Prayer Book.'[1981] Savery received this letter on 30 November.

On 4 December, the old missionary from China came and read a shortened form of Evening Prayer over Flecker, at his request. Also on 4 December he wrote to Cheesman who was in training with the Hampshires in Ireland.

Maison Baratelli
My Dear Leonard.

Very glad to hear from you – how splendid. I'm not allowed to write long letters. But take my old baccy pouch – since I never shall smoke again and let me think of your pulling him out in Ireland and in France – he is a good old friend.

Let me know about all old Oxford friends; and who you have with you and give my love to anyone I know. Do write again. I feel rottenly sentimental and long to be with you.

I'm darn tired of life and what's the use of Fame and money that my writing can bring me now.[1982]

He enclosed with this letter some poems, including 'The True Paradise' and 'The Burial in England', 'with stage directions inserted to show how it could be recited at an actual graveside or even a recruiting meeting with the speaker 'pointing towards the British flag proudly waving.'

Cheesman, in his reply,[1983] told Flecker 'I'm sure no recruiter has ever waved a flag, and my troops when marching deliberately bar any song which refers to the matter in hand.'

Flecker had no need to think in terms of sending anything to Savery at this time. Savery arrived on a week's visit next day, travelling from Berne. Hellé did not refer to Savery's visit in her reminiscences and the visit gets only a brief mention in the LIFE: 'During December, Mr. Savery managed another visit to him. They went through his last poems together, and Flecker confided certain literary arrangements to him.'[1984]

Flecker's parents had to learn from Hellé's letters about the joy, and later exhaustion, brought on by Savery's visit. A more detailed account of the week spent when his old friend 'was visibly dying' was given by Savery in the introduction to the first edition of Flecker's *Collected Poems*.

Not only did Savery recall that, during his visit, he could see that Flecker's death was not far away, but 'at time growing weakness numbed his faculties'. But Flecker was sufficiently determined to want to complete his poem 'The Burial in England', and to put his affairs into the care of a competent literary agent. He dictated letters to Savery; a task usually performed by Hellé. One evening Flecker, Hellé and Savery went through 'The Burial in England' line by line. Flecker had hoped for publication of this poem in December, but dissatisfaction and the opportunity to revise the poem in detail with Savery must have delayed this publication plan. The longer version was never finished. One of the alterations to 'The Burial in England' was that the line 'Toledo-wrought neither to break nor bend' replaced the original line of 'Damascus-wrought for rich men's sons of old.'

The version published in *The Sphere* contains lines not in the version published in *Collected Poems*. The manuscript[1985] has amendments made in Savery's hand. But an amendment of a different sort was needed to the notion that Flecker had returned to his religious roots, if heed is paid to the views of Savery, which he gave to Hellé in 1925.[1986]

Savery had contributed to the first edition of the *Collected Poems* in 1916 and his view (as has been seen) was that Flecker's faculties were numbed at this time. In 1925, Savery wrote: 'As long as his faculties remains unimpaired, Roy had no use for religion.'

The implication in this sentence seems to be that it was Flecker's 'numbed faculties' that had made him turn back to what Savery described (in 1925) 'the ideal of revealed religion'. But Savery was not merely expressing his own opinion, because at Davos, when Savery made his December visit, Flecker asked him to see a Catholic priest on his behalf and it was Savery who told the Catholic Priest that he 'did not think Roy had really experienced conversion in any satisfactory sense'.[1987]

Savery, who stated (in 1925) that he 'would have done anything to mitigate the sufferings of his deathbed', may still have recollected Flecker's attacks on the Catholic Church and its breakaway from the Eastern Church. The Catholic Church did not allow 'married clergy, English Church service, English Bible, (don't you miss 'em?) .....'[1988]

The early days of December were not all filled with literary and religious matters. Christmas presents had to be selected and Flecker sent his sister Joyce a brooch, which also was a token of appreciation for the books she had sent and she was told: 'Opals are unlucky unless you are born in March. Then they are lucky. In any case, there's no fear between brother and sister. This is true magic.'[1989]

Other Flecker family members were also under consideration for Christmas gifts when Flecker instructed his family to visit the Japanese shop 'just past Tottenham Circus on the right' and they were to get 'anything jolly from a carving to a toy, from a book of drawings to a colour print.'[1990]

His brother, Oswald, (invalided out of the army) was to have for Christmas his purple-bound *Salammbô*. This was on condition that his father permitted him to do so. Flecker described the book as 'a great, famous and beautiful classical French novel about Carthage of old – written of course for men – but not a patch as shocking as the Latin and Greek fellows he reads for his Schol.' [1991,1992] Oswald and Joyce both helped out at Dean Close, as teachers, during the war. Oswald taught classics; Joyce, science.

To a young cousin, Hubert, who had also enlisted and whom he had not seen for about nine years, he sent a trench lantern with a letter telling him how to use it. 'You hang it on your buttonhole to light your trench.' Flecker wished he was with his cousin and told him that he was thought 'by good critics to be about the greatest poet in England, and I'm famous enough for anything.' He boasted of a 'war poem of mine', which would be in the *Times* or *Sphere*, which he predicted would 'make England jump'.

This letter was found in the pocket of the cousin when he was later killed in the war.

Flecker included a gift for 'our good old Agnes,' the maid at school who was said to have had to clean up after him. In the letter to Hubert he enclosed: 'The box is for Gladys – who is for me now a pretty shadow I but half-remember – how I adored her when I was a boy.'

His old friend Mr. Cooper did not appear to have been sent a present, but in a last letter Flecker let him know that he was envious of him: 'Remember, man, here lies one who would give his right hand to be able to do your work, and to have a Virgil or a French class before him – to schoolmaster on £100 a year and food... Go to France for the Xmas holidays...'.

Flecker now seemed to have lowered his sights on the amount he would have been prepared to live on if a job had been available to him as a schoolmaster in England prior to his having to come back to Beirut. His statement made to Savery, in July 1912, that he would not live on less than £350 a year could have been one he now regretted. Now his literary works were beginning to pay, he could have thought that, with a schoolmaster's job and time to do literary work, he might, after all, have been able to survive financially in England. But that left out of the dream the fact that he would also be struggling against consumption, which the climate in England would not have helped him overcome.

Flecker's health had rallied at this point, which may have made him over-optimistic, because of a new remedy sent to him from Paris by his brother-in-law. This new remedy, [1993] although details are not given about what it contained, was said 'had an astonishing effect on his health, and, naturally, on his spirits.' [1994,1995]

He wrote to his father with the news: 'God bless you, dear Father. Your disappointing son is getting rapidly better, and once he is well enough to write a reasonable amount, which, pray God, will be in the spring, will probably support myself six months every year from literature alone – if not more.'

Then his father was given the same sort of news about Flecker's standing in the literary world: 'Do you realise your son is thought by Gosse, Yeats, Gilbert Murray, and also, thank God, by some editors, to be far the greatest poet of his day, barring Yeats? Is it not worth a year's illness to be great? I think so.'[1996]

Flecker sent his father a cheque for his birthday on 10 December (a fact omitted from the LIFE, but the fact of Flecker having received a cheque from his father for his birthday a month before was not). This cheque to his father indicated that not only was praise forthcoming for Flecker's work but hard cash was already in his pocket. His article 'Paul Fort, The Prince of Poets', which (it is to be supposed, thanks to the efforts of Mavrogordato whose help in getting it published had been asked for in a letter of a few months previous) paid the author £20 and was to be published in *The Nineteenth Century and After* in the January 1915 edition. This £20 was £2 more than the sum received from the publication in the United States for *The King of Alsander*. Despite the money and fame, Flecker could not resist telling his father: 'I know you still dream of a successful son in the FO.'

(This was omitted from the letter when it was published in the LIFE. Also omitted was 'rotten' before 'your son is thought by Gosse,' etc. and 'other fools' after 'Gilbert Murray'[1997]).

The money also was useful in purchasing a small glass elephant, which he sent to his mother with the parcel of family Christmas presents and a message: 'A real elephant would not weigh my love.'[1998]

This note was not mentioned in the LIFE, but reference is made to 'a tiny wee carved elephant fit for your glass cupboard'. This elephant was given to him by his doctor, who came to tea around the time of Flecker's birthday. It is explained in a note that Flecker had started collecting this sort of carved elephant while at Cambridge and he sent many of them for his mother's cupboard in the Dean Close drawing-room. Flecker also sent his mother, for her birthday on 3 January, his own Tauchnitz New Testament (Authorised Version).

On December 24 Flecker dictated the following letter to Hellé to send to Monro.[1999]

Dictated Maison Baratelli, Davos-Platz
December 24

My dear Monro,

Nothing will give me greater pleasure than you should take over all my poetical work and publish the following volumes in succession.

1/ Broadsheet containing

a/ New version of God Save the King (this I have sent to the *Sphere* to be published; it is quite rewritten and a verse longer. I told Clement Shorter you had given me full copyright a liberty I hope I was justified in taking – By the way if MacMillans is making money out of that patriotic Anthology there is no reason why he should not give a guinea or two for the use of my poem –)

b/ The Old Battleship which I suppose will be published in the *Sphere* by the time this reaches you.

c/ My magnificent war poem in blank verse a hundred and sixty miles long described by a friend as much the best thing written since the War began, called at present The Burial in England but which I shall prefer to call Heroism: a Funeral Oration at a British Grave. This poem is in possession of the Authors' Alliance to whom I want to entrust all my work for the future especially as far as publications in magazines and American rights go.

I would be writing to them instead of to you about this matter were it not for the fact that 1) I have not received yet an answer from them as to whether they will take me up. 2) I do not happen to have sent them any of my poetry, except the above mentioned war poem which must be in a magazine before being broadsided for obvious pecuniary reasons. Now if these people are going to take me up I don't offend them and I rely on your tact to go round and talk the matter over with them [?] amiably [word unclear] and read the great war poem.

Next by the time the broadsheet is out and I don't see why it shouldn't sell a million like the work of a young admirer of mine from Nottingham whose name I forget, I shall have sent you 'The Rose Tree in the Garden of Time'[2000] a volume about the length of Samarkand containing all my work up to date. But if I send you this my dear Monro I shall be constrained by severe necessity to ask you for as large an advance on royalty as you can manage. For Samarcand I got 10£. It has sold over 1100 copies so Goschens must have made about 70£ over it. Please put my increased fame against the war risk and discount with the probable success of the war poem broadsheet. There is also a lot to be done with my *Forty Two Poems* which are my own copyright and now rotting at Dents' and with an Edition de luxe containing my Eastern poems only. But enough for the present as I am just recovering from a severe attack of nervous prostration and only want to add that I liked your poems so much that I cut out several of them out of the *Westminster* and stuck them in my book of Victorian verse. I am glad to have your jolly volume.

Ever yours

James Elroy Flecker

I haven't written to the Authors' Alliance: show them this.

'The Burial in England' was published in 1915 in dark blue wrappers and printed by Clement Shorter, acknowledging that the poem was first published in *The Sphere* of 27 February 1915. 'That patriotic anthology' referred to was *War Poems*, edited by H.B. Elliott, with a Foreward by Baroness Orczy (1865–1947), author of *The Scarlet Pimpernel.* Flecker's 'God Save The King' was published with a note saying that the representatives of the late Mr. James Elroy Flecker granted permission to reprint 'God Save the King' '(one of the last compositions from the pen of this gifted author)'. Jarrold & Sons published the anthology in 1915 and it was published reprinted in April 1915.

The Edition deluxe 'containing my Eastern Poems only' was published in 1922. It was a large book containing fourteen poems. *Eastern Poems* was also the title of the volume. It was illustrated with lithographs by Charles Freegrove Winzer, fourteen full page plates. Five hundred copies, fifty copies in old Japanese vellum. Printed by Maurice Darantiers in Dijon for the Poetry Bookshop.

The poems published were:

'Golden Journey to Samarkand Prologue. Epilogue'
'Destroyer of Ships, Men, Cities'
'Gates of Damascus'
'Santorin'
'Yasmin'
'The Hamman Name'
'War Song of the Saracens'

'The Princess'
'Pillage'
'The Queen's Song'
'The Ballad of Iskander'
'The Lover of Jalalu'ddin'
'The Old Ships'
'Saadabad'

After writing this letter, Flecker sent for the barber and asked for the short Van Dyke beard, which he had sported since the days in Montana, to be shaved off. Hellé could hardly bear to realise how much this changed his looks, revealing to her how in a year he had grown so emaciated.

On Christmas Day the chaplain was too ill to bring Flecker Communion. Christmas presents were opened and he enjoyed the plum pudding from Dean Close.

On 29 December he received the second volume of *Sinister Street* and he read it. Hellé felt cautiously optimistic about her husband's progress but on New Year's Day, 1915, at three o'clock in the afternoon, he had yet another relapse. He coughed for several hours to the point of utter exhaustion. He was so weak that the doctor came on Sunday 3 January, and sounded his patient's heart. Hellé was told that her husband's end would come in a matter of hours. This news shocked Hellé , but she knew she had to send for the clergyman. Rev. Watt arrived to give Flecker Communion. The tall clergyman, himself near death, said Flecker's prayers for him and left. Hellé told her husband that they would go the Italian lakes shortly. But he knew that she was only trying to cheer him up as she had done so often in the past, with success. He told the nurse to leave and after loving words to Hellé he rested for a time. After a burst of delirium and singing, he murmured 'Lord, have pity on my soul'.

At 3.20 in the afternoon he died peacefully. Afterwards the snow fell heavily.

Last Love

(From Novalis – adaptation of his last words)

Now for a last glad look upon life: my journey is ending:
Now this door that is Death quietly shuts me behind.
Thankful I hear Love's call – the faithful call of a comrade:
Then all joyful am I, ready to give her my heart.
All through life it is Love hath been my counsellor only:
Hers be the praise alway if I have followed aright.
For as a mother awakes with kisses her slumbering baby,
As she first has a care – as she alone understands –
So has Love been mine, has watched and tended and kissed me:
Near me when I was a child: near me till I was a man.
Thus, mid sorrow or doubt, I have clung to her, learning her lesson:
Now she has made me free – free to rejoice evermore.

1904?
James Elroy Flecker
C.P.

NOTES

CHAPTER ONE

[1] In adulthood, he exchanged 'Herman' for James.

[2] Charles Williams, *Flecker of Dean Close*, the Canterbury Press, 1946, p.38.

[3] LIFE, p.14

[4] LIFE, p.15

[5] Williams, p.37

[6] Williams, p.37

[7] Harry Verrier Holman Elwin: *The Tribal World of Verrier Elwin. An Autobiography* OUP 1964, p.11

[8] Williams, p.15

[9] Williams, p.11

[10] LIFE, p.81

[11] Williams, p.18

[12] Donald Thomas, *Lewis Carroll, A Portrait with Background*, John Murray, 1996, p.87

[13] Williams, p.18

[14] Williams, p.18

[15] Williams, p.20

[16] '*British Opium Policy, and its results to India and China*', by F.S. Turner, B.A., formerly of the London Missionary Society. Sampson Low, London, 1876

[17] p.174/5

[18] Ibid p.180

[19] Williams, p.20

[20] Williams, p.23

[21] Williams, p.17

[22] Rev R.F. McNeile, *A History of Dean Close School*, Wilding, 1966, p.14

[23] Katherine, born 1838. Frederick, born 1840. Theo, born 1844. Alice, born 1845. Ettie (Het), born 1850, Olive, born 1855. William, born 1857

[24] NGJ, p.1

[25] Williams, p.20

[26] Battels Ledger, W.W. Flecker. October 1879 to June 1880, Durham University Library

[27] Williams, p.22

[28] Williams, p.19

[29] [Photo]: Findlay papers, University of Witwatersrand. Olive Schreiner Letters Vol.1 1871–1899 OUP 1988

[30] Williams, p.20

[31] Claire Draznin. 'My Other Self', p.506

[32] S.C. Cronwright-Schreiner. *The Life of Olive Schreiner*. Fisher-Unwin, 1924, p.142

[33] Ibid. p.142. Also *Mrs. John Brown* (1847–1935) edited by Angela James and Nina Hills. John Murray 1937 Part III xxiii 'Recollections of Olive Schreiner' by Mary Brown

[34] Draznin, p.46

[35] Draznin, p.44

[36] Williams, p.29

[37] Cronwright-Schreiner, p.151

[38] Williams, p.35

[39] *My Other Self. The Letters of Olive Schreiner and Havelock Ellis, 1884–1920.* Edited by Yaffa Claire Draznin. Peter Lang. New York. No.5, p.72 1992

[40] Draznin, above.

[41] *Olive Schreiner, a Biography* by Ruth First and Ann Scott. Andre Deutsch 1980, p.63. Also in unpublished papers Ellis, Havelock: Works Olive Schreiner, Ams./draft fragments and notes with A revisions. 25pp 1884, 6 June, Ellis writes: 'She [OS] was going to call *The African Farm Mirage* with a motto of her own "Life is a series of abortions" but found there was another book of that name and thought the motto revealed the ending of the book too plainly.'
Havelock Ellis, a medical student, may be using the reference to 'abortions' to mean a pregnancy that ended naturally, not as a result of an unqualified person terminating the pregnancy illegally. In later life, after OS gave birth to her daughter, who only survived a few hours; she had three miscarriages.

[42] Draznin p,72, who takes the information from Havelock Ellis A biography by Arthur Calder-Marshall Rupert. Hart-Davis 1959, p.90. A.C-M mistakenly places New College in the Isle of Wight.

[43] S.C.C.S. p.151

[44] S.C.C.S. p.151

[45] Ibid p.152

[46] 'His vocation lay in the instruction of the young.' Williams, p.32

[47] Henry Havelock Ellis was a medical student when he met OS. After *The Story of an African Farm* was published in two volumes, under the nom de plume 'Ralph Irons', in 1883, Ellis wrote to OS in 1884. He told the author how much he admired the work but also criticised it. Ellis and OS

met three months later, and went on to write to each other frequently, as well as spend time together. A sexual relationship never developed, but their close friendship remained until OS's death. Ellis made his name as an author of over 50 books. *Psychology of Sex* was one of his best known books, a work of 7 volumes

48 Karl Pearson, academic, qualified in mathematics, physics and law. Post in mathematics at University College, London. He was introduced to OS in 1885 and OS was much in love with him, but he did not return her feelings. This rejection (although Pearson had deep feelings for OS, these were not those of love) brought OS to the point of mental illness. OS was much helped in this emotional crisis by Bryan Donkin

49 H. Bryan Donkin was OS's own doctor and also doctor of Karl Marx's family. Eleanor Marx was a friend of OS. Donkin fell in love with OS and wanted to marry her, but OS wanted a stronger man to marry

50 Williams, p.30

51 Williams, p.24

52 Williams, p.22

53 'Oak and Olive'

CHAPTER TWO

54 The word 'Memorial' was eventually dropped from the name of the school. Francis Close was a leading evangelical, a former Rector of Cheltenham, and, before his death in 1882, was greatly involved in education. The school was a memorial to him.

55 McNeile, p.9

56 The Rev. R.F. McNeile, OD. *A History of Dean Close School*, Wilding, 1966, p.10

57 The use of physical punishment is not recorded, but Sherwood in NGJ, pp. 4 and 5, states that 'Mrs. Flecker was young and inexperienced and had no chorus of child psychologists to guide her'. On the strength of her own Notes for the LIFE she stands self-convicted of having done all the things they would have advised against. There were 'many battles of will, she records, many of them brought on by her son's obstinacy over quite unimportant things'. In describing her son's refusal to pronounce '5' in counting she recounts that 'neither coaxing nor punishment would cure him'. Exactly what punishment is not given.

58 Annual Dinner of Dean Close Old Boys, 12 Jan. 1899

59 Flecker of Dean Close, p.53

60 Flecker of Dean Close, p.54

61 The First Hundred Years, p.31

62 NGJ, p.9

63 LIFE, p.23

64 LIFE, p.16

65 NGJ, p.6

[66] NGJ, p.6

[67] LIFE, p.17

[68] LIFE, p.15

[69] *Flecker of Dean Close*, p.11

[70] LIFE, p.214, letter dated June 1914 from Davos to Mr. Cooper

[71] NGJ, p.14

[72] LIFE, p.16

[73] LIFE, p.23

[74] LIFE, p.23

[75] 'November Eves'

[76] LIFE, p.21

[77] This fascination with railway engines is at odds with some notes about railways Roy Flecker made in one of his early notebooks (*Olla Podrida*) when he complained of the 'black battered railway' and 'black loathsome smoke' although he thought that little trains were 'rather picturesque'. The adult Flecker's love was to be for the magic of the journey, rather than an appreciation of the trains themselves.

[78] NGJ, p.7

[79] NGJ, p.9

[80] TSM, p.39

[81] LIFE, p.26

[82] LIFE, p.195

[83] p.23

[84] p.23

[85] LIFE, p.23

[86] LIFE, p.23

[87] LIFE, p.139

[88] LIFE, p.23

[89] LIFE, p.25

[90] Life, p.25

[91] LIFE, p.19

[92] NGJ, p.8

[93] Some aspects of these biblical stories enacted in the plays of his childhood appear to have been replayed in the work of the adult playwright James Elroy Flecker. In *Hassan* the main character and others sit in a basket to be drawn up in the 'house with the balcony' in the Street of Felicity.

[94] LIFE, p.22

[95] NGJ, p.8

[96] GILL, vol.1, p.3

[97] LIFE, p.32

[98] LIFE, p.32

[99] McNeile, p.14

[100] '*The First 100 Years* p.25

[101] McNeile, p.17

[102] LIFE, p.101

[103] TMS, p.35

[104] In his notebook *Olla Podrida* Roy Flecker told potential readers (tongue in cheek) that Mr. Phil May sent him a cheque for £100 asking that he may be allowed to illustrate the book. Roy Flecker was compelled to refuse the offer because he thought that the purity of the poetry would be clouded by the illustrations.

[105] Photograph (p.33 facing) LIFE, entitled 'On the shore at Southbourne'.

[106] LIFE, p.26

[107] LIFE, p.33

[108] LIFE, p.35

[109] LIFE, p.35

[110] *The First Hundred Years*, p.23

[111] *The Grecians*, p.21

[112] NGJ, p.12

[113] LIFE, p.26

[114] The poet Frederick Locker-Lampson (1821–95) whose works inclu ded '*London Lyrics*' (1st edition 1857) and '*Patchwork*' (1879), had four children by his second marriage to Hannah Jane, only daughter of Sir Curtis and Lady Lampson. The marriage took place in 1874. When Sir Curtis Lampson died in 1885, Locker and his wife and four children took the name Locker-Lampson. The four children were Godfrey, Dorothy, Oliver and Maud. Godfrey (no christian name is given in the LIFE, but as the elder he is the son who would be of an age to be the 'Mr. Locker-Lampson' referred to on p.26), went to Eton, and letters were published from his father to Godfrey in '*Frederick Locker-Lampson*' A Character Sketch composed and edited by his son-in-law The Right Hon. Augustine Birrell Constable 1920. Godfrey is advised by his father (after Locker-Lampson senior has read his son's poems) to read Macaulay's Poems. In the next letter (dated 17 June 1888), Godfrey is given thirteen rules that must be obeyed if the son is to write a good sonnet. Another letter discussed 'Solitude' and advises the reading of Milton, and another letter advises the son against difficult or too abstract subjects. Locker-Lampson senior advises on writing in a very simple metre in order to 'get a power of expressing your thoughts, clearly and forcibly'. A complete poem is quoted in the letter:

> Mrs. Boem
> Wrote a poem
> In praise of Teignmouth air,
> Mr. Boem
> Read that poem,
> And built a cottage there.* p.152

Another poem printed was:

FINAL EFFORT OF THE SON AGED SEVENTEEN ON THE OCCASION OF THE DEATH OF HIS GODFATHER, LORD TENNYSON. [1892]

The poem begins:

> The sorrowing nations weep and mourn for thee,
> And voices of the dead cry from their graves,
> And send sad echoes sighing thro' the sea
> Of dark eternity; and shadowy waves
> Roll on the ocean of men's minds...

Frederick Locker's daughter, Eleanor by his first marriage married in 1878 Lionel, son of the Poet Laureate, Alfred Lord Tennyson. She had three sons and after Lionel's death she married Augustine Birrell, widower, a barrister, politician and man of letters. Their son Francis Frederick Locker Birrell (1889–1935) became a friend of James Elroy Flecker at Cambridge (see Chapter Six).

Two poems of Frederick Locker-Lampson ('To My Grandmother' and 'At her window') were published in *The Oxford Book of Victorian Verse.* Oxford Press 1912 (chosen by Sir Arthur Quiller-Couch,) as well as two poems by James Elroy Flecker: 'Riouperoux' and 'War Song of the Saracens'.

[115] LIFE, p.26

[116] Frederick Locker-Lampson, a Character Sketch, p.61

[117] *A Character Sketch*, p.69

[118] *A Character Sketch*

[119] 'Phaon, A Tale of Days gone by in Twelve Idylls' (see Chapter 3)

[120] LIFE, p.24

[121] The Queen, as Princess Elizabeth, accepted a first edition of Flecker's *Hassan* when visiting Dean Close School in 1951. Cecil Roberts, in his book *Sunshine and Shadows* refers to Winston Churchill quoting Flecker [p.384] and in another book by Roberts, *The Pleasant Years,* relates how the British Ambassador, Sir John Balfour, who had known Flecker, has a specially illustrated book of Flecker's poems on the grand piano in the Embassy in Madrid. [p.108]

[122] NGJ, p.12

[123] LIFE, p.58

[124] Observer Colour Supplement 'Visions of Byzantium'. Anna Pavord, 21 June 1987, p.55

[125] LIFE, p.58

[126] In his adult years Flecker was to describe some of his poems, which others took seriously, as 'a jest'.

[127] LIFE, p.58

[128] E.S. Turner. *Boys will be Boys.* Michael Joseph, 1948 p.18

[129] NGJ, p.12

[130] Auto to Kalon: Beauty and Goodness which is central to the philosophy of Plato.

[131] The *Decanian,* August 1908 (see also Chapter 6)

[132] In TMS 'flaked' is 'flanked'. LIFE refers to 'flashing white' in this context.

[133] These lines are republished in the LIFE, p.27 and also by Mercer p.11. He omits lines 1 and 4. Sherwood p.13 omits lines 6, 7 and 8.

Chapter Three

[134] LIFE, p.36

[135] LIFE, p.36

[136] *The Grecians,* p.63

[137] Byrd. p.94 N quoting Parkin

[138] LIFE, p.43

[139] George Douglas R.D. Lindeman. Twaynes English Author Series p.83 George Norman Douglas (1868–1952) left Uppingham in 1883. [It was Dr. Selwyn, who did not come to Uppingham until 1887, who was credited with the chapel before breakfast regime.]

[140] *The Grecians,* p.18

[141] *The Grecians,* p.27. Flecker finally used 'moral prig' in his published version of *The Grecians,* but 'religious prig' was his original choice, and he altered it to moral prig when referring to compulsory vice. (Mss. in the BOD.)

[142] NGJ, p.15

[143] LIFE, p.36/7

[144] *The Grecians,* p.97

[145] LIFE, p.37

[146] *The Grecians,* p.121

[147] Gill, p.188

[148] *The Grecians,* p.121

[149] LIFE, p.54

[150] LIFE, p.37

[151] *A Wanderer's Way,* C.E. Raven Hopkinson, 1928. p.16

[152] *The Grecians,* p.61

[153] NGJ, p.16

[154] *Looking Back,* Norman Douglas, Autobiography, Chatto & Windus, 1934, refers to 'accounts swindled and food so vile' although an earlier period than that of Flecker's, the situation would not be greatly improved.

The Life of Edward Thring by George Parkin, gives many instances of Thring's financial difficulties, Vol. II p.312, Parkin describes Thring as overwhelmed by debt through the greater part of his life. Parkin, Vol. II p.310, describes Thring as having been brought up in an affluent way and Thring never understanding the rigid economy in the use of money.

[155] LIFE, p.52

[156] LIFE, p.45

[157] LIFE, p.60

[158] Knighted 1902, elected Unionist MP for East Hull, 1895

[159] *The Grecians*, p.70 [Flecker began *The Grecians* at Oxford and continued it while at Cambridge. Firbank was at Cambridge, at the same time as Flecker, and Firbank was also friendly with Rupert Brooke. In *Prancing Novelist – In Praise of Ronald Firbank* by Brigid Brophy, Macmillan, 1973, p.131/2 the author associates Firbank with a satire of himself. 'Firbank, in the remark his delusion has attributed to Sitwell, is the boot-button boy, the buttons who cleans the boots.']

[160] Firbank had accused Sitwell of spreading the rumour that the Firbank fortune had been founded on boot-buttons.

[161] Raven's piece for the LIFE, p.60

[162] Raven's autobiographical writings: *A Wanderer's Way*, Martin Hopkinson, London 1928; *Evolution and the Christian Concept of God*, 1936

[163] *A Wanderer's Way*, C.E. Raven, Martin Hopkinson, 1928 p.28

[164] *Norman Douglas, A Biography*. Mark Holloway, Secker and Warburg, 1976, p.40. [The master referred to was the Revd. J.H. Skrine, and the school he went to Glenalmond.] In his book *A Memory of Edward Thring* MacMillan & Co. 1889, John Huntley Skrine, Warden of Glenalmond, states in his preface that he was for seven years a pupil at Uppingham and for five a pupil in Thring's class and for fourteen a worker at his side, in ties of nearest intimacy. Skrine states that Uppingham, under Thring was known as the school where they whip the boys so, and one incident, where he flogged boys who had been late back to school, but had good reasons for being late, got into the papers. Thring held the papers in contempt.

[165] NGJ, p.21

[166] NGJ, p.21

[167] *Charles Raven* by F.W Dillistone, Hodder & Stoughton, 1975, p.30

[168] *The Grecians*, p.63/64

[169] *The Grecians*, p.64

[170] *The Grecians*, p.63

[171] *The Grecians*, p.61

[172] *The Grecians*, p.62

[173] *The Grecians*, p.54

[174] *Poet of Expressionist Berlin. The Life and Work of Georg Heym*, Patrick Bridgwater, 1992, Libris p.22

[175] *The Grecians*, p.61

[176] *Norman Douglas*, Mark Holloway, Secker Warburg, London 1976, p.48

[177] *Life of Edward Thring*, G.R. Parkin, Macmillan & Co. 1898, Vol. I, p.53

[178] *Life of Edward Thring*, G.R. Parkin, Macmillan & Co., 1898 Vol. II, p.154

[179] *Life of Edward Thring*, G.R. Parkin, Macmillan & Co., 1898 Vol. II, p.154

[180] *The Grecians*, p.132

[181] *The Grecians*, p.132

[182] LIFE, p.38

[183] *The Grecians,* p.60

[184] LIFE, p.38

[185] *The Grecians,* p.49

[186] LIFE, p.38

[187] LIFE, p.39

[188] MS f.42 BOD. Inscription (a version) also is in Flecker's *Olla Podrida* (p.243) notebook dated March 1901. ('Phaon' dated in 'O.P.' March 1902). Inscription published LIFE, p.25

[189] This last sentence was omitted from the letter published in the LIFE, p.39, giving the impression that '700 lines' was the end of the letter. NGJ, p.25 is the source of the sentence.

[190] The Burial of Areios, MS. f42 p.18

[191] p.6 MS. f42 (also LIFE, p.55)

[192] LIFE, p.38

[193] Notebook D.244, p.42

[194] LIFE, p.51/2

[195] *Evolution and the Christian Concept of God,* C. Raven, Oxford, 1936, p.7 Reprinted in *Charles Raven & F.W. Dillistone* Hodder & Stoughton, 1975, p.31

[196] LIFE, p.39

[197] In February 1901, he added to his poem 'The Brook' written in 1899, verses dated February 1901. (In both notebooks D243, 244)

[198] Truth (D244), To 'On' (D243), March 1901

[199] D244, p.20

[200] LIFE, p.49

[201] D243

[202] D244

[203] Sherwood reprints this poem in full. NGJ, p.18 Byrd, p.16n, refers to this poem in relation to Catullus' 'Attis', and in her text to poems which Flecker wrote after Uppingham, which include the image of the 'fatal woman'.

[204] D243, 244, 245, (BOD) BKJ (BL)

[205] *The Collected Poems of James Elroy Flecker,* edited with an Introduction by Sir John Squire, first published in 1916, contains translations of Catullus in the Juvenilia section. In NGJ p.14n, Sherwood points out the incorrect dating of Catullus III. Byrd, p.23, states that the same is true of three other translations. Gill p.186, makes the point about later polished versions appearing in *Collected Poems,* and different versions in the LIFE.

[206] D243

[207] Gill p.186, makes this point, but indicates the difference between Byron's translations and Flecker's. Gill refers to Catullus in English Poetry by E. S. Duckett Smith Classical Studies, Northampton, Mass USA 1925 where both Byron's and Flecker's translations are quoted.

[208] Gill, p.187

[209] Gill, p.188

[210] (CP Dates given: 1901-4) (BKJ: 1900)

[211] D245

[212] *The Grecians*, p.127. 'But I will at all events give no countenance to the foolish and vulgar hostility with which so-called classical men too often treat science and her followers.'

[213] *The Grecians*, p.134

[214] *The Grecians*, p.134

[215] LIFE, p.60

[216] This point is made in *Charles Raven* by F.W. Dillistone, Hodder & Stoughton, 1975, p.30

[217] The Wanderer's Way, p.17

[218] LIFE, p.47

[219] LIFE, p.47

[220] LIFE, p.47

[221] LIFE, p.47

[222] LIFE, p.49

[223] LIFE, p.48

[224] LIFE, p.47

[225] LIFE, p.40

[226] LIFE, p.41

[227] LIFE, p.50

[228] LIFE, p.41

[229] LIFE, p.60

[230] LIFE, p.52

[231] Byrd, p.22n

[232] The cause of the death of Lewis is not given in published school records [in the BL]. It is possible that he was consumptive, as Flecker refers to 'compulsory cricket and compulsory vice. From the first of these evils a boy can only escape by being consumptive....'

[233] *The Grecians*, p.27

[234] LIFE, p.48

[235] LIFE, p.49

[236] LIFE, p.49

[237] LIFE, p.49

[238] LIFE, p.43

[239] LIFE, p.44

[240] LIFE, p.44

[241] LIFE, p.44

[242] LIFE, p.45

[243] LIFE, p.53

[244] LIFE, p.54

[245] LIFE, p.58

[246] LIFE, p.59

[247] *The Grecians*, p.101

[248] *Edward Thring Headmaster* by George Parkin, London, Macmillan & Co. 1898, Vol. II, p 164/5

[249] LIFE, p.51

[250] The Eye Brook reservoir was opened in 1940, and later Rutland Water brought a landscape with stretches of water to the area.

[251] K of A, p.5

[252] LIFE, p.54 and NGJ, p.26. In the LIFE the sentence 'Not that I have been misjudged' was left out.

[253] *Edward Thring Headmaster of Uppingham School, Life and Letters* by George Parkin, London Macmillan & Co., 1898, Vol. II p.134/5

[254] LIFE, p.43

[255] This master is identified only as 'T', which could be John Gale Thring (b. 1854) son of Edward Thring, who had been a pupil at Uppingham and a master in Flecker's time.

[256] GIll, p.187

[257] GIll, p.185

[258] LIFE, p.40

[259] Selwyn retired 1907. David retired 1908. Haines retired 1905.

[260] NGJ, p.25

[261] LIFE, p.62

[262] NGJ, p.25. This letter is published in the LIFE, p.54, with the first part of the sentence omitted: 'I don't think many people here' etc., given as the start of a sentence.

[263] LIFE, p.54

[264] LIFE, p.54

[265] LIFE, p.61.

[266] BKJ, July 1903, also D245 BOD 1902.

[267] BKJ, July 1902. Also D245, BOD 1902. (In this notebook the second last line reads: 'With its clanging, clashing, crashing, slow reverberated knell,')

CHAPTER FOUR

[268] A fellow undergraduate, Humbert Wolfe, described meeting a visitor off the train at Oxford, who asked to borrow sixpence to tip the porter. A friend who was with him produced a shilling, and was told by the visitor that a shilling was too much. *The Upward Anguish* by Humbert Wolfe. Cassell and Co., p.106

[269] He took the matter of tipping into his artistic consciousness: in the novel he began at Oxford, *The King of Alsander*, he featured the aptly named Norman Price, the hero, carrying his luggage 'painfully' back from the station. Later, the same hero received a letter with £100 in it, and tipped

the postman 2d., a sum his parents would have approved of, even if the author displayed a certain amount of mean spirit.

[270] *King of Alsander* p.18 'I'm an Oxford man myself and understand that curious world.'

[271] The 'Volunteers' were the Oxford University Volunteers. A contemporary, Humbert Wolfe, in his *Upward Anguish*, Chapter VI, Soldiers in Oxford, described a meeting in the JCR when: 'An amiable Brigadier, under the guidance of Major Dixey, a most military don, addressed the College on the desirability of fitting themselves for the inevitable war.' (p.116) Wolfe went on to relate: 'A wave of enthusiasm swept through the room.' .... 'The officer who was taking names all but escaped writer's cramp.' (p.117). Humbert Wolfe gives a long and detailed and amusing story of his unsatisfactory attendance at camp. Wolfe acknowledged the part played by former members of the Oxford University Volunteers in the Great War.

[272] In a letter (NGJ p.29) Flecker wrote to his parents: '(there are a sub. or two to be paid yet – musical, bike, cleaning 7/-d etc.,)'. Trinity College records show that he did not join the Savoyards Society, so exactly what 'Musical' he joined or did not join, is not clear. There were two, the Oxford University Musical Union, and the Oxford University Musical Club.

[273] The fact that he found the Logic lecture 'incomprehensible' was something he shared with 'Tommy Lascelles'(Sir Alan Lascelles) (1887–1981) who had come up to Trinity in 1903, and read Greats. He wrote in his book *End of an Era, Letters & Journals of Sir Alan Lascelles from 1887–1920* Hamish Hamilton, p.25, 'Cook Wilson, on Logic, was inaudible, inane, and quite unable to convey any meaning to me at all.' 'Tommy' Lascelles visited Flecker who is described as having rooms in Trinity, in Harold Nicolson's *A Biography, volume 1, 1886–1929*, Hamish Hamilton by James Lees-Milne: p.208. 'Harold had once met Flecker when they were at Oxford together. Flecker had a marked Levantine appearance. He liked people to come to his rooms in Trinity where he gave them marsala. He was hospitable in his way, and his rooms were known as "The Saracen's Head". Harold only visited him once in the company of Alan Lascelles.' In Humbert Wolfe's book *The Upward Anguish* he refers to 'Cooke-Wilson', p.135, ' "You know about Cooke-Wilson? The old boy who rides about on a bicycle in golfing breeches, and would write a book on metaphysics if he hadn't lost the alphabet in his long white beard." Flecker was not amused. "Cooke-Wilson has constructed a balcony at his house in North Oxford designed to refute Idealism." "Has it fallen through?" enquired the Scholar. Flecker was not prepared to continue a conversation on these lines.' John Cook Wilson (1849–1915) was a tutorial fellow of Oriel College before he was elected Wykeham Professor of Logic in 1889, a post attached to New College. Cook Wilson had married in 1876 and had a son, his wife's health was said to have worn him out, which may have

contributed towards his appearance of being an old man, although in Flecker's Oxford years Cook Wilson was in his mid-fifties.

[274] LIFE p.86

[275] References to the Oxford student magazines all come from a typescript of a letter to Cheesman, undated, in the BOD

[276] LIFE p.86

[277] The notebook (MS. Eng. Poet. D245 BOD) and *The Book of Kara James* (BM), which survive as a record of Flecker's poetry during his Oxford years, span the years 1902–06, with the year 1903 not represented. Both books contain drafts and different versions of the same poems, some with the titles altered. BKJ alone contains typewritten versions of his poetry, which point to these being the final versions, as he did not appear to compose poetry on the typewriter. BKJ alone contains prose, and it is of the two, more likely to contain direct references to people he was mixing with at Oxford. Many poems, especially in BKJ, remain unpublished.

[278] Humbert Wolfe published two books that contain recollections of Flecker. He published in 1934, *Portraits by Inference* and in 1938, *The Upward Anguish*. The Flecker/Wolfe paths had an opportunity to cross at the Freshers' Dinner and at the Volunteers, but he implied in *Portraits by Inference*, that he first met Flecker in 1904. On p.9 of *Portraits by Inference*, he states: 'It was Gabriel Woods who first told me that there was a poet at Trinity called John Flecker.' [sic] Wolfe was invited to meet Flecker in Exeter College by Gabriel Woods. Wolfe, publishing his account of meeting Flecker, thirty years after the event, could easily have not realised that he knew Flecker before the formal introduction by Gabriel Woods, who mentioned '*The Red-Man*' (which was '*The Best Man*', which did not come out until 1906) in the course of a meeting that came about 1904. John Sherwood makes a similar point about Humbert Wolfe's recollections, in NGJ p.47

[279] *The Upward Anguish*, Humbert Wolfe, Cassell & Co., 1938, p.132

[280] *My Life and Times Octave Three* 1900–07, Compton Mackenzie, Chatto & Windus, 1964

[281] *The Upward Anguish*, p.133

[282] *The Upward Anguish*, p.139

[283] *The Upward Anguish*, p. 140

[284] Geoffrey Grigson 'Coming To London VII', *The London Magazine*, June 1956, Vol.3, No.6, p.43. W.H. Auden, Verse-Letter to C. Day-Lewis –

> 'While Wolfe, the typists' poet, made us sick
> Whose thoughts are dapper and whose lines are slick.'
> One poem of Wolfe's which is still well-known is:
> 'You cannot hope
> to bribe or twist
> thank God! the
> British journalist.
> But seeing what

the man will do
unbribed, there's
no occasion to.'

[285] The exact date of Flecker changing his name from Herman to James is not known. His name remained Herman for official purposes. Usually, to his family and others close to him, he was 'Roy'. But, as his father was also William Herman, this could lead to confusion. In NGJ Sherwood relates (p.51) how Dr. Flecker opened letters addressed to his son c/o Dean Close and on one occasion found to his distress that his son was 'associating with an Oxford shopgirl'. This sort of discovery would be avoided if letters were addressed to James Elroy Flecker, instead of Herman Flecker. The reason for the choice of James is not clear, but his father's brother was named James and that may have been part of the reason for the choice. Sherwood does not explain why it was necessary for Dr. Flecker to open his son's letters, and as it was in this case obviously a private letter, the chances are that he opened it by accident, because of the similar Christian names.

[286] Wolfe entered the Board of Trade 1908 and became Department Secretary in the Ministry of Labour.

[287] *The Upward Anguish,* p.133

[288] *The Upward Anguish,* p.137

[289] *The Student's Prayer-Book,* published by Methuen & Co. Reviewed by Oxford Magazine, 20 Nov. 1903.

[290] McKelvie became a chaplain in India.

[291] 'Savery left Uppingham in the middle of Flecker's first term, after a violent row. NGJ p.15

[292] JEF pp. 18/19

[293] JEF p.19

[294] *Book of Kara James* p.50 no.26

[295] *The Grecians* (begun at Oxford) p.106 CP

[296] *The Grecians* p.96

[297] LIFE p.68

[298] In the notebook in which Flecker wrote *The Grecians* (now in the BOD) there are the following alterations from the original mss: 'decadents' for 'aesthetes' 'dim, scarlet' for dim, reddish' and 'half suggested' for 'suggested'.

[299] *The Grecians* p.97

[300] The poet Thomas Chatterton (1752–70), whose life inspired English Romanticism. He committed suicide, destitute, in London.

[301] Guidebook of the day

[302] Before he could enter the Taylorian, which was given every year for modern languages, it was abolished.

[303] LIFE, p.72

[304] LIFE p.72

[305] Letter to Cheesman – undated – BOD. Also quoted in *James Elroy Flecker. Unpublished Poems and Drafts*. Martin Booth 1971.

[306] LIFE, p.86

[307] *King of Alsander* p.4 and p.12

[308] Jack Beazley's maternal grandfather, John Davidson, was born in Montrose, Scotland in 1824 (or 1825) and his maternal grandmother, Mary Robertson, was born in Glasgow in the same year: his maternal grandparents married on 6 July 1854. Their daughter, Mary Catherine (named after her paternal grandmother Katherine Ritchie) was born in Glasgow on 5 April 1855, at 120 Renfrew Street, Glasgow, her father was then employing one man, four boys and a girl, and by the time his eldest daughter, Jack Beazley's mother, was in her teens, his brother-in-law, John Robertson was a lithographer, successful enough to employ six men and a boy and fifteen girls. The business John Davidson carried on was at 170 Buchanan Street, and as well as his four daughters, who included Mary Catherine, aged 15 in 1870, there were Jack Beazley's aunts, Jessica then aged 11, and Jemima and Luisa Ann aged 10 and 8, and a domestic servant was employed.

Mary Catherine Davidson, when she was 28, married Mark John Murray Beazley, from 21 High Street, Belfast, a Club Secretary, on 18 September 1883, in the Church of Scotland Church, at St. George's-in-the-fields. Jemima Davidson was a witness, and so was Arthur Gaffikin. (A friend of Norman Price, had a similar surname in *The King of Alsander*, he was John Gaffekin.)

Also an Uppingham fellow pupil, G.H. Gaffikin who won an Open Scholarship to Oxford also in 1902.

A change in family fortunes took place: at the time of his daughter's marriage, John Davidson was a Commercial Traveller. Mary Beazley's in-laws, Jack Beazley's grandparents, were James Murray Beazley, a Club Steward, and Rosina Beazley, who was Miss Holland before her marriage. Mary Beazley by her marriage did not appear to have stepped up the social ladder.

[309] As Mark James Robertson Beazley had the same Christian name as his father, he could have been called James to avoid confusion, and this gave Flecker the idea of changing his name to James, so that in a sense, he and Beazley became brothers.

[310] A.C. Haden (1885–1940), an anthropologist, formerly zoologist, made the move from his father's stationery business. J.G. Frazer, author of *The Golden Bough*, although from a middle-class background, but not one where it would be expected that he would go to university, made the transition to Glasgow University and Trinity College, Cambridge.

[311] K of A, p.6/7

[312] NGJ, p.34

[313] Sir John Squire, in his introduction to *The Collected Poems* (p.XXII), stated that 'An influence still more marked is that of Sir Richard Burton.

Flecker, when still a boy, had copied out the whole of his long *Kasidah*, and its rhythms and turns of phrase are present in several of his Syrian poems. It was in *The Kasidah* that Flecker found Aflatun and Aristu, and the refrain of "the tinkling of the camel-bells" of which he made such fine use in *The Golden Journey*.'

Flecker's notebook entitled *Olla Podrida* (d. 243 BOD) which contains details of original and translated verse (1898–1901) has under the heading 'Sendings' the following information:

Kasidah – *Gentleman's* [a magazine that was published between 1713–1907]

Flecker's notebook that contains fair copies of Flecker's poems (1901–05) with some drafts of original poems and a version of *The Kasidah* by Richard Burton is D.245 notebook in the BOD. Flecker had noted in his copybook (D.245) that 'Aflatun and Aristu' are Plato and Aristotle, he wrote this in the margin, after he had copied out *The Kasidah*.

He went on to use Aflatun and Aristu in his 'Ballad of Iskander'.

GILL points out (p.210) that: Flecker need not have derived the names 'Aflatun and Aristu from Burton's *Kasidah*. He could have found them in Persian, where they are the well-known forms for the Greek names, and where he found the name "Iskander" for Alexander.'

GILL also points out that Flecker referred to the silver sound of the camel-bells but does not use Burton's word 'tinkling'. p.211

In her Epilogue for the LIFE Hodgson stated '*The Kasidah* being difficult to obtain, Flecker copied it out.' p.256

[Nowhere is there an indication as to where Flecker obtained the original copy of Burton's *Kasidah*.]

Another source for the camel-bells refrain is revealed in a letter T.E. Lawrence wrote to Flecker from Aleppo, which is dated 18 Feb. (1912), when Lawrence wrote:

'Aleppo is all compact of colour, and sense of line: you inhale Orient in lungloads, and glut your appetite with silks and dyed fantasies of clothes.* To-day there came through the busiest vault in the bazaar a long caravan of 100 mules of Baghdad, marching in line rhythmically to the boom of two huge iron bells swinging under the belly of the foremost. Bells nearly two feet high with wooden clappers, introducing 100 mule-loads of the woven shawls and wine-coloured carpets* of Bokhara: such wealth is intoxicating: and intoxicated I went and bought the bells. "You hear them", said the mukari, "a half-hour before the sight." And I marched in triumph home, making the sound of a caravan from Baghdad: "Oah, Oah", and the crowd parted the ways before me.'

From the *Letters of T.E. Lawrence,* Selected and Edited by Malcolm Brown 1988, Dent. p.45/6

* The Golden Journey to Samarkand
Epilogue: 'Turbans and sashes, gowns and bows and veils,'
* The Golden Journey to Samarkand
Epilogue: 'Have we not Indian carpets dark as wine,'

An attempt is made in the Epilogue to the LIFE (p.256–7) to link the stanza of the camel's bell with Flecker's poem. Also Hodgson pointed out what she feels is some influence on Flecker's early verse of *The Kasidah*. She also (p.273) linked *The Kasidah* to *Hassan*.

Savery's brief and tidy memory of what took place at the lunch with Beazley and Savery, when the focus was on one poem of Burton's, which was presented to show that it was possible for one line to fall into Flecker's artistic consciousness, so that a fragment came to the surface in one of Flecker's best known works, is also rather neat and tidy.

What Savery and Hodgson were trying to do, was to make sure that nobody thought that any of Burton's works, or his philosophy of life, was in any way an influence on Flecker. Hodgson does admit in her Epilogue: 'Besides the works of (p.257) Sir Richard Burton, Flecker had studied the *Arabian Nights* in the Mardrus' version' *The Kasidah* was a poem that could be read without embarrassment, which could not be said for some of Burton's other works.

Burton's main influence on Flecker was the picture he presented of a man, who, although he had failed at Oxford, nevertheless went on to be a figure who gained fame in the world beyond Oxford.

Savery did not refer to Francis Thompson's poem mentioned by Flecker in a letter dated 5 July 1913, when he wrote to Savery: 'FRANCIS THOMPSON. Jack utterly loathes him as a quack. I have been forced to admire 'The Hunchèd Camels' … *

The poem referred to was:

> Arab Love-Song
> The hunchèd camels of the night*
> Trouble the bright
> And silver waters of the moon.
> The Maiden of the Morn will soon
> Through Heaven stray and sing,
> Star gathering.
>
> Now, while the dark about our loves is strewn,
> Light of my dark, blood of my heart, O come!
> And night will catch her breath up, and be dumb.
>
> Leave thy father, leave thy mother
> And thy brother;
> Leave the black tents of thy tribe apart!
> Am I not thy father and thy brother,
> And thy mother?

†*Letters of J.E. Flecker to Frank Savery*, The Beaumont Press, 1926
* Cloud shapes observed by travellers in the East.
†'Arab Love-Song' was first published in *The Dome* magazine, in January 1899. Then in Eyes of Youth, 1910.

> And thou – what needest with thy tribe's black tents
> Who has the red pavilion of my heart?

314 It was obvious that neither Hodgson nor Savery wanted their readers to think that Flecker was in any way influenced by such a book (see previous footnote). It was difficult to prove that Flecker came across *The Kasidah* and read it without any curiosity about anything else that Burton had written, and he had written a great deal. But Flecker, writing to Savery, 5 July 1913, from Leysin, stated: 'Concerning a saying of yours implying no decent man would care to get to know Malays and wandering Arabs – don't follow Chesterton into that anti-Oriental fallacy. Eastern races are worth knowing – or we should never have had either Burton or Kipling, both very decent men.'
The Letters of J.E. Flecker p.41/2

315 Gill, p.187 also puts Flecker's translation above Burton's.

316 Der duftende Garten des Scheik Nefzaui, Ein arabische Bearbeitung von H. Conrad. Privatdruck de Verlages 'Der Spiegal' zu Leipzig. (1905) Burton also translated with F.F. Arbuthnot *The Kama Sutra of Vatsyayana*. With a Preface and Introduction.

317 *No Golden Journey*, pps.35/36

318 *King of Alsander*, p.9

319 *King of Alsander*, p.10

320 *King of Alsander*, p.9

321 *King of Alsander*, p.9

322 John Davidson Beazley died on 7 May 1970, his certificate gives his date of birth, but the place of birth has a line through it. Balliol's published record describe Beazley's father as 'Mark Beazley of Brussels', although he did live in Brussels, he was not born there or brought up in Brussels.

323 LIFE, p.88/89

324 LIFE, p.89

325 [BKJ, facing p.51]

326 Clerk to the House of Lords (1907–44) became Granville Proby; his father changed his name to Proby by Deed Poll.

327 LIFE, p.89

328 LIFE p.90

329 LIFE, p.90

330 LIFE, p.90

331 *King of Alsander*, p32/3

332 In a letter to Sedgwick (July 1904, p.91/2 LIFE) Flecker wrote: 'parted from J. last Monday, after having seen him almost every day ever since I first met him in March.' He sent this letter with another version of his poem 'Song', also another poem which he eventually called 'Dream-Song'; neither of the versions sent to Sedgwick had titles: they were published later.

[333] *Book of Kara James*, p.59 Typewritten with alterations (another version in black notebook)

[334] *My Life and Times*, Octave Three 1900–07 Compton Mackenzie, Chatto & Windus, 1964, p.178

[335] LIFE, p.80

[336] LIFE, p.80

[337] NGJ, p.24

[338] The Rev. H.E.D. Blakiston (1862–1942) Senior Tutor. President of Trinity (1907–38). 'He is a funny, nervous little man, but quite interesting when you get him going. He expressed an opinion that G.K. Chesterton, Kipling and Bernard Shaw should be transported to a desert island for life.' *End of an Era – Sir Alan Lascelles*. Hamish Hamilton. p.19

[339] Flecker's examination papers are no longer preserved at Trinity College, or the Bodleian, although examination questions are preserved; these are unlikely to reveal the reasons why Flecker did so badly in them. (Letter to HW from Bodleian, 8.3.91)

[340] LIFE, p.81

[341] LIFE, p.90/91

[342] Flecker himself does not elaborate in any great detail why he hated philosophy, although he recognised that it was an excellent mental training. 'Tommy' Lascelles, in his book in which he describes the life and work of himself and fellow undergraduates around the same time as Flecker was also an undergraduate, says of philosophy:
'Great works kept me fairly busy, though I did not do enough, I still find that in the majority of philosophic works there are whole pages from which I can extract no meaning whatever. J.S. Mill is especially absolutely unintelligible for the most part. Berkeley I can fathom; and also Kant, more or less. Aristotle is fairly clear, but for his infernal brachylogy [condensed expression]. But men like T.H. Green, Lotze and H. Spencer should never have been allowed within six feet of an inkstand.
I had an extraordinarily good Aristotle lecturer in Henry Hadow of Worcester; he is v. musical and has composed several songs.' *End of an Era*, p.25
(Henry Hadow (1859–1937) composer and author of many books on music. Knighted 1918.)

[343] *Sartor Restartus* The Life and Opinions of Herr Teufelsdrockh by T. Carlyle describes the spiritual crisis such as Carlyle himself had experienced.
Thomas Carlyle (1795–1881) early critical work first appeared in magazines.
Sartor Resartus in *Frazer's Magazine* in 1840, later in a collected edition.

[344] Flecker wrote a poem 'The Mycenaeans' in April 1905, typewritten p.61 B of KJ XXXVI. The poem consisted of 8 lines, last verse four lines, the French form of ballade.
The refrain: 'Older than Homer's oldest song.'

[345] Jane Harrison (1850–1928) was born in Yorkshire (9.9.50) but educated at Cheltenham College. She was among the original intake of women students at Newnham. While studying at the British Museum she gave lectures in Greek Art to boys in the great public schools. She met Gilbert Murray in 1900.

[346] *Jane Ellen Harrison, A Portrait from Letters* by Jessie Stewart. London Merlin Press, 1959. *Reminiscences of a Student's Life*, originally published by Hogarth Press, London, 1965. Jane Ellen Harrison *The Mask and the Self*, Sandra J. Peacock, Yale University Press, p.182.
Harrison's feeling were echoed by Edwinson when he talked to Hofman in Flecker's *Grecians*, p.23
'You see, the grand old classics are waking up, Hofman. During the last few years the scientific treatment of art and archaeology has made tremendous strides; while the study of folk-lore and comparative mythology is revolutionising our ideas upon Roman and Greek religion. Our comprehension of the classics has advanced more between the year 1880 and the present time than between the years 1600 and 1880.'

[347] Ernest Renan (1823–92) published *The Life of Christ* in 1863, and it had been an immediate success. Renan, a Breton, a Protestant, a Professor of Hebrew, used his own experience of living for a year in the Holy Land, to help him write his book

[348] LIFE, p.91

[349] This particular sentence appears twice in the same chapter in the LIFE, once in the letter to Sedgwick, and again to introduce the subject of Flecker's professed agnosticism, which indicated that had Sedgwick's letter not been preserved, and offered for publication in the LIFE, the fact of Flecker professing agnosticism would not have gained such prominence, when it came to write Flecker's life. The letter to his father, and any memory of how it was expressed, beyond the reference in the letter to Sedgwick, dated May 1904, does not now exist. Mrs. Flecker was as effective in removing selected letters from publication, as she had been in her supervision of the old nurse who had the job of deciding what to pack in Flecker's luggage, before he set off for Oxford. He wanted Viyella shirts replaced by white ones, but because, it was said, her son would not promise to wear a vest, his mother 'suppressed' the linen ones. (LIFE, p.91) His mother thought she knew better during her son's life and after his death. She certainly thought she knew better than the old nurse, who, like Hodgson, was only a hired hand, however devoted to their jobs and not lacking expertise in the matter. Mrs. Flecker always had to have the last word.
Mrs. Flecker and Beazley may have had differing views on the meaning of agnostic, which was coined by T.H. Huxley and meant:
'One who believes that the existence of anything beyond material phenomena is unknown and probably unknowable.' To Mrs. Flecker it meant that Beazley was 'against Christ'.

[350] LIFE, P.79

351 NGJ, p.35

352 LIFE, P.77

353 LIFE, P.77

354 LIFE, P.77

355 Letter dated 13 May 1917, to Cecil Roberts, from Sarah Flecker, Churchill College, Cambridge.

356 NGJ, p.30

357 In a letter dated 13 May 1917, to Cecil Roberts, Mrs. Flecker wrote, when referring to Beazley: 'The "other friend" had risen from the ranks by his great gifts, and Roy had shown him kindness at Oxford when he was lonely. He grew to admire the friend's talent, and then love him in an almost extravagant manner." Letter Churchill College, Cambridge.

358 NGJ, p.63

359 Another version of this poem is dated September 1904, in the leathercloth copybook (D245) BOD. Flecker gave this version the title 'Salutory Advice Given to Poets of this Generation'. Sherwood published this version in full (NGJ p.42). In the BKJ version Flecker changed 'Bards have lost all Heavens' good mercies' to 'Bards have lost all God's good mercies.'

360 NGJ, p.38

361 Gill, p.187

362 BKJ, p.40/3

363 In the LIFE, p.92, Hodgson prints the two poems together, only separated by a row of dots which give the impression that the two poems are one. The first 'Launch the galley sailors bold;' eventually became the poem 'Dream Song' after having been given the title 'Desire' in the black copybook D245. 'Song' was the title of the poem that began with the lines 'Not the night of her Wild Hair'. Sherwood, p.40, gives 'Song' as one title for the poem 'Desire', which is not the case.

364 BKJ, p.53

365 He struggled with the word shipless or shiftless to use in this line.

366 D245, July 1904, XV

367 The first verse (above) of 'The Little Song of her Sorrow' is quoted by J.C. Squire in *The Collected Poems of James Elroy Flecker*, p. xiv. Squire makes no reference to the BKJ version of the poem. Squire does not date it with the month, simply states that it is '1904'. Squire points out that the rhythm and language of Flecker's 'Danae's Cradle Song for Perseus' (1902) is Tennysonian and so is the first line of the 'Song' of 1904.
In *Notes and Queries*, Feb. 1972 S.W. Parry reprints the poem 'The Little Song of her Sorrows', and points out that nobody had drawn attention to the publication of this poem (meaning Squire, Hodgson and Goldring). The BKJ version of 'Little Song of her Sorrows' was not available to S.W. Parry, when he wrote his piece for *Notes and Queries*.

368 A great deal of space is taken up in the LIFE, to account for this changing of Flecker's plans, and it is used as an example to explain that Flecker

always expected that things would go right for him, even if he had made different and conflicting arrangements. The comment was made: 'The sagacious and prudent are often vexed when this peculiar kind of improvidence is justified as it is occasionally of its child.' (LIFE, p.82) But amid all argument, so that blame is put on their son, it is possible that it was not the whole story. Beazley was to be included in the Swiss holiday with a visit to Dean Close beforehand.

[369] LIFE, p.82

[370] Book of Kara James, p.56 August 1904 XXXI

[371] Book of Kara James [facing p.56]

[372] There is another version of this verse (Also in his black notebook.)
Yet rather seem those lands below
From Glion at the close of day.
As vivid as a Cameo
Graved by the Poet Gautier.

[373] 'vapours' is replaced by 'spirits' in the D240 version

[374] BKJ XXXV, p.55, August 1904. Both verses. For these poems D245 has the date 7/04

[375] LIFE, p.93

[376] LIFE, p.93

[377] LIFE, p.93

[378] LIFE, p.82

[379] See Footnote 495

[380] LIFE, p.78

[381] LIFE, p.71

[382] LIFE, p.83

[383] LIFE, p.83

[384] LIFE, p.83

[385] LIFE, p.66

[386] *James Elroy Flecker Unpublished Poems and Drafts.* Martin Booth, Keepsake Press, 1971

[387] LIFE, p.62

[388] Unpublished Biography of Cheesman in New College, Oxford

[389] Typescripts of letters in BOD

[390] Sherwood p.36 NGJ, gives the Easter vacation of 1904 as the date of a 'sexual honeymoon' of Beazley and Flecker

[391] Facing page 51 BKJ

[392] LIFE, p.84

[393] *John Maynard Keynes*, Vol.1 (1883–1920). Robert Skidelsky, Macmillan, p.168, 1983.

[394] Robert ('Robin') Hamilton Dundas (1884–1960), Scottish background, educated at Eton and New College, Oxford. Classics Don. Lecturer in Greek History and Censor, Christ Church, Oxford, 1909. Student of Christ Church, 1910–57

[395] *The Life of John Maynard Keynes* (Penguin Books) R.F. Harrod
p.105/7, 1972

[396] *The Life of John Maynard Keynes* (Penguin Books) R.F. Harrod
p.105/7, 1972

[397] In Flecker's notebook (D245) BOD, there is another version of 'South,
East, and North', and it is this version that has been published in SLA
(p.130) and NGJ (p.42/3). Neither Hellé Flecker nor John Sherwood
makes any reference to the state of Flecker's mind, when he wrote the
poem. As the version published in NGJ and SLA has the date 6 November
1904, and the BKJ version is dated November 1904, it is difficult from this
information alone, to decide with certainty which is the original version
and which is the final. But as the BKJ version is typewritten with pencil
alterations, this points to it being his final version. There is no reference
in either SLA or NGJ to the BKJ version.
Flecker's most important alteration from the D245 version to the BKJ
version is 'cold white desert' to 'empty' desert. In the D245 version, 'cold'
is an afterthought, and so is 'white'.
Hellé Flecker stated that these lines indicated to her that her husband
had a strange intuition where his last years were to be spent. But it
is far from certain that the lines about the cold, white desert refer to
Switzerland, where he did die. He did not have happy recollections of his
time in Switzerland, and thoughts of death could have been in his mind
when he wrote the poem, although not his own death in particular, and
where he would die. He knew (unpublished essay, in the BOD) that the
Swiss exacted a tax on foreigners dying in Switzerland; he may not have
known this when he wrote the poem.
Flecker's original referral to 'cold white desert' could be due to his
fascination with the tragic end of the balloonist Andree, who planned, in
1897, to be carried to the North Pole, by balloon. Andree took off but he
and his companions never reached their destination. Their bodies were
not found until 1930, and their tragic journey was pieced together when
diaries were found. Flecker mentioned Andree in his poem 'Ballade',
which was published in 1907. Alterations besides the 'cold white desert'
to 'empty desert' in the BKJ version of 'South, East, and North' were
'languorously monotoned' to 'softly monotoned'. Flecker had written,
opposite his poem on 'Captain Savery' in the BKJ copybook, 'And Beazley
languorous with divine despair'. Beazley had a hand in altering some
of the words in poems by Flecker in BKJ, and 'softly' would disguise any
hidden references in the poem to Beazley. Mary Byrd Davis described
'South, East and North' as Flecker expressing in non-Christian terms,
a longing for spiritual rebirth, and as he first entitled the poem 'The
Everlasting Yea', the death in the desert is the annihilation of the self
which Carlyle discussed in 'The Everlasting Yea' of Sartor Restartus. Byrd
refers to a line deleted from stanza one, which states that Flecker wishes
to be called 'From hope that trembles and from thought that kills.' which
is in the D245 notebook, now in the BOD. Davis does not make any

references to the BKJ version, as it was not available to her at the time she wrote her critical study of Flecker (1977).

398 p.47 BKJ

399 This version is published in full in NGJ, p.43 (It differs slightly from the BKJ version)

400 BKJ, p.48 dated March 1905 and April 1905

401 CPr p.191

402 Details of an unpublished and unfinished play entitled *The Poet's Tragedy* are in DAVIS, p.39. Flecker's play is about Dick who remains cheerful despite the fact that 'only his play separates him and his family from eventual starvation'.

403 CPr p.201

404 CPr p.204

405 'A Woman and her Son' from *New Ballads* by John Davidson, The Bodley Head, 1897.

406 LIFE, p.93

407 Typescript of letter in BOD

408 *James Elroy Flecker, Unpublished Poems and Drafts*. Martin Booth, Keepsake Press 1971

409 In the draft sent to Cheesman 'groans" is 'swathed' 'muddy blood' is 'dullness' and 'inevitably meet' is 'interminably' and 'formless, faceless' is 'nebulous' and 'friends and fires' is 'friends and foes'. There are other small alterations.

410 Original: 'thhonging' [typing error?]

411 F.O. Mann (b. 1885) of Balliol, who took a first-class degree in 1909, and although not mentioned as being a member of the Beazley/ Flecker/Cheesman circles, it is possible he was on the fringe, as he had Gloucestershire ancestors. In Mann's *Poems*, published by Basil Blackwell in 1924, he wrote a poem: 'Ancestry' about his forefathers. In his second volume of poems: *London & Suburban*, 1925, published by G. Bell & Son, his poem 'The Typist' has the lines:

Days of dullness, doubtful eves
Up and down the gaslit street;
One of half a million leaves
Blown about the casual feet.

Mann became an Inspector of Schools and was said to have influenced John Betjeman whose work was also said to have been influenced by Douglas Goldring's book of poems *Streets*. (*Young Betjeman*, Bevis Hillier, Cardinal 1988, p.340).

412 This point is made about other works, in *Sexual Anarchy Gender & Culture of the Fin de Siècle*. Bloomsbury, 1991, by Elaine Showalter, p.113.

413 Typescript of letter in BOD

414 p.45 NGJ and JEF p.22

[415] *Odd Man Out* by Douglas Goldring, Chapman & Hall Ltd., 1935

[416] Dayrell-Reed published: *The Battle for Britain in the 5th century, An Essay in Dark Age History*, Methuen 1943, and *The Rise of Wessex. A Further Essay in Dark Age History*, Methuen 1945

[417] LIFE, p.91

[418] BKJ, p.61 xxvi

[419] *Book of Kara James* XVII, p.27

[420] [bay]

[421] [let me decry]

[422] BKJ, p.64

[423] There appears to be more than one version of this play, as DAVIS states p.37, that there 'is a homemade booklet containing Nero', there is also a group of 'obscene poems with the title, *Jardin Impudique*'. Davis felt that Flecker must have realised that Nero was more than a scurrilous joke. She describes the rough draft of three scenes, which deals with murder and homosexuality and an attack on religion. DAVIS, as had been noted, did not have access to the *Book of Kara James*. Sherwood makes a reference to Nero, a Masterpiece, NGJ, p.54, but does not give as much detail as DAVIS. The version which DAVIS and Sherwood refer to is not in Flecker's papers at the BOD. [My reference is to the version in BKJ.]

[424] NGJ, p.54

[425] Cheesman won in 1911 the Arnold Prize with an essay on the 'Auxilia of the Roman Army', which was published as 'The Auxilia of the Roman Imperial Army' by the Clarendon Press in 1914.

[426] BKJ, p.85

[427] In March 1904, Keynes, on his first trip to Germany, had seen a performance of Ibsen's *Wild Duck* in Berlin, and written to Swithinbank about it. Beazley had also written 'Peer Gynt Come Home' (in his notebook in the BOD, p.16)

[428] Example given

[429] NGJ, p.51

[430] *The Grecians*, p.35

[431] SNM was Miller, Steuart Napier, first son of David George Miller, Lecturer, Established Church Normal School, Glasgow, born 2 June 1880, Aberlour, Banffshire. Educated at Glasgow University, admitted Exhibitioner Trinity, 12 October 1901. Miller had a third in Mods in 1903, and a second in final degree, in 1905

[432] NGJ, p.48

[433] BKJ, pp. 86–87

[434] BKJ, p.83

[435] BKJ, p.83

[436] NGJ, pp. 51–2

[437] BKJ, p.88, signed HEF

438 If the Beazley/Swithinbank connection had been known to his parents, Swithinbank would not have subsequently been allowed to contribute to the LIFE; he would have been consigned to the 'flatterers' section. The fact that he was the son of an Anglican priest, and went on to enjoy a secure career, would be all in his favour.

Swithinbank's Oxford career followed a similar pattern to Flecker's. Swithinbank got a poor second in classics, and in consequence planned to go to Fiji. He came third in the Indian Civil Service Examinations and decided on a career in Burma.

439 NGJ, p.54

440 NGJ, p.52

441 NGJ, p.53

442 Bridge of Fire Copybook, p.119

443 BKJ, p.82

444 BKJ, p.63

445 BKJ, p.94

446 BKJ, p.184

447 BKJ, p.91

448 In *Meredith A Change of Masks A Study of the Novels* by Gillian Beer, The Athlone Press, 1970, p.124, RL Stevenson reports that when a young friend complained that Meredith had based Sir Willoughby on him, Meredith replied, 'No, my dear fellow, he is all of us.' from 'Books which have influenced me. Essays in the Art of Writing.' London, 1905.

449 'Where are there some women like Meredith's?' Letter from Flecker to Savery, 2 August 1910, portion omitted from letter. University of Texas at Austin. The letters of J.E. Flecker, Beaumont Press, 1926.

450 LIFE, p.95

451 LIFE, p.95

452 LIFE, p.95

453 LIFE, p.95

454 Walter Pater (1839–94) published *Appreciations* in 1889

455 NGJ, p.51

456 In the version sent to Sedgwick the second line of this poem is 'Nor the star-sparkle of her eye,'. In the *Book of Kara James* version (which he wrote in March 1904) it is 'Nor remembrance of her eyes.' The chorus of the poem in the version sent to Sedgwick, and published in the LIFE is: 'Good-bye' while in the *Book of Kara James* version it is: 'As her echoing good-byes.'

457 NGJ, p.65

458 NGJ, p.65

459 BKJ, p.96

460 BKJ, p.53

461 NGJ, p.63

[462] BKJ, p.80

[463] CP. First published in *The Bridge of Fire*.

[464] CP. First published in *The Bridge of Fire*.

[465] Hedley Vicars Storey was also a social reformer. In 1907 he brought out the *Oxford Herald*, a Literary Monthly Guide for Social Reform, which cost 1p. It was advertised in *The New Age* magazine.

[466] LIFE, p.97

[467] LIFE, p.97

[468] 'rising' changed to 'conquering' for publication in *36 Poems*

[469] BKJ, p.97

[470] BKJ typewritten, p.31

[471] BKJ typewritten, p.32

[472] *Flecker of Dean Close*. Charles Wilson. Canterbury Press 1946, p.18

[473] *Flecker of Dean Close*. Charles Wilson. Canterbury Press 1946, p.18

[474] *Flecker of Dean Close*, Charles Wilson, Canterbury Press 1946 p.18

[475] NGJ, p.59

[476] NGJ, p.59

[477] This letter was not published in the LIFE, but in NGJ. Sherwood states (p.60) after publishing the letter in NGJ, that Dr. Flecker commented, during the drafting of the LIFE, on his son complaining about his not discussing religious matters with him, which he admitted that after a time was true. [There is no comment on the accusations of lack of affection, that if his son was not his son, he would hate him.]

[478] The *Academy* of 9 November 1907, published a reply of Flecker's, in which he set out why he had written as he had done in 'Oxford Canal' and he had made reference to *Sartor Restartus*.

[479] Byrd, p.33, states that this line suggest the Crucifixion

[480] *The Best Man*, p.2

[481] *A Wiltshire Village*, A. Williams, Duckworth 1912, p.165

[482] *Cotswolds of One Hundred Years Ago*, Alan Sutton, Alan Sutton Publishing 1991, p.43 [Unable to get the precise date of this suicide verified - HW]

[483] *Portraits by Inference*, H. Wolfe, p.18

[484] *Portraits by Inference*, H. Wolfe, p.18

[485] *Portraits by Inference*, H. Wolfe, p.18/19

[486] *The Upward Anguish*, p.135

[487] *The Upward Anguish*, p.135

[488] *Portraits by Inference*, H. Wolfe, p.19

[489] *The Upward Anguish*, p.191

[490] 'The Potato Ghoul', *The Best Man*, p.4

[491] DAVIS, p.19, suggests that Flecker may have been drawing on Keats' 'The Fall of Hyperion' for 'The Potato Ghoul'. If this is so, DAVIS says 'he has turned a symbol of tragedy of human life into a symbol of its own emptiness.'

492 DAVIS suggests that Flecker's 'mists' could be a comment, serious or otherwise, on his own writing, p.19

493 T.M.A. Cooper had stated 'In these Oxford years and afterwards, Roy was, I think in a good deal of distress.' [LIFE, p.101]

494 *Erewhon*, Samuel Butler (first published 1872) edition Cape 1960, p.192

495 As usual when trying to piece together the battle between Dean Close and Flecker, it is difficult to get all the pieces to fit into a convincing picture. Sherwood, in NGJ p.60, tells of visits by Beazley and Savery, but does not give a precise date for the visits, which must have taken place behind JEF's back. Sherwood ties the visits to a paragraph when he mentions the visits and 'Long before the final showdown'. In the LIFE, p.107, it is stated that 'a somewhat unusual circumstance' took place, namely that both Beazley and Savery wrote to Mrs. Flecker about the question of JEF's future career, which had been put to them by Mrs. Flecker, but no mention is made of actual visits.
Reference is made on p.78 of the LIFE about asking Beazley to Dean Close again and that the letter was written soon after a letter of Flecker's in the Trinity term of 1904, but in this letter reference is made to Beazley going in for the Hertford, which was in 1905.

496 Raleigh wrote in a letter to H.H. Turner 9.12.12. 'Very many thanks for your kindness to Flecker I hope Lindsay understood him. His appearance and impression disaffects all disciplinarians. But he's all right, in the wide world.'

497 *A Selection of the letters of Sir Walter Raleigh, 1880–1922.* Methuen 1922

498 *The Upward Anguish*, p.152

499 *King of Alsander*, p.10

500 *King of Alsander*, p.9

501 *King of Alsander*, p.99

502 *Life*, p.99

503 *The Grecians*, CPR p.162

504 C.P.

505 *The Grecians*, p.38

CHAPTER FIVE

506 Nat. Library of Scotland. (Acc.8264). The letter has written on it: 'This is part of a letter James wrote to me about 1908. Dayrell-Reed.'
The drawing in *Ballooning and Aeronautics*, has Reed's initials and the date 1906 printed on it. This points to 1906 rather than ('about 1908') as suggested in the note on Flecker's letter.

507 '*Song*' in September 1905 and 'The Little Song of Her Sorrow' in November 1905. Both published under the pseudonym of Kara James.

508 'Desire' was also published in the *Eclectic* magazine in New York in April 1907.

In *Notes and Queries*, 1972. Three Poems in the *Idler* magazine. Stephen Parry refers to 'Desire' and the reference to it in *The Collected Poems* and the inclusion of it in a letter to Sedgwick. (LIFE p.92). Parry reprints 'The Little Song of Her Sorrows' in *Notes and Queries*.

In the copy sent to Sedgwick there is (following on) the poem 'Song', which begins:

'Not the night of her wild hair,'

The version in *The Book of Kara James* begins:

'Not the remembrance of her eyes'

and the last line of the first verse is 'As her echoing good-byes.'

[509] Goldring's book, which came out before the LIFE, referred to the publication of 'Desire', and he mentioned other poems getting into print at this time, but there are no exact details.

Goldring p.30/31 JEF states: ' think that the first set of verses which Flecker ever got into print in a London paper was the poem called 'Desire' which appeared in the *Idler* in January 1907'. He goes on to say that Flecker 'probably had several little poems in the *Idler*, and other early work was printed in a motor journal, of which a friend was editor.' It is not clear which motor journal Goldring was referring to, as there were at least seven, which as well as extolling the joys of the open road, also explained the mechanics of the motor car. Not many motor journals published poetry. T.S. Mercer who was a schoolfriend of Flecker's at Dean Close, became assistant editor of *The Automobile Engineer*, but had no knowledge until Flecker was dead, that his old schoolfriend was Flecker the poet.

[510] LIFE, p.113

[511] This statement is made in the index of NGJ

[512] NGJ, p.61; also LIFE, p.107

[513] His essay 'N'Jawk' CPR p.35

[514] From the notebook Flecker used to copy out two dozen or more of Beazley's poems. p.1 (BOD)

[515] It is possible that although he was not satisfied with his attempted translation of Baudelaire's poem, the idea remained in his mind and gave him the basis for the inspiration for one of his most successful poems: 'Areiya' the first line of which is 'This place was formed divine for love and us to dwell;'. 'Areiya' is in a notebook that contains published and unpublished verse (1910/11) BOD E186

[516] Revised as 'The Translator and the Children'.

[517] 'children' altered to 'babies'.

[518] LIFE, p.82

[519] A letter signed 'Distracted', which appeared in *The Academy* 10 August 1907, under the heading 'A Question for Literary workers', if not written by Flecker, certainly deals with the subject of noise in a way he would agree with wholeheartedly. The writer of the letter wrote from a house in the suburbs, which he said stood in its own grounds. If his windows were open, the 'romping of children', amongst other noises disturbed

his thoughts, while noise, however great, if it was continuous, did not. He asked the readers of *The Academy* if they could tell him where to obtain 'ear caps'.

[520] Hodgson writes: p.243 'Flecker might, and often did, suffer and suffer acutely. But he always suffered vigorously. His was not the de-humanised, sardonic pain which shivers like a thin, dry, drear wind through *Les Fleurs du Mal.*'

[521] *James Elroy Flecker From School to Samarkand* by T.S. Mercer. The Merle Press 1952 p.14, Mercer states that the letter was signed H.E. Flecker and Mr. Mathews' name was spelled with two tt's. (There was another writer at this time with the surname Matthews, which might be the reason for Flecker's confusion: also Matthew Arnold.)

[522] National Library of Scotland

[523] The rough draft of The Two Sonnets of Bathrolaire, which dealt with sin and punishment and a view of Hades with 'mad lovers' eventually had a few alterations before publication in *The Bridge of Fire.*

[524] NGJ p.64. In a letter of Flecker's written on his birthday, 1906, Sherwood refers to 'a Cambridge friend turned publisher', which may be a reference to Mavrogordato, although Mavrogordato was at Oxford.

[525] Harvard

[526] In *Compton Mackenzie A Life*, Andro Linklater Chatto & Windus 'Mathews would only publish if he were guaranteed against loss'.

[527] T.S. Mercer made this point in his book on Flecker. P.43 *James Elroy Flecker From School to Samarkand*, The Merle 1953.

[528] 'Moreover his desire to rewrite famous works and his translations of other men's conceptions had a parallel to the Eastern poets who attempted to emulate earlier writers by revising their themes and materials;' *Aspect of Islamic Civilisation* p.350. Mary Davis makes this reference in her book: *James Elroy Flecker – A Critical Study.*

[529] *The Grecians*, p.160 CPr

[530] *For What We Are About to Receive'*, Francis Toye, p. 47, 1950

[531] The LIFE stated:
'When the project showed itself to be intolerably unsuccessful, he wrote to his father about the Foreign Consular Service.' LIFE, p.114

[532] The LIFE just stated that they were published 'during 1907', which implied a later period. p. 120.

[533] *The King of Alsander* is not referred to in the LIFE until much later; if they knew he was writing a novel and hoping to get it published at this stage, it was not considered to be of sufficient importance to mention.

[534] The information about Torrington Square in 1917, comes from *Jean Rhys*, Carole Augier, Deutsch, 1990, p.96. Information about Christina Rossetti and Torrington Square from *Christina Rossetti*, Frances Thomas, 1992, Self-Publishing. *Orpen – Mirror to an Age* Bruce Arnold, Jonathan Cape, 1981. The artist Orpen lived in lodgings at No.52 Torrington Square until 1900.

[535] *Author Hunting*, Grant Richards, Hamish Hamilton 1934, p.219

[536] *Author Hunting,* Grant Richards, Hamish Hamilton 1934, p.217

[537] *Author Hunting,* Grant Richards, Hamish Hamilton 1934, p.99

[538] *Author Hunting,* Grant Richards, Hamish Hamilton 1934, p.100

[539] *James Joyce,* Richard Ellman, OUP New and Revised edition, 1982, p.191

[540] LIFE, p.93

[541] *Author Hunting,* Grant Richards, Hamish Hamilton 1934, p.219

[542] *Arthur Symons, Selected Letters 1880–1935* edited by Karl Beckton and John Munro, Macmillan, 1989.

[543] Maurice Woods is described in SLA, p.187, as 'M.H. Woods who was at Trinity with Roy but a year senior to him: at the time this letter was written he was by way of being in politics.' Letter was undated but written Sept./ Oct. 1908.

Humbert Wolfe in *The Upward Anguish* p.102, gives details of the friendship between himself and Gabriel Woods, brother of Maurice Woods. Wolfe gives the impression that Gabriel Woods, of Exeter, was the brother, who was interested in Flecker, the poet.

[544] Princeton University Library

[545] Isabel Davidson is simply mentioned by name by Goldring in his books about Flecker and exactly who she was in relation to Reed is unclear. A poem Flecker wrote in his *Second Book of the Prophet James*, which has no title, has these lines:
Helen of Troy rose up from Hell
Some have hidden life
To live for her alone.
This version is dedicated to I.D. A different version is published in *The Bridge of Fire* (with the dedication). The title the poem was given was 'Destroyer of Ships, Men, Cities'.

[546] Alice Head (1886–1981), daughter of F.D. Head, who was born and died in London, gave an account of her working life in periodicals in her autobiography *It Could Never Have Happened* published by Heinemann, 1939. She was born in Notting Hill Gate, the daughter of a building contractor; her father was a strict Baptist, and her mother a teacher. She had a sister three years older, and a brother who was killed in the Great War. She went on to work for *Woman and Home, Good Housekeeping* and William Randolph Hearst.

[547] Ronald Firbank was said to have been 'mildly victimised by the other pupils, who included an uncle of Miss Nancy Mitford's.' [*The Complete Ronald Firbank* with a preface by Anthony Powell, Gerald Duckworth, 1961, p.6]

[548] LIFE, p.115

[549] LIFE, p.115

[550] The play thus begins like Davidson's *Smith*, which Flecker outlined and quoted in 'John Davidson: Realist'. Davidson's tragic farce, Flecker

described as 'opens in a public-house'. Brown, from Oxford, James and Robertson are discussing the characters of Hallowes, a poet.

551 As the fragment of Flecker's play *The Poet's Tragedy* has no precise date, and it was not written all in one version, it is possible that Cambus could have been based on some of the editorial staff encountered by Goldring at *The Academy*, or later on when he encountered Ford Maddox Ford as editor of *The English Review.*

552 PUL

553 '*Odd Man Out*', Chapman 1935 p.61

554 JEF, p.32

555 Urbana

556 PUL

557 PUL

558 *Reputations*, D. Goldring, Chapman & Hall, p.5, 1920

559 *Collected Poems*

560 Geoffrey George Knox (subsequently Sir Geoffrey George Knox) appeared in books about Flecker as 'J.J. Knox'. In *Reputations – Essays in Criticism* by Goldring (1920) Chapman & Hall Ltd., he was 'a friend in the Foreign Office'. In JEF, Goldring referred to 'J.J. Knox', who afterwards went (I think) to Teheran.' p.36. But in his autobiography *Odd Man Out*, Chapman & Hall, Goldring referred to 'G.G. Knox – who has since acquired fame as Governor of the Saar.' p.72, when recalling a last meeting with Flecker and Knox.
G.G. Knox's education was finished in 1906. (No details are given of this education, in *Sources of British Political Life 1900–51*, vol. 2). He went as student-interpreter to Trinity College in 1906, and two years later he was appointed student-interpreter in the Levant. Transferred to the diplomatic service, became Chairman, Governing Commission of the Saar, 1932–35. Published in 1942 *The Last Peace and the Next*. Died 6 April 1958. Unmarried.

561 Francis Toye, born John Francis Toye on 27.1.83. Went on to Trinity College, Cambridge, as student-interpreter in 1904. Gave up this career and came to London to pursue his interest in music. His autobiography *For What We Have Received* published by Heinemann.

562 *The Athenaeum*, 29 Oct. 1904, Obituary of Laurence Hope by Thomas Hardy.

563 The expedition with Knox is not mentioned in the LIFE. Goldring mentioned the expedition in JEF, which was published in 1922, before the LIFE, in 1925. Also published in *Reputations – Essays in Criticism* by Goldring (1920) Chapman & Hall Ltd.

564 PUL

565 Harvard

566 *The Grecians*, p.118 CPr

567 PUL

568 PUL

569 PUL

570 'to those' is in the original notebook in BOD, omitted from CPr.

571 *The Grecians*, p.142

572 *The Grecians*, p.142

573 'Looking Eastwards' published in the Nation 29ᵗ February 1908

574 SLA, p.177

575 The precise date of *The Bridge of Fire*'s publication is not given; reference
to *The Bridge of Fire* in the LIFE was:
'It appeared, during 1907, in a red paper cover.' [LIFE, p.120]
[*The Bridge of Fire* was first published in September 1907.]
Further mention of *The Bridge of Fire* was made in the LIFE by outlining
the poems that were not republished or republished with a new title.
'Anapaests' is the only poem discussed, it is described as:
'..tinged with anything which can be called decadence, though the word
is used so vaguely that it is difficult to know what some who use it really
mean.'
Flecker crossed through the title and wrote 'Decadent poem', in his own
edition of *The Bridge of Fire*.
The last verse of 'Anapaests' read:
Songs breathed to the tremulous ditties
Of broken and harsh violins
Songs hinting the rose and the vine,
Half drowned in the roar of red cities
And youthfully pleased at their sins,
These songs I adore: they are mine.
The last line the LIFE felt 'was glaringly untrue'.

576 CPr, p.35

577 *Théophile Gautier*, R. Snell. Clarendon Press. Oxford 1982 p.65 quoting
article in La Presse, 18th Dec. 1843

578 Sir John Suckling (1609–42). One of the Metaphysical poets. Gentleman
Poet. His play *Aglaura* produced 1637.

579 Penguin Classics *Charles Baudelaire Selected Poems* Chosen and Selected by
Joanna Richardson 1975

580 University of Texas, at Austin

581 Arthur Symons, a critic, poet and prolific writer, influenced by Browning,
admirer of Walter Pater, member of the Rhymers' Club, friend of Yeats,
Joyce, Olive Schreiner, Symons published in 1900 *The Symbolist Movement
in Literature*. In late September 1908, he suffered a mental breakdown and
was certified insane, but he recovered and continued writing and getting
published.

582 SLA, p.179

583 SLA, p.176

584 Davis, p.11. Gillanders p.35

585 Letter in the Bod. from Flecker to Alice Head, refers to exchanging words with both Miss Head and Lord Alfred Douglas. [Could have been by telephone.]

586 Arthur Machen (1863-1947)

587 *The Life of Lord Alfred Douglas, Spoilt Child of Genius*, by Wm. Freeman, Herbert Joseph Ltd. 1948

588 Edgar Jones, University College of Wales, Aberystwyth, in his '*La Giocosa: James Elroy Flecker's Aesthetic Academy*' (Part 1), June 1973, Durham University Journal 1973 p.271, makes a convincing case for Flecker's poem 'The Young Poet' as a posthumous tribute to Ernest Dowson (1867–1900), basing his case on the fact that there was an article on Dowson by Edgar Jepson (1863–1938) in which in the article 'The Real Ernest Dowson', Jepson described Dowson as 'one of the most distinguished lyric poets of our generation' and went on to say 'I was forced to the conclusion that one of the worst misfortunes which befell that most unfortunate poet was that he found his biographer in Mr. Arthur Symons.'

[It was Arthur Symons (1865–1945) who had praised *The Bridge of Fire*, and it was *The Academy* of whom it could now be said, was the worst misfortune that befell James Elroy Flecker, that his book of poems was reviewed by *The Academy*. A review by Arthur Symons would have served him much better.]

589 In *The Bridge of Fire* – 'the' silent homes

590 GILL page 21, when referring to 'The Young Poet' states 'The Young Poet, for instance was a youth who:
'Loved and sang and sinned
With roses on his brow'
but is now dead, his sins expiated by death and his singing glorified, for his fame survived the wreck of his body. This poem might almost be taken as an epitaph on the poets of the decadence, some of whom had died quite young a few years before.'
GILL gives as examples Dowson and Lionel Johnson (1867–1902)

GILL also states that the poem was possibly intended as an epitaph for Francis Thompson. Francis Thompson died on 13 November, after the publication of 'The Young Poet'. Thompson's epitaph was published in *The Academy* by Wilfred Scawen Blunt on 23 November 1907.
The case for the poem being inspired by the death of Laurence Hope in 1904, is less obvious, although she died on 6 October 1904, at the age of 39, but in his article on Hope, Flecker does refer to her as 'this woman who died so young' in the article he published on her in *The Monthly Review*.
Mary Byrd Davis stated p.28 when referring to 'The Young Poet': 'he created a lyric effect using three-foot lines and occasional feminine rhymes.'
Flecker's poem 'The Poet Francis Thompson' was first written in September 1904 (notebook in BOD)

[591] NEW BOD

[592] Carducci and Heine, published by *The Academy* 29.8.08

[593] The poem called 'A Dream' with the line 'The sun upclomb' was published in *The Academy* on 4 January 1908. The poem is by 'XYZ'.

[594] Stephen Phillips (1864–1915) - published by Elkin Mathews '*New Poems*', published 1907. He had been awarded 100 Guineas by *The Academy*, in January 1898 for his volume of poems published in 1897.

[595] SLA, p.179

[596] A month had elapsed since the publication of Goldring's review but Flecker's response did show great skill.

[597] JEF, p.63

[598] Lord Alfred Douglas

[599] JEF p.62, published 1922

[600] *Arthur Machen*, Reynolds and Charlton, The Richards Press 1963

[601] *Arthur Machen*, Reynolds and Charlton, The Richards Press 1963

[602] '*Odd Man Out*'

[603] SLA, p.179 - Postmarked 5 Nov. 1907

[604] To JACK BEAZLEY
Poetæ, meo sodali

> Gentle Poet, only friend
> Lover of the stars and sun,
> Since our days are at an end,
> Since the older days are done;
>
> Since it seems that nevermore
> May I hope to trail my gown
> Rapturously., as before,
> With my friend in Oxford Town;
>
> Since I so regret a time
> So unprofitably spent,
> Let me send a little rhyme
> From a king in banishment, –
>
> Send a wish that we may see
> Better days, and braver days:
> *Floreas, amico mi!*
> *Floreat Praxiteles.*

The dedication, if nothing else, enabled Jack Beazley to get his proper recognition in the LIFE. P.120 LIFE says that *The Bridge of Fire* is dedicated to his greatest friend.

[605] SLA, p.180

[606] JEF, p.62

[607] SLA, p.185

[608] SLA, p.185

[609] In *Odd Man Out*, p.68 Goldring stated:

'His eyes were always sad eyes, and there was a certain sadness latent in his smile which added to his charm. It has been asserted particularly by critics who never knew him, that the occasional undernote of melancholy was purely factitious. This to my mind, is a very superficial view, based not only on ignorance of Flecker but ignorance of the human heart as well. ... When he described himself as "the lean and swarthy poet of despair," it was probably a joke, but like all jokes worth making there was a substratum of truth in it.'

[610] SLA, p.178

[611] CPr. p.39

[612] CPr. p.45

[613] LIFE, p.115

[614] *Pentheus* published in *The Academy*, 9 April 1910 There is reference in '*The Best Man*' to 'The Passionate Door' by Lilac V. Smith, Library of Modern Masterpieces, vol.1, p.4

[615] SLA, p.179

[616] *The Albany* was advertised in *The Academy*, 5 October 1907: Now Ready - The October issue of *The Albany*, Review p.983, Edited by Charles Roden Buxton, 2s.6d., John Lane, Vigo Street, W. Contents included: Current events; The Working of Universal Suffrage in Austria and In Prison, Maxim Gorki. All subjects dealt with, but a very high literary standard required.

[617] Collected Prose, p.218

[618] PUL

[619] University of Illinois

[620] PUL

[621] PUL

[622] This was the one act play written in 1905. Davis outlines and comments on this play pages 37-42. Typescript in Beinecke Rare Books. Yale University.

[623] PUL

[624] SLA, p.180/1

[625] Reference is made in *The Academy*, 5 October 1907 edition, to '*From the Hills of Dream*', and '*Later Poems*' by Fiona Macleod, under the heading Mr. William Heineman, p.979 'Fiona Macleod' was William Sharp (1855–1905).

[626] A review of '*The Son of the Bondwoman*' by Emilia Pardo Bazan, translated from the Spanish by Ethel Harriet Hearn, published by Lane, appeared in *The Academy*, 26 October 1907, p.68. The opening sentence of the review reads:

'The picture of life in this novel is crude and at times brutal, but it is convincing, in spite of the translation, which is not good.'

[627] From the 'Hills of Dream Threnodies, Sons and Later Poems' by Fiona Macleod was published by Heinemann, 1901. (Unable to trace any review of work by Fiona Macleod in The Academy for this period.)

[628] BOD The letter written to Alice Head, is on Dean Close stationery, but it is a sheet that he must have first used for a letter to aunt and uncle, as it ends:
'when you next see me!
With best wishes for the New Year.
Your loving nephew Roy F.'

[629] 'A Christmas Carol' was revised as 'Masque of the Magi' it was set to music by Heller Nicholls the music master at Dean Close and performed in Canterbury Cathedral. (SLA, p.186)

[630] 'To the World and a Poet a Thousand Years Hence' was published in the *Living Age*, 29 February 1908, and revised as 'To the Poet a Thousand Years Hence'.

[631] Mary Davis makes this point p.63

[632] See Chapter Six, p.220

[633] NGJ p.84, Sherwood states:- 'His own letters in the early month of 1908 suggest that he was finding life as a schoolmaster very tiring. he was "utterly worn out" when he left Mill Hill. A month later he complained of being "rather ill and feverish".'

[634] PUL

[635] LIFE, p.118

[636] PUL

[637] LIFE, p.118

[638] NGJ, p.75

[639] This Hodgson stated in a footnote to be *The Bridge of Fire*, published in 1907, which is interesting, as on the next page of the LIFE, in order to account for Flecker's great weariness at this time, she suggested that it 'was soothed by the coming of that unique moment in a writer's life – the appearance of his first book of importance.' This statement gave the impression that Flecker's book of importance came out in the spring of 1908, instead of September the year before. Hodgson thus placed more importance on '*The Last Generation*' (which was published in an expanded form, in 1908) than the two previous Flecker books.

[640] NGJ, p.76

[641] PUL

[642] PUL

[643] Foreign Office Directory

CHAPTER SIX

[644] John Sherwood (NGJ) p. 76 outlines proposals that would have meant that Flecker would never have to ask his father for money again.

Sherwood states that Dr. Flecker's replies are missing, and it is difficult to decide where faults lay when proposals did not work out.

[645] SLA Undated letter postmarked at Cambridge 1 May 1908, p.182–3

[646] He wrote to Frank Savery on 8 April 1910 (SLA) p.189, and explained to him that the cost of typing a manuscript could be had for 6d. per thousand words, which would mean that even at five pounds, the cost of typing *The King of Alsander* was a more expensive estimate than it need be, and he could have got the job done much more cheaply.

[647] *The New Age* was an independent weekly review of politics, literature and art; the circulation by the autumn of 1908 had risen to more than 20,000 a week (price 1d.). Contributors (who got no payment) included G.B. Shaw (a financial backer), G.K. Chesterton (whose brother Cecil, a freelance journalist, worked mainly for the *New Age* between 1907–1912). An ambitious woman journalist, Beatrice Hastings, who lived with the editor, was on the staff. The editor was, from the end of 1907, Alfred Richard Orage (1873–1934). Other contributors were Arnold Bennett and John Davidson. In *John Davidson; Poet of Armageddon* by J. Benjamin Townsend (Yale University Press) 1961: page 469 states:
'On another occasion the *New Age*, an advanced socialist organ, accepted one of his poems for publication. The poet accompanied his contribution with a letter in which he said he had read the journal for some weeks with great pleasure and profit.
Subsequently discovering its close affiliation with the Socialist movement, he wrote a letter in a towering rage, withdrawing his endorsement. He objected in the strongest terms to the appearance of his poem under such a flag and declared that had he known that the *New Age* supported such an "advanced view" nothing on earth would have induced him to write a line for it. His anger was not allayed when the editor gently hinted to him that he was in all probability the only man in Great Britain who could read the journal for weeks on end and not discover its political views.'
(*The Manchester Courier*, 29 March 1909). By that date Davidson was already dead.

[648] JEF, p.38. Goldring refers to 'some review', not mentioning *Country Life*, where he had worked as a sub-editor.

[649] John Mavrogordato, in his diary (BOD) Jan. 21st (1904), when having dinner with Compton McKenzie, mentions that '*The Napoleon of Notting Hill*' was delightful.
'I have been reading Max Nordau's *Degeneration*, a splendid work, very mistaken in parts, but wholesome as an antidote;' (letter to Sedgwick from Oxford, dated 14 March 1904 (LIFE) p.90.
'Unquestionably, however, the immediate source of Flecker's inspiration was Max Nordau's once famous book, *Degeneration*.' Gill, Vol.2, p.346.
'At this time he became violently anti-Christian. Ostensibly, this change was due to the works of Max Nordau whom he used to quote to me.' (LIFE, p.68). Piece by Stanley McKelvie.

[650] C. Pr., p.3

[651] C. Pr., p.4

[652] C.Pr. p.22

[653] C.Pr. p.24

[654] C.Pr. p.32

[655] C.Pr. p.27

[656] *Book of Kara James* (BL)

[657] SLA letter postmarked 21 April 1908, Cambridge, written at Dean Close, p.182

[658] Peckham – promoted to be an Assistant on 7 September 1908 – was still in Cambridge. His college was Corpus. He arrived in Constantinople at the end of summer, 1908.

[659] Flecker wrote of the 'menace of solitude'. 'This sent him moving and set him longing – longing very definitely for human companionship. Thus he fell short of the self-sufficient man recommended by Aristotle, for which the reader may devoutly praise the Lord'. *King of Alsander* p.34–5 G.P. Putnam's Sons, New York & London, 1914.
He wrote from Capel Curig (Easter, 1903), 'With a companion is one thing, solitude is another. Yet I enjoy it, because I enjoy everything....' LIFE, p.73

[660] He wrote to Sedgwick: 'But, of course, Switzerland, seen under whatever drawbacks of tourists and solitude, is an opener of the eyes to the Nature lover.' LIFE, p.93

[661] Flecker wrote to his father: 'I don't care if Chamonix is as flat as a pancake. I want to work and to be with someone...' LIFE, p.81

[662] He wrote to his parents: 'There is something very desolate about these Eastern Counties, and I often wonder how the garden is getting on. Are there any flowers yet about?' He had been shutting himself up and working all day, when he wrote about the desolation of his surroundings. LIFE, p.131. Feb. 1909

[663] LIFE, p.124 (letter to mother)

[664] In *The Camels Must Go* (Faber & Faber 1961) Sir Reader Bullard writes: 'we all started on Arabic, Turkish and Persian the first day. This was a bad method. The best way would have been to devote one term entirely to Arabic, which entered largely (and still, in spite of linguistic nationalism, enters to a considerable extent) into Turkish and Persian; then to begin the language of the country to which one was to be posted; and to leave the third language until the last two or three terms. This however would have meant that in some terms the lecturers in Turkish and Persian (unhappy refugees both of them) would have had no work to do since the Student Interpreters were their only pupils, and we were sacrificed to administrative convenience.' p.46

[665] Charles Raven left Uppingham for Caius in 1904 and by the time he and Flecker were reunited in 1908, he had obtained a BA and he was then a research student. Raven had already won prizes and he had been editor

of his College Magazine, *The Caian,* and then editor jointly with R.M. Pattison-Muir of the most famous Cambridge magazine, *The Granta.*

[666] During the course of his editorship of *The Granta* he commissioned three men from Trinity to write a piece exposing the selling of laboratory slides before examinations. Raven was threatened with a libel action but was able to prove his case. (*Charles Raven,* F.S. Dillistone, Hodder and Stoughton, 1975). He was able to prove what he had written was true.

[667] Goldsworthy Lowes Dickinson, 1862–1932, Philosopher, Fellow of King's. Wrote: *A Greek View of Life* (1896), *Letters to John Chinaman* (1901)

[668] George Gilbert Aime Murray, 1866–1957. Elected Fellow of New College, Oxford 1905; elected Oxford Professor of Greek, October 1908

[669] LIFE, p.124

[670] Gillanders, Vol.2, p.35

[671] It was Jane Harrison's *Prolegomena to the study of Greek Religion* that Jack Beazley was studying during the Easter vacation with Flecker at Capel Curig, LIFE, p.73

[672] *Jane Ellen Harrison, A Portrait from Letters* by Jessie Stewart, London. Merlin Press 1959. *Reminiscences of a Student's Life,* originally published Hogarth Press, London, 1965.

[673] In the LIFE, p.124, in a tactful piece, Raven wrote: 'The literary Society which Flecker originated, and which included Rupert Brooke ... was typical of the time. Several of its members were genuinely original, men of free and fearless outlook prepared to test life faithfully and tell the truth about it; Flecker belonged to this group. But others were mere poseurs, bundles of rather nasty affectation ... I am afraid that the effect of the society on all its members was bad.'

[674] NGJ, p.32. This reference to scandal is omitted when quoting McKelvie's piece in the LIFE, p.68.

[675] In his book *A Wanderer's Way,* Hopkinson, 1928, Raven made the following observation: [pp. 55–6]
'The aesthetic movement was still strong, and in my fourth year, I was one of the original members of a society which has since achieved a reputation. [Although not mentioned by name, the society is most likely to be the Fish and Chimney.] We met to read plays and started decorously enough with the *Playboy of the Western World.* Next week it was a Shaw, and then, I think *Ghosts.* So far splendid, if not very constructive. Then we lapsed into Congreve, whose indecency is at least subtle and graced by wit. And so to Wycherley – and my departure ......
To read such stuff in company makes me hot and uncomfortable; ......
For the homosexual I have a vast sympathy and often a warm affection, though his peculiarity despite the Freudians is utterly outside my experience. But when he runs riot in a university and all sorts of dirty souls catch the cult, the consequences are neither refined nor enlightening.'

676 *Jane Ellen Harrison The Mask and The Self.* Sandra J. Peacock. Yale New Haven and London, 1989, p.101

677 Kenneth Woollcombe was born on 11.7.1888, son of William Frederick Reynolds Boyce and Sarah Louise Boyce (formerly Griffiths) at 1 Warwick Road, London. By the time he came to Cambridge, he used the name Woollcombe-Boyce.

678 Letter 25 May 1908, LIFE, p.124. Boyce identified only as K, but in NGJ Sherwood refers to Boyce when quoting reference to dullard.

679 *The Scholar's Italian* Book, 1911 – An Introduction to the Study of the Latin Origins of Italian; published by David Nutt, 1911.

680 LIFE, p.134

681 As he became editor of *The Caian* in 1909 it is reasonable to assume he was already involved in the running of the magazine itself in 1908.

682 *The Caian,* Easter 1910 Review of *Thirty-Six Poems.* Also Flecker's 'A Visit and an Invitation' (which was reprinted in the LIFE, p.135, to which Boyce contributed his memories of Flecker and himself together at Cambridge).

683 PUL

684 LIFE, p.124–5

685 16 January 1909

686 *Ronald Firbank.* Miriam B. Benkovitz. Weidenfeld, 1969. p.98–9

687 *The Granta's* Review continued: 'But he still has to perfect his instrument whereby he expresses poetic thoughts. The lines 'To Francis Thompson' and 'The Ballad of Hampstead Heath' are, to our thinking, the most real expressions of the author's self in the book.'
The Granta and Its Contributors (1889–1914) compiled by F.A. Rice, introduced by A.A. Milne, Constable 1924, refers to the conflicting views of *The Granta's* admiration for the poet and the mockery of his appearance and dislike of his personality, p.43. Raglan Spencer is described as 'the Heavy Villain from Queens whose lash has spared neither friend or foe', in a further quotation from *The Granta* of 16 Jan. 1909, when Spencer was relinquishing the editor's chair.

688 *Life and Letters*, volume II, January 1929–June 1929, Sybil Pye, p.373

689 Frances Darwin (1886–1960) perhaps best known now for her poem 'To A Lady Seen From The Train: O Why do you walk through the fields in gloves, /Missing so much and so much?/ O fat white woman whom nobody loves,'. Her grandfather was Charles Darwin, and she married Francis Cornford (1874–1943), a classical scholar (who played the part of Comus) who was a close scholar friend of Jane Harrison, who was in love with him and devastated by his marriage.

690 *Rupert Brooke* by C. Hassell, Faber and Faber 1964.

691 'Edwinson, meanwhile, gazed intently on the young man, and since he held ['he held' originally was 'he was the lover'] the neo-pagan idea of Greece, mentally raved about Apollo. Yet no one could have been more unlike the swarthy, straight-nosed Greeks than this merry-eyed young

man, with long, light hair, high cheek-bones, and vivid colouring'. (The Three Englishmen, p.95, *The Grecians*) (CPr)

[692] Brooke had met Lytton Strachey (1880–1932) and his younger brother James (1887–1967) during his schooldays, and at the age of six he had played cricket on the beach at St. Ives with the eleven-year old Virginia Stephen (later Woolf). Christopher Hassall states in his *Life of Rupert Brooke* that the families came to St. Ives in 1899, but by this time Virginia Stephen's mother had died and the St. Ives holiday home had been given up in favour of one in the Isle of Wight.

[693] Hugh Dalton (1887–1967), the same age as Brooke, son of Canon Dalton of Windsor (former tutor to the Royal Princes), Etonian and future Socialist politician.

[694] Gerald Frank Shove (1887–1947) also educated at Uppingham (arrived after Flecker had left) and King's. Changed from classics to economics. Married a cousin of Virginia Stephen.

[695] Philip Noel-Baker (1889–1982), later Lord Philip Noel-Baker, M.P., winner of Nobel Peace Prize.

[696] Francis Birrell (1889–1935)

[697] Reference to Francis Birrell was given in the LIFE as 'I have made a great friend of Augustine Birrell's respected son', p.131, but this was in the Lent term of 1909. It would seem that Dean Close or Flecker thought it important to mention Birrell was the son of a well-known politician rather than a step-grandson of Tennyson (see Chapter Two).

[698] Richard Deacon, *The Cambridge Apostles, A History of Cambridge University's elite Intellectual Secret Society*. Robert Boyce Ltd., 1985, p.65

[699] Professor Giles's anthology of Chinese poems (*Chinese Poetry in English Verse* Herbert A. Giles, MA LLD (Aberd.) Professor of Chinese, University of Cambridge, Quaritch 1898) was much admired by James Strachey and his brother Lytton. Lytton wrote an appreciation of Professor Giles's anthology in the *New Quarterly* and the *Living Age* in the autumn of 1908. *The Living Age* had published 'To The World and A Poet 1,000 Years Hence' by Flecker on 29 February 1908 and 'Looking Easterwards' in April 1908.
Also the *New Age* on 11 July 1908, whose publishing house had published Flecker's '*The Last Generation*' in May 1908, published an article by a young poet, F.S. Flint, who declared (11 July 1908): 'To the poet who can catch and render, like these Japanese, the brief fragments of his soul's music, the future lies open.'
Michael Holroyd refers to James Strachey's reading of Professor Giles's book, in *Lytton Strachey, The Unknown Years 1880–1910* Wm. Heinemann p.317

[700] Lytton Strachey's jealous character, and the reasons for it, are outlined in *Maynard Keynes*, De Moggridge. Routledge, 1992, p.109.

[701] 'James Elroy Flecker, who made no particular impression' on him; 'he lunched with Swithinbank on strawberries and cream, and saw Jack

Beazley resplendently beautiful with high complexion, curling red-golden hair and charming affectionate manners;' p.320–21.

Lytton Strachey, The Unknown Years 1880–1910 Michael Holroyd Wm. Heinemann. 1967.

Lytton Strachey took a dislike to Arthur Schloss 'and could see nothing good in his poetry. He declared that the translations were not grammatical and greatly inferior to Giles' version etc., etc., *Great Friends* p.176, David Garnett, Macmillan 1979. Garnett goes on to refer to a personal quarrel 'among the older Bloomsburries'. This indicates that Flecker was not alone in being the object of Strachey's dislike, as he was not alone in being disliked by Raglan Spencer. In a letter to Lytton Strachey, dated 5 March 1906 from J.M. Keynes:

'have just come away from tea with Beazley and it is plain that he is quite unspoilt....'

A man called Flecker was there and, according to Swithin, is always there ... I am not enthusiastic about Flecker, – semi-foreign, with a steady languid flow and, I am told, an equally steady production of poems and plays which are just not bad ....'

The Life of John Maynard Keynes, R.F. Harrod, p.132–3, Pelican Biographies, first published 1951, Pelican Books 1972

[702] JEF, p.39

[703] Brigid Brophy in *Prancing Novelist, In Praise of Ronald Firbank*, Macmillan, 1973 p.110-114, explains the reasons why Firbank caricatured Rupert Brooke, in his novel *Vainglory*. Brophy explains that Winsome Brookes cannot be seen as a caricature of Brooke alone, but that Winsome Brookes is both Brooke and Firbank, and the choice of 'Winsome' not only was a reference to Brooke's looks, but can be seen as a reference to Marsh and the Churchill family. Brophy quotes from *Vainglory* also to explain Firbank's feelings towards Rupert Brooke, when Mrs. Shamefoot says about Winsome Brookes:

'Without any positive reasons for disliking him, she found him perhaps too similar in temperament to herself to be altogether pleased.'

From information about the Brooke/Firbank/Winsome Brookes/Marsh connections, it is possible to see a Flecker/Firbank/Guy Fawkes/Nicolson/Marsh connection. Mr. Guy Fawkes is a character in *Vainglory* and Flecker's birthday was 5 November, which makes Guy Fawkes an obvious choice of name, but Vyvyan Holland, a friend of Firbank's, thought that his birthday was 5 November, and not 3 November, the date his birth was registered. Holland, a son of Oscar Wilde, had been at Scoones, also studying to be a diplomat; a career, he chose not to follow. Another friend, Harold Nicolson, did follow a diplomatic career, was in Constantinople as Third Secretary, in 1912, where Firbank met up with him. Firbank, like Holland, had not followed up his original career as a would-be diplomat. Mr. Guy Fawkes was the son of Mrs. Guy Fawkes, who in *Vainglory* read aloud a letter from her son 'a dutiful diplomat who, even when fast asleep, it was said, suggested the Court of St. James.' 'Just now,'

she read, 'the Judas trees are coming in to flower. They are neither red nor violet, and at evening they turn into a sort of agony of rose.'
Reader Bullard wrote to Constantinople being at its best in spring when 'the Judas trees challenging the cypresses' in *The Camels Must Go.*
Flecker's maternal grandmother's maiden name was Fox.
Vainglory was published in the spring of 1915, too late for Brooke or Flecker to read the published version, but Brooke at least could have known about Winsome Brookes before publication, and Brooke kept in touch with Flecker, after leaving Cambridge.
It is also possible to see an element of Flecker in Winsome Brookes as Flecker and Firbank were also similar in temperament, they both had joined the Fabians, and both had sado-masochistic tendencies. Flecker invented the character Winsome Torment in his poem 'The Hamman Name'. In *The Grecians*, p.71, Flecker wrote 'You can tell a boy that the word we pronounce fewsha is connected with the German for a fox even if he hasn't read and could not read the second part of Faust.' Firbank had a German governess as a child, and was supposed to be taking German classes at Cambridge, but failed to master German to any degree. (*Prancing Novelist*, p.228). So this could be a dig at Firbank by Flecker because Firbank was obsessed with flowers and flower names (which is dealt with in Brophy's book). So with the similar sounds of Fawkes and Fox this could be seen as a reference to Firbank; Nicolson caricatured Firbank under the name Lambert Orme in his book *Some People.*
One reason why no Flecker connection is made to any of Firbank's characters is the lack of documentary evidence (apart from Winsome Torment) of Firbank and Flecker meeting at Cambridge, but with an Uppingham, Scoones, Fabian Cambridge connection and as they shared connections or friendships with Brooke, Marsh, Nicolson they had ample opportunity to meet or at least know about each other.
Hassall, in order to show how Brooke made casual callers his excuse for neglected work, used as examples:
'.. now [it was] Ronald Firbank, leaning against the chimneypiece and looking witty, and now it was the poet Flecker, looking swarthy, who had dropped over from Caius. It was maddening.' [RBH, p.174]
Flecker's name crops up in *Some People*, p.50, when Nicolson writes:
'While I dabbled in Bakst and Flecker, Lambert had already reached the van.'
Brophy in *Prancing Novelist*, pps.107-9, gives reasons for the choice of the name Lambert Orme for Firbank. Lambert from Lambert Simnel and Orme from the French for Elm. [Firbank was converted to Catholicism, and Orme also could be seen as an anagram of Rome.]
A further clue to the use of Winsome Torment is in Flecker's poem 'The Hamman Name', which is about Winsome Torment in a Turkish Bath. Firbank was sent after Uppingham to Buxton, which had natural mineral and thermal baths. Buxton was chosen by his parents so that Firbank's health would benefit, as well as his studies, from attending a

cramming establishment. *Ronald Firbank, A Biography*, Miriam J. Benkovitz, Weidenfeld & Nicolson, 1970, p.26

[704] *Albert in Oxford, The Upward Anguish.* Humbert Wolfe, Cassell 1938, p.109–110

[705] Humbert Wolfe refers to Albert Rothenstein who 'trumped everybody's tricks. From Victor Hugo to Monet there was not a European name that did not figure in his personal acquaintance'. (*Portraits by Inference*, Humbert Wolfe, Methuen, p.18)

[706] Frederic Hillersdon Keeling (born 28.3.86), whose late father had been a solicitor, was educated at Winchester and entered Trinity on a Major Scholarship in 1904; his mother by that time was also dead. He was already a socialist at this time, and one influence, not surprisingly was a mother figure – Emily Townshend (1849–1934) – at whose flat in Earl's Court, 'Ben' Keeling used to meet and discuss Guild Socialism.* She was also a friend of C.P. Scott of the *Manchester Guardian*, and she married a first cousin of the wife of G.B. Shaw. Keeling eventually married her daughter Rachel, and a book was published after Keeling's death in the Great War (1916) on the Somme. He wrote to Emily Townshend, and these letters were of a very personal nature and reveal much about the tortured spirit of Keeling. H.G. Wells wrote the introduction. Keeling became the first assistant editor of *The New Statesman*.

Keeling was asked to organise a Fabian meeting in the Lent Term of 1906 by 'Dicky' Coit of King's. John Collings Squire was appointed Secretary. Jack Squire (born 2.4.86) History Scholar, St. John's College. Author of *Poems and Baudelaire Flowers*, which Squire published at his own expense in 1909, The New Age Press did the printing. Squire came to London with Keeling in 1906. He married Eileen Wilkinson, a niece of E.W. Hornung (educated at Uppingham, creator of Raffles) who was a member of the Fabians; Squire did not know Flecker well, he had met him only once or twice in undergraduates' rooms at Cambridge, but was an important factor in the establishment of Flecker's posthumous fame. Squire was described by his biographer Patrick Howarth as the 'most generous of men', a quotation from a letter to Squire from Clifford Bax, who was quoting Siegfried Sassoon. Squire's biography was published in 1936 by Hutchinson. Squire was the future editor of James Elroy Flecker's *Collected Poems*, published in 1916.

Amber Reeves was the first Treasurer. The Fabian Society of Cambridge was addressed by Beatrice Webb and Sydney Webb, G.B. Shaw, H.G. Wells and Keir Hardie. There were joint meetings with the Oxford Fabians founded in 1895.

Squire's generosity extended towards Raglan Spencer who was best man at Squire's wedding, and Squire named his first son Raglan.

* Guild Socialism was a rival to Fabianism and was outlined in a series of articles in the *New Age* by S.G. Hobson. Guild Socialism 'broadened the attacks on the economic system by moving the emphasis of criticism from

bad conditions and unemployment to the notion of employment itself.'
Lives and Letters, John Carswell, Faber & Faber, 1978

[707] JEF, p.39

[708] JEF, p.39–40

[709] JEF, p.39–40

[710] He had spoken against Socialism at an Oxford Society

[711] JEF, p.40

[712] In the original manuscript of *Don Juan* these lines are:
Man at the Foreign Office I suppose. No, but I
shouldn't fit in to Politics; you've got to hold
other people's ideas. The diplomatic now –
there you needn't have any ideas at all.
No, I shouldn't fit in. For instance, I don't like
the idea of this war.
(MSS. Cheltenham, p.44)

[713] LIFE, p.95–96

[714] JEF, p.40

[715] *Portraits by Inference*, Humbert Wolfe, Methuen 1934, p.15

[716] Leah Tappin writing of her time at Cambridge, when she was eighteen, in
her book *A Life for Education*, Gollancz 1970: 'I had only been in residence
a few days when I received a note on King's College paper signed by
Hugh Dalton, of whom I had never heard. It gave his credentials and said
that the Rev. Stewart Headlam had asked him to call in the hope that my
college authorities would allow him to introduce me to the University
Fabian Society. Later, I saw that note from Stewart Headlam. It said that I
came from a rather stuffy middle-class family – Methodist and Liberal in
politics – but I had the makings of a good Socialist, provided I did not slip
back into the atmosphere of a Women's Training College.' p. 34.
Leah Tappin went on to relate (p.37):
'The Fabian Society taught me a thing or two – it certainly knocked off
some of my spots of innocence. Many things discussed left me a trifle
bewildered. I had never heard of homosexuality, but a frank, open debate
on the subject, which sixty years ago followed exactly the same lines as
Wolfenden, made me understand suddenly my grandfather's outraged
feelings at the sentence on Oscar Wilde.'
Leah Tappin married Will Manning in July 1914, and stayed on as a
married teacher; an unusual event in 1914. She became a member of the
Labour National Executive and a MP.

[717] The Fabian Summer School was opened at the end of July 1907 at Pen-
yr-Allt, Merioneth, N. Wales. It was started independently of the Fabian
Society as six members put up capital and had the financial responsibility
and the Fabians arranged the lectures and the administration of the
buildings.

[718] Brooke was also a book reviewer and in particular he had reviewed (in *The Cambridge Review*) *The Oxford Book of French Verse*, which had been brought out by his mentor W. St. John Lucas in 1907.

In *The Grecians* p.164 CPr: Referring to *The Oxford Book of French Verse*, Flecker writes 'it is a tolerable anthology, not much superior in anything but length to that admirable sixpenny *Cent Meilleurs Poemes* and woefully inferior to that splendid collection, *The Oxford Book of English Verse.*'

Lucas had already published a prose fantasy called *The Marble Sphinx*, which Brooke had read in manuscript while still at Rugby School. The publisher was Elkin Mathews.

Hassall suggests that this book was the origin of Flecker's *Hassan*. But, as has already been seen, *The Marble Sphinx* was reviewed in *The Academy*, of 18 January 1908, possibly by Flecker himself.

Hassall writes: 'Within a few months, early in 1908, Elroy Flecker came up to Cambridge as an advanced student in Oriental Languages attached to Caius, and began his acquaintance with Brooke. He would certainly have been told all about *The Marble Sphinx* and if he bought or borrowed it he would have discovered a writer of "jewelled" language who was intrigued with sadism and the idea of a gross and corpulent man associating with a girl of delicate youth and beauty such as, not long after, Flecker himself was to portray with more artistry in the love of Hassan for Yasmin.' RBH, p.131

If this is possible, it could be also true that, whilst this idea was intriguing him, Flecker was also fascinated by the real life adventures of Auriel Stein, which were being reported in *The Times* that same year, as he lead the Central Asian Expedition to the Caves of the Thousand Buddhas on The Journey to Samarkand.

If *The Marble Sphinx* can be taken as an influence on the origin of *Hassan*, then the No plays of Japan, eventually translated by Arthur Waley, a member of the Brooke circle, could be taken as a similar sort of influence on the conception of *Hassan*. That is if Waley brought the No plays to Flecker's attention in the same way as Brooke was assumed to have brought *The Marble Sphinx* to his attention. The No plays are described as revealing the tragedies of dispossessed or thwarted lovers. As in so many ways the formality and lyric freshness of the words belie the horrors they describe; (Introduction to *A Half of Two Lives – A Personal Memoir* by Alison Waley, Weidenfeld and Nicolson, 1982. Hilary Spurling.

[719] Brooke's father, William Parker Brooke, was a schoolmaster at Fettes College in Edinburgh and married the sister of another master, the Rev. Charles Cotterill, Ruth Mary, who held the post of matron in her brother's House, Glencorse. Her uncle, the Bishop of Edinburgh, married the couple in 1879.

[720] This argument is outlined in *Great Friends*, David Garnett, Macmillan, 1979.

[721] From letter in King's College Library.

[722] JEF, p.39

[723] *Carbonari Ball and Change – A Bibliography of Arthur Waley.* Allen and Unwin, 1966, by Francis John.

[724] Goldsworthy Lowes Dickinson: 'It was in a very different spirit that he approached China. He came to her as a lover, who worshipped afar for years.' *E.M. Forster.* Goldsworthy Lowes Dickinson, Edward Arnold, 1934, p.142.

[725] *Memoirs of an Aesthete,* Harold Acton, Hamish Hamilton Paperback 1984, pp.140–1

[726] In one version of Flecker's poem 'Invitation', written to Beazley, he ended the poem with the line 'That you are mute and have no tales to tell.' (B. of Fire Copybook).

[727] University of Illinois at Urbana-Champaign

[728] LIFE, p.257–8

[729] English renderings of these are given in Captain Cranmer Byng's *A Lute of Jade.*

[730] English renderings of these are given in Captain Cranmer Byng's *A Lute of Jade.*

[731] '...'stalk of jade' was the male member, the 'golden lily' the female; that peach flowers are sexual images;' *Stalks of Jade* Renderings of Chinese Erotic Verse, Martin Booth, The Menard Press, 1976

[732] Ivy Compton Burnett eventually embodied in her novel *Pastors and Masters,* published in 1927, the experience and feelings she absorbed in these prewar years and the life the young men enjoyed but which was denied to her in the same way.

[733] *The Secret River* by Rose Macaulay was published by John Murray in 1909. Subsequent novels of Rose Macaulay, such as *Views and Vagabonds* published in 1912, use the writer's experiences of her friendship with Rupert Brooke.
Rose Macaulay, a Writer's Life, Jane Emery, John Murray 1991, outlines Rose Macaulay's relationship with Rupert Brooke and his circle.

[734] *The Grecians,* C.P., p.107

[735] It is likely that Birrell, as a member of the Brooke circle, had met Flecker before 1909 (the date given in the LIFE) and the relationship deepened from 1909. Birrell contributed in length, details of his friendship for the LIFE.

[736] Birrell in later years contributed to a long piece for the LIFE, p.147 and also in *The Nation* and *The Atheneum* 29 Sept. 1923. V. Sackville-West in her review of *The Life of James Elroy Flecker,* 7 Feb. 1925, says: 'The five pages of Mr. Francis Birrell's letter contain more real information than the whole of the book put together.'

[737] LIFE, p.149

[738] *The Academy,* 9 November 1907.

[739] *Maynard Keynes, An Economist's Biography,* D.E. Moggridge, London and New York, 1991, Routledge, p.838

740 But a brief footnote in the LIFE, p.148, contradicts this statement of Birrell's. 'As a matter of fact there was no sign of consumption till 1911. He contracted the disease in Constantinople.' In the obituary in Cheltenham's *The Looker On* on 9 Jan. 1915, it is stated: 'in the Turkish capital he seems to have contracted the disease from which he died'. John Sherwood (NGJ, p.84) states with medical hindsight, that Flecker showed signs of undiagnosed TB as early as 1908 after leaving Mill Hill school.

741 LIFE, p.125

742 LIFE, p.125

743 Birrell referred to this in his piece for the LIFE.

744 The double standard extended in some ways to Brooke's life at King's where his father had been, and his father's brother was Dean. Brooke did not live with his Uncle Alan, but friction resulted between them. Brooke enjoyed more freedom in his rooms in the Fellows' Buildings, as these were also lived in by the young, and unmarried dons. One was Oscar Browning (1837–1923), an eccentric College Lecturer and University Lecturer in History. H.E. Wortham in *Victorian Eton and Cambridge* wrote: 'OB took up with young men either because it flattered his vanity to detect unsuspected genius – the same sort of pleasure some people get from backing an outsider – or because their youth and good looks attracted him.' By 1908, aged 71, he had lost his posts but remained a Fellow of King's.
Brooke and Dalton, after a late evening at The Carbonari, had continued the discussion at the bottom of the staircase that led to their rooms and Lowes Dickinson had told them to get to bed as he could not sleep because of the noise they were making. Next day, when they apologised and the subject of their discussions disclosed, Brooke and Dalton were told that Dickinson would have joined them. (*Rupert Brooke*, C. Hassall, Faber and Faber Ltd.)

745 LIFE, p.125 letter to his mother .... 'Lunched with my tutor yesterday. Dull. He doesn't teach me anything, only looks after my morals. It is a Cambridge custom.'

746 Son of Sir Benjamin Chapman Browne, Engineer.

747 Formerly Alice Caroline Blackburne Daniell (daughter of Francis Henry Blackburne Daniell, Barrister), aged 26 when she married Browne, aged 44.

748 *Last of the Dragomans* (Turkey 1899–1908), Sir Andrew Ryan, Bles, 1951, p.50

749 LIFE, p.125

750 LIFE, p.133, letter to his parents: 'Letter from J. who is being frozen with cold at Athens.'

751 Carducci and Heine. Review of *Poems by Carducci*, translated by M. Holland and Heine's *Book of Songs* HEINE'S translated by J. Todhunter. The Academy, 29th August, 1908, p.204.
Gio Sue Carducci (1835–1907), Italian poet, Nobel Prize 1906

Heinrich Heine (1797–1856), German Romantic poet. Some of the poems set to music by Schubert and Schumann.

752 Although when putting this fact in the LIFE, Jack remains 'J' in the text.

753 SLA letter from 10 Jesus Lane, which F.S. thinks was October 1908 or Sept., but it is most likely the latter, p.183.

754 SLA, p.183

755 The poem that was eventually given the title (p.75, p.150 revised) 'To a Poet a Thousand Years Hence', started life in the *Bridge of Fire Copybook* with the title 'To a Friend a Thousand Years Hence'. Also 'To an Unknown Friend, Dedication of a Story' was first published in *The Nation* on 11 January 1908, and on 4 April in *Living Age*. Savery refers to a version of this poem being sent to him in November 1907. Frank Savery was sent the first version of this poem in the autumn of 1907.

756 Published in *Collected Poems*.

757 Published in *Collected Poems*.

758 'Love, the Baby' was first published as 'Baby Love' in *The Nation* 25 January 1908.

759 Before republishing it in his anthology *Thirty-Six Poems*, the last two verses were crossed through and a third and final verse inserted.

760 The repetition of hands in this line is a similar idea to the one he liked in Dollie Redford's poem, reviewed by him in 'More Recent Poetry', *The Academy*, 6.11.07, p.83, see Chapter Five. Mary Byrd Davis, p.74, mentioned that Gautier was fascinated by hands.

761 original 'found' *Bridge of Fire Copybook* p. 82

762 Goldring, (p.133) JEF writes that: 'Up to 1910 he still wanted, for some unknown reason, to write poems about London, and he retained enough affection for his failures in this direction to print two of the worst. 'The [sic] Ballad of the Londoner' does not come off'. Goldring does not attach much importance it seems, to the fact that Flecker was born a Londoner, and he had happy memories of times in London with Beazley and Goldring too, when they crossed the Thames and met often in the Brixton flat of a lady who appreciated young poets, and this as well as the influence of Davidson could have been the inspiration of 'Ballad of the Londoner'.

763 Gillanders writes 'The [sic] Ballad of the Londoner' on the other hand does not come off because of the feebleness of its subject matter. It has only three stanzas, two of which evoke a scene and promise a theme which is allowed to fizzle out in a vague and wavering third stanza. One is impatient with this slight poem because the opening lines are perfect in their rhythm and realism' [he quotes the first two lines]. 'These,' he writes, 'might be the opening lines of a T.S. Eliot *Prelude*'. GILL, Vol.1, p.58

Of 'Ballad of the Londoner' Mary Davis states: '... by removing one of the more musical stanzas and by eliminating the anapaests from the final stanza, but even in its altered form this poem has a more pronounced lyric movement than have any of the other poems in simple stanzas.' Byrd Davis, p.79

'Ballad of the Londoner' appealed to a later generation. Michael de Larrabeiti reprinted the poem in his book *A Rose Beyond the Thames*, published in 1978 which took its title from Flecker's poem.

[764] Two versions of 'Vox in Desertis' also appear in the *Second Book of the Prophet James* (BOD) p.28, next to 'Ballad of the Student in the South' dated April 1907. Sherwood, NGJ p.65, relates 'Vox in Desertis' to an unhappy period in Flecker's life in Oxford, February 1907. 'Vox in Desertis', like 'The Ballad of the Queen's Bouquet' and 'Mes Manes a Clytie', remains unpublished.

[765] Another version of 'The Ballad of the Queen's Bouquet' exists in papers in the BOD with notes that verses were revised in July (3rd and 5th) 1910 and December 1910 (C81). He states the poem is 'from the French'. Last verse re-written.

[766] London County Council

[767] From the Minute Book of the Cambridge Fabian Society 1906–1913 in Elizabeth Houghton Collection, Dept. of Special Collections and University Archives. Memorial Library, Marquette University.

[768] In his letter to Sedgwick (LIFE, p.93) he writes: 'And I have an entire scheme of education: of course, immature as yet, but different to all others. I will not dilate on it, simply saying that its main idea is to make each boy "know something about everything, and everything about something".'

[769] In a letter to *The Nation* and *The Athenaeum* published on 21 February 1925, Professor Browne wrote:

JAMES ELROY FLECKER

Sir, - In reading the interesting review of *The Life of James Elroy Flecker* in your issue of to-day (February 7th), I cannot help wondering why no attempt has been made by his biographers to study in greater detail the traces in his work of the Oriental studies which he pursued at Cambridge in 1908–1910, preparatory to his appointment to a Consulate in the Near East. Such traces are very evident in his spirited 'War Song of the Saracens' in *Hassan* (ed. 1923, pp.104-5), of which the form, rhyme, and metre were certainly suggested by Dr. R.A. Nicholson's verse translation of an ode of Shams-i-Tabriz occurring on p.344 of his *Selected Poems from the Diwan* of that great mystical poet, published in 1898 by the Cambridge University Press. Flecker's lines:

From the lands where the elephants are to

the forts of Merou [i.e. Merv] and Balghar [i.e. Bulghar]

Our steel we have brought and our star to shine

on the ruins of Rum,

are, I think, evidently suggested by Nicholson's:

I was born not in China afar, not in Saqsin,

and not in Bulghar,

Not in India, where five rivers are, nor Iraq

nor Khorasan I grew.

So much for form: now, as regards substance. The Oriental studies of Student Interpreters (now called 'Consular Probationers') in this University, designed mainly for practical ends, do not include much Arabic, Persian, or Turkish poetry. With one Arabic poem occurring in the 'Romance of 'Antara' they were, however, familiar in Flecker's time, since it was one of the best phonographic records which I obtained in Cairo in 1902 from a Muhaddith, or professional story-teller, who nightly delighted his audience in a certain coffee-house in the Shari' Bayt al-Qadi with recitations from that pleasing tale. In order to enable the students to follow the intonation of this record, each was supplied with the Arabic text in the proper character and in Romanized transcript, and with an English prose translation. The poem in question beginning, 'Idha Kashafa 'z-zamanu laka 'l-qina'a,' evidently suggested by the following lines in Flecker's 'War Song of the Saracens':

Not in silk nor in samet we lie, nor in curtained
solemnity die
Among women who chatter and cry and children who
mutter a prayer.

and:

A mart of destruction we made in Yalula [i.e., Jalula]
where men were afraid,
For death was a difficult trade, and the sword
was a broker of doom;
And the Spear was a Desert Physician, who cured
not a few of ambition,
And drove not a few to perdition with medicine
bitter and strong:

The literal translation of the passage in the above-mentioned Arabic poem, which, as I have no doubt, suggested these verses, is as follows:

And do not choose a bed of silk whereon to pass
the night fearful of the battle,
While round about thee women wail in terror,
casting aside their veils and coverings,

and:

We set up in Zawabil a mart of War (Suqa harbin)
wherein [human] souls supplied the wares.
My spear was the Broker of Dooms (Dallalu'l-Manaya),
plunging into their hosts, buying and selling,
And my sword was a Physician in the Desert, curing
the heads of all who complained of headache.

Thinking that these evidences of the influence of Flecker's Oriental studies on his later literary work may be of interest to some of his admirers, I have ventured to trouble you with this letter.

Yours, &c.,

Edward G. Browne.

Cambridge.
Browne, who died the following year, appeared not to have read the book, only the review, or he would have noted that in the Epilogue of the LIFE Dr. Hodgson stated, p.257–8:
'Again, as a natural result of his Interpretership, Flecker gradually acquired, at Cambridge, and in the following years in the East, a considerable knowledge of Oriental languages and literatures.'
She then goes on to say: 'The 'War Song of the Saracens', which Mr. Goldring published* in 1910 in a magazine he was then editing, seems a little solitary among the rest of Flecker's work, and perhaps a trifle irrelevant in *Hassan* itself. The reader of this Anthologie may wonder if it did not owe its existence to a particularly fine Chant de Guerre which M. Thalasso found in Altai, and rendered in stirring verse. The following stanzas must suffice'. Hodgson then quotes 17 lines.
Gillanders in his *James Elroy Flecker*, Vol.1, p.226, states:
'There may be something in Dr. Hodgson's suggestion that Flecker had the idea of this poem from a Chant de Guerre in Adolphe Thalasso's *Anthologie de l'Amour Asiatique*, which was in Flecker's possession. She quotes for comparison'. Gillanders reprints 6 lines. 'The idea is certainly very similar to that of Flecker's second and third 'bayt's' in the first stanza, but the possibility of both Thalasso and Flecker deriving the idea from original oriental sources, most likely Arabic, cannot be ruled out.'
'War Song Of The Saracens' was published in *The Tramp*, March 1918. There is a musical arrangement of 'War Song of the Saracens', chorus for men's voices unaccompanied: (words) Music by Granville Bantock, London. Curwen c.1920

770 Savery in *Collected Poems* p.xii, states:
'I only visited him once there [referring to Cambridge] – in November, 1908, I think – but I have the distinct impression that he was more independent than he had been at Oxford. He was writing his first long version – that is to say, the third actual draft of *The King of Alsander*. Incidentally he had spoilt the tale, for the time being, by introducing a preposterous sentimental conclusion, a departure to unknown lands, if I remember rightly, with the peasant-maid, who had not yet been deposed, as she was later on, from her original position of heroine.'

771 'Looking Eastwards' was published in *The Nation* on 29 February 1908 and in *The Living Age* on 4 April 1908

772 'Flecker never reprinted the poem, perhaps finding its sentiment embarrassing in the light of the hard realities of the Levant Consular Service' NGJ, p.74

773 The *Second Book of the Prophet James*, p.41–2 (BOD) contained his first jottings (many scored through) of Dulce Lumen: 'God has made'
The sun beats down upon the world, the deeper mystery begins
The darkness of our mysteries
In the city where stones
In that sweet city of the carven stones

I know lies a famous city where the flowers
are all of stone and rivers of
Do you remember
The city where the flowers are all of stone
And rivers of
Never shall forget how Pan (for I saw him)
we walked in the city of bright stone flowers

Another poet of Flecker's age was travelling in Italy and visiting Venice at this time. He was Ezra Pound. He had reference in *The Cantos*: 'Stone trees, white and rose-white in the darkness,' which seem reminiscent of Flecker. Flecker did not know Pound, or like his work. Mary Byrd Davis states: 'However Flecker did not need to steal from Pound' p.248 Note

It was not possible for any 'stealing' to take place at this point as Dulce Lumen preceded *The Cantos.* If there is any accusation of stealing, then Pound may have 'stolen' from Flecker, or Pound may have forgotten where he 'borrowed' the image from, or simply the same image came to the minds of both poets, or from earlier poets.

Rupert Brooke's Review of *Personae* by Ezra Pound was in the *Cambridge Review,* 2 December 1909.

Brooke wrote of Pound's work: 'He is blatant, full of foolish archaisms, obscure through awkward language, not subtle thought, and formless; he tastes experiences keenly, has an individual outlook, flashes into brilliance, occasionally, and expresses roughly a good deal of joy in life.'

774 LIFE, p.41, 'have been reading a lot of Ruskin lately – *Stones of Venice, Modern Painters,* etc. The more I read, the more I love and admire the man.'

775 *Bridge of Fire,* p.23

776 LIFE, p.133

777 'Masque I. was sung in Canterbury Cathedral: when I imagine some good-voiced pork-chopper singing about:
my children who are *very* wise
stand by a tree with shutten eyes
and *seem* to meditate *or* pray
I rejoice in my heart. Surely it is a jolly well-written verse exercise. And those splendid asses trailing along their robes in the snow. O for a picture by Aubrey!' SLA, p.186

778 An early version of 'Joseph and Mary' is titled 'A New Carol', and is in Flecker's papers in the Bodleian.

779 Line 5 of 'Resurrection' in the Copybook reads instead of 'There's a sharp movement in this shivering morn' reads 'There's a sharp magic', with the word 'moment' written above it with a question mark.

Housman's 'Easter Hymn' has the same image of the sleeping Christ as 'Resurrection':
If in that Syrian garden, ages slain,
You sleep, and know not you are dead in vain,
Nor even in dreams behold how dark and bright

Ascends in smoke and fire by day and night
The hate you died to quench and could but fan.
Sleep well and see no morning, son of man.

780 *Bridge of Fire Copybook*, p.94

781 In Persian, a ghazel, an ode of between four and fifteen couplets.

782 NGJ, p.36, and LIFE, p.89

783 GILL, Vol.1, p.220

784 Gillanders states, p.222
'For the "mad songs without a name" there is no justification and "the sons of pleasure" & "children of desire" are Swinburthian touches quite contrary to the spirit of the original and cannot be said to be "in the mode of Iraq" either. The choice of the epithet in "moonbright boy" on the other hand is a close translation of the original "mahru" (moonfaced).' GILL, Vol.1
'mad songs without a name' line four of 'The Lover of Jalalu'ddin is similar to 'my mad singing startles the valleys and the hills' which appears in Arthur Waley's translations of poems by P-Chu-I. 'Madly Singing in the Mountains' from *Chinese Poems* by Arthur Waley, Unwin Paperbacks, published 1946.

785 GILL, Vol.1, p.220

786 'Corrumpus' *Bridge of Fire Copybook*, Jan. 1909, p.96

787 Mary Byrd Davis states: 'There are similarities to Wilde's 'Harlot's House', but Flecker's speaker, unlike Wilde's girl, resembles the house's occupants.' Byrd Davis, p.75

788 Notebook (BOD) Poem in Flecker's handwriting (p.6)

789 This line was altered at one time in the notebook to: 'I have know families who .....' but stet written in margin.

790 Hodgson states that the letter telling his mother of his weekend in Paris is undated, but the letter explaining what had happened, is according to Hodgson dated November 1908. J. Sherwood NGJ, p.87,says that the visit to Paris took place in the following summer term. Postcard to Rupert Brooke, 11 Nov. 1908, Berg Collection [unseen].

791 The French version of Flecker's enlarged version of '*The Last Generation*', was entrusted to Pimodan a year previously, to go into a French paper but there is no evidence that this was actually done, so how wise he was to rely on Pimodan for help with a tutorship is open to question.

792 LIFE, p.132

793 Andrew Ryan in *The Last of the Dragomans*, G. Bles 1952, writes: p.24 'The répétiteur indigène whom I knew best was Khalil Bey Khalid, who had fled to England from the Hamidian tyranny in Turkey, and whom Browne befriended. He was a man of fair intelligence and education, very good-looking, rather vain and inclined to laziness. He would have liked to marry an English wife. His failure to achieve this may have helped to sour him later. If ever liberty spoiled a man who had

suffered for it, it spoiled him. Returning to Constantinople after the Revolution of 1908, he went into Parliament. He was afterwards for a time Turkish Consul-General in Beirut. As the War of 1914–1918 approached, he went strongly and ungratefully anti-British. He died comparatively young. Poor Khalid! One could not admire him much, but I always had an affection for him. For one thing, he was the first Turk I knew, and I knew him in the easy atmosphere of Cambridge.'

Also

Francis Toye writes in his book *For What We Have Received*, Heinemann, 1950 p.57–8

'... Turkish was in the hands of a lackadaisical, somewhat indolent, but very pleasant and good-looking Turk called Halil Halid. The wisest thing Halid ever did was to retire mysteriously for a term or two and hand over his duties to a fiery, podgy compatriot, Nazim Bey, then living in exile in Paris. Not only was Nazim a better teacher, but also he was a very stimulating person, who subsequently played an important part in the Young Turk Revolution by raising the army at Salonica against the Sultan.'

[794] LIFE, p.133

[795] *For What We Have Received*, Francis Toye, Wm. Heinemann 1950 p.70

[796] *'The Camels Must Go*, Reader Bullard, p.43

[797] The Foreign Office was only bringing into line a practice which enquiries revealed went on in the India Office, NGJ, p.81. By coincidence in October 1906, Maynard Keynes started as a junior clerk in the Military Department of the India Office at a salary of £200 a year and then moved in 1907 to the Revenue Statistics and Commerce Department, in which everything came to him to read and he read it. (Quoted in *John Maynard Keynes*, Robert Skildersky, Macmillan). Keynes failed to get elected a Fellow of King's but he helped Rupert Brooke to get elected as Apostle in January 1908. He himself resigned from the India Office and returned to King's in July 1908. The Foreign Service Students' Committee was established on 15 June 1905. Previously the Board of Indian Civil Service Studies established on 12 March 1896, to promote the study of living languages, supervised the training of student-interpreters sent by the Foreign Office, but in 1905, this was transferred to the FSSC. In 1909 Keynes was elected to the Special Boards of Studies, for Economics and Politics and for the Indian Civil Service Courses.[*Maynard Keynes, An Economist's Biography*, D.E. Moggridge Routledge, 1992.]

[798] LIFE, p.126

[799] LIFE, p.134

[800] Letter dated 4 May 1908, to Jacques Raverat from King's. *The Letters of Rupert Brooke* Chosen and edited by G. Keynes. Faber & Faber, 1968

[801] Edward Marsh (1872–1953) was educated at Westminster School, and Trinity College, Cambridge, where he studied Classics. Entered the Civil Service, interested in painting, drama, and the life of literary London. In 1905 he was appointed Private Secretary to the Parliamentary Under-

Secretary for the Colonies, Winston Churchill, who became a life-long
influence and close friend. Marsh met Brooke in 1907, and they were
able to continue meeting through membership of The Apostles' Society.
Brooke stayed with Marsh in London. Marsh was more than patron to
many young writers, including Flecker.

A letter to Richard Gilcrest Potter, dated 5 December 1924. (Dartmouth
College Library, Hanover, New Hampshire, U.S.A.). In it he (Marsh) notes
that he first learned of Flecker's poetry through Rupert Brooke.

[802] 'He was', said Brooke, 'for ever talking about his own poetry. However the
conversation began that was how it ended'. 'We used' Brooke told me 'to
argue for hours which one of us wrote the better poems. But you know'
he added with a touch of self-consciousness and laughing naivete, 'I could
always see that he did think his were better'. Second Essays in Literature.
Edward Shanks. W. Collins 1927

In a letter to Edward Marsh, from Calgary dated 16 August 1913, Brooke
writes 'I don't THINK I should value Flecker's volume so highly as you
seem to ... I expect I'd find him too fluid.' p.500 - *The Letters of Rupert
Brooke*, Geoffrey Keynes. Faber & Faber 1968.

[803] *Hanging On*. Diaries December 1960 to August 1963. Frances Partridge.
Collins 1990

[804] 'He tossed over a letter which bore the address "On a hill". It was signed
R.B., and indicated that if the writer were not detained by Dryads he
might join Morrison in a cup of wine on Saturday night. "Who is R.B.?"
asked the Scholar. "A man called Rupert Brooke, as beautiful and lonely
as a cloud, and thought to be a better poet even than Flecker."
Here were two astounding phrases.'

The Upward Anguish by Humbert Wolfe, Cassell & Co., 1938, p.154

More evidence of the J.H. Morrison/Brooke friendship is contained in a
letter to Brooke:

12, King's Parade,

Cambridge.

Wed. Jan.27th 09

Dear Brooke,

Albert Rothenstein is coming to me for this week-end. Will you lunch with
us on Sunday at 1.30 and let theory (or superstition) take a holiday in the
contemplation of the arts. There will also Beazley & Co.

Letter (56) (King's College, Cambridge)

[805] 'Brooke discovered himself at once. He leaped straight to an eminence
he deserved. But thereafter he steadily declined. The reason for that
decline is not hard to seek. His poetic development was concurrent with
a growth of self-consciousness. The impersonal quality, the objective
reality of his vision gradually narrowed and obscured, and replaced by a
particular consciousness usurping the universal. Just as this stress upon
a self-conscious usurping expression transformed him into an inspired
and talented poet. With Flecker the increasing thing is that the process is
precisely in the opposite direction.'

Letters to X p.254 H.J. Massingham, Constable & Co., 1919.
'But all allowances being made, the immense popularity of Rupert Brooke is clearly being permitted to wane, while a truer value tends to be set on his friend and contemporary, Flecker.'
Alex Macdonald – 'James Elroy Flecker'.
The Fortnightly Review, February 1924

[806] Two poems written by Brooke, before he met Flecker. 'The Song of the Pilgrims' (halted around the fire by night, after moon-set, they sing this beneath the trees) and 'Pine Trees and the Sky: Evening', apart from the titles, have no real resemblance to two poems subsequently written by Flecker, i.e. 'The Golden Journey to Samarkand' Prologue, which begins 'We who with songs beguile your pilgrimage,' and his poem with the theme of pine trees. 'Brumana' has little in common with Brooke's poem on the theme of homesickness, 'The Old Vicarage, Grantchester', so Beazley's poetry remains much closer to poems by Flecker, than Brooke.

[807] In *The Camels Must Go – An Autobiography* by Sir Reader Bullard, Faber & Faber 1961, p.47 'in our second term we were permitted, though not obliged, to take up a fourth language, Russian or Modern Greek. C. and I decided to do Russian; the other three felt that one could have too much of a good thing and refused to make yet another visit to the Tower of Babel. Russian was little studied at Cambridge, but there was a lecturer in Russian, who eked out a minute salary with a small allowance from the Fishmongers' Company. We were hampered by the lack of books in English for the study of Russian, and we had to learn it through German: a German grammar of Russian and the dullest of reading books with notes and vocabulary in German. Only a few years later Nevill Forbes of Oxford was to publish his excellent Russian grammar and one of the best language books ever written, on the Russian verb.'
[One person who later studied Russian at Cambridge was Jane Harrison, but she had a romantic attachment to Russia, *Jane Ellen Harrison*, S.J. Peacock, Yale. p.230.]

[808] 'Donde Estan?' (pp. 97-101) comes between 'Corrumpus', Jan. 1909 and 'Town Without a Market' (p.105) finished in April 1909. There are few alterations in the *Book of Fire Copybook*, except that in the second last line of the second last verse 'Dryads' replaces 'Bacchus'.

[809] FO/369/261

[810] NGJ, p.86

[811] *Maynard Keynes*, D.E. Moggridge, Routledge 1992, p.194

[812] J. Sherwood NGJ, related 'The Town Without a Market' to a poem among Flecker's papers which is written in Beazley's hand and is untitled and undated and begins:
Light at our ears the evening air
Can hardly stir a stem;
And the soft grey line over there
Is where they bury them: (p.85)

[813] 'The Town Without a Market' was published in *The Nation* on 8 May 1909. A letter to Savery, which is undated but postmarked in England on 4 April 1910. SLA, p.185 says:

'Jack, who saw them all and dislikes 'Western Voyage' most of 'The Town Without a Market' – as it appeared in the *Nation* it had a lot of literary phrases which I have struck out – Jack is a meticulous critic: you want the spirit of the thing.'

The number of changes to the version which appeared in the *Thirty-Six Poems* and *The Nation* version bear this out.

[814] These lines were altered before the poem was republished. He changed 'dense' habitations to 'small' habitations, his original choice in the *Bridge of Fire Copybook*.

[815] These lines were altered before the poem was re-published. He changed 'dense' habitations to 'small' habitations, his original choice in the *Bridge of Fire Copybook*.

[816] The soul and the Deity are often used by Oriental writers, imagined by the lover and his beloved one.

[817] Yellow Springs = Hades

[818] *Chinese Poetry in English verse.* Herbert A. Giles, Professor of Chinese in the University of Cambridge, Quartich 1898

[819] But that line was changed when republished to 'I used to sing and play.'

[820] In the proofs of *Thirty-Six Poems* this line is: 'lovely strength', in future printed versions it is 'manly strength'.

[821] Previously (*B. of F. Copybook*) 'The hills of gold' (p.107)

[822] 'Laurence Hope', James Elroy Flecker, *The Monthly Review*, April 1907

[823] Money had not saved John Davidson; his health and his fortune had not been improved by £250 given to him by Bernard Shaw, so that Davidson, in 1906, could write the great work that was within him. This money was to be repaid out of possible half royalties. Shaw did not think the play Davidson wrote performable, so there would be no royalties and Davidson would be left with a debt he could not repay. The existence of the play, Shaw suggested to the publisher John Lane, should not be mentioned, unless the continuation of Davidson's pension was refused to his widow. The matter of Davidson's pension was taken up in March 1923.

The two letters from Shaw about Davidson are published in *Author Hunting* by Grant Richards, Hamish Hamilton, 1934.

Also Mary O'Connor has written 'Did Bernard Shaw kill John Davidson?', *Shaw Review* 21 (1987) p.108-23.

The facts about Shaw's £250 and Davidson are outlined in Mary O'Connor's book: *John Davidson*, Scottish Writers Series, Scottish Academic Press, 1987, p.9

[824] Lines in loose leaf paper in the Bodleian. (Reminiscent of the Anonymous Poem 'Winter Roses' published in *The Idler* in Jan. 1907 (see Chapter V).

[825] Note on the page reads: 'I walked in the Town of Rest at noon on a hot calm day.'

826 RBH

827 Letter to Jacques Raverat dated 3 November 1909. *The Letters of Rupert Brooke* 1968, Faber and Faber.

828 Testament of John Davidson

829 *The Book of Kara James* (BL)

830 'The Westward Voyage' (four verses) was published in *Country Life*, 23 October 1909

831 This point is taken up by A.L. Rowse in:
'A Buried Love; Flecker and Beazley'. *The Spectator* 21/28 December 1985, who says 'Flecker's poetry blurts out the truth in the way poets have – for in verse one can say anything; most people won't know what is being said.' Rowse also states: 'the inner nature of that relationship is fully revealed only in Flecker's poetry.'

832 Poem entitled 'Waste' in notebook in the Bodleian. First poems in the notebook of poems by Jack Beazley, but in Flecker's handwriting.

833 'Got a letter asking if I was Flecker's archaeologist. He wrote the poem about ten years ago back about one Beazley a don at Ch.Ch.' (10 Nov. 1912). Home, *Letters of T.E. Lawrence* Blackwell, 1954, p.243

834 original only

835 This last line with its reference to 'broken vases widowed of their wine' is puzzling. 'Widowed' in its literal sense cannot be used to describe broken vases and lost wine; it is more likely that widowed refers to menstruation [*The Wise Wound*, Shuttle and Redgrove. New and Revised edition. Paladin. Grafton 1986, p.171] and it is a hidden reference to women such as Jane Harrison, who at the time the poem was written was 60, and although unmarried, she had close relationships with fellow male academics, such as Francis Cornford and D.S. MacColl.
It was as if Flecker was saying to Beazley, that his deep interest in archaeology had not brought him into contact with young men or even young women, as would a continuing interest in poetry.

836 There is no reference in the LIFE to Flecker and Beazley having spent a holiday together in Scotland but there is a reference in a letter to Sedgwick to: 'I have walked up many mountains in Scotland.' [LIFE, p.96 – Letter dated 9 September 1905]
The LIFE tells of part of the Easter Vacation being spent with a French family in Neuilly, but no mention is made of his being joined in Paris by Beazley.

837 Proof copy in BL

838 Proof copy in BL

839 The original Spanish poem is on p.430 *James Elroy Flecker*, Salzburg, Vol.2, Gillanders. 1983

840 Stephen Parry in *James Elroy Flecker. Poems – a new selection*. Autolycus 1980, says of Lord Arnaldos, p.56 'A translation of a famous Spanish (originally Catalan) ballad which is the subject of Longfellow's 'The Secret of the Sea' and has also been translated by Robert Graves. St. John's Eve is

midsummer's day and in the original Catalan version the mysterious sailor tempts Arnaldos to leave the world for fairyland. This is not clear in the Spanish ballad, and Flecker may only have understood the point intuitively.'

'Lord Arnaldos' was published in *Literary Digest*, 2 June 1917

[841] *Bridge of Fire Copybook*, p.72

[842] *Henry James in Cambridge*, Geoffrey Keynes. W. Heffer & Sons. Cambridge 1967

[843] LIFE, p.132

[844] LIFE, p.132

[845] LIFE, p.133

[846] *Rupert Brooke*, C. Hassall. Faber & Faber, 1964 p.188
Hassell attributes the complaint about Flecker's lunch to Brooke, (also NGJ p.86). But in *Friends and Apostles* the correspondence of Rupert Brooke and James Strachey 1905–1914 edited by Keith Hale, Yale University Press New Haven and London 1998 p.70 attributes the complaint about the lunch to James Strachey in a letter dated 16 July 1909 which James Strachey wrote to Brooke.

[847] In December 1910, Brooke moved from The Orchard to the Old Vicarage next door and rented two rooms on the ground floor and on the first floor, and also paid 30 shillings for full board. Reginald Pole of King's recorded in his *To An Unknown God*, a fictionalised account of his friendship with Brooke, the litter of books and manuscripts in Brooke's study at the Old Vicarage. 'Rupert Brooke and The Old Vicarage, Grantchester'
Mary Archer, Silent Books, 1989, p.13

[848] *Second Essays in Literature*. Edward Shanks. W. Collins 1927

[849] Brooke, who himself had already seen the effectiveness of dressing the part to pole a punt for Henry James, might have felt that Flecker was imitating him, or even doing it better, hence the accusation of 'creeping'. Or, as the episode of Flecker coming up the river to Grantchester is not given a date, it could be that Brooke imitated Flecker.

[850] From the Minute Book of the Cambridge Fabian Society, 1906–13. In Elizabeth W. Houghton Collection, Dept. of Special Collections and University Archives, Memorial Library, Marquette University.

[851] 'Song of Love', p.15 *Letters of Rupert Brooke and Noel Oliver*. Bloomsbury 1991. Letter post-marked 25th July, 1909

[852] NGJ, p.80

[853] *Bridge of Fire Copybook*, p.124

[854] James Elroy Flecker. S. Parry, Poems - a new selection. Autolycus 1980. 'The Parrot' was published in *The Cambridge Review* 4 November 1909, p.56

[855] *Bridge of Fire Copybook*, p.122

[856] A similar theme is worked out by Francis Thompson in his poem 'Sister Songs Part of the First' - 275-295, with the lines:
And of her own scant pittance did she give,

That I might eat and live;
Then fled, a swift and trackless fugitive.
His relationship with a street-girl who cared for him when he attempted
suicide and who inspired the poem is referred to in *Between Heaven and
Charing Cross* Brigid Boardman. Yale 1988, p.89. 'She had played her part
and it ended in a perfect exit at a turning point in his life when she knew
her presence could have done harm.' Also, 'Francis's gratitude was such
that he never forgot her. Years later he still longed to see her again.'
(Much of the information about Francis Thompson's relationship with
the street-girl and suicide is given by Wilfrid Meynell to Wilfred Scawen
Blunt, friend of Professor Browne.)

[857] *Thirty-Six Poems.* Negative microfilm in Houghton Library, Cambridge,
Mass.

[858] 'And yet' alongside the first line of the verse corresponds to a line on its
own but crossed out – 'And yet I walk to Primrose Hill.'

[859] This verse has 'Keep' in Beazley's handwriting in *Bridge of Fire Copybook.*

[860] breathes is substituted for 'takes' in the second line of the revised version

[861] p.18 of the Notebook in the Bodleian had a poem by Beazley called
'Johnnie and Maisie' (although Maisie is altered to Masie). Maisie is the
name of the educated grocer's daughter in Flecker's unpublished 'An
Evening Tale'.* Maisie could be a name associated with girls of this class.
* MSS. Yale (one version)

[862] SLA, p.186, postmarked 4 April 1910

[863] LIFE, P.136

[864] LIFE, P.136

[865] An early version of this poem is 'Cross Country' (*B. of F. Copybook*) which
has the lines:
Farewell, O young and friendly coast
Old love The East no more prevails;
Farewell! I journey Westermost
And ride on shining rails,
Along the road to Wales. ('The Welsh Sea', p.131)
In this poem 'The East' referred to the east coast of England.

[866] Poetry Collection Lockwood Memorial Library – JEF's Rough Copybook

[867] Poetry Collection Lockwood Memorial Library – JEF's Rough Copybook

[868] Poetry Collection Lockwood Memorial Library – JEF's Rough Copybook

[869] He published the poem under the title 'The Welsh Sea' separately in five
line stanzas in *The Nation* in November 1909. The poem was revised in the
Bridge of Fire Copybook in January 1910, p.154

[870] He wrote to Mr. Cooper from the British Consulate in Beirut 23.11.11.
(BL) and reminded him: 'Surely you know the legend of the drowned
lands of Wales or rather that large parts of Carnarvon Bay were
submerged.'

[871] *Bridge of Fire Copybook*, p.130 – 'filth and fire' is altered to 'filth and smoke'.

872 John Sherwood refers to 'filth and smoke' in NGJ There are two versions of this poem, one in the *Bridge of Fire Copybook* and the other in the Rough Copybook in the Poetry Collection, Lockwood Memorial Library from which the 'filth and fire' quotation is taken.

873 *Bridge of Fire Copybook*, Opp. p.130 – 'Low hung the fiery noon.'

874 MS. of *Thirty-Six Poems*

875 *Collected Poems*

876 *The Wise Wound.* Shuttle and Redgrove. Paladin 1986 Quoting APH Scott

877 LIFE, p.190

878 When referring to Flecker's holiday in North Wales with Cyril Roberts, Sherwood states: 'Years later its powerful magic distilled itself into 'The Welsh Sea'.' ......' p.36.

879 LIFE, p.139

880 LIFE, p.90

881 The Brooke contingent, which included Birrell, attended the Fabian Summer School in North Wales in late July. At the end of August, Brooke's parents rented the vicarage at Clevedon, Somerset, with large grounds and sufficient bedrooms to have a lot of the Brooke circle to stay including Birrell, Maynard Keynes and Edward Marsh. It seemed a superior residence to the rectory in Norfolk that the Flecker parents had taken for their break.

882 *Frederic Keeling*, E.T. Townshend. 1918 Allen and Unwin.

883 Jessie Holliday, artist Limner to the Summer School, from Harrow, married E.T. Dana, Professor of Philosophy, grandson of Longfellow. Information about this incident is contained in a letter, now in The Huntington Library and Art Gallery, San Marino, California. The letter was to introduce Conrad P. Aiken (1889–1973), poet, essayist, novelist, short story writer and dramatist who had been reading Flecker's work in *The New Statesman.* Conrad Aiken was born in the USA and left for his first trip to Europe in 1911.

884 William R. Titterton, from Hampstead, had not thought fit to advertise the fact that he was a poet when he signed the Visitors' Book (now at Nuffield College, Oxford). He simply wrote that he was an author and journalist, although he had had poems previously published by the New Age Press and Elkin Mathew, *River Music and Other Poems* in The Vigo Cabinet Series, Elkin Mathews, 19 April 1909. *Love Poems: Studies in Solitary Life.* He was a regular contributor to the *New Age.*
'Titterton eventually became a left-wing poet and journalist of immense persuasion who had met Flecker during a Fabian Summer School and had been accounted the better poet.' Basil Dean, *Seven Ages*, Hutchinson, p.207. Titterton, according to Dean, was involved in 'admirable publicity' for the production of *Hassan.*

885 NGJ, p.92

886 LIFE, p.137

887 *The Time Traveller, The Life of H.G. Wells*, p.225 Weidenfeld & Nicolson

888 *King of Alsander*, p.113

889 LIFE, p.137

890 LIFE, p.138

891 Mary Hankinson is mentioned in *History of the Fabian Society* by E.R. Pearse, Cassell & Co., p.196

892 University of Texas. Flecker, James Elroy. ALS to Hankinson, Miss.

893 'Flecker's letter to his parents is, in its abrupt and comprehensive sweeping of past and present into one whole, entirely in keeping with his life-long capacity for total absorption in a given moment and set of conditions.' LIFE, p.137

894 'Opals are unlucky unless you are born in March' LIFE, p.225. Letter to his sister, when sending his sister a brooch.

895 LIFE, p.137

896 LIFE, p.138

897 SLA, p.184 – some lines not published – (see note 988).

898 His translations 'From the Gulistan of Sa'di' could be described under the same heading; these were half-prose and half-verse. 'Mansur' also contains verse translations of the fifteenth-century Baghdad poet, Nesimi, who died for his religion. His story, 'Mansur', like the Gulistan, was based on Flecker's own Cambridge Oriental studies, and both of his works appeared in *The Cambridge Review*. The first instalment of the Gulistan appeared in *The Cambridge Review* of 25 November 1909, and More Gulistan in the 14 February 1910 edition. Mansur appeared in the 20 January 1910 edition.
Flecker's source for one of two stories, interwoven in 'Mansur', one serious, one humorous, was Gibb's *History of Ottoman Poetry*. The Gulistan also has touches of humour in the Flecker style.
Referring to the tale as 'a beauty' may not have been entirely due to the beauty of the tale and words, as the tale contains a description of Nesimi being flayed alive. The beauty is more the beauty of achievement, as Gillanders says:
'Without exception it can be said that Flecker's verses are improvements upon the literal versions of Gibb, for while retaining as far as possible the original rhyme pattern Flecker aims at a simplicity of statement which helps to clarify the often obscure point of the mystical Ottoman poet. This is particularly true of the lines from the ghazel of Nesimi which Flecker includes in the story, Mansur.'
GILL, Vol.1, p.238

899 In a letter to Hugh Dalton Brooke wrote on 8 September 1909, from Rugby to say 'I am sorry if everyone is turning against that good poet, that gaunt, sorrow-stricken zany (his own description), my friend James Elroy Flecker. I love him yet. He has seen life.' *The Letters of Rupert Brooke* chosen and edited by Geoffrey Keynes, K.C., Faber & Faber, 1968.

900 Dodd is not given a Christian name. Frederick Lawson Dodd (1868–1962), dentist and Fabian, who had suggested the idea of the Fabian

Summer School. He is described in *The Diary of Beatrice Webb,* Vol.3 Virago, 1984, as 'Quaker-like' and as 'ruling the roost' at the Fabian Summer Schools. Or 'Francis Dodd, artist', '*Lawrence of Arabia*', J. Wilson, Heinemann 1989, p.125.
Francis Dodd (1874–1949). Art training Glasgow, Paris, Italy. Portrait painter; war artist.

901 *The Letters of Rupert Brooke* (chosen and edited by G. Keynes) Faber & Faber, 1968, p.20

902 GILL, Vol.1, p.236

903 CPR, p.47

904 'He was content to sink to be a dragoman',[Dragoman – corruption of Arabic word for translator.] *Portraits of Inference,* Humbert Wolfe, Methuen 1934, p.20

905 C.Pr. pp.47–48

906 Gillanders says: 'Nesimi means that Man is a microcosm in which the Universe, which is God, is reflected as in a mirror. He was drawing upon an ancient tradition according to which the Universe consists of eighteen thousand worlds. Flecker uses this phrase to represent man as a reflection of God but by changing "worlds" to "aeons" gives the idea of an eternity of Time rather than the infinity of Space in the universe.'
Gillanders also says: 'There is a more striking alteration in a line which Flecker made his own and used again with great effect in 'The Gates of Damascus':
My body is the holy glass where eighteen thousand aeons pass.'
GILL, Vol.1, pp.238–9

907 NGJ, p.92

908 Flecker, when writing to Savery to announce his engagement, refers to Eleanor having a very pale face and blue eyes. SLA p.184 Also in NGJ Sherwood refers to a note for the LIFE which mentions 'Eleanor's strange blue eyes.' p.93

909 K of A, p.41

910 K of A, p.53

911 The description of Peronella's mother fits in with descriptions of an old aunt in Gautier's *Mlle. de Maupin* Chapter XII:
'Nevertheless, this old woman had retained some plain and impressive traces of her former beauty which had saved her from lapsing into that shrivelled ugliness which is the fate of women who have been only pretty or just rosy-cheeked; her eyes, though they were flanked by a network of wrinkles, and had slack and heavy lids, still retained a few sparks of their original fire, and anybody could see that when the other king was on the throne, the flashes of passion which had darted from them must have been downright dazzling. Her thin and delicate nose, somewhat curved like the beak of a bird of prey, imparted to her profile a certain dignity on her Hapsburg lips, which were painted carmine, in the style of the last century.'

Mademoiselle de Maupin, translated from the French by Paul Silver, Hamish Hamilton, 1948, p.272.

[912] K of A. p.56

[913] K of A, p.21

[914] K of A, p.72

[915] LIFE, pp.144–5

[916] NGJ, p.93

[917] JEF, p.65

[918] Goldring makes no comment at all in his published recollections about the fact that Flecker had got engaged and that his change of dress, appearance and social activities might have had some connection with that particular event. Nor did Birrell, who was keen on being best man at the proposed wedding. It is much more likely that the person Goldring encountered was Ronald Firbank.

[919] *South Lodge,* D. Goldring. Constable, 1943

[920] Robert Ferguson *The Short Sharp Life of T.E. Hulme* Allen Lane 2002 p.52

[921] Frank Flint was the poet who had written in the *New Age* on 11 July 1908 about Japanese poetry. Another member of the breakaway group, Edward Storer, published a book: *Mirrors of Illusion,* in which he wrote of good poetry as 'made up of scattered lines, which are pictures, descriptions, or something at present incapable of accurate identification.' This as-yet-unnamed infant called growing up at the Poets' Club to be known as Imagism would have been of interest to Flecker had he made his way there, but he would not have blended into the background, even in 'Society Man' dress.

Rupert Brooke in his lecture 'Democracy and the Arts' delivered to the Fabians on 24 November 1910, refers to a group of poor and ill-educated cockney writers he had met in London. If ill-educated refers to Frank Flint then Brooke could not have known of Flint's knowledge of the literature of many languages. In using the term ill-educated Brooke may have meant either self-educated or those poets who had not been to a public school or Oxford or Cambridge. Brooke said: 'Their poems give fuller value when pronounced as they thought or felt them than in the old-world passion and mellifluous despair of any gentleman's.' (did he mean Flecker?) *Rupert Brooke* by Christopher Hassall, p.244, quoting from Democracy and the Arts, Rupert Brooke, with a preface by Geoffrey Keynes. Rupert Hart-Davis, 1946

[922] JEF, p.66

[923] NGJ, p.95

[924] 'Two days after the announcement of my appointment as "Dean at twenty-four" I received an ingenious missive from an address in East London. It commended a moustache-grower, and guaranteed that the use of one bottle would add ten years to my age. That had warned me (for I smelt a forgery in it) of the difficulties that might await me. Twelve months before I had been a fairly well-known and by no means devout bachelor of arts, a

friend of Flecker and Rupert Brooke and of the Sunday Games Club and other unecclesiastical circles. Now I was a parson and a don, responsible for the religion and morals of men who had been at school with me. I fully expected to be unmercifully ragged. At Caius I most certainly would have been.'

A Wanderer's Way by Charles E. Raven DD, London, Martin Hopkinson & Co. Ltd., 1928, Chapter IV, p.120

[925] LIFE, p.149

[926] Flecker quotes the lines from Shakespeare in his copybook.

[927] K. of A. p.120

[928] Revised as 'A Western Voyage'.

[929] 'The Ballad of the Student in the South' has six stanzas finally in the *Collected Poems* version, the verse which was originally from his poem 'Dorothy' is the fourth verse. In the proofs for *Thirty-Six Poems* it is the fifth verse, and the fifth verse, in the *Collected Poems* version which begins 'Darling a scholar's fancies sink', is the fourth verse in the proofs of *Thirty-Six Poems*. (Houghton)

[930] NGJ, p.65

[931] *The Bridge of Fire Copybook*, p.140, has a reference to this poem with the lines:

Listen, the half-mile distant sea

Is saying we are wise,

Look for the morn in majesty

Is shining in your eyes.

which seems to rule out Grenoble, if this verse had been inserted. The *Second Book of Prophet James* has a version of this poem dated April, '07, 5 verses.

[932] Gillanders [Vol.1, p.35] states that it may only be a coincidence that the girl in Flecker's ballad is found by her lover 'Up to her breast in Southern corn' as Thompson's Daisy was also 'Breast deep 'mid flower and spine.' [Vol.1, p.35]

It may also be a coincidence that Beazley was a student in the South and had golden hair, and subsequent revisions made to disguise the Beazley factor more carefully, were also unsatisfactory.

[933] p.140 *Bridge of Fire Copybook*, and p.11 *Bridge of Fire*.

[934] CP

[935] Published in *Collected Poems*.

[936] The title of his piece in *The Cambridge Review* was from the Gulistan of Sa'di. In a manuscript of this translation which survives, it is entitled 'The Rose-Garden of Sa'di.' The manuscript is in the Houghton Library, Harvard University, Cambridge, Massachusetts, U.S.A.

[937] 'The Gulistan' or 'Rose-Garden of Shekh Muslihu'd-Din Sadi of Shiraz' was translated into prose and verse by Edward B. Eastwick of Merton College, Oxford and published by Stephen Austin in 1852. He gives details of other translations in his preface. The Gulistan was written in

the first half of the thirteenth century by Sa'di, who lived in Baghdad, where Arabic was spoken and Arabic was scattered throughout his work. 'The Gulistan' is the best known of his works, and it is written in a simple and beautiful style, with great wit, and had great popularity in the East. The grotesque runs through the stories, which are concerned with ethics. Sa'di preached the gospel of acceptance and resignation and was contemptuous of riches. Also, the 'Gulistan or Rose Garden of Sa'di' Faithfully Translated into English by the Kama Shastra Society for Private Subscribers. (Translated by Edward Rehatsek with Burton supervising the editing. 1888)

[938] *Translation of Eastern Poetry.* R.A. Nicholson 1922 CUP

[939] 'In accordance with this my master, the august and felicitous Mir Ali Mushtakm used to call Sa'di the "Nightingale of a thousand songs"' intending to convey in every branch of poetry he displayed the perfection of his genius.'
From Sa'di, Eastwick 1852, Stephen Austin.
Francis Birrell (LIFE, p.150) says that Flecker was very proud of two lines in one of his poems ('No Coward's Song')
I know dead men are deaf and may not hear
The singing of a thousand nightingales.
Birrell says that 'what was wrong with dead men was that they could not hear one nightingale, and if they could hear a thousand it would be extremely disagreeable.' Birrell obviously did not know the reference to Sa'di, and he was applying 'what we dubbed the Johnsonian method of criticism' which Flecker did not appreciate.
Flecker's pride in these lines and his frustration at not being able to explain exactly what he meant may also have been because he had read what is stated in Eastwick's 'Sa'di', p.6 Preface:
'As the nightingale for all its warblings, is not a true moth, which perishes in the brilliance it adores without a sigh; so the truly devout are not those who speak of their devotion, but those who are wrapt into silent ecstasy.'
Flecker saw himself as the moth, his parents' devoutness as the nightingale he would not hear when he himself was dead.

[940] *Literary History of Persia.* E.G. Browne, 1906

[941] 'It is, indeed, his skill in rendering Sa'di's verse passages that is Flecker's chief claim to consideration before other translators. Where others have not attempted to translate Sa'di's verse into English verse form, or have been content to mark the difference between the prose and verse by putting the latter into simple quatrains, Flecker has endeavoured in many ways to preserve at least a semblance of the original style by imitating the rhythmic and rhyme pattern.'
GILL, Vol.1 1983, p.215

[942] NGJ, p.95

[943] LIFE, p.140

[944] LIFE, p.140

[945] LIFE, p.143

[946] LIFE, p.141

[947] *The Retreat of Tuberculosis 1850–1950*, F.E. Smith Croom Helm, 1988

[948] LIFE, p.141

[949] The new title had a kinship with Baudelaire's 'Spleen', the first line is: 'I have more memories than a thousand years.' Also the second line of the third verse 'a bright-eyed love' is akin to 'quick-eyed love', from George Herbert's (1593–1632) poem 'Love'.

[950] LIFE, p.141

[951] *The Tramp* published 'War Song of the Saracens' in its issue of March 1910, and a poem 'The Visit' by J.D. Beazley illustrated by T. Dayrell-Reed. Goldring makes no mention of the May 1909, Vol.1 issue of *The Tramp*, which published Flecker's poem 'Tramps'

[952] The persuasion would have been difficult as the proprietor condemned Goldring for publishing poems by Flecker and Beazley and T. Dayrell-Reed's drawings. Also 'The Ghost Road' by L. Cranmer-Byng Rendered from the Chinese of Tu-Fu (712–770), p.64

[953] RBH, p.116

[954] *Letters of Rupert Brooke*, Ed. Geoffrey Keynes, Faber & Faber 1968, p.217

[955] particularly hoping 'Mr. Flecker will not abandon the intoxicating lyricism of the third stanza.'

[956] Letter p.184 SLA Undated, but postmarked Neuilly on 23 March 1910

[957] Letter p.185 SLA Undated, but postmarked in England on 4 April 1910.

[958] Masque 1 was set to music. It was originally 'A Christmas Carol', and revised as 'The Masque of the Magi'. He told Savery: 'Criticise the masques as poetry if you like. But they are not void of the true spirit of me which is hugeous humour.' SLA, p.186

[959] *Gloucestershire Echo*, 16 March 1910.

[960] 'The Ballad of Iskander' was published in Flecker's *Forty-Two Poems*, and in *The English Review*, March 1911, p.

[961] Letter p.185 SLA Undated, but postmarked in England on 4 April 1910

[962] JEF, p.38

[963] C.L. Freeman, LIFE, p.105 and SLA, p.185. Freeman – editor of *Varsity Magazine*, worked on *The Times Literary Supplement* (Compton Mackenzie)

[964] C.Pr. p.54

[965] GILL, Vol.1, p.240

[966] Mary Davis states 'the philosophy of the Sufis, according to which every earthly object has an archetype in the ideal world.' (Nicholson, *Divan Shamsi*).
Byrd Davis, pp.114–5

[967] *Portraits by Inference*, Humbert Wolfe, Methuen, p.21

[968] *Portraits by Inference*, Humbert Wolfe, Methuen, p.22

[969] Wolfe related the same incident in *The Upward Anguish*, Cassell, although the poem Flecker is reciting is 'Rioupéroux' in this version, pp.155–6, first published in *The Bridge of Fire*.

[970] JEF, p.37

[971] JEF, p.37

[972] K of A., p.238

[973] When Brooke's poem 'Grantchester' was published in *Georgian Poetry 1911/12* and Flecker reviewed it (unpublished ms c81 BOD) he praised the poem and mentioned 'the charming passage about Byron's pool' and quoted the lines.

[974] SLA, p.188. Letter undated but postmarked in England, 4 April 1910.

[975] LIFE, p.141

[976] Reference to *Thirty-Six Poems* is made in *The Scotsman*, Monday 14 March 1910

[977] LIFE, p.141

[978] LIFE, p.142

[979] LIFE, p.143

[980] LIFE, p.143

[981] K of A., p.122

[982] K of A., p.123

[983] LIFE, p.142

[984] K. of A. p.120–2

[985] 'we bored each other' he wrote to his parents. K of A. p.69–70

[986] Omitted portion of letter to Savery p.184 SLA.

[987] LIFE, p.140

[988] This is borne out by a portion of the letter written to Savery (undated, but postmarked in Cheltenham on 30 September 1909) omitted from the published letter on p.184 SLA;
Before the published sentence: 'We shall not marry unless we find we are still suited to each other in the spring.' The omitted portion reads: 'She has a profile, a figure, a good taste, a superb talent for playing the violin, no general information at all. (Praise God she knows nothing of literature [????] about life. £400 a year, rich relatives, and above all a sense of humour. She is half German, and bilingual: talks also very nice French. This sounds like the catalogue of an impassioned lover: She is also full of faults. She is not robustious, she has the devil of a [pigheaded?] will, she is a [goddess?] flirt with a passion for handsome men, worldly, irreligious, yet, with rather too violent an objection to coarseness.' (The University of Texas at Austin, Harry Ransom Humanities Research Centre, Copy sent) The half German reference is not borne out by the information in the 1901 census for the Finlayson's residence 60 Cornwall Gardens, Kensington. Eleanor's father, John was born in Scotland in 1849, her mother, Edith, was born in Manchester in 1860, John Finlayson's occupation is given as Director of Public Companies, and the household

employed a Cook and three more domestic servants, which bears out
the Society people image. Eleanor was born in Straits, Settlements in
1887 and her sister, Mignon, in 1885. Also in the Household is Blanche
Finlayson, born in Switzerland in 1881, who could be another sister of
Eleanor. Blanche's occupation is given as Governess, but no relationship
to the Head of the household (John Finlayson) is given.

[989] Taylor Institute, Oxford.

[990] Alterations to the poems in this copy:
'A Western Voyage' p.39
'And wake the hills of long ago' crossed out and inserted 'I used to know'
'The Queen's Song' p.49, the verse which begins 'Thus is my love'
On page 68 there is also an alteration to the poem 'The Blind Man'
'For nations yet unborn' is crossed out and
'Beyond is mist, when the mist clears
Enough. Away! O friend I would be there.'
Written in: 'And mountains straight as spears.'
In J.D. Beazley's book of poems in the Bodleian, his poem (p.4)
'The Ballad of My Friend' contains the lines:
'I have been to the court of the Emperor of Rome,
Seen Prester John who lives in a tomb,
And where Indian mountains rise like spears,
~~Brown men~~ ['Brown men' altered to 'negroes'] with coral in their ears.'

[991] 'Moonlight bearers of wine' is altered to 'moon browed bearers of wine'
in later version.

[992] Copy, Princeton University Library

[993] Sir John Squire in *The Collected Poems of James Elroy Flecker*, Secker &
Warburg, p.xxii, gives reasons for the alterations in sex in the poem.
Referring to Sir John Squire's comments Gillanders states:
'At the same time the change of sex in the subject of the poem for the
sake of a better rhyme indicates how little personal feeling entered the
poem. Although written in the first person, the poem is completely
objective. It is the craftsmanship of the poem and not the emotion
expressed which interested Flecker.'
GILL, Vol.1, p.56
Stephen Parry states in *James Elroy Flecker, a new selection*, Autolycus 1980:
'The Queen's Song'. Written 1906-7. In the original version (entitled 'The
Golden Head') the 'boy' is a 'maid' and the speaker (presumably) male.
Some of Flecker's contemporaries assumed that the female persona was
adopted as a camouflage, taking the poem as 'the amorous description of
a boy'.
The queen is not a straightforward mouthpiece, however; she is treated
ironically, in the mention of Midas, whose gift brought him no good, in
an echo of Milton ('nations yet unborn' see 'Paradise Lost', v.263) and in
what one may call an excessive delicacy of diction (e.g. 1.29).'

[994] John Lehmann in his book: *His Life and Legend, Rupert Brooke*, Quartet
Books, 1981, refers to 'a more serious moral fault' in relation to 'The

Queen's Song' He writes: 'Whatever the rather obscure fault (the ambiguous meaning of Queen in 1910?) it went into *Georgian Poetry*.' p.65

995 Davis, p.81

996 Mary Byrd Davis, p.31, when referring to the 'Queen's Song' states: 'The play on words may be obscene.'
'The Sanskrit word "jani' is an origin for the word "Queen'. [*The Wise Wound*, p.174] 'The Queen is *cwen* or wife with the *quim*, which is *combe* or *cwm*, the *gune* (woman) is a goddess when she is *gana* and *jani* (woman) with a *yone*, or cunt. *Gens* is wife, as in generation, or great tribe. This is all natural, as all human being are born from a womb, and without this first "magic" there would be no consciousness, and therefore no human religion, or anything else.' [*The Wise Wound*, p.169]
Flecker was interested in languages. In *For What We Have Received* by Francis Toye, Toye writes:
'There were teachers of other less important languages too, and of course Dons who specialised in more or less theoretical knowledge of more or less obscure Indian dialects but with the exception of the Russian teacher none of these came my way.' p.58
The 'Dons' could have come Flecker's way, or he could obtain books on Sanskrit from the Cambridge Library.
Also, Sedgwick was studying Sanskrit.

997 Brooke obviously had not heard, or read, or if he had he did not agree with Flecker's statement in his article on Laurence Hope, p.167, *Monthly Review*.
'The true lover of art, confronted with this straightforward verse, should not let speculations about the weak rhyme or some possible imitation of Swinburne interfere with his admiration and pleasure.'

998 *The Gownsman* Review is reprinted in *The Prose of Rupert Brooke*, Sidgwick & Jackson 1956, p.111, but the poem is not included.

999 'Presume a joyously amusing review of me in *The Gownsman* was by your pen'. Extract from letter to Brooke, King's College Cambridge, postmarked Stroud, Glos., 5 Nov. 1910. Copy PUL

1000 The examinations (without the Russian papers) comprised 20 sheets, 11 in English and 9 in Turkish, Arabic and Persian. There is a note on the examination papers in PUL: Professor Browne, whose protégé he had become, carefully preserved the papers until 1920, when he gave them to Sir Sydney Cockerell, who had written a short note on the envelope.

1001 SLA, p.190

1002 NGJ, p.99

1003 John Sherwood in NGJ, p.99 states: 'The Sentimentalist', despite one false clue deliberately planted in it, is clearly his farewell to Eleanor Finlayson. Mary Byrd Davis states that it is a farewell to Beazley. Byrd Davis, p.114

1004 Copy Book. Lockwood Library, Buffalo, New York.

1005 Charles Baudelaire, *Selected Poems*, Penguin Classics Translated by Joanna Richardson

[1006] Stephen Parry, *James Elroy Flecker*, Autolycus 1980 'The Sentimentalist' is apparently an entirely 'sentimental' poem – callow musings on the photograph of a lost friend; but it incorporates an echo of Donne's 'A Valediction; forbidding mourning'. Again the parallel is not exact, but again the context enforces the allusion; Donne proclaims what Flecker's sentimentalist denies, love's independence of physical presence. The effect is to separate the authorial voice and the persona of the poem, to substitute self-directed irony dramatically presented for straightforward 'sincerity'.pp.8-9

[1007] NGJ, p.99

[1008] There is a reference to the cinema in *The Grecians*.

[1009] GILL, p.63 and Byrd Davis, p.115 'Although Pavlova in London is more ambitious in theme then anything he had hitherto attempted Flecker has really little to say. It philosophises vaguely upon the text that beauty is transient and that dancers have their day. From the melancholy of "all the world's stage" he drifts into ancient Greek associations of dancing nymphs and fauns and into a style elaborately rhetorical.' Byrd Davis states that 'Pavlovna' has its sources in Keats 'Ode on a Grecian Urn' but concludes that the poem does not have the intensity of Keats' Ode. But however transient the theme of 'Pavlova in London' it endured for a wider audience until at least 18[t] August 1936 when the BBC broadcast it in its Empire programme for the usual fee of 5 shillings for the reading. (From the A.P. Watt Records #11036 Folder 375.12, Manuscripts Department, Wilson Library, The University of North Carolina at Chapel Hill, USA)

[1010] *Collected Poems.*

[1011] *The Golden Journey to Samarkand.* Prologue

[1012] 'Pavlovna' was published in *The Cambridge Review*, 24 November, 1910. It was revised as 'Pavlova in London'. Published in Flecker's *Forty-Two Poems*.

[1013] LIFE, p.153

[1014] The extract from the letter published in the LIFE is as follows: 'I am so desperately hard at work doing this play of mine and so forth. I am only going away for fifteen months after all... Thank you both ever so much for all the great kindness you have shown me, and for the outfit, which is a splendid one, and for the parting gifts.'
In NGJ, Sherwood quotes what appears to be the same letter but places it in a later period, after Flecker's return from Constantinople, in March 1911.
'I am so very sorry,' he replied, 'but I do not see how it can possibly be managed. I am absolutely pledged to go to Paris Thursday night, having put it off once already – and till then I have not a single moment to myself. I am so desperately hard at work doing this play of mine. Also one can't afford a pound – neither I nor you – and also I am only going away for fifteen months after all. But I am very sorry not to be able to see you again.' NGJ, p.126

In both cases the letter (or letters?) is quoted to show Flecker's reply to his parents when they request one last farewell visit, when he is already in London.

[1015] K of A, pp.239–40

[1016] 'The most brilliant in that very talented group of young poets up at Cambridge in the years just preceding the Great War.' *The Poetry of James Elroy Flecker*, Dublin Magazine, January, 1924.

[1017] K of A, p.239

[1018] K of A, p.239

Chapter Seven

[1019] Omitted portion of letter published in LJEF p.12, also SLA p.7. Supplied by University of Texas in Austin

[1020] SLA p.1

[1021] K of A, p.40

[1022] Hellé quoted four lines of D.G. Rossetti in SLA:
'O heart that neither beats nor heaves/in that one
darkness lying still,/What now to thee my love's great will/Or the fine
web the sunshine weaves.'

[1023] C.Pr. 240

[1024] Peronella to Norman, p.40 K of A

[1025] SLA p.2

[1026] CP

[1027] SLA, p.4, omitted from LJEF, p.12

[1028] GILL, p.227

[1029] This reference to five years was not explained, but in practical terms it could refer to the time he had to stay in the service, without forfeiture of Dr. Flecker's £500 bond. [Five years was about the length of time Hellé and Flecker were together.]

[1030] Omitted portion of letter sent to Savery March 1911, Paris. TS supplied by University of Texas at Austin. Published in LJEF p.20; SLA, p.36

[1031] Omitted portion of letter sent to Savery from The British Consulate 2 Aug. 1910, Constantinople. TS supplied by University of Texas at Austin. Letter published LJEF, p.14 and SLA, p.8

[1032] SLA, p.8; LJEF, p.14

[1033] K of A, p.124

[1034] SLA, p.7; LJEF, p.12

[1035] Portion of letter omitted from letter to Frank Savery published in LJEF p.12, SLA p.7 supplied by University of Texas at Austin.

[1036] K of A, p.123

[1037] K of A, p.125

[1038] K of A, p.125

[1039] K of A, p.126

[1040] K of A, p.127

[1041] K of A, p.126

[1042] K of A, p.42
[1043] Notebook Poetry Collection, Lockwood Memorial Library, New York. Byrd, p.116, refers to this fragment.
[1044] Notebook Poetry Collection, Lockwood Memorial Library, New York. Byrd, p.116, refers to this fragment.
[1045] *Don Juan*, Act 1, Scene 2, p.16.
[1046] TSDJ, p.9
[1047] Rupert Brooke, Hassall, pp.167, 230
[1048] K of A, p.124
[1049] K of A, p.44
[1050] SLA, p.3
[1051] TSDJ, p.83
[1052] TSDJ, p.84
[1053] GILL, p.77
[1054] SLA, p.2
[1055] NGJ, p.108
[1056] NGJ, p.164
[1057] LJEF, p.12; SLA, p.7
[1058] LIFE, p.153
[1059] Later Sir Reader Bullard, K.C.B., K.C.M.G.
[1060] CMG, p.56
[1061] LIFE, p.155
[1062] CMG, p.58
[1063] LIFE, p.155
[1064] LD, p.71
[1065] CMG, p.56
[1066] SLA, p.4
[1067] CMG, p.71
[1068] NGJ, p.103
[1069] Preface to *Letters From Tehran: A British Ambassador in World War II Persia.* Reader Bullard, I.B. Tauris & Co. Ltd. London, 1991, p.xii
[1070] LIFE, p.153
[1071] NGJ, p.105
[1072] LJEF, p.14
[1073] CMG, p.70
[1074] Bullard was said by his son, in *Letters from Tehran* to have no interest in the natural world. It was Flecker's influence that made Bullard enjoy this day. Although Bullard always enjoyed books and the company of friends.
[1075] Another unpublished poem may also have resulted from the day spent with Reader Bullard. *In Inside Stalin's Russia: the Diaries of Reader Bullard, 1930–1934*, edited by Julian and Margaret Bullard, Day Books 2000, p.123, reference is made to: 'I felt it was fortunate that the Alcibiades of Flecker's unpublished poem was not there:
When Alcibiades
Met naiades
He would remove the bodices

From those delightful goddesses.'

[1076] BYRD, p.118

[1077] C81 Bod. Byrd prints the rest of this poem p.118, also p.108 refers to it. NGJ, p.119 quotes a line of this poem in a letter to Hellé dated Dec. 1910.

[1078] C.Pr. p.58

[1079] NNY, Lockwood

[1080] NNY, Lockwood

[1081] NNY Lockwood

[1082] CP

[1083] NNY Lockwood

[1084] SLA, p.4

[1085] LIFE, p.154

[1086] LIFE, p.154

[1087] LJEF, p.14; SLA p.8 portion omitted from letter supplied by University of Texas

[1088] SLA, p.4

[1089] NGJ, p.107

[1090] NGJ, p.105

[1091] Act 2, Scene 3 Anna's speech, p.135

[1092] *Tramp*, p.498. March 1911
Byrd, p.124.
NGJ, p.107

[1093] Poetry Collection, Lockwood Memorial Library MS.

[1094] FO Directory

[1095] Omitted portion of letter to Savery, LJEF, p.106. Also SLA p.171

[1096] CPr. p.61

[1097] CPr. p.62

[1098] CPr. p.57

[1099] CPr. p.59

[1100] LIFE, p.154

[1101] NGJ, p.106

[1102] *Letters from Tehran*, p.274

[1103] NGJ, p.110

[1104] LIFE, p.155

[1105] SLA, p.33, refers to meeting again a British Consul who had been aboard and had been in the expedition to Athens.

[1106] SLA, p.99; LJEF p.47

[1107] Lockwood

[1108] LJEF, p.44; SLA, p.98

[1109] K of A, p.134

[1110] LIFE, p.156

[1111] LIFE, pp.163–4

[1112] LIFE, p.157 and NGJ, p.108

[1113] FO Memo

[1114] NGJ, p.110

[1115] LIFE, p.164

1116 *The Greatest Story Never Told*. Frank Ryan, Swift Publishers 1992, p.18 refers to an outbreak of TB in a primary school. Uppingham Br. Medical 291 1039-40, Lancet 1 1141- 3 Br 5 DIS 81 193-4. Outbreak discovered in 1978, the source traced to a teacher.

1117 *The Grecians*, p.53

1118 LIFE, p.28

1119 K of A, p.144

1120 CMG, p.71

1121 2nd Dragoman, later Sir Andrew Ryan (1876–1949)

1122 LD, p.70

1123 FO memo

1124 James Elroy Flecker in Constantinople, Sir Reader Bullard *The Listener*, 15 February 1951, p.268

1125 CMG, p.66

1126 Lockwood

1127 Lockwood

1128 *Baudelaire*, Pichois & Zeigler. Trans. Graham Robb. 1989 Vintage, p.99

1129 *Baudelaire*, Pichois & Zeigler. Trans. Graham Robb. 1989 Vintage, p.99

1130 *Baudelaire*, Pichois & Zeigler. Trans. Graham Robb. 1989 Vintage, p.100

1131 SLA, p.6

1132 K of A, pp.128–9

1133 TSDJ, p.6

1134 *Don Juan*, Act 1, Scene 2, p.55

1135 The Public as Art Critic, CPr.p.248.

1136 C81 BOD. Byrd, p.117 refers to this poem.

1137 Omitted portion of letter to Savery, Paris, March 1911. Supplied by University of Texas at Austin, published in LJEF, p.20; SLA, p.36

1138 CP

1139 NGJ, p.169

1140 Originally Flecker used 'want' instead of 'hope', but scored out 'want', and 'finished' instead of 'polished'. TSDJ, p.39

1141 DJ Heinemann, p.57

1142 LIFE, p.157

1143 SLA, p.5

Chapter Eight

1144 LIFE, p.157

1145 LIFE, p.157

1146 LJEF, pp. 15–16. SLA, pp.8–9

1147 LJEF, pp. 15–16. SLA, pp.8–9

1148 NGJ, p.113

1149 Names from omitted portion of letter supplied by University of Texas

1150 Names from omitted portion of letter supplied by University of Texas

1151 Omitted portion only – no names
1152 Omitted portion only – no names
1153 LJEF, p.17 and SLA, p.10
1154 FO 369/332
1155 C.Pr., p.264
1156 LIFE, p.213, reference made in letter June 1914
1157 JEF, p.73
1158 BL
1159 *Odd Man Out*, p.105
1160 *Odd Man Out*, p.105
1161 NGJ, p.113
1162 NGJ, p.113 first sentence only of this letter published p.6 SLA.
1163 NGJ, ps. 112, 113.
1164 See The 'other girl' could have been a man, Ronald Firbank
1165 SLA, p.6
1166 From omitted portion of letter supplied by University of Texas
1167 LJEF, p.17; SLA, p.10
1168 portion omitted from letter
1169 NGJ, p.112
1170 Charles Murray Marling (1862–1933), transferred to Constantinople 1 Oct. 1909. Chargé d'affaires from 23 Oct. 1909–1 Jan. 1910. Later Sir Charles Marling, CMG. Retired 1926
1171 LD, p.70
1172 FO 369/417
1173 NGJ, p.115
1174 Lockwood
1175 SLA, p.6
1176 Lockwood
1177 NGJ, p.115
1178 NGJ, p.115
1179 Preface DJ, p.v
1180 Don Giovanni
1181 *Don Juan*
1182 This poem is not with the letter now in the University of Texas at Austin. (Letter to HW, 1994 from Research Library.)
1183 NGJ, p.118
1184 NGJ, p.118
1185 Byrd, p.122 (quoting from a version in the Berg collection)
1186 JEF, p.63
1187 *Odd Man Out*, p.63
1188 T.S. Mercer makes this point p.26. [Goldring's copy sent to Flecker on his birthday was auctioned in 1992 in London.]
1189 Hassall, p.258
1190 Copy of this letter obtained from PUL. Original seen in King's College Library, Brooke's papers.

[1191] This is a line from Ernest Dowson's poem 'Cynara'
'And I was desolate and sick of an old passion'.

[1192] Original seen in King's College Library, Brooke's papers.

[1193] word unclear

[1194] word unclear

[1195] Copy of PC obtained from PUL Original in King's College Library,
Brooke's papers

[1196] Hassall, p.224 quotes some of this postcard, saying that Flecker had a
habit of 'shooting off exclamatory postcards.' Hassall assumes that the
letter/postcard arrived a week or two after Brooke's review of *Thirty-
Six Poems* in *The Gownsman*, but the date indicated that Flecker only
acknowledged the review on his return from Turkey. Hassall quotes
Brooke's remark about Flecker 'dying of syphilis' p.44 without giving it a
date or source, but uses it to illustrate Brooke's never giving up this form
of affectation.

[1197] NGJ, p.118

[1198] Hassall, p.243

[1199] NGJ, p.119 Sherwood refers to a weekend in Cambridge early in
December,but does not refer to arrangements to meet Rupert Brooke

[1200] NGJ, p.119

[1201] NGJ, p.120

[1202] *The Faith of Edward Wilson*, G. Seavor Murray, 1948, p.2

[1203] LIFE, P.158

[1204] LIFE, p.204

[1205] LIFE, p.204

[1206] LIFE, p.204

[1207] GILL, pp.384–413, Vol.II

[1208] NGJ, p.121

[1209] NGJ, p.121

[1210] This poem was later revised as 'A Sacred Incident' and included in
Flecker's Book of Verse *The Golden Journey to Samarkand*, published by
Max Goschen Limited, 1913. In a letter to Savery in July 1913, Flecker
described it as one of the two rotten poems in the book 'harmless rather
than offensive'. (SLA, p.98. LJEF, p.43)

[1211] The BL, Dept. of Manuscripts Add.Mss. 41295 ff22 gives the date the
poem was written, which was Feb., 1913. Byrd p.155 n discusses the
mis-dating of the writing of 'Oak and Olive'. She states that the position
in Flecker's notebook (BOD) supports the Feb. 1913 date. *Hassan's*
preface written by Squire states that 'Oak and Olive' was written in
Corfu and GILL, p.110 also puts the writing of 'Oak and Olive' in Corfu.
Misunderstandings about the exact date could have come about first from
the LIFE, as on pp.158–9, when two verses of 'Oak and Olive' are quoted,
it is also stated that it 'belongs to this time so far as it is concerned with
his own country; and the time could not have been one of undiluted
boredom and fretting'. Hodgson is writing about Flecker's time in the
sanatorium in Cranham and reference is made to Cranham in 'Oak and

Olive'. As Flecker's first visit to Athens is not mentioned in the LIFE, Squire could have taken the reference to Athens as the time of Flecker's marriage in Athens, which was not a happy time and not a time of hot weather; it was still spring. Squire, like Gillanders, could have concluded that the Athens wedding was the important and lasting memory, but Gillander's work was first written before NGJ revealed how unhappy had been the time of the Athens wedding. Gillander's work he tells us, when republished in 1983, was not altered.

[1212] SLA, p.99. LJEF, p.45

[1213] NGJ, p.169

[1214] Chapter 5.

[1215] LIFE, p.158, refers to Cranham being four or five miles from Painswick Beacon

[1216] *The Victorians and Ancient Greece.* Richard Jenkyns, Blackwell, Oxford. 1980, pp.185–7, reference to 'Oak and Olive' and 'The Ballad of Hampstead Heath'.

[1217] CPr., p.246

[1218] SLA, p.12

[1219] K of A, pp.56–57

[1220] NGJ, p.124

[1221] LOCKWOOD

[1222] MS. Eng. Poet C81. Article: 'Liberalism and Youth'.

[1223] Notebook MS. Eng. Poet. e 186 BOD.
Poem: 'We are Young British Liberals...'

[1224] NGJ, p.123.

[1225] FO 369/416

[1226] Unison and Part Songs, 'The Princess', J.E. Flecker SSC and piano Stainer and Bell Ltd. Composition by Thomas Wood

[1227] TS DJ, p88

[1228] DJ Heinemann, p.142

[1229] SLA, p.36. LJEF, p.20

[1230] republished CPr., p.229

[1231] This letter is published in full in DJ pp.ix, x, 1925. A copy in Hellé's hand is in the BL, but it differs from the extract quoted by Flecker in a letter to Savery, which is also published in DJ, LJEF, p.22; SLA, p.38

[1232] LIFE, p.161

[1233] *Don Juan* by Flecker was eventually performed on Sunday, April 26 1926, at the Court Theatre, Three Hundred Club, *Don Juan* was performed by The Adelphi Players in the autumn/winter of 1942, Cecil Davies, *The Adelphi Players The Theatre of Persons*, introduced and edited by Peter Billingham. Routledge Harwood, London and New York, 2002. *Contemporary Theatre Studies* A series of books edited by Franc Chamberlain and on 6–17 January 1947 at the St. George's Hall, WC1, by the Elroy Players (RADA). GILL, p.293 gives this information in a footnote, and also gives details of reviews that appeared at the time i *The New Statesman* etc. on p.294.

Esther Menasce, in her book *Minor Don Juans in British Literature*, Cisalpino
– Goliardica, 1986, which reprints for the first time since 1925, the
full text of Flecker's *Don Juan* play, states that Flecker's play was never
produced, p.7, but this is incorrect.
Edward Shanks in his *Second Essays on Literature*, published by Collins in
1927, states p.99, that *Don Juan* by Flecker is not likely to be produced
'except by misguided fanatics'. Shanks also states that the play 'may never
be printed'. But Shanks has to tell his readers, in a footnote, that *Don Juan*
has been printed and produced.
Don Juan was first published by Wm. Heinemann Ltd. in 1925. The *Times
Literary Supplement*, in its review of Thursday 26 November, described the
play as brilliantly contrived and full of gorgeous passages. The reviewer
was able to make comparisons with Flecker's *Hassan*. Ten years had
elapsed since the death of Flecker and the writer of the review stated that
England kills its poets by neglect. Discussion of how much Flecker's work
influenced Shaw is outlined in Timothy Kidd's *A Wolf in the Conservatory
Essays in Criticism*, Park Press, 1998, p.87, 'James Elroy Flecker and George
Bernard Shaw.' Also there is reference to Flecker's 'Hassan' and Shaw's
'St. Joan' in Herbert Palmer's 'Post-Victorian Poetry'

[1234] *Bernard Shaw*, Michael Holroyd, Vol.2, 1898–1918 Chatto & Windus, p.280
[1235] The exact wording of the record of Flecker's time in London trying to
get someone interested in his play was that he had five appointments on
the day he saw Trench and that he knew Trench would not agree to 'do
the play'.[letter to his parents, LIFE, p.161] In his letter to Savery, Flecker
states: 'I finished my play *Don Juan* on Tuesday, revised it Wednesday, had
it typed Thursday, gave it to Bernard Shaw to read Friday, got it back and
got a letter to Trench, Lessee of the Haymarket Theatre Monday, sent it to
Trench Tuesday, for an appointment with Trench Thursday and found he
had read it and went off to Paris the same night.' [SLA, p.38]
In NGJ Sherwood states that the typescript (of *Don Juan*) was delivered
to Shaw on Friday, March 3rd and Shaw read it over the weekend and
returned it on Monday with some opinions and advice. Sherwood states
that Flecker had a letter of introduction from Shaw, p.126
[1236] All these points are covered by GILL, pp.292–3
[1237] BL, Dept. of Manuscripts. Add. Mss. 60666
[1238] Omitted portion of letter published LJEF, p.20. SLA p.36
[1239] NGJ, p.130
[1240] NGJ, p.130
[1241] NGJ, p.131
[1242] DJ, p.136
[1243] SLA, p.13
[1244] SLA, p.42; LJEF, p.27
[1245] LIFE, p.162
[1246] LJEF, p.25 (that letter omitted from SLA)
[1247] NGJ, p.132

[1248] Arthur James Mason DD, *Life of William Edward Collins Bishop of Gibralter*, 1912, p.184, Longmans

[1249] LIFE, p.163

[1250] NGJ, p.134

[1251] Andrew Ryan, in LD p.81, describes the difficulties of wedding in the Embassy, Constantinople, when he was Catholic and his wife was not. The wedding took place in 1912.

[1252] NGJ, p.138

[1253] NGJ, p.135 and LIFE, p.163 ('no money' and 'going to see Hellé in Athens' omitted from publication of letter in LIFE)

[1254] John Sherwood in NGJ, p.134, states that Flecker saw the Consulate doctor on 20 April and wrote to Hellé the same day with the news of his relapse. But a letter to Mavrogordato, dated 20 April [SLA, p.43] tells Mavrogordato he is going to get married on 10 May. On receipt of a letter from Savery, Flecker replied that same day, 21 April, [SLA, p.43] now giving the date of the wedding as 15 May, and this letter is Savery's formal announcement of his wedding to Hellé. This change of date indicated receiving a letter from Hellé on 20 or 21 April which gave a change of wedding date, and also her would-be date of departure from Paris. Hellé [SLA, p.13] states that she got the news of Flecker's health giving him trouble when she reached Athens, where he joined her a week later. The fact of Hellé receiving the letter about her future bridegroom's breakdown in health, after she had arrived in Athens for the wedding, made postponement at that stage by her, much more unlikely.

[1255] SLA, p.14

[1256] NGJ, p.138

[1257] NGJ, p.153

[1258] LIFE, p.162

Chapter Nine

[1259] Sacred to Venus and the Goddess of Love

[1260] K of A, p.236

[1261] '*An Artist in Corfu*' by Sophie Atkinson in *The English Review* of May, 1912

[1262] In '*Artist in Corfu*', Sophie Atkinson writes: 'The marriage includes the exchange of rings, and three interchangings of the gold and silver wreaths on the heads of the bride and bridegroom. Finally a little procession round the inside of the church with many pauses for blessing'.

[1263] K of A, p.162

[1264] NGJ, p.143

[1265] When Hellé died, fifty years later, on 27 October 1961, her age on the death certificate was given as seventy-seven, although she must have been eighty. Byrd Davis, p.112, refers to Hellé insisting that some references to her were cut from letters printed in the LIFE. Also references were cut from Flecker's published letters to Savery. But some of the references in the omissions from the letters to Savery refer to her age being thirty at the time of her first meeting with her future husband in June 1910, (which, if strictly accurate, would add another year or two to her age) and also some unflattering references to her appearance were omitted from LJEF. A flattering passage was also omitted from LJEF but Hellé did not omit this passage when she herself published the same letters in 1930, after the publication of LJEF in 1926. The sentence that was previously left out was the one where Flecker described Hellé to Savery as 'a fair Greek maiden called Hellé of extraordinary intelligence and taste , knowing all the poetry in the world. She took me round Athens .....' [SLA, p.7]

[1266] *Letters from Tehran*, Bullard, p.274

[1267] SLA, p.14

[1268] SLA, p.19

[1269] *Letters from Tehran*, p.274

[1270] Bullard, in his *Letters from Tehran*, p.233, states that Hellé was given a Civil List pension of £90.

[1271] Note to Herr Freissler (unpublished) enclosed in letter to Savery, SLA p.140. Supplied by University of Texas.

[1272] Omitted note to Herr Freissler (unpublished) enclosed in letter to Savery, SLA p.140. Supplied by University of Texas.

[1273] SLA, p.18

[1274] Omitted note to Friessler, Texas, SLA. p.140

[1275] Omitted note to Freissler, Texas, SLA. p.140

[1276] SLA, pps.43-44

[1277] SLA, p.46

[1278] Omitted note to Freissler, Texas, SLA. p.140

[1279] BYRD DAVIS, p.180

[1280] J.M. Munro, JEF pps.64–5

[1281] CP

[1282] NNY LOCKWOOD

[1283] *Japanese Noh Dramas*, edited and translated by Royall Tyler, Penguin Books, 1992, p.238

[1284] *Japanese Noh Dramas*, edited and translated by Royall Tyler, Penguin Books, 1992, p.238

[1285] SLA, p.99

[1286] GJ, p.x

[1287] J.M. Munro, pp.64–5 in his book *James Elroy Flecker* explains that familiarity with de Régnier's writings 'helps to clarify Flecker's intentions.' Munro thinks that 'A Ship, an Isle' was the poem that 'gave symbolic expression to his sense of disillusionment.' Byrd Davis, p.179–180 describes Munro's analysis of 'A Ship, an Isle' as ingenuous but prefers not to assign it a specific message. GILL discusses the poem on pp.84–85 Vol.I, and states that Flecker elaborates an idea from his poem 'Fountains'. Hodgson in LIFE, p.253 compares the poem 'A Ship, an Isle' to a poem by Samain. Hodgson states that these 'are more than beautiful verses; they plunge through the surface to the depths of emotion. But they cannot be analysed for the unseeing any more than a proof that the whole is greater than its part could be furnished for the mathematically deficient.'

[1288] SLA, p.114

[1289] NGJ, p.168

[1290] *Ronald Firbank: Memoirs and Critiques.* Edited by Mervyn Horder. Duckworth, 1977, pp. 9, 90.

[1291] Unpublished article in the BOD.

[1292] SLA, p.114

[1293] C.Pr., p.71

[1294] Munro, p.66

[1295] C.Pr., p.58

[1296] C.Pr., p.58

[1297] K of A, p.203

[1298] Richard Jenkyns. *The Victorians and Ancient Greece,* Blackwell pp.40–1

[1299] NGJ, p.133

[1300] NGJ, p.131

[1301] Flecker's review in *The English Review,* May 1912 of Sophie Atkinson's '*An Artist in Corfu*'

[1302] *Edward Lear,* edited by Humbert Wolfe, Augustan Books of Modern Poetry, 1927.

[1303] 1938

[1304] Later Lord John Proby

[1305] SLA, p.49, August 11th, 1911

[1306] LIFE, p.165

[1307] NGJ, p.137

[1308] Omitted portion of letter, published SLA, p.146 from original in the BOD

[1309] SLA, p.46

[1310] 'James Elroy Flecker' by Alec Macdonald. *The Fortnightly Review,* New Series, Feb. 1924.

[1311] *Marco Polo's Travels* (Newnes, 3s.6d., leather) one of Flecker's favourite books. LIFE, p.195

[1312] Act III, Scene 4, *Hassan.* Epilogue of *The Golden Journey to Samarkand.*

[1313] Epilogue to *The Golden Journey to Samarkand.* Act III, Scene 4, Hassan.

[1314] Sarah Searight, *The British in the Middle East,* East-West Publications, 1979, pp.64, 252, 268, 271

[1315] CP

[1316] MS. C.81 BOD.

[1317] FO 369/513

[1318] Dorina L. Neave, *Twenty-Six Years on the Bosphorus,* Grayson & Grayson, 1933, p.161. Also mentioned in 'James Elroy Flecker in Constantinople' by Sir Reader Bullard, *The Listener,* February 15th, 1951

[1319] Dorina L. Neave. *Twenty-Six Years on the Bosphorus,* Grayson & Grayson, 1933, p.161. Also mentioned in 'James Elroy Flecker in Constantinople' by Sir Reader Bullard, *The Listener,* February 15th, 1951.

[1320] Dorina L. Neave. *Twenty-Six Years on the Bosphorus*, Grayson & Grayson, 1933, p.161. Also mentioned in 'James Elroy Flecker in Constantinople' by Sir Reader Bullard, *The Listener*, February 15th, 1951.

[1321] SLA, p.4

[1322] SLA, p.48

[1323] SLA, p.48

[1324] GILL, Vol.2, p.307, gives references to the unanimous praise from critics, among them 'the perfection of phraseology' quoting *The Times*.

[1325] Act III, Scene 1.

[1326] Act III, Scene 3.

[1327] Act III, Scene 1

[1328] GILL, Vol.2, pp.370–1

[1329] Patric Dickinson. *James Elroy Flecker. Literature and Life.*

[1330] LIFE, p.128

[1331] Arthur Waley wrote the Introduction to the Collected 1929 edition of Firbank's Works. Firbank had made arrangements just before he died in May 1926, for the issue at his own expense of a Collected edition of his work. '*Ronald Firbank: A Memoir* by Ifan Kyrle Fletcher' was reproduced in full in *Ronald Firbank: Memoirs and Critiques* edited with an introduction by Mervyn Horder. Duckworth, 1977. Arthur Waley's Introduction and a Critique by E.M. Forster was published alongside many others.

[1332] GILL, Vol.2, p.334

[1333] Arthur Waley. *Introduction to the Noh Plays of Japan*, Allen & Unwin. First published 1921. p.53

[1334] Brigid Brophy in *Prancing Novelist* draws attention to the Chinese influence of Firbank's work that attracted Waley, and Evelyn Waugh wrote about Firbank's comedy and the Chinese wit.

[1335] *Hassan*, Act 1, Scene 1.

[1336] CP

[1337] Act 1, Scene 1.

[1338] CP

[1339] In Firbank's play *The Princess Zoubaroff: A Comedy*, which was published by Grant Richards at Firbank's expense in 1920, contains a character, Lord Orkish, who says: 'I'm never bored. I enjoy everything.' This has an echo of Flecker writing to his mother from Wales in the Easter vacation of 1903, when he is referring to his solitude, 'Yet I enjoy it, because I enjoy everything ...'. The character Lord Orkish was speaking to, agrees and says 'Alone with my shadow I'm soon depressed.', which also echoes a Flecker sentiment (and not Firbank's). The Princess Zoubaroff herself is disappointed with mountains which irritate her and she says that 'I should like to shake Switzerland', which is reminiscent of Flecker's feelings about that country and the anguish transmitted in his poem 'South, East and North' of which he wrote two versions and more than one interpretation. The Princess goes on to recall a death that occurred 'just as the clock was striking mid-day.... He begged me to mourn him Chinese fashion – White.'

[1340] Ellis Waterhouse writing about Ronald Firbank in *Alta: the University of Birmingham Review*, No.3 Summer 1967. Reprinted in *Ronald Firbank: Memoirs and Critiques*, p.217 suggested that in *Inclinations* Firbank had parodied some very silly literature of the period he says that Professor T.J.B. Spencer has suggested Firbank is referring to *Three Sons and a Mother*, 1916. Firbank later rewrote a dinner scene which takes place in Part 2 of *Inclinations*, but the typescript of *Inclinations* was in the hands of the publisher in the first week of 1916, the year that Gilbert Cannan's novel was also published.

[1341] E 186 BOD

[1342] Act 1, Scene 1

[1343] SLA, p.10. LJEF, p.17

[1344] Ch.6, p.130

[1345] Act 1, Scene 1

[1346] Act 1, Scene 2.

[1347] Act II, Scene 1

[1348] Donald Keene, *The Pleasures of Japanese Literature*, Columbia University Press, New York, 1988.

[1349] Act IV, Scene 1.

[1350] LIFE, p.138

[1351] Act V, Scene 1

[1352] 'The orientals in *Hassan* are Edwardians in fancy dress pretending to be orientals and the audience is meant to realize this.' *The Victorians and Ancient Greece*, Richard Jenkyns, Basil Blackwell, 1980, p.327

[1353] Byrd Davis, p.213

[1354] Act 1, Scene 1

[1355] C.Pr., p.45

[1356] Act II, Scene 1

[1357] Alec Macdonald. 'James Elroy Flecker'. *Fortnightly Review*, Feb. 1924.

[1358] GILL, vol.2, p.309

[1359] Hassan denies when challenged by Ishak that he is a poet. Ishak answers that he is Ishak the poet, a man of no repute. [Act I, Scene 4]

[1360] Act I, Scene 2

[1361] SLA, p.21

[1362] SLA, p.98

[1363] SLA, p.98

[1364] NGJ, p.141 (part of poem quoted)

[1365] GILL, Vol.1, p.128

[1366] NGJ, p.169

[1367] Some confusion exists about Flecker actually reading the poems of Beazley's when they were published in *The English Review*, the April edition. In April 1911, in a letter to Mavrogordato, Flecker asks for a copy of *The English Review* if Beazley's poems are to be in that edition. SLA, p.42. In a letter to Mavrogordato at *The English Review* office, from Corfu on 25 July, Flecker tells Mavrogordato that he had got the April number of the *E.R.* But in a postcard to Mavrogordato dated 11 August, Flecker states that he has got the July *English Review* but not the April No. 'for which I yearn.' SLA, p.49. Sherwood, NGJ p.141, does not refer to the published version of Beazley's poem. Byrd Davis, p.260, states that Flecker had read the published version of Beazley's poem and this may have prompted him to write his own version.

[1368] GILL, vol.I, p.129 in a footnote states:
'The poetic image of the cloths of heaven is found in William Morris's poem 'The Defence of Genevere'. A variation of this theme is also found in Stevenson's poem 'I will make you brooches.'

[1369] CP

[1370] SLA, p.81

[1371] NGJ, p.165

[1372] SLA, p.99

[1373] NGJ, p.141

[1374] LIFE, p.246

[1375] Hodgson states that Flecker does not appear to be aware of 'this other use and meaning of the image'. LIFE, p.246

[1376] SLA, p.49.

[1377] E 186 BOD

[1378] It is not clear from the notebook whether 'Fairy Story' is a poem or prose. Records of Flecker's work in magazines do not mention *Nash's Magazine* publishing any of his works.

[1379] Flecker does not indicate in this notebook that he sent 'The Ballad of the Queen's Bouquet' for publication. The inclusion of this poem at this time when Flecker was writing a new poem 'The Hamman Name', another poem with a hidden reference to Ronald Firbank, indicates it was influenced by 'The Queen's Bouquet' in which the references to Firbank are even more carefully hidden. 'The Queen's Bouquet' includes the use of such words as 'fragrant flower de luces' and 'such a winsome scent they had'. John Anthony Kiechler in ' *The Butterfly's Freckled Wings*: A study of Style in Novels of Ronald Firbank' Swiss Studies in English, p.114, comments on the unusual form of 'fleur de lys' in the works of Firbank, and 'Flower-de-luce' was a pre-nineteenth century anglicised form. But in using this, Flecker was using a word similar to 'fleur de luce', which according to Kiechler was common only to Beardsley and Firbank. The use of 'winsome scent' can also be seen as a hidden reference to Ronald Firbank. In 'The Hamman Name' Flecker uses the more obvious 'Winsome Torment'.

[1380] *Journey to Samarkand*, which Flecker put alongside 'Dream Afloat' – *Spectator* in his notebook, could be the pair of poems about which he wrote to Mavrogordato 'I have written a joyous and Eastern poem which I have sent to America (I'll copy it out for you if you send me a nice reply. It's 4 pages).' [SLA, pp.47–8] He enclosed another poem in this letter (dated 25 July) and asked Mavrogordato's opinion and told him if the *E.R.* did not want it, he had 'contracted the habit of sending my work to America.'

[1381] While in Corfu, Flecker wrote, in July, a translation of Mistral's 'La Contigo', which he gave the title 'Denis and Antonia' From the Provençal.' [Ms C81 BOD]

[1382] A reference to 'A Miracle in Bethlehem'.

[1383] BL Add. Mss. 60666

[1384] The Houghton Library, Harvard University

[1385] The deleted stanza is reproduced on p.10 of *The Golden Road to Samarkand* by Wilfrid Blunt. Hamish Hamilton. 1973 Holograph of *The Golden Journey to Samarkand* by JEF is in the Fitzwilliam Museum. The deleted stanza is also reproduced in *James Elroy Flecker* in The Small Book Series, published by J.L. Carr of poets from Matthew Arnold to William Wordsworth. In *The Last Englishman. The Life of J.L. Carr* by Byron Rogers Aurum Press 2003 the stanza is reproduced again (p.7) to illustrate that The Small Book Series had enabled J.L. Carr to publish 'his own favourite[poet]' and to put the deleted stanza in the introduction to the booklet which contained some of Flecker's poems including *The Golden Journey to Samarkand*.

[1386] SLA, p.48 – 28 July 1911

[1387] Ch.6, p.27

[1388] SLA, p.99 – Letter to Savery, July 1913

[1389] CP

[1390] GILL, Vol. II, p.233

[1391] GILL, Vol. II, p.233

[1392] K of A, p.144

[1393] 'Eddy' was based on the Honourable Evan Montague whom Firbank thought had a face resembling the mummy of Rameses. Firbank, who met Montague after leaving Cambridge, was said to be infatuated or in love with Montague.

[1394] Cyril W. Beaumont. *Bookseller at the Ballet. Memoirs 1891–1929*. C.W. Beaumont, 1975, p.180

[1395] K of A, p.193,

[1396] K of A, p.260

[1397] CP

[1398] 'In Phaecia'

[1399] SLA, p.24

[1400] SLA, p.127

[1401] SLA, p.81

[1402] SLA, p.81

[1403] LIFE, p.168, letter dated 16 August.

[1404] SLA, p.58

[1405] Humbert Wolfe. *The Upward Anguish*

[1406] Jocelyn Brook, *Ronald Firbank*, Arthur Barker, 1952, p.36

[1407] NGJ, p.227

[1408] K of A, p.260

[1409] Publication of *Vainglory* was a new beginning for Firbank as a writer, who had not got his work published for eight years, and it coincided with the end of Flecker's life. *Vainglory* had been submitted to Martin

Secker, who rejected it in December 1914. Grant Richards read *Vainglory* over Christmas and refused it on 28 December. Richards accepted the manuscript next day because Firbank agreed to pay for publication. 5 January 1915 was the date of a specimen page being seen in Richard's office. [6 January was the day that Flecker's obituary appeared in *The Times.*] 7 January the day that Firbank began to take an active interest in the production of *Vainglory.* M.J. Benkovitz, *Ronald Firbank*, Weidenfeld and Nicolson, 1969, p.134

[1410] Cleopatra is also the title of a poem by Beazley, published in *The English Review*

[1411] NGJ, p.55

[1412] Brigid Brophy in *Prancing Novelist*, Macmillan 1973, p.366–7 refers to Firbank's character Mrs. Thoroughfare singing in his novel *Valmouth* of 'White Mit-y-lene,' (and of Geraldine O'Brookomore and Mabel Collins in *Inclinations* going to Greece) as a tribute to Natalie Clifford Barney, poetic-dramatist on the subject of Sappho and Renee Vivien (née Pauline Tarn, in 1877, she had lived as a young girl for a time in Chislehurst, where Firbank's parents had their home), poet and translator of Sappho. Renee Vivien and Natalie Clifford Barney stayed at the villa Renee Vivien which Renee Vivien owned in Mytilene. Renee Vivien died in 1909 of drink and starvation.

Flecker's article 'Forgotten Warfare', which was published in *The New Statesman* of 24 October 1914, contains references to Mytilene in Flecker's description of the battle of Lemnos.

'Forgotten Warfare' was republished in C.Pr.

[Firbank (and as a result Brophy) use the spelling Mitylene. Flecker uses the more usual Mytilene.]

[1413] NGJ, p.120

[1414] Jocelyn Brooke, *Ronald Firbank*, Arthur Barker 1951, p.67

[1415] SLA, p.30

Chapter Ten

[1416] Private letter to Lord Dufferin from Cumberbatch. Dated 21 November 1913

[1417] Forgotten Warfare, C.Pr.

[1418] Forgotten Warfare, C.Pr.

[1419] Forgotten Warfare, C.Pr.

[1420] K of A, p.45

[1421] K of A, p.75

[1422] K of A, p.79

[1423] The Houghton Library, Harvard University, Cambridge, Mass. Published in instalments. First instalment in *The Cambridge Review*, 25 November 1909

[1424] LIFE, p.171

[1425] LIFE, p.167 and NGJ, part p.144, Original BL

[1426] Professor George Saintsbury

[1427] Ch.6, p.143

[1428] SLA, p.186

[1429] The version of 'The Dying Patriot' published in *The Golden Journey to Samarkand* in 1913 differs from *The English Review* version. The latter version is the same as the speech by the dying Lord Framlington in Act 2, Scene 1 of *Don Juan* published in 1926. The manuscript version of *Don Juan* in Cheltenham differs in some respects to the published version.

[1430] T. Stanley Mercer, *James Elroy Flecker. From School to Samarkand*. The Merle Press, 1952.

[1431] T. Stanley Mercer, *James Elroy Flecker. From School to Samarkand*. The Merle Press, 1952.

[1432] NGJ, p.144

[1433] pp.115–7

[1434] LIFE, p.169

[1435] SLA, p.186

[1436] Munro, p.84, makes a similar point

[1437] SLA, p.46

[1438] CP

[1439] *Dean Close School: The First Hundred Years.* Cheltenham, 1986, p.58.
A Book of Memoirs edited by M.A. Girling and Sir Leonard Hooper, printed at the Holywell Press Ltd., Oxford

[1440] BYRD DAVIS, pp.102–104

[1441] BYRD DAVIS, pp.103–104

[1442] BYRD DAVIS, p.101. MBD outlines 'The Tale of Grasso' partly from Flecker's MS. which is not present in Flecker's unpublished papers in the Bod.

[1443] *Home Letters of T.E. Lawrence.* Blackwell, 1954, p.243 (Letter dated 10 November 1912)

[1444] SLA, p.64

[1445] In *Lawrence of Arabia*, Heinemann 1989, p.97, Jeremy Wilson states that Lawrence and Flecker met early in August 1911. This statement is based on the letter from TEL to Noel Rieder [DG *The Letters of T.E. Lawrence* edited by David Garnett, Cape 1938.] published in DG p.120. [Noel Rieder was married to Andre Rieder and taught languages at the American School at Jebail.] This letter is given the postmark 12.8.11. The letter (published with eight lines omitted at the start and sixteen at the end) informs Noel Rieder that Mr. and Mrs. Flecker are coming out to Jebail next weekend. The reference to meeting Mr. and Mrs. Flecker could not have been written in August 1911, as during August 1911, (the early part before Lawrence sailed from Beirut) the Fleckers were on honeymoon in Corfu. The letter was written by Lawrence from the German Hotel, where he and the Fleckers were both living. The Fleckers made their home in the German Hotel from October 1911, until February 1912. It is more likely that Lawrence's letter was postmarked

12.10.1911. Malcolm Brown in *The Letters of T.E. Lawrence*, which he selected and edited in 1988, published by Dent, p.44, states that another letter to Flecker which is only dated 'Feb. 18th' was assigned to 1914 in the documentation of the Houghton Library at Harvard, but it shows clearly that it belongs to 1912. Another suggested dating of the Rieder letter could be 8 February 1912, when Lawrence was again in Beirut, en route for Damascus, and the Fleckers were in the German Hotel.

[1446] Knightly and Simpson *Secret Lives of Lawrence of Arabia*, Nelson 1969

[1447] 'Beazley is a very wonderful fellow, who has written almost the best poems that ever came out of Oxford: but his shell was always hard, and with time he comes to curl himself tighter and tighter into it. If it hadn't been for that accursed Greek art he'd have been a very fine poet.'
Letter to Sydney Cockerell 27.v.27 [Karachi] *The Letters of T.E. Lawrence*, edited by David Garnett, London 1938, p.519.

[1448] K of A, p.6.

[1449] NGJ, p.153

[1450] SLA, p.52

[1451] Henry Savage, *Richard Middleton. The Man and his work.* Cecil Palmer, 1922, p.175

[1452] Bibliography Savage p.199

[1453] Richard Holmes in his *Sidetracks – Explorations of a Romantic Biographer*, Harper Collins, 2000 argues that Thomas Chatterton's death was due to his trying to cure himself of some form of venereal disease by taking by mistake both opium and arsenic at the same time. Chatterton did not intend to kill himself. Thomas Chatterton The Case Reopened p. 5-50

[1454] Monologues, p.67

[1455] *Life of Richard Middleton*, p.188

[1456] *The Home Letters of T.E. Lawrence and his Brothers*, p.229–30

[1457] *The Complete Fairbank*, p.237

[1458] p.305

[1459] NGJ, p.149

[1460] SLA, p.35

[1461] Frontispiece to SLA.

[1462] NGJ, p.148

[1463] NGJ, p.150

[1464] Sherwood does not give a precise reason for the 'risked scandal' but the dictionary definition is burnous(e) Arab, Moorish and lady's hooded cloak. For a man, especially a foreigner, to dress up as a woman in the Middle East would certainly be a scandal.

[1465] FO/369/513

[1466] FO/369/513

[1467] FO/369/513

[1468] FO/369/261

[1469] Lawrence. Essay on Flecker.

[1470] LIFE, p.173

[1471] SLA, p.63

1472 LIFE, p.176

1473 NGJ, p.144

1474 'The clerical colleague' is not named in NGJ. In the LIFE, p.176 a reference is made to the Bishop of London 'coming to stay with some friends of the Fleckers', that they were to meet him at dinner; the 'Orthodox Patriarch of Antioch and the Bishop of Beirut being also invited.' LIFE, p.176. The Bishop of London, an evangelical, could have been described as a clerical colleague, but there is no record of his having been in Beirut in the spring of 1912.

The Bishop of London from 1901–35 was Arthur Foley Winnington-Ingram (1858–1944). In one of the biographies of Winnington-Ingram by S.C. Carpenter, published in 1949, although a chapter is devoted to the travels of the Bishop of London, no mention is made of his going to Beirut. (Winnington-Ingram was a teetotaller and a non-smoker and unmarried; not an obvious person to select, in any case, to pronounce on the suitability of a bride at a dinner party.)

1475 LIFE p.76

1476 Original Houghton Library. Published in the *Letters of T.E. Lawrence*, Malcolm Brown. Dent. 1989 Wilson, p.101 [the lines to Mrs. Flecker not published]

1477 Original Houghton Library. Published in the *Letters of T.E. Lawrence*, Malcolm Brown. Dent. 1989 Wilson, p.101 [the lines to Mrs. Flecker not published]

1478 Richard Aldington. *Lawrence of Arabia*. Pelican Biographies 1971, p.94–5

1479 *The Golden Journey to Samarkand* Epilogue: 'Turbans and sashes, gowns and bows and veils,'

1480 *The Golden Journey to Samarkand* Epilogue: 'Have we not Indian carpets dark as wine,'

1481 This letter was published in the LIFE, p.174–5 and NGJ, p.151–2, in both cases only partly: it is necessary to read the two copies to get a full pictures.

1482 Sherwood, p.145, quotes from a *Manchester Guardian* review of *Forty-Two Poems* (the date given for this review on p.231 is 26 February 1912). [Unable to trace the review in the Newspaper Library's copy of the *Manchester Guardian* but there will have been more than one edition of the newspaper.]

1483 First published, after he had left the service, in *The New Statesman* of 24 October 1914. Originally entitled 'On War, Some Memories by J.E. Flecker.'

1484 FW

1485 FW, p.71

1486 FW, p.71

1487 SLA, p.166, letter to Savery 21 Sept. 1914.

1488 The letter of Brooke's is published in full in SLA, p.17 and also on p.337 of Hassall's biography of Brooke, in part in Lehmann's Brooke biography, p.65. The original letter was sent to Edward Marsh by Hellé, and it is now in the Berg. Philip Milito, Technical Assistant of the Berg collection where the letter has been deposited, explains that a sentence of Brooke's which in the published version reads: 'among toads I am very hodmandod.' has been altered by EM to 'bards' instead of 'toads', 'hodmandod' appears as 'hodmanclod' in Hassall's biography of Brooke.

[1489] Unpublished BOD. This letter is preserved in Mavrogordato's papers and may account for the fact that Harrison did not reply to it.

[1490] 'An Essay on Flecker' by T.E. Lawrence.

[1491] 'An Essay on Flecker' by T.E. Lawrence.

[1492] NGJ, p.154-5

[1493] The flower-loving Firbank has been compared to a butterfly. Butterflies flit through his work. Brigid Brophy in *Prancing Novelist*, p.132-5, details the references to butterflies in Firbank's work and the comparison is made to the butterfly as being 'an obvious self for Firbank'. Brophy also refers to the monograph by John Anthony Kiechler about Firbank which is called '*The Butterfly's Freckled Wings*', which lists butterflies in Firbank works. Comparison of Firbank to a butterfly is made in Osbert Sitwell '*Noble Essences*' and Sitwell's contribution to the '*Memoir*' [of Firbank].

[1494] NGJ, p.154

[1495] NGJ, p.155

[1496] J.M. Munro in *James Elroy Flecker*, Twayne Publishers 1976, quotes from 'James Elroy Flecker', in 'An-Nahar', 14 January 1968, in which those who could recall the Fleckers' short stay in Areiya, remembered that the Fleckers were always quarrelling. p.132n.

BYRD DAVIS, p.112n, states: 'If the villagers of Areiya remembered anything at all after fifty odd years, they may have recalled some evidence of the sadomasochistic activities in which the two chose to share.'

In SLA, p.58, Hellé wrote about Angela: 'She did not get on with my husband, whom she bullied, and they screamed at each other without understanding what the other said, ...'

Hellé, in SLA, p.57, states that the neighbours [at Areiya] were noisy or quarrelsome.

[1497] NGJ, p.153

[1498] LIFE, p.177

[1499] Norman Douglas, *Looking Back: Autobiographical Excursion*, Chatto and Windus, 1934.

[1500] NGJ, p.154

[1501] CP

[1502] MS.Eng. e 186, p.70

[1503] *Selected Letters of T.E. Lawrence*, Edited by David Garnett World Books, p.56

[1504] SLA, facing p.64

[1505] SLA, facing p.64

[1506] *T.E. Lawrence by His Friends*, Edited by A.W. Lawrence, Cape 1937, pps.86–92

[1507] *Seven Pillars of Wisdom*

[1508] Lawrence's Essay on Flecker

[1509] *Home Letters of TEL* 12 September 1912.

[1510] 'An Essay on Flecker', by Lawrence. First published 1937

[1511] 'An Essay on Flecker', by Lawrence. First published 1937
Viola Tree did not become involved with *Hassan* until Dec. 1914 It is possible that Flecker and Lawrence discussed *King of Alsander*, not *Hassan*.

[1512] FW

[1513] LIFE, p.175

[1514] In the original MS. entitled 'On War, some memories' by J.F. Flecker, the descriptive parts are written first in the margin.

[1515] Munro, p.41
In Footnote to p.41, Munro quotes from an Arabic newspaper, when Farida Ali Akl, who knew Flecker and Lawrence, was interviewed, and spoke of Flecker's taking walks to the tomb

[1516] Letter to Sir G.A. Lowther, British Ambassador in Constantinople from Fontana, 15.6.13.
FO.371/1812 fos.101-2. Published in Jeremy Wilson's *Biography of Lawrence*, p.997

[1517] FO 369/25

[1518] NGJ p157

[1519] FO/369/518

[1520] SLA, p.67

[1521] FO 369/518

[1522] p.18, Ch.8

[1523] Lady Dorina L Neave, *26 years on the Bosphorus*. Grayson and Grayson, London, 1933, p.90. She was Cumberbatch's niece.

[1524] Christopher Hassall. *Edward Marsh*. Longmans, Green & Co. Ltd. p.197.

[1525] BYRD DAVIS, p.167 fn:
In his review of *Georgian Poetry*, not published, Flecker wrote 'The eternal gloom of the social question hangs over all literature nowadays – some poets turn their faces away attempting to avoid it like Mr. Sturge Moore with somewhat lifeless and lengthy reconstructions of Arcady; some plunging into it and trying to turn it into poetry like Mr. Gibson and Mr. Masefield; but all show the tormented spirit of the age by that lack of form which comes of lack of faith.' [Quoted from unpublished ms C 81 BOD] Marsh gave more space to Sturge Moore in *Georgian Poetry 1911/12* than any other poet, although Moore was forty-two and above the general age limit of thirty-five, which applied to Georgian poets and Moore was dropped from later editions of *Georgian Poetry* on the grounds that he was 'an anachronism'.

[1526] Joy Grant. *Harold Monro and The Poetry Bookshop*. Routledge and Kegan Paul, 1967.

[1527] The editions were:-

Georgian Poetry	1911/12
Georgian Poetry	1913/15
Georgian Poetry	1916/17
Georgian Poetry	1918/19
Georgian Poetry	1920/22

[1528] Sherwood, NGJ p.159, states that 'The Painter's Mistress' was written on the voyage from Beirut in November 1912 because that is the date of the MS.[ms in the BOD has no date.] But as the poem was published in *The Poetry Review* of November 1912, it is more likely that Flecker wrote the poem before he left Beirut because of the time needed to send the poem to London for it to be set up in print for the November issue of *The Poetry Review*. In a letter to Savery, SLA p.98, dated July 1913, Flecker wrote: 'Damn clever of me to write a poem far out of myself as the 'Painter's Mistress'. My wife has not ceased wondering. Suggested by a play of Bataille's and written on the Lebanon.' 'The Painter's Mistress' was published in *The Golden Journey to Samarkand* anthology.

[1529] LIFE, p.176

CHAPTER ELEVEN

[1530] Published SLA, p.70 dated 21 November [1912] (PS unpublished)

[1531] SLA, p.70

[1532] FO/369/518.

[1533] NGJ, p.161

[1534] EMH, p.200

[1535] *The Poetry Bookshop* A Bibliography, J. Howard Woolmer 1912–1935 Woolmer/Brotherson 1988

[1536] *Arundel del Re.* Studies in English Literature, Vol. XIVI Georgian Reminiscences, p.31 (1932)

[1537] NGJ, p.161

[1538] SLA, p.67

[1539] *The Diary of Arthur Christopher Benson*, Ed. Percy Lubbock, Hutchinson & Co. 1926, p.214

[1540] NGJ, p.162

[1541] An amended autograph copy of 'A Sacred Dialogue' dated December 1912 is in MS. C 81 BOD. 'A Sacred Dialogue' was published in CP

[1542] Martin Booth JEF, *Unpublished Poems and Drafts.* Keepsake Press 1971

[1543] Martin Booth JEF, *Unpublished Poems and Drafts.* Keepsake Press 1971

[1544] The poem in CP is accompanied by a note from J.C. Squire, which reads: 'Originally written for Christmas 1912, and referring to the first Balkan War, this poem contains in the last speech of Christ words that ring like a prophecy of events that may occur very soon. *December, 1914.*'

[1545] *Letters of Sir Walter Raleigh*, vol.1.

[1546] EMH, p.200

[1547] A.C. Wood, *A History of the University College of Nottingham 1881–1948*, Blackwell Oxford 1953

Also in biographies of D.H. Lawrence, who followed a two-year course
of study for a teacher's certificate at University College Hospital
between 1906 and 1908. Lawrence eloped with the wife of Professor
Weekley. Weekley, Professor of Modern Languages at University College
Nottingham, sold his house there and commuted from Chiswick to
Nottingham.

[1548] SLA, pp.67–8

[1549] SLA, p.70, Letter dated [December, 1912]

[1550] NGJ, Foreword p.x

[1551] BKJ, p.88

[1552] LIFE, facing p.42

[1553] *Inclinations*, p.294 *The Complete Firbank*

[1554] The Complete Firbank, p.299

[1555] SLA, p.71

[1556] EMH, p.201

[1557] SLA, p.63

[1558] NGJ, p.163

[1559] FO/369/626

[1560] NGJ, p.6

[1561] LIFE, p.181

[1562] NGJ, p.165

[1563] Charles Wilson. *Flecker of Dean Close*, p.64, 1946 The Canterbury Press

[1564] LIFE, p.181

[1565] LIFE, p.181

[1566] *Inclinations.* 'In Italy have they Brussels sprouts – like we have?' A question
put to Mabel Pastorelli on her return to England.

[1567] LIFE, p.178

[1568] LIFE, p.183

[1569] NGJ, p.120

[1570] LIFE, p.178

[1571] SLA, p.82n

[1572] SLA, p.82

[1573] Brophy, p.274

[1574] *The Complete Firbank*, p.82

[1575] MS University of Edinburgh Library. In Sar. Coll.15

[1576] FO/369/261

[1577] SLA, p.63

[1578] NGJ, p.167

[1579] SLA, p.73

[1580] SLA, pp.73–4

[1581] NGJ, p.166

[1582] NGJ, p.166

[1583] NGJ, p.166

[1584] LIFE, p.183

[1585] This letter is published in part in both the LIFE, p.183 and NGJ, p167. In
the LIFE the word is 'tried' but in NGJ it is 'lived'.

[1586] The reference to '£150' is omitted from the part of the letter published in the LIFE. All the items of expenditure are omitted from the LIFE.

[1587] Would this amount be two guineas in the original letter?

[1588] In SLA, p.81–2 there are two letters written to Marsh, one dated [Paris, January 2] 1913 and the second, Sunday January 1913, but from the content of the letters they appear to have been published in reverse order to Flecker's writing them.

[1589] Hassall, p.200

[1590] NGJ, p.166

[1591] NGJ, p.204

[1592] Catalogue of the Berg Collection. The New York Public Library. *Hassan*. Holograph synopsis of play. Signed, undated 18p (mutilated) first draft. Came with Sir Edward Marsh's correspondence.

[1593] p.9

[1594] Byrd, p.204, quoting from the complete TS of Act I of *Hassan* in Texas

[1595] Introduction to *Hassan*, written by J.C. Squire, p.12

[1596] NGJ, p.167

[1597] 'Forgotten Warfare', C.Pr. p.75

[1598] 'Forgotten Warfare', C.Pr. p.75

[1599] 'Forgotten Warfare', C.Pr. p.75

[1600] 'Forgotten Warfare', C.Pr. p.76

[1601] NGJ, p.168

[1602] LIFE, p.183

[1603] SLA, p.76

[1604] SLA, p.99

[1605] Ch.9

[1606] FO/369/626

[1607] JEF, p.74

[1608] NGJ, p.168

[1609] In 1920 this became the American University of Beirut. [Munro, p.45]

[1610] NGJ, p.168

[1611] NGJ, p.171

[1612] NJG, p.169

[1613] Published (two verses) in NGJ, p.169, original D250 dated February 1913

[1614] SLA, p.75

[1615] NGJ, p.168

[1616] NGJ, p.171

[1617] SLA, p.83

[1618] SLA, p.186

[1619] NGJ, p.171

[1620] SLA, pp.83–84

[1621] Hassall, p.201

[1622] NGJ, p.172

[1623] NGJ, p.172

[1624] NGJ, p.172
LIFE, p.184

[1625] NGJ, p.172–3

[1626] JEF, p.76

[1627] JEF, p.76

[1628] *Harold Monro and 'The Poetry Bookshop'*, p.61

[1629] EMH, p.684

[1630] Letter, Houghton Library.

[1631] Letter MS. University of Edinburgh

[1632] NGJ, p.174

[1633] LIFE, p.184

[1634] NGJ, p.174

[1635] NGJ, p.173

[1636] FO/369/626

[1637] NGJ, p.175

[1638] D 250 BOD

[1639] revised as 'snowy'

[1640] LIFE, p.184

[1641] revised as 'of rain'

[1642] revised as 'whistling'

[1643] *Chinese Poems*, Arthur Waley. First published 1946, George Allen & Unwin

[1644] revised as 'minutes'

[1645] revised as 'so'

[1646] p.174

[1647] MS D250 Bod, dated 14 April, 1913

[1648] MS D250 Bod, dated May–June, 1913. 'China' published as 'Taoping'

[1649] MS D250 Bod, dated 14 April, 1913

[1650] CP

[1651] Gill, p,201

[1652] Gill, p,202

[1653] 'Pannyra of the Golden Heel' was published in *The New Statesman*, 14 March 1914 edition. Also in Flecker's 'The Old Ships' published by The Poetry Bookshop in 1915.
In Firbank's novel *Vainglory,* published in 1915, reference is made to 'the poet's 'With Golden Ankles', for instance' (*Complete Firbank*, p.92). Firbank could be poking fun at the title of Flecker's translated poem and substituting 'ankles' for 'heel'. The audience watching the whirling, dancing Pannyra would have the illusion that not only were her heels golden (their 'eyes are all in a trance' in Flecker's translation), but her ankles also. Brophy p.442 suggests that 'With Golden Ankles' could be a slip of the pen or a 'sly Firbankian joke'.

[1654] Gill, p,201-4

[1655] D 252 BOD, dated April [19]13 - Notebook of verse 'The Rose Tree in Time's Garden'.

[1656] SLA, p.97, July 1913

[1657] *Golden Journey to Samarkand*, p.29 revised version of the original *Bridge of Fire Copybook*, p.70. Not published in CP

[1658] misprint 'mountain' in this line should be 'mountains'

[1659] misprint 'mountain' in this line should be 'mountains'

[1660] 'Brumana' is a revised version of Flecker's poem published in *The Nation* 10 May 1913 edition with the title 'The Pines'. 'The Pines' was published in the *Literary Digest* in July 1919 edition and the *Living Age* 30 August 1919 edition.

The MS. of 'Brumana' is in the Poetry Collection. Lockwood Memorial Library, Buffalo NY. Also MS d 250 Bod. An early version of 'The Pines' is published in NGJ, p.177, from loose pages among Flecker's papers.

[1661] Byrd, p.181 states that the version of 'Brumana' published in NGJ, p.177, contains the lines:

> When I find the maid of my heart
> I will take her into the pine trees
> Out on the open hills
> And saying no word of love will look into her eyes
> And see if she dreams such dreams as me. [original D249 BOD]

Byrd suggests that these lines indicate that the version was written during Flecker's Cambridge years. Byrd states this because matching sheets contain notes from Flecker's Eastern studies and a portion of Flecker's translation of 'The Golden Ass'. The translation of 'The Golden Ass' was begun by Flecker in 1906. Byrd refers to Douglas Goldring reading Flecker's translation of 'The Golden Ass', which he said Flecker never finished. Goldring goes on to write: 'I'm afraid my criticism of detailed points discouraged him, which was the last thing I meant.' In JEF, Goldring later quotes 12 lines of 'Brumana', p.136, but does not say he ever read an earlier version of 'Brumana'.

In HRHRC, there is a list of manuscripts relating to Flecker, the following details are given:

– Brumana. Ams. Nd. Written on this: Flecker, James Elroy
'My ship had spread her phantom sail...' Ams. Nd.

Also,

– My ship had spread her phantom sail...' Ams. Nd. Written on:
James Elroy Flecker Brumana Ams. Nd.

[1662] MS. Lockwood 'bluer'

[1663] MS. Lockwood 'break'

[1664] MS. Lockwood 'sweet pain'

[1665] Arthur Waley's translation from the Chinese of 'The Pine-Trees in the Courtyard' was first published in Arthur Waley. *Chinese Poems* by George Allen & Unwin, 1946

Sherwood states that the early version of 'Brumana', which he published in NGJ, p.177, is 'in a different emotional context' when he refers to the theme of pine trees. The emotional context of 'The Pine-Trees in

the Courtyard' is closer to the early version of 'Brumana' than the final
version. There is nothing resembling the feelings of Flecker in 'Brumana'
when he wrote:

O traitor pines, you sang what life had found

The Falsest of fair tales. [CP]

in either the Chinese translation or the early version when both poets love
the pine trees.

The relationship between these two poets further reinforces Byrd's
statement that the lines from the early version were written during
Flecker's Cambridge years. Waley's interest in translations from the
Chinese and Flecker's interest in the pine trees of his childhood could
have come together at one time.

Byrd also, on p.181 in a note, refers to Régnier's boyhood at Honfleur
and his love there of sea and forest. Byrd cites Régnier's 'Un Vieillard'
and 'Echo marin'

[1666] SLA, p.85. Original MS. PUL

[1667] MS. Houghton Lib.

[1668] NGJ, p.180

[1669] FO/369/626

[1670] LIFE, p.185

[1671] Houghton Library

[1672] The poem's relationship with the version Sherwood prints on p.177,
NGJ, which Sherwood says 'The theme of the ubiquitous pine trees in a
different emotional context (The translation of 'The Pine-Trees in the
Courtyard' contains the line: 'They have only loosened the shackles that
bind my heart,' which is in keeping with the verse of Flecker's in NGJ
about 'taking the maid of my heart to the pine trees'.)

Chapter Twelve

[1673] NGJ, p.182

[1674] NGJ, p.173

[1675] SLA, p.80

[1676] SLA, p.79

[1677] John Addington Symonds and his daughter Margaret, *Our Life in the Swiss
Highlands*, Adam and Charles Black, London and Edinburgh, 1892, p.7

[1678] LIFE, p.190

[1679] LIFE, p.189

[1680] NGJ, p.182

[1681] MS. 972 and 972.1 Houghton

[1682] MS. Eng MS. 972 and 972.1

[1683] 'a little bit improper' is written in the margin and it is not indicated
precisely where it is to be inserted.

[1684] this is 'lines' in CP

[1685] Houghton MS.972 and 972.1

[1686] Houghton

[1687] JEF, p.81

[1688] This included an unpublished poem 'Golden', which Sherwood [NGJ, p.188] states that Flecker first planned to include in *The Golden Journey*, the poem of eight couplets. The first draft, which contains many alterations, is in Princeton.

He wrote the poem in 1912; a mocking poem about using the word 'golden', a word he removed from 'The Welsh Sea' and 'The Ballad of the Student in the South'.

[1689] SLA, pp.85–86 original PUL

[1690] *John Davidson*, Mary O'Connor, Scottish Writers Series, Scottish Academic Press, Edinburgh 1987 (Chapter 7, Reputation)

[1691] CPr

[1692] SLA, pp.87–88

[1693] SLA, pp.87–88

[1694] SLA, p.89

[1695] Berg Collection, published with omissions JEF pp.83–7,

[1696] GJ S and CP

[1697] GJS and CP

[1698] Name omitted from published letter, supplied by Berg Collection, New York Public Library

[1699] Omitted portion of letter supplied by Berg Collection, New York Public Library

[1700] Name omitted from published letter, supplied by Berg Collection, New York Public Library

[1701] JEF, p.89

[1702] SLA, p.89

[1703] This version of *Hassan* is known as the Leysin version. It was published in the Salzburg Studies in English Literature under the direction of Professor Erwin A. Sturzl. The Leysin Version is edited by James Hogg, in 1976. The Bodleian Library MSS. Don d.30 contains the Leysin version of *Hassan*.

[1704] Information about MS. of '*Les Extravagants*' received from Vincent Giroud in letter to HW (7 July 1994)

[1705] The Agreement between the publishers and James Elroy Flecker author of *The King of Alsander* was drawn up on 3 July 1913 and signed on behalf of Max Goschen on 8 July. The publishers agreed to publish the work entirely at their own expense and pay the author on the published price of twelve out of every thirteen copies sold Ten(10) per centum. In the event of cheaper editions of the work being issued, the royalty shall be Five(5) per cent.

The publishers shall have the right to sell or assign the American, Colonial, Continental, Foreign translation, serial, dramatic rights and they shall credit the AUTHOR with 50 per centum of all profits arising.

Copy of Agreement (From A.P.Watt Records, #11036.Folder 208.6) from the Manuscripts Department, Wilson Library. The University of North Carolina at Chapel Hill. NC USA

[1706] MS. Eng. 972 and 972.1

[1707] JEF, p.88

[1708] By the time Goldring's novel *Margot's Progress* was published in 1916 by Eveleigh Nash Company, two previous novels are listed *It's an ill wind* and *The Permanent Uncle*. Goldring had also published two books of verse and three books of *Travels and Essays*.

[1709] JEF, p.91

[1710] Information supplied by HRHC, Office of the Research Librarian

[1711] *Lives and Letters*, John Carswell, Faber & Faber, London, 1978.

[1712] EMH, p.684

[1713] This reference to 'violence and rawness' was later connected to Flecker's *Hassan*. Hassall wrote: [EMH, p.684]

'Looking back, the "violence" and the "rawness" which Gosse was quick to detect, seem characteristic of the first Georgians, whose typical figures were Abercrombie, Bottomley, and Brooke. The "violence" in Flecker's *Hassan* and Brooke's play *Lithuania* is of the same early Georgian order.' *Hassan* was not performed until a decade after Gosse (if he had *Hassan* in mind when he wrote his review of *Georgian Poetry* and made the reference to 'violence' and 'rawness') made the statements Hassall connected with *Hassan*. Gosse could have gained the feeling of 'violence and rawness' from Marsh's reading of the MS. of *Hassan* and discussing it with him. Or from reading such poems of Flecker's as 'The War Song of the Saracens' or 'Pillage', which Marsh rejected as contributions to *Georgian Poetry*. Flecker had sent Gosse a copy of *The Bridge of Fire* and he would , if he cared to do so, and had the opportunity, been able to read *Thirty-Six Poems* and *Forty-Two Poems* but like Brooke's poems, Flecke's poems were brought to Gosse's attention by Marsh.
Gosse was to become an admirer of Flecker, he later wrote:
'The success of the venture [*Georgian Poetry 1911-12*] was immediate and prolonged. Poets whose isolated productions had been unnoticed woke up to find themselves famous beneath the aegis of 'E.M.'. Rupert Brooke and James Elroy Flecker were the main ornaments of the first collection, and when a second instalment came (in 1916) it was inscribed to their memory.' [*More Books on the Table*, Heinemann, London, 1923, p.227]
Gosse admired in particular Flecker's 'The Dying Patriot'. Alec Waugh remembers Edmund Gosse 'reading Flecker's 'The Dying Patriot' in his mellifluous voice'. [*The Early years of Alec Waugh*, Cassell, London, 1962, p.80]
Gosse told Marsh after Flecker's death: 'There always seemed to be a worm slumbering at the root of his talent.' [EMH, p.304]

[1714] MS. Eng. 972 & 972.1

[1715] MS. 972 and 972.1

[1716] MS.972 and 972.1

[1717] The deluxe edition was limited to 50 copies numbered and signed by the author. Certificate pasted inside front cover. (Bibliography TSM)

[1718] MS.972 and 972.1

[1719] MS. 972 and 972.1

[1720] EMH, p.233

[1721] EMH, p.244

[1722] EMH, p.246

[1723] SLA, p.94

[1724] SLA, pp.93–94

[1725] SLA, p.125

[1726] CMG, p.70

[1727] CMG, p.78

[1728] *The Listener*, 15 February 1951

[1729] MS.972 and 972.1

[1730] SLA, p.97

[1731] Manuscript by and relating to James Elroy Flecker in the HRHRC. Subject Edward John Morton Drax Plunkett Dunsany, 18th Baron AMs (pp. 172A–175) 1946 April 1 Bound.

[1732] Gill p.86, makes a similar point.

[1733] CP

[1734] SLA, p.80

[1735] Listed in: 'Dr. James Hogg. *On Poets and Poetry*. Salzburg studies in English literature. James Elroy Flecker. Some sources For a Study of His Poetry' 1974, p.33

[1736] LIFE, p.199 and JEF, p.113.

[1737] NGJ, p.185

[1738] SLA, p.99

[1739] Flecker had written:
'Good poetry has been full of high moral sentiments, like Wordsworth's, or highly amoral sentiments like Herrick's.'

[1740] SLA, p.98

[1741] LIFE, p.199

[1742] LIFE, p.196

[1743] LIFE, p.208

[1744] NGJ, p.188

[1745] SLA, p.101

[1746] SLA, p.103

[1747] SLA, p.104

[1748] CP

[1749] Houghton, MS.Eng.972, MS.Eng.972:1

[1750] NGJ, p.185

[1751] *Books on the Table*. Heinemann Ltd. 1923

[1752] SLA, p.105

[1753] NGJ, p.189

[1754] FO 369/626

[1755] SLA, p.107

[1756] SLA, p.110

[1757] JEF, p.102

[1758] FO 369/626

[1759] NGJ, p.189

[1760] LIFE, p.189

[1761] FO memo

[1762] MS.972 and 972.1

[1763] This word not clear, but if it is a reference to *The Athenaeum* a review of *The Golden Road* was published in its 26 July 1913 edition.

[1764] JEF, p.113

[1765] Frank Swinnerton, *The Georgian Literary Scene, 1910–1935*, Hutchinson & Co. (Publishers) Ltd., 1935, p.212

Also JEF, p.126

[1766] SLA, p.108

[1767] SLA, p.107

[1768] When *Hassan* was first produced in Darmstadt on 1 June 1923, Herr Hartung 'had unfortunately to leave out the ghost scene...' [Letter from Hellé to Basil Dean 5 June 1913, Dawn Redwood *Flecker and Delius – the Making of Hassan* Thames Publishing 1979, p.43]

[1769] Edinburgh. University of Edinburgh, Library. In Sar. coll. 15. Correspondence between JEF (2 letters) and C. Sarolea (1 letter, copy) [1913 and undated].

[1770] LIFE, p.81

[1771] SLA, p.110

[1772] 'The *Near East* also published on 26 September 1913, 'The Drowned Women of Janina' by J.E. Flecker and Hellé Flecker. This article contains the themes Flecker outlined in his published letters admired by the Greek Minister. Flecker wrote to Savery, 7 November 1914, LJEF, p.117, '.... I am prouder of that letter than all of my poems'.

[1773] SLA, p.112

[1774] SLA, pp.112–3

[1775] LIFE, p.209

[1776] LIFE, p.209

[1777] MSS. Eng.971 and 972.1 Houghton

[1778] *Selected Letters of T.E. Lawrence.* Edited by David Garnett. World Books, p.66

[1779] SLA, p.115

[1780] MS.Eng. 972 and 972.1 Houghton.

[1781] MS. Eng. 972 and 972.1 Houghton.

[1782] LIFE, p.203

[1783] SLA, p.116

[1784] *The Golden Journey* was published in four editions of 250 each, the first 6 advance copies came out on 1.7.13. The second impression was printed on 4.7.13 and the 3rd on 14.10.13 and the 4th on 7.1.15. Production Card for *The Golden Journey*. Houghton

[1785] MS.Eng. 971 and 972.1 Houghton

[1786] SLA, p.117

[1787] MS.Eng.972. MS. Eng. 972.1

[1788] SLA, p.118

[1789] JEF, p.111

[1790] SLA, p.120

[1791] SLA, p.120

[1792] NGJ, p.227

[1793] LIFE, p.252

NGJ, p.192

[1794] NGJ, p.192

[1795] GILL, p.171

[1796] *Hassan*, James Elroy Flecker, The Chaucer Press Ltd., 1966, Introduction p.3

[1797] Introduction to *Hassan*, p.3

[1798] NGJ, p.193

LIFE, p.207

[1799] LIFE, p.200

[1800] JEF, p.111

[1801] The letter is printed in full in the LIFE, pp.200–203, and also in part in *The Poetry Review* for September 1917. The fact of this letter, when published, using 'write' instead of 'right' indicates that Flecker dictated it to Hellé. Hodgson would not be aware, at the time, of what Flecker's handwriting looked like and at the time of publication the elder Fleckers may not have even seen it.

[1802] SLA, p.123

[1803] SLA, p.123

[1804] SLA, p.122 Original postcard PUL

[1805] SLA, p.123

[1806] SLA, p.126

[1807] LIFE, p.209

[1808] Princeton not published in SLA

[1809] SLA, p.137

[1810] SLA, p.137

[1811] Martin Booth. *James Elroy Flecker. Unpublished Poems and Drafts*. The Keepsake Press. 1971

[1812] NGJ, p.194

[1813] Dr. Flecker, when he visited Switzerland in 1885, remarked on the grandeur of the Swiss hotels. He told of 'pianos' and 'grand assembly rooms'. Charles Williams, *Flecker of Dean Close*, The Canterbury Press, p.38

[1814] LIFE, p.210

[1815] LIFE, p.210

[1816] SLA, p.131. The date of this letter is 17.1.14 when a letter from Beazley must have been received. Sarah Flecker in her letter to Cecil Roberts from Dean Close on May 13th 1917 told him. 'The friend he loved so dearly was worthless in the base return of affection. It was one of the griefs of Roy's last days to have been convinced of this against his will He was singularly

faithful to all his friends.'
Churchill Archives Centre. Cecil Roberts Papers.

[1817] Cheesman's visiting Flecker in a sanatorium at Montana is referred to in a portion of the Cheesman unpublished biography in New College and the date is given as 1914. Because the Fleckers left Montana at the end of March 1914, his visit must have taken place in the first three months of 1914.

[1818] SLA, p.131

[1819] SLA, p.96

[1820] D.H. Lawrence, writing to Edward Garnett on 14 July 1913, refers to a cheque for £3 (one seventeenth of the profits of the *Georgian Poetry*). *The Letters of D.H. Lawrence*, CUP 1981, p.38. Lawrence, whose poem 'Snap-Dragon' was included in *Georgian Poetry* thanked Marsh profusely in a letter written the day before, p.35. On 10 January 1914, Lawrence wrote to Arthur McLeod from Italy and told him he was expecting Marsh. On 24 January, after Marsh's visit, Lawrence wrote and thanked him for a cheque of £4, p.140.

[1821] EMH, p.265

[1822] SLA, p.132

[1823] NGJ, p.30

[1824] SLA, p.134

[1825] SLA, p.135

[1826] EMH, p.265

[1827] SLA, p.135

[1828] GILL, p.170

[1829] W.H. Auden, writing in *The Nation* (26 April 1947) quoted in David J. Gordon. *D.H. Lawrence as a Literary Critic*, New Haven and London/Yale University Press/ 1966

[1830] SLA, p.140

[1831] SLA, p.82

[1832] CP

[1833] EMH, p.243

[1834] *The Letters of DHL, Vol.II*. Letter to Marsh dated 18 November 1913, pp.102–4

[1835] EMH, p.243, quoting a letter from DHL. Lawrence began the argument about *The Golden Journey* in another letter to Marsh dated 18 August 1913, and to Cynthia Asquith dated 20 August 1913. *The Letters of DHL. Vol.II*, p.61 and 62

[1836] David J. Gordon, *D.H. Lawrence as Literary Critic*. Yale University Press. New Haven and London, 1966, p.65

[1837] J. Markowitz *J.E. Flecker. The Roles of Tuberculosis in English Poetry*. The Canadian Forum April 1937
BYRD DAVIS comments on this article, pp.100–111.
GILL, in Appendix C, writes on 'Characteristic Traits in Certain Other Poets who Suffered from Tuberculosis'. GILL discussed D.H. Lawrence and Flecker's work from the point of view of their having TB.

A. Banerjee edited D.H. Lawrence's Poetry: '*Demon Liberated*'. Macmillan. 1990. In this book Gregory's article discusses the Flecker/Lawrence conflict (but not the fact that both had TB) on p.140.

Allan Ingram in *The Language of D.H. Lawrence*, Macmillan 1990, discusses the Flecker-Lawrence conflict but also without mention of the fact that both had TB.

Susan Sontag in *Illness as Metaphor*. Allen Lane 1979, discusses in general the TB patients' disintegration and the help thought to be afforded to TB patients by a change of air.

[1838] SLA, p.136

[1839] BL Department of Manuscripts Ashley B 3229

[1840] SLA, p.144

[1841] Leeds, Brotherton Library. Brotherton Collection

[1842] BYRD DAVIS, p.236.
GILL, p.155

[1843] SLA, p.114

[1844] Published as 'Paul Fort, 'The Prince of Poets.' in *The Nineteenth Century and After* (January 1915) and also reprinted in C.Pr

[1845] SLA, p.137

[1846] SLA, p.137

[1847] The Production Card for *The King of Alsander* indicates that the printers were instructed to print 1,000 copies on 19.2.14 Houghton

[1848] SLA, p.138

[1849] NGJ, p.195

[1850] SLA, p.128

[1851] SLA, p.142

[1852] BOD MS. Gilbert Murray 435, fols.201-216 Aeneid/ translated into English Verse by James Elroy Flecker. With [MS. Gilbert Murray 24, fols.24-25] a letter 1914, from James Elroy Flecker to Gilbert Murray.

[1853] SLA, p.143

[1854] SLA, p.145

[1855] SLA, p.146

[1856] SLA, p.146

[1857] SLA, p.145

[1858] SLA, p.147

[1859] JEF, p.113

[1860] JEF, p.113

[1861] Masters letter to Flecker PUL. The ultimate fate of the proposed popular play is not known. The proposal to make *The King of Alsander* into a film met the same sort of unknown fate. The proposal for the popular play was made not long before the outbreak of the First World War. The proposal for making the book into a film was made three years before the outbreak of the Second World War. A letter to Curtis Brown Ltd., Film Department, dated 24 April 1936, to H. Watt of the Literary Agents A.P. Watt & Son about *The King of Alsander* refers to an offer of agreement to be drawn up between Miss Clemence Dane and Mrs. Flecker. Clemence

Dane was said to have been very busy with the preparation of her play and also with film work for Mr. Korda. Clemence Dane was said to have been very glad to proceed on a fifty-fifty basis. A fact not mentioned in this letter was that problems had arisen ten years earlier on 26 June 1926 (letter from solicitors, Field, Roscoe & Co., Lincoln's Inn Fields to H. Watt of A.P. Watt & Son) when the question of who had 'the right to authorise a cinematograph of the novel itself'. The matter was open to doubt. The publishing house of Max Goschen who had published *The King of Alsander* in 1913, having passed to George Allen & Unwin. Copy from the Manuscripts Department, Wilson Library, The University of North Carolina at Chapel Hill, NC.

[1862] JEF, p.113

[1863] both names supplied by HRHRC and 'Samarkand' to 'Clarence Johnson, Esq. c/o S.S. Carpathia.'

[1864] JEF, p.115–6

[1865] JEF, p.116

[1866] SLA, p.148 AM 16159 PUL

[1867] CP p.XIII

[1868] Introduction to CP, First Edition, published 1916.

[1869] CP p.XIII

[1870] LIFE, p.211

[1871] LIFE, p.212

[1872] NGJ, p.200

[1873] LIFE, p.212, quoting a letter sent to Hodgson from Savery, 7 March 1924. Also in a letter to Savery, received 30 November 1914, Flecker makes a similar statement.

[1874] FO 369/626

[1875] John M. Munro, *James Elroy Flecker* Twayne Publishers 1976, p.41

[1876] SLA, p.150

[1877] John Addington Symonds *Our Life in the Swiss Highlands*, Black 1892 (Published in collaboration with his daughter, Margaret)

[1878] John Addington Symonds *Our Life in the Swiss Highlands*, Black 1892 (Published in collaboration with his daughter, Margaret), p.25

[1879] John Addington Symonds *Our Life in the Swiss Highlands*, Black 1892 (Published in collaboration with his daughter, Margaret), p.25

[1880] John Addington Symonds *Our Life in the Swiss Highlands*, Black 1892 (Published in collaboration with his daughter, Margaret), p.4

[1881] W.G. Lockett, *Robert Louis Stevenson*, Hurst & Blackett Ltd. pp. 160 and 216. Also LJEF p.125, letter to Savery received 30 November 1914, refers to 'a toy printing press as Christmas present. Thus Stevenson when here.'

[1882] SLA, p.150

[1883] SLA, p.151

[1884] 29 January 1938, letter from Hellé Flecker to A.W. Lawrence (BOD) replying to A.W. Lawrence after reading a draft (much-corrected) found amongst T.E. Lawrence's papers of 'A Note on James Elroy Flecker', published in *Lawrence of Arabia, Strange Man of Letters. The Literary Criticism and Correspondence of T.E. Lawrence*, edited by Harold Orlands, Associated University Presses, Inc.1993

[1885] JEF, p.117

[1886] LIFE, p.200, Facsimile facing p.200 LIFE

[1887] Princesse Edmonde de Polignac (1865–1943) provided the money for the Royal Society of Literature to award £100 each November for an imaginative work which had been published in the previous year. Walter de la Mare was the first winner in 1911. John Masefield was the winner in 1912 and James Stephens in 1913. Ralph Hodgson was the winner in 1914.

[1888] JEF, p.119

[1889] *Hassan* by James Elroy Flecker, An Acting Edition and introduced by Basil Dean, p.xiv.

[1890] Basil Dean Acting Edition '*Hassan*'. Heinemann, first published 1922, p.xv

[1891] SLA, p.155

[1892] SLA, p.154

[1893] SLA, p.153

[1894] *Selected Letters of T.E. Lawrence*, edited by David Garnett, World Books, London, first published 1938. Letter No.38: The first part of the letter dealing with the conflict at Carchemish is published. The remaining part of Lawrence's letter dealing with Lawrence's views on *The Golden Road* and *Alsander* is omitted. Original Houghton.
The description of the conflict at Carchemish is published in C. Leonard Woolley's *Dead Towns and Living Men*, being pages from an Antiquary's Notebook. Cape, 1932. This fact gives the opportunity to compare the two descriptions and realise that Lawrence's was not embellished just to impress Flecker.

[1895] *Selected Letters of T.E. Lawrence* edited by David Garnett, p.286

[1896] RBH p.65) with a memoir by Arthur Symons, with four illustrations by Aubrey Beardsley and a Portrait by William Rothenstein, was published by John Lane, The Bodley Head, in 1905.

[1897] p. vii

[1898] Jad Adams. *Madder Music Stronger Wine*, The life of Dowson, Poet and Decadent. I.B.Tauris. London 2000, p.47

[1899] Lawrence James *The Golden Warrior The Life and Legend of Lawrence of Arabia*. Weidenfeld and Nicolson, p.218

[1900] K of A, p.159

[1901] Edited by Harold Orlans, *Lawrence of Arabia, Strange Man of Letters. The Literary Criticism and Correspondence of T.E. Lawrence*, Associated University Presses Inc. 1993

[1902] Robert Payne. *Lawrence of Arabia, a Triumph* (Revised edition) Robert Hale 1966. First published by Pyramid Books. Almat Publishing Corp., New York 1962

[1903] First published in 1936

[1904] T.E. Lawrence '*The Mint*', Panther Books, Hamilton and Co., 1962, p.19

[1905] *Minorities,* edited by J.M. Wilson with a preface by C. Day Lewis, Cape 1971. Note on 'The Pensive Prisoner' points out the similarities between the paragraph in 'The *Mint*' and 'The Pensive Prisoner'.

[1906] Edited by Christopher Palmer. *The Collected Arthur Machen.* Duckworth 1988 p.236

[1907] Edited by A.W. Lawrence. *T.E. Lawrence by His Friends.* Cape 1937

[1908] Wilson, p.147, quoting J.E. Flecker to T.E. Lawrence 27.7.14 LTEL, p.57

[1909] SLA, p.157

[1910] *Dean Close School: The First Hundred Years.* Cheltenham 1986, p.32

[1911] SLA, p.156

[1912] EMH, p.293

[1913] SLA, p.158

[1914] SLA, p.160

[1915] SLA, p.161

[1916] SLA, p.166

[1917] CP

[1918] MSS. Don 155 BOD

[1919] RBH, p.483

Hassall quotes these six lines but suggests that the influence of these lines for Brooke was 'The Old Vicarage, Grantchester', rather than 'The Soldier'

[1920] NGJ, p.214

[1921] EMH, p.299

[1922] John Lehmann. *Rupert Brooke: His Life and His Legend.* Quartet Books, 1981 p.126

[1923] Act II, Scene 1

[1924] EMH, p.300

[1925] SLA, p.170 (amended lines published.)

[1926] RBH, p.481

[1927] SLA, p.171

[1928] omitted portion of letter SLA, p.171 supplied by HRHRC

[1929] Introduction to *Hassan* p. xvi

[1930] LJEF, p.110

[1931] LJEF, p.109

[1932] LJEF, p.113

[1933] SLA, p.172

[1934] SLA, p.174

[1935] BL Ms Department of Manuscripts Ashley b.3229(1)

[1936] The illustration was carried out by Harold Nelson Published in *The Sphere* on 26 December 1914

[1937] LIFE, p.215

[1938] *New Statesman*

[1939] Photograph facing p.215 LIFE,

[1940] LIFE, p.221

[1941] Mary O'Connor *John Davidson.* Scottish Writers Series, editor David Daiches 1987, p.32

[1942] SLA, p.174

[1943] 'its dead': the non-fertilized seed.

[1944] Lynd does not name the poem, but it is 'Dirge in Woods' from *A Reading of Earth* published in 1888. 'Dirge in Woods' was first published in the *Fortnightly*, 1 August 1870. It was written on the death of Meredith's second father-in-law, and is a close imitation of Goethe's 'Uber allen Gipfeln' ('Wandrers Nachtlied II'). [*George Meredith Selected Poems* edited by Keith Hanley, Carcanet Fyfield Books. 1983]

GILL, p.176, states that Flecker may have found a hint of the idea of the association of death with the falling leaves of autumn in a poem 'Feuilles Mortes' by Paul Fort. Also that after death the spirit might return to beloved places of boyhood. GILL quotes a passage from *Hassan* to support this and also compares the idea with those in the poems of the Georgian Poets, particularly Brooke, and also de la Mare, and Hilaire Belloc's poem 'Duncton Hill'.

BYRD DAVIS, p.236 mentions Verlaine and de la Mare when writing about 'November Eves'.

The poem by Verlaine which BYRD-DAVIS may have had in mind is 'Chanson d'Automne', which contains the lines:

> Les sanglots longs
> Des violins
> De l'automne
> Blessent mon coeur
> D'une longueur
> Monotone.

LIFE, p.238, Hodgson in her Epilogue states:

'.... it is interesting to notice that the only considerable portion of the planned *Aeneid*, left fit for publication, was the descent of Aeneas, under Hecate's guidance, to Avernus, in the sixth book:

'They went obscure in lowering, lone night
Through lodges of King Dis, untenanted.'

Hodgson then goes on to state: 'he [Flecker] handled beautifully the description of the multitude of drifting souls'

The lines of the translation by Flecker of Virgil's *Aeneid*: Book VI which embody the 'drifting souls' and autumn leaves are:

All a great multitude came pouring down,
Brothers and husbands, and the proud-souled heroes,
Life's labour done: and boys and unwed maidens
And the young men by whose flame-funeral
Parents had wept. Many as leaves that fall
Gently in autumn when the sharp cold comes
Or all the birds that flock at the turn o' year
Over the ocean to the lands of light. [CP]

[1945] *Fortnightly Review*, New Series 1924 Jan– Jun James Elroy Flecker by Alec Macdonald.

[1946] *Fortnightly Review,* New Series 1924 Jan–Jun James Elroy Flecker by Alec Macdonald.

[1947] *Portraits by Inference,* pp.16–17

[1948] Byrd, p.237, when discussing 'Narcissus', states: 'If we consider that the poem still contains a homosexual note, the speaker could be saying farewell to a beloved friend.'

[1949] CP

[1950] CP

[1951] CP

[1952] LIFE, p.221

[1953] LIFE, p.221

[1954] LIFE, p.219

[1955] LIFE, p.221

[1956] LIFE, p.221

[1957] NGJ, p.215

[1958] NGJ, p.215. The article by Bernard Shaw was entitled 'Common Sense about the War,' published in *The New Statesman*: Special Supplement (14 November 1914). Flecker (who had been thinking along the same lines as Shaw before the article appeared [LIFE, p.117]) was not entirely in agreement with what Shaw had put in his article. He outlined where he parted company with Shaw in a letter to his father [NGJ, p.215] and to Savery when he wrote from Davos on 24 November 1914:
'I send Bernard Shaw on War ..... I agree with three quarters of B.S., all except the Hyde Park tosh. I am a democrat.' [LJEF, p.120]

[1959] SLA, p.173

[1960] MS. Eng. Poet c.81 two incomplete copies in Hellé Flecker's hand amended by Flecker. BOD

[1961] SLA, p.172

[1962] LIFE, p.119

[1963] SLA, p.175

[1964] MS. Don. 155 BOD

[1965] NGJ, p.218. Also in a letter to Savery [received 30 November 1914] LJEF p.121, Flecker wrote '(b) enclosed poem which return; written 5.45 a.m. in twenty minutes and hardly altered.'

[1966] A.748 BL Dept. of Manuscripts, Ashley

[1967] SLA, p.128. Also LJEF, p.118 [Davos 17 Nov. '14] Flecker wrote to Savery 'I dreamt a wonderful poem about Jerusalem new and old – my only mystic vision. 'Hellé also mentions the dream of the New Jerusalem'. SLA p.128

[1968] NGJ, p.219

[1969] In the LIFE [LIFE, p.223] the first sentence is slightly different:
'It will please you to know that I intend to take Communion this Xmas.' And the next sentence is: 'Please just mention your pleasure in your next letter.'

[1970] LIFE, p.223

[1971] Princeton, AM 16159

[1972] BYRD DAVIS, p.241

[1973] CP

[1974] CP

[1975] NGJ, p.217

[1976] CP

[1977] CP

[1978] p.xviii Introduction to *Hassan*.

[1979] EMH, p.303

[1980] SLA, p.175

[1981] LJEF, p.122

[1982] MS Don d.155

[1983] NGJ, p.219

[1984] LIFE, p.228

[1985] MS Eng Poet d.249, BOD

[1986] NGJ, p.219

[1987] NGJ, p.220

[1988] LJEF, p.120

[1989] LIFE, p.225

[1990] LIFE, p.226

[1991] LIFE, p.227

[1992] In a letter to Savery 7 November from Davos Platz [LJEF, p.115] Flecker wrote:
'How ripping of you to send me *Salammbô* (one of those books I think I have read and haven't) in so magnificent an edition! I am not going to read it for a few days for I think that I want to complete my delight in it and have it bound. I have just had some books bound at Geneva (parchment with corners and sides brown paper) and the result has been excellent.'
[*Salammbô* was published in 1862 and earned the author, Gustave Flaubert, the Legion of Honour in 1866.]

[1993] In a letter from Davos which Savery received on 30 November 1914 [LJEF, p.123] Flecker refers to his brother-in-law:
'.... thousands have magnificent old titles my brother-in-law is a count a Venetian [?] title & too lazy (he says too poor) to get the papers. He has never got a copy of his arms but has seen them – his titles not old & the arms are a[??] asleep under a tree (shadow pleases, okia d'apeoes [?]) skiadaressi.' [omitted portion of letter supplied by HRHRC]

[1994] LIFE, p.225

[1995] The spirits of Dr. Flecker and his wife, during the war, were under great strain. Hundreds of former Dean Close pupils volunteered for the armed forces. Many never returned, and all were known to their old headmaster and his wife. Many Dean Close masters left to go to the war. Food was short, and at times Dr. Flecker and his wife were mistakenly thought to be Germans, and ostracised. Flecker was a German-sounding name. Olive Schreiner also found because her name was German that people in the hotel at which she was staying alone in London also ostracised her during the war. [*My Other Self* The Letters of Olive Schreiner and Havelock Ellis 1884–1920 edited by Yaffa Claire Drazin. Peter Lang. 1992 p.488] She had insisted on keeping her maiden name after marriage. Her husband changed his name to Crownwright-Schreiner. In the autumn of 1916 Dr Flecker was apprehended on leaving the Army and Navy Stores, Victoria, London, with several items for which he had not paid. he gave a false name and tried to bribe the police-officer who arrested him. Dr. Flecker made a public confession before the school and resigned his post. The jury at the trial accepted his defence submission about Dr. Flecker's 'mental prostration' and dismissed the charges. Dr. Flecker was prevailed to stay in his post but was given leave of absence lasting a term, to recover. Dr. Flecker remained at Dean Close until 1924.

Dean Close School. The First One Hundred Years. edited by M.A. Girling. Cheltenham 1986

[1996] LIFE, p.225

[1997] NGJ, p.220

[1998] NGJ, p.221

[1999] Princeton, AM 16150

[2000] 'The Rose Tree in the Garden of Time' is a reference to a notebook in Flecker's verse (MS.Eng.Poet d.252. BOD). After Flecker's death the Poetry Bookshop, in 1915, published some of the poems, in *The Old Ships*. 'The Rose Tree in Time's Garden', was the title Flecker gave his notebook and the sections were titled:

'Poems of the First White Rose' (prewar unpublished verses)

'Poems of the War-Rose' (Poems written after August 1914).

It is interesting that in 'Poems of the War-Rose' Flecker has to include 'November Eves'.

He also planned to have a section 'Poems of the Second White Rose', which would be works written after the war.

PRINCIPAL WORKS

The Best Man	Oxford	1906
The Bridge of Fire	London	1907
The Last Generation	London	1908
Thirty-Six Poems	London	1910
The Grecians	London	1910
Forty-Two Poems	London	1911
The Scholar's Italian Book	London	1911
The Golden Journey to Samarkand	London	1913
The King of Alsander	London	1914
The Old Ships	London	1915
Hassan	London	1922, 1923, 1951
Don Juan	London	1925

Main Sources with Abbreviations

THE LIFE OF JAMES ELROY FLECKER – LIFE
From letters and materials
Provided by his mother.
By Geraldine Hodgson
Basil Blackwell, OXFORD, 1925

NO GOLDEN JOURNEY – NGJ A biography of James Elroy Flecker.
By John Sherwood Heinemann, LONDON 1973

JAMES ELROY FLECKER – JEF
An appreciation with some
biographical notes.
By Douglas Goldring
Chapman and Hall, LONDON, 1922

SOME LETTERS FROM ABROAD of – JAMES ELROY FLECKER
WITH A FEW REMINISCENCES SLA by Hellé Flecker and an
Introduction by Sir J.C. Squire Heinemann, LONDON, 1930

RUPERT BROOKE – RBH A biography By Christopher Hassall Faber
and Faber, LONDON, 1964

JAMES ELROY FLECKER, A CRITICAL STUDY – BYRD DAVIS by
Mary Byrd Davis Salzburg Studies in English Literature, 1977

JAMES ELROY FLECKER – GILL, Vol. 1 By Ronald A. Gillanders –
Vol.2 Salzburg Studies in English Literature Vol.1 and Vol. 2, 1983

THE LETTERS OF RUPERT BROOKE – RBL Chosen and edited by
Geoffrey Keynes,
Faber and Faber, LONDON, 1968

THE KING OF ALSANDER – K of A
G.P. Putnam's Sons
NEW YORK & LONDON, 1914

BOOK ABBREVIATIONS

THE LAST OF THE DRAGOMANS – LD
By Sir Andrew Ryan,
With a forward by the editor,
Sir Reader Bullard.
Geoffrey Bles, LONDON, 1951

THE CAMELS MUST GO – CMG An autobiography
By Sir Reader Bullard
Faber & Faber, LONDON, 1961

HAROLD NICOLSON, Vol.1, 1886-1929 – HN
By James Lees-Milne,
Hamish Hamilton paperback First published LONDON, 1981

THE LETTERS OF J.E. FLECKER – TO FRANK SAVERY LJEF
Forward by Hellé Flecker
The Beaumont Press, LONDON, 1926

DON JUAN, DJ
(one of 380 copies)
Wm. Heinemann, LONDON, 1926

EDWARD MARSH, PATRON OF THE ARTS – EMH A biography by
Christopher Hassall. Longmans, LONDON, 1959

LETTERS TO T.E. LAWRENCE – LTEL A.W. Lawrence (ed.,)
(LONDON, Jonathan Cape, 1962)

THE GOLDEN JOURNEY TO SAMARKAND – GJS
By James Elroy Flecker
Max Goschen Ltd., LONDON, 1913

FLECKER OF DEAN CLOSE – WILLIAMS
By Charles Williams The Canterbury Press LONDON, EDINBURGH,
1946

THE LIFE OF OLIVE SCHREINER S.C.C-S.
By S.C. Cronwright-Schreiner
T. Fisher Unwin Ltd., LONDON, 1924

JAMES ELROY FLECKER: FROM SCHOOL TO SAMARKAND TSM
By T.S. Mercer Merle Press, Richmond, 1952

POEMS AND PROSE ABBREVIATIONS

COLLECTED POEMS – CP, p... Edited with an Introduction by
Sir John Squire, Secker & Warburg, London, 1946 (CP contains
misprints)

COLLECTED PROSE – CPr, p... William Heinemann. London, 1922

CONTENTS
Tales and Sketches – The Last Generation, N'Jawk, Pentheus, Mansur,
Candilli, The 'Bus in Stamboul, Translations from the Gulistan,
Forgotten Warfare, Philanthropists, The Grecians: A Dialogue on
Education.

Critical Studies – John Davidson: Realist, John Davidson, The New
Poetry and Mr. Housman's 'The Shropshire Lad', Two Critics of
Poetry, Preface to The Golden Journey to Samarkand, The Public as
Art Critic, Paul Fort, The Prince of Poets

FORGOTTEN WARFARE – FW, CPr (Collected Prose)

MANUSCRIPTS ABBREVIATIONS

BOOK OF KARA JAMES – BKJ

DON JUAN – By James Elroy Flecker in Cheltenham Public Library,
TSDJ

Notebook of JEF Poetry Collection – NNY
LOCKWOOD
Lockwood Memorial Library
State University of New York
at Buffalo

Bridge of Fire Copybook – B of F Copybook

Abbreviations

Berg Collection The New York Public Library   Berg
The Huntington Library. San Marino, California   Huntington
Princeton University Library   PUL
University of Texas at Austin Harry Ransom Humanities Research
Centre   HRHRC
Houghton Library at Harvard University   Harvard
British Library   Library Reproductions (Western Manuscripts)   BL
John M. Munro   Munro
James Elroy
Flecker Twayne
Publishers Boston
Mass., 1975

The Golden Journey to Samarkand
Flecker's Original Manuscripts

When those long caravans that cross the plain
With dauntless feet & sound of silver bells
Put forth no more for glory or for gain,
Take no more solace from the palm-girt wells.

When the great markets by the sea shut fast
All that calm Sunday that goes on and on:
When even lovers find their peace at last,
Earth is but a star, that once had shone.

———————

The Golden Journey

~~Prologue~~ to SAMARCAND ? K/

3 8

At the gate of the Sun, Bagdad, in olden time.

The merchants:

Away, for we are ready to a man!
Our camels sniff the ~~morning~~ & are glad
Lead on, O master of the Caravan:
Lead on the merchants of divine Bagdad

The Chief ~~from~~ Draper

Have we not Indian Carpets dark as wine,
Turbans & ~~sashes~~, gowns & tows locels,
Broideries of intricate design,
& printed hangings in enormous bales.

The Chief Grocer

We have rose-candy, we have ~~spikenard~~,
mastic and ~~terebinth~~ & ~~mandragora~~ & oil & spice,
& such sweet Jams meticulously jarred
As gods own Prophet eats in Paradise

The Chief ~~Merchant~~

We have bags of ~~nuts~~ of special kinds,
white, brown & black, fragile or fair or strong:
Their bosoms shame the rose: their behinds
Impel the ~~admiring~~ nightingales to song

4

The Principal Jews

And we have manuscripts in Peacock styles
By Ali of Damascus: we have swords
Engraved with storks and apes & crocodiles,
And heavy beaten necklaces, for lords

The Master of the Caravan
writing out – lot of Jews
But you are ~~only Jews as one can see~~

The Principal Jews
~~Sir~~ Sir, even deep ~~buy~~ day of the ~~the~~ true pay
~~we~~ miserable Jews. but ~~die code~~ pay

The Master of the Caravan
~~with, even deep have daylight, None we~~
But who are ye with in rags & rotten shoes
You dirty bearded, blocking up the way?

The Pilgrims
We are the Pilgrims, master: we shall go
Always a little further: ~~sometimes~~ it may be
Beyond that last blue mountain barred with snow
Across that angry or that glimmering sea.

While on a throne or guarded in a cave
There lives a prophet who can understand
Why we were born: but surely we are brave,
Who make the Golden journey to Samarcand

? K

47

The Chief Merchant

We know the sail of hurry. Master, away!

One of the women

O turn your eyes to where your children stand.
Is not Bagdad the beautiful? O stay!

The merchants, in chorus,

We take the Golden Road to Samarkand.

An old man

Have you not girls & garlands in your houses,
Eunuchs and Syrian boys at your command?
Seek not excess: God hateth him who roams!

The merchants, in chorus

We take the golden journey to Samarkand

A Pilgrim with a beautiful voice

Sweet to ride forth at evening from the wells
When shadows pass gigantic on the sand,
And softly through the silence beat the bells
Along the golden road to Samarkand

A merchant

We travel not for trafficking alone:
By hotter winds our fiery hearts are fanned:
For lust of knowing what should not be known
We take the golden journey to Samarkand

The master of the caravan

Open the gate, O watchman of the night!

6

The Watchman.

To, travellers, I open. For what land
Leave you the dim-moon city of delight
The Merchants (with a shout)
We make the golden journey to Samarkand
The caravan passes through the gate
The Watchman (watching the women)
What would ye, ladies? It was ever thus.
Men are unwise and curiously planned.
A woman
They have their dreams and so not think of us
Voices of the Caravan, in the distance, singing
We make the golden journey to Samarkand.

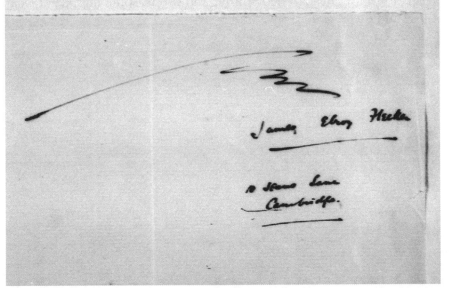

James Elroy Flecker

10 Stone Lane
Cambridge.

OBITUARIES

The Times on 6th January, 1915 published Flecker's obituary (unsigned). It was written by Rupert Brooke.

The *Academy, Athenaeum, Nation* and *Daily Express* published obituaries of Flecker. The *Sphere* in January 1915 published a sympathetic article by Clement Shorter

The *New Statesman*'s obituary of January 9th 1915 was written under the name of Solomon Eagle (J.C.Squire) and took up a whole page.

Cheltenham's *The Looker-On* of January 30th 1915 published Flecker's obituary, also a photograph and his poem 'God Save the King' and details of Flecker's funeral. In the paragraph about the funeral 'on Thursday last' it was explained how Flecker's body was brought to Cheltenham from Switzerland via Paris, Havre and Southampton. After a preliminary service at the Chapel of Dean Close School his body was interred in Cheltenham Cemetery. Among the mourners were listed Flecker's widow, his parents, brother and sisters, some masters of Dean Close and the Servants.

Flecker's Legacy

Some writers whose work (and life) owe a debt to Flecker

Herbert Haworth *Notes on Some Figures behind T.S. Eliot* Chatto & Windus London 1968 Flecker pp 24, 108

Robert Payne *Lawrence of Arabia A Triumph* Robert Hale London 1962
The chief influence on his determination to be a writer may have been James Elroy Flecker, the poet.'

Frank Kermode *Romantic Image* Routledge-Kegan Paul London 1957 (and Munro) refer to Flecker's possible influence on W.B.Yeats's poem 'Byzantium'.

Bevis Hillier *Young Betjeman* John Murray London 1988

Betjeman's poems and some of Flecker's discussed under the heading 'Later Influences'.

In *The Lost Club Journal* by R.B. Russell outlines details of the life and work of the writer,Sarban the pen-name of John William Wall (1910-1989) whose decision to join the Levant Consular Service and who was appointed vice-Consul at Beirut was influenced to some extent by the life of James Elroy Flecker. homepages.pavilion.co.uk

C.E. Bosworth, *James Elroy Flecker: Poet, Diplomat, Orientalist* The John Rylands University of Manchester 1987 p. 374.

Hassan is therfore a landmark pointing the way to more recent successes in this field by authors like T.S. Eliot and Christopher Fry.

HASSAN

James Elroy Flecker's *Hassan*
The Story of Hassan of Bagdad and how he came to make the Golden
Journey to Samarkand. A Play in Five Acts.

Bibliography and Notes

T.Stanley Mercer *James Elroy Flecker From School to Samarkand.* The Merle Press.
Thames Ditton. 1952 contains a bibliography which includes details of
editions of *Hassan* and published musical scores of *Hassan.*

Dawn Redwood *Flecker and Delius – the Making of Hassan* Thames Publishing
London 1978

Timothy Kidd *A Wolf in the Conservatory – Essays in Criticism* Park Press
London 1999 contains *Hassan: The Road to the Haymarket* Also published in
Theatre Research International New Series Volume IV Number 3 May 1979

James Hogg *James Elroy Flecker's Hassan:* A Near Master-Piece? Salzburg
Studies in English English Literature 1975

The Leysin Edition of James Elroy Flecker's *Hassan* edited by James Hogg
Salzburg Studies in English Literature 1976

Edward Shanks *James Elroy Flecker* and A H Fox Strangways MUSIC *Hassan:*
in *The London Mercury* edited by J.C. Squire November 1923 Volume IX
no 49

Hassan was translated into Persian and staged in Tehran in June 1945.
The translation was published by the British Council in Tehran, in
1946.

James Elroy Flecker Poet, Diplomat, Orientalist C.E. Bosworth MA Ph.D. The John Reylands University Library of Manchester 1987 p. 378.

Performances of Hassan

World Premiere
Darmstadt Germany The Heische Landes-Theater First Night 1st June then ran for two weeks. The German translation of *Hassan* was made from the Leysin version.

First Performance in English

London His Majesty's Theatre First Night September 20th 1923 Arranged for production by Basil Dean Music composed by Frederick Delius The Ballets arranged by Michel Fokine. Hassan played by Henry Ainley Yasmin by Cathleen Nesbitt Performed to packed houses for 281 performances.

Hassan was performed at the Knickerbocker Theatre, New York in September 1924 and ran for ten days. *Hassan* was staged at The Royal Dramatic Theatre, Stockholm, and directed by Olof Molander, on 28th March 1925 and ran for 20 performances until 5th May, 1925. The translation was made by Prins Wilhelm, brother of King Gustav VI. Hellé Flecker wrote to Douglas Goldring on March 30th, 1925 from the Grand Hotel, Stockholm telling Goldring of her meeting with Prins Wilhelm and her impression of the performance of *Hassan.* She thought that the actor who played Hassan was secondary with no personality so that Ravi-Pervaneh pair dominate. She approved of the ghost-scene. Hellé mentioned that J.C. Squire was hoping to see the performance, in April. She failed to meet Goldring in person at that time.
(University of Victoria, Canada, Archives and Special Collections).

Hassan was performed at the Maddenmarket Theatre, Norwich 1931
More performances of Flecker's *Hassan* were staged at: South Africa (1951) Festival of Britain (1951) at Canterbury (1954) by Rose Bruford students at the Scala Theatre (1958) Dublin (1960) then transferred to Belgrave Theatre, Coventry.
The Windward Theatre Company staged *Hassan* Adapted and Arranged by Andrew Potter at South Street Theatre, Reading, December 2002

Hassan was on radio on 21st November 1926
Hassan was broadcast on the Third programme on November 22nd 1946
Hassan was produced on BBC Television in 1970

A silent film based on *Hassan* entitled *The Lady of the Harem* was released in London in 1926

The Golden Journey Scenes from the life of James Elroy Flecker was broadcast on the Home Service on January 12th 1951 by Derek Patmore, produced by D.G.Bridson

Hassan by James Elroy Flecker Introduction by Basil Dean. Costume Designs (in colour) by Peter Bucknell The Folio Society. London 1966

Hassan first published in September 1922 by Heinemann Ltd., was in five acts.Basil Dean made a three -act version in 1951.

The complete music of *Hassan* was broadcast by the BBC on December 23rd 1973 Played by the BBC Welsh Orchestra, with the play.
Delius Incidental Music to *Hassan* words by James Elroy Flecker Bournemouth Sinfonietta Chorus was recorded by EMI Records Ltd., 1979 ASD 3777 also available on CD

Earlier music scores for *Hassan* are given in: TSM and *Flecker and Delius* by Dawn Redwood

Select Bibliography

Jad Adams *Madder Music, Stronger Wine. The Life of Edward Dowson, Poet.* IB Tauris London and New York 2000

Flora Armitage *The Desert and the Stars* Faber and Faber London 1956

Bruce Arnold *Orpen Mirror to an Age* Cape London 1989

Joyce Avrech Berkman *The Healing Imagination of Olive Schreiner Beyond South African Colonialism.* The University of Massachusetts Press Amherst 1989

Philip Bagguley *Harlequin in Whitehall* A Life of Humbert Wolfe Poet and Civil Servant Nyala

Mary Beard *The Invention of Jane Harrison* Harvard University Press, Cambridge, Mass., London 2000

Cyril W. Beaumont *Anna Pavlova* C.W.Beaumont London 1945

Cyril Beaumont *Bookseller at the Ballet Memoirs 1891–1929* C.W. Beaumont London 1975

Fiona Beckett *DH Lawrence – The Thinker as Poet* St Martin's Press Inc., First published in USA 1997

Gillian Beer *Meredith A Change of Masks A Study of the Novels* The Athlone Press London 1970

Brigid M. Boardman *Between Heaven and Charing Cross The Life of Francis Thompson* Yale London 1988

Martin Booth *Dreaming of Samarkand* Hutchinson London 1989 (Novel based on a relationship between James Elroy Flecker and TE Lawrence)

Martin Booth *OPIUM A History* Simon and Schuster London 1996

Martin Booth *Stalks of Jade* Renderings of Early Chinese Erotic Verse The Menard Press London 1976

Vera Buchanan-Gould *Not Withour Honour* The Life and Writings of Olive Schreiner Hutchinson & Co., London 1948

Julian and Margaret Bullard Editors *The Diaries of Reader Bullard* Day Books, Oxfordshire 2000

Sir Reader Bullard *James Elroy Flecker in Constantinople The Listener* February 15th 1951

Reader Bullard *Letters From Tehran – A British Ambassador in World War 11 Persia* I.B.Tauris & Co., London and New York 1991

Arthur Calder-Marshall *Havelock Ellis* Rupert Hart-Davis London 1959

Hymphrey Carpenter *A Serious Character The Life of Ezra Pound* Faber & Faber London 1988

John Carswell *Lives and Letters 1906–1957* Faber & Faber London 1978

John Davidson *New Ballads* John Lane, The Bodley Head, London and New York 1897

Richard Deacon *The Cambridge Apostles* – A History of Cambridge University's Elite Intellectual Secret Society Robert Royce Ltd., London 1985

Basil Dean *Seven-Ages* Hutchinson & Co Ltd., Lodon 1970

Paul Delaney *The Neo-Pagans Friendship and Love in the Rupert Brooke Circle* Macmillan London 1987

F.W.Dillistone *Charles Raven* Hodder & Stoughton London 1975

Yaffa Claire Drazin *The Letters of Olive Schreiner and Havelock Ellis* 1884–1920 Peter Lang London 1992

Havelock Ellis *My Life* Wm Heinemann Ltd., First Published 1940

Gilbert Frankau *Eve, Blanche and Prynette (With apologies to the Spirit of James Elroy Flecker) The Somme Times* No1 Vol 1 31st July 1916

Christoher Fry *Can You Find Me A Family History* OUP Oxford 1978

Douglas Goldring *Life Interests* Macdonald London 1948

Frederick L Gwyn *Sturge Moore and the Life of Art* Richards Press Ltd., and the University of Kansas Press 1952

Christopher Hassall *Edward Marsh Patron of the Arts* Longman's London 1959

Christopher Hassall *Rupert Brooke* A Biography Faber & Faber London 1964

Dominic Hibberd *Harold Monro – Poet of the New Age* Palgrave 2001

Susan Hill *The Spirit of the Cotswolds* Michael Joseph London 1988

Vyvyan Holland *Son of Oscar Wilde* Rupert Hart-Davis London 1954

Richard Holmes *Sidetracks Explorations of a Romantic Biographer* Harper Collins London 2000

A.E. Housman *Collected Poems and Selected Poems* edited by Christopher Ricks Penguin Books London 1989

A.E.Housman *Last Poems* Grant Richards Ltd., London 1922

Allan Ingram *The Language of DH Lawrence* Macmillan Education Ltd., London 1990

Richard Jenkyns *The Victorians and Ancient Greece* Basil Backwell Oxford 1980

Alan Judd *Ford Maddox Ford* Collins London 1990

Rana Kabbani *Europe's Myths of Orient: Devise and Rule* Macmillan London 1986

Guy Kendall *Charles Kingsley and his Ideas* Hutchinson & Co., London 1947

Geoffrey Keynes *The Letters of Rupert Brooke* Faber & Faber London 1968

T.E. Lawrence *The Mint* Cape, London 1955

Leigh Hatts *The Bournemouth Coast Path* Countryside Books Newbury 1985

Peter Levy *Edward Lear A* Biography Macmillan London 1995

Mary S.Lovell *A Rage to Live* A Biography of Richard and Isabel Burton Little, Brown & Co., London 1998

Sarah Macdougall *Mark Gertler* John Murray London 2002

Thomas Mann *The Magic Mountain* With a postscript by the author on: The Making of the Novel. Translated from the German by H.T. Lowe-Porter Seeker and Warburg London Reprinted 1971

J.Markowitz *The Canadian Forum* April 1937 Article J.E. Flecker The Role of Tuberculosis in English Poetry

Edward Marsh *A Number of People* Heinemann Ltd., London 1939

Arthur James Mason DD *Life of William Edward Collins, Bishop of Gibraltar* Longman's Green & Co., London 1912

Frank McLynn *Burton-Snow upon the Desert* 1821–1890 London 1990

Frank McLynn *Robert Louis Stevenson* Hutchinson London 1993

Alex Mezey *Muse in Torment* The Book Guild Lewes 1994

D.E. Moggridge *Maynard Keynes An Economist's Biography* Routledge London 1992

Dorina Neave *Twenty-Six Years On The Bosphorus* Grayson & Grayson London 1933

James G.Nelson *Elkin Mathews Publisher to Yeats, Joyce and Pound* The University of Wisconson Press 1989

R.A.Nicholson *Translations of Eastern Poetry and Prose* CUP Cambridge 1922

Mary O'Connor *John Davidson* Scottish Writers Series Scottish Academic Press Edinburgh 1987

Richard Ollard *A Man of Contradictions* A Life of A.L.Rowse Allen Lane London 1999

Norman Page *A E Housman* A Critical Biography Macmillan Press Ltd., London 1983

Frances Partridge *Hanging On Diaries December 1960 to August 1963* Collins London 1990

Anna Pavord *Visions Of Byzantium, The Observer,* 21 June 1987

Stephen Phillips *Christ in Hades* John Lane The Bodley Head London 1917

Claude Pichois *Baudelaire* Hamish Hamilton London 1989

George Pickering *Creative Malady* George Allen & Unwin London 1974

Ben Pimlott *Hugh Dalton* Cape London 1985

Roy Porter *The Greatest Benefit to Mankind – A Medical History from Antiquity to the Present* Fontana Press Edition London 1999

F.A.Rice *The Granta and its Contributors 1889–1914* Constable London 1924

Grant Richards *Author Hunting By an Old Literary Sporstman. Memories of Years spent Mainly in Publishing 1897-1925* Hamish Hamilton London 1934

Joanna Richardson *Baudelaire* John Murray London 1994

Richard Rive Editor Russell Martin *Olive Schreiner Letters* Vol 1 1871–1899 OUP 1989

Jane Emery Rose *Macauley – A Writer's Life* John Murray London 1991

A.L.Rowse *Oxford – In the History of the Nation* Weidenfeld & Nicolson London 1975

Dr. Frank Ryan *Tuberculosis; The Greatest Story Never Told.* Swift Publishers London 1992

Max Saunders *Ford Madox Ford A Dual Life* Vol 1 The World Before the War OUP 1996

Sarah Searight *The British in the Middle East* East West Publications 1979

F.B.Smith *The Retreat of Tuberculosis 1850 to 1950* Croom Helm London New York and Sydney

Robert Snell *Théophile Gautier A Romantic Critic of the Visual Arts* Clarendon Pess Oxford 1982

Hilary Spurling *Ivy* The Life of Ivy Compton-Burnett Richard Cohen Books London 1995

Noel Stock *The Life of Ezra Pound* Routledge & Kegan Paul London 1970

Alan Sutton *The Cotswolds of 100 Years Ago* Alan Sutton Publishing, Glos., 1990

Philip E Tennent *Théophile Gautier* University of London The Athlone Press London 1975

Francis Toye *For What we Have Received-An Autobiography* Heinemann Ltd London1950

Mark Valentine *T.E. Lawrence An Essay on Flecker, Forgotten Warfare* by James Elroy Flecker published by Mark Valentine 1988

Annabel Walker *Ariel Stein: Pioneer of the Silk Road* John Murray London 1995

G.Turquet-Milnes *The Influence of Baudelaire in France and England* Constable & Co., London 1913

Alison Waley *Half of Two Lives* Weidenfeld & Nicolson London 1982

Eric Walker *W. P. Schreiner A South African* OUP 1937

Heather Walker *The Arcadian* Issue no 5 Spring 1993 Article James Elroy Flecker

Heather Walker *Journal of the Eighteen – Nineties Society* Double issue Nos. 17 & 18 1989 Article; Remembering John Davidson 1857–1909 James Nelson ditto Article Elkin Mathews, Publisher to Lionel Johnson

Heather Walker *Poetic Hours* Autumn 1993 Issue no 1 Article James Elroy Flecker

Heather Walker *Poetic Hours* Spring 1994 Issue no 2 Article TB or not TB?

Heather Walker *Poetic Hours* Autumn 1996 Issue no 7 Article Scandal in Bohemia The Life and Times of Richard Middleton

Heather Walker *Poetic Hours* Spring 1997 Issue no 8 Article, No Bed of Roses

Heather Walker *Poetic Hours* Autumn 1997 Article: Chapter or Verse? Ronald Firbank

Heather Walker *The New Writer* February 1998 no 15 Article Sorrow in Sunlight The Novels of Ronald Firbank

Heather Walker *Poetic Hours* Autumn 1999 Article Bring me Sunshine. On holiday with Flecker

Heather Walker *Poetic Hours* Autumn 2000 Issue no 15 Article I have been faithful to thee Dowson! In my Fashion

Theresa Whistler *Imagination of the Heart The Life of Walter de la Mare* John Murray London 1993

Peter Whitebrook *William Archer* A Biography Methuen London 1993

A.Williams *A Wiltshire Village* Duckworth London 1912

Duncan Wilson *Gilbert Murray OM* Clarendon Press Oxford 1987

Jeremy Wilson *Lawrence of Arabia* Heinemann London 1989

H.V.F. Winstone *Gertrude Bell* Cape London 1978

Humbert Wolfe *Portraits by Inference* Methuen London 1934

Humbert Wolfe *Requiem Poems* Ernest Benn Ltd., London 1927

Humbert Wolfe *The Upward Anguish* Cassell & Co., London 1958

Humbert Wolfe *This Blind Rose, Poems* Gollancz London 1928

J.Howard Woolmer *The Poetry Bookshop 1912–1935* Bibliography Woolmer/Brotherston Winchester 1988

Mark Yardley *Backing into the Limelight Biography of TE Lawrence* Harrap London 1985

Charles Baudelaire – Selected Poems Chosen and Translated with an Introduction by Joanna Richardson Penguin Books London First Published 1975

Frederick Locker-Lampson – A Character Sketch Edited by The Right Hon. Augustine Birrell Constable & Company, London, 1920

R.L.Megroz *Francis Thompson The Poet of Earth in Heaven. A study in Poetic Mysticism and the Evolution of Love-Poetry.* Faber & Gwyer London 1927

Monologues – Richard Middleton T.Fisher Unwin London 1913

My Life and Times Octave Three 1900–07 Compton McKenzie Chatto & Windus London 1964

My Other Self – Draznin The Letters Of Olive Schreiner And Havelock Ellis 1884–1920 Edited by Yaffa Claire Draznin, Peter Lang, New York, 1992

Ronald Firbank: Memoirs & Critiques Edited by Mervyn Horder, London 1977

The Collected Arthur Machen Edited by Christopher Palmer Duckworth London 1988

The Complete Poems of Rupert Brooke Sidgwick & Jackson London 1939 Publishing London 1997

The Diary of Arthur Christopher Benson edited by Percy Lubbock Hutchinson & Co 1926

The House of Dent 1888–1938 J.M. Dent & Sons Ltd., London 1938

The Works of William Collins Edited by Richard Wendorf and Charles Ryskamp The Clarendon Press Oxford 1979 (Collins general source for his Ecologues was Thomas Salmon's *Modern History* published in 31 volumes between 1725 and 1738 p 107)

George Meredith Selected Poems edited by Keith Hanley Carcenet Press Ltd., Manchester 1988

The Complete Ronald Firbank Preface by Anthony Powell Duckworth 1961

Translating Poetry The Double Labyrinth edited by Daniel Weissbort Macmillan London 1989

Frederick Locker-Lampson *An Autobiographical Sketch Addressed to My Descendents* Smith Elder & Co., London, 1896

E.S. Turner *Boys Will Be Boys* Michael Joseph London 1948

Compiled by The Rev. R.F. McNeile, OD *A History of Dean Close School (1886–1895)* Wilding Shrewsbury London 1966

Edited by M.A. Girling & Sir Leonard Hooper *The First Hundred Years – Dean Close School 1886–1986* The Holywell Press Ltd. Oxford, Cheltenham 1986

EPILOGUE

Hellé Flecker brought her husband's body back to England for burial at Cheltenham. Later, the question of how James Elroy Flecker's life and work should be presented to the public caused rifts to develop between Hellé Flecker and her parents-in-law[1]. Much the same sort of rifts that resulted after the death of Rupert Brooke between Edward Marsh and Rupert Brooke's mother.

Hellé Flecker spent the years before the stage production of *Hassan* in 1923 behind the scenes endeavouring as tactfully as she could to get Basil Dean, Delius and others to set a date to stage her late husband's play. Hellé attended the first night of *Hassan* at Darmstadt. She had hoped that some of her late husband's friends, such as Jack Beazley would attend, but none of them was able to do so. Hellé was at the first night (in english) of *Hassan* at His Majesty's Theatre on 20th September, 1923, with her parents-in-law. Amongst many famous people in the audience were Ivor Novello, J.M. Barrie, Arnold Bennett and Compton Mackenzie. Also in the audience were Flecker's friends, Edward Marsh, Douglas Goldring, 7875698 Private T.E. Shaw alias T.E. Lawrence[2] and Francis Birrell who wrote a review of *Hassan* in *The Nation and Athaeneum's* September 29th edition under the heading *On Getting Muddled.*

Hellé Flecker spent the years of the Second World War in the south of France, caring for her brother, Spiro. She died on 27th October, 1961, in London. Her health had failed so completely she was unable to look after herself in her last years. The sale of one of her husband's poetry notebooks to a library in the USA would (it is to be hoped), enable her to have some financial security, in her remaining years. Financial security was not something she had enjoyed during her marriage. On her death certificate she was described as 'widow of James Elroy Flecker, a Poet'[1]. (Her husband's death certificate did not give his occupation as, Poet). Hellé is buried beside her husband in the grave at Cheltenham.

AFTERWORD

On Tuesday, January 12th John Mavrogordato wrote in his diary[3] after reading about Flecker's death at Davos:

> 'I was afraid from his last letter that he wouldn't last the winter. Long word of praise in the *Times*. But when he was alive editors wouldn't answer his letters.'

On January 13th Mavrogordato wrote:

> 'dreaming about Flecker....'

Jack Beazley (1885–1970)

John Beazley (later Sir John Beazley) Lincoln Professor of Classical Archaeology and Art from 1925–1956. The Beazley Archive after his death was brought to the Ashmolean Museum, Oxford where it is housed in several rooms and has been enlarged and enhanced, for the use of scholars, (www.beazley.ox.ac.uk)

Frank Savery (1883–1965)

Frank Savery, CBE spent most of his official career in Warsaw (1919–1945) first as British Consul and then as Consular General. He had a wide knowledge of Polish literature. He retired in 1949. He is buried at Silverton, Devon.

Francis Birrell (1889–1935)

Francis Birrell, critic and journalist worked in France for the War Victims Relief Committee of the Society of Friends 1915–1919.

---

[1] NGJ p xv
[2] The T.E.Lawrence Society Newsletter no 44, Winter 1997/8
[3] BOD

INDEX